The great
book of
Desserts

THUNDER BAY
P·R·E·S·S

The great book of
Desserts

Small Desserts
Creams, Custards and Mousses • Crepes and Omelettes
Pies and Cakes • Ices and Frozen Desserts • Fried Desserts

By
GIANNA BROCATO

Translation by
ANDREA JOURDAN

THUNDER BAY
P·R·E·S·S

First published in 2000 by
Thunder Bay Press
An imprint of the Advantage Publishers Group
5880 Oberlin Drive, San Diego, CA 92121-4794
www.advantagebooksonline.com

Direction: Marco Drago, Andrea Boroli
Editorial Director: Cristina Cappa Legora
Editorial Coordinator: Valeria Camaschella
Graphic Coordinator: Marco Volpati

Editorial collaboration: Fenice 2000 s.r.l., Milan
Graphic Design: Paolo Leveni
Graphic Layout: Twister s.r.l., Milan
Jacket: Paola Piacco

Research into iconography by the Centro Iconografico
at the Istituto Geografico De Agostini
directed by Maria Serena Battaglia

Photos: Archivio I.G.D.A. (N. Banas, L. Chiozzi, I. Feroldi,
K. Kissov, Kissov-Banas, G. Losito, P. Martini, U. Marzani,
G. Pisacane, Prima Press, F. Reculez, L. Rizzi, C. Ruggiero,
M. Sarcina, G. Ummarino, Visual Food)

First published in Italy by Istituto Geografico De Agostini
under the title:
Il libro d'oro dei dolci e delle decorazioni

Library of Congress Cataloging-in-Publication Data
Great book of desserts
    p.cm.
    Includes index.
    ISBN 1-57145-249-4
    1.Desserts

    TX773.G697 2000
    641.8'6--dc21

Printed in Italy.

1 2 3 4 5 00 01 02 03 04

Contents

Welcome to the kitchen

For most amateur cooks and even those with developed skills, the idea of preparing a dessert is unthinkable. They can spend hours creating delicious and even complicated dishes, but a simple dessert would leave them terrorized in front of an empty bowl. They generally know where the best pastry shops are in their neighborhood. In reality, there are all kinds of desserts and some, although extremely simple to prepare, can still impress your guests. And, once you pass the first terrorizing moments, you find; yourself trying more difficult recipes and even decorating cakes without any panic or fear. Some will say that I had an edge, being born with a pastry chef father. Granted, I grew up with wedding cake for my birthdays and extravaganza desserts for my simple meals. My dreams were made of sugar flowers and whipped cream, so maybe they are right. I sure never feared any dessert. But that is pure luck. If you are not that lucky, all you really need is good equipment. Nowadays, everyone owns the basics, such as whisks and electric beaters, food processors and other fancy tools my dad never knew. The other thing you'll need, and that my dad knew all about, is to respect cooking times and oven temperatures. For example, the secret for a perfect meringue is a very low oven temperature. The rest is... just plain luck.

This book will help build your courage by offering an exceptional variety of recipes for all kinds of desserts, from the easiest to the most difficult ones. For breakfast or tea time, snacks or dinners, you will be able to satisfy the most demanding of your gourmet guests. It has been designed as a guide for those who start and also as a helpful reference for those who like desserts and look for new recipes. In the first pages, you will find suggestions to help you go through all recipes with more ease. In the book, the recipes are divided into small pastries, puddings and mousses, crepes and omelettes, pies and cakes, ice cream and fried desserts, to help you select the right dessert. Every type of dessert can find its place on the right table. Small pastries can be eaten at any moment of the day or with coffee, after an elegant meal. Pralines, marzipan, nougat and candied fruits can be used to enrich many cakes and preparations.

The puddings and mousses are generally served after a more important dinner: bavarois, charlottes, mousses, crèmes and aspics are not difficult to prepare but require a long preparation. Their light textures and elegant look can bring inspiration to a whole meal. Inspired by a summer fruit, you might make a light strawberry mousse. To end a fish dinner on a perfect note, you might prefer a lemon cream tart. With surprising fillings, crepes and omelets will end a lighter dinner on a beautiful note. Sure, the first time you offer a fruit and cream filled sweet omelet to your guests, they will be surprised. But the sight of the flambéed dish arriving on the table will have prepared them well for this exquisite dish.

Simple cakes, soft ones and dry ones, pies filled with fresh fruits or other delicacies, cheese or yogurt cakes – all can be served for tea time, snacks, desserts and even, if there are any left over, for a sinful breakfast. Think of the irresistible meringue pies or the lighter fruit pies of our childhood. Bring those to your dinner table and you will immediately transport your friends to some of their best memories. When they close their eyes after the second bite, expect a moment of silence as their faces illuminate with a smile. Everyone's absolute favorite dessert is, of course, ice cream. Summer is the best season to propose sorbets and ice creams, but a rhubarb or raspberry iced dessert in the middle of the winter can evoke summer pleasures in a flash. The good part in preparing frozen desserts is that they are made in advance, even several days in advance, taking away any panic attack from the cook: dessert is ready and delicious; you can relax. Fried desserts, instead, need to be eaten hot. Therefore they have to be prepared in front of your guests; but this can be turned into a fun kitchen party. Everyone can participate.

You will find the basic preparations, recipes and tips at the beginning of the book. You can come back to them at any moment. At the end, will you will find basic recipes and tips for decoration. How you present your dessert is, of course, important. It is the last dish your guests will see, taste… and remember. Don't disappoint them. Look into your pockets, your drawers and your cupboards, and try to find a little… courage. Just remember when you were small, making patties and sand cakes on the beach. It is not really more difficult to concoct a great finale for your meals. After all, you hold the whisk. Welcome to the beautiful world of sweet dreams.

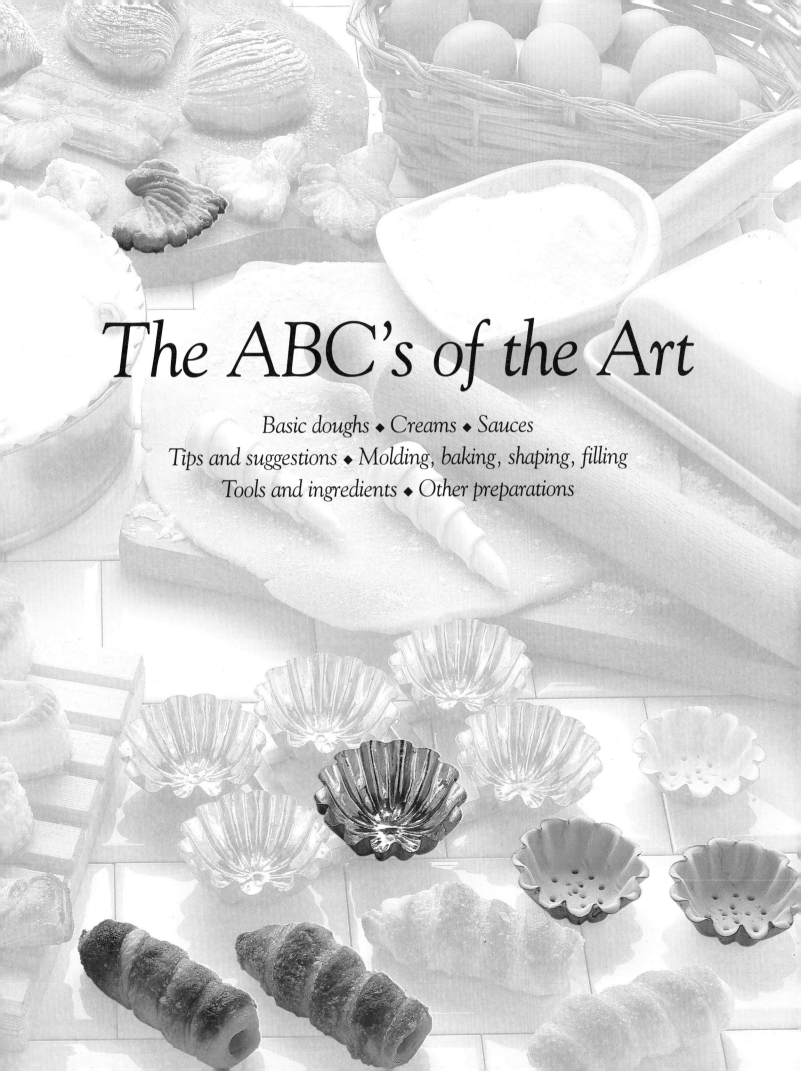

The ABC's of the Art

Basic doughs ◆ Creams ◆ Sauces
Tips and suggestions ◆ Molding, baking, shaping, filling
Tools and ingredients ◆ Other preparations

Basic sponge cake

Time needed: *50 minutes*

INGREDIENTS FOR **6** SERVINGS
1 cup of flour
1/2 cup of sugar
3 eggs
2 tablespoons of butter
1 teaspoon of vanilla

◆ Grease and flour an 8-inch round cake pan. Preheat the oven to 350°F.
◆ Melt the butter in a small pan.
◆ In a bowl, mix the eggs and the sugar with an electric mixer until smooth, thick and foamy **(1)**. Add the vanilla, the sifted flour **(2)** and the melted butter **(3)**, blending delicately (for a lighter cake, whisk egg yolks with butter and sugar, and fold in the egg whites, beaten with a pinch of salt to firm peaks, and the flour).
◆ Pour the preparation in the cake pan **(4)** and bake in the preheated oven for 35-40 minutes.
◆ To verify the cooking time, when the top of the cake is golden and raised, insert a cake tester or a wooden skewer in its middle. If it comes out clean,

remove the cake, turn onto a cake rack and let cool.
◆ If this cake is to be filled, it is better to bake it the day before. It will be easier to slice without crumbling too much.
◆ To make a chocolate sponge cake, you only need to add 1/2 cup of unsweetened cocoa to the ingredients and remove 1/2 cup of flour.

Raised dough

For this type of dough, several ingredients are mixed with a whisk to add air to the batter, to insure the end result will be soft and spongy. It can be made easier by using an electric mixer, which will save you some time and guarantee excellent results. The batter is poured into a buttered cake pan and baked in the oven.

Margherita cake

Time needed: *1 hour*

INGREDIENTS FOR **8-10** SERVINGS
6 eggs
1 cup of sugar
12 tablespoons of softened butter
1 cup of potato starch
1 cup of flour
2 teaspoons of baking powder
1 teaspoon of vanilla
a pinch of salt

◆ Grease and flour a 10-inch cake pan. Preheat the oven at 325°F.
◆ In a bowl, whisk the butter and the sugar with an electric mixer. When mixture is creamy, add the egg yolks and continue mixing.
◆ Sift the flour, the potato starch and the baking powder; add to the mixture. Delicately fold in the vanilla and the egg whites, beaten with the salt to stiff peaks
◆ Pour the preparation in the cake pan and bake in the preheated oven for 40-45 minutes. The cake is ready when a cake tester or skewer, inserted in the middle, comes out clean. Turn the cake on a rack and cool.

Genoise

Time needed: *1 hour*

INGREDIENTS FOR **6-8** SERVINGS
4 eggs
2/3 cup of sugar
1 1/3 cup of flour
4 tablespoons of butter
a pinch of salt

◆ Grease and flour an 8-inch round cake pan. Preheat the oven at 325°F.
◆ In a bowl, placed over boiling water, whisk the eggs, salt and sugar with an electric mixer until the mixture has tripled in volume (15-20 minutes). Remove the bowl from heat and slowly add the melted butter; delicately fold in the flour, being careful to not deflate the preparation.
◆ Pour the batter in the cake pan and bake in the preheated oven for 35-40 minutes. The cake is done when a cake tester or a skewer, inserted in the middle, comes out clean. Turn onto a rack and cool completely.

Rolled biscuit or savoyard

Time needed: *45 minutes*

INGREDIENTS FOR 2 ROLLS, CIRCLES, SAVOYARDS
*1 1/2 cup of flour
1/2 cup of sugar
6 eggs
1 teaspoon of vanilla
a pinch of salt*

◆ Grease 2 cookie sheets, line with parchment paper. Preheat the oven at 425°F.
◆ In a large bowl, whisk the egg yolks, sugar and vanilla with an electric mixer. When mixture is pale and creamy, slowly add the sifted flour. Beat the egg whites with salt to stiff peaks and fold into the batter.

◆ Transfer the batter to a pastry bag, fitted with plain tubes; distribute batter in rectangles **(1)** and level batter with a spatula; or form circles or long cookies with the batter. Bake for 10-12 minutes.
◆ Delicately remove circles or cookies and place on rack. Use circles as base for other desserts. For the rolled cakes, roll the biscuit in a humid kitchen towel **(2)**. Set aside to cool completely. Unroll the biscuit and cover with chosen filling **(3)**. Roll the biscuit onto itself **(4)**, cover with plastic wrap and refrigerate until time to decorate or serve. If biscuit is filled with ice cream, keep it in freezer.
◆ To make a chocolate biscuit, simply add 1/2 cup of unsweetened cocoa to the ingredients.

Raised dough

How to store them
The basic cakes can be kept for a few days before being used for dessert preparations but it is always important to follow a few basic and simple rules.
As soon as the genoise or Margherita or sponge cake are completely cool, they need to be covered with aluminum foil.
The rolled biscuit can be kept a few days in the refrigerator, rolled in a humid towel to keep it fresh and moist. The circles and cookies will retain their freshness wrapped in aluminum foil.
Once cooled and dry, the choux can be kept hermetically closed in an airtight container. Placed in the refrigerator, they would become soggy; left to the air, they would dry up quickly.

Nota bene
With the batter for "choux," you can prepare several desserts such as "profiteroles" (choux filled with cream and covered with chocolate sauce), "croquembouche" (a pyramid of filled choux held together with caramel), "Saint-Honoré," "eclairs" (oblong choux filled and covered with coffee or chocolate cream) and diverse "crowns," split and filled with various creams.

Pâte à choux

Time needed: *40 minutes*

INGREDIENTS FOR 6-8 SERVINGS
*1 1/2 cup of flour
9 tablespoons of butter
6 eggs
1 vanilla bean
1 tablespoon of vanilla sugar
a pinch of salt*

◆ Grease a cookie sheet. Preheat the oven to 400°F. In a saucepan, bring to boil _ cup of water, the salt, the butter in pieces and the split vanilla bean **(1)**.
◆ Remove from heat and, all at once, add the flour **(2)** and mix vigorously until all absorbed. Return the saucepan to the heat and stir with a wooden spoon for a few minutes, until the dough detaches itself from the sides of the pan and forms a mass with a film forming at the bottom **(3)**.
◆ Remove from heat, discard vanilla bean and add the vanilla sugar. Add the eggs, one at a time, making sure the first one has been completely absorbed before adding the next one **(4)**. To do this more rapidly, you can use an electric mixer.
◆ Transfer the dough in a pastry bag and make the "choux," or puffs, of the required size on the cookie sheet. Bake in the preheated oven for 20 minutes or until golden. Pierce the side of every choux with a little knife. Leave the oven door half-open and turn off the heat, but leave the choux in for another 5 minutes to dry inside.

Pie doughs

Time needed: *15 minutes*
(plus refrigeration time)

INGREDIENTS FOR 2 MEDIUM SIZE PIES

2 1/2 cups of flour

8 tablespoons of butter
1/2 cup of sugar ◆ 1 egg yolk
grated peel of 1/2 lemon
1/2 teaspoon of vanilla

◆ Bring the butter to room temperature.
◆ On a work surface, sift the flour and make a well. Add the butter in pieces, the vanilla, the sugar, the egg yolk and lemon peel (1). Quickly work the ingredients with your fingers into a firm dough. Shape into a ball, cover in plastic wrap and refrigerate for 30 minutes to 2 hours. This resting time is necessary, or else the dough would shrink during the baking.
◆ If you add 1 teaspoon of unsweetened cocoa to the ingredients (2), you will get a chocolate dough, to use together with the plain dough for bi-colored cookies (3) or to decorate (4).
◆ The pasta will be lighter if the sugar is replaced by powdered sugar. This dough is better used for smaller pies.
◆ When the pie dough needs to be baked before filling it, it should be lined with a piece of parchment paper and filled with beans or rice. Then it can be baked at 370°F for 20 minutes. Remove from oven; discard beans and paper. You could also push down on the dough after baking it for 10 minutes, but the results will definitely not be as good.

All ingredients are mixed together, rapidly or for a longer time, depending on the type of dough, whether elastic or flaky. After a period of rest, the dough will be flattened with a rolling pin to different thicknesses. And it will be used as the base for pies, quiches or tartlets.

Nota bene
Puff pastry requires time and elaborated skills. Fortunately, today, you can also find ready-made and frozen puff pastry of excellent quality.

Puff pastry dough

Time needed: *1 hour*
(plus refrigeration time)

INGREDIENTS FOR 2 LBS OF DOUGH

5 cups of flour ◆ 1 lb of butter
1/2 cup of water
1 teaspoon of salt

◆ Sift the flour on a work surface. Quickly mix it with salt and water to make a soft dough. Make a small ball; with a knife, cut a cross on its top, cover it with a kitchen towel and set aside for 30 minutes..
◆ Work the butter into a square brick, cover it with plastic wrap and refrigerate.
◆ Flour your work surface. Roll your dough in a square. Remove the butter from the refrigerator; beat it lightly with the rolling pin to soften it a

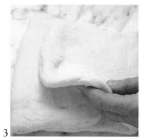

little; place it in the middle of the dough square (1). Fold all sides of the dough over the butter to enclose it completely.
◆ With the rolling pin, press the dough into a rectangle (2). Give a first turn to the dough, folding it in three (3). Turn it a quarter and roll it again. Fold it again in 3 (second turn) and refrigerate for 1 hour, covered with plastic wrap.
◆ Return the dough to the work surface and re-

peat the operation (third turn) and return to the refrigerator for at least 2 hours. One hour before using the dough, give it another 2 turns.

◆ Once rolled and cut in the required shapes, always let the dough rest for 20 minutes, so it won't move during the baking. The ideal oven temperature for baking puff pastry should be 400°F. The baking sheet should always be brushed with water.

◆ To make "vol-au-vent," cut circles with a fluted cookie cutter. With a smaller cutter, cut off the center of half the circles (4) and keep them aside for other use. Brush the circles with beaten egg whites and place circles with wholes on top of the first ones (5). Set aside to rest for 15-20 minutes before baking. In the oven, the dough will raise, leaving a hole in the middle for the filling.

◆ In the preparation of a "napoleon" (layers of puff pastry alternated with layers of cream), it is necessary to prick the dough with the points of a fork so it will become light and flaky.

◆ To make "palmiers" or "fans," roll the dough in a very thin rectangle, sprinkle with sugar and roll dough from both sides towards the middle. Flatten and slice (6). During the baking, the dough will open into a lovely puff pastry fan.

Strudel dough

Time needed: *25 minutes*
(plus refrigeration time)

INGREDIENTS FOR 1/2 LB OF DOUGH

2 1/2 cups of flour

a pinch of salt
1 tablespoon of sugar ◆ 1 egg
4 tablespoons of softened butter
5-6 tablespoons of chilled water

◆ Sift the flour on a work surface. Make a well and add the salt, the sugar, the egg, the butter in pieces and the water. Mix all ingredients vigorously well. Beat the dough on the work surface several times until the dough is smooth and elastic. Make a ball. Heat a saucepan and turn it over the dough (cover it completely) and let rest for 30 minutes.

How to store them

The pie dough, covered with plastic wrap, can be kept refrigerated for a week and can be frozen for several months.

The puff pastry dough, covered with plastic wrap, can be kept a few days in the refrigerator. Before using it, give it 1 or 2 turns. It can also be frozen for several weeks, well wrapped. It is better to freeze it in small batches, to thaw only the necessary quantities when needed. When thawed, give the dough 1 or 2 turns before using it.

The strudel dough can be kept 1 day in a cool place but is definitely better used immediately.

The "pate brisée" can be kept refrigerated for 3 to 4 days, tightly covered with plastic wrap. Divided in half-pound packs, it can be frozen for several months. In this case, it can be thawed quickly at room temperature or in the refrigerator 12 hours.

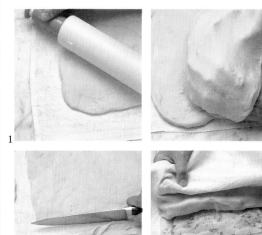

◆ Flour a large sheet. Over it, roll the dough until very thin (1). Flour your hands, put them under the dough and start stretching it. The movement should be from the inside out to extend the dough without breaking it (2) until you have a large rectangle of thin, almost transparent dough. Cut off the borders of thicker dough (3).

◆ To form the strudel, cover with the filling and roll onto itself, with the half of the sheet (4). Fold in the extremities (5), pressing them well to seal.

◆ To bake, place the strudel on a buttered cookie sheet, sealed sides down (6). Brush the strudel with melted butter and bake in a preheated oven at 350°F for about 1 hour.

Pâte brisée

Time needed: *15 minutes*
(plus refrigeration time)

INGREDIENTS FOR 2 PIES

*5 cups of flour ◆ 1/2 lb of butter
1/2 cup of milk ◆ 1 egg yolk
2 tablespoons of sugar
a dash of salt*

◆ Sift the flour and the salt on a work surface (1). In the middle, put the butter (2), the sugar and the egg yolk (3). Work the ingredients rapidly with the tips of your fingers to obtain a rough sandy mixture (4). Add the milk (5) and mix rapidly until smooth. Wrap dough in plastic (6) and refrigerate for at least 1 hour.
◆ A quicker way to prepare this dough is to put the flour, the cold butter in pieces, the sugar and the salt in a food processor. Mix until the mixture is coarse; add the egg yolk and the milk slowly, mixing until the dough is smooth and forms a ball
◆ With a rolling pin, spread the dough thinly. If you line a pie plate with dough that is too thick, it will not cook correctly because of the humidity of the filling. It is important to bake pies in the lower third of the oven.

Nota bene
Pâte brisée is used for pies, tarts and quiches.
To make a light, flaky dough, use very cold butter and work rapidly. When worked for a long time, butter melts and blends into the other ingredients, resulting in a heavier dough.

◆ When the pie needs to be pre-baked, line the mold, prick the dough all over with the tips of a fork and cover the dough with parchment paper. Fill top of paper with beans; it will prevent the dough from raising or moving during baking time. Transfer the pie in a preheated oven at 375°F for 20-30 minutes or until pie crust is lightly golden. Discard beans and paper; fill pie crust with chosen preparation.
◆ Pate brisée can also be made without addition of egg yolk. In this case, substitute the egg yolk and the milk by ice water. In a food processor, mix flour, sugar, salt and cold butter in pieces until mixture is coarse. Add ice water, drop by drop, and mix until the dough forms a ball.

Brioche dough

Time needed: *1 hour*
(plus raising time)

INGREDIENTS FOR 1 LB OF DOUGH
*2 1/2 cups of flour
8 tablespoons of softened butter
1/2 cup of sugar
2 eggs
2 tablespoons of milk
2 teaspoons of yeast
a pinch of salt*

◆ Dissolve the yeast in the warmed milk.
◆ On a work surface, pour the flour and make a well in the middle. Add the dissolved yeast, the eggs, the sugar, the salt and the butter in small pieces. Mix all ingredients very well. Work the dough for about 15 to 20 minutes, lifting it and beating on the work surface, until it is smooth and elastic. If, when you lift a small part of the

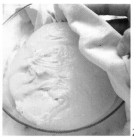

dough, it does not break but rather stretches thinly (1), it is a sign that your dough is ready. Cover with a cloth and set it aside to raise in a warm place for 30 minutes

Yeast base dough

◆ Work the dough a few minutes and transfer it to a large bowl (the dough should fill only 1/3 of it). Cover it with a humid kitchen towel and put it in the lower part of the refrigerator for 12 hours (2).

◆ Transfer the dough in a mold or on a cookie sheet in any form you wish. Let it raise at room temperature, away from any drafts for 1 hour.

◆ Just before putting it in the oven, delicately brush the dough with a beaten egg. Transfer to the preheated oven at 375°F. There are several types of crust you can get: for a darker golden effect, brush the dough with beaten egg yolk and for a lighter effect, brush it with beaten whole egg.

Croissant dough

Time needed: *1 hour*
(plus raising time)

INGREDIENTS FOR ABOUT 2 LBS OF DOUGH
5 cups of flour
1/2 cup of water
1 tablespoon of yeast
1/2 lb of butter
1/2 cup of sugar
1/2 cup of milk
a pinch of salt

◆ Dissolve the yeast in warm water. In a saucepan, heat the milk with the sugar, 1/3 of butter and the salt, until all ingredients have melted.

◆ On a work surface, put the flour and make a well in the middle. Add the dissolved yeast and the milk mixture. Mix all ingredients well, making a smooth dough. Make a little loaf, cover with a towel and set aside in a cool place for 30 minutes.

◆ Mold the leftover butter into a square brick and refrigerate, covered with plastic wrap.

All ingredients of the recipe are mixed and worked together for a long time. Then, set aside to raise in a warm place so the dough doubles in volume. For the brioche, after the final shaping of the dough, it is left to raise a second time before baking it.

How to store it
Brioche dough can be kept, refrigerated, for a few days. It will need to be reworked a little to get its elasticity back. You can also shape it ready to bake and leave it in the freezer for a few months. From the freezer, the dough should be left to raise at room temperature for at least 3 hours before baking it.

Croissant dough can be kept for a few days in the refrigerator. It will need a few turns to give it back its elasticity before shaping and baking. It can also be kept frozen for up to 2 months. In this case, it should be set aside to raise for at least 3 hours before baking.

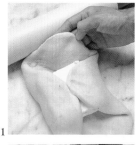

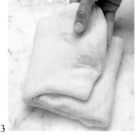

◆ Flour the work surface and roll out the dough in a thin square. Put the cold butter in the center of the dough; beat it lightly with the rolling pin to soften a little. Fold the four sides of the dough over the butter to close completely (1).

◆ Roll out this dough packet in a rectangle (2). Fold dough in 3 parts (3), give it a 1/4 turn and roll it out again. Fold the dough again in 3 pieces and set aside in the refrigerator for 1 hour, in a large bowl covered with plastic wrap.

◆ Roll the dough again, in a rectangle. Fold it in 3 parts and return it to the bowl. Refrigerate for at least 2 hours or, better, overnight.

◆ With the roll-out dough, form croissants (4) and set aside to raise for 1 hour on a greased cookie sheet. Bake in a preheated oven at 375°F.

Pastry cream

Time needed: *20 minutes*

INGREDIENTS FOR 6 SERVINGS

1/2 cup of sugar ◆ *5 egg yolks*
2 cups of whole milk
1/2 cup of flour
1/2 teaspoon of vanilla
1 lemon

◆ Rinse the lemon and cut off the peel in a thin long strip. Bring the milk and lemon peel to a boil.
◆ In a saucepan, mix the egg yolks with the sugar (**1**) until creamy. Slowly add the vanilla and flour, stirring (**2**). Discard the lemon peel and add the boiling milk, little at a time, stirring carefully (**3**). Bring to boil on low heat, stirring to prevent lumps. Lower the heat and cook the cream for 7-8 minutes, stirring from time to time.
◆ Pour into a bowl (**4**), sprinkle with a little sugar (**5**) so no crust or skin will form on the cream, and set aside to cool.
◆ To make a lighter pastry cream, mix 2 egg whites beaten until firm peaks, into the warm preparation. To make it smoother, add 3-5 tablespoons of whipped cream to the cold preparation.

How to keep them

Pastry cream and crème anglaise can be kept refrigerated for 2-3 days, in a bowl covered with plastic wrap.

Nota bene

If you prefer to not sprinkle the top of the pastry cream with sugar, to keep the cream from forming a hard skin you can stir the cream until completely cool.

For rum pastry cream
◆ Incorporate 2 tablespoons of good quality Jamaican rum to the cold pastry cream (**6**). You can use other liquors such as Grand Marnier, Cointreau or Kirsh to flavor the cream.

For chocolate pastry cream
◆ Add 3 tablespoons of unsweetened cocoa passed through a sieve (**7**) to the warm pastry cream. Or add 2 tablespoons of finely grated unsweetened chocolate and stir to blend perfectly.

For almond, pistachio or hazelnut pastry cream
◆ Scald 3/4 cup of almonds in boiling water. Drain and cool. Peel the almonds and toast them in the oven at 375°F for a few minutes. Finely chop them and stir into the cold pastry cream (**8**). To prepare a pistachio or hazelnut cream, the ground pistachios or hazelnuts can be incorporated to the cold cream.
◆ You can also add chopped praline hazelnuts or almonds (see page 21) to the pastry cream.

For coffee pastry cream
◆ Melt 1 teaspoon of coffee in the warm milk and prepare the pastry cream with the coffee-flavored milk

For fruit flavored pastry cream
◆ Mix 1/2 cup of fruit jam into the cold pastry cream (**9**) or stir in chopped fresh fruits (or wild berries) soaked in a little sugar and lemon juice.

Crème Anglaise

Time needed: *20 minutes*

INGREDIENTS FOR 6 SERVINGS
1 cup of milk

1 cup of heavy cream
6 egg yolks
3/4 cup of sugar
1 vanilla bean

◆ Bring milk and cream to a boil with 1/2 sugar and split vanilla bean. In another saucepan, whisk the egg yolks and the remaining sugar until frothy; add the milk and cream mixture slowly. Discard the vanilla bean.
◆ Put the saucepan on low heat and, whisking, bring almost to boil without ever letting it boil. If, by error, the mixture would start to boil and separate, add 1 teaspoon of cornstarch. Remove from heat, pass through a sieve and let it cool completely, stirring from time to time

Zabaglione

Time needed: *20 minutes*

INGREDIENTS FOR 4 SERVINGS
4 egg yolks

1/2 cup of Marsala
2 tablespoons of dry white wine
4 tablespoons of sugar

◆ In a bowl, whisk the egg yolks with the sugar until pale, thick and creamy (**1**). Stir in the Marsala and the wine; pour into a heavy saucepan (or better, a clean copper bowl or saucepan).
◆ Cook the cream in a double boiler, on low heat, whisking constantly. Make sure the preparation never boils. Whisk until mixture becomes thick and has doubled in volume (**2**).
◆ Pour the zabaglione immediately into individual serving bowls.
◆ Zabaglione can be prepared using only Marsala, or a rich red wine, or a different wine (Vinsanto,

Butter creams

Butter creams are best for covering and decorating a cake. They can be replaced by lighter preparations or mousse but, for spectacular results, nothing can replace them.

Nota bene
Butter creams can be flavored with vanilla, chocolate, citrus extracts, or liquors.

Port, Madeira, Malaga) or even with champagne. If you wish to prepare it with alcohol like Cognac, Whisky or rum, use 3 tablespoons of alcohol and 3 tablespoons of dry white wine.

For cold zabaglione
◆ If you wish to serve the zabaglione cold, pour it into a bowl and mix until completely cool. At that point, mix in a few tablespoons of unsweetened whipped cream.

Butter cream

Time needed: *30 minutes*

INGREDIENTS FOR 2 CUPS OF CREAM
1/2 lb of unsalted butter
1/2 cup of sugar
3 egg whites
a pinch of salt

◆ Soften the unsalted butter at room temperature.
◆ In a bowl, mix the egg whites and salt. Add 1 tablespoon of sugar and beat, with an electric mixer, for 2-3 minutes to stiff peaks.
◆ In a saucepan, bring to boil the sugar and 1 teaspoon of water; cook for 6-7 minutes. Delicately add it to the egg whites (**2**), beating slowly with the electric mixer. Continue mixing until mixture is cold.
◆ At this point, add the butter (cut in small pieces), mixing with a whisk (**3**) until the cream is smooth.

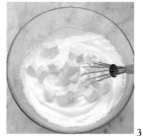

Classic coffee butter cream
Dissolve 1 tablespoon of instant expresso in 1 tablespoon of hot milk; whisk into the butter cream.

Classic chocolate butter cream
In a bain-marie, melt half a cup of chopped bittersweet chocolate and mix with the butter cream.

Cold butter cream

Time needed: *20 minutes*

INGREDIENTS FOR A BOUT 2 CUPS OF CREAM
8 tablespoons of unsalted butter
1 cup of powdered sugar
1/2 teaspoon of vanilla

◆ Soften the unsalted butter to room temperature.
◆ In a bowl, whisk the butter until creamy. Always whisking, slowly incorporate the vanilla and the sugar, a little at a time.
◆ This cream can be flavored by adding 2 teaspoons of any liquor or coffee or 2 tablespoons of melted chocolate or chestnut purée.

French butter cream

Time needed: *30 minutes*

INGREDIENTS FOR 4 CUPS OF BUTTER CREAM
1/2 lb of unsalted butter
3 egg yolks
a few drops of vanilla
1/2 cup of sugar

◆ Soften the butter, bringing it to room temperature.
◆ In a saucepan, bring to boil the sugar with 1 teaspoon of water and let cook for 7 minutes.
◆ In a bowl, whisk egg yolks with an electric mixer. Slowly mix in the sugar syrup at little at a time. Add the vanilla and continue to whisk until the mixture is cool.
◆ In another bowl, whip the butter with the electric mixer until creamy. Stir into the egg preparation. Add flavoring to taste.

Nota bene
The fresher and cold the cream, the easier it will be to whip it. It is also better to use a stainless steel bowl set in the freezer for at least 20 minutes. You can also beat cream in a stainless steel bowl set over a large bowl filled with ice cubes.

How to store it
The ganache can be kept in the refrigerator for several days, covered with plastic wrap. Before using it, bring it to room temperature.

Chantilly

Time needed: *10 minutes*

INGREDIENTS FOR ABOUT 2 CUPS OF CREAM
1 cup of whipping cream
2 tablespoons of powdered sugar
1 teaspoon of vanilla

◆ Put a stainless steel bowl in the freezer for 20 minutes.
◆ Pour the cold whipping cream into the cold bowl. Whisk the cream and vanilla with an electric mixer, slowly adding the sugar, until it forms stiff peaks. Keep refrigerated.

Ganache

Time needed: *30 minutes*

INGREDIENTS FOR ABOUT 4 CUPS
1 lb of bittersweet chocolate
1 1/2 cup of whipping cream
4 tablespoons of butter

◆ Chop the chocolate and melt in a double boiler, with the butter cut in pieces. Remove from heat and set aside to cool. Beat the cream to soft peaks and delicately mix into the melted chocolate.
◆ Another way to make ganache is to melt the chocolate with the butter in the cream. Set aside to cool and whip until the mixture is cold and thick.

Brazilian cream

Time needed: *20 minutes*

INGREDIENTS FOR ABOUT 3 CUPS OF CREAM
3 ripe bananas ◆ *1 1/2 cups of whipped cream*
1/2 cup of Maraschino
1/2 cup of powdered sugar

◆ Put a stainless steel bowl in the freezer for 20 minutes.
◆ Pour the cream and sugar into the cold bowl; whip with an electric mixer to stiff peaks. Refrigerate.
◆ Peel the bananas, slice them and purée in a food processor with the Maraschino. Delicately fold the banana purée into the whipped cream. Refrigerate until ready to use.
◆ This Brazilian cream can be used to fill tartlets.

Vanilla sauce

Time needed: *20 minutes*

INGREDIENTS FOR 4 SERVINGS
*1 cup of milk ◆ 3 egg yolks
1/2 cup of sugar
1 vanilla bean*

◆ In a saucepan, bring milk and split vanilla bean to boil.
◆ In a bowl, stir the egg yolks and the sugar with a wooden spoon until well blended (**1**). It is better to not use a whisk: You would get a frothy mixture and the foam would make it difficult to control the cooking of the sauce. Remove the vanilla bean and slowly incorporate the milk into the egg yolks (**2**).
◆ Return the preparation to the saucepan and cook on low heat. Bring it almost to boil (do not let it boil), stirring until the sauce coats the wooden spoon (**3**). Remove from the heat and pour into a bowl, through a sieve. Sprinkle with 1 teaspoon of sugar and set aside to cool.

Hazelnut sauce
◆ In a food processor, grind 1/2 cup of praline hazelnuts and mix into the cold vanilla sauce.

Almond sauce
◆ Lightly toast 1/2 cup of almonds and peel them. In a food processor, mix to a paste with 1 teaspoon of sugar. Mix into the cold vanilla sauce.

Sauces are used to accompany pies, cakes, puddings, soufflés and ice creams.

How to store them
Vanilla and chocolate sauces can be kept refrigerated for a few days, in closed airtight containers. Fruit sauces can also be kept a few days in the refrigerator or in a freezer for up to 2 months, closed in airtight containers. To thaw, bring to room temperature or leave in refrigerator overnight.

Caramel
In a saucepan, melt 1/2 cup of sugar in 2 tablespoon of water. Cover and cook it on low heat. When it starts to color, remove the cover and stir with a wooden spoon until caramel is smooth. To get a darker caramel, simply cook a few more minutes; this will also develop a more bitter flavor. Be careful not to burn the caramel, which would give the sauce an unpleasant bitter taste

Walnut sauce
◆ In a double boiler, melt 1/2 cup of grated bittersweet chocolate. Finely chop 1/2 cup of walnuts. Stir the melted chocolate and the chopped walnuts into the vanilla sauce until well blended.

Rum sauce
◆ Add 2 tablespoons of a good Jamaican rum to the cold vanilla sauce.

Coffee sauce
◆ To the hot vanilla sauce, add 1/2 cup of espresso coffee or 1 tablespoon of instant coffee.

Caramel cream sauce

Time needed: *20 minutes*

INGREDIENTS FOR 4 SERVINGS
*1/2 cup of sugar
1/2 cup of heavy cream*

◆ In a saucepan with high sides, cook sugar with 1 tablespoon of water (**1**) on low heat until it becomes golden (see photo).
◆ Remove from heat and very slowly add the cream (**2**), rapidly stirring with a wooden spoon (**3**).
◆ Return the saucepan to low heat and stir until caramel is completely melted.
◆ Set aside to cool.

Caramel sauce (variation)

Time needed: *30 minutes*

INGREDIENTS FOR 4 SERVINGS

1/2 cup of milk ◆ *3 egg yolks*
3 tablespoons of sugar
1/2 teaspoon of cornstarch
1/2 teaspoon of vanilla

Syrup:
3 tablespoons of sugar

◆ In a saucepan, mix the egg yolks and the sugar with a wooden spoon. Add the cornstarch, vanilla and the warm milk a little at a time. Stir until all ingredients are blended. On medium heat, bring the mixture just to boil. Remove from heat and cool the sauce, stirring from time to time.
◆ For the caramel syrup: In a saucepan, melt the sugar in 1 tablespoon of water. Cook until caramel is golden. Remove from heat and set aside to cool lightly. Add 1/2 cup of water and melt the caramel on medium heat. Stir this caramel into the egg preparation until blended.

Chocolate sauce

Time needed: *15 minutes*

INGREDIENTS FOR 6 SERVINGS

1/2 lb of bittersweet chocolate
2 tablespoons of butter
5 tablespoons of heavy cream
3/4 cup of milk

◆ Chop chocolate and melt in a double boiler with butter. Whisk in milk and heavy cream; bring to a boil, remove from heat and cool.

Chocolate sauce (variation)

Time needed: *15 minutes*

INGREDIENTS FOR 6 SERVINGS
2 cups of milk
1/4 lb of bittersweet chocolate
1/4 cup of sugar
2 tablespoons of potato starch

Cooking sugar

While cooking, sugar passes through different stages. The most important ones are: the thread (when liquid sugar may be pulled into brittle threads between the fingers); pearl (when the thread formed by pulling liquid sugar between fingers may be stretched); soft ball (when syrup dropped in ice water may be formed into an elastic ball which flattens on removal from water); hard ball (when syrup dropped into ice water may be formed into a hard ball which holds its shape when removed from water when sugar reaches 244 to 250°F); and caramel, when the liquefied sugar turns golden, and then brown.

How to temper chocolate

Tempering is necessary when melted chocolate has not been mixed with cream, butter or other ingredients, in order to keep its glossy sheen.
Melt chocolate in a double boiler until it reaches no more than 120°F (always use a thermometer). Transfer saucepan onto a bowl filled with ice cubes. Cool to 70°F for milk and dark chocolate and 72°F for white chocolate. Return to heat on the double boiler and bring to 90°F for milk and bittersweet chocolate and to 85°F for white chocolate.
Tempered chocolate is used to cover cakes and pastries, and in the preparation of individual chocolates

◆ Dissolve the potato starch in 1/3 of the milk. In a saucepan, melt the chocolate and sugar in the remaining milk.
◆ On low heat, bring the mixture to a boil and add the dissolved potato starch. Cook on low heat for 2 minutes, stirring.

Strawberry sauce (or other fruit)

Time needed: *15 minutes*

INGREDIENTS FOR 4 SERVINGS
1 lb of strawberries
juice of 1/2 lemon
1/2 cup of sugar

◆ Rinse the strawberries, dry them and slice them. In a saucepan, mix the strawberries, the sugar and the lemon juice. Cook for 6-7 minutes on medium heat. Set aside to cool.
◆ In a food processor, mix the preparation until you have a thick sauce with tiny pieces of strawberry.
◆ Instead of strawberries, you can use raspberries, peaches or apricots for a delicious sauce.

Pralined hazelnuts

Time needed: *30 minutes*

INGREDIENTS FOR 4 SERVINGS
1/2 cup of hazelnuts
1/2 cup of sugar
1 tablespoon of almond oil

◆ In an oven, preheated at 375°F, toast the hazelnuts for 3 minutes. Transfer them to a kitchen towel and rub to remove the skin.
◆ In a saucepan, melt the sugar in 4 tablespoons of water (**1**) and bring it to boil on moderate heat. Cook for 6-7 minutes until it reaches 240°F (control this with a sugar thermometer). Remove from oven and add the hazelnuts (**2**); rapidly mix until hazelnuts are covered by a grainy substance (**3**).
◆ Return to stove and, on medium heat, melt the caramel (**4**). Brush a cookie sheet or a marble slab with the almond oil. Pour the hazelnut mixture on the slab. Separate all hazelnuts from each others with a fork. Set aside to cool.

Pralines and brittles

Pralines
Making pralines is basically dipping almonds, hazelnuts or walnuts into a thick sugar syrup. This layer of sandy sugar keeps the nuts separated.

Pralined nuts can be kept in a dry cool place. It should not be refrigerated for it will become sticky, but it can be frozen.

Brittles
Almonds, hazelnuts, nuts, pistachios or pine nuts are not dipped but cooked in the sugar without any water added. When caramelized, the sugar coats the nuts and forms a compact mass. It is then transferred to an oiled marble slab. This chopped brittle can be mixed into creams, ice creams or cake batters.

Brittles should be kept in a dry cool place. Do not refrigerate or it will become sticky. It can be frozen.

Pralined almonds
◆ Replace the hazelnuts by 1/2 cup of almonds. Scald for a few seconds in boiling water, peel and toast in a preheated oven at 375°F. Use as the hazelnuts.

Almond or hazelnut brittle

Time needed: *40 minutes*

INGREDIENTS FOR 6 SERVINGS
2 cups of almonds or hazelnuts
1 cup of sugar
1 teaspoon of lemon juice
2 teaspoons of almond oil

◆ Scald the almonds in boiling water for a few minutes, peel them and dry them in an oven preheated at 350°F. Coarsely chop the almonds (**1**) and shake them in a colander (**2**) to eliminate any dust or powder.
◆ In a saucepan, melt the sugar in lemon juice until golden. Remove from heat and add the chopped

almonds **(3)**. Return to the heat. Stir with a wooden spoon until the sugar is caramelized again. If you cook too long, you will have a darker and bitter caramel.

◆ Brush a marble surface (or a cookie sheet) with 1/2 the almond oil. Pour the preparation on the surface; turn and fold it with a spatula **(4)** to cool it, preventing the sugar from falling at the bottom. Oil the surface again and spread the mixture quickly with an oiled rolling pin. Cut the almond brittle with a sharp knife or with cookie cutters **(5)**.

Royal icing

Time needed: *5 minutes*

INGREDIENTS FOR COVERING
ONE MEDIUM-SIZE CAKE
*1 cup of powdered sugar
1 egg white
a few drops of lemon juice*

◆ In a bowl, mix the egg white and the lemon juice **(1)**. Add the sifted powdered sugar a little at a time **(2)**. Whisk until mixture is smooth, creamy and dense.

◆ On waxed paper, design with a pencil the decorative shapes you need. Cover the drawings with icing and set aside to harden. Remove the waxed paper delicately and decorate the cakes **(3)**.

Icing
Water-based icing is the easiest to do and is used when you want a light transparent coating to cover or decorate a savarin, a baba, a donut or a cake, on which you sprinkle colored sugar. If you want this icing to be white, the coated cake or pastry should be placed in a hot oven for 2-3 minutes; drying, the icing becomes white.

When a cake requires a thicker and richer icing, royal icing is ideal. Easy to make, it can be colored using natural colorant. It is also used to make different types of cake decorations.

Fondant
Fondant is used to cover donuts and petits-fours. Unlike icing, it can be kept refrigerated for a long time, covered with a humid towel or plastic wrap. Before using, slightly reheat the fondant on very low heat with a few drops of sugar syrup and work it until it becomes smooth and shiny.

If you do not have a sugar thermometer, you can use the old method of the "soft ball." Dip a skewer in boiling sugar, dip your fingers in ice water and work sugar between fingers. If you can make a sugar ball that is elastic, the sugar temperature probably reached 240°F.

Water-based icing

Time needed: *5 minutes*

INGREDIENTS TO COVER
ONE MEDIUM-SIZE CAKE
*1 1/2 cups of powdered sugar
2 tablespoons of water*

◆ In a bowl, sift the powdered sugar over the water, a little at a time. Stir until mixture is smooth and creamy.

Fondant

Time needed: *45 minutes*

INGREDIENTS ENOUGH
TO DECORATE A CAKE OR
SMALL CAKES FOR **8** SERVINGS

1 1/2 cups of sugar ◆ *1/2 cup of corn syrup
1/2 cup of water* ◆ *a little almond oil*

◆ In a saucepan, mix the sugar, the water and the corn syrup. Cook until it reaches 220°F. Use a sugar thermometer for exact temperatures. Clean the sides of the saucepan with a wooden spatula, so the sugar does not caramelize. The syrup should remain clear.

◆ Brush a marble work surface (marble is essential with almond oil). Pour the syrup on the marble **(1)** and stir it with a spatula until it becomes white, soft and smooth **(2, 3)**. Work into a ball

and transfer to a bowl; cover it with a humid kitchen cloth or plastic wrap to prevent drying **(4)**.

Coffee fondant
◆ On low heat, dissolve 1 tablespoon of instant coffee in 1 teaspoon of sugar syrup and add it to the white fondant. Work with the spatula until fondant is soft and smooth. It may be necessary to dilute it with a little sugar syrup.

Chocolate fondant
◆ In a double boiler, melt 1/2 cup of chopped bittersweet chocolate. Delicately stir into the white fondant, a little at a time. If necessary, dilute it with a little sugar. Work the mixture until smooth and soft with a matte glow.

Hazelnut paste

Time needed: *30 minutes*

INGREDIENTS FOR 1/2 LB OF PASTE

1 lb of shelled hazelnuts ◆ *1 cup of sugar*

◆ Preheat the oven to 375°F.
◆ Place the hazelnuts on a cookie sheet and put in the preheated oven for 10 minutes until light-

Marzipan and hazelnut paste

Fondant can be colored for decoration: make it pink with a few drops of alchermes, yellow with orange liquor, green with mint extract.

Before covering a cake with fondant, always brush it with melted strained apricot jam.

Marzipan
Almond paste, or marzipan, is often used to cover cakes and small pastries, to flavor creams or fillings and to decorate. It can be found ready made in most fine food shops. Marzipan can be colored with alchermes, mint liquor, saffron, ground pistachios, etc. Homemade almond paste always has more taste since it generally contains less sugar, thus permeating more of the almond flavors.

Before spreading the almond paste with a rolling pin, you must always dust your work surface with powdered sugar.

Since marzipan tends to dry out rather quickly, it should be kept in a cool place. Covered in plastic wrap, it can be stored for a few weeks. It can also be frozen with excellent results.

Hazelnut paste
Easy to prepare, it is used to flavor creams, ice creams, cakes and custards. Hazelnut paste has a more delicate taste than almond paste. It can be kept, refrigerated, for up to 2 weeks in an airtight container. It can also be frozen for a few months.

ly toasted. While still hot, rub the hazelnuts with a towel to eliminate the skin.
◆ In a food processor, grind hazelnuts and mix with the sugar until the oil is released from the hazelnuts and the mixture turns into a smooth paste.

Marzipan or almond paste

Time needed: *45 minutes*

INGREDIENTS FOR 1 LB OF PASTE
1 lb of shelled almonds
1/2 cup of powdered sugar
1 egg white

◆ Preheat the oven at 350°F.
◆ Scald the almonds in boiling water for 5 minutes. Drain, peel and transfer to a cookie sheet. Place in the oven for 5 minutes to dry them without toasting.
◆ In a food processor, grind the almonds to a powder. Add sugar. In a bowl, beat the egg whites to stiff peaks and blend in the almond-sugar mixture a little at a time.
◆ Mix until all ingredients are blended and paste is smooth. Pass this thick paste in a pasta machine to roll out a thin layer of paste (you can also roll it with a rolling pin).

Raw meringue, ready to bake

Time needed: *20 minutes*

INGREDIENTS TO COVER AN 8-INCH CAKE
3/4 cup of egg whites
1/2 cup of sugar
a few drops of lemon juice
grated peel of 1/2 orange
1 teaspoon of powdered sugar
a pinch of salt

◆ In a large bowl, lightly beat the egg whites. Stir in salt and lemon juice (1). With an electric mixer, whisk at high speed to soft peaks. Add the sugar (2) and the grated orange peel (3). Continue beating to firm peaks.
◆ Transfer the mixture to a large pastry bag, fitted with a star tube. On the ready-to-serve cake, pipe out rosettes of meringue to cover the whole cake. Sprinkle with the sifted powdered sugar (4) and bake it in the preheated oven, at the highest temperature possible, until golden (5).

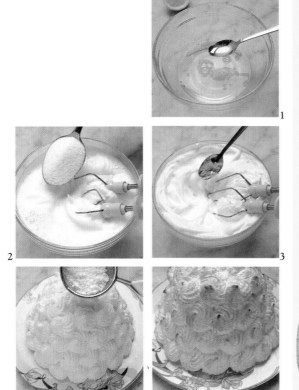

Nota bene
Recipes for classic meringue, baking meringues or Italian meringues, all have one ingredient on which they depend: egg whites. And the secret to fluffy and perfectly stable beaten egg whites is their freshness. They should also be separated without a trace of egg yolk, preferably at room temperature and mixed in a glass or ceramic bowl for optimum results.

Any fat substance is a foam inhibitor and will keep the egg whites from becoming stiff. Plastic bowls should never be used for meringue. For faster results, it is preferable to use an electric mixer (a classic whisk can also be used). Most recipes call for the addition of a pinch of salt, although salt will decrease the foam stability; but, it is not necessary.

Italian meringue is prepared with sugar syrup, and used in the preparation of butter creams or for icing small pies or cakes.

How to store it
Once completely cold, meringues can be kept for a week in a covered metal bowl. If used to cover or decorate a cake, it is better to use the meringue as soon as it is whipped.

Italian meringue

Time needed: *20 minutes*

INGREDIENTS TO COVER A CAKE OR PIE
FOR **6** SERVINGS
1/2 cup of egg whites
1/2 cup of sugar
a pinch of salt

◆ In a saucepan, heat 2/3 of sugar in a teaspoon of water (1), brushing the sides of the saucepan to remove any sugar crystals (2). Check sugar syrup temperature with a sugar thermometer. When it reaches 248°F, remove from the heat.

◆ Beat the egg whites with the salt and remain-

ing sugar. Add the sugar syrup in a steady stream (3), beating at a high speed until the mixture is cool and thick (4).

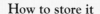

Meringue

Time needed: *30 minutes*

INGREDIENTS FOR **50** SMALL MERINGUES
3 egg whites
a pinch of salt
a few drops of lemon juice
1 teaspoon of vanilla
3/4 cup of sugar

◆ Line two large cookie sheets with parchment paper. Preheat the oven to 225°F.
◆ With an electric mixer, beat the egg whites until foamy. Add the salt, the vanilla and the lemon juice; beat to soft peaks. Add the sugar, one spoon at a time, and continue beating at the same speed for 1 minute between each spoonful. Continue beating until stiff and glossy peaks form.
◆ Transfer meringue in a pastry bag, fitted with a star tube and pipe out small rosettes onto the lined cookie sheets, leaving 1/2 inch between each rosette.
◆ Transfer cookie sheets to oven, lower heat to 200°F and dry the meringue for 1 1/2 hours or until meringue can easily be removed from the baking sheet. Transfer to a rack and cool.

Meringue circles
◆ Put meringue preparation in a pastry bag, fitted with a straight tube. On a lined cookie sheet, pipe out in concentric circles and spread lightly with a spatula. Dry in the oven at 200°F for 1 1/2 hours.

Nota bene
Fruit compotes are not to be confused with jams and marmalades. In marmalades, fruits are puréed. In jams, fruits are used sliced or whole. And in both cases the fruits are cooked for a long time. Compotes, on the other hand, are prepared by boiling pieces of fruit in a sugar syrup for a short time. This leaves the flavors of the fruit intact. Dried fruits must be soaked in warm water for 1 hour before being cooked in syrup.
Avoid using aluminum pans to make compotes; they seem to give an unpleasant taste to the fruits. Compotes are used for pies, tarts or cake fillings or even as a sauce.

How to store it
Melon or strawberry compotes can be kept in covered glass jars, in the refrigerator for up to 2 days.

Melon compote

Time needed: *30 minutes*

INGREDIENTS FOR ABOUT **8** CUPS OF COMPOTE
2 lb of peeled melon
1 cup of sugar
juice of 1/2 lemon

◆ Slice the peeled lemon and chop in large cubes **(1)**. In a bowl, marinate the melon in the lemon juice and the sugar for 30 minutes, stirring occasionally.
◆ In a saucepan, cook the melons **(2)** for 5 minutes, on medium heat. Set aside to cool completely. Transfer the compote to a glass jar or in a bowl, covered with plastic wrap.

Apple compote

Time needed: *30 minutes*

INGREDIENTS FOR ABOUT **8** CUPS OF COMPOTE
2 lb of apples
3/4 cup of water
juice and grated peel of 1/2 lemon
1 cup of sugar

◆ Rinse and peel the apples, core and cut in small cubes. In a bowl, soak the apples in the lemon juice. In a saucepan, bring the sugar and the water to boil. Add grated lemon peel and apples. Cook for 15 minutes, stirring occasionally with a wooden spoon.
◆ Set the compote aside to cool. Transfer to a bowl and cover with plastic wrap. This compote can be kept, refrigerated, covered, for 2 to 3 days.

Strawberry compote

Time needed: *20 minutes*

INGREDIENTS FOR ABOUT 8 CUPS OF COMPOTE

2 lbs of strawberries ◆ *1 1/2 cups of sugar*
juice of 1 lemon ◆ *1 1/2 cups of water*

◆ In a saucepan, bring sugar and water to a rolling boil, and cook for 5 minutes.
◆ Rinse strawberries in ice water, dry and remove stems. Slice large strawberries **(1)**, halve or leave small strawberries whole. Mix strawberries in boiling syrup **(2)**. Cook for 5 minutes, add the lemon juice and continue cooking for 5 minutes. Cool in the saucepan or in a serving bowl.

Quince jelly

Time needed: *30 minutes*
(plus marinating time)

INGREDIENTS

4 lbs of ripe quince
sugar ◆ *juice of 1/2 lemon*

◆ Rinse the quince, slice in half, core and chop in large cubes. Wrap the quince in cheese cloth, place in a saucepan and cover them with cold water.
◆ Cook on medium heat until quince are soft and let them marinate in cooking liquid overnight.
◆ Pour the marinating liquid in a bowl; press the quince in its cheesecloth to extract as much juice as possible. Discard the quince. Weigh the juice and add the same weight in sugar; add the lemon juice.
◆ In a stainless steel saucepan, cook the mixture skimming often for 10 minutes or until it becomes gelatinous.

Fruit jellies

Fruit jellies are used often in desserts. They are used to brush cakes before covering them with almond paste, fondant or candied fruits; they are brushed on the bottom of pie crusts to protect from humidity; brushed on fresh fruits to keep them from darkening, and to make them shinier, more appetizing.

Nota bene
The best fruits to make jelly are those with a high quantity of natural pectin, an organic agent present in raspberries, blueberries, strawberries, quince, blackberries, apples and other fruits.

For cooking fruits, always use stainless steel bowls and pans; never use aluminum pans.

How to store jelly
Fruit jellies should be poured hot in clean, dry, hot jars. Close with airtight covers, turn upside down a few minutes, return to normal position and cool completely. Jars of jelly should be kept in cool, dry places.

Raspberry jelly

Time needed: *20 minutes*
(plus time to press juices)

INGREDIENTS

2 lbs of raspberries ◆ *3 1/3 cups of sugar*
1 cup of water

◆ Rinse raspberries in ice water, dry and place in a stainless steel saucepan. Add sugar **(1)** and water **(2)**.
◆ Place a cheese cloth over a large bowl. Pour in the raspberry mixture **(3)**. Let the mixture in the cheese cloth pass its juices, through a sieve suspended over the bowl **(4)**, for 12 hours. Press and wring the cloth to press out any remaining juices.
◆ Return the juice to a saucepan and cook on moderate heat for 10 minutes, skimming the top often until the mixture becomes gelatinous. It should read 220°F. If you do not have a sugar thermometer, you can pour a teaspoon of mixture on a plate to verify the density **(5)**.
◆ Pour the hot gelatin in a clean, dry, hot glass jar **(6)**. Close with airtight lids and set aside to cool. Store in a cool and dry place.

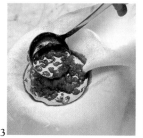

Light candied fruit

Time needed: *20 minutes*
(plus macerating time)

INGREDIENTS
1 lb of citrus fruits (oranges, lemons)
1/2 cup of sugar
3/4 cup of water

◆ Rinse and dry the fruits. In a saucepan, bring the water and the sugar to a boil; cook for 2 minutes.
◆ Cut the oranges and the lemons in thin slices **(1)**, transfer to a bowl and cover with the boiling syrup **(2)**. Let macerate for 6 hours.
◆ For the candied zest, remove strips of citrus peel in fine julienne **(3)**, transfer to a bowl and proceed as indicated before.
◆ For zest spirals, remove strips of citrus peel in fine julienne, turn around metallic tubes and place in a large dish. Cover with the boiling syrup **(4)** and proceed as indicated before.
◆ After 6 hours of maceration, drain the citrus slices, zest or spirals. Place on a kitchen towel and give it any decorative form you like.

Light candying softens and sweetens fruits and fruit peel. The light sugar syrup keeps the bright and brilliant color of the fruits. Classic candying prepares the fruit peel for cake decoration or for fillings.

Nota bene
Candied fruit peel can be bought in specialty shops. Home-made ones are softer and have a more delicate taste. Always use organic fruit, brush them under running water and dry carefully before using them.

How to store
Lightly candied fruits can be kept refrigerated for a few days in their syrup. Classic candied fruits can be kept for several months in a cool dry place, in their syrup or, drained, in jars.

Classic candied fruit

Time needed: *40 minutes*

INGREDIENTS
5 oranges
5 lemons
3/4 cup sugar
1/2 cup water

◆ Rinse and dry the fruits. With a sharp potato peeler, remove the strips of peel **(1)**. Cut the peel in thin julienne strips or any other shapes **(2)**. Place in a saucepan, covered with cold water, and bring to a boil. Drain. Repeat this operation two more times to eliminate the bitterness.
◆ Return the drained peels to a saucepan with the sugar and 1/2 cup of water **(3)**. Bring to boil on moderate heat and cook for 20 minutes, stirring constantly. Remove from the heat when the peels are bright and shiny, and the liquid is almost completely evaporated.
◆ Drain **(4)**. Separate the peels and place on a rack to dry.

Sugar syrup

◆ Sugar syrup, used to soak biscuits, cakes and charlottes is generally made of 50% sugar, 40% water and 10% liquor. The most commonly used syrups are made with Grand Marnier, Maraschino or rum.
◆ In a saucepan, melt the sugar in the water, remove from the heat, skim and stir the liquor in.

Preparation of molds and pans

◆ Preparing a pan to bake a simple cake is easy enough : If you are using a springform pan, grease it and flour it. If you are using a classic cake pan, it is better to grease it, line it with parchment paper to be greased again, floured. It is most important to line the bottom of the pan; the sides can be greased only. When the cake is cooked, pass a knife around the edges of the cake and turn it onto a rack.

◆ Some desserts - pies, quiches or zuccotti - need to be baked in filled cooked pastry doughs.

◆ Quiches and pies require a pate brisée or puff pastry base. Line a pie dish with a thin sheet of dough, prick with the tip of a fork, cover with the filling and bake in a preheated oven.

◆ If the pie base needs to be precooked, line the pie dish, prick and cover with parchment paper, covered with beans, and bake in a preheated oven at 350°F for about 20 minutes. Remove from the oven; discard the beans and the paper. Brush the hot pie crust with a beaten egg white and then cover with filling.

◆ For zuccotti or charlottes, the molds will be lined with savoyard cookies or a sponge cake.

Lining a pan with sponge cake

◆ To line a 4- to 6-cup zuccotto mold, you will need 1 lb of sponge cake. The sponge cake should be baked 1 or 2 days before assembling so that it will not crumble when sliced. Slice it vertically in 1/2 inch thick pieces (1).
◆ Use the longest pieces to line the middle of the mold the shortest for the sides (2). Brush the sponge cake with sugar syrup, pour filling in cavity and top with the remaining sponge cake to close.

Peeling citrus fruits
Many recipes ask to peel the citrus fruits. This means to remove all peel, including the bitter white pith beneath the skin and even to remove all skin between fruit segments. This easy operation is suited when citrus fruits are to be used in fruit salads or to decorate. It should be done over a large bowl to pick up any juices.

Peeling almonds, hazelnuts and pistachios
*To peel almonds, scald them in boiling water for a few minutes. Drain and peel them. Place the almonds on a cookie sheet and dry them in a preheated oven, without letting them turn gold.
To peel hazelnuts, place them on a cookie sheet and toast in a preheated oven. Remove and immediately scrub in a clean kitchen towel to remove the skins.
To peel pistachios, scald them in boiling water for 2 minutes. Drain, peel and dry them in the oven for a few minutes only.*

All nuts can be kept in airtight glass jars.

Lining a mold with biscuit

◆ For a 4-cup zuccotto mold, you will need 2 circles of biscuit. These should be baked just before using them so it is elastic, or prepared the day before and covered with plastic wrap.
◆ In the first circle, cut off 1/4 (1). Place the cut circle in the mold, pressing to make it stick to the mold and bring the cut sides together (2). Pour the filling in and close top with other circle.

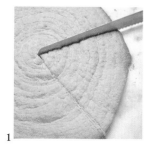

1   2

Lining a mold with savoyard cookies

◆ With a sharp knife, remove 1 rounded edge of cookies. Slice some cookies in triangles, the length of 1/2 diameter of the mold bottom (1). Place the sliced cookies in the bottom of the mold in sections (2). Place long cookies around the sides (3) and slice off the extremities (4). Pour the filling into the mold and close with remaining cookies.

1   2

3   4

1   2

Lining a pan with chocolate

◆ Puddings, ice creams and mousses can be attractively served in a chocolate case or box.

◆ Prepare a circle of parchment or wax paper to line the bottom of a pan. Prepare a long strip of parchment or wax paper to line the sides.

◆ Use a springform pan; brush the bottom and the sides of the pan with butter. Carefully line the bottom and the sides with the prepared paper.

◆ In a double boiler, melt 1 cup of grated chocolate. Brush all the interiors of the pan with 1/2 of the melted chocolate (1), carefully covering the paper with a thin coat.

1   2

◆ Place the pan in a refrigerator until the chocolate is solid. Brush with the remaining melted chocolate and return to the refrigerator. When the chocolate is firm, cold and solid, delicately open the springform pan. Remove the chocolate base and carefully discard the paper (2).

Baking

◆ Electric ovens are preferable to get the best results when baking. A good gas oven can also be used but in any case, if you are not sure that your oven maintains the indicated temperature, control it with an inexpensive tool: a portable oven thermometer.

◆ The first important step, when baking, is that the oven must be at the required temperature before putting the cake in. Cake batters do not wait and will not raise properly if the oven is not hot enough. In most recipes, the necessary temperature of the oven is indicated at the beginning of the recipe, in order to get ready.

◆ While baking, it is better to not open the oven door. When necessary, it is better to do it quickly and without slamming the door.

Whipping cream
Pour the cold whipping cream into a very cold bowl (left in the freezer for 15 minutes). If the bowl is not cold, place it on a larger bowl filled with ice cubes. Cream can be beaten with or without the addition of sugar. Slowly beat the cream with an electric mixer, slowly raising the speed, until it forms firm peaks. Be careful not to overheat or the cream will turn to butter. Refrigerate until ready to use.

Beating egg whites
Egg whites are beaten with a pinch of salt, at room temperature, in a round bottom bowl. The bowl can be stainless steel or copper, but never of plastic. Bowl and whisk or beaters should be absolutely clean. Egg whites need to be free of any trace of egg yolk.

The beaten egg whites are delicately folded into the batter or other preparations, a little at a time.

Raisins
When added to a cake batter, raisins need to be soaked in warm water or liquor, drained, dried and passed in flour. This will prevent them from falling to the bottom of the pan during the baking.

Cooking with a bain-marie

◆ Bain-marie is an ingenious way to bake. The batter is poured into a pan, itself placed in boiling water. You do not need special pans to do this: The cake pan can be placed in another pan, slightly larger, filled with boiling water. The level of water must reach half of the batter-filled pan.

Deep frying

◆ To deep-fry pastries, peanut oil is generally used. It is better to use a pan with high sides so the dough is completely immersed and the boiling oil does not splatter all over. For best results, the oil should be very hot, otherwise the results would be a heavy and soft dough, and not light and crispy as desired.

Slicing cakes

◆ Slicing a cake in several layers to spread with filling is not very difficult. Place cake on parchment paper, to be able to turn cake easily. With a long serrated knife, slice off layers, starting at the top of the cake. Place layers one next to the other on work surface, to spread the filling.

Filling

◆ Start with the layer that is the least perfect (generally the top layer). Place it on a serving plate, with the sliced part on top. Spread with a layer of filling. Cover with another layer of cake and a layer of filling and so on. Top with the last layer, sliced side down and cover the entire cake with the cream or icing, spreading it with a spatula.

Main ingredients

Citrus. It is common to use the peel and the juice of citrus fruits in dessert recipes. When the peel is used, it is important to use only untreated organic fruits, since any chemicals used on citrus tend to concentrate on the peel. Aromatic essence comes from the colored part of the peel (yellow for lemons, orange for oranges, green for limes). It is necessary to carefully slice the peel and discard any white pith.

Butter. Generally, butter is composed of 80% fat and 20% water. Do not replace butter in baking, for it gives a delicate taste and lightness to all preparation. Butter should be very fresh. Keep it refrigerated, wrapped for up to 2 weeks or frozen for up to 3 months.

Cocoa. Powdered cocoa is one of the purest forms a chocolate: 1/2 of its cocoa butter has been removed. For baking, use the Dutch-processed cocoa, which has a mellow flavor and is more soluble.

Chestnuts. Chestnuts are sweet and floury. Often used in pastries, fresh chestnuts must first be boiled, peeled and puréed. They keep very well in covered jars for 1 week, refrigerated in plastic bags for 1 month. Chestnut purée can be kept in a freezer for up to 8 months.

Chocolate. Its scientific name (theobroma cacao) means "food for the Gods." Chocolate is produced from cocoa beans and cocoa butter. The best ones contain no less than 35% of cocoa butter. The types of chocolate used in baking are milk chocolate, bittersweet chocolate and white chocolate. The later one having a very high percentage of cocoa butter is deprived of any cocoa. Couverture chocolate is used for dipping or to cover cakes. Due to its high percentage of cocoa butter (up to 50%), it melts easily and rapidly. Chocolate should be kept in a dry and cool place.

Flour. For baking, all-purpose flour is generally used. It has a higher starch level and is lighter than other flours. Flour should be kept in an airtight container, away from the heat.
◆ Whole wheat flour, which contains wheat germ, rich in oils, can be kept for about 2 months.
◆ Corn flour is often used for baking and can be found fine or coarsely ground.

American and German recipes often include sour cream. It can be prepared by mixing 1 tablespoon of lemon juice in 1 cup of heavy cream; refrigerate for a few hours. The cream will become thick with a tangy flavor.

Gelatin
Gelatin in sheets or in powder is used in many preparations. Soak or dissolve the gelatin in a little water before incorporating with other ingredients. It is used as a stabilizer that gives creams and mousses the density required for fillings or to stand up. If gelatin solidifies, heat lightly and mix. Before adding preparations with whipped cream or meringue, cool gelatin completely.

Agar-agar is a vegetal gelatin made of algae. It can be used to replace traditional gelatin.

Cooling custards
When cooling pastry creams or custards, always mix often so a "skin" does not form on top. Warm custards can also be sprinkled with sugar to protect them until cold.

Potato starch. This powder form starch is used to thicken sauces and custards. Its "lightness" permits it to be part of cake recipes, alone or mixed with all-purpose flour.

Fresh cheese. Sometimes, fresh cheese adds a delicate flavor to baked goods. Ricotta, cottage cheese, cream cheese, "fromage frais," quark or mascarpone are different versions that are all used for their sweet flavor. Used for various desserts or to accompany fruits, it can generally be kept refrigerated for 1 week.

Fruits. For any dessert with fruits as a main ingredient, always choose them ripe and perfect. ▶

Tools

◆ To be a perfect baker, some "tools of the trade" can be very useful, others necessary. Some are on the next page, from top to bottom: 1) springform cake pan; 2) animal shape cake pan; 3) springform cake pan; 4) heartshape pan; 5) low cake pan; 6) fluted tube pan; 7) loaf pan; 8) pie pan (for quiches or pies); 9) rounded loaf pan; 10) pie pan; 11) flour sifter; 12) sifter; 13) sugar duster; 14) rolling pin; 15) pastry bag; 16) decorating tubes; 17) serrated knife; 18) small kitchen knife; 19) fluted pasta cutters; 20) paper liners; 21) tartlet molds; 22) wooden spatula; 23) Pierced spatula; 24) wooden spoon; 25) steel spatula; 26) grater; 27) slicer-grater; 28) Whisk; 29) whisk; 30) rubber spatula; 31) rubber spatula; 32) brush; 33) double brush.

◆ You also need stainless steel bowls and glass bowls in various sizes. Plastic bowls are never good, since, after some time, they develop odors and are difficult to clean properly. It is good to have several molds for Charlottes and soufflés made of pyrex or ceramic, a saucepan with a long handle with copper bottom to cook creams and sauces, individual molds, a mortar and a pestle, an ice cream scooper and metal molds to fry Sicilian cannoli.

◆ Modern kitchens should have electric mixers, blenders, a food processor, an ice cream machine, a pasta machine, a juice presser, a sugar thermometer, etc.

When sliced, pears, bananas and apples should be soaked in lemon juice so they do not darken. To peel apricots or peaches, scald them in boiling water, drain and peel. All small fruits should quickly be rinsed in ice water and then dried on a clean towel.

Dried fruits. They hold a large place in baking. The fruits need to be soft and their color dense. When using raisins, soak them in warm water for 10-15 minutes, drain and dry them on a towel.

Gelatin. You can find gelatin in supermarkets;

generally in powder form or in sheets. One teaspoon of gelatin is normally enough for 2 cups of liquid. For creamy preparations, the gelatin proportion is always higher. Gelatin should first be dissolved or soaked in cool water, then melted or mixed into a warm mixture. Fresh pineapple contains an enzyme that prevents gelatin from thickening.

Glucose. An invert sugar present in fruits, honey and especially in corn, glucose is manufactured in syrup form and found in bakery supply shops. It can be replaced by corn syrup.

Milk. Whole milk is generally used in baking. It is of outmost importance to use fresh milk (always

Roll dough without problems
First, the dough should be softened at room temperature. The work surface should be clean and lightly floured. Dough should be pushed down by hand, then rolled, with a flour dusted rolling pin, from the center out.
It can also be rolled on a piece of waxed paper so it can easily be transferred to a pie pan.

A perfect soufflé
To prevent the soufflé from deflating before being served, professional chefs cook it in a bain-marie. Put a folded kitchen towel on the bottom of a baking dish; put the soufflé dish on top. Add cold water in the baking dish to half the height of the soufflé. On moderate heat, bring to boil and cook for 20-30 minutes; 10 minutes before serving the soufflé, put it in an oven preheated to 400°F to raise and brown. When filling the soufflé dish, always fill to 3/4 only so the soufflé can rise without overflowing.

check the expiration date). Some recipes require evaporated or condensed milk; you can find those in cans. Fresh milk can be kept refrigerated up to a week.

Raising agents. Fresh or dry yeast is used for baking breads and brioche-type dough, which require extensive handling of the dough. It permits the dough to raise, transforming the sugars of the flour into carbon dioxide. Fresh yeast is a live organism and makes the dough light and tasty and should be kept refrigerated. For optimum results, the fermentation temperature is around 90°F. Fresh and dry (powdered) yeast are available in supermarkets.
◆ Baking powder is a chemical type yeast made from baking soda and cream of tartar. It works especially well in cake batters and with flours with a low gluten content. It gets its leavening power when in contact with liquids. It should be added last to recipes because its energy and power last about 10 minutes.

Cornstarch. A white starch with twice the thickening power of flour, it is used most in creams and puddings.

Honey. Depending on the flowers used, this natural sweetener takes different colors and tastes. The lighter the color, the lighter the flavor. Honey does not add more sugar to desserts, but adds more humidity and also acts as a preservative.

Nuts. Almonds, nuts, hazelnuts, pine nuts, peanuts, pistachios, etc. are often used in desserts. Freshly shelled nuts have the best flavor. Badly stored or old nuts develop a rancid flavor that can ruin any dish. Nuts can be kept 2-3 months in a dry and cool place. Unshelled nuts can be kept in airtight containers, refrigerated for 3 to 6 months, or well wrapped, in a freezer for up to 1 year.

Coconuts. To control the freshness of a coconut, shake it next to your ear. If the coconut is fresh, you will hear the liquid inside, which is not true with an old coconut. The meat of the coconut is generally grated for use in pies and cakes, or as decoration for desserts. When open, the coconut keeps for 1 week under refrigeration or it can be frozen for 9 months.

Oils. Extra virgin olive oil, which has less than 1% acidity, is used only in a few regional desserts such as the "castagnaccio" (or chestnut tart). Peanut oil is preferred for deep frying. It is almost tasteless and can be heated to high temperatures without burning. To oil pans and molds for puddings and mousses, or to brush work surfaces, the light and flavorful almond oil is preferable.

Tips and suggestions

Cream. For desserts, heavy cream or whipping cream are generally used. It should be fresh and can be kept refrigerated for a few days. Cream can be frozen up to 3 months, but will be unsuitable for whipping.

Spices. Among all the spices, those most used in desserts are the following:
◆ CINNAMON is the spice obtained from the bark of the cinnamon tree. It is used in sticks or in powder form.
◆ CARDAMOM, the seed of an Asian plant, has a strong flavor. It is used in fruit compotes.
◆ CLOVES, the dried flower buds of an equatorial tree, are often used in apple desserts (as is cinnamon), but should be used in moderation because of its intense flavor.
◆ JUNIPER, a berry from a Northern European shrub, is often used in spiced cakes and other desserts.
◆ NUTMEG and MACE, both from the same aromatic seed, are the size of a walnut. The dried, ground covering or aril of the nutmeg is the mace.
◆ VANILLA. The pods (or beans) from tropical orchids accentuate other flavors. The beans are rather expensive and add a subtle sweet taste. The extract is commonly used to flavor sweet preparations. Artificial vanilla flavor should be avoided for it imparts a bitter taste and has less flavor.
◆ GINGER, the root of a plant, is used fresh, powdered or crystallized to transfer its highly perfumed flavor. In desserts, powdered and crystallized ginger are most used.
Most of these spices can be stored in airtight jars, stored in a dark and cool place. Vanilla beans can be kept indefinitely at room temperature. Fresh ginger is kept refrigerated for up to 2 weeks and the crystallized one can be kept indefinitely.

Eggs. They need to be very fresh and should be used within 3 weeks of buying them.
An old method of checking the freshness of an

A well baked cake
Even when following recipes precisely, cakes can require different baking times. Ovens often are unreliable and cake pans made of different materials can affect the cooking time. To check if a cake is ready, it is always good to verify by inserting a toothpick in its middle. If it comes out clean, the cake is cooked; if not, the cake should go back in the oven.
If the cake top browns too much too rapidly, cover it with aluminum foil, piercing a hole in the middle of the foil to let any steam out. If the cake browns too much on the bottom, put a pan filled with some cold water in the lower part of the oven.

egg is to immerse it in water: if the egg goes to the bottom, it is fresh; if it floats vertically, it is 2-3 weeks old; if it floats at the top, it is a few months old and should be thrown out. Eggs should be stored in the refrigerator. Egg yolks should be sprinkled with a little water and stored refrigerated in an airtight container. Egg whites can be stored covered in the refrigerator for up to 2 weeks or frozen for up to 1 year. Once thawed, they can be beaten to firm peaks like the fresh ones.

Yogurt. It is made from milk curdled by particular bacteria. Used as an ingredient in cake batters with baking powder, yogurt helps the raising of the cakes and makes them lighter. For baking

recipes, always use plain yogurt (not fat-free).

Sugar. It is obtained from sugar beets or sugar cane, and found in supermarkets in various forms:
◆ REFINED SUGAR is the type of sugar commonly used in cooking and baking.
◆ POWDERED SUGAR is also called confectioner's or icing sugar; it is sold mixed with 3% cornstarch to avoid humidity.
◆ VANILLA SUGAR is best if homemade. In a large covered jar of sugar or powdered sugar, add one or several vanilla beans. Vanilla beans previously used in sauces are perfect for this.
◆ PEARL SUGAR and its large granules are used to sprinkle brioche and pastries.
◆ BROWN SUGAR is a refined sugar with a part of the molasses added to it. It is darker and adds a different taste but it is not sweeter than regular sugar.

Small Desserts

Choux ◆ Cookies ◆ Sweets and finger pastries ◆ Brioches ◆
Marzipan ◆ Meringues ◆ Chocolates and pralines
Nougats and brittles ◆ Fruits and candies
Gelatins ◆ Wafers

Chocolate profiteroles

Butter a cookie sheet. Preheat the oven to 370°F.

◆ To make the pate à choux, bring 3/4 cup of water with the butter, salt and split vanilla bean to a boil. Pour in the flour, all at once, remove from heat and stir vigorously. Continue to stir for a few minutes until dough forms a ball and comes away from sides of saucepan.

◆ Remove the vanilla bean and cool. With an electric mixer, whisk in the powdered sugar and eggs, one at a time.

◆ Put the mixture into a pastry bag, fitted with a straight tube and pipe out onto the

Time needed:
50 minutes
Difficulty: medium
INGREDIENTS FOR 6 SERVINGS

2 cups of whipping cream
3 tablespoons of powdered sugar
1/2 teaspoon of vanilla
7 oz of grated dark chocolate

Pate à choux:
1 1/2 cups of flour
1/2 cup of butter
6 eggs
1 vanilla bean
1 tablespoon of powdered sugar
a pinch of salt

cookie sheet in tiny mounds (the size of a hazelnut), one separated from each other.

◆ Bake for 20-25 minutes until fluffy and golden. Turn the oven off and leave the profiteroles inside for 5 minutes to let them dry; transfer onto a rack to cool. Melt the chocolate in a double boiler with 1/3 cup of water and cool.

◆ Whip the cream with the sugar and vanilla, put it in a pastry bag, fitted with a small tube. Make a hole in the profiteroles and fill them with the whipped cream. Put them on a serving dish in a pyramid and pour over the melted chocolate. Serve cold.

Pineapple profiteroles

Time needed: *50 minutes*
Difficulty: medium

INGREDIENTS FOR 6 SERVINGS
3/4 lb of pineapple ice cream (see page 280)
4 slices of fresh pineapple
1 cup of whipping cream

Pate à choux:
1 1/2 cups of flour ◆ 1/2 cups of butter
6 eggs ◆ 1 vanilla bean
1 tablespoon of powdered sugar
a pinch of salt

◆ Butter a cookie sheet. Preheat the oven to 375°F.
◆ Prepare the pate à choux with the above listed ingredients. (See page 11). Put the mixture into a pastry bag, fitted with a smooth tube and pipe out onto the cookie sheet in tiny mounds (the size of a hazelnut), separated from each other. Bake for 25 minutes until puffed up and golden. Let the profiteroles cool on a rack.
◆ Cut the choux into half horizontally, leaving them attached on one end, and fill one half with the pineapple ice cream; fill the other half with 2/3 of the whipped cram. Close them and put them on a serving dish in a pyramid. Fill a pastry bag, fitted with a star tube, with

Pineapple profiteroles

the remaining whipped cream and pipe rosettes in between each profiterole. Garnish with the diced pineapple. Serve immediately.

Cream puffs

Time needed: *45 minutes*
Difficulty: medium

INGREDIENTS FOR 8-10 SERVINGS
1 1/2 cups of flour ◆ 1/2 cups of butter
6 eggs ◆ 1 vanilla bean
1 tablespoon of vanilla sugar
1 1/4 cups of whipping cream
1 tablespoon of powdered sugar
3 tablespoons of granular sugar
a pinch of salt

◆ Butter a cookie sheet. Preheat oven to 375°F.
◆ Prepare the pate à choux with the flour, butter, eggs, vanilla, powdered sugar and salt (see page 11). Put the mixture into a pastry bag, fitted with a straight tube and pipe out onto the cookie sheet in tiny mounds (the size of a hazelnut), separated from each other. Sprinkle with the granular sugar and bake for about 30 minutes until puffed up and golden. Let the puff pastry cool on a rack.
◆ Whip the cream with the sugar and refrigerate.
◆ Cut the top off the pastry. Fill them generously with whipped cream, piped out of the pastry bag, fitted with a star tube. Cover with the cut-out top. Keep in a cool place until ready to serve.

Cream puffs

Chocolate profiteroles

Glazed cream puffs

Time needed: *1 hour and 30 minutes*
Difficulty: *medium*

INGREDIENTS FOR 6 SERVINGS

Pate à choux:
1 1/2 cups of flour ◆ 1/2 cups of butter
6 eggs ◆ 1 vanilla bean
1 tablespoon of vanilla sugar
a pinch of salt

Pastry cream:
4 egg yolks ◆ 2/3 cup of sugar
grated peel of one organic lemon
2 cups of milk
2 tablespoons of butter

Caramel:
1/2 cup of sugar

◆ Butter a cookie sheet. Preheat the oven to 370°F.
◆ Prepare the pate à choux with the above listed ingredients (see page 11). Put the mixture into a pastry bag, fitted with a straight tube and pipe out on the cookie sheet in hazelnuts sized mounds, one separated from the other. Bake for 25 minutes until fluffy and golden. Let the puffs cool completely.
◆ Prepare a pastry cream (see page 16) with the above listed ingredients and let it cool, stirring occasionally to avoid the forming of a skin on the surface. Make a small hole in the puffs and fill them with the pastry cream.
◆ Prepare the caramel (see page 19), dip in the top part of the puffs and place them in a pyramid on a serving dish.

Glazed cream puffs

Profiteroles with strawberries and whipped cream

Profiteroles with strawberries and whipped cream

Time needed: *45 minutes*
Difficulty: *medium*

INGREDIENTS FOR 6 SERVINGS
1 cup of strawberries
1 1/2 cups of whipping cream
1/4 cup of sugar
a liquor glass of Grand Marnier or Framboise
1 tablespoon of powdered sugar

Pate à choux:
1 1/2 cups of flour ◆ 1/2 cup of butter
6 eggs ◆ 1 vanilla bean
1 tablespoon of powdered sugar
a pinch of salt

◆ Butter a cookie sheet. Preheat the oven to 370°F.
◆ Prepare the pate à choux with the above listed ingredients (see page 11). Put the mixture into a pastry bag, fitted with a straight tube and pipe out on the cookie sheet in tiny mounds (the size of a hazelnut), separated from each other. Bake for 25 minutes until fluffy and golden. Let the puffs cool completely.
◆ Rinse the strawberries in ice water and dry. Soak them in the liquor for 20 minutes. Set 10 strawberries aside and puree the remainder with the sugar in a food processor.
◆ Whip the cream with powdered sugar and put 3/4 of it in a pastry bag, fitted with a small tube. Make a hole in the puffs, fill them with whipped cream and place them in a pyramid onto a serving dish. Mix the remaining cream with the strawberry purée and pour over the puffs, garnish with the remaining strawberries cut in halves.

Coffee eclairs

Time needed: *1 hour*
Difficulty: *medium*

INGREDIENTS FOR 6 SERVINGS
Pate à choux:
1 1/2 cups of flour ◆ 1/2 cup of butter
6 eggs ◆ 1 vanilla bean
1 tablespoon of powdered sugar
a pinch of salt

Cream:
6 eggs ◆ 3/4 cup of sugar
2 cups of milk ◆ 1 1/2 oz of flour
1/2 teaspoon of vanilla
1 teaspoon of instant coffee

Icing:
3 1/2 oz of powdered sugar
about 2 tablespoons of very strong espresso coffee

◆ Butter a cookie sheet. Preheat the oven to 390°F.
◆ Prepare the pate à choux with the above listed ingredients (see page 11). Put the mixture into a pastry bag, fitted with a large straight tube and pipe out onto the cookie sheet in sticks 1 inch wide and 2 inch long. Bake for 25-30 min-

Coffee eclairs

utes until puffed up and golden.
◆ Let the eclair sticks cool on a rack and make a little hole with a small sharp knife.
◆ Make a custard (see page 16) with the above listed ingredients and mix in the instant coffee while the custard is still hot. Let it cool, and with it fill a pastry bag, fitted with a small and smooth nozzle. Pipe into the eclairs through the hole.
◆ To make the icing, mix the powdered sugar with the espresso coffee a little at a time until dense but smooth. Using a teaspoon, put a little coffee icing on each eclair and keep in a cool place.

Hazelnut cream puffs

Time needed: *1 hour*
Difficulty: *medium*

INGREDIENTS FOR 6-8 SERVINGS

Pate à choux:
1 1/2 cups of flour ◆ 1/2 cup of butter
6 eggs ◆ 1 vanilla bean
1 tablespoon of vanilla sugar
a pinch of salt

Pastry cream:
1 cup of milk ◆ 3 egg yolks
1 tablespoon of flour
1/4 cup of sugar
1 1/2 oz of toasted hazelnuts
1/2 cup of whipping cream

Glaze:
3 1/2 oz of powdered sugar
1 egg white ◆ drops of lemon
1/2 cup of toasted hazelnuts

◆ Butter a cookie sheet. Preheat the oven to 370°F.
◆ Prepare the pate à choux with the above listed ingredients (see page 11). Put the mixture into a pastry bag, fitted with a straight tube and pipe out onto the cookie sheet in tiny mounds (the size of a hazelnut), separated from each other. Bake for 25 minutes until puffed up and golden. Let the choux cool completely.
◆ Prepare a pastry cream (see page 16) with the milk, egg yolks, flour and sugar. Mix in the finely chopped hazelnuts and cool completely. Fold in the whipped cream and put the mixture in a pastry bag, fitted with a straight tube. Make a hole in the choux and fill with the hazelnut mixture.

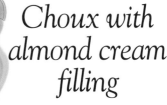

Hazelnut cream puffs

Choux with almond cream filling

◆ To make the glaze, coarsely chop 8 hazelnuts and grind the remainder. In a bowl, whisk the egg whites with the lemon juice and powdered sugar until thick and creamy. Blend in the ground hazelnuts.
◆ Dip the top of the choux in the glaze and garnish with the chopped hazelnuts. Put the choux in mini paper dollies, and place them onto a serving dish.

Choux with almond cream filling

Time needed: *1 hour*
Difficulty: *medium*

INGREDIENTS FOR 6-8 SERVINGS

1 1/2 oz of chopped praline almonds
1 tablespoon of powdered sugar

Pate à choux:
1 1/2 cups of flour ◆ 1/2 cup of butter
6 eggs ◆ 1 vanilla bean
1 tablespoon of vanilla sugar
a pinch of salt

Pastry cream:
1 cup of milk ◆ 3 egg yolks
1/3 cup of flour ◆ 1/3 cup of sugar
2 1/2 oz of toasted ground almonds
1 cup of whipping cream

◆ Butter a cookie sheet. Preheat the oven to 370°F.
Prepare the pate à choux with the above listed ingredients (see page 11). Put the mixture into a pastry bag, fitted with a straight tube and pipe out onto the cookie sheet in 1-inch-long sticks, leaving a little space between each one. Bake for 25 minutes until puffed up and golden. Let the choux cool completely.
Prepare a prepare cream (see page 16) with the milk, egg yolks, flour and sugar. Stir occasionally to avoid forming a skin on the surface. When cold, blend in the ground almonds and gently fold in the whipped cream.
Make a hole in each choux. Put the almond cream into a pastry bag, fitted with a small straight tube and pipe it into the choux. Place them onto a serving dish and sprinkle with powdered sugar. Keep them in a cool place until ready to serve.

Coconut cookies

Butter and flour a cookie sheet. Put the flour in a mound onto a work surface, make a well in the center and place the butter in pieces, coconut, powdered sugar, egg and egg yolk. Knead rapidly with your fingertips, form a ball and refrigerate for 2 hours, covered with plastic wrap.

◆ Unwrap the dough, cut into pieces and roll out into several 2-inch-long cylinders. Cover each cylinder with plastic wrap and refrigerate for 3 hours.

Time needed:
30 minutes
(plus resting time)
Difficulty: easy
INGREDIENTS
FOR 6 SERVINGS

2 cups of flour
1 oz of grated coconut
7 tablespoons of softened butter
1 egg
1 egg yolk

◆ Preheat the oven to 360°F.

◆ Unwrap the cylinders and roll them repeatedly in sugar. Slice into 1/2-inch-thick rounds. Put them onto the prepared cookie sheet and bake for 15-20 minutes. Let the cookies cool on a rack and place them on a serving dish.

◆ To keep the cookies fresh and crispy, put them in a tightly closed cookie jar.

Pine nut and chocolate sticks

Time needed: *50 minutes*
(plus resting time)
Difficulty: medium

INGREDIENTS FOR 6 SERVINGS
2 cups of flour
7 tablespoons of softened butter
1/2 cup of sugar
1/2 teaspoon of baking powder
1 teaspoon of vanilla flavored powdered sugar
1 egg ◆ *a pinch of salt*
2 1/2 oz of pine nuts
2 tablespoons of raspberry jelly
3 1/2 oz of grated dark chocolate

◆ Butter a cookie sheet.
◆ Put the sifted flour and baking powder in a mound onto a work surface, make a well in the center and put the sugar, vanilla flavored powdered sugar, butter in pieces, salt and egg, keeping half the egg white aside.
◆ Knead rapidly with your fingertips and refrigerate the dough for 1 hour, covered with plastic wrap.
◆ Preheat the oven to 350°F.
◆ Thinly roll out the dough and cut it into rectangular strips, 1-inch wide and 2 1/2-inch-long. Place them onto the cookie sheet, brush with the remaining, lightly beaten egg white and sprinkle with pine nuts.
◆ Bake for 10-12 minutes. Remove cookies from the cookie sheet and let cool completely.

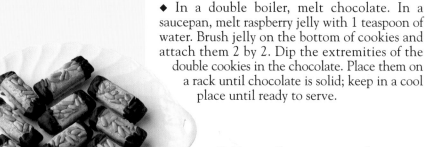

Pine nut and chocolate sticks

◆ In a double boiler, melt chocolate. In a saucepan, melt raspberry jelly with 1 teaspoon of water. Brush jelly on the bottom of cookies and attach them 2 by 2. Dip the extremities of the double cookies in the chocolate. Place them on a rack until chocolate is solid; keep in a cool place until ready to serve.

Hazelnut and almond cookies

Time needed: *40 minutes*
Difficulty: easy

INGREDIENTS FOR 4-6 SERVINGS
1 cup of toasted hazelnuts
1 1/2 tablespoons of sugar
2 egg whites

◆ Butter and flour a cookie sheet. Preheat oven to 450°F.
◆ In a food processor, mix the almonds, hazelnuts and 1 1/4 cups of sugar until smooth. Blend in egg whites and put mixture into a pastry bag, fitted with a straight tube. Form 1-inch long sticks and put on the cookie sheet, spaced away from each other; lightly crush them with a moistened fork and bake for 4-7 minutes.
◆ On low heat, cook the remaining sugar in 2 tablespoons of water for 2 minutes. Brush the hot cookies with this syrup, remove from cookie sheet and let them cool completely before serving.

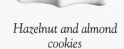

Hazelnut and almond cookies

Coconut cookies

"Crumiri" from Piedmont

Time needed: *40 minutes*
(plus resting time)
Difficulty: easy

INGREDIENTS FOR 6 SERVINGS
1/2 cup of very fine corn flour
1 1/2 cups of flour
4 egg yolks
1 teaspoon of vanilla
3/4 cup of softened butter
1/2 cup of sugar

◆ Butter a cookie sheet. Line with parchment paper. Mix both the flours and place them in a mound on a work surface. Make a well in the center, in it place the butter cut into pieces, sugar, egg yolks and vanilla. Knead rapidly, form a ball and set aside in a cool place for 30 minutes, covered with plastic wrap.
◆ Preheat the oven to 340°F.
◆ Fill a pastry bag, fitted with a star tube, with the cookie dough mixture, and pipe onto the cookie sheet, forming 3-inch-long half moons. Bake for about 15 minutes until golden. Cool and place onto a serving dish.

"Crumiri"
from Piedmont

Little almond croissants

Time needed: *40 minutes*
Difficulty: medium

INGREDIENTS FOR 6 SERVINGS
1 cup of sugar
1 cup of chopped, peeled almonds
1/3 cup of slivered almonds
1 medium apple

◆ Butter and flour a cookie sheet. Preheat the oven to 360°F.
◆ In a saucepan, dissolve 3/4 cup of sugar in 2 ta-

blespoons of water. Add the almonds and stir rapidly until smooth; set the mixture aside.
◆ Peel the apple, core and dice. Put it with the remaining sugar in a non-stick saucepan and cook it for about 20 minutes until you have a thick applesauce. Cool.
◆ In a bowl, mix the almond mixture with the applesauce. With this mixture form cylinders of 1/2 inch in diameter and cut into 1 1/2 inch long sticks. Lightly crush them, shape into half moon and roll on both sides in the chopped almonds.
◆ Place the cookies onto the cookie sheet and bake for about 7 minutes. Let them cool completely before transferring onto a dish.

Little almond
croissants

Lady kisses

Time needed: *1 hour*
(plus resting time)
Difficulty: medium

INGREDIENTS FOR ABOUT 20
1/2 cup of flour
1/8 cup of peeled almonds
1/8 cup of toasted hazelnuts
1/4 cup of sugar
4 tablespoons of softened butter
2 oz of grated dark chocolate
1 teaspoon of vanilla

◆ Butter and flour a cookie sheet. Grind the almonds and hazelnuts together.
◆ In a bowl, mix the butter in pieces, sugar, salt and vanilla with the ground almonds and hazelnuts. Add the flour, knead rapidly and refrigerate the dough for 4 hours, covered with plastic wrap.
◆ Preheat the oven to 320°F.
◆ Unwrap the dough and cut into pieces of about 2 oz inch. Form into little balls and put onto the cookie sheet. Bake for about 25-30 minutes, until golden. Cool completely.
◆ Melt the chocolate in a double boiler and with a teaspoon, spread a little on the flat side of each cookie. Stick another cookie to this chocolate covered side. Place onto a serving dish.
◆ These cookies keep well if sealed in a tin can. Their taste will get better after 3 or 4 days.

Lady kisses

Scottish cookies

Time needed: *1 hour*
(plus resting time)
Difficulty: *medium*

INGREDIENTS FOR **6** SERVINGS

2 1/2 cups of flour
1/2 cup of butter
1/3 cup of sugar
a pinch of salt
1 egg white

◆ Butter and flour a cookie sheet.
◆ Put the flour in a mound on a work surface and make a well in the center. Place the butter in pieces, sugar and a few tablespoons of water. Knead until dough is firm. Roll out into a long and thin rectangle. Fold over in 3 parts to have 3 thickness of dough and let it rest for 5 minutes.
◆ Roll out once more into a rectangle and fold into 2 parts. Repeat this last processes another 3 times.
◆ Wrap into a cloth and put in a cool place for 3 hours.
◆ Preheat the oven to 400°F. Roll out the dough into a thin sheet and cut out dough with a cookie cutter. Roll out further sheets with the trimmings and continue to cut out cookies. Place them onto the cookie sheet; brush with the lightly beaten egg white for about 20 minutes until golden. Remove from the cookie sheet and cool before serving.

Scottish cookies

Cookies from Provence

Time needed: *40 minutes*
Difficulty: *medium*

INGREDIENTS FOR **6** SERVINGS

1/2 cup of peeled almonds
1/3 cup of sugar
2 tablespoons of flour
2 3/4oz of candied orange
2 egg whites
a pinch of salt
1 tablespoon of powdered sugar

◆ Butter and flour a cookie sheet. Preheat the

Cookies from Provence

oven to 325°F.
◆ Finely chop 1 oz of candied orange peel and cut the remainder into small circles. Grind the almonds with 1/3 cup of sugar; mix in with the flour and chopped orange peel.
◆ Beat the egg whites with the salt to stiff peaks and gently fold into the almond and flour mixture. Pour mounds of 1 tablespoon of this mixture onto the cookie sheet, each mound spaced from the other. With your moistened fingertips, flatten lightly the cookies put a candied orange circle on each and sprinkle with powdered sugar.
◆ Bake for 20-25 minutes, remove from the cookie sheet with a spatula and cool on a rack before serving.

Sesame rings

Time needed: *40 minutes*
Difficulty: *easy*

INGREDIENTS FOR **4-6** SERVINGS

3 cups of flour
2 3/4 tablespoons of softened butter
1/2 cup of sugar
1/2 teaspoon of baking powder
4 eggs
3 tablespoons of milk
grated peel of 1/2 organic lemon
1 1/2 oz of sesame seeds

◆ Butter and flour a cookie sheet. Preheat an oven to 400°F.
◆ With an electric mixer, whisk the butter until creamy; blend in the sugar and then the eggs, one at a time; add the lemon peel; add a little at a time, the sifted flour and baking powder alternating it with the milk. Should the mixture be too stiff, add a little more milk.
◆ Form sticks just a little thinner then a pencil and 12 inch long, fold them in two and twist the ends, bringing the two ends together to form rings.
◆ Sprinkle the rings with sesame seeds, place them on the cookie sheet and bake for 18-20 minutes. Remove from the cookie sheet and cool completely before serving.

Sesame rings

Coffee shortbread cookies

Time needed: *45 minutes*
Difficulty: *easy*

INGREDIENTS FOR 6 SERVINGS
3 cups of flour
8 tablespoons of softened butter
1/3 cup of sugar
1/2 teaspoon of baking powder
1 egg ◆ a pinch of salt
1 tablespoon of instant coffee
1oz of coffee beans
1 1/2 oz of grated dark chocolate

◆ Butter and flour a cookie sheet. Preheat the oven to 360°F.
◆ Put the flour with the baking powder in a mound on a work surface and make a well in the center. Place the sugar, salt, butter in pieces, egg and the coffee dissolved in 1 tablespoon of warm water. Knead rapidly with your fingertips and roll out the dough into a thin sheet.
◆ Cut the dough with a cookie cutter (kneading the trimmings and rolling them out into a sheet). Bake the cookies for about 15 minutes until golden. Transfer to a plate and cool.
◆ Melt the chocolate in a double boiler and pour it into a parchment paper cone. Let one drop of chocolate fall on each cookie, top with 3 coffee beans and let another chocolate drop fall in between the 3 coffee beans.

Whole-wheat cookies

Time needed: *40 minutes*
Difficulty: *easy*

INGREDIENTS FOR 4 SERVINGS
3/4 cup of whole-wheat flour
1/4 small cup of sugar
3 tablespoons of softened butter
grated peel of 1/2 organic lemon
2 egg yolks ◆ 4 tablespoons of milk
a pinch of salt

◆ Butter and flour a cookie sheet. Preheat the oven to 375°F.
◆ Put the flour mixed with the sugar and salt in a mound on a work surface and make a well in the center. Place the lemon peel, milk, egg yolks and butter in pieces. Knead until smooth, put it in a pastry bag, fitted with a large star tube and

pipe it onto the cookie sheet in S-shaped cookies, one cookie separated from the other.
◆ Bake for 10-12 minutes, remove from the cookie sheet, cool and place on a serving dish.

Bean-shaped cookies

Time needed: *1 hour*
Difficulty: *easy*

INGREDIENTS FOR 4 SERVINGS
1 1/2 cups of flour ◆ 3/4 cup of sugar
3 cups of peeled, ground almonds
1/2 cup of pine nuts ◆ 2 eggs
grated peel of 1/2 organic lemon
1 tablespoon of brandy
a pinch of cinnamon ◆ 1 egg white

◆ Butter and flour a cookie sheet. Preheat the oven to 325°F.
◆ Put the flour in a mound on a work surface and make a well in the center. Add the sugar, eggs, chopped almonds, pine nuts, lemon peel, brandy and cinnamon. Knead until smooth.
◆ Form rolls of about 1/2 inch in diameter; cut them into pieces the size of a lima bean. In the middle of each piece, make a small indentation. Whisk one egg white; dip every "bean" in it. Place on the cookie sheet and bake for about 30 minutes. Cool completely.

Honey amaretti

Time needed: *1 hour and 10 minutes*
Difficulty: *easy*

INGREDIENTS FOR 6 SERVINGS
2 egg whites ◆ 5oz of honey
1/2 small cup of peeled almonds
1/2 small cup of toasted hazelnuts
a pinch of salt

◆ Butter and flour a cookie sheet. Preheat the oven to 300°F.
◆ Finely chop almonds and hazelnuts together.
◆ Beat the egg whites with the salt to stiff peaks; gently fold in the honey. Add the almond and hazelnut mixture. Place onto a cookie sheet in mounds the size of a walnut, separately from each other. Bake for about 50 minutes until they easily detach from the cookie sheet. Cool and transfer onto a plate.

Piedmontaise cookie twists

Time needed: *40 minutes*
(plus rising time)
Difficulty: medium

INGREDIENTS FOR **6-8** SERVINGS
2 1/2 cups of flour
7 tablespoons of softened butter
1/2 a teaspoon of yeast
1 tablespoon of sugar
a pinch of salt

◆ Butter and flour a cookie sheet. Dissolve the yeast in 4-5 tablespoons of warm water. Put the flour with the salt in a mound on a work surface and make a well in the center. Place the yeast and knead until well blended. Put the dough in a bowl, cover it and let it rise in a warm place for at least 1 hour.
◆ Turn dough onto work surface and knead it again. Blend in the butter, cut in pieces. Let it rest once more, covered for 30 minutes.
◆ Preheat an oven to 360°F.
◆ Knead the dough again for a few minutes, form strings just a bit thinner than a pencil. Cut them 4 in. long and roll them in sugar. Fold them over and secure the ends together, forming oval rings. Put the cookies on the cookie sheet and bake for 12-15 minutes, until golden. Cool completely.

French biscuits

Time needed: *40 minutes*
(plus resting and rising time)
Difficulty: medium

INGREDIENTS FOR **6-8** SERVINGS
2 1/2 cups of flour
12 tablespoons of butter
4 eggs ◆ *1/4 cup of sugar*
1 teaspoon of yeast

◆ Butter and flour a cookie sheet. Put the sifted flour in a mound on a work surface and make a well in the center. Place the yeast dissolved in 1/2 cup of warm water. Add the sugar, and 3 eggs; knead vigorously, lifting and slamming it onto the work surface until smooth and elastic; it will detach from your hands easily. Put the dough in a bowl, cover with a humid kitchen towel and refrigerate for 12 hours.

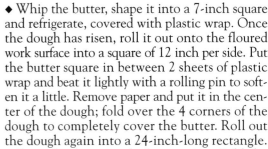

◆ Whip the butter, shape it into a 7-inch square and refrigerate, covered with plastic wrap. Once the dough has risen, roll it out onto the floured work surface into a square of 12 inch per side. Put the butter square in between 2 sheets of plastic wrap and beat it lightly with a rolling pin to soften it a little. Remove paper and put it in the center of the dough; fold over the 4 corners of the dough to completely cover the butter. Roll out the dough again into a 24-inch-long rectangle.
◆ Start the first round of processing: Fold the dough into 3, then place a short side in front of you and roll out again to a length of 24 inch and fold into 3 once more. Cover with plastic wrap and refrigerate for at least 2 hours.
◆ Remove it from refrigerator and give the dough another 2 processing (fold it and roll it out twice), then roll it out into a thin sheet. Cut 2 1/2 x 1 1/2 inch rectangles and place them onto the cookie sheet, each separated from the other. Lightly indent the sides with a small knife and set aside in a warm place for 30 minutes to rise. Preheat the oven to 360°F.
◆ Brush the rectangles with the remaining beaten egg and bake for 15-20 minutes. Remove the biscuits with a spatula and serve cold.

Beaked cookies

Time needed: *45 minutes*
Difficulty: easy

INGREDIENTS FOR **4** SERVINGS
5 cups of corn flour
2/3 cup of raisins ◆ *1 cup of pine nuts*
4 oz of walnut kernels
1 2/3 cups of peeled almonds
1 2/3 cups of dried figs ◆ *1/4 cup of sugar*
4 tablespoons of olive oil
a pinch of salt

◆ Brush a cookie sheet with oil. Preheat the oven to 300°F.
◆ Soak the raisins in warm water. Scald the almonds and walnuts; finely chop with the dried figs.
◆ Put the flour in a mound on a work surface and make a well in the center. Add 3 tablespoons of oil, the strained raisins, pine nuts, chopped dried fruit mixture, sugar and salt, adding enough boiling water to knead into a rather soft dough.
◆ Make small balls out of the dough, press them lightly and put them onto the cookie sheet, separated from each other. Bake for about 20 minutes. Remove from the cookie sheet and cool on a rack before serving.

Licorice cookies

Time needed:
1 hour and 15 minutes
Difficulty: easy
INGREDIENTS
FOR 4 SERVINGS

1 3/4 cups of flour
1 cup of sugar
1/2 oz of aniseeds
5 eggs
1/2 teaspoon of baking powder
a pinch of salt

Line a rectangular cake pan with parchment paper. Preheat the oven to 320°F.

◆ With an electric mixer, whisk the egg yolks with the sugar (keeping 2 tablespoons aside) until light and creamy.

◆ Blend in the flour, aniseeds and baking powder. Beat the egg whites with the salt to stiff peaks; gently fold into the mixture.

◆ Pour into the cake pan and bake for about 30 minutes. (Put a skewer through the dough; if it comes out clean, the preparation is ready.) Turn over on a rack, remove the paper and let it cool. Raise the oven temperature to 360°F.

◆ Cut the cake into 1-inch-wide slices. Place them onto a cookie sheet and return to the oven for 8-10 minutes, until crisp and dry.

Spiral cookies

Time needed: *30 minutes*
(plus cooling time)
Difficulty: medium

INGREDIENTS FOR 8 SERVINGS
4 cups of flour
1 1/4 cups of softened butter
3/4 cup of sugar
2 egg yolks
1 teaspoon of vanilla
grated peel of one organic lemon
2 tablespoons of unsweetened cocoa

Spiral cookies

◆ Butter and flour a large cookie sheet.
◆ Put the flour and vanilla in a mound on a work surface and make a well in the center. Place the butter in pieces, sugar, egg yolks and lemon peel. Knead rapidly and briefly. Divide the dough into 2 equal portions. In one portion, blend in the cocoa and refrigerate for at least 1 hour, covered with plastic wrap.
◆ Roll out both balls into thin sheets and cut out from each sheet two 8x4 inch rectangles. Put each dark rectangle over a light one, folding the dark one 1/4 inch under, then roll it up. Cover each roll with plastic wrap and refrigerate for at least 30 minutes.
◆ Preheat the oven to 360°F.
◆ Unwrap the rolls, cut into 1/4 inch slices and place onto the cookie sheet. Bake the cookies for 10-12 minutes, remove with a spatula and cool on a rack.

Viennese pretzels

Time needed: *50 minutes*
(plus resting time)
Difficulty: medium

INGREDIENTS FOR 6 SERVINGS
2 1/2 cups of flour
3/4 cup of softened butter
6 egg yolks
1/4 cup of sugar
grated peel of an organic lemon
1 tablespoon of cocoa
3 1/2oz of grated dark chocolate

◆ Butter and flour a cookie sheet. Put the sifted flour in a mound on a working bench and make a well in the center. In it place the butter cut into pieces, the sugar, egg yolks and lemon peel. Knead with your fingertips, form a ball and refrigerate for at least 1 hour, covered with plastic wrap.
◆ Preheat the oven to 360°F.
◆ With the dough, form 8-inch long sticks a little thinner than a pencil. Fold them into circles, twist the ends, turning them toward half way and gently press to make them stick. Put the pretzels onto the cookie sheet and bake until golden. Cool completely.
◆ Melt the chocolate in a double boiler. Put 1/3 of the pretzels onto a rack, placed over a cookie sheet. Cover pretzels with the melted chocolate and let it harden in a cool place. Sprinkle half of the remaining cookies with the cocoa.
◆ Place the pretzels onto a dish, alternating them according to color.

Viennese pretzels

Licorice cookies

Spicy madeleines

Time needed: *40 minutes*
(plus resting time)
Difficulty: easy

INGREDIENTS FOR 8 SERVINGS
4 eggs
3/4 cup of sugar
2 1/2 cups of flour
1/2 cup of butter
3 tablespoons of milk
1 teaspoon of vanilla
1/2 teaspoon of powdered cardamom seeds
1/2 teaspoon of cinnamon
a pinch of nutmeg
a pinch of ground cloves

◆ Butter and flour indented Madeleine moulds. Melt the butter on low heat.
◆ In a bowl, mix the sugar, flour, vanilla and ground spices. Mix in the eggs, one at a time; stir in the milk and the melted butter. Refrigerate 3 hours.
◆ Preheat the oven to 370°F.
◆ Put the mixture into a pastry bag, fitted with a straight tube and fill the molds. Bake for about 20 minutes, until lightly golden. Remove from the oven and cool on a rack. Transfer them onto a plate.

Skpicy madeleines

Whole-wheat date cookies

Time needed: *50 minutes*
Difficulty: easy

INGREDIENTS FOR 6 SERVINGS
1 1/4cups of flour
1 1/4cups of whole-wheat flour
3/4 cup of softened butter
3/4 cup of sugar
1 egg
1 teaspoon of baking powder
1/4 cup of dates
1 tablespoon of powdered sugar

◆ Butter and flour a cookie sheet. Preheat the oven to 400°F.
◆ Pit the dates and chop them finely. In a large bowl, using an electric mixer, whisk the butter and sugar until creamy; add the egg and the sift-

Whole-wheat date cookies

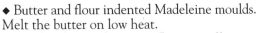

Cookies from Merano

ed flour (both kinds) with the baking powder. Add the dates, mix, shape into walnut sized balls and put onto the cookie sheet.
◆ Bake for 15-20 minutes; remove the cookies from the cookie sheet with a spatula and let them cool on a rack.
◆ Lightly dust with the powdered sugar and transfer onto a dish.

Cookies from Merano

Time needed: *50 minutes*
(plus resting time)
Difficulty: easy

INGREDIENTS FOR 6 SERVINGS
1 1/2 cups of flour
1 tablespoon of peeled ground almonds
6 tablespoons of softened butter
1/3 cup of sugar
1/2 teaspoon of baking powder
1 egg yolk
grated peel of 1/2 organic lemon
a pinch of salt
1 tablespoon of powdered sugar
3 tablespoons of red currant jam

◆ Butter and flour a cookie sheet.
◆ Put the sifted flour and baking powder in a mound on a work surface and make a well in the center. Add the butter in pieces, salt, almonds, sugar, egg yolk and lemon peel. Rapidly knead with your fingertips and refrigerate for 30 minutes, covered with plastic wrap.
Preheat the oven to 360°F.
◆ With a rolling pin, thinly roll out the dough. With a cookie cutter, cut circles of 3 inch in diameter. (Knead the trimmings and roll out again to cut more circles until all the dough has been used.)
◆ Make 3 holes of 1 inch in diameter with a cutter in half of the circle. Put the circles onto the cookie sheet and bake for 10-15 minutes, gently remove them; place onto a rack and let them cool.
◆ Heat the jam with 1 tablespoon of water and brush it onto the circle without holes. Sprinkle the circles with the holes with powdered sugar and put these on top of the ones with the jam. Pour the remaining jam in a parchment paper cone and distribute it into each hole to completely fill them.

Amaretti

Time needed: *1 hour and 15 minutes*
Difficulty: easy

INGREDIENTS FOR **6** SERVINGS
1 3/4 cups of powdered sugar
1 1/3cup of peeled almonds
1 1/2 oz of bitter almonds
3 egg whites
30 wafers

◆ Butter a cookie sheet and preheat the oven to 400°F.
◆ Grind the almonds in a mortar to a fine powder and fold in the two egg whites. Mix and knead the ingredients by hand, adding half the sugar and, little by little, the remaining egg whites and remaining sugar (keeping aside two tablespoons); keep working the mixture until you have a soft dough.
◆ Form the dough into thirty uniform pieces. Form into balls and lightly press between the hands to make small circles of 1/3 inch thick. Place these circles individually on top of the wafers and put them onto the cookie sheet. Sprinkle with powdered sugar and bake for a few minutes until crispy. Remove from the oven and cool.

"Not so pretty but good"
cookies

Almond crisps

"Not so pretty but good" cookies

Time needed: *50 minutes*
Difficulty: easy

INGREDIENTS FOR **6** SERVINGS
1 1/3 cup of toasted coarsely chopped almonds
1 cup of powdered sugar
3 1/2 oz of stiff egg whites
1/3 cup of sugar
a pinch of salt

◆ Butter a cookie sheet and preheat the oven to 250°F.
◆ In a bowl, mix the almonds with the powdered sugar. In another bowl, whisk the egg whites with salt to soft peaks, add the sugar and continue whipping. Gently fold in the mixture of almonds and powdered sugar.
◆ Drop walnut size mounds on the cookie sheet, leaving a space between each one. Bake for 30-40 minutes until golden. Remove with a spatula and cool on a rack.

Savoyard cookies

Almond crisps

Time needed: *50 minutes*
Difficulty: medium

INGREDIENTS FOR **6** SERVINGS
1/2 cup of sugar
2 tablespoons of flour
1 1/2tablespoons of melted butter
1 1/2 oz of thinly sliced almonds
2 egg whites

◆ Butter a cookie sheet and preheat the oven to 350°F.
◆ In a bowl, mix the egg whites with the sugar, flour and melted butter. Add the thinly sliced almonds and drop the mixture by tablespoons directly onto the cookie sheet, leaving enough space between each one. Flatten each mound of mixture with wet fingertips until very thin. You may need to use several cookie sheets or to bake in several batches.
◆ Bake the cookies for about 15 minutes until the edges become brown in color. Remove with a spatula and immediately lay them around a rolling pin, then press slightly and shape them into tiles. Serve cold.

Savoyard cookies

Time needed: *30 minutes*
Difficulty: easy

INGREDIENTS FOR **6-8** SERVINGS
3 eggs
3/4 cup of flour
1/2 teaspoon of vanilla
2 tablespoons of powdered sugar
a pinch of salt

◆ Butter and flour a cookie sheet and preheat the oven to 350°F.
◆ In a bowl, using an electric mixer, whisk the sugar, vanilla and egg yolks, until the mixture is light and creamy. Add the sifted flour and mix. Fold in the egg whites, beaten to stiff peaks.
◆ Place the mixture in a pastry bag, fitted with a straight tube and pipe out directly onto the cookie sheet 2 inches long sticks. Sprinkle with one tablespoon of powdered sugar and bake for 10-12 minutes until the edges become light brown.
◆ Remove with a spatula and cool. Set on a dish and sprinkle with powdered sugar.

Norman sand cookies

Time needed: *40 minutes*
(plus resting time)
Difficulty: easy

INGREDIENTS FOR 6-8 SERVINGS
2 1/2 cups of flour
3/4 cup of softened butter
3 1/2 oz of powdered sugar
1/2 cup of pine nuts
1/4 cup of sugar
3 egg yolks
1/2 teaspoon of vanilla

◆ Butter a cookie sheet and line with parchment paper.
◆ In a food processor, mix together the pine nuts and sugar into a paste. In a bowl, whisk the butter, powdered sugar and vanilla. Add the egg yolks, pine nuts mixture and flour; mix well. Refrigerate for 2 hours.
◆ Preheat the oven to 350°F.
◆ Roll out the mixture on a floured work surface. Cut into even 1-inch squares. Place on a cookie sheet and bake for 15 minutes until slightly browned. Cool. Remove with a spatula and transfer to a serving dish.

Peanut cookies

Time needed: *35 minutes*
(plus cooling time)
Difficulty: easy

INGREDIENTS FOR 6 SERVINGS
1 3/4 cups of flour
7 oz of finely chopped peanuts
3/4 cup of sugar
6 tablespoons of softened butter
1/3 cup of whipping cream
1/4 cup of chopped candied citron
2 egg yolks
a pinch of salt
2 oz of grated dark chocolate
1 1/4 oz of peeled peanuts
1 oz of candied lime cut in small pieces

◆ Butter and flour a cookie sheet and preheat the oven to 340°F.
◆ In a bowl, mix the chopped peanuts, sifted flour, sugar, salt and chopped citron. Add the egg

yolks, butter in pieces and cream. Mix all the ingredients together and form nut sized balls with the mixture. Place them on the cookie sheet with much space between each one and bake for 15 minutes. Cool.
◆ Halve the peanuts. In a double boiler melt the chocolate. Pour it into a paper cone and trace a diagonal stripe on each cookie. While the chocolate is still soft, add a half peanut and a triangle of candied citron to decorate.

Brussels cookies

Time needed: *40 minutes*
(plus resting time)
Difficulty: easy

INGREDIENTS FOR 8 SERVINGS
2 1/2 cups of flour
3/4 cup of softened butter
1 cup of brown sugar
1 teaspoon of baking soda
1 teaspoon of vanilla sugar

◆ Butter and flour a cookie sheet and preheat the oven to 325°F.
◆ In a bowl, mix the butter in pieces with 1/2 cup of brown sugar, 1 tablespoon of water, the baking soda, the vanilla sugar and the sifted flour.
◆ On a work surface, roll the mixture into cylinders of 3/4 inch in diameter. Cover with plastic wrap and refrigerate for 3 hours. Cut the cylinders into thick rounds. Place them on the cookie sheet, leaving much space between each one. Sprinkle them with the remaining brown sugar.
◆ Bake for about 15 minutes and remove with a spatula. Cool on a rack and serve.

Viennese angel's kiss cookies

Time needed: *2 h;ours*
Difficulty: medium

INGREDIENTS FOR 4 SERVINGS
1 cup of peeled chopped almonds
2 egg whites
3/4 cup of sugar
grated peel of 1/2 organic lemon
2 teaspoons of lemon juice
a pinch of salt

◆ Butter and line a cookie sheet with parchment paper. Preheat the oven to 220°F.

◆ In a bowl, whip the egg whites with the salt to soft peaks. Slowly add the sugar and continue whipping to stiff peaks. Gently fold in 1 tablespoon of almonds, the peel and juice of the lemon.

◆ Drop the mixture onto the cookie sheet with a spoon, leaving much space between each mound. Bake until slightly golden and cookies easily detach themselves from the paper.

◆ To keep them fresh and dry put them in a tin cookie box.

Cinnamon daisies

Time needed: *45 minutes*

Difficulty: **easy**

INGREDIENTS FOR 6 SERVINGS
2 cups of flour
11 tablespoons of softened butter
1 tablespoon of cinnamon
1/3 cup of sugar
1 egg yolk
1 teaspoon of vanilla
3 1/4 oz of chopped dark chocolate

◆ Butter and flour a cookie sheet and preheat the oven to 350°F.

◆ On a work surface, put the sifted flour, the cinnamon and vanilla, make a well in the center and add the butter in pieces, sugar and egg yolks. Knead the ingredients rapidly with your fingertips and place the mixture into a patisserie bag, fitted with a large star tube. Pipe 3/4-inch flowers onto the cookie sheet.

◆ Bake for 10-12 minutes. Remove the cookies with a spatula and let them cool completely.

◆ In a double boiler, melt the chocolate. Transfer to a pastry bag, fitted with a small tube and pipe out chocolate all along the edges of the cookies; place a drop in the middle of each. Let the chocolate harden in a cool place before serving.

Malaysian cookies

Time needed: *45 minutes*

Difficulty: **easy**

INGREDIENTS FOR **6-8** SERVINGS
1/2 cup of coconut cream

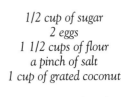

1/2 cup of sugar
2 eggs
1 1/2 cups of flour
a pinch of salt
1 cup of grated coconut

◆ Butter a cookie sheet and preheat the oven to 320°F.

◆ In a saucepan, cook the coconut cream with the sugar, stirring until completely dissolved.

◆ To the cream, add the eggs, the flour and salt. Turn onto a work surface and knead the mixture until it becomes smooth.

◆ Roll out to 1/3-inch thickness. Cut the dough into diamond shapes and place onto the cookie sheet. Spread the grated coconut evenly on the cookies and bake for 8-10 minutes, or until they are golden. Cool completely before serving.

Banana cookies

Time needed: *30 minutes*

Difficulty: **easy**

INGREDIENTS FOR **6** SERVINGS
2 1/2 cups of flour
1 tablespoon of potato starch
1 teaspoon of baking powder
a pinch of salt
2 bananas
1 cup of sugar
9 tablespoons of softened butter
2 eggs
1 teaspoon of vanilla
1 teaspoon of cinnamon
2 tablespoons of rum

◆ Butter and flour a cookie sheet. Preheat the oven to 350°F.

◆ Peel the bananas, cut them into pieces, mash them with a fork and mix them with the rum. In a bowl, using an electric mixer, whisk the butter and sugar (keeping 1 tablespoon aside) until creamy. Blend in the eggs, one at a time, the vanilla, the sifted flour with the potato starch and the mashed bananas in rum.

◆ Drop the mixture onto the prepared cookie sheet in walnut sized mounds, lightly separated from each other. Sprinkle the cookies with the remaining sugar mixed with the cinnamon and bake for about 15 minutes.

◆ Remove the cookies with a spatula and let them cool on a grid, then transfer them onto a plate.

Pear tartlets

Time needed:
40 minutes
Difficulty: complex
**INGREDIENTS
FOR 4 SERVINGS**

*5 oz of puff pastry
(see page 12)
2 pears
1/4 cup of sugar
juice of 1 lemon
1 tablespoon of powdered
sugar*

Preheat an oven to 375°F. Thinly roll out the dough and cut out four 5-inch circles.

◆ Brush four 4-inch molds with water. Line them with the circles of dough and prick the dough with a fork.

◆ Refrigerate the molds so the puff pastry will keep its shape better during baking.

er, onto the cookie sheet. Bake for 15-18 minutes. Cool completely before serving.
◆ Rinse, peel and core the pears. Cut them into thin slices and brush with lemon juice to preserve their color. Place the pear slices into the molds in concentric circles, overlaying them slightly. Sprinkle with the sugar and bake for 20-25 minutes.

◆ Sprinkle the tartlets with powdered sugar and serve warm.

Hazelnut filled puff pastry ravioli

Time needed: *1 hour*
Difficulty: medium

INGREDIENTS FOR 6 SERVINGS
*2 1/2 cups of flour
1/2 cup of sugar
6 tablespoons of softened butter
2 egg yolks
1 1/2 teaspoon of baking powder
grated peel of 1/2 organic lemon
6 tablespoons of milk
a pinch of salt*

Filling:
*1/3 cup of chopped toasted hazelnuts
1/4 cup of sugar ◆ 1 egg ◆ 1 egg yolk
1 tablespoon of rum*

Scones

◆ Butter and flour a cookie sheet. Preheat the oven to 360°F.
◆ To make the filling, mix the chopped hazelnuts with the sugar, the egg and the rum. Set the mixture aside.
◆ To make the pastry dough, put the flour on a work surface in a mound; make a well in the center. Add the sugar, salt, baking powder, butter in pieces, lemon peel and warm milk. Mix and knead well; roll out into a thin sheet. Cut out circles with a 3-inch indented cookie cutter. Brush them with the remaining egg yolk, lightly beaten with 1 tablespoon of water, and put 1 tablespoon of the filling on each circle.
◆ Fold the circles over and press on the edges to seal. Place the raviolis, separated from each oth-

*Hazelnut filled
puff pastry ravioli*

Scones

Time needed: *30 minutes*
Difficulty: easy

INGREDIENTS FOR 4 SERVINGS
*2 cups of flour ◆ a pinch of salt
1/2 teaspoon of baking soda
1 teaspoon of cream of tartar
2 3/4 tablespoons of cold butter
4 tablespoons of milk*

◆ Butter and flour a cookie sheet. Preheat the oven to 400°F.
◆ In a food processor, put the flour, salt, baking soda, cream of tartar and butter cut in pieces; pulse until the mixture resembles coarse meal.
◆ Continue mixing, slowly adding a mixture of 4 tablespoons of milk and 4 tablespoons of water.
◆ When blended, roll out the dough onto a floured surface into a 1/2-inch-thick sheet. Cut the sheet into 2-inch circles a round cutter.
◆ Knead the trimmings, roll out again and cut into more circles. Continue until the dough has been completely used.
◆ Place the circles onto the cookie sheet and bake for 10-15 minutes, or until the scones have risen and are golden in color.
◆ Serve scones hot with butter and jam. You may serve them for breakfast or to accompany tea. You can also serve them as a dessert at the end of a meal.

Pear tartlets

Fig and chocolate sweets

Time needed: *30 minutes*
(plus resting time)
Difficulty: medium

INGREDIENTS FOR 6 SERVINGS
10 soft dried figs
2 tablespoons of Maraschino
1/2 cup of grated dark chocolate
1 tablespoon of butter
2 tablespoons of powdered sugar
candied violets

◆ Finely chop the dried figs and soak them in the Maraschino. With the resulting mixture, form walnut sized balls and put them in the fridge for at least 30 minutes.
◆ Melt the chocolate and butter in a double boiler, dip in the fig balls, remove them with the aid of a cocktail stick. Place them on a rack to dry.
◆ Mix the powdered sugar in 1/4 teaspoon of water, added drop by drop until dense and creamy. Transfer to a pastry bag, fitted with a star tube and pipe out a rosette over every cake. Garnish with the candied violets, put the cakes in paper dollies and then onto a dish.

*Fig and chocolate
sweets*

Coffee delights

Time needed: *50 minutes*
(plus resting time)
Difficulty: medium

INGREDIENTS FOR 6 SERVINGS
3 cups of flour ◆ 3/4 cup of butter
3/4 cup of sugar ◆ 2 egg yolks
1 tablespoon of instant-coffee powder
1/2 cup of chopped toasted hazelnuts
3 1/2oz of chopped dark chocolate

Cream filling:
9 tablespoons of softened butter
1 tablespoon of instant coffee powder
1/2 cup of sugar
2 egg whites ◆ a pinch of salt

◆ Butter and flour a cookie sheet.
◆ With an electric mixer, whisk the butter and the sugar until creamy. Blend in the egg yolks, the coffee dissolved in 1 tablespoon of warm water, the chopped nuts and the sifted flour. Let the mixture rest in the refrigerator for about 30 min-

Coffee delights

utes. Preheat the oven to 360°F.
◆ To make the coffee cream, follow the recipe on page 17 for a classic butter cream. Blend in the instant coffee dissolved in 1 tablespoon of warm water.
◆ Thinly roll out the dough onto a floured surface. On 3/4 of dough, cut out 2-inch circles, and with the remaining dough, cut out the same amount of 1-inch circles. Place them onto the prepared cookie sheet and bake for 10-15 minutes until lightly golden. Remove them from the cookie sheet with a spatula and cool completely.
◆ Transfer the coffee cream in a pastry bag, fitted with a star tube and pipe out a crown all along the edge of the larger circles, pipe a rosette in the center. Melt the chocolate in a double boiler, dip in the smaller circles, let them cool, lay them in the center of the larger circles and let them harden before serving.

Fig and almond cookies

Time needed: *1 hour*
Difficulty: easy

INGREDIENTS FOR 4 SERVINGS
1 cup of sugar ◆ 1 tablespoon of honey
2 1/4 cups of flour
3/4 cup of softened butter
2 1/2oz of soft dried figs
1/4 cup of toasted peeled almonds
4 eggs ◆ almond essence

Decoration:
2 tablespoons of chopped almonds
1 tablespoon of honey

◆ Preheat the oven to 360°F. In a bowl, using an electric mixer, whisk the butter until light and creamy. Blend in the sugar, honey, eggs (one at a time) and sifted flour.
◆ Finely chop the dried figs and almonds and add to mixture. Stir in, adding a few drops of almond essence.
◆ Butter and flour 20 miniature muffin molds. Fill them 3/4 full with the mixture and place on a cookie sheet.
◆ Bake for about 20 minutes until raised and golden. Remove from the oven onto a rack and let cool. Brush the surface of each cake with honey and sprinkle with chopped almonds.

*Fig and almond
cookies*

Pine nut nougat

Time needed: *1 hour*
Difficulty: medium

INGREDIENTS FOR **6** SERVINGS
2 1/2 cups of sugar
1/2 cup of pine nuts
1 cup of flour
grated peel of one organic lemon
2 drops of vanilla

◆ In a heavy bottom stainless steel saucepan, cook the sugar in 1/2 cup of water on low heat for 12-15 minutes until syrupy and dense.
◆ Lightly flour the pin nuts and mix them into the syrup with the remaining flour, lemon peel and vanilla. Continue to cook for another 10-15 minutes.
◆ Pour the mixture onto a marble surface or a lightly greased cookie sheet. Spread it to 1-inch thickness. When cool, cut into diamond shapes.
◆ Let cool completely and, when nougat is firm, place on a serving dish.
◆ They can be kept for about 1 month, wrapped in aluminum foil in a cool and dry place.

Pine nut nougat

Kiwi tartlets

Time needed: *1 hour*
(plus resting time)
Difficulty: medium

INGREDIENTS FOR **8** SERVINGS
1 1/2 lb of ripe Kiwi
5 tablespoons of apricot jelly

Shortbread pastry:
2 1/2 cups of flour
9 tablespoons of butter
1/3 cup of sugar
1 egg yolk
grated peel of an organic lemon
a pinch of vanilla

Pastry cream:
1/3 cup of sugar ◆ *3 egg yolks*
1 1/4 cups of milk
1/3 cup of flour
grated peel of 1/2 organic lemon
a pinch of vanilla

Kiwi tartlets

◆ Butter and flour eight 4-inch tartlet molds.
◆ Prepare the shortbread pastry (see page 12) and refrigerate for 1 hour, covered with plastic wrap.
◆ Prepare the pastry cream (see page 16) and cool, stirring occasionally.
◆ Preheat the oven to 400°F.
◆ Thinly roll out the shortbread pastry dough and cut it into eight 5-inch circles. Line the molds with the dough. Prick the dough with a fork, cover it with aluminum foil and fill with rice or beans. Bake for about 20 minutes, until lightly golden. Remove and discard the rice and aluminum foil; let the tartlets cool.
◆ Peel the kiwis and slice them thinly. Fill each tartlet with a spoonful of pastry cream and top with the kiwi slices. Brush with the jelly, melted in a double boiler.

Raisin cookies

Time needed: *35 minutes*
Difficulty: easy

INGREDIENTS FOR **4** SERVINGS
2 cups of flour
4 tablespoons of butter
1/2 cup of sugar ◆ *1 egg*
3 tablespoons of dry white wine
1/4 cup of milk
grated peel of 1/2 organic lemon
1/2 cup of raisins
1/2 teaspoon of baking powder

◆ Preheat the oven to of 390°F. Butter and flour a large cookie sheet. Soak the raisins in warm water.
◆ Place the sifted flour with the baking powder and sugar in a mound on a work surface and make a well in the center. Add the butter in pieces, the egg, white wine and grated lemon peel. Knead until smooth. Blend in the strained dried raisins.
◆ With a rolling pin, roll out the dough to 1/2-inch thickness and cut into circles with a round mold, or with the edge of a glass. Knead the trimmings and continue to cut our disks until all of the dough has been used up.
◆ Put the circles onto the cookie sheet and bake for about 15 minutes.
◆ Gently remove the cookies onto a rack to cool. Place them onto a serving dish.

Raisin cookies

Ginger candies

Time needed: *40 minutes*
(plus soaking and refrigeration time)
Difficulty: medium

INGREDIENTS FOR 6 SERVINGS
1 1/2 oz toasted, finely chopped hazelnuts
1/3oz of dried apricots ◆ 1 egg white
2/3 oz of finely chopped candied ginger
2 tablespoons of powdered sugar
1 teaspoon of lemon juice

For the outer candy:
2/3 cup of peeled, finely chopped almonds
1 1/4oz of sugar ◆ 1/2 egg white
1 tablespoon of lemon juice
2/3oz of peeled almonds

◆ Soak the apricots in warm water for 30 minutes.
◆ To make the outer candy, mix the chopped almonds with the sugar, lemon juice and egg white, until smooth. Place in the refrigerator for 2 hours, covered with plastic wrap.
◆ Dry and finely chop the apricots. Mix them with the hazelnuts, candied ginger and powdered sugar. Put in the refrigerator for about 1 hour.
◆ Remove both mixtures from the refrigerator. Make the same amount of little balls with both mixtures. Lightly press the balls of almond mixture, and making a small cavity, put in the hazelnut balls.
◆ Coarsely chop the remaining almonds and put a piece on each candy.

Frou-frou

Time needed: *50 minutes*
Difficulty: medium

INGREDIENTS FOR 6-8 SERVINGS
7 oz of marzipan
1 tablespoon of powdered sugar
2 tablespoons of apricot jelly

Filling:
6 tablespoons of softened butter
1/4 cup of sugar
1/3oz of egg white ◆ a pinch of salt

Glaze:
3 1/2oz of powdered sugar
1 tablespoon of alchermes
1 egg white ◆ lemon juice
2 tablespoons of peeled pistachios

◆ Preheat the oven to 225°F.
◆ On a work surface dusted with powdered sugar, roll out the marzipan into a thin sheet. With a cookie cutter, cut out as many 2-inch circles as possible and line 1-inch molds with these circles. Bake for 30 minutes; let them cool.
◆ With the filling ingredients, prepare a classic butter cream (see page 17).
◆ To make the glaze, mix the egg white with the lemon juice and alchermes, add the powdered sugar a little at a time until mixture is thick and smooth.
◆ Brush the inside of the marzipan tartlets with the apricot jelly, melted in a double boiler. Put the butter cream in a pastry bag, fitted with a straight tube and pipe out a large mound on each tartlet. Pour the pink glaze into a parchment paper cone and completely cover the tartlet filling. Place in a cool place until glaze is hard and garnish with the pistachios.

Semolina delights with raisins

Time needed: *1 hour and 10 minutes*
Difficulty: easy

INGREDIENTS FOR 6 SERVINGS
2 cups of milk
2/3 cup of semolina
1/2 cup of sugar
2 tablespoons of butter
3 eggs ◆ 1/2 cup of raisins
grated peel of one organic lemon
a pinch of salt
2 oz of chopped bittersweet chocolate
1/4 cup of raisins

◆ Butter and flour 6 1/2-cup molds. Preheat the oven to 360°F.
◆ Soak the raisins in warm water. Bring the milk to a boil and slowly add the semolina, stirring constantly with a wooden spoon. Cook for 20 minutes; remove from heat and mix in the butter in pieces; add the sugar, lemon peel, drained raisins and salt.
◆ Pour the mixture into the molds and bake for 30-35 minutes. Remove from the oven, slide the blade of a knife around the edge of the molds and turn cakes onto a serving dish.
◆ In a double boiler, melt the chocolate. Pour into a parchment paper cone and draw chocolate sunbursts on top of each cake. Garnish with the raisins.

Coconut cones

Time needed: *25 minutes*
(plus resting time)
Difficulty: easy

INGREDIENTS FOR **6-8** SERVINGS
7 oz of fresh or dried coconut
1/3 cup of sugar
1/3 cup of powdered sugar
2 eggs
1 egg yolk
1 teaspoon of vanilla flavored powdered sugar

◆ Butter a cookie sheet. Preheat the oven to 360°F.
◆ Grate the coconut and mix with the eggs, egg yolk and all 3 types of sugar, keeping 1 tablespoon of powdered sugar aside. Let the mixture rest for at least 30 minutes.
◆ Shape the mixture into many egg-sized balls. Lightly press the bottom a little, to shape each egg into a cone. With a sharp knife, make some light vertical cuts from top to bottom. Place cones onto the cookie sheet and bake for 15-20 minutes until golden.
◆ Let them cool completely and serve sprinkled with the remaining powdered sugar.

Little chocolate baskets

Time needed: *50 minutes*
(plus resting time)
Difficulty: medium

INGREDIENTS FOR **6** SERVINGS
Shortbread pastry:
1 1/2 cups of flour
4 tablespoons of butter
1 egg yolk
grated peel of 1/2 organic lemon
1/3 cup of ground toasted hazelnuts

Cream:
7 oz of chopped bittersweet chocolate
1/3 cup of whipping cream
8 tablespoons of butter

Topping:
3 1/2oz of milk chocolate

◆ Butter and flour 12 small muffin molds.
◆ Prepare shortbread pastry dough (see page 12) with the above listed ingredients. Refrigerate for 1 hour, covered with plastic wrap.
◆ Preheat the oven to 360°F.
◆ Thinly roll out the shortbread pastry dough, cut out 3-inch circles with an indented cutter. Line the 12 molds with the circles. Prick dough with a fork; cover with a sheet of aluminum foil and fill the molds with rice. Bake the tartlets for about 15 minutes. Remove and discard rice and aluminum foil, and transfer onto a dish. Let them cool.
◆ To make the cream, melt the chocolate in a double boiler; pour it in a bowl with the butter cut into pieces. Bring the whipping cream to a boil; pour it into the chocolate and whisk with an electric mixer until thick and frothy.
◆ Fill the cold pastry baskets with the chocolate cream and garnish with shaved milk chocolate curls.

Monferrato small cakes

Time needed: *40 minutes*
(plus resting time)
Difficulty: easy

INGREDIENTS FOR **8-10** SERVINGS
2 lb of Golden apples
1 cup of crumbled amaretti
2 tablespoons of breadcrumbs
1/4 cup of raisins
3 tablespoons of Marsala
1/4 cup of strong espresso coffee
1 tablespoon of unsweetened cocoa
3 eggs
1 tablespoon of acacia honey
grated peel of 1/2 organic lemon
10 small amaretti
2 tablespoons of apricot jelly

◆ Butter and flour a few miniature muffin molds. Soak the raisins in warm water.
◆ Mix the amaretti with the breadcrumbs, Marsala, eggs and coffee until well blended. Let the mixture rest for about 30 minutes, stirring occasionally.
◆ Preheat the oven to 325°F.
◆ Peel the apples and grate them. Mix them into the amaretti mixture together with the strained raisins, honey, lemon peel and cocoa. Pour this mixture into the molds and bake for 20-25 minutes.
◆ Transfer the cakes onto a serving dish, let them cool completely. Brush cakes with the apricot jelly, melted in a double boiler. Garnish with the amaretti brushed with jelly.

Cortemilia small cakes

Grind the hazelnuts in a mortar or in a food processor. Put the flour in a non-stick oven pan and toast it lightly until golden: be careful to not toast it too much, or it will have a bitter taste.

◆ In a small saucepan, mix the minced hazelnuts, half the sugar, the toasted flour, the egg and softened butter cut into pieces.

◆ Cook the mixture on a low heat for 5 min-

Time needed:
30 minutes
Difficulty: easy
INGREDIENTS
FOR **4-6** SERVINGS

1/3 cup of flour
1/2 cup of toasted, peeled hazelnuts
2 tablespoons of butter
1 egg ◆ *1 egg yolk*
1/4 cup of sugar
1 tablespoon of cocoa

utes, stirring continuously. Remove from the heat and blend in the remaining sugar and egg yolk. Spread the mixture onto a marble surface or onto a cookie sheet, brushed with water. Let it cool completely.

◆ Form small even sized balls with the cold mixture and sprinkle them with cocoa. Place them onto a serving dish as they are, or in miniature paper baking cups.

Strawberry tarts

Time needed: *1 hour*
(plus time in the refrigerator)
Difficulty: medium

INGREDIENTS FOR **6** SERVINGS
Shortbread pastry:
1 1/2 cups of flour
4 tablespoons of butter
1/4 cup of sugar ◆ *1 egg yolk*
grated peel of 1/2 organic lemon
1 1/4 oz of ground toasted almonds

Pastry cream:
3 egg yolks ◆ *1/3 cup of sugar*
1 cup of milk ◆ *2 tablespoons of flour*
1/2 teaspoon of vanilla
grated peel of 1/2 organic lemon

Topping:
1 1/4 cups of strawberries
2 tablespoons of strawberry jelly

◆ Butter and flour six 4-inch tartlet molds.
◆ Prepare a shortbread pastry dough (see page 16) with the above listed ingredients and refrigerate for 1 hour, covered with plastic wrap.
◆ Prepare a pastry cream (see page 16) with the above listed ingredients and let it cool, stirring occasionally.
◆ Preheat the oven to 360°F.
◆ Thinly roll out the shortbread pastry dough and line the molds. Prick dough with a fork, cover it with aluminum foil and fill with rice or beans. Bake for 10-15 minutes, remove and discard rice and foil, and let the tartlets cool before removing them from the molds.
◆ Rinse the strawberries in ice water, dry them and slice them thinly. Fill the tartlets with pastry cream and cover with the strawberry slices. Brush

Strawberry tarts

strawberries with the jelly, melted in a double boiler.

Blackberry puff pastry tarts

Time needed: *1 hour*
(plus time in the refrigerator)
Difficulty: complex

INGREDIENTS FOR **6-8** SERVINGS
7 oz of puff pastry (see page 12)
3 cups of blackberries
2 3/4oz of apricot jelly

Pastry cream:
1 cup of milk ◆ *2 egg yolks*
1/4 cup of sugar ◆ *1/2 oz of potato starch*
grated peel of 1/2 organic lemon
1 tablespoon of Kirsch

◆ Thinly roll out the puff pastry. Cut it into 5-inch circles. With them, line as many 4-inch tartlet molds as there are circles. Refrigerate for about 30 minutes.
◆ Prepare the pastry cream (see page 16) with the above listed ingredients, blend in the kirsch and let it cool, stirring occasionally.
◆ Preheat the oven to 390°F. Line the dough, in the molds, with aluminum foil and fill them with rice or beans. Bake for 15 minutes. Remove and discard rice and foil; transfer tartlets onto a dish and let them cool.
◆ Rinse the blackberries in ice water and dry them. Fill the tarts with pastry cream and cover with a layer of blackberries. Brush the berries with the jelly, melted in a double boiler.

Blalckberry puff pastry tarts

Cortemilia small cakes

Raisin cupcakes

Time needed: *40 minutes*
Difficulty: *easy*

INGREDIENTS FOR **6** SERVINGS
1 1/2 cups of flour
12 tablespoons of softened butter
1/2 cup of sugar
1/2 teaspoon of baking powder
2 eggs ◆ *1/3 cup of raisins*
1 1/4 oz of candied lime and orange peel, diced

◆ Butter and flour 2-1/2-inch muffin molds. Preheat the oven to 360°F.
◆ Soak the raisins in warm water.
◆ In a bowl, using an electric mixer, whisk the butter until creamy; blend in the sugar, the eggs, one at a time, the sifted flour and baking powder, the drained raisins and candied fruit.
◆ Pour the mixture into the molds, filling them up to half and bake for 15-20 minutes. Serve them cold.

Raisin cupcakes

Baba au rhum

Time needed: *1 hour*
(plus rising time)
Difficulty: *medium*

INGREDIENTS FOR **6-8** SERVINGS
2 1/2 cups of flour
8 tablespoons of softened butter
1/3 cup of sugar ◆ *1 teaspoon of yeast*
4 eggs ◆ *3 tablespoons of milk*
a pinch of salt
grated peel of half an organic lemon

Syrup:
1 cup of sugar
1 organic orange and 1 organic lemon
3 tablespoons of rum
1 vanilla bean ◆ *1 clove*
3 tablespoons of apricot jelly

◆ Butter and flour 8 individual baba molds.
◆ Dissolve the yeast in warm milk. Sift the flour into a large bowl, add the dissolved yeast and mix well. Blend in the butter, cut in pieces, the sugar, salt, lemon peel and the eggs, one at a time. Thoroughly knead the ingredients until dough is smooth and elastic. Cover with a kitchen towel and let the dough raise in a warm place until doubled in size.
◆ Preheat the oven to 400°F.

Babà au rhum

◆ Distribute the dough into molds, filling to 3/4. Let the dough raise again, in a warm place, until it has reached the edge of the mold. Bake for about 30 minutes.
◆ To make the syrup, cut the lemon and orange peel, carefully removing the pith. In a saucepan, bring 2 cups of water and the sugar, the citrus peel, the vanilla bean and clove to a boil. As soon as the sugar is dissolved, remove from heat and mix in the rum, keeping 1 tablespoon aside.
◆ Remove the babas from the molds and immediately dip them into the hot syrup. Drain them on a rack. Heat the jelly with the remaining rum and 2 tablespoons of water; brush it over the babas. Serve them cold.

Apple and custard bundles

Time needed: *1 hour*
Difficulty: *complex*

INGREDIENTS FOR **4** SERVINGS
7oz of puff pastry (see page 12)
2 large golden delicious apples
2 tablespoons of butter
4 teaspoons of sugar
1 teaspoon of cinnamon
1 teaspoon of powdered sugar

Pastry cream:
1 1/4 cups of milk
2/3 cup of flour ◆ *1/4 cup of sugar*
1 teaspoon of powdered sugar
1 egg yolk ◆ *1 teaspoon of vanilla*
1 tablespoon of slivered almonds

◆ Preheat the oven to 375°F.
◆ Prepare a pastry cream (see page 16) with the above listed ingredients (except for the almonds). Remove from heat and mix in the slivered almonds.
◆ Peel, core and dice the apples. In a non-stick pan, cook them for 10 minutes.
◆ Thinly roll out the puff pastry and cut into four 6-inch squares. Place a tablespoon of pastry cream and 1/4 of the applesauce in the middle of each square; fold the 4 edges towards the center; pinch the sides to seal.
◆ Put the bundles onto a buttered cookie sheet and bake for about 25 minutes. Transfer onto a plate, sprinkle with powdered sugar and remaining cinnamon; serve warm.

Apple and custard bundles

Norwegian sweet cakes

Time needed: *1 hour*
Difficulty: medium

INGREDIENTS FOR 6-8 SERVINGS
7 oz of marzipan
2 tablespoons of potato starch
1 tablespoon of peeled chopped pistachios
1 tablespoon of chopped candied lime
1 egg ◆ *2 egg whites*
a pinch of cinnamon ◆ *a pinch of salt*

Decoration:
3/4 cup of chopped bittersweet chocolate
2 tablespoons of powdered sugar
1 egg white ◆ *1 teaspoon of mint syrup*
a pinch of saffron

◆ Butter and flour six 2-inch molds. Preheat the oven to 350°F.
◆ Crumble the marzipan into a bowl and mix in the egg, pistachios, candied lime, cinnamon and potato starch, until well blended. Beat the egg whites with the salt to stiff peaks and gently fold into the mixture. Pour into the molds and bake for about 20 minutes. Transfer the cakes onto a rack and cool completely.
◆ Place the cakes onto a sheet of parchment paper. In a double boiler, melt the chocolate. Pour it over the cakes to cover them completely. Place cakes in a cool place until the chocolate is hard.
◆ Mix the egg white with the powdered sugar until thick and smooth. Divide it into 3 portions: To the first portion add the mint syrup; to the second portion add the saffron. Pour the yellow glaze into a parchment paper cone and draw vertical lines on the sides of the cakes, a circle on the top edge and a cross over the top. Fill opposite triangles on the top of the cakes with the green glaze and fill the other 2 with the white glaze. Let this glaze become hard before serving the cakes.

Mirlitons

Time needed: *1 hour*
Difficulty: complex

INGREDIENTS FOR 6 SERVINGS
5 oz of puff pastry (see page 12)
3/4 cup of sugar ◆ *3 eggs*
6 tablespoons of butter
1 tablespoon of Maraschino
2 tablespoons of powdered sugar

Norwegian sweet cakes

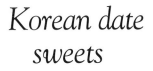
Mirlitons

Decoration:
4 oz of powdered sugar
1/2 cup of chopped bittersweet chocolate
lemon juice ◆ *1 egg white*
1 tablespoon of alchermes
1 tablespoon of mint syrup

◆ Preheat the oven to 360°F.
◆ Thinly roll out the puff pastry and with a dough cutter, cut six 5 1/2-inch circles. Brush six 5-inch tartlet molds with water, line them with the circles of dough and prick with a fork.
◆ Mix the sugar, Maraschino, eggs, and melted butter until well blended, fill the molds with this mixture to 1/4 inch from the edge. Sprinkle with powdered sugar and bake for about 20 minutes. Let the tartlets cool. Sprinkle them with powdered sugar.
◆ In a double boiler, melt the chocolate and spread it in a thin layer onto a sheet of parchment paper. Let it harden in a cool place. Cut out six 2-inch circles with a cookie cutter.
◆ In a bowl, mix the egg white with the lemon juice and powdered sugar until thick and smooth. Divide it into 3 bowls: Mix the alchermes in one and the mint syrup in another. Fill 3 parchment paper cones with the 3 glazes and decorate the chocolate circles, alternating colors. Let the glaze dry and top the tartlets with the chocolate circles.

Korean date sweets

Time needed: *20 minutes*
Difficulty: easy

INGREDIENTS FOR 4 SERVINGS
5 oz of dates
3 tablespoons of honey
1/2 teaspoon of cinnamon
3 1/2 oz of pine nuts

◆ Preheat the oven to 360°F. Toast the pine nuts in the oven until lightly golden and coarsely chop 2/3.
◆ Pit the dates, chop them finely and mix with the honey and cinnamon until well blended. Divide the mixture into small oval balls and, in each one, insert 1 whole pine nut. Roll each cake in the chopped pine nuts until covered and put them in miniature paper baking cups. Place them onto a serving plate.

Korean date sweets

Neapolitan "sfogliatelle"

Time needed: *1 hour and 40 minutes*
(plus resting time)
Difficulty: *complex*

INGREDIENTS FOR 6 SERVINGS
5 cups of flour
2 cups of vegetable shortening (or lard)
a pinch of salt
1 tablespoon of powdered sugar

Filling:
2 1/2 oz of very fine semolina
1/2 cup of ricotta
1/2 cup of powdered sugar
1 cup of chopped mixed candied fruit
a pinch of cinnamon
a pinch of salt ◆ *1 egg*

◆ Butter a cookie sheet.
◆ Put the flour into a mound onto a work surface and make a well in the center. Add 2/3 of shortening and the salt. Pass the ingredients through your fingers until the lard has absorbed the flour and mixture is coarse. Add enough cold water to make a rather firm dough. Knead for 15 minutes, beating it with a rolling pin and folding it with the palm of your hand, being careful not to tear it. Shape it into a ball, grease it with a little shortening and let it rest in a cool place for 1 hour, covered with plastic wrap.
◆ To make the filling, bring to a boil 1 1/2 cups of water with the salt, sprinkle with semolina and cook for 5 minutes, stirring constantly. Pour mixture into a bowl and let it cool; mix in the candied fruit, powdered sugar, cinnamon and ricotta. Set aside in a cool place for 30 minutes.
◆ Melt the remaining shortening. Roll the pastry dough into a very thin rectangular sheet and trim the sides to obtain a rectangle of 20x37 in. Cut it in 2 lengthwise, and in 2 again, obtaining 4 equal strips. Brush them with a little shortening, lay them one on top of the other and let them rest in a cool place for 1 hour.
◆ Preheat the oven to 450°F.
◆ Starting from one end, roll the dough forming a 5 1/2-inch roll. Cut the roll in 12 slices about 1/2-inch thick; place them onto a floured work surface and roll them out with a rolling pin, starting from the center to obtain oval shapes. Turn them over with a spatula and put a little filling in each.
◆ With a little lightly beaten egg, brush the pastry around the filling. Fold the oval into a half moon, pressing the edges to seal the pastry. Place

the Sfogliatelle on the cookie sheet; brush them with leftover shortening. Bake for 40 minutes until golden, lowering the heat by 50 degrees every 15 minutes, first to 400°F then to 350°F.
◆ Serve the Sfogliatelle hot, sprinkled with powdered sugar.

Almond sandwich

Time needed: *1 hour*
(plus rising time)
Difficulty: *medium*

INGREDIENTS FOR 6-8 SERVINGS
3 cups of flour ◆ *3 eggs*
8 tablespoons of softened butter
3 tablespoons of sugar
1/2 teaspoon of yeast
1/3 cup of milk
a pinch of salt
2/3 cup of praline almonds

Pastry cream:
3 egg yolks
1/3 cup of sugar
1 cup of milk
2 tablespoons of flour
1/2 teaspoon of vanilla
grated peel of 1/2 organic lemon

◆ Prepare a Brioche pastry dough (see page 14) with the flour, 2 eggs, butter, sugar, yeast, milk and salt. Let it rise, covered, in a warm place for 30 minutes.
◆ Knead the dough a little more, put it in a bowl (it should fill 1/3 of it), cover with a humid kitchen towel and refrigerate for 12 hours.
◆ Butter and flour a cookie sheet. Preheat the oven to 350°F.
◆ Knead the dough a little more on a lightly floured surface and roll it out into a thin rectangle. Put it onto the cookie sheet and brush it with the remaining egg, lightly beaten. Coarsely chop the praline almonds and sprinkle them onto the rectangle of dough. Let it rise in a warm place for 15-20 minutes; bake for about 20 minutes.
◆ Prepare the pastry cream (see page 16) and let it cool, stirring occasionally.
◆ Remove the brioche pastry from the oven and let it cool. Trim it to obtain an 8x5-inch rectangle. Cut it in 2, lengthwise; spread with the custard and cover with the second half of brioche. Slice the cake in rectangles and place on a serving dish.

Rice muffins

Time needed: *40 minutes*
Difficulty: medium

INGREDIENTS FOR 6 SERVINGS
1/4 cup of rice, cooked al dente
1 cup of milk ◆ *3 eggs*
1 3/4 tablespoons of melted butter
1 1/2 cups of flour ◆ *1 tablespoon of sugar*
1/2 teaspoon of salt
2 tablespoons of raisins
2 tablespoons of rum

◆ Butter and flour 12 small muffin molds. Preheat the oven to 400°F. Soak the raisins in rum.
◆ In a large bowl, using an electric mixer, whisk the flour, milk, egg, melted butter, sugar and salt. Blend in the boiled rice and drained raisins. Pour the mixture into the molds and bake for 20-25 minutes.
◆ Let cool slightly before serving.

Moka tartlets

Time needed: *50 minutes*
(plus resting time)
Difficulty: medium

INGREDIENTS FOR 6 SERVINGS
Shortbread pastry:
1 1/2 cups of flour
6 tablespoons of butter
1/3 cup of sugar ◆ *1 egg yolk*
grated peel of 1/2 organic lemon

Pastry cream:
1 cup of milk ◆ *3 egg yolks*
1/3 cup of sugar ◆ *1/3 cup of flour*
1/2 tablespoon of instant-coffee powder
1/2 teaspoon of vanilla

Topping:
1 tablespoon of powdered sugar
1 1/4 oz of candied cherries cut in stripes

◆ Butter and flour individual barquette molds.
◆ Prepare shortbread pastry dough (see page 12) with the above listed ingredients and refrigerate for 1 hour, covered with plastic wrap.
◆ Make a coffee pastry cream (see page 16) with the above listed ingredients and let it cool, stirring occasionally.
◆ Preheat the oven to 350°F.
◆ Thinly roll out the shortbread pastry dough and line the molds. Prick the dough with a fork, cov-er it with aluminum foil and fill the molds with rice or beans. Bake for 10-15 minutes. Remove and discard the rice and foil. Fill the tartlets with the coffee pastry cream. Raise the oven temperature to 400°F.
◆ Sprinkle the tartlets with powdered sugar and place them in the oven for a few minutes. Remove from the oven, garnish with the candied cherries and them onto a dish. Serve cold.

Pineapple mini cakes

Time needed: *1 hour*
(plus time in the refrigerator)
Difficulty: complex

INGREDIENTS FOR 6 SERVINGS
9 oz of puff pastry (see page 12)
1 lb of fresh pineapple
2 tablespoons of butter ◆ *1/4 cup of sugar*
1 tablespoon of powdered sugar
1 teaspoon of cinnamon powder

Pastry cream:
2 egg yolks ◆ *1/4 cup of sugar*
1 cup of milk ◆ *2 tablespoons of flour*
1/2 teaspoon of vanilla
grated peel of 2 organic lemons

◆ Prepare a pastry cream (see page 16) with the above listed ingredients and let it cool, stirring occasionally.
◆ Roll out the puff pastry dough into a very thin rectangle, pricking it with a fork. Place it onto a cookie sheet and refrigerate for about 1 hour.
◆ Preheat the oven to 420F. Line the rectangle with aluminum foil, place another cookie sheet over the rectangle, and place some weights on it to keep the dough flat. Bake for 15 minutes; remove from oven; remove weights, foil and top cookie sheet. Raise oven temperature to 450°F.
◆ With a cookie cutter, cut the sheet into eight 4-inch circles; sprinkle them with powdered sugar and replace in the oven for a few minutes until cara-melized.
◆ Dice the pineapple and in a non-stick pan, roast in butter for 5 minutes. Halfway through the cooking, add the sugar, stirring often until caramelized. Remove from heat and stir in the cinnamon.
◆ Pour the pastry cream over the 4 puff pastry circles and put over the diced pineapple, keeping 1 tablespoon aside. Cover with the remaining circles and garnish with the remaining diced pineapple. Serve warm.

Little "dobos"

Butter 3 cookie sheets and line them with buttered parchment paper. Preheat the oven to 350°F.

◆ In a bowl, beat the egg yolks with half the sugar, vanilla, and heavy cream until mixture is creamy. Blend in the flour and potato starch. Whisk the egg whites with the salt to soft peaks; continue whisking, adding the remaining sugar a little at a time. Gently fold into the egg yolk mixture.

◆ Pout the mixture 2-inch thick onto the cookie sheets. Bake for about 15 minutes. Remove from the oven and let the cake cool completely.

◆ To make the mousse, melt both chocolates in a double boiler, with 1 tablespoon of water and the butter. Whisk the egg yolks with half the sugar; add melted chocolate and rum.

Time needed: *1 hour*
(plus time in the refrigerator)
Difficulty: complex
INGREDIENTS
FOR 6-8 SERVINGS
1/4 cup of sugar
1 teaspoon of heavy cream
1 oz of potato starch
1/3 cup of flour
a pinch of vanilla
a pinch of salt

Mousse:
1/2 cup of chopped bitter-sweet chocolate
1/2 cup of chopped milk chocolate
1 1/2 tablespoons of butter
2 eggs ◆ 1 teaspoon of rum
1/4 cup of sugar
a pinch of salt

Decoration:
4 tablespoons of strawberry jelly
1/4 cup of chopped bitter-sweet chocolate
1 tablespoon of crystallized sugar
mint leaves

Whisk the egg whites with the salt to stiff peaks; continue whisking, adding the remaining sugar a little at a time. Fold into the cold chocolate mixture.

◆ Put 1 cake layer on a cookie sheet, spread it with half of the chocolate mousse, cover with a second layer of cake; spread the remaining mousse and cover with the third layer of cake. In a double boiler, melt the strawberry jelly in 1 tablespoon of water; brush it over the top of the cake (1). Refrigerate for 2 hours.

◆ Remove the cake from the cookie sheet with a spatula and cut it into many rectangles of equal size (2). In a double boiler, melt the chocolate. Pour it into a parchment paper cone and pipe out a flower onto each rectangle (3). Finish decorating with a piece of sugar and a mint leaf (4).

Chocolate hedgehogs

Time needed: *40 minutes*
(plus time in the refrigerator)
Difficulty: medium

INGREDIENTS FOR 6-8 SERVINGS
1/2 cup of chopped milk chocolate
1/2 cup of chopped bittersweet chocolate
1/2 cup of whipping cream
1 tablespoon of sugar ◆ 2 tablespoons of rum
5 oz of dry cookies
3 tablespoons of unsweetened cocoa

Decoration:
3 oz of pine nuts ◆ 1/2 oz of candied cherries
1 oz of chopped white chocolate
3/4 oz of chopped milk chocolate

◆ Coarsely chop the dry cookies.
◆ In a saucepan, dissolve sugar in 1 tablespoon of

Chocolate hedgehogs

water, mix in whipping cream and bring to a boil. Remove from heat, add both chocolates and stir until completely dissolved. Blend in crumbled cookies, add rum and let the mixture cool. Stir again and refrigerate until mixture is hard.

◆ Put the mixture onto a work surface, form it into a 1 1/2-inch roll and cut into 1 1/2-inch long pieces. Shape each piece into a hedgehog and roll each one in the unsweetened cocoa.

◆ Insert the pine nuts into the hedgehogs to simulate spines, leaving the snout free. Cut the candied cherries into small pieces. In a double boiler, separately melt the white and milk chocolate and pour them into 2 parchment paper cones. Let 2 drops of white chocolate fall on each hedgehog's snout and stick 2 cherry pieces to form the eyes. Trace a little milk chocolate triangle on the tip of the snout to form the nose.

◆ Place the hedgehogs onto a serving dish and keep in a cool place until ready to serve.

Little "dobos"

Little fruit "savarins"

Time needed: *1 hour*
(plus rising time)
Difficulty: *medium*

INGREDIENTS FOR 6-8 SERVINGS
2 1/2 cups flour
9 tablespoons of softened butter
1/3 cup of sugar
1 teaspoon of yeast
4 eggs ◆ *2 cups of milk*
grated peel of one organic lemon
a pinch of salt
2 tablespoons of apricot jelly

Syrup:
1 cup of sugar
one organic orange
one organic lemon
1/3 cup of rum
1 vanilla bean
2 cloves

Filling:
1 cup of milk ◆ *3 egg yolks*
1/3 cup of sugar
2 tablespoons of flour
1/2 teaspoon of vanilla
grated peel of 1/2 organic lemon
1 teaspoon of unsweetened cocoa
2 tablespoons of Kirsch
1 cup of mixed berries
1/2 cup of whipping cream

◆ Butter and flour 6-8 individual savarin molds.
◆ Dissolve the yeast in warm milk. In a large bowl, sift the flour and mix in the milk, the butter in pieces, sugar, salt, lemon peel and the eggs, one at a time. Knead vigorously until dough is smooth and elastic. Cover with a cloth and let it rise in a warm place until it doubles in size.
◆ Preheat the oven to 400°F.
◆ Fill the molds up to 3/4 with the dough. Let it rise again until it reaches the edges of the molds. Bake for about 30 minutes.
◆ To make the syrup, cut off the orange and lemon peel. Cook the sugar in 2 cups of water with the citrus peel, vanilla bean and cloves on a low heat for a few minutes until the sugar dissolves. Remove from the heat and add the rum.
◆ Remove the savarins from the oven and with a slotted spoon, dip them completely into the hot syrup. Drain them onto a rack and brush them with the apricot jelly, melted in a double boiler.
◆ Prepare a pastry cream (see page 16) with the

milk, egg yolks, sugar, flour, vanilla and lemon peel. Divide it into 2 bowls. Add the cocoa to one and the Kirsch to the other.
◆ Rinse the berries in ice water and dry them. Put the chocolate pastry cream in a pastry bag and fill half the savarins. Transfer the Kirsch-scented pastry cream to a pastry bag and fill the remaining savarins. Put both kinds of savarins on a serving dish and garnish with berries and rosettes of whipped cream.

Candied fruit cakes

Time needed: *1 hour*
(plus soaking time)
Difficulty: *medium*

INGREDIENTS FOR 4 SERVINGS
1/2 cup of flour ◆ *1/4 cup of sugar*
1 egg ◆ *2 egg yolks*
2 oz of candied mixed fruit, diced
2 tablespoons of Maraschino

Decoration:
9 oz of marzipan
2 tablespoons of mint syrup
1 1/2 oz of candied mixed fruit, diced
3/4 cups of whipping cream
1 teaspoon of powdered sugar
2 tablespoons of apricot jelly

◆ Butter and flour four 5-inch molds.
◆ Soak the diced candied fruit in the Maraschino for 20 minutes.
◆ Preheat the oven to 350°F.
◆ In a large bowl, using an electric mixer, whisk the egg, egg yolks and sugar until thick and frothy. Blend in the sifted flour and candied fruit. Pour the mixture into the molds and bake for about 30 minutes. Remove from the oven and let the tarts cool completely.
◆ To decorate, mix the marzipan with the mint syrup until absorbed; sprinkle a work surface with the powdered sugar and thinly roll out the marzipan.
◆ Brush the cold tarts with the apricot jelly, melted in a double boiler. Cover tarts with marzipan, gently pressing with your hands to make the marzipan stick. Trim the excess marzipan and place the tarts onto a serving plate.
◆ Whip the cream; transfer to a pastry bag, fitted with a star tube and pipe out a crown around the border of each tart. Garnish with candied fruit.

Mini petits fours

Time needed: *2 hours*
(plus cooling time)
Difficulty: *complex*

INGREDIENTS FOR 10 SERVINGS

WITH HAZELNUTS
1 cup of chopped bittersweet chocolate
1 cup of ground toasted chopped hazelnuts
1/2 cup of powdered sugar
5 tablespoons of whipping cream

Decoration:
1 tablespoon of toasted hazelnuts
5oz of chopped milk chocolate

WITH MARZIPAN
6 oz of marzipan
1 tablespoon of alchermes
2 tablespoons of powdered sugar

Decoration:
1/2 cup of chopped white chocolate
2 tablespoons of chopped bittersweet chocolate

WITH PISTACHIOS AND CHOCOLATE
12 oz of marzipan
2 tablespoons of peeled chopped pistachios
2 tablespoons of powdered sugar
1/2 cup of chopped milk chocolate
1/2 cup of chopped bittersweet chocolate
3 tablespoons of whipping cream
2 tablespoons of butter ◆ *1 tablespoon of rum*

Decoration:
1/2 cup of chopped bittersweet chocolate
peeled pistachios

◆ To make the hazelnut petits fours, line a cookie sheet with parchment paper. In a double boiler, melt the chocolate. Mix in the hazelnuts, sugar and whipping cream, pour it onto the cookie sheet and spread it evenly with a spatula. Refrigerate until mixture is hard, turn it on a work surface and remove the paper. With a ruler, cut the chocolate mixture into 1/2-inch squares.
◆ To decorate, put the chocolates onto a grid and top each one with a hazelnut. In a double boiler, melt the milk chocolate. Pour it into a parchment paper cone and pipe out to cover the chocolates. Refrigerate until hard.
◆ To make the marzipan petits fours, mix the marzipan with the alchermes. Line a cookie sheet with parchment paper. Sprinkle a work surface with powdered sugar; roll out marzipan mixture the same dimension as the cookie sheet. Place the marzipan on cookie sheet.
◆ As for the hazelnut petits fours, divide the marzipan into 1/2-inch squares.
◆ To decorate, put the squares on a rack. In a double boiler, melt the white chocolate. Pour into a parchment paper cone and pipe out to cover marzipan squares. In a double boiler, melt the dark chocolate. Pour into another parchment paper cone and top each petit four with a drop of dark chocolate. Set aside until chocolate is hard.
◆ To make the pistachio and chocolate petits fours, working with your hands, blend the chopped pistachios into the marzipan. Line a cookie sheet with parchment paper. Sprinkle a work surface with powdered sugar; roll out the marzipan the same dimension as the cookie sheet. Place the marzipan on cookie sheet.
◆ Bring the whipping cream and the butter in pieces to a boil. Remove from heat and mix in both chocolates and rum until well blended. Spread the mixture onto the marzipan and refrigerate until hard. Turn it onto a work surface and remove the paper. As for the previous chocolates, cut into 1/2-inch squares.
◆ To decorate, put the squares onto a rack. Melt the dark chocolate in a double boiler; pour it into a parchment paper cone and pipe over the chocolates to cover. Top each chocolate with a pistachio and set aside in a cool place until hard.

Chestnut cakes

Time needed: *1 hour and 40 minutes*
Difficulty: *medium*

INGREDIENTS FOR 4 SERVINGS
1 1/2 lbs of chestnuts
1 1/4 cups of whipping cream
1 tablespoon of rum ◆ *1 teaspoon of vanilla*
1/4 cup of sugar ◆ *1 tablespoon of cocoa*
30 candied violets

◆ Boil the chestnuts in plenty of water and when almost cooked, drain carefully. Peel them and cut into pieces.
◆ Put chestnuts in a saucepan with 1 cup of whipping cream, the vanilla, rum, sugar and cocoa, keeping 1 tablespoon aside. Cook on moderate heat for 30 minutes, stirring continuously and adding a little water, if necessary, to avoid sticking. In a food processor, purée the mixture and cool completely.
◆ Shape the mixture into many walnut sized balls, press them lightly into circles and sprinkle them with the remaining cocoa.
◆ Put them in miniature paper baking cups; place them onto a serving dish and garnish with the remaining whipped cream and candied violets.

Almond and zucchini muffins

Time needed: *50 minutes*
Difficulty: easy

INGREDIENTS FOR 4-6 SERVINGS

2 cups of flour
1/2 teaspoon of baking powder
1/2 teaspoon of cinnamon
1 cup of sugar ◆ *2 eggs*
8 tablespoons of extra virgin olive oil
1/2 lb of zucchini ◆ *1 teaspoon of vanilla*
1/3 cup of peeled, ground almonds
1/4 cup of raisins ◆ *a pinch of salt*

◆ Butter 6 large muffin molds. Preheat the oven to 360°F.
◆ Soak the raisins in warm water. Rinse the zucchini, trim and coarsely grate them.
◆ In a large bowl, beat the eggs with the sugar until frothy; blend in the oil, drop by drop. Add the zucchini, vanilla, almonds, strained raisins, baking powder, cinnamon and flour a little at a time. Blend well; pour the mixture into the molds (filling them 3/4 full) and bake for 15-30 minutes. Remove from the oven.
◆ Let the muffins rest for 10 minutes before turning them onto a rack to cool completely.

Almond and zucchini muffins

Polish tartlets

Time needed: *40 minutes*
Difficulty: complex

INGREDIENTS FOR 6 SERVINGS

11 oz of puff pastry (see page 12)
1 egg
1/2 cup of grated bittersweet chocolate
1 oz of candied orange peel
1 tablespoon of powdered sugar

◆ Preheat the oven to 375°F.
◆ Thinly roll out the pastry dough and cut into four 3-inch squares. Brush with the lightly beaten egg.
◆ In each square, put 1/4 of the grated chocolate, folding the corners of each square toward the center and pinching to seal. Brush the bundles with the beaten egg, place them onto a cookie sheet and bake for 20-25 minutes.
◆ Remove the cookie sheet from the oven and raise the oven temperature to 450°F.

Polish tartlets

◆ Sprinkle the bundles with the powdered sugar and let them caramelize in the oven for a few minutes. Remove; transfer them onto a dish and serve cold, each topped with a candied orange peel circle.

Brazilian tartlets

Time needed: *1 hour*
(plus time in the refrigerator)
Difficulty: medium

INGREDIENTS FOR 6 SERVINGS

Shortbread pastry:
2 cups flour ◆ *5 tablespoons of butter*
1/3 cup of sugar ◆ *1 egg yolk*
1/2 teaspoon of vanilla

Pastry cream:
6 egg yolks ◆ *1 cup of milk*
3/4 cup of sugar ◆ *1/3 cup of flour*
1/2 teaspoon of vanilla
1/2 tablespoon of instant coffee powder

Glaze:
1 1/2 oz of powdered sugar
1 1/2 tablespoons of butter
1-2 tablespoons of milk
3 1/2 oz of chopped chocolate

Decoration:
1/3 cup of whipping cream
coffee beans

◆ Butter and flour eight 3-inch tartlet molds.
◆ Prepare a shortbread pastry dough (see page 12) with the above listed ingredients and put it in the refrigerator for 1 hour, covered with plastic wrap.
◆ Preheat the oven to 360°F. Thinly roll out the dough and with a cookie cutter, cut into eight 4-inch circles. Line the molds with the circles of dough; prick with a fork, cover with aluminum foil and fill with rice. Bake for about 15 minutes; remove the rice and foil and cool before transferring to a dish.
◆ Prepare a coffee pastry cream (see page 16) with the above listed ingredients and cool, stirring occasionally.
◆ Fill the tartlets to 2/3 with the coffee pastry cream. For the glaze, melt the chocolate in a double boiler with the butter, milk and powdered sugar. Spread the glaze over the custard and top each tartlet with a rosette of whipped cream and a coffee bean.

Brazilian tartlets

Date and almond puff pastries

Time needed: *1 hour*
Difficulty: complex

INGREDIENTS FOR 8 SERVINGS
1 lb of puff pastry (see page 12)
1/2 cup of sugar
1 egg yolk
2/3 cup of slivered almonds
1 teaspoon of vanilla
grated peel of half an organic lemon
1 lb of dates

◆ Butter a cookie sheet. Preheat the oven to 360°F.
◆ In a saucepan on low heat, cook the dates in 1 cup of water with the sugar, lemon peel and vanilla for 15 minutes. Drain the dates and pit.
◆ Roll out the puff pastry dough into a thin sheet and cut it into 3-inch circles with a cookie cutter. Top each circle with 2 dates and a few almonds slivers and cover with a second circle, pressing the edges to seal.
◆ Put the puff pastries onto the cookie sheet; brush them with the egg yolk, mixed with 1 tablespoon of water and bake for 30 minutes. Serve hot.

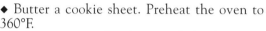

Date and almond puff pastries

Spanish petits fours

Time needed: *1 hour*
(plus time in the refrigerator)
Difficulty: medium

INGREDIENTS FOR 6 SERVINGS
Shortbread pastry:
1 1/2 cups of flour
7 tablespoons of butter
1/4 cup of sugar
2 egg yolks
grated peel of an organic lemon

Filling:
2 egg whites
2/3 cup of sugar
grated peel of one organic lemon
1 tablespoon of powdered sugar
1/2 cup of peeled ground almonds
1 tablespoon of apricot jelly
a pinch of salt

Spanish petits fours

◆ Butter and flour 2-inch tartlet molds.
◆ Make a shortbread pastry dough (see page 12) with the above listed ingredients and put it in the refrigerator for 1 hour, covered with plastic wrap. Preheat the oven to 375°F.
◆ Thinly roll out the dough. Cut it into circles with a 2-inch cookie cutter. Line the molds with the dough. Prick them with a fork, cover with aluminum foil and fill with rice. Bake for about 10 minutes.
◆ To make the filling, whisk the egg whites with the salt to stiff peaks; keep whisking, adding the sugar a little at a time. Add half of the ground almonds and the lemon peel.
◆ Remove molds from the oven and discard the rice and foil. Transfer the tartlets onto a dish and brush with the apricot jelly melted in a double boiler. Fill the tartlets with the almond mixture. Sprinkle with powdered sugar and remaining almonds. Replace in the oven at 400°F for 5-6 minutes until golden on top. Serve cold.

Irish apple cakes

Time needed: *1 hour*
(plus resting time)
Difficulty: medium

INGREDIENTS FOR 6 SERVINGS
2 1/2 cups of flour
1 1/2 teaspoon of baking powder
12 tablespoons of softened butter
3/4 cup of sugar ◆ *1 egg*

◆ Preheat oven to 400°F. Rinse apples, core and place in an oven dish. Bake for 15-20 minutes.
◆ Put the flour in a mound on a work surface and make a well in the center. Add the baking powder, sugar, butter in pieces and the egg. Knead rapidly and shape into a ball; put the dough in a cool place for 1 hour, covered with plastic wrap.
◆ Remove the apples from the oven, peel and purée. Lower the oven temperature to 360°F.
◆ Thinly roll out the dough and with a cookie cutter, cut into 2-1/2-inches circles. Drop spoonfuls of apple purée in the middle of the circles and fold them over into half moons. Place them on a cookie sheet and bake for 15-20 minutes until golden.
◆ Serve warm or cold, sprinkled with powdered sugar.

Irish apple cakes

White chocolate cakes

Time needed: *1 hour*
Difficulty: easy

INGREDIENTS FOR 6-8 SERVINGS
1/4 cup of grated white chocolate
4 tablespoons of butter
2 eggs ◆ 1/2 cup of sugar
1 teaspoon of vanilla
1 1/4 cups of flour ◆ a pinch of salt
1/2 cup of chopped bittersweet chocolate
1 tablespoon of powdered sugar

◆ Butter a 10-inch square cake pan and line the bottom with buttered parchment paper. Preheat the oven to 370°F.
◆ In a double boiler, dissolve half the white chocolate with the butter. In a bowl, using an electric mixer, whisk the egg yolks with the sugar, until light and creamy. Mix in the melted chocolate, vanilla, flour and the remaining white chocolate. Whisk the egg whites with the salt until stiff and gently blend into the mixture.
◆ Pour into the cake pan and bake for about 30 minutes. Let it cool and cut into 2-inch squares.
◆ Sprinkle with the powdered sugar. In a double boiler, melt the dark chocolate. Pour it into a parchment paper cone and pipe out on each cake a design of your choice.

Pàrdulas

Time needed: *50 minutes*
(plus resting time)
Difficulty: medium

INGREDIENTS FOR 4 SERVINGS
2 cups of flour
3 tablespoons of softened butter
a pinch of salt

Filling:
1 lb of Sardinian fresh pecorino cheese
1/2 cup of sugar
1 sachet of saffron ◆ 2 egg yolks
grated peel of 1/2 organic orange
1 tablespoon of raisins

◆ Butter a cookie sheet. Soak the raisins in warm water.
◆ Put the sifted flour into a mound on a work surface and make a well in the center. Add the butter in pieces and enough water to obtain a smooth and elastic dough. Cover it with a cloth and let

it rest for 30 minutes. Preheat the oven to 340°F.
◆ In a bowl, mix the pecorino cheese with the sugar and saffron, dissolved in 1/2 teaspoon of warm water. Mix in the egg yolks, orange peel and strained raisins until well blended.
◆ Roll out the dough into a thin sheet and cut out 2-1/2-inch circles with a cookie cutter. In the middle of each circle, put a little pecorino mixture and lift the edges of the dough, pinching them to obtain little dough cups or bowls. Place them away from each other, on the cookie sheet. Bake for 15-20 minutes. Let them cool completely before transferring onto a serving dish.

"Moulin Rouge" Tartlets

Time needed: *1 hour*
(plus resting time)
Difficulty: complex

INGREDIENTS FOR 6 SERVINGS
Shortbread pastry:
1 1/2 cups of flour ◆ 4 tablespoons of butter
1/4 cup of sugar ◆ 1 egg yolk
grated peel of 1/2 organic lemon
1oz of peeled, chopped almonds

Pastry cream:
3 egg yolks ◆ 1/3 cup of sugar
1 1/4 cup of milk
2 tablespoons of flour
1/2 teaspoon of vanilla
1 oz of dark chocolate

Decoration:
2 egg whites ◆ 1 1/4 cups of flour
a pinch of salt ◆ 2/3 cup of sugar
grated peel of 1/2 organic lemon
1 tablespoon of powdered sugar
1 oz of candied lime cut into strips

◆ Butter and flour miniature tartlet molds.
◆ Prepare the shortbread pastry dough (see page 12) with the above listed ingredients blending in the chopped almonds and refrigerate for 1 hour, covered with plastic wrap.
◆ Preheat the oven to 360°F.
◆ Make a pastry cream (see page 16) with the egg yolks, sugar, milk, flour and vanilla; remove from heat and mix in the chocolate. Let the pastry cream cool, stirring occasionally.
◆ Thinly roll out the shortbread pastry dough and with an indented cookie cutter, cut it into 2-1/2-inch circles. Line the molds with the circles and prick with a fork. Cover with aluminum foil and

fill with rice or beans. Bake for about 15 minutes; remove the rice and foil. Let the tartlets cool before transferring them onto a serving dish.

◆ Pour the chocolate pastry cream into a pastry bag and pipe it into the tartlets. Whisk the egg whites with the salt to stiff peaks, and continue whisking, adding the sugar a little at a time and the lemon peel. Fill the tartlets with the meringues, leveling with a spatula. Put the remaining beaten egg whites into a parchment paper cone and pipe rosettes to cover the tartlets. Put the candied lime strips in between the rosettes and place in the oven for a few minutes until lightly golden on top.

Flames

Time needed: *2 hours*
(plus time in the refrigerator)
Difficulty: *complex*

INGREDIENTS FOR 6 SERVINGS
Shortbread pastry:
1 cup of flour
4 tablespoons of butter
1/4 cup of sugar ◆ *1 egg yolk*
grated peel of 1/2 organic lemon

Filling:
1 lb of chestnuts ◆ *1 cup of milk*
1/2 cup of sugar
1 teaspoon of unsweetened cocoa
a pinch of cinnamon ◆ *1 tablespoon of rum*
4 tablespoons of softened butter
a pinch of salt

Topping:
1 cup of chopped bittersweet chocolate

◆ Butter and flour a cookie sheet.

◆ Prepare the shortbread pastry dough (see page 12) with the above listed ingredients and refrigerate for 1 hour, covered with plastic wrap.

◆ With a sharp knife, make a cut into the skin of the chestnuts and boil them for 15 minutes. Peel them, remove the internal skin and place them in a saucepan with milk, salt and sugar. Cook on low heat for about 1 hour, stirring occasionally. Purée. If it comes out too soft, dry mixture out on high heat. With an electric mixer, whisk the chestnut purée with the butter in pieces, cocoa, cinnamon and rum.

◆ Preheat the oven to 360°F.

◆ Thinly roll out the shortbread pastry dough and with a cookie cutter, cut it into 2-inch circles. Place circles onto a cookie sheet and bake them for about 15 minutes. Let them cool and place

them onto a rack.

◆ Put the chestnut cream into a pastry bag, fitted with a large star tube. Pipe out a high mound of cream over each circle, forming a "flame." In a double boiler, melt the chocolate. Pour it into a parchment paper cone and pipe it over the flames, to cover. Set aside in a cool place until chocolate is hard.

Viennese tartlets with lemon mousse

Time needed: *50 minutes*
(plus resting time)
Difficulty: *medium*

INGREDIENTS FOR 6 SERVINGS
Shortbread pastry:
1 1/2 cups of flour ◆ *4 tablespoons of butter*
1/4 cup of sugar ◆ *1 egg yolk*
grated peel of 1/2 organic lemon
1oz of peeled, finely chopped almonds

Mousse:
3/4 cups of heavy cream
1/2 cup of lemon juice
4 eggs ◆ *1 cup of sugar*
1/4 oz of unflavored gelatin
1 organic lemon ◆ *a pinch of salt*

◆ Butter and flour six 3-inch tartlet molds.

◆ Prepare the shortbread dough (see page 12), adding the almonds and refrigerate for at least 1 hour, covered with plastic wrap. Preheat the oven to 360°F. Soak the gelatin in a little cold water.

◆ Thinly roll out the dough and with an indented cookie cutter, cut it into six 5-inch circles. Line the tartlet molds with circles and prick with a fork. Cover the circles with aluminum foil and fill with rice. Bake for about 15 minutes; remove the rice and foil. Let the tartlets cool completely before transferring them onto a dish.

◆ Bring the heavy cream to a boil; remove from heat and stir in the gelatin. In a bowl, using an electric mixer, whisk the egg yolks with 3/4 cup of sugar; slowly add the hot whipping cream a little at a time; add the lemon juice. Let it cool.

◆ Whisk the egg whites with the salt to stiff peaks and continue whisking, adding the remaining sugar, a little at a time. Gently fold meringue into the egg and cream mixture and fill the tartlets with this mousse.

◆ Rinse and dry the lemon. Cut 1/2-inch triangles from the lemon peel and scald them for 2 minutes in boiling water. Garnish the tartlets with the dried lemon peel triangles.

Butter a cookie sheet. Preheat the oven to a high temperature of 400°F. Melt the butter on very low heat.

◆ In a bowl, mix the sifted flour with the sugar and egg whites. Blend in the melted butter, a little at a time. Add vanilla. Refrigerate batter for about 20 minutes.

◆ After the batter has rested, using a tablespoon, drop mounds of batter on the cookie sheet. With the back of a spoon, flatten the mounds into 6 oval forms, 6 inches long and 3 inches wide. Bake the wafers for 7-8 minutes until the edges start to brown. Open the oven door, and pull the cookie sheet half way out, to keep the wafers as hot as possible. Detach them one by one, with a spatula and put them over 6 upside down glasses or bowls.

◆ Shape the wafers into a boat, pressing with

Wafers with strawberry mousse

Time needed:
40 minutes
(plus resting time)
Difficulty: medium
INGREDIENTS
FOR 6 SERVINGS
Wafer:
1 cup of flour
1/2 cup of butter
1/2 cup of sugar
2 egg whites
1 teaspoon of vanilla

Mousse:
1 cup of strawberries
3/4 cups of whipping cream
3 1/2 oz of powdered sugar

Decoration:
1 1/2 oz of strawberries
a few mint leaves

the palm of you hand and pinching the ends. Work fast to make sure the wafers do not get cold. If they become to hard to shape, put them back in the hot oven for a few minutes, to soften. When cold, gently detach them and keep them in a dry place until ready to fill.

◆ To make the mousse rinse the strawberries in ice water, dry them and purée with powdered sugar. Whip the cream; gently fold into the strawberry purée and refrigerate until ready to serve.

◆ To decorate, rinse the strawberries in ice water, dry them, cut 6 in halves and slice the remainder. When ready to serve, distribute the mousse into the wafers; garnish with the halved strawberries at the ends of the boat and form a flower on the top with the sliced strawberries and mint leaves.

Apple crisps

Time needed: *45 minutes*
Difficulty: medium

INGREDIENTS FOR 4 SERVINGS
2 tablespoons of flour
1/3 cup of sugar
1 1/2 oz egg whites
4 tablespoons of butter
1 lb of golden apples
a pinch of salt

◆ Butter twelve 4-inch molds. Preheat the oven to 350°F.
◆ In a bowl, quickly mix the flour, egg whites, salt and 1/4 cup of sugar. Blend in 1 1/2 tablespoons of melted butter and 1/2 cup water to obtain a rather liquid mixture. Pour a thin layer of the mixture into each mold and bake until golden. Carefully detach the wafers from the molds and let them cool.
◆ Peel the apples, core and slice thinly. In a non-stick pan, cook them with remaining butter for 5 minutes. Add the rest of the sugar half way through. Place a little applesauce on each wafer; cover with a second wafer, layer with a little more apple purée and cover with a third wafer. Continue this way until all the wafers and filling have been used. Serve warm.

Chestnut cream cones

Chestnut cream cones

Time needed: *50 minutes*
Difficulty: medium

INGREDIENTS FOR 6-8 SERVINGS
1 cup of flour
8 tablespoons of softened butter
1/2 cup of powdered sugar
4 egg whites
1 teaspoon of vanilla

Filling:
5 oz of mashed chestnuts
1/2 cup of powdered sugar
1 cup of whipping cream
4 tablespoons of rum

◆ Butter and flour a cookie sheet. Preheat the oven to 450°F.
◆ With an electric mixer, whisk the butter cut into pieces and the sugar, until smooth and creamy. Blend in the sifted flour, a little at a time, the vanilla and egg whites. Drop spoonfuls of the mixture into mounds on the cookie sheet. With the back of a spoon, press the mounds into thin 2-1/2-inch long ovals.

Wafers with strawberry mousse

◆ Bake them for 7-8 minutes until the edges start to brown.

◆ Open the oven door and folding the sheet half way out, detach the wafers with a spatula and while still hot, roll each one around the handle of a ladle to shape into a cone. Continue working rapidly, until all the wafers are rolled up and let the cones cool completely.

◆ To make the filling, mix the chestnut purée with the sugar and rum; gently fold in the whipped cream. Put the mixture into a pastry bag, fitted with a star tube. Pipe out into the cones. Place them onto a dish and keep in a cool place until ready to serve.

Coils

Coils

Time needed: *50 minutes*
Difficulty: *medium*

INGREDIENTS FOR 6 SERVINGS
8 tablespoons of softened butter
2/3 cup of powdered sugar
4 egg whites ◆ *3/4 cup of flour*
1 teaspoon of unsweetened cocoa

◆ Butter a cookie sheet.

◆ In a cardboard, cut out a 12-inch long and 2-inch wide rectangle. In the middle of it, trace a 9-1/2-inch-long and 1-1/2-inch wide rectangle. Also trace 2 triangles, one at each edge, with the vertex towards the inside and shaped like a swallow's tail. Cut out the drawings, keeping the shape of the cardboard intact.

◆ Preheat the oven to 375°F.

◆ In a large bowl, using an electric mixer, whisk the butter and the powdered sugar until creamy and light. Blend in the egg whites, one at a time and the sifted flour. If the mixture separates, warm it up in a double boiler and mix again.

◆ Mix the cocoa with 2 tablespoons of the egg mixture. Put the cardboard onto the cookie sheet and with a spatula, put a little of the light mixture into the cuts, forming a strip. Repeat until all mixture has been used. Put the dark mixture into a parchment paper cone and border each strip with a thread of dark mixture.

◆ Bake the strips for 8-10 minutes. They should not brown. Open the oven door and take the sheet half way out of the oven, detach each strip with a spatula and while still warm, roll it up on a 1-inch tube. Repeat the process with remaining strips. Let strips cool and place on a serving dish..

Rich rolls

Rich rolls

Time needed: *45 minutes*
(plus rising time)
Difficulty: *medium*

INGREDIENTS FOR 4 SERVINGS
1/8 lb of bread dough
1/4 cup of sugar
3 cups flour
1/2 cup of pine nuts
1/2 cup of candied citron
2/3 cup of raisins
2 eggs
6 tablespoons of extra virgin olive oil
a pinch of salt

◆ Oil a cookie sheet.

◆ Knead the bread dough with 1 cup of flour, 1 egg, 1 tablespoon of olive oil and the salt until well blended. Form a ball and let it rest, covered, in a warm place for 4 hours.

◆ Soak the raisins in warm water.

◆ Knead the dough again, adding the remaining flour, sugar, remaining egg, 3 tablespoons of oil and a little warm water until smooth; blend in the drained raisins, pine nuts and chopped candied citron. Knead another 5 minutes; divide into oval rolls and put them onto the cookie sheet, well separated from each other. Let them rise in a warm place for 6 hours.

◆ A quarter of an hour before the end of the rising time, preheat the oven to 375°F.

◆ Bake the rolls for 15-20 minutes, until golden. Serve warm or cold.

Cigarettes

Time needed: *1 hour*
Difficulty: *medium*

INGREDIENTS FOR 6 SERVINGS
8 tablespoons of softened butter
4 tablespoons of powdered sugar
4 egg whites
3/4 cup of flour
1 teaspoon of unsweetened cocoa
2 tablespoons of apricot jelly
2 tablespoons peeled chopped almonds

◆ Butter a cookie sheet.

◆ Cut a cardboard sheet into a 5-inch-long and 3-inch-wide rectangle. In this rectangle, trace another one, 3-1/2-inch-long and 1-1/2-inch-wide. Trace a line 1 inch away from the short sides. Cut the inside of both rectangles, leaving the traced line attached. Preheat the oven to 400°F.

◆ In a large bowl, using an electric mixer, whisk the butter cut into pieces with the powdered sugar until very creamy; blend in the egg whites, one at a time and the sifted flour. If the mixture separates, warm it up in a double boiler and mix again.

◆ Mix the cocoa in 1/3 of the mixture.

◆ Place the cardboard onto the cookie sheet. With a spatula, spread a thin layer of the light mixture inside the larger part of the rectangle; spread a thin layer of dark mixture into the smaller part. Detach the cardboard with a spatula; attach the light mixture to the dark mixture. Continue this way, forming many two-colored rectangles. Bake them for 8-10 minutes; do not brown.

◆ Open the oven door and take the cookie sheet half way out; detach each wafer and while still warm, roll it around a smooth pencil. Slide the pencil out and continue the process until all the wafers are rolled up. Let the cigarettes cool. Brush the light end with the apricot jelly, melted in a double boiler; press in the chopped almond. Place the cigarettes onto a serving dish.

Cigarettes

Brioches with pine nuts and raisins

Time needed: *50 minutes*
(plus rising time)
Difficulty: medium

INGREDIENTS FOR **6** SERVINGS
5 cups flour ◆ 3 eggs
8 tablespoons of softened butter
1 teaspoon of yeast
1/2 cup of sugar
1oz of pine nuts
1/3 cup of raisins
grated peel of one organic lemon
1 cup of milk ◆ a pinch of salt

◆ Butter and flour a cookie sheet. Soak the raisins in warm water.

◆ In a large bowl, using an electric mixer, whisk the butter with the sugar until creamy; blend in the salt and the eggs, one at a time, the lemon peel, sifted flour (except for 1 tablespoon) and the yeast dissolved in lukewarm milk. Knead the dough thoroughly on a work surface. Put the dough in a bowl and let it rise, covered in a warm place for 3-4 hours.

Brioches with pine nuts and raisins

◆ Drain the raisins, dry them and roll them into the remaining flour. Knead the dough again, blend in the raisins and pine nuts. Divide it into oval rolls and place them, each separated from the other, onto the cookie sheet. Let the rolls rise in a warm place for a further 2 hours.

◆ A quarter of an hour before the end of the rising time, preheat the oven to 375°F.

◆ Bake the Brioches for about 20 minutes, until golden.

◆ The Brioches are particularly tasty sliced and filled with whipped cream.

Puff pastry croissants

Time needed: *1 hour*
(più il tempo di riposo e di lievitazione)
Difficulty: complex

INGREDIENTS FOR **10-12** SERVINGS
5 cups flour ◆ 1/2 cup of milk
1/2 lb of softened butter
3 tablespoons of yeast◆ ◆ 1/4 cup of sugar
a pinch of salt ◆ egg

◆ Dissolve the yeast in 1/3 of a cup of warm water; dissolve the sugar and salt in the milk. Put the flour in a mound on a work surface, make a well in the middle and add the dissolved yeast, 4 tablespoons of butter and the milk. Knead until dough is smooth and elastic; let the dough rest for 30 minutes, covered.

◆ Roll out the dough in a 24-inch-long rectangle; spread 2/3 of the length with 13 tablespoons of butter cut into thin slices. Fold the sheet of dough into 3, starting from the unbuttered end. Turn the dough round a 1/4 turn; roll it out again to a 24-inch-long rectangle and fold it into 3 (as for puff pastry). Refrigerate for 2 hours, covered with plastic wrap. Repeat the 2 preceding operations with the remaining butter and refrigerate for at least 4 hours or, even better, overnight.

◆ Butter and flour a cookie sheet. Roll out the dough 1/4-inch thick and cut it into 2-1/2-inch-wide strips. Cut them diagonally to obtain equal-size triangles. Roll triangles towards the point, forming many croissants. Press the points slightly downwards; place the croissants onto a cookie sheet and let them rise in a warm place for about 40 minutes.

◆ Preheat the oven to 360°F.

◆ Brush the croissants with the lightly beaten egg and bake for 20-25 minutes. Serve warm or cold.

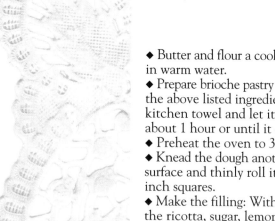

Viennese apple rolls

Time needed: *40 minutes*
(plus rising time)
Difficulty: *medium*

INGREDIENTS FOR 6 SERVINGS
2 1/2 cups flour ◆ *1 teaspoon of yeast*
8 tablespoons of softened butter
1/3 cup of sugar ◆ *4 eggs*
3 tablespoons of milk
3 Golden Delicious apples ◆ *a pinch of salt*

◆ Butter and flour a cookie sheet.
◆ Dissolve the yeast in warm milk. Mix the yeast with 1/4 of the flour and let it rise for 30 minutes in a warm place. In a bowl, whisk the butter with 3 eggs, 1/8 of a cup of sugar, remaining flour and salt. Blend in the yeast dough and knead on a work surface until dough is smooth and elastic. Cover and let the dough rise in a warm place for at least 1 hour.
◆ Peel the apples, core and slice thinly. Divide the dough into small pieces. In the middle of each piece, place 2 or 3 apple slices, sealing well. Brush each roll with the remaining lightly beaten egg and sprinkle with remaining sugar. Place the rolls on the prepared cookie sheet and let them rise in a warm place for 45-50 minutes.
◆ A quarter of an hour before the end of the rising time, preheat the oven to 360°F.
◆ Bake the rolls for about 20 minutes. Serve warm.

Danish rolls with ricotta

Time needed: *1 hour*
(plus rising time)
Difficulty: *medium*

INGREDIENTS FOR 6-8 SERVINGS
Brioche pastry:
3 cups flour ◆ *2 eggs*
8 tablespoons of softened butter
3 tablespoons of sugar ◆ *1 teaspoon of yeast*
6 tablespoons of milk ◆ *a pinch of salt*
Filling:
9 oz of ricotta ◆ *3 egg yolks*
1/2 cup of sugar ◆ *1/2 cup of raisins*
grated peel of one organic lemon ◆ *1 egg*
Topping:
2 tablespoons of apricot jelly

◆ Butter and flour a cookie sheet. Soak the raisins in warm water.
◆ Prepare brioche pastry dough (see page 14) with the above listed ingredients. Cover dough with a kitchen towel and let it rise, in a warm place for about 1 hour or until it doubles in size.
◆ Preheat the oven to 375°F.
◆ Knead the dough another 5 minutes, on a work surface and thinly roll it out. Cut it into little 5-inch squares.
◆ Make the filling: With an electric mixer, whisk the ricotta, sugar, lemon peel and egg yolks, add the strained raisins.
◆ Spread 2 tablespoons of filling on each square, leaving 1/4 in. empty around the edges. Fold the edges inward, making the angles square. Brush the pastry with the lightly beaten egg; place the cakes onto the cookie sheet and bake for 15-20 minutes.
◆ While still warm, brush the cakes with the jelly, melted in a double boiler. Serve cold.

Buccellato

Time needed: *1 hour and 10 minutes*
(plus rising time)
Difficulty: *medium*

INGREDIENTS FOR 6 SERVINGS
4 cups of flour
2/3 cup of sugar
8 tablespoons of softened butter
2/3 cup of raisins ◆ *2 eggs*
1/2 teaspoon of aniseeds
1/4 cups of milk
a pinch of salt

Topping:
1 teaspoon of thinly sliced almonds
1 tablespoon of lemon juice
1 tablespoon of powdered sugar

◆ Butter and flour a cookie sheet. Soak the raisins in lukewarm water.
◆ Dissolve the yeast in warm milk and mix in 1/4 cup of sugar and a little flour; stir until smooth. Let it rise in a warm place for 20 minutes.
◆ Put the remaining flour in a mound on a work surface, make a well in the center and add remaining sugar, salt, strained raisins, ground aniseeds, 1 egg and the butter cut into pieces. Knead vigorously until dough is smooth and soft. Blend in the yeast mixture and continue to knead for about 10 minutes. Cover and let dough rise in a warm place for about 20 minutes.
◆ Knead another 5 minutes; divide into 6 portions, shape into 6 rings and make a circular cut

on each one. Place rings on the cookie sheet and let them rise in a lukewarm place for at least 30 minutes. Preheat the oven to 350°F. Brush the rings with the remaining lightly beaten egg. Bake for 40-50 minutes.

◆ Mix the powdered sugar with the lemon juice; brush on the surface of the rings. Sprinkle them with the almonds and return to the oven for 5-6 minutes. Serve cold.

Brioches and croissants

Time needed: *1 hour*
(plus rising time)
Difficulty: *medium*

INGREDIENTS FOR ABOUT 12 BRIOCHES
2 1/2 cups flour
8 tablespoons of butter
1/4 cup of sugar ◆ *2 eggs*
3 tablespoons of milk ◆ *1 teaspoon of yeast*
a pinch of salt ◆ *egg yolk*

◆ Prepare a brioche pastry (see page 14) with the flour, butter, sugar, eggs, milk, yeast and salt. At the end of the second rising (12 hours in the re-frigerator), knead the dough a little and set 1/5 aside. With the remainder, form egg-sized balls. Place them on a buttered cookie sheet, well sep-arated from each other and make a cavity press-ing with your index finger. With the dough set aside, make hazelnut-sized balls, one for every large ball. Put a small ball in each cavity.
◆ Let the brioches rise in a warm place for about 1 hour, or until doubled in size.
◆ Preheat the oven to 375°F.
◆ Brush the brioches with the beaten egg yolk and bake for about 20 minutes, or until lightly golden.

INGREDIENTS FOR ABOUT 12 CROISSANTS
2 1/2 cups flour
8 tablespoons of butter
1/4 cup of sugar
2 eggs ◆ *1 teaspoon of yeast*
a pinch of salt ◆ *1 egg yolk*
3 tablespoons of any jam

◆ Prepare a brioche pastry (see page 14) with the flour, butter, sugar, eggs, milk, yeast and salt. At the end of the second rising (the 12 hours in the refrigerator), roll out the dough into a 1/4-inch-thick rectangle. Cut it in equal-size triangles and in each one, put a teaspoon of jam.
◆ Roll the dough up, starting from the base. Fold

ends and place the croissants on a buttered cook-ie sheet, separated from each other.
◆ Let them rise, in a warm place, for 1 hour, or until doubled in size.
◆ Preheat the oven to a 375°F. Brush the crois-sants with the beaten egg yolk and bake for about 20 minutes.

Danish wheels

Time needed: *1 hour and 30 minutes*
(plus rising and resting time)
Difficulty: *medium*

INGREDIENTS FOR 6-8 SERVINGS
Brioche pastry:
3 cups flour ◆ *2 eggs*
8 tablespoons of softened butter
3 tablespoons of sugar ◆ *1 teaspoon of yeast*
6 tablespoons of milk ◆ *a pinch of salt*
grated peel of one organic orange

Filling:
3/4 lb of apricots ◆ *1/4 cup of sugar*
1 tablespoon of apricot liqueur
1 tablespoon of toasted chopped hazelnuts

Topping:
1 egg ◆ *1 tablespoon of cloves*

◆ Prepare a brioche pastry (see page 14) with the above listed ingredients. Let the dough rise, cov-ered in a warm place for 30 minutes. Knead it an-other 5 minutes; put it in a large bowl (it needs to fill 1/3 of it), cover it with a humid kitchen towel and refrigerate for 12 hours.
◆ Make the filling: Rinse the apricots, pit and cut into small pieces. In a saucepan, cook apricots with sugar and liquor for about 20 minutes, stir-ring often. Let the mixture cool; mix in the hazel-nuts.
◆ Butter and flour a cookie sheet. Preheat the oven to 375°F.
◆ Roll out the dough into a thin rectangle. Cut the rectangle into 4-inch squares and brush them with the lightly beaten egg. Put a spoonful of fill-ing in the middle of each square. From each cor-ner, make a cut, diagonally, 1/3 of the way into the square. Fold 4 points of dough to the center, over the filling, alternating, and press points light-ly to form windmills.
◆ Place pastries away from each other on the cookie sheet and let them rise in a warm place for 1 hour or until doubled in size. Brush with the re-maining egg; insert a clove in the center and bake for about 20 minutes. Serve cold.

To make the marzipan, toast the almonds in the hot oven for a few minutes, without letting them brown. Let them cool and grind them.

◆ Beat the egg whites to stiff peaks, mix in sugar and ground almonds. Put this dough through a pasta maker, passing it repeatedly through the rollers until very thin (or roll it with a rolling pin on a work surface).

◆ Divide the dough into 4 equal portions. Blend the coffee, dissolved in 1 tablespoon of warm water, into the first portion. Blend the alchermes into a second portion. Blend the orange peel into a third portion and the pistachio paste into the last portion. Divide each portion into 3 balls and cut each ball in half. Place them onto a sheet of parchment paper and let them rest in a cool place for 24 hours..

◆ To make the coffee flavored marzipan flowers, insert the coffee beans around the half balls of coffee flavored marzipan. Melt the white chocolate in a double boiler, pour it in

Marzipan bouquet

Time needed: *1 hour (plus resting time)*
Difficulty: *complex*

INGREDIENTS FOR 24 FLOWERS

Marzipan:
1/2 cup of sugar
3 cups of peeled almonds
1 egg white
2 teaspoons of instant coffee
2 tablespoons of alchermes
grated peel of 3 organic oranges
1 tablespoon of peeled pistachios ground into a paste

Decoration:
a few coffee beans
2/3 cups of thinly sliced almonds
3 tablespoons of pistachios
1 teaspoon of pine nuts
1 tablespoon of chopped white chocolate
1 tablespoon of chopped bittersweet chocolate

a parchment paper come and pipe points on the flowers (**1**).

◆ To make the orange flavored marzipan flowers insert almond slivers around the half balls of orange flavored marzipan. Melt the dark chocolate in a double boiler; pour it into a parchment paper cone and pipe points on the flowers (**2**).

◆ To make the alchermes marzipan flowers, insert pine nuts around the half balls of the pink half balls (**3**).

◆ To make the pistachio flavored marzipan flowers, insert pistachios around the green half balls (**4**).

◆ Cut out 8 x 5 inch crepe paper rectangles (pink, green, yellow and orange). Wrap each one around a stick, open the paper into a funnel and in it, insert a marzipan flower. Make sure the paper sticks to the flower and forms bouquets wrapped in larger pieces of crepe paper. Use the bouquet as a centerpiece.

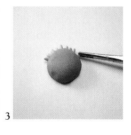
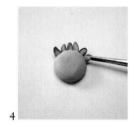

Almond pearls

Time needed: *35 minutes*
Difficulty: *medium*

INGREDIENTS FOR 4-6 SERVINGS
3 cups of peeled almonds
3 tablespoons of powdered sugar
1 egg white
14 candied cherries

Topping:
2/3 cup of peeled almonds
1 tablespoon of powdered sugar

Almond pearls

◆ Butter a cookie sheet. Preheat the oven to 375°F. Dry out the almonds in the oven without letting them brown. Grind them and mix them with the sugar and the egg white beaten to stiff peaks, blend the ingredients well. Pass the dough through a pasta maker's rollers or roll it with a rolling pin on a work surface. Form small 2-inch balls and in each, insert a candied cherry.
For the topping, coarsely chop the almonds and lightly toast them in the oven. Remove them from the oven, let them cool and roll the balls in, pressing lightly to make the nuts stick. Sprinkle with powdered sugar.
Put the pearls on a cookie sheet and bake them at 450°F for 2-3 minutes. Place them in miniature paper baking cups and serve cold.

Marzipan bouquet

Almond paste or marzipan

Time needed: *45 minutes*
Difficulty: *medium*

MAKES 14 OZ OF MARZIPAN
3 cups of peeled almonds
5 tablespoons of powdered sugar
1 egg white

♦ Preheat the oven to 325°F.
♦ Scald the almonds in boiling water, drain and peel them.
♦ Place them on a cookie sheet in the oven for a few minutes; do not let them brown. Grind them in a food processor (or in a mortar). Beat the egg whites to stiff peaks; fold in the sugar and the ground almonds until well blended.
♦ Put this dough through a pasta maker, passing it repeatedly through the rollers until very thin (or roll it with a rolling pin on a work surface).
♦ The marzipan can be used to make sweets of different shapes or to cover or decorate a variety of cakes.

Marzipan cakes

Marzipan cakes

Time needed: *1 hour and 20 minutes*
(plus time in the refrigerator)
Difficulty: *medium*

INGREDIENTS FOR 6 SERVINGS
Shortbread pastry:
33 cups flour
4 egg yolks
2/3 cup of sugar
1/2 cup of butter
grated peel of one organic lemon

Marzipan:
1 1/4 cups of peeled almonds
2 peeled bitter almonds
3/4 cup of sugar
1 1/2 tablespoons of diced candied orange peel
2 tablespoons of butter
1 egg yolk
1 tablespoon of powdered sugar

♦ Butter and flour 20 miniature molds. Prepare shortbread pastry dough (see page 12) with the above listed ingredients. Refrigerate for about 1 hour, covered with plastic wrap.
♦ Put the almonds in a hot oven for a few minutes; do not let them brown. Grind them with the sugar in a mortar (or in a food processor). Mix the almond paste with the candied orange, the butter and egg yolk, adding 3-5 tablespoons of ice water, until smooth.
♦ Preheat the oven to 400°F.
♦ Roll out the shortbread dough into a very thin sheet. With a 2-1/2-inch cookie cutter, cut out 20 circles, large enough to cover the molds and go over the edges. Cut 20 smaller circles with a 1-1/2-inch cookie cutter.
♦ Line the molds with the larger circles; distribute the marzipan over the dough; fold the excess dough toward the inside. Brush dough with a little water and cover with the smaller circles.
♦ Bake pastries for 15-20 minutes until golden. Cool completely and transfer onto a serving dish, sprinkled with powdered sugar.

Russian marzipan rolls

Time needed: *20 minutes*
Difficulty: *easy*

INGREDIENTS FOR 6-8 SERVINGS
11 oz of marzipan
1 tablespoon of instant coffee
1 tablespoon of milk
2 tablespoons of toasted slivered almonds

Russian marzipan rolls

♦ Butter and flour a cookie sheet. Preheat the oven to 375°F.
♦ Dissolve the coffee in the warm milk and mix it into the marzipan until completely absorbed.
♦ Roll out the marzipan 1-inch thick. Dice it and roll each cube into your hands to form even sized balls. Roll balls into the slivered almonds, pressing lightly to make them stick evenly.
♦ Place the marzipan balls on a cookie sheet and bake for about 5 minutes, or until golden. Let them cool. Place them in miniature paper baking cups; transfer to a serving dish.

Marzipan diamonds with pistachios

Time needed: *50 minutes*
(plus time in the refrigerator)
Difficulty: *medium*

INGREDIENTS FOR **6-8** SERVINGS
7 oz of marzipan
1 tablespoon of Maraschino
5 oz of chopped dark chocolate

Hazelnut chocolate:
1/2 cup of chopped milk chocolate
1/2 cup of chopped bittersweet chocolate
1/2 cup of chopped praline hazelnuts
3/4 cup of powdered sugar
5 tablespoons of whipping cream

Decoration:
1/2 cup of powdered sugar
1 egg white
a few drops of lemon juice
1 tablespoon of peeled chopped pistachios

◆ Line an 8-inch square cake pan with parchment paper.
◆ To make the hazelnut chocolate, melt both types of chocolate in a double boiler, mix in the sugar, the chopped hazelnuts and the whipping cream until well blended. Pour the mixture into the cake pan in an even layer and refrigerate for several hours.
◆ Melt the bittersweet chocolate in a double boiler. Blend the Maraschino into the marzipan and knead a little with your fingertips. Roll it out into a square the size of the cake pan and place it over the cold hazelnut chocolate. Cover evenly with the melted chocolate and return to the refrigerator.
◆ As soon as the chocolate has hardened, turn the preparation onto a work surface, remove the paper and, with a sharp knife, cut into small diamonds. Place them onto a serving dish with the dark chocolate side upwards.
◆ To decorate, scald the pistachios, remove the skin with the tip of a knife and cut them in half lengthwise. In a bowl, mix the powdered sugar with the egg white and lemon juice until thick and smooth. Pour this mixture into a parchment paper cone and decorate each diamond with 2 rectangles at the sides (or other drawings of your choice). Pipe a drop of glaze in the middle of each diamond and top it with half a pistachio.

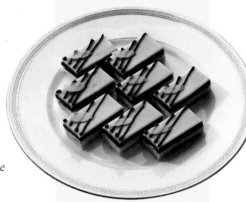

Marzipan slices with chocolate

Marzipan diamonds with pistachios

Marzipan slices with chocolate

Time needed: *45 minutes*
(plus cooling time)
Difficulty: *medium*

INGREDIENTS FOR **6-8** SERVINGS
3/4 lb of marzipan
5 oz of chopped white chocolate
5 oz of chopped dark chocolate
1 oz of slivered almonds
3 tablespoons of whipping cream
1 tablespoon of powdered sugar

Decoration:
3 oz of chopped dark chocolate
2 teaspoons of thinly sliced almonds

◆ Line an 8 x 4 inch cookie sheet with parchment paper.
◆ Knead the marzipan a little with your fingertips to soften it. On a work surface sprinkled with powdered sugar roll the marzipan out into a thin sheet. Cut out 2 rectangles, the same size as the cookie sheet and place one rectangle onto it.
◆ In a double boiler, melt the white chocolate with a tablespoon of whipping cream. Spread it evenly onto the marzipan in the cookie sheet, let it harden a little and sprinkle it with the slivered almonds.
◆ In a double boiler, melt the dark chocolate with the remaining whipping cream. Pour it over the slivered almonds. Let the dark chocolate harden a little and cover with the second marzipan rectangle. Set aside in a cool place until the chocolate is hard.
◆ Turn the cookie sheet over on the work surface, remove the paper and with a sharp knife, cut into 2-inches long rectangles.
◆ To decorate, melt the dark chocolate in a double boiler, pour it into a parchment paper cone and pipe 3 strips and a point on each rectangle. Top with almonds sliver.
◆ For a less sweet taste, you can replace the white chocolate with 10 oz of dark chocolate, melted in a double boiler with a tablespoon of strong coffee and 3 tablespoons of dark rum. This filling can be poured over the first and second marzipan sheets. Decorate the marzipan squares with coffee beans.

Copacabana meringue

Time needed: *2 hours*
Difficulty: *complex*

INGREDIENTS FOR **6** SERVINGS
3 egg whites ◆ *1/2 cup of sugar*
4 tablespoons of powdered sugar
a pinch of salt

Custard:
3 egg yolks ◆ *3oz of powdered sugar*
1 tablespoon of cornstarch
1/2 cup of milk ◆ *14 tablespoons of butter*
1 tablespoon of chopped dark chocolate
1 tablespoon of rum

◆ Butter a cookie sheet and line it with parchment paper.
◆ In a large bowl, using an electric mixer, whisk the egg whites with the salt to stiff peaks. Mix the sugar with the powdered sugar and blend it into the beaten egg white, a teaspoon at a time, beating for 1 minute between each addition.
◆ Preheat the oven to 200°F.
◆ Put the meringue mixture into a pastry bag, fitted with a star tube and pipe out twelve 2-1/2-inch long meringues onto the cookie sheet, leaving much space between each meringue. Bake for 1 3/4 to 2 hours. Do not let the meringues brown.
◆ To make the custard, mix the egg yolks with the sugar, add the cornstarch and hot milk, a little at a time. Cook on a moderate heat for 7-8 minutes, stirring constantly until the custard thickens. Melt the chocolate in a double boiler and blend it into the custard with the butter. Let it cool completely.
◆ Distribute the custard onto the flat side of 6 cold meringues, cover with the remaining meringues and place onto a serving dish.

Meringue sticks

Time needed: *2 hours*
Difficulty: *complex*

INGREDIENTS FOR **10** SERVINGS
4 egg whites ◆ *1/2 cup of sugar*
4 tablespoons of powdered sugar
a pinch of salt
1/2 cup of chopped bittersweet chocolate

◆ Butter a cookie sheet and line it with parchment paper.

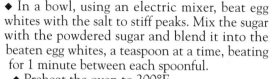

Meringue sticks

◆ In a bowl, using an electric mixer, beat egg whites with the salt to stiff peaks. Mix the sugar with the powdered sugar and blend it into the beaten egg whites, a teaspoon at a time, beating for 1 minute between each spoonful.
◆ Preheat the oven to 200°F.
◆ Put the meringue mixture into a pastry bag, fitted with a straight tube and pipe out 1-1/2-inch-long sticks onto the cookie sheet, leaving much space between each meringue. Sprinkle them with powdered sugar and let them rest for 10 minutes. Bake for about 2 hours. Do not let the meringues brown. In a double boiler, melt the chocolate; diagonally dip in the meringue sticks and place them onto a rack until chocolate is hard.

Meringue swans

Time needed: *2 hours and 30 minutes*
Difficulty: *complex*

INGREDIENTS FOR **6-8** SERVINGS
4 egg whites
1/2 cup of sugar
1/2 cup of powdered sugar
a pinch of salt
1 1/4 cups of whipping cream
3 tablespoons of chopped bittersweet chocolate

◆ Butter a cookie sheet and line it with parchment paper.
◆ In a large bowl, using an electric mixer, whisk egg whites with the salt to stiff peaks. Mix the sugar with powdered sugar and blend into the beaten egg whites, a teaspoon at a time, beating for 1 minute between each spoonful.
◆ Preheat the oven to 200°F.
◆ Put 1/3 of meringue mixture into a pastry bag, fitted with a straight tube and pipe out 3-inch long ovals onto the cookie sheet to make the body of the swans; also pipe out a backward S. To obtain the swans' neck, let a little meringue drop on one end of the S. Put the remaining meringue mixture into the pastry bag, changing the tube to a star one. On the cookie sheet, pipe wavy ovals, as large as the preceding ones but twice as large. They will become the swan's wings.
◆ Sprinkle the meringues with the remaining sifted powdered sugar and let them rest for 10 minutes. Bake for about 2 hours. Do not let the meringues brown. As soon as they are done, gently remove them from the paper and let them cool completely.

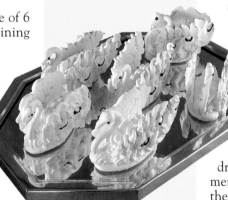

Meringue swans

◆ Whip the cream and transfer to a pastry bag with a star tube. Pipe out a layer of cream onto the swan's body and pipe a strip of cream in the center. Laterally insert, in the cream, the meringue wings and complete by inserting the necks in the center. Melt the chocolate and pour it into a parchment paper cone. Lightly decorate the wings with a few chocolate curls and trace the eyes with 2 chocolate drops.
◆ Place on a dish and serve.

Meringue kisses

Time needed: *2 hours*
Difficulty: *complex*

INGREDIENTS FOR 6-8 SERVINGS
6 egg whites ◆ *1/2 cup of sugar*
1/2 cup of powdered sugar ◆ *a pinch of salt*

Cream:
1/2 cup of mascarpone cheese
1 tablespoon of powdered sugar
1 teaspoon of instant coffee ◆ *1 tablespoon of milk*

◆ Butter a cookie sheet and line it with parchment paper.
◆ Mix the sugar with 3 oz of powdered sugar. With an electric mixer, whisk the egg white with the salt to stiff peaks. Blend the sugar into the beaten egg white, a teaspoon at a time, beating for 1 minute between each spoonful, until mixture is thick and shiny.
◆ Preheat the oven to 200°F. Transfer the meringue mixture into a pastry bag with a smooth or star tube and pipe small meringues of different shapes onto the cookie sheet; make 2 of every shape so you can pair them later. Sprinkle them with the remaining powdered sugar and set aside for 10 minutes.
◆ Bake for 60-65 minutes. The meringues should dry but not brown; they are done when they can easily be detached from the cookie sheet with a spatula. Let cool on a rack.
◆ To make the cream, mix the mascarpone cheese with the sugar and the coffee dissolved in the warm milk until well blended. Transfer the cream to a pastry bag, pipe out a little on the flat side of half the meringues and stick to the other halves, making sure the shapes match. Place them onto a serving dish.
◆ If you prepare the meringues ahead of time, it is preferable to keep them in a metal box and fill them just before serving. Avoid keeping them in the refrigerator or they will become soggy.

Meringue kisses

Fruit meringues

Fruit meringues

Time needed: *2 hours*
Difficulty: *complex*

INGREDIENTS FOR 6-8 SERVINGS
2 egg whites ◆ *1/4 cup of sugar*
2 tablespoons of powdered sugar
a pinch of salt
2 tablespoons of peeled, ground almonds
2 tablespoons of puréed apricots
1/2 cup of slivered almonds

◆ Butter a cookie sheet and line it with parchment paper.
◆ Mix the sugar with powdered sugar. In an electric mixer, whisk egg white with salt to stiff peaks. Blend the sugar into the beaten egg white, a teaspoon at a time, beating for 1 minute between each spoonful. When the mixture is thick and shiny, gently fold in the ground almonds and apricot puréed apricots.
◆ Preheat the oven to 200°F.
◆ With a pastry bag, distribute small mounds of meringue onto the cookie sheet. Sprinkle them with almonds and bake for about 2 hours. The meringues should dry without browning. They are done when they can be easily removed from the cookie sheet with a spatula. As soon as they are cold, place them in miniature paper baking cups.

Chocolate meringues

Time needed: *2 hours*
Difficulty: *complex*

INGREDIENTS FOR 6-8 SERVINGS
4 egg whites ◆ *1/2 cup of sugar*
2 1/2 tablespoons of powdered sugar
a pinch of salt
1 cup of unsweetened cocoa

◆ Butter a cookie sheet and line it with parchment paper.
◆ Mix the sugar with the powdered sugar. In an electric mixer, beat the egg white with the salt to stiff peaks. Blend the sugar into the beaten egg whites, a teaspoon at a time, beating for 1 minute between each spoonful. When mixture is thick and shiny, blend in the cocoa.
◆ Preheat the oven to 200°F. Transfer the mixture into a pastry bag, fitted with a star tube and pipe out small meringues onto the cookie sheet. Bake for 25-60 minutes, watching carefully for the meringues need to dry without browning. They are done when they can be easily removed from the cookie sheet with a spatula.

Two color ground cherries

Time needed:
15 minutes
(plus resting time)
Difficulty: easy
INGREDIENTS
FOR 6-8 SERVINGS

30 ground cherries
1 1/4 cups of chopped white chocolate
2 tablespoons of whipping cream
1 cup of chopped dark chocolate

Ground cherries are berries with a golden orange color, covered with a straw-color paper-thin skin. Its lovely, lightly acidulous taste marries well with chocolate.

◆ Delicately break the ground cherries' covering, and turn it backwards along the stem, forming a little handle.

◆ In a double boiler, melt the white chocolate with 2 tablespoons of whipping cream. Holding the berries by their "handles," dip them, one at a time into the chocolate and place them on aluminum foil to dry. In a double boiler, melt the dark chocolate with 2 tablespoons of water and dip in the berries half way to coat their bottom only in the dark chocolate.

◆ Let them dry again on aluminum foil. When the chocolate has hardened, place the ground cherries in miniature paper baking cups.

Half-moon truffles

Time needed: *1 hour*
(plus time in the refrigerator)
Difficulty: medium

INGREDIENTS FOR 6-8 SERVINGS
1/2 cup of chopped milk chocolate
1 cup of chopped bittersweet chocolate
10 tablespoons of heavy cream
4 tablespoons of butter
5 oz of white chocolate
1 1/4 cups of unsweetened cocoa

◆ Butter a small cookie sheet and line it with parchment paper.
◆ In a double boiler, melt both milk and bittersweet chocolates with the butter cut into pieces in 6 tablespoons of heavy cream. Pour the mixture onto the prepared cookie sheet in a 1/4-inch even layer. Refrigerate until hard.
◆ In a double boiler, melt the white chocolate with the remaining heavy cream, stirring until smooth and well blended. Set aside in the refrigerator for 1 hour.
◆ Form 1-inch balls with the white mixture and place them onto a small cookie sheet in the refrigerator.
◆ Take the cookie sheet with the layer of dark chocolate, turn it over on a work surface and remove the paper. Cut out 2 1/2-inch circles with a cookie cutter. Prepare as many pieces of plastic wrap as there are circles; place a circle on each piece of plastic wrap. Put a white chocolate ball over each dark chocolate circle and fold the plastic wrap, in order to wrap each ball in dark chocolate forming even sized balls.

Half-moon truffles

◆ Remove the film, roll the balls in cocoa; cut each in 4 segments. Put each segment in a miniature paper baking cup and refrigerate until ready to serve.

Cognac truffles

Time needed: *30 minutes*
(plus soaking time and time in the refrigerator)
Difficulty: complex

INGREDIENTS FOR 10 SERVINGS
7oz of chopped bittersweet chocolate
1/2 cup of whipping cream
1/2 cup of chopped prunes
1/4 cup of Cognac
3 tablespoons of unsweetened cocoa
1 teaspoon of sweet paprika

◆ In a bowl, soak the prunes in the cognac for 1 hour.
◆ In a saucepan, bring the whipping cream to a boil, remove from heat and blend in the chocolate; set aside for 2 minutes and stir.
◆ Let the mixture cool completely. Once it starts to set, mix in the prunes with the Cognac and refrigerate. Using a teaspoon, divide the mixture into hazelnut sized balls, place them on a tray lined with parchment paper and replace in the refrigerator for 1 hour.
◆ Roll the truffles in the cocoa, sifted with sweet paprika. Place them in miniature paper baking cups onto a serving dish and keep them in a cool place until ready to serve.

Cognac truffles

Two color ground cherries

Chocolate hazelnuts

Time needed: *40 minutes*
(plus time in the refrigerator)
Difficulty: medium

INGREDIENTS FOR 6 SERVINGS
1 cup of toasted peeled hazelnuts
1/2 cup of sugar
1 cup of chopped bittersweet chocolate
1 1/2 oz of chopped white chocolate
2 tablespoons of almond oil

◆ In a saucepan, cook the sugar with 2 tablespoons of water for 3 minutes, stirring continuously. Remove from heat and add the hazelnuts, stirring to wrap them in a layer of sandy sugar. Return saucepan to moderate heat and stir the hazelnuts until caramelized.
◆ Pour them onto an oiled marble surface and with 2 forks or small tongs, put them in mounds of three, with a fourth on top. Let them cool.
◆ In a double boiler, melt the dark chocolate, dip in the hazelnut mounds and place them on a rack to drain. Transfer them to the refrigerator on a sheet of parchment paper until the chocolate is hard.
◆ In a double boiler, melt the white chocolate. Pour it into a parchment paper cone and decorate the hazelnuts with white drops.

Chocolate hazelnuts

Fondants

Fondant candies

Time needed: *30 minutes*
(plus time in the refrigerator)
Difficulty: medium

INGREDIENTS FOR 6 SERVINGS
1/2 cup of toasted finely chopped hazelnuts
3/4 cup of peeled finely chopped almonds
4 1/2oz of assorted candied fruit
14 teaspoon of vanilla
2 tablespoons of icing sugar
1 cup of chopped bittersweet chocolate
1 1/2 oz of chopped white chocolate

◆ Cut half the assorted candied fruit into tiny circles and finely chop the remainder.
◆ In a double boiler, melt the icing sugar; mix in the almonds, hazelnuts, vanilla and finely chopped candied fruit. Form walnut-sized balls with this mixture and refrigerate them for at least 1 hour.
◆ In a double boiler, melt the bittersweet choco-

late and dip the balls, one at a time. Place them on a sheet of parchment paper and refrigerate until chocolate is hard. In a double boiler, melt the white chocolate, pour it into a parchment paper cone and let 3 drops fall on the top of each chocolate ball. Place 3 candied fruit circles of different colors on the chocolate. Keep the fondants refrigerated until ready to serve.

Walnut wonders

Time needed: *30 minutes*
(plus time in the refrigerator)
Difficulty: easy

INGREDIENTS FOR 8 SERVINGS
10 1/2 oz of walnuts
5 oz of honey
5 oz of chopped bittersweet chocolate

◆ In a double boiler, melt the bittersweet chocolate and let it cool lightly. Coarsely chop the walnuts and mix them with the honey. Blend into the melted chocolate and let the mixture cool completely.
◆ With the mixture, form walnut-sized balls, put them onto a sheet of parchment paper and refrigerate for about 1 hour. Put the chocolates in miniature paper baking cups and transfer onto a serving dish.

Coconut truffles

Time needed: *30 minutes*
(plus time in the refrigerator)
Difficulty: easy

INGREDIENTS FOR 8-10 SERVINGS
1 1/3 cups of chopped bittersweet chocolate
3 oz of chopped Novara cookies
1/3 cup of hazelnuts
2 tablespoons of rum
2 tablespoons of milk
2 tablespoons of grated fresh coconut

◆ Preheat an oven to 360°F.
Lightly toast the hazelnuts in the oven; peel, rubbing them with a cloth and finely chop.
◆ Melt 1 cup of chocolate with the milk. Remove from heat; blend in the rum, hazelnuts, and chopped cookies. Refrigerate until cold.

Coconut truffles

◆ With the mixture, form walnut-sized oval balls; roll them in the coconut, pressing lightly so it sticks. Return to refrigerator for at least 30 minutes.

◆ In a double boiler, melt the remaining chocolate. Dip the two ends of each truffle in the chocolate and set aside in the refrigerator on a sheet of parchment paper until ready to serve.

Boer liquor balls

Time needed: *40 minutes*
(plus time in the refrigerator)
Difficulty: medium

INGREDIENTS FOR 6 SERVINGS
1 1/2 cups of chopped bittersweet chocolate
1/3 cup of whipping cream
1 tablespoon of Kirsch
25-30 cherries in brandy
1 tablespoon of powdered sugar

◆ In a double boiler, melt 1 cup of chocolate with the whipping cream. Remove from heat and blend in the Kirsch. Refrigerate the mixture until hard.

◆ On a work surface, sprinkled with the powdered sugar, form 3-inch cylinders. Cut them into 1-inch-long pieces and in each one, insert a cherry. Wrap the cherries with the chocolate, forming balls and place them on a sheet of parchment paper. Refrigerate for at least 1 hour.

◆ In a double boiler, melt the remaining chocolate. Insert a skewer in the cherry balls and dip them in the chocolate. Place them onto a rack to dry. Transfer chocolates in miniature paper baking cups; place onto a serving dish.

Chocolate chestnuts

Time needed: *30 minutes*
(plus time in the refrigerator)
Difficulty: medium

INGREDIENTS FOR 8-10 SERVINGS
1 1/4 cups of chestnut purée
1/2 cup of powdered sugar
8 tablespoons of softened butter
1 1/4 cups of cocoa
1 cup of chopped bittersweet chocolate

Boer liquor balls

Milk truffles

Chocolate chestnuts

◆ In a bowl, using an electric mixer, whip the butter and sugar. Mix the cocoa with the chestnut purée and blend in the whipped butter. Put the mixture into a pastry bag, fitted with a straight tube and pipe chestnut sized mounds onto a sheet of parchment paper. Refrigerate for at least 4 hours.

◆ In a double boiler, melt the dark chocolate. With a skewer, dip in the chestnut balls, leaving top part free of chocolate. Line them onto a sheet of parchment paper and return to the refrigerator. Once the chocolate is hard, remove the stick from the chestnuts; put them into miniature paper baking cups and place onto a dish. Keep them in the refrigerator until ready to serve.

Milk truffles

Time needed: *40 minutes*
(plus time in the refrigerator)
Difficulty: easy

INGREDIENTS FOR 6 SERVINGS
9 oz of chopped milk chocolate
1/3 cup of whipping cream
1 tablespoon of sugar

Coating:
3/4 cup of chopped milk chocolate

◆ Dissolve the sugar in 1 tablespoon of water in a stainless steel saucepan on a low heat. Add the whipping cream and bring to a boil, stirring. Remove from the heat, add the chocolate, let the mixture rest for a few minutes, stir and let it cool completely. When the mixture starts to set, mix again and refrigerate until completely hard.

◆ With a teaspoon, take little portions of the mixture and from irregular hazelnut sized balls. Replace in the refrigerator for about 1 hour on a sheet of parchment paper.

◆ For the coating, melt the chocolate in a double boiler. Insert a skewer in the truffles and dip them into the chocolate; drain them on a rack. Roll truffles over the rack to create lots of little crevaces on the surface.

◆ Put the truffles on a tray in the refrigerator, and let them rest for at least 2 hours. When ready to serve, put them in petit paper dollies and onto a serving dish.

Two color chocolates

Time needed: *1 hour*
(plus time in the refrigerator)
Difficulty: *medium*

INGREDIENTS FOR **10** SERVINGS
14 oz of marzipan
1 1/4 cups of chopped bittersweet chocolate
1/4 cup of whipping cream
1 tablespoon of ground peeled pistachios
1 tablespoon of alchermes
a pinch of saffron

◆ Divide the marzipan into 4 equal portions. With your fingertips, blend in each separate portion, the ground pistachios, the alchermes and the saffron, dissolved in a drop of water. Keep the last portion natural.
◆ Roll out the marzipan into 12 in. long thin strips. Cut them into 1 1/2 in. in width. Melt 1 cup of chopped chocolate in the whipping cream; pour into a pastry bag, fitted with a straight 1/2-inch tube and pipe a string of chocolate along the whole length of each marzipan strip. Put the strips onto a tray and refrigerate for at least 30 minutes until the chocolate is hard.
◆ Roll up every marzipan strip around the chocolate cylinder. Melt the remaining chocolate in a double boiler, brush a thin layer over every cylinder and replace in the refrigerator for at least 30 minutes. Just before serving, slice the rolls and place them onto a dish..

Fudge

Time needed: *20 minutes*
Difficulty: *easy*

INGREDIENTS FOR **6** SERVINGS
1 1/2 cups of chopped bittersweet chocolate
3 3/4 cups of sugar
3/4 cup of whipping cream
6 tablespoons of butter
1 teaspoon of vanilla

◆ Line the bottom of 18 round molds of 3/4 inch in diameter with parchment paper.
◆ On very low heat, using a heat-resistant chinaware pan with a heat diffuser; melt the chocolate with sugar, whipping cream and butter. Stir until everything is dissolved, bring to a boil and cook very slowly for about 10 minutes. Remove from the heat and blend in the vanilla.
◆ Pour this tick mixture into the molds and let it cool at room temperature.

◆ Turn the molds over; remove the paper and put the fudge onto a serving dish.

Chestnuts in their husks

Time needed: *50 minutes*
(plus time in the refrigerator)
Difficulty: *medium*

INGREDIENTS FOR **8-10** SERVINGS
1 1/4 cups of chestnut purée
1/2 cup of powdered sugar
8 tablespoons of softened butter
1 1/4 cups of chopped dark chocolate
1/2 lb of marzipan
1/2 cup of ground, peeled pistachios

◆ In a bowl, beat the butter with the sugar until creamy, blend in the chestnut purée and refrigerate for about 30 minutes. Divide the mixture into hazelnut size balls and replace in the refrigerator for at least 3 hours.
◆ In a double boiler, melt 3/4 cup of dark chocolate. Dip in the chestnut balls, place them on a sheet of plastic wrap and set aside in a cool place until hard.
◆ Knead the marzipan with the pistachios, roll it out into a thin layer and cut out 1-1/2-inch circles with a cookie cutter.
◆ Place 1 chestnut ball on each circle and wrap the disk up thus forming larger marzipan balls. In a double boiler, melt the remaining chocolate. Dip the marzipan balls in the chocolate and place them on a sheet of plastic wrap. Let them set a little, then roll them over a rack, forming the spikes of the husk. Place the chestnuts onto a tray lined with parchment paper and refrigerate for 2 hours before serving.

Rum chocolates

Time needed: *30 minutes*
(plus time in the refrigerator)
Difficulty: *complex*

INGREDIENTS FOR **6** SERVINGS
1 1/4 cups of finely chopped milk chocolate
1/2 cup of finely chopped dark chocolate
1/2 cup of whipping cream
1 tablespoon of sugar
2 tablespoons of rum

◆ In a saucepan, dissolve the sugar in 1 table-spoon of water, add the whipping cream and bring to a boil. Remove from the heat, add 1 cup of milk chocolate and the dark chocolate; let the mixture rest for a few minutes, then stir. Blend in the rum and let the mixture cool. When it starts to set, stir and refrigerate until chocolate is hard.
◆ With a teaspoon, divide the mixture into hazel-nut-sized balls; place them on a sheet of parchment paper and return to refrigerator for about 1 hour.
◆ Roll the chocolates into the remaining chopped milk chocolate; place them in miniature paper baking cups and transfer onto a serving dish. Keep in a cool place.

Coffee flavored chocolates

Time needed: *20 minutes*
(plus time in the refrigerator)
Difficulty: easy

INGREDIENTS FOR **6** SERVINGS
1/2 cup of chopped dark chocolate
3 tablespoons of heavy cream
1 tablespoon of instant coffee

◆ Heat the heavy cream and dissolve the coffee in it. In a double boiler, melt the chocolate. Mix in the coffee-flavored cream and let it cool slightly.
◆ Pour the mixture into a pastry bag, fitted with a large star tube and pipe out small mounds into miniature paper baking cups. Refrigerate the chocolates for a few hours to set.

Maraschino chocolates

Time needed: *1 hour*
(plus time in the refrigerator)
Difficulty: medium

INGREDIENTS FOR **6-8** SERVINGS
7 oz of chopped milk chocolate
Filling:
1 1/4 cups of chopped milk chocolate
1/2 cup of softened butter
3 tablespoons of Maraschino

◆ In a double boiler, melt milk chocolate. Pour it into 18-20 chocolate molds. Rotate around molds to form thick cups. Turn them over to drain excess chocolate. Pass a spatula over the border of the molds to even out and refrigerate until set and hard. Set the remaining chocolate aside.
◆ ITo make the filling, melt the chocolate in a double boiler. In a bowl, whisk the butter until creamy, add the warm melted chocolate and blend. Add the maraschino. Put the filling into a pastry bag, fitted with a straight tube and pipe it into the cold molds. In a double boiler, melt the chocolate. Pour it onto the molds to cover the chocolates with a thin layer. Refrigerate until chocolate is hard.
◆ IOn a work surface, turn the molds and remove the chocolates by lightly banging the molds. Place the chocolates in miniature paper baking cups and keep in a cool place.

Hazelnut pralines

Time needed: *45 minutes*
(plus time in the refrigerator)
Difficulty: medium

INGREDIENTS FOR **6-8** SERVINGS
1 cup of chopped milk chocolate
1 cup of toasted finely chopped hazelnuts
1/2 cup of powdered sugar
5 tablespoons of heavy cream

Coating:
2 tablespoons of toasted hazelnuts
3/4 cup of chopped dark chocolate

◆ Butter a shallow cake pan and line the bottom with parchment paper.
◆ In a double boiler, melt the milk chocolate. Mix in the chopped hazelnuts, powdered sugar and heavy cream. Pour the mixture into the cake pan, spread it evenly and refrigerate until hard.
◆ Turn the chocolate layer onto a work surface. Remove the paper and with a ruler, cut it into small 3/4-inch squares. Roll the squares into balls.
◆ To make the coating, place a hazelnut over each ball, pressing lightly to make it stick. In a double boiler, melt the dark chocolate. Dip the prepared chocolate balls in the melted chocolate. Drain them over a rack and refrigerate until hard.
◆ These pralines, like all chocolates in general, need to be kept in a cool place (if necessary in the refrigerator). Before serving them, place them in miniature paper baking cups and onto a serving dish. If you let them rest for 1 or 2 hours at room temperature before serving, they will be tastier.

Pistachio brittle

Time needed:
30 minutes
Difficulty: medium
INGREDIENTS
FOR 6 SERVINGS
*3 3/4 cups of shelled
pistachios
1 cup of sugar
1/2 tablespoon of lemon juice
2 tablespoons of almond oil*

Preheat the oven to 300°F. Briefly scald the pistachios in boiling water and peel them. Dry them in the pre-heated oven without letting them brown.

◆ Oil a marble surface and a rolling pin.

◆ In a saucepan, cook the sugar with the lemon juice and 1 tablespoon of water. Add the pistachios and continue to cook on a moderate heat, stirring constantly until the sugar turns golden.

◆ Pour the mixture onto the marble surface and with the rolling pin, roll it out to 1/8-inch-thick, while mixture is still hot.

◆ Cut into 1-inch-wide strips and into 1 1/2-2-inch-long rectangles. Cool completely.

Candied almonds

Time needed: *45 minutes*
Difficulty: medium

INGREDIENTS FOR 16 ALMONDS
*16 peeled almonds
1 cup of sugar
2 tablespoons of corn syrup*

◆ Place the almonds in warm water for 5 minutes, drain and dry them well.
◆ In a saucepan, mix the sugar and corn syrup; place on moderate heat and bring to boil; cook until mixture is thick.
◆ Pour the syrup into a bowl and let it cool. With a wooden spoon, stir until it thickens. Pour the mixture onto a marble surface; knead it with your hands, forming 16 balls; insert an almond in each ball. Wrap each candied almond in aluminum foil or place them in miniature paper baking cup.

Pine nut brittle

◆ Pour the mixture onto the marble surface and with the rolling pin, roll it out to a 1/8-inch thickness, while still hot. Cut into 1-inch-wide strips and then into 1-inch squares. Cool completely.
◆ The pine nut brittle can be kept in airtight glass jars.

Chocolate nougats

Time needed: *3 hours*
Difficulty: complex

INGREDIENTS FOR 8 SERVINGS
*1 cup of honey
2 egg whites
a pinch of salt
1 cup of sugar
6 cups of finely chopped almonds
1 cup of grated bittersweet chocolate
grated peel of one organic orange
1 tablespoon of corn syrup
1 tablespoon of almond oil*

◆ Oil a cookie sheet.
◆ Stirring occasionally, cook the honey and corn syrup in a double boiler for about 2 hours until it reaches 220°F. With a sugar thermometer, check the temperature.
◆ In a saucepan, cook the sugar with 1/2 teaspoon of water, stirring occasionally, until it reaches 220°F on the thermometer.
◆ Beat the egg whites with the salt to stiff peaks and fold into the cooked honey. Add the cooked sugar, a little at a time and continue to cook until mixture starts to harden. Add the almonds, ▶

Pine nut brittle

Time needed: *30 minutes*
Difficulty: medium

INGREDIENTS FOR 6 SERVINGS
*3 3/4 cups of pine nuts
1 cup of sugar
1/2 a tablespoon of lemon juice
2 tablespoons of almond oil*

◆ Oil a marble surface and a rolling pin. In a saucepan, dissolve the sugar in the lemon juice and 1 tablespoon of water. Add the pine nuts and continue to cook on a moderate heat, stirring continuously, until the sugar turns golden.

Chocolate nougats

Pistachio brittle

chocolate and orange peel, stirring vigorously to blend the ingredients.

◆ With a spatula, spread the mixture to 1-inch thickness onto the cookie sheet. Cut it into little slabs and cover with plastic wrap.

Pralined almonds or hazelnuts

Pralined almonds or hazelnuts

Time needed: *30 minutes*
Difficulty: *medium*

INGREDIENTS FOR **6-8** SERVINGS
*1 cup of whole peeled almonds
(or toasted and peeled hazelnuts)
1/3 cup of sugar
1 tablespoon of almond oil*

◆ Put the sugar in a saucepan with 3 tablespoons of water. Bring it to boil on moderate heat and cook for 3 minutes, or until thick. Remove from heat and add the almonds (or hazelnuts); stir until almonds are covered with a layer of sandy sugar.

◆ Continue to cook until the sugar caramelizes. Brush a marble surface or a cookie sheet with a little oil, pour over the almonds on an oiled surface and quickly separate them, using 2 forks. Let them dry completely before putting them in a bowl.

Hazelnut nougat

Hazelnut nougat

Time needed: *1 hour and 20 minutes*
Difficulty: *complex*

INGREDIENTS FOR
ABOUT **3 LBS 9 OZ** OF NOUGAT
*1 cup of toasted, peeled hazelnuts
3/4 cup of sugar
1 cup of honey
2/3 cup of chopped bittersweet chocolate
3 egg whites
a pinch of salt
1 box of rice paper*

◆ Cover a cookie sheet with a layer of slightly overlapping rice paper.

In a double boiler, dissolve 1/8 cup of sugar and the chocolate in 2 tablespoons of water, stirring constantly.

◆ In a medium size stainless steel saucepan, slowly bring the honey to boil and cook, stirring constantly with a wooden spoon, for about 1 hour and 30 minutes, until a little honey crystallizes immediately when drooped in a glass of cold water.

◆ In another stainless steel saucepan cook the remaining sugar in 1/4 cup of water, stirring constantly until lightly caramelized. Add the cooked honey, melted chocolate and whole hazelnuts; stir mixture for 8-10 minutes. Remove from heat and fold in the egg whites, whisked with the salt to stiff peaks.

◆ Pour the mixture onto the rice paper and let it cool lightly; cut into rectangles. When cold, wrap the nougat in aluminum foil and keep in airtight tin boxes.

Almond brittle

Time needed: *1 hour*
Difficulty: *medium*

INGREDIENTS FOR **4** SERVINGS
*1 cup of whole peeled almonds
1 1/2cups of sugar
3/4 cup of water
1 tablespoon of almond oil*

◆ Preheat the oven to 360°F. Oil a marble surface or a cookie sheet and a rolling pin with the almond oil.

◆ Spread the almonds on a cookie sheet and lightly toast them. Chop them.

◆ In a saucepan with a thick bottom, cook the sugar and water on low heat until it starts to turn golden. Add the almonds and continue to cook, stirring until the caramel has turned dark golden.

◆ Pour the mixture onto the marble surface and with an iron spatula dipped in cold water, spread it out to a 1/2-inch thickness.

◆ Let the mixture cool lightly; cut it into little squares, diamonds or triangles. Let them cool completely, before transferring onto a serving dish.

Almond brittle

Chestnuts in liquor

Time needed: *2 hours and 40 minutes*
Difficulty: *complex*

INGREDIENTS FOR 4 LBS OF CHESTNUTS

4 lb of large chestnuts
4 1/2 cups of sugar
1 3/4 cups of rum, Cognac or brandy
2 bay leaves
4 cloves

Chestnuts in liquor

◆ Peel the chestnuts leaving the internal skin intact. Put them in a saucepan with the bay leaves and cloves; cover with cold water. Cook on low heat for 25 minutes.
◆ With a slotted spoon, gently drain chestnuts; cool. When cold, remove the skin using a small knife, making sure you do not cut into the chestnuts.
◆ In a large saucepan, bring 4 cups of water and the sugar to boil, repeatedly skimming the foam. After 8 minutes add the chestnuts, without stirring, and cook on low heat for 5 minutes. Let the chestnuts cool in their syrup; drain them with a slotted spoon and put them in a glass jar with an airtight lid.
◆ Bring the syrup back to a boil, skimming the foam repeatedly; mix in the liquor and let it cool. When cold, pour it, through a sieve, onto the chestnuts. If there is not enough syrup to cover the chestnuts, add some more liquor.
◆ Close the jar and wait at least 2 weeks before using the chestnuts.

Majestic grapefruit

Time needed: *1 hour*
Difficulty: *medium*

INGREDIENTS FOR 4 SERVINGS

4 large grapefruits
2 oranges
1/2 cup of pitted cherries in liquor
1/2 cup of kirsch
4 half peaches in syrup
1 tablespoon of sugar
1 egg white
2 tablespoons of powdered sugar
a pinch of salt

Majestic grapefruit

◆ Cut the grapefruits to 3/4 of their height and extract the pulp. Peel the segments, discard the skin and cut half of the segments into small pieces.
◆ Peel the oranges to the fruit and cut the segments in pieces. Dice the apricots, peaches and cherries (setting 4 whole cherries aside). In a bowl, mix the fruits with the sugar and the kirsch and let it rest for 30 minutes.
◆ Transfer the fruit salad into the emptied grapefruits. Whisk the egg whites with the salt to stiff peaks, add the sugar a little at a time, and continue whisking until all sugar is added. Put the mixture into a pastry bag, fitted with a star tube and pipe a large rosette on each grapefruit. Put the grapefruits under the grill for 4-5 minutes; decorate with the remaining cherries.

Apricots with zabaglione

Time needed: *50 minutes*
Difficulty: *medium*

INGREDIENTS FOR 6 SERVINGS

12 large, ripe apricots
4 tablespoons of sugar
4 tablespoons of butter
a pinch of cinnamon
3/4 cup of peeled, toasted almonds
1 teaspoon of vanilla

Zabaglione:

4 egg yolks
4 tablespoons of sugar
1/3 cup of dry Marsala
2 tablespoons of Moscato wine

Apricots with zabaglione

◆ Thoroughly rinse the apricots, cut them in half and pit. Line them, with the cavity upwards, in an oven dish large enough to hold them all. Sprinkle them with cinnamon, vanilla, butter cut in small pieces and 1/4 cup of water. Cover and cook until apricots are tender and the liquid has reduced to a syrupy film. Set aside to cool.
◆ Preheat the oven to 400°F.
◆ Prepare the zabaglione (see page 17) with the above listed ingredients. Pour it into the halved apricots. Bake for about 15 minutes.
◆ Garnish the apricots with lightly toasted and coarsely chopped almonds. Transfer onto a dish and serve warm.

Glazed pineapples

Cut the pineapple into segments. In a double boiler, dissolve the royal icing on very low heat (1) and stir in the maraschino. Using tweezers, delicately dip in 2 or 3 pineapple segments. (2) Pull them out using the edge of the pan to remove any excess coating. (3) Place them onto a sheet of parchment paper to set. In a double boiler, melt the chocolate in a double boiler and dip in the pineapple to cover half the icing (4).

◆ Let the pineapple segments dry on a sheet of parchment paper; transfer them to a dish and serve.

Time needed:
40 minutes
Difficulty: easy
INGREDIENTS
FOR 6 SERVINGS
7 oz of candied pineapple slices
1/2 cup of royal icing
1/2 cup of chopped dark chocolate
1 tablespoon of Maraschino

Peach Melba

Time needed: *1 hour*
Difficulty: *easy*

INGREDIENTS FOR 6 SERVINGS
3 firm, medium size yellow peaches
3/4 lb of raspberries
1 1/2 lb of vanilla ice cream (see page 282)
1 teaspoon of vanilla
3 tablespoons of sugar
2 tablespoons powdered sugar
1/2 cup of whipped cream

◆ Dip the peaches in boiling water for a few seconds. Drain and peel them. Cut them in half, pit and place them in an oven dish, large enough for the peaches.
◆ Add enough water to cover them, sprinkle with the sugar, add vanilla and cook on very low heat to reduce the liquid, until syrupy. Let the half peaches cool in the syrup.
◆ Quickly rinse the raspberries in ice water, drain them well and purée with powdered sugar.
◆ Put the half peaches in individual cups with the cavity upwards. Fill each cavity with a scoop of ice cream; top with the raspberry purée.
◆ Put the whipped cream into a pastry bag, fitted with a star tube nozzle and pipe a large rosette on each dessert.

Apples flambé

Apples flambé

Time needed: *45 minutes*
Difficulty: *easy*

INGREDIENTS FOR 4 SERVINGS
4 Golden Delicious apples
2 tablespoons of chopped walnuts
2 tablespoons of pitted and chopped dates
2 tablespoons of raisins ◆ *4 candied cherries*
1 tablespoon of chopped candied orange peel
1 tablespoon of powdered sugar
1 cup of white wine
1/2 cup of rum

◆ Butter around baking dish that can be taken to the table. Soak the raisins in warm water.
◆ Rinse and dry the apples, core with an apple corer and enlarge the cavity, scraping with a teaspoon.
◆ In a bowl, mix the walnuts, dates, drained raisins, cherries and orange peel. Add the powdered sugar and mix well.
◆ Fill the apples with some of the mixture; place them in the baking pan and surround them with the remaining fruit mixture. Add the wine and cook on moderate heat for about 20 minutes, or until the wine has evaporated.
◆ When ready to serve, pour a little boiling rum over the apples, flambé and bring to the table immediately.

Glazed pineapples

Orange glazed bananas

Time needed: *25 minutes*
Difficulty: *easy*

INGREDIENTS FOR 4 SERVINGS
4 bananas
2 1/2 tablespoons of butter
1/3 cup of orange juice
2 tablespoons of Grand Marnier
1/3 cup of chopped walnuts
1/4 cup of brown sugar
12 oz of vanilla ice cream (see page 282)

◆ Thoroughly butter a Pyrex dish. Preheat the oven to 425°F.
◆ Peel the bananas, cut in half lengthwise and put them into the dish. Cover with a mixture of orange juice and Grand Marnier; sprinkle with butter, cut in small pieces.
◆ Bake for 10 minutes, basting them occasionally with their cooking liquid. Sprinkle the bananas with the walnuts and sugar and continue to cook for 5 minutes until top is browned.
◆ Serve the glazed bananas hot, with vanilla ice cream.

Orange glazed bananas

Stuffed kiwis

Time needed: *45 minutes*
Difficulty: *easy*

INGREDIENTS FOR 6 SERVINGS
10 medium size kiwis
2 egg yolks
1/4 cup of sugar
1/4 cup of flour
3/4 cup of milk
3/4 cup of whipping cream
1 teaspoon of vanilla

◆ Prepare a pastry cream (see page 16) with the sugar, flour, milk and vanilla. Let it cool, stirring often.
Peel 1 kiwi, slice it and cut each slice in 4. Cut the remaining kiwis in half lengthwise and empty them with a teaspoon. Purée the kiwis; mix it in the cold pastry cream and gently fold in the whipped cream. Fill the empty kiwis with this mixture and garnish them with the kiwi slices.
Serve the kiwis accompanied with savoyard cookies or biscotti.

Stuffed kiwis

Peaches with pastry cream

Time needed: *30 minutes*
Difficulty: *easy*

INGREDIENTS FOR 6 SERVINGS
6 peaches, ripe and firm
1/2 cup of sugar
1 vanilla bean
1/3 cup of peel, chopped almonds

Pastry cream:
2 egg yolks
1/4 cup of sugar
1 cup of milk ◆ *1/3 cup of flour*
1/2 teaspoon of vanilla
grated peel of 1/2 organic lemon

◆ Lightly butter a cookie sheet.
◆ Rinse the peaches, scald them for a few seconds in boiling water, drain and peel them.
◆ Cook the sugar with the vanilla in 3/4 cup of water for 10 minutes. Add the peaches to soak until the syrup has cooled.
◆ Make a pastry cream (see page 16) with the ingredients listed above and let it cool, stirring often.
◆ Drain the peaches, cut them into halves and pit. Fill each half peach with the cold pastry cream, sprinkle with the chopped almonds and place them under the grill until top is golden and crisp. Serve immediately.

Frosted grapes

Time needed: *15 minutes*
Difficulty: *easy*

INGREDIENTS FOR 4 SERVINGS
3/4 lb of white or red grapes
1/2 cup of sugar ◆ *1 egg white*

◆ Rinse the grapes under running water, drain, and cut each grape from the bunch with scissors, keeping the stalk attached. Dry each grape with a kitchen towel.
◆ In a bowl, lightly beat the egg white; dip in the grapes, a few at a time. Roll them in sugar until completely covered and place them on a sheet of parchment paper to dry.
◆ Place the grapes in miniature paper baking cups, on a serving dish.

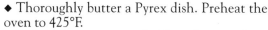

Frosted grapes

Caramelized figs

Time needed: *15 minutes*
(plus time in the refrigerator)
Difficulty: medium

INGREDIENTS FOR **4** SERVINGS
16 white ripe figs
1 cup of sugar

◆ Delicately clean the figs with a humid towel, keeping the peel intact. Place in the refrigerator for 24 hours.
◆ In a saucepan, cook the sugar in 4 tablespoons of water on low heat, until you have a light caramel. Put the figs on a rack, placed over a large cookie sheet. With a spoon, pour caramel over figs to cover them completely. Keep in a cool place until ready to serve.

Caramelized figs

American caramelized apples

Time needed: *45 minutes*
Difficulty: medium

INGREDIENTS FOR **4** SERVINGS
4 red, firm apples (1 1/2 -2 lb)
1 1/4 cups of sugar
2 3/4 tablespoons of butter
1/4 cup of whipping cream
a pinch of cream of tartar

◆ Rinse and dry the apples. Preheat the oven to 325°F.
◆ In a deep and narrow ovenproof saucepan, slowly bring to boil the sugar and 1/4 cup of water, stirring until the sugar dissolves completely. Add the cream of tartar, the butter and whipping cream and stir until well blended. Bake in the oven for 20-25 minutes until mixture is creamy and sticky like soft toffee.
◆ Put the apples on four 5 1/2-inch-long wooden sticks; remove the pan from the oven and dip the apples in the syrup until completely coated.
◆ Put the apples onto a lightly buttered cookie sheet and set aside until caramel is hard.

Pompadour strawberries

Chocolate dipped cherries

Pompadour strawberries

Time needed: *20 minutes*
(plus resting time)
Difficulty: easy

INGREDIENTS FOR **6** SERVINGS
18 medium size strawberries
1 egg white
1 cup of powdered sugar
1 tablespoon of lemon juice
1/4 cup of sugar

◆ In a bowl, beat the egg white with the lemon juice. Add, a little at a time, the sifted powdered sugar and whisk until mixture is thick and smooth.
◆ Sprinkle a work surface with the sugar. Rinse the strawberries in ice water and dry them. Holding them by the stalk, dip them in the egg-white-sugar glaze. Drain them well and place on the sugared work surface. Let them rest for about 2 hours until the glaze has hardened.
◆ Put the strawberries in miniature paper baking cups and onto a dish. Serve.

Chocolate dipped cherries

Time needed: *30 minutes*
(plus cooling time)
Difficulty: easy

INGREDIENTS FOR **6** SERVINGS
1/2 lb of firm cherries
1 cup of royal icing
1 cup of chopped dark chocolate
1 tablespoon of Kirsch or Maraschino

◆ Rinse and dry the cherries without removing the stalks. Melt the royal icing in a double boiler on low heat. Remove from heat and mix in the Kirsch or Maraschino. Holding the cherries by their stalks, dip them in mixture, one at a time. Let them dry on a sheet of parchment paper.
◆ When the icing has hardened completely, melt the chocolate in a double boiler and dip in the cherries. Let them dry on a sheet of parchment paper; put them in miniature paper baking cups, on a serving dish.

Cut and discard the 2 ends of the oranges. Cut the remaining peel in 4 parts, keeping a little pulp attached and divide the peel into 1/8-inch-wide strips. Put them in a saucepan, cover with cold water, bring to a boil and drain. Repeat the process twice to remove any bitterness.

◆ Drain the peels; replace them in the saucepan with 1 cup of water and the sugar. Bring to boil and cook for 30 minutes, stirring

Chocolate dipped orange sticks

Time needed: *1 hour*
Difficulty: medium
INGREDIENTS
FOR 6 SERVINGS
4 organic oranges with thick peel
1 cup of sugar
1 cup of chopped dark chocolate

occasionally until the peels are shiny and transparent and the liquid has evaporated. Put the peels onto a rack, separated from each other and let them cool and dry.

◆ In a double boiler, melt the chocolate in a double boiler. Dip in the peels one at a time, coating them on 3/4 of their length. Put the sticks of orange peel onto a sheet of parchment paper in a cool place, until the chocolate has hardened.

Custard filled apples

Time needed: *1 hour*
Difficulty: easy

INGREDIENTS FOR 4 SERVINGS
4 apples
2 tablespoons of sugar
2 tablespoons of butter

Pastry cream:
1 cup of milk ◆ *1/4 cup of flour*
1/3 cup of sugar ◆ *2 egg yolks*
a few crumbled amaretti
2 tablespoons of Kirsch
2 tablespoons of butter

Decoration:
4 candied cherries

◆ Butter a small Pyrex pan. Preheat the oven to 360°F.
◆ Prepare a pastry cream (see page 16) with the milk, flour, sugar and eggs. Let it cool, stirring occasionally to prevent the forming of a skin.
◆ Mix the crumbled amaretti, Kirsch and melted butter into the cold custard.
◆ Rinse and dry the apples. Core, using a knife and a teaspoon, keeping the bottom of the apples intact. Enlarge the cavity of the apples and fill with pastry cream. Put the apples into the pan, sprinkle with sugar and a few pieces of butter. Bake for 30 minutes.
◆ Serve the apples warm or cold, topped with a candied cherry.

Custard filled apples

Bananas flambé

Time needed: *25 minutes*
Difficulty: easy

INGREDIENTS FOR 4 SERVINGS
4 medium size bananas
(not too ripe)
juice of 1 orange
4 tablespoon of apricot jelly
2 tablespoons of peeled and toasted almonds
3 tablespoons of butter
1/2 cup of sugar
1/4 cup of rum

◆ Coarsely chop the toasted almonds. Peel the bananas and cut them in half lengthwise.
◆ In a heat-resistant dish, dissolve the butter and sugar on low heat, without stirring until the sugar starts to change color. Add the orange juice and apricot jelly, stirring gently and slowly until all ingredients have dissolved.
◆ Place the half bananas into the baking dish, keeping them whole. Lower the heat and cook them for 3 minutes.
◆ Heat the rum in a small saucepan; pour it, boiling, onto the bananas and flambé until the flame dies.
Remove from heat and sprinkle the bananas with the chopped almonds. Serve immediately.

Bananas flambé

98

Chocolate dipped orange sticks

Orange delight

Time needed: *40-45 minutes*
(plus time in the refrigerator)
Difficulty: *medium*

INGREDIENTS FOR **6** SERVINGS
6 oranges of equal size
2 eggs and 1 egg yolk
3/4 cup of sugar
grated peel of one organic lemon
6 drops of orange water
1/2 cup of flour
6 candied cherries
3 tablespoons of apricot jelly

◆ Rinse and dry the oranges, cut them in half, squeeze juice and remove any white internal skin.
◆ In a saucepan, mix the eggs and egg yolk with the sugar, lemon peel and sifted flour; add 1/2 cup of strained orange juice. Cook on a low heat, stirring constantly until the custard starts to thicken. Remove from heat and mix in the orange water. Pour into half of the scooped out oranges and refrigerate until the custard has set.
◆ Detach the custard from the oranges with a grapefruit knife and turn it over into the remaining emptied half oranges. Melt the apricot jelly in a double boiler and pour it gently over the cream.
◆ Top each orange with a candied cherry, place on a serving dish and refrigerate until ready to serve.

Orange delight

Chocolate covered pears

Time needed: *1 hour*
Difficulty: *medium*

INGREDIENTS FOR **4** SERVINGS
4 large pears
4 oz of dark chocolate
3 tablespoons of honey
1 egg
2 tablespoons of softened butter
a pinch of salt

◆ Rinse the pears and peel them, leaving the stalk

Chocolate covered pears

intact. Put them in a saucepan, just large enough for them and add 1/2 cup of water. Cover the saucepan and cook on moderate heat for about 30 minutes, or until done. Drain and place them on a serving dish.
◆ In a saucepan, dissolve the honey in 1 tablespoon of water; brush on the pears and let them cool completely.
◆ Chop chocolate in small pieces and melt it in 3 tablespoons of water on low heat.
◆ Remove from heat and cool lightly. Add the butter, cut into pieces and the egg yolk; stir until well blended.
◆ Beat the egg white with salt to stiff peaks; gently fold into the chocolate. Pour the sauce over the cold pears and serve.

Jamaican pineapple with double rum

Time needed: *30 minutes*
(plus soaking time)
Difficulty: *medium*

INGREDIENTS FOR **4** SERVINGS
1 ripe pineapple
1/4 cup of white rum
1/4 cup of dark rum
6 tablespoons of butter
3/4 cup of sugar
4 egg yolks

◆ Peel the pineapples, slice thinly and cut out center, using an apple corer. Put the slices into a bowl, sprinkle with 1/4 cup of sugar, add the white rum and set aside in a cool place for about 2 hours.
◆ Prepare the sauce. Melt the butter in a double boiler. Mix in the remaining sugar. Add the dark rum and the egg yolks. Keep whisking on very low heat, until mixture starts to thicken.
◆ Drain the pineapple slices and place them on fruit plates or desert bowls.
◆ Pour the hot rum sauce over pineapples. Serve immediately. If you wish, you can top each portion with a candied cherry.

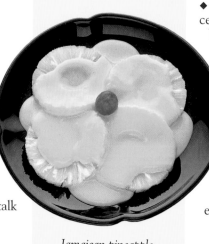

Jamaican pineapple with rum

Dried fruit pyramids

Time needed: *30 minutes*
(plus time in the refrigerator)
Difficulty: easy

INGREDIENTS FOR **6** SERVINGS
2 1/2 oz of chopped dried figs
2 1/2 oz of pitted chopped dates
2 1/2 oz of chopped pine nuts
2 1/2 oz of dried apricots
1 1/4 oz of chopped candied cherries
2 tablespoons of lemon juice
1/4 cup of powdered sugar
1/4 cup of grated dried coconut

◆ Soak the apricots in boiling water for 5 minutes. Drain, dry and chop them. In a bowl, mix all dried fruits, candied cherries, sugar and lemon juice. Knead with your fingertips until firm and smooth, adding a little lemon juice if too dry.
◆ In a non-stick pan, lightly toast the coconut, stirring with a wooden spoon. Divide the dried fruit mixture into walnut sized balls, roll them into the coconut and shape them into pyramids. Place them on a serving dish and refrigerate for at least 1 hour.

Dried fruit pyramids

Apricots with chocolate

Time needed: *1 hour and 20 minutes*
Difficulty: medium

INGREDIENTS FOR **6** SERVINGS
12 large, ripe apricots
1 1/4 cups of whipping cream
3 1/2 oz of crumbled amaretti
3 1/2 oz of chopped dark chocolate
2 tablespoons of flour
2 egg yolks
1 1/4 cups of milk
1/2 cup of sugar

◆ Butter a cookie sheet and preheat the oven to 360°F.
◆ Rinse the apricots, divide them into halves, pit and place them on the cookie sheet. Sprinkle with 1/8 cup of sugar and bake until just tender. Let cool completely.

Apricots with chocolate

◆ Whip the cream and blend in the amaretti. Place the apricots into serving cups and fill the cavities with the whipped cream mixture.
◆ In a bowl, whisk the egg yolks with the remaining sugar until light and creamy, mix in the flour and milk, a little at a time. Cook in a double boiler, stirring continuously until the custard films a spoon. Remove from heat, add the dark chocolate and mix until completely melted. Let the custard cool.
◆ Pour the cold chocolate custard over the apricots and serve.

Royal pears

Time needed: *30 minutes*
Difficulty: easy

INGREDIENTS FOR **6** SERVINGS
3 Kaiser pears
4 oz of amaretti
4 tablespoons of lime (or orange) marmalade
1/4 cup of amaretto liquor
grated peel of 1/2 organic lemon

◆ Preheat the oven to 360°F.
◆ Peel the pears, cut them in half and core. Scoop out some of the pulp in the center, forming a cavity.
◆ Crush the amaretti in a mortar. In a bowl, mix amaretti, marmalade and half the liquor until well blended. Fill the pears with this mixture; line them in a baking dish, just large enough to hold them one next to the other. Add the sugar, white wine, lemon peel and remaining liquor.
Bake for 20 minutes until top is golden. Serve warm or cold.
◆ A variation to this recipe consists in baking the pears inthe oven with a little sugar and Marsala. When cooled, the pears can be filled with zabaglione (see page 17).

Royal pears

Venetian caramelized fruit

Time needed: *35 minutes*
Difficulty: *medium*

INGREDIENTS FOR 4 SERVINGS
1 1/4 cups of powdered sugar
1 tablespoon of corn syrup
a few white grapes
a few pitted firm cherries
a few slices of peeled peach
4 pitted apricots cut in half
4 pitted prunes
a few walnuts
4 pitted dates

◆ Soak the prunes in warm water, drain and dry them. Rinse and dry all the fruit.
◆ In a casserole with a heavy bottom dissolve the sugar with 1 tablespoon of water and corn syrup on high heat until the sugar caramelizes.
◆ Place the various fruits on skewers and carefully dip them in the caramelized sugar until completely coated; set aside vertically into the holes of a sieve until caramel is hard.
◆ Trim any caramel dribbles with a pair of scissors and place the fruits onto a serving dish.

Stuffed dates

Time needed: *50 minutes*
Difficulty: *medium*

INGREDIENTS FOR 40 DATTERI FARCITI
40 dates
1 tablespoon of alchermes
1 tablespoon of rum
1 teaspoon of peeled pistachios
grated peel of one organic orange
2/3 lb of marzipan

Decoration:
1 oz of candied orange peel
3 candied cherries
10 raisins

◆ Knead the marzipan lightly and divide it into 4 equal portions.
◆ Set 5 pistachios aside for decoration and grind the remaining pistachios. Mix 1 portion of marzipan with the alchermes, a second portion with the rum, a third portion with the ground pistachios and the fourth one with the orange peel. Knead marzipan with your fingertips to blend the ingredients.
◆ Cut the dates lengthwise and pit. Form 1/2-inch-thick rolls, in diameter with the 4 types of marzipan and cut in 1-inch-long pieces.
◆ Fill 10 dates with the alchermes flavored marzipan, fill a further 10 dates with the rum flavored marzipan, fill a further 10 dates with the pistachio marzipan and the last 10 dates with the orange peel marzipan. Place all dates onto a serving dish.
◆ Garnish the green marzipan dates with the pistachios divided in halves, the rum flavored marzipan dates with the raisins, the pink marzipan dates with the candied cherries and the yellow marzipan dates with pieces of candied orange peel.
◆ To keep the stuffed dates, cover with plastic wrap and set aside in a cool place.

Candied grapefruit peels

Time needed: *1 hour*
Difficulty: *medium*

INGREDIENTS FOR 8 SERVINGS
4 organic grapefruits
1 1/2 cups of sugar

◆ Cut the two ends of the grapefruits and discard them. Cut the remaining peel in 4 parts with 1/3 of the pulp attached and divide it in 3/4-inch-wide strips.
◆ Place the peels in a saucepan, cover with cold water, bring to boil and drain them. Repeat this process for a further 2 times to eliminate the bitter taste (as well as any impurities).
◆ Replace the drained peels in the saucepan with 1 1/4 cups of sugar and 1 cup of water. Bring to boil and cook on moderate heat for 30 minutes, stirring occasionally until the peels are shiny and transparent and the liquid has evaporated. Drain on a rack, separated from each other and let them dry completely.
◆ Roll peels into the remaining sugar; put them in miniature paper baking cups and transfer to a serving dish.
◆ You may vary this recipe by replacing the grapefruits with 6 large lemons, using the same quantity of sugar. The procedure is identical.

Chocolate candies

Time needed: *45 minutes*
Difficulty: *medium*

INGREDIENTS FOR 2 LBS OF CANDIES
1 cup of brown sugar
3/4 cup of butter
2/3 cup of honey
2/3 cup of chopped dark chocolate
3 tablespoons of whipping cream
2 tablespoons of almond oil

◆ Oil a marble surface or cookie sheet.
In a saucepan, cook the sugar with the butter, the honey, chocolate and whipping cream, on low heat for 10-15 minutes, stirring constantly.
◆ Pour the mixture onto the oiled marble surface. As soon as it is cool, with a sharp knife, trace small 3/4-inch squares on top of mixture. Let it cool completely; break of the squares and wrap each in plastic.

Coffee candies

Time needed: *35 minutes*
(plus resting time)
Difficulty: *medium*

INGREDIENTS FOR ABOUT 1 LB OF CANDIES
1 1/4 cups milk
1 1/4 cups of sugar
3 oz of corn syrup
1 tablespoon of instant coffee
1 tablespoon of butter
1 tablespoon of almond oil

◆ Brush an 8 x 4-inch cookie sheet with oil.
◆ In a saucepan, bring the milk with the coffee to boil; add the sugar and glucose, stirring continuously, to prevent mixture from sticking. As soon as it starts to boil, dip a cooking thermometer into the mixture. Lower the heat and continue to cook until it reaches 220°F. Add the butter and continue to cook until it reaches 250°F. Remove from heat.
◆ Pour the mixture into the cookie sheet and let it rest for 8 hours. Turn over onto a work surface and cut it into 2 x 1/2-inch bars. Wrap each bar in plastic.
◆ Keep the candies in a glass jar.

Coconut gelatins

Time needed: *25 minutes*
(plus infusion and refrigeration time)
Difficulty: *medium*

INGREDIENTS FOR 6-8 SERVINGS
12 oz of fresh coconut (or 3 oz of dried coconut)
1 1/4 cups of milk
1 tablespoon of sake
2 teaspoons of unflavored gelatin

Decoration:
3 tablespoons of coconut

◆ Bring 1/2 cup of water to a boil. Finely chop the coconut and soak it in the boiling water for 30 minutes. Dissolve the gelatin in cold water.
◆ Pass the coconut infusion through a sieve; squeeze the coconut pulp. Mix the milk and sake to the coco water.
◆ In a double boiler, heat 2 tablespoons of the coconut milk with the gelatin; mix well. Pour into the remaining coconut milk mixture, stirring. Pour into a small cookie sheet to a 1-inch thickness. Refrigerate for 1 hour until the gelatin has set.
◆ Cut out into shapes of your choice with a cookie cutter and decorate with slivers of coconut.
◆ Keep in the refrigerator until ready to serve.

Sugar candies

Time needed: *40 minutes*
Difficulty: *medium*

INGREDIENTS FOR 1 LB OF CANDIES
2 1/2 cups of sugar
1 tablespoon of almond oil
1/2 lemon

◆ Oil a marble surface or a coolie sheet.
◆ Put the sugar in a copper saucepan and cook it on low heat, stirring, with a wooden spoon, until golden. Once it starts to smoke, add 3 tablespoons of cold water. The sugar will build in volume and it will darken. Remove it from the heat immediately, stir and pour it onto the oiled surface. Press it lightly with half a lemon to spread it evenly to a 1/2-inch thickness.
◆ Cut into the surface to trace many little squares. When cool, break in small pieces.

Strawberry gelatins

Time needed:
20 minutes
(plus time in the refrigerator)
Difficulty: medium
INGREDIENTS
FOR 4-6 SERVINGS

7 oz of strawberries
2/3 cup of sugar
2.5 g of agar-agar

Quickly rinse the strawberries in ice water, dry, cut off the stems and purée in a food processor.

♦ Strain through a sieve to discard the seeds and pour into a saucepan.

♦ Bring the purée to boil, remove from heat and add 1/8 cup of sugar and the agar-agar. Bring back to boil and cook for 1 minute, stirring constantly. Add 1/3 cup of sugar and continue to cook for 2 minutes, stirring until dissolved.

♦ Pour the mixture into a moistened 3/4-inch deep, 6x5-inch cookie sheet. Refrigerate until set.

♦ Cut the gelatin in shapes of your choice and roll some of them in the remaining sugar. Place in miniature paper baking cups, onto a serving dish. Keep in the refrigerator.

Home style candies

Time needed: *1 hour*
Difficulty: medium

INGREDIENTS FOR ABOUT 3/4 LBS OF CANDIES
1 1/4 cups of sugar
2 tablespoons of honey
4 tablespoons of butter
a few tablespoons of almond oil

♦ In a small copper saucepan, cook the sugar and honey on low heat, stirring gently to prevent from sticking.
♦ Keep a bowl with ice water, a brush and a long skewer nearby. Brush the walls of the saucepan with cold water often, to prevent the sugar from burning, which would alter the taste of the candies.
♦ When all the sugar has dissolved, add the butter, stirring to blend well. After 20 minutes, check the sugar by dipping the stick first in ice water, then into the mixture: if the sugar on the tip of the stick comes out in a ball that hardens immediately, the sugar is ready.
♦ Oil a marble work surface or a cookie sheet; pour the mixture, letting it spread naturally. As soon as it begins to cool, cut into it tracing diamonds or squares, in order to break it off into candies easily, once the mixture has cooled completely.

Orange and wild berry gelatins

Home style candies

Orange and wild berry gelatins

Time needed: *25 minutes*
(plus time in the refrigerator)
Difficulty: medium

INGREDIENTS FOR 6 SERVINGS
2 lbs of juicy oranges
2/3 cup of sugar
1 tablespoon of agar-agar
3/4 cup of assorted berries

♦ Quickly rinse the berries in ice water, dry and keep them in the refrigerator.
♦ Squeeze the oranges to get 1 1/3 cups of juice. Strain it; pour it into a saucepan with 1/8 cup of sugar and the agar-agar. Cook for 1 minute on a low heat. Add the remaining sugar and cook for a further 2 minutes, stirring often.
♦ Pour the mixture into a medium size oven dish and with tongs, distribute the berries over it, 1 inch away from each other.
♦ Being careful to not move the berries, bring the dish to the refrigerator and leave for at least 1 hour or until the gelatin is set.
♦ Cut the gelatin in different shapes with cookie cutters. Each piece of gelatin should have a berry in the middle.
♦ Place the gelatins onto a dish and keep in the refrigerator until ready to serve.

Strawberry gelatins

Creams, Custards and Mousses

Bavarois ◆ Charlottes ◆ Puddings ◆ Soufflés ◆ Aspics
Creams and Other Desserts

Raspberry bavarois

Time needed
*1 hour and 15 minutes
(plus cooling time)*

Difficulty media

**INGREDIENTS
FOR 6-8 SERVINGS**
*1/3 of almond cookie dough
1 cup of milk
9 oz of raspberries
1 cup of sugar
4 egg yolks
1 1/2 cups of whipping cream
2 teaspoons of unflavored
gelatin sheet*

Decoration:
*5 oz of raspberry
1 tablespoon of apricot jam*

Grease and flour an oven tray and trace a 4 x 8 inch rectangle onto the tray. Spray a 4 x 8 inch loaf pan with water. Preheat an oven to medium temperature of 370°F.

◆ Prepare almond cookie dough (see page 11) and place on the oven tray on the 4 x 8 in trace. Bake in the preheated oven for 18-20 minutes, turn over on a kitchen towel and let cool.

◆ Dissolve gelatin in a teaspoon of cold water. Quickly rinse the raspberries in ice water, dry them and mash before putting them through a sieve.

◆ Bring the milk to a boil. In a saucepan, mix the egg yolks with the sugar, add the boiling milk a few drops at a time, and almost bring to a boil on low heat, stirring continuously (the mixture should not reach the boiling point, or it will curdle irreparably). Remove from the heat, add the strained gelatin, and carefully stir until completely dissolved. Once lukewarm, add the raspberry purée and whipped cream to the mixture. Pour into the loaf pan, distributing evenly with the aid of a spatula. Place the almond cookie rectangle over the mousse and cover with a sheet of aluminum foil. Refrigerate for at least 3 hours.

◆ Rinse the raspberries for the decoration in ice water and dry well . Dip the mold in lukewarm water to remove the bavarois, turn onto a serving dish and top with the raspberries. Dissolve the apricot jam in a double boiler and brush over the raspberries. Refrigerate until ready to serve.

Traditional bavarois

Time needed: *30 minutes
(plus cooling time)*
Difficulty: *medium*

INGREDIENTS FOR 4 SERVINGS

*3 egg yolks ◆ 1/2 cup of sugar
1 1/2 cups of milk
1 1/2 cups of whipping cream
1 1/2 teaspoon of unflavored gelatin sheet
a few candied cherries*

◆ Spray a 9-cup fluted tube pan with water. Dissolve gelatin in cold water.
◆ Bring the milk to a boil. In a saucepan, work in the egg yolks with the sugar until smooth, light and creamy. Add the boiling milk a few drops at a time. Almost bring the preparation to a boil on low heat, stirring continuously ensuring the mixture never reaches the boil. Remove from the heat, add the gelatin, and carefully stir until completely dissolved. Let it cool completely.
◆ Fold the whipped cream into the cold mixture, and pour into the moistened tube pan. Cover with a sheet of aluminum foil and place in the fridge for at least 4 hours. Dip the mold in lukewarm water to remove the bavarois. Turn it on a serving dish and top with the candied cherries.

Traditional bavarois

Vanilla bavarois

Vanilla bavarois

Time needed: *40 minutes
(plus cooling time)*
Difficulty: *medium*
INGREDIENTS FOR 6-8 SERVINGS

*1 cup of milk ◆ 1/2 cup of sugar
4 egg yolks ◆ 1 teaspoon of gelatin
1 1/2 cups of whipping cream
1 vanilla bean
1 teaspoon of vanilla extract*

◆ Spray a 9-cup fluted tube pan with water.
◆ Dissolve gelatin in a little cold water. Bring the milk with the split vanilla bean to a boil.
◆ In a pan, whisk the egg yolks with the sugar and the vanilla extract. Add the boiling milk a few drops at a time, whisking. Place on low heat and almost bring to a boil, stirring continuously. Remove from heat, add the gelatin, and carefully stir until completely dissolved. Set aside to cool.
◆ Whip the cream until it forms stiff peaks and fold into the cold mixture, pour into the tube pan. Cover with a sheet of aluminum foil and place in the fridge for at least 4 hours.
◆ Dip the mold in lukewarm water to remove the bavarois and turn on a serving dish.

Raspberry bavarois

Fig bavarois

Time needed: *1 hour and 15 minutes*
(plus cooling time)
Difficulty: *medium*

INGREDIENTS FOR 6-8 SERVINGS

1 1/4 lbs of fresh figs ◆ *1 cup of milk*
1 cup of sugar ◆ *4 egg yolks*
2 teaspoons of gelatin ◆ *1 1/2 cups of*
whipping cream

◆ Moisten a 6-cup fluted pudding mold with water.
◆ Dissolve gelatin in a little cold water. Peel the figs (leaving a few aside for decorating), wash them, using a fork, and place in a saucepan with half the sugar. Bring to a boil on low heat and cook for a few minutes until dense. Let cool completely.
◆ Bring the milk to a boil. In a saucepan, whisk in the egg yolks with remaining sugar; add the boiling milk a few drops at a time, almost bring to a boil on low heat, stirring continuously. Remove from heat, add gelatin and stir until dissolved. Let cool. Add the cold fig mixture and fold in the whipped cream. Pour into mold and refrigerate for at least 4 hours.
◆ Peel remaining figs and cut into segments. Turn the bavarois onto a serving dish and top with the fig segments. Refrigerate until ready to serve.

Fig bavarois

Mint bavarois

Time needed: *40 minutes*
(plus cooling time)
Difficulty: *medium*

INGREDIENTS FOR 6-8 SERVINGS

1 cup of milk ◆ *1 small bunch of mint*
1 small glass of mint syrup
1/2 cup of sugar ◆ *4 egg yolks*
2 teaspoons of unflavored gelatin sheet
1 cup of whipping cream
1 teaspoon of vanilla extract

Decoration:
Confectioner's chocolate leaves
1 small bunch of fresh mint

◆ Brush a 6-cup fluted pan with water. Dissolve gelatin in a little cold water. Rinse and dry the mint leaves.
◆ Bring the milk to a boil and let it infuse with the mint for about 30 minutes.
◆ In a saucepan, whisk egg yolks with sugar and

Mint bavarois

vanilla extract. Add milk through a sieve a few drops at a time, and almost bring to a boil on low heat, stirring continuously. Remove from heat, add gelatin and the mint syrup; stir and let cool.
◆ Whip the cream and fold into the cold mixture. Pour into the moistened mold and refrigerate for at least 4 hours. To serve, dip the mold in lukewarm water to help remove the bavarois. Turn onto a serving dish and decorate with the confectioner's chocolate leaves and fresh mint leaves.

Pistachio bavarois

Time needed: *1 hour*
(plus cooling time)
Difficulty: *medium*

INGREDIENTS FOR 6-8 SERVINGS

1 1/2 cups of milk ◆ *1 1/2 cups of*
whipping cream
5 egg yolks ◆ *1 cup of sugar*
1/2 cup of shelled and skinned
pistachios
1 teaspoon of gelatin
the peel of one organic lemon

Decoration:
6 kumquats
3 tablespoons of whipped cream
shelled and peeled pistachios
1 tablespoon of apricot jam

◆ Spray a shallow 8 inch glass mold with water.
◆ In a food processor, mix pistachios into a paste. Dissolve gelatin in a little cold water.
◆ Bring milk and lemon peel to a boil. In a saucepan, whisk in the egg yolks with sugar. Add the pistachio paste and boiling milk a few drops at a time. Almost bring to a boil on low heat, stirring continuously. Remove from heat, add gelatin, and carefully stir until completely dissolved. Let the preparation cool, stirring occasionally. Whip the cream until firm and gently fold into the cold mixture. Pour into mold and refrigerate for at least 4 hours.
◆ To decorate, rinse and dry the kumquats. Make 6 incisions from the top to the bottom of the fruit and peel the skin, ensuring you leave it attached at the bottom. Roll it inward to form petals. In a double boiler, warm up the apricot jam and use it to brush the kumquats. Slice the pistachios in half. Dip mold in warm water to remove the bavarois. Turn onto a serving dish.

Pistachio bavarois

◆ Decorate the edge of the bavarois with the halved pistachios, and place the kumquat 'roses' on top. Fill a pastry bag, fitted with a star tube, with whipped cream and pipe around the bottom edge of the bavarois to make a crown. Refrigerate until ready to serve.

Bavarois with peaches in syrup

Time needed: *25 minutes*
(plus cooling time)
Difficulty: easy

INGREDIENTS FOR 8 SERVINGS

12 oz of drained peaches in syrup
1/2 cup of sugar
1 cup of whipping cream
2 teaspoons of gelatin
juice of 1 orange
confectioner's sugar leaves and sugar flowers

◆ Spray a 5-cup fluted pudding mold with water.
◆ Dissolve gelatin in a little cold water. In a food processor, mix peaches with sugar until smooth. Add orange juice. In a saucepan, bring to a boil on medium heat. Remove, add gelatin, let cool. Fold the whipped cream into mixture, and pour into mold. Refrigerate for at least 4 hours.
◆ Dip mold in warm water to remove the bavarois, turn onto a serving dish and decorate with confectioner's sugar leaves and sugar flowers. Refrigerate until ready to serve.

Tangerine bavarois

Time needed: *40 minutes*
(plus cooling time)
Difficulty: medium

INGREDIENTS FOR 6-8 SERVINGS
1 cup of milk
juice and grated rind of 3 organic tangerines
1/2 cup of sugar
4 egg yolks
2 teaspoons of gelatin
1 cup of heavy cream
segments of 2 tangerines

Bavarese alle pesche sciroppate

Bavarese di mandarini

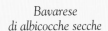

Bavarese di albicocche secche

◆ Brush a 6-cup fluted, pudding mold with water. Soften the gelatin in a little cold water.
◆ Bring the milk and half the grated tangerine rind to a boil. In a saucepan, whisk in the egg yolks with the sugar. Add the boiling milk and almost bring to a boil on low heat, stirring continuously. Remove from the heat, add the gelatin, mix well and let cool. Add the tangerine juice, the remaining rind, and gently fold in the whipped cream. Pour into the moistened mold and place in the refrigerator for at least 4 hours.
◆ Dip the mold in warm water to remove the bavarois, turn it on a serving dish and decorate with the skinned tangerine segments. Refrigerate until ready to serve. You can replace the tangerines with oranges.

Dried apricot bavarois

Time needed: *30 minutes*
(plus cooling time)
Difficulty: medium

INGREDIENTS FOR 6-8 SERVINGS

1 cup. of dried apricots ◆ 1 cup of milk
1 cup of sugar ◆ 4 egg yolks
1 1/2 cups of whipping cream
1 1/2 teaspoons of gelatin

◆ Brush a 6-cup fluted pudding mold with water. Soak 3/4 of the dried apricots in warm water. Dissolve gelatin in a little cold water.
◆ Drain the apricots and process into a smooth purée. Bring milk to a boil. In a saucepan, whisk in the egg yolks with sugar. Add boiling milk a few drops at a time. Almost bring to a boil on low heat, stirring continuously. Remove from heat, add gelatin, stir well and let cool.
◆ Add the apricot purée and fold the whipped cream into the mixture. Pour into mold and refrigerate for at least 2 hours.
◆ Rinse and dry remaining apricots; cut in half, keeping one whole. Dip mold in warm water to remove the bavarois. Turn onto a serving dish and decorate, placing the whole apricot in the middle and the halved apricots around the sides. Refrigerate until ready to serve. You can replace the apricots with prunes.

Chocolate bavarois

Time needed
50 minutes
(plus cooling time)

Difficulty: medium

INGREDIENTS
FOR 6-8 SERVINGS
*1/2 cup of grated bittersweet
chocolate
4 egg yolks
1/2 cup of sugar
1 cup of milk
1 1/3 cups of whipping cream
2 teaspoons of gelatin
1 thin layer of sponge cake
2 tablespoons of rum*

Decoration:
*1/2 cup of grated dark
chocolate
1/2 cup of grated white
chocolate*

Brush an 8-inch springform pan with water.

◆ Dissolve gelatin in a little cold water. Bring the milk to a boil. In a saucepan, whisk in the egg yolks with sugar; add boiling milk, a few drops at a time, almost bring to a boil on low heat, stirring continuously. Remove from heat, add gelatin and grated chocolate, and carefully stir until completely dissolved.

◆ Cut a thin 8-inch circle of sponge cake (see page 11). Brush it with rum and place into the spring form. Whip the cream and fold into the cold mixture. Pour preparation into the springform, over the sponge cake. Refrigerate for at least 4 hours. Transfer onto a serving dish.

◆ Trace two 3 x 3 inch squares on waxed paper. Melt the dark and white chocolate separately in a double boiler.

◆ Coat the wax paper squares with dark chocolate (**1**). Once hardened, cover with white chocolate (**2**) and once this hardens, coat again with dark chocolate (**3**). Let rest in a cool place for an hour, then evenly trim the sides of the chocolate squares (**4**). Peel off the paper and place one on top of the other, in the center of the bavarois crosswise. Refrigerate until ready to serve.

Lemon bavarois with blueberry sauce

Time needed: *40 minutes*
(plus soaking and cooling time)
Difficulty: medium

INGREDIENTS FOR 6 SERVINGS

*3/4 cup of strained lemon juice
4 egg yolks ◆ 1 cup of sugar
2 teaspoons of gelatin
grated peel of 1 lemon
1/2 teaspoon of vanilla
2 cups of whipped cream
2 egg whites ◆ 1 pinch of salt
2 slices of candied lemon*

Salsa:
*1 lb of blueberries ◆ 2 tablespoons of sugar
1 1/4 cups of Moscato wine
3 tablespoons of brandy ◆ 1 tablespoon of butter
1 teaspoon of corn starch ◆ 1 pinch of cinnamon*

*Lemon bavarois
with blueberry sauce*

◆ Line a 4 x 8 inch rectangular loaf pan with parchment paper letting it come over the edges of the mold. Dissolve gelatin in a little cold water.

◆ In a saucepan, whisk in the egg yolks with sugar. Add the lemon juice and 4 tablespoons of water. Cook on low heat for about 10 minutes, stirring continuously. Remove from heat, add gelatin and carefully stir. Let cool. Add the lemon rind and vanilla. Beat egg whites and salt to stiff peaks and fold into the cold mixture. Fold in the whipped cream and pour preparation into the mold. Refrigerate for at least 4 hours.

◆ Rinse blueberries and soak for 1 hour and 30 minutes in the Moscato wine with cinnamon and sugar. In a saucepan, bring to boil on low heat; add the brandy and cornstarch mixed with butter. Simmer for 10 minutes. Remove from heat. Keep a tablespoon of blueberries and blend the rest of the sauce into a smooth consistency, in a food processor.

◆ Turn the bavarois onto a large serving dish and remove the parchment paper. Decorate with the candied lemon slices topped with remaining blueberries. Cover with the sauce or serve it on the side.

Chocolate bavarois

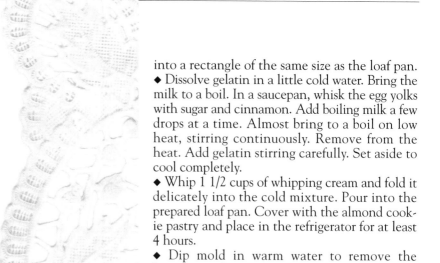

Hazelnut bavarois

Time needed: *30 minutes*
(plus cooling time)
Difficulty: medium

INGREDIENTS FOR 8 SERVINGS
1/2 cup of toasted hazelnuts
1 cup of milk ◆ 3/4 cups of sugar
5 egg yolks ◆ 2 teaspoons of gelatin
1 1/2 cups of whipping cream
8 praline hazelnuts

◆ Brush a 6-cup fluted pudding mold with water. Dissolve gelatin in cold water.
◆ Bring milk to a boil. In a saucepan, whisk in the egg yolks with sugar. Add boiling milk a few drops at a time and almost bring to a boil on low heat, stirring continuously. Remove from heat. Add gelatin and carefully stir. Let cool. Add chopped hazelnuts and fold 1 cup of whipped cream into the cold mixture.
◆ Pour into the mold and refrigerate for at least 4 hours. Dip mold in warm water to remove the bavarois and carefully turn onto a serving dish. Fill a pastry bag, fitted with an indented nozzle, with the remaining whipped cream and decorate the center of the bavarois.
◆ Top with the praline hazelnuts and refrigerate until ready to serve.

Cinnamon bavarois

Time needed: *1 hour*
(plus cooling time)
Difficulty: medium

INGREDIENTS FOR 6-8 SERVINGS
1/2 a recipe of almond cookie dough (see page 11)
3/4 cup milk ◆ 1/4 cup sugar
4 egg yolks ◆ 2 teaspoons of gelatin
1 3/4 cups of whipping cream
2 teaspoons of ground cinnamon
1 cinnamon stick

◆ Line a cookie sheet with parchment paper. Grease and flour. Preheat the oven to 360°F. Spray a 4 x 8 inch rectangular loaf pan with water.
◆ Prepare the almond cookie dough, spread on the cookie sheet and even out. Bake in the preheated oven for 15- 20 minutes. Turn onto a kitchen towel, remove the waxed paper and cut

into a rectangle of the same size as the loaf pan.
◆ Dissolve gelatin in a little cold water. Bring the milk to a boil. In a saucepan, whisk the egg yolks with sugar and cinnamon. Add boiling milk a few drops at a time. Almost bring to a boil on low heat, stirring continuously. Remove from the heat. Add gelatin stirring carefully. Set aside to cool completely.
◆ Whip 1 1/2 cups of whipping cream and fold it delicately into the cold mixture. Pour into the prepared loaf pan. Cover with the almond cookie pastry and place in the refrigerator for at least 4 hours.
◆ Dip mold in warm water to remove the bavarois and turn it onto a serving dish. Whip the remaining cream and, with a knife, make chips out of the cinnamon stick. Fill a pastry bag, fitted with a flat tube, with the whipped cream, and top the bavarois with little squares of cream. Place the cinnamon chips in between the cream squares and heap some in the center. Refrigerate until time to serve.

Wild strawberry bavarois

Time needed: *30 minutes*
(plus cooling time)
Difficulty: medium

INGREDIENTS FOR 6-8 SERVINGS
1 cup of milk
2 1/2 cups of wild strawberries
(or cultivated strawberries)
1 cup of sugar ◆ 4 egg yolks
2 teaspoons of gelatin

◆ Brush a 6-cup fluted tube pan with water. Dissolve gelatin in cold water. Rinse wild strawberries in ice water, dry and purée half in a food processor. Strain through a sieve. Keep the rest aside for decoration.
◆ Bring milk to a boil. In a saucepan, whisk in the egg yolks with sugar. Add boiling milk a few drops at a time, almost bring to a boil on low heat, stirring delicately. Remove from heat, add gelatin, stir carefully and let cool completely.
◆ Add strawberry purée to the mixture and delicately fold in the whipped cream. Pour into tube pan and place in the refrigerator for at least 2 hours.
◆ Dip the mold in warm water to remove the bavarois. Turn onto a serving dish and top with the remaining strawberries. Refrigerate until serving time.

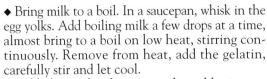

Almond bavarois

Time needed: *1 hour*
(plus cooling time)
Difficulty: *medium*

INGREDIENTS FOR 6-8 SERVINGS
1 1/2 cups of milk

1 1/3 cups of whipping cream
5 egg yolks ◆ *1 cup of sugar*
3 tablespoons of blanched, chopped almonds
2 teaspoons of unflavored gelatin
grated peel of 1 organic lemon
confectioner's chocolate leaves
5 blanched almonds

◆ Brush a shallow rectangular glass cake pan with water. Dissolve the gelatin in cold water.
◆ Bring milk with lemon rind to a boil. In a saucepan, whisk in the egg yolks with sugar. Add chopped almonds and boiling milk a few drops at a time through a sieve. Almost bring to a boil on low heat, stirring continuously. Remove from heat, add gelatin and stir carefully. Let cool completely.
◆ Whip 1/2 cup of cream and delicately fold into the cold mixture. Pour into cake pan and refrigerate for at least 2 hours.
◆ Dip mold in warm water to remove the bavarois and turn onto a serving dish. Fill a pastry bag, fitted with a star tube, with the remaining whipped cream and top the bavarois with little squares of cream. Form a crown of cream around the top of the pudding and one around the bottom. Place the confectioner's chocolate leaves in the center and top with the blanched almonds. Refrigerate until serving time.

Walnut bavarois

Time needed: *30 minutes*
(plus cooling time)
Difficulty: *medium*

INGREDIENTS FOR 8 SERVINGS
1 cup of milk
1/2 cup of sugar
5 egg yolks ◆ *2 teaspoons of gelatin*
1 cup of whipping cream
1 walnut (whole)

◆ Spray a deep square cake pan with water. Dissolve the gelatin in a little cold water.

◆ Bring milk to a boil. In a saucepan, whisk in the egg yolks. Add boiling milk a few drops at a time, almost bring to a boil on low heat, stirring continuously. Remove from heat, add the gelatin, carefully stir and let cool.
◆ Add chopped walnuts into the cold mixture. Fold in the whipped cream delicately, keeping 1 tablespoon aside. Pour preparation into the cake pan and refrigerate for at least 2 hours.
◆ Dip mold in warm water to remove the bavarois and turn onto a serving dish. Fill a pastry bag, fitted with a star tube, with the remaining cream. Decorate the center of the bavarois. Chop the whole walnut and sprinkle on the whipped cream.

Bavarois with Cointreau

Time needed: *40 minutes*
(plus cooling time)
Difficulty: *medium*

INGREDIENTS FOR 6-8 SERVINGS
1 cup of milk
1/2 cup of sugar
4 egg yolks
2 teaspoons of gelatin
2 cups of whipping cream
1 vanilla bean
3 tablespoons of Cointreau
6 strawberries
a few sprigs of mint

◆ Brush a 6-cup fluted cake pan with water. Dissolve the gelatin in a little cold water.
◆ Bring milk with split vanilla bean to a boil. In a saucepan, whisk in the egg yolks with sugar. Remove and discard vanilla bean from boiling milk; add milk to the egg mixture a few drops at a time. Almost bring to a boil on low heat, continuously stirring. Remove from the heat, add the gelatin and carefully stir. Let cool completely.
◆ Add the Cointreau to the cold mixture and fold 1 1/2 cups of whipped cream. Pour into the cake pan and refrigerate for at least 2 hours.
◆ Dip mold in warm water to remove the bavarois and turn onto a cold serving dish. Rinse strawberries in ice water, dry and cut each into 4 segments. Fill a pastry bag, fitted with a smooth long tube, with the remaining whipped cream and decorate the base and center of the bavarois. Place the strawberry segments at the base of the bavarois and the sprigs of mint in the center. Refrigerate until ready to serve.

Pear charlotte

Time needed *1 hour*
(plus cooling time)
Difficulty: complex

**INGREDIENTS
FOR 4 SERVINGS**
*1 recipe of almond cookie
dough
1 1/2 lbs of pears
1/2 cup of milk ◆ 6 egg yolks
2 tablespoons of pear flavored
Grappa ◆ 1/2 cup of sugar
1/2 cup of whipping cream
2 1/2 teaspoons of gelatin
1 lemon ◆ 1 tablespoon of
butter*

Sauce:
*1/2 lb of apricots
1/2 cup of sugar
1 tablespoon of dry white
wine*

Decoration:
*2 tablespoons of sugar
2 tablespoons of grated dark
chocolate
a few sprigs of mint*

Grease and flour a cookie sheet. Preheat the oven to 360 F.

◆ Prepare the almond cookie dough (see page 11) and put into a pastry bag fitted with a smooth nozzle. On the cookie sheet, form a 4 inch diameter disc and with the remainder, make 2 inch long sticks. Bake in the oven for 15-20 minutes. Remove from oven. Detach the disc and sticks from the tray and let cool on a rack.

◆ Dissolve gelatin in cold water. Peel pears and sprinkle with lemon juice. Cut 1 vertical slice of the central part of 1 pear, discard the seeds, moisten with lemon juice and set aside. Dice remaining pears and sauté in a pan with butter for a few minutes in a food processor. Purée half the pears and set aside.

◆ Bring milk to a boil. In a saucepan, whisk in the egg yolks with sugar. Add boiling milk a few drops at a time. Stir in the pear purée. Almost bring to a boil on low heat, stirring continuously. Remove from heat, add the gelatin, and carefully stir until completely dissolved. Let it cool. Add the Grappa and fold gently in the whipped cream.

◆ Place the almond cookie disc at the bottom of a charlotte mold about 4.5 inches in diameter. Line the sides with the almond cookie sticks. Pour the mixture into mold and refrigerate for at least 4 hours.

◆ Rinse the apricots and scald in boiling water for 1 minute. Peel, pit and purée together with sugar and white wine in a food processor.

◆ Turn the charlotte on a serving dish. Place a 4 inch cardboard disk on the charlotte and sprinkle with confectioner's sugar to cover only the sides. Carefully remove the cardboard disk. Caramelize 2 tablespoons of sugar (see page 19) in a little water and cook the pear slice in it for 2 minutes on each side. Let cool and top the charlotte with it.

Strawberry charlotte

Time needed: *45 minutes*
(plus cooling time)
Difficulty: medium

INGREDIENTS FOR 6 SERVINGS

*10 strawberries
9 oz of lady fingers (savoyard cookies)
1/2 cup of sugar
5 egg yolks
1 cup of milk
1 cup of whipping cream
2 1/2 teaspoons of gelatin
2 tablespoons of Maraschino liquor
grated peel of 1 lemon*

Decoration:
*8 strawberries
2 tablespoons of strawberry jam
1/3 cup of fresh cream*

◆ Line a medium charlotte mold with cookies. Dissolve gelatin in a little cold water.
◆ Quickly rinse the strawberries in ice water, dry and purée in a food processor.

Stsrawberry charlotte

◆ Bring milk with lemon peel to a boil. In a saucepan, whisk in the egg yolks with sugar. Add the boiling milk a few drops at a time. Almost bring to a boil on low heat, stirring continuously. Remove from heat, add the gelatin and carefully stir. Let cool completely.
◆ Whip the cream. Add the Maraschino and strawberry purée to the cold mixture and delicately fold in the whipped cream. Pour half of mixture into the mold; cover with a layer of cookies, pour over the remaining mixture and cover with another layer of cookies. Refrigerate for at least 4 hours.
◆ Rinse strawberries for the decoration in ice water, dry them and slice lengthwise, keeping one whole aside.
◆ Turn the charlotte on a serving dish. In a double boiler, melt the strawberry jam and brush the charlotte with it. Cover the charlotte with sliced strawberries, starting from the bottom. Whip the cream; place it in a pastry bag, fitted with an indented nozzle and crown the top of the charlotte. Place a crown of strawberry slices over it and top with a knob of whipped cream. Refrigerate until ready to serve.

Pear charlotte

Raspberry charlotte

Time needed: *1 hour*
(plus cooling time)
Difficulty: *medium*

INGREDIENTS FOR **8** SERVINGS
1 recipe of almond cookie dough
1 1/2 lb of raspberries
1/2 cup of sugar
1/2 cup of whipping cream
3 teaspoons of gelatin

♦ Preheat the oven to 360 F.
♦ Prepare the almond cookie dough (see page 11) and put into a pastry bag, fitted with a smooth nozzle. On a cookie sheet, form 2 inch long sticks. Bake for about 15 minutes. Remove, detach the sticks from the tray and let cool on a rack.
♦ Dissolve gelatin in a little cold water. Rinse raspberries in ice water, dry well, set 9 aside for decoration and purée the rest. In a double boiler, mix gelatin, sugar and raspberry purée. Whip the cream, set 3 tablespoons aside and carefully fold the rest into the mixture.
♦ Line a 7 inch diameter charlotte mold with the almond cookie sticks; trim them to the edge of the mold. Pour the raspberry mixture and cover with a layer of shortbread sticks. Refrigerate for at least 4 hours.
♦ Turn onto a serving dish, top with whipped cream and the raspberries.

Raspberry charlotte

Chocolate charlotte

Time needed: *40 minutes*
(plus cooling time)
Difficulty: *medium*

INGREDIENTS FOR **8** SERVINGS

5 oz of bittersweet chocolate
9 oz of milk chocolate
2 tablespoons of butter
4 eggs
3 tablespoons of Jamaican rum
1/2 cup of sugar
20 ladyfingers (savoyard cookies
a pinch of salt
1 teaspoon of unsweetened cocoa
Syrup:
1 tablespoon of sugar
2 tablespoons of rum

♦ Line a deep round mold with savoyard cookies.

Chocolate charlotte

Grate the dark chocolate and mix with 5 oz of milk chocolate.
♦ Melt chocolate with butter and rum. In a bowl, whisk the egg yolks with sugar (except for one tablespoon) until pale and creamy. Add melted chocolate, stirring to mix well. Beat the egg whites with salt to soft peaks. Add the tablespoon of sugar set aside and beat to firm peaks. Fold gently into the chocolate mixture. Pour into the mold and refrigerate for 4 hours.
♦ For the syrup, dissolve the sugar in 3 tablespoons of boiling water and add the rum.
♦ Turn charlotte onto a serving dish, brush with the rum syrup and dust with cocoa. Top with curls of milk chocolate. Refrigerate until ready to serve.

Pistachio and gianduia cream charlotte

Time needed: *1 hour*
(plus cooling time)
Difficulty: *medium*

INGREDIENTS FOR **6-8** SERVINGS

1/2 a recipe of almond cookie dough
1 cup of milk
1 cup of whipping cream
1/2 cup of sugar
5 egg yolks
2 teaspoons of gelatin
1 vanilla bean
1/2 cup of skinned and chopped pistachios
1/2 cup of toasted and minced hazelnuts
2 tablespoons of grated dark chocolate
2 tablespoons of grated milk chocolate
3 tablespoons of rum
Decoration:
1 tablespoon of confectioner's sugar
1/2 cup of vanilla sauce
a little melted dark chocolate

♦ Grease a cookie sheet. Line it with parchment paper. Grease again and flour. Preheat the oven to 370 F. Dissolve the gelatin in a little cold water.
♦ Prepare the almond cookie dough (see page 11), place on the tray and bake for 18-20 minutes in the preheated oven. Turn the pastry onto a kitchen towel, roll up the pastry in the towel and

rest for a while.

◆ Bring milk with split vanilla bean to a boil. In a saucepan, whisk in the egg yolks with sugar. Add boiling milk through a sieve, a few drops at a time, almost bring to a boil on low heat, stirring continuously. Remove from heat, add gelatin and carefully stir. Divide the preparation into 2 bowls. In one, add the grated dark and milk chocolate, stirring until completely melted; add minced hazelnuts and Rum. To the second bowl, add minced pistachios. Let the custard cool.

◆ Unroll the almond cookie pastry from the cloth. With 2/3 of it, line a 10 inch long rectangular mold with an arched bottom. Whip the cream delicately; fold into the pistachio custard, pour into the mold and refrigerate. Fold the remaining cream into the chocolate custard and place, spoon by spoon over the pistachio custard.

◆ Cover the charlotte with an almond cookie rectangle and refrigerate for at least 4 hours.

◆ Turn onto a serving dish, sprinkle with confectioner's sugar and serve sliced, surrounded by vanilla sauce (see page 19) topped with a few melted dark chocolate drops.

Pistachio and gianduia cream charlotte

Chocolate and orange charlotte

Time needed: *1 hour*
(plus cooling time)

Difficulty: complex

INGREDIENTS FOR **16-20** SERVINGS

9 oz of savoyard cookies
1 1/2 cups of grated dark chocolate
2 cups of milk
8 egg yolks
3/4 cup of sugar
2 cups of whipping cream
2 teaspoons of unflavored gelatin
2 tablespoons of rum

Cream:

juice of 4 oranges and 1/2 lemon
4 egg yolks
1/2 cup of powdered sugar
1 teaspoon of unflavored gelatin
1 cup of whipping cream
grated peel of 1 orange

Syrup:

1/2 cup of sugar
grated peel of 1 organic orange
2 tablespoons of orange liquor

Chocolate and orange charlotte

Decoration:

candied orange peel
4 oz of bittersweet chocolate
1 tablespoon of powdered sugar

◆ Line 9-cup charlotte mold and also a 3-cup mold with waxed paper. Dissolve gelatin in a little cold water. Coarsely chop dark chocolate.

◆ Bring the milk to a boil. In a saucepan, whisk in the egg yolks with sugar until pale and smooth. Add boiling milk a few drops at a time, almost bring to a boil on low heat, stirring continuously making sure the mixture never boils or the custard will curdle.

◆ Remove from heat, add gelatin and carefully stir until completely dissolved. Let cool completely. Fold the whipped cream into the cold mixture; add rum and stir.

◆ To make the syrup, simmer sugar with orange peel in 1/2 cup of water for about 2 minutes. Let cool and add the orange liquor. Set aside.

◆ Line the 2 molds with savoyard cookies, trimming if necessary, and brush them with syrup. Pour 2/3 of the custard into the large mold, and the remaining 1/3 into the small mold. Cover both molds with a sheet of aluminum foil and refrigerate.

◆ To make the orange cream, dissolve gelatin in a little cold water. Bring orange and lemon juice, with grated orange peel to a rolling boil. In a saucepan, whisk in the egg yolks with the sugar. Add boiling juice, a few drops at a time. Almost bring the preparation to a boil on low heat, stirring continuously. Remove from heat, add the gelatin, and carefully stir until completely dissolved. Let cool. Fold the whipped cream into the cold mixture.

◆ Remove molds from refrigerator. Pour 2/3 of this cream into the large mold and the remainder into the small mold. Cover the molds with a layer of cookies, wrap once more with aluminum foil and refrigerate for at least 4 hours.

◆ To decorate, coarsely chop the dark chocolate, melt in a double boiler, and pour onto a waxed paper. With a spatula, even it out very thinly. As soon as it hardens, cut into small triangles. Cut the candied orange peel into small discs. Turn the large charlotte onto a serving dish; remove the aluminum foil. Turn the small charlotte, with delicately onto the large charlotte.

◆ Remove aluminum foil and sprinkle with confectionery sugar. Place chocolate triangles and orange discs on the bottom, edges and top, forming garlands. Refrigerate until ready to serve.

Crème caramel

Time needed:
*1 hour and 15 minutes
(plus cooling time)*
Difficulty: medium

INGREDIENTS
FOR 4 SERVINGS

*2 cups of milk
3 eggs
2 egg yolks
1 vanilla bean
1 cup of sugar
1 tablespoon of raisins
2 tablespoons of pine nuts*

Preheat the oven to 360°F. In a saucepan, bring the milk with the split vanilla bean to a boil and set aside. In a saucepan, whisk in the egg yolks with the sugar until well blended. Remove the vanilla bean from the milk and add milk to the mixture, a few drops at a time. Set aside.

◆ Prepare the caramel: In a small pan on low heat, caramelize the sugar with 2 tablespoons of water.

◆ When golden in color, pour into a mold, turning it and making sure it covers the whole surface. Through a sieve, pour the egg and milk mixture in the mold.

◆ Place the mold in an oven pan (used as a bain-marie) and put into a preheated oven being careful that the water in the pan does not exceed 1/3 of the height of the mold. Bake the cream for about 1 hour. The crème caramel will be ready when firm. Remove from the oven, let cool completely and refrigerate.

◆ To remove the crème caramel from its mold, pass a knife in between the crème caramel and the edge of the mold and turn onto a serving dish; pour over the caramel left at the bottom of the mold.

◆ To decorate, alternate the raisins and the pine nuts along the edge and in the center of the crème caramel.

◆ If you prepare this dessert one day in advance, leave it in the refrigerator in its mold all night, the caramel will detach from the bottom with ease.

Bread pudding with whisky sauce

Time needed: *1 hour and 30 minutes*
Difficulty: medium

INGREDIENTS FOR 8 SERVINGS

*1 lb of day-old bread
4 cups of milk ◆ 3 eggs
1/2 cup of sugar ◆ 1 teaspoon of vanilla
1/2 cup of raisins*
Sauce:
*1 cup of milk ◆ 3 egg yolks
1/2 cup of sugar ◆ 1 vanilla bean
4 tablespoons of bourbon ◆ 1/3 cup of whipping cream*

◆ Butter and flour a deep charlotte mold 8 inches in diameter. Preheat oven to 320°F.
◆ Soak the raisins in warm water. Remove crust from bread and cut in small pieces. Soak in the milk for 10-15 minutes.
◆ In a bowl, lightly whisk the eggs with the sugar, vanilla and strained raisins (keeping 5 on the side). Mix the bread until smooth and add to the egg mixture.
◆ Pour this preparation into the mold and bake in oven for about 1 hour. Let cool completely before serving.
◆ To make the sauce, bring the milk with the split vanilla bean to a boil. In a saucepan, whisk in the egg yolks with the sugar until smooth, light and creamy. Add the boiling milk through a sieve a few drops at a time, almost bring to a boil on very low heat, stirring continuously ensuring that the mixture never boils. The sauce, when ready, will lightly cover the back of a spoon. Remove from heat, add gelatin and carefully stir until completely dissolved. Let cool; add the whisky and stir.
◆ Turn onto a serving dish and decorate with whipped cream and the raisins; serve accompanied by the whisky sauce.

*Bread pudding
with whisky sauce*

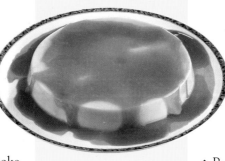

Panna cotta

Panna cotta

Time needed: *20 minutes
(plus cooling time)*
Difficulty: medium

INGREDIENTS FOR 4 SERVINGS

*2 cups of whipping cream
2 cups of sugar
1 tablespoon of cornstarch ◆ 1 vanilla bean*

◆ Put half the sugar and 2 tablespoons of water (see page 19) in a pan. Caramelize until golden on low heat. Pour the caramel into an 8-cup mold and turn to completely cover all sides.

Crème caramel

◆ In a saucepan, dilute the cornstarch in the whipping cream; add the remaining sugar and the split vanilla bean; bring to a boil on low heat. As soon as the mixture becomes dense, pour into the mold, let it cool to lukewarm and refrigerate.
◆ When ready to serve, turn onto a dish, pouring over the caramel left in the bottom of the mold.

Rice pudding with raspberry sauce

Time needed: *40 minutes*
(plus cooling time)
Difficulty: medium

INGREDIENTS FOR **6** SERVINGS
2 tablespoons of raisins
2 tablespoons of Grand Marnier
1 cup of uncooked rice ◆ *1 1/2 cups of milk*
1 cup of sugar
1 tablespoon of grated lemon peel
1 vanilla bean ◆ *2 teaspoons of gelatin*
2 tablespoons of butter ◆ *4 egg yolks*
2 oz of candied lime and orange (in small pieces)
1 1/3 cups of whipping cream ◆ *a dash of salt*
1 lb of raspberries ◆ *1 oz of candied orange*

◆ Soak the raisins in Grand Marnier and dissolve the gelatin in cold water. Scald the rice in salted boiling water for 2-3 minutes, drain and put under cold running water.
◆ Bring to boil the milk with half the sugar, the grated lemon peel, the split vanilla bean and salt. Once the sugar has dissolved, add the rice and cook on medium heat until the milk has been completely absorbed. Discard the vanilla bean.
◆ Add the gelatin to the hot milk, stirring until completely dissolved; add 1/2 the drained raisins, butter in pieces, candied fruit and egg yolks. Blend well and let cool completely.
◆ Whip 1/2 the cream, fold into the rice mixture, pour into a 6-cup fluted mold, cover with plastic wrap and refrigerate for at least 6 hours.
◆ To make the sauce: Rinse the raspberries in ice water, dry and purée with the remaining sugar in a food processor.
◆ Briefly dip the mold in warm water and turn the pudding onto a serving dish. Whip the remaining cream, put in a pastry bag, fitted with and indented nozzle, and decorate around the pudding. Top with the candied orange and remaining raisins. Serve accompanied by the raspberry sauce.

Apricot donut

Time needed: *1 hour and 15 minutes*
Difficulty: easy

INGREDIENTS FOR **4-6** SERVINGS
2 lb of apricots (ripe and firm)
2 cups of sugar ◆ *1/2 cup of Moscato wine*
4 eggs ◆ *2 tablespoons of apricot jam*

◆ Butter a tube pan. Preheat the oven to 360°F.
◆ Rinse and pit the apricots. Set a few aside to decorate. On low heat, simmer the apricots with the sugar and wine for about 15 minutes, stirring occasionally. Pass through a sieve and cook until almost dry, stirring. Let it cool a little and add the eggs one at a time, mixing.
◆ Pour the mixture into the mold, cover with aluminum foil and bake in a bain-marie in the oven for 45-50 minutes. Turn onto a serving dish and let cool.
◆ In a double boiler, dissolve the apricot jam. Brush some over the pudding. Cut the remaining apricots into segments and place on the pudding and around its internal base. Brush with the remaining jam.

Apple pudding

Time needed: *1 hour and 30 minutes*
Difficulty: easy

INGREDIENTS FOR **6** SERVINGS
1 1/2 lbs of apples ◆ *1/2 cup of sugar*
3 tablespoons of dry white wine
1/2 cup of raisins ◆ *2 tablespoons of potato starch*
1 cup of crumbled Amaretti ◆ *2 eggs*
1 tablespoon of breadcrumbs
1 tablespoon of powdered sugar ◆ *a pinch of salt*

◆ Butter a deep mold 7 inches in diameter. Line with breadcrumbs. Preheat the oven to 320°F.
◆ Soak the raisins in warm water. Peel, core and dice the apples. Cook with the wine and sugar for 7-8 minutes until the fruit is soft and the wine evaporated.
◆ In a large bowl, mix the apple sauce with the drained raisins, potato starch, amaretti and egg yolks; beat egg whites with salt to firm peaks. Add to the apple mixture. Pour into the mold and bake in oven for about 40 minutes.
◆ Let the pudding cool. Turn onto a serving dish and serve warm, sprinkled with powdered sugar.

Turkish pudding

Time needed: *50 minutes*
(plus cooling time)
Difficulty: easy

INGREDIENTS FOR 8 SERVINGS

1 cup of blanched, chopped almonds
2 cups of milk
1/2 cup of sugar
2 teaspoons of gelatin
2 cups of whipping cream
1 cup of candied pineapple
1 slice of fresh pineapple
1 small bunch of mint
1 candied cherry

◆ Dissolve the gelatin in a little cold water.
◆ In a saucepan, bring milk, sugar and almonds to a boil, stirring occasionally. Remove from heat; add the gelatin stirring carefully. Set aside to cool. Strain the milk through a muslin cloth, squeezing well; add the diced candied pineapple. Set aside.
◆ Whip the cream to firm peaks. Fold into the cold mixture. Brush a 6 inch diameter Zuccotto mold with water and pour in the preparation. Refrigerate 4 hours.
◆ To serve, dip mold in warm water for a few minutes and turn onto a serving plate. Top with the mint leaves, pineapple slice and candied cherry.

Hazelnut rose

Time needed: *1 hour*
Difficulty: medium

INGREDIENTS FOR 6 SERVINGS

1 cup of toasted, chopped hazelnuts
5 oz of bittersweet chocolate, in small pieces
1/4 lb of softened butter
8 eggs ◆ *1/2 cup of sugar*
1/3 cup of powdered sugar
1/4 lb of chocolate sponge cake

Decoration:

1/2 cup of whipping cream
3/4 cup of hazelnuts
1 tablespoon of sugar
1 tablespoon of almond oil

◆ Grease an 8-cup fluted tube pan and sprinkle with sugar. Preheat the oven to 360°F.
◆ Crumble sponge cake and pass it through a sieve. Melt chocolate in a double boiler.

◆ In a large bowl, whisk butter and powdered sugar until smooth and creamy. Add egg yolks, one at a time, always whisking. Add melted chocolate, hazelnuts and sponge cake crumbs. Beat egg whites with sugar, to stiff peaks; gently fold into the mixture. Pour all the mixture into the tube pan, filling 2/3 of it and bake in a bain-marie in the oven for 35-40 minutes. Let it cool completely.
◆ To decorate, toast the hazelnuts for 4-5 minutes in the oven at 360°F. To remove the skin, rub them with a clean kitchen cloth.
◆ Bring sugar and 2 teaspoons of water to a boil and simmer for 3 minutes. Remove from heat, add hazelnuts and stir until they are all coated with a layer of granular sugar. Return to heat and stir until the sugar caramelizes. Pour hazelnuts onto an oiled marble surface and detach the coated hazelnuts one at a time. Let cool and coarsely chop.
◆ Turn the pudding onto a serving plate. Whip the cream; put in a pastry bag, fitted with an indented nozzle and form knobs at the center of the pudding and along the fluted sides. Top with praline hazelnuts.

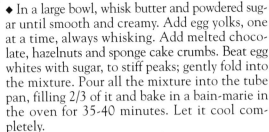

Almond pudding

Time needed: *1 hour and 20 minutes*
(plus cooling time)
Difficulty: medium

INGREDIENTS FOR 4 SERVINGS

1/2 cup of peeled and toasted almonds
3 cups of milk ◆ *1 cup of sugar*
1/4 cup of crumbled savoyard cookies
3 eggs ◆ *1/2 teaspoon of vanilla*
1/3 cup of whipping cream
8 cherries in syrup

◆ Preheat the oven to 370°F.
◆ In an 8-cup pudding mold, cook half the sugar in 2 tablespoons of water until caramelized (see page 19); turn the mold to completely cover it with caramel. Finely chop the almonds into a paste, in a food processor.
◆ Bring milk, vanilla, remaining sugar, and savoyard cookies to a boil. Add almond paste, stir and cook for 10 minutes. Sift the mixture, stir in the beaten eggs and pour into the mold.
◆ Bake in a bain-marie in the oven for 45-50 minutes. Let cool for 2 hours, turn onto a serving dish and pour the remaining caramel over. Whip the cream and place in knobs on the pudding with a pastry bag. Garnish with cherries.

Roman ricotta pudding

Time needed: *1 hour*
Difficulty: easy

INGREDIENTS FOR 6-8 SERVINGS

3/4 lb of ricotta
3/4 cup of powdered sugar ◆ *3 eggs*
2 egg yolks ◆ *a pinch of cinnamon*
grated peel of 1 organic lemon
1 pinch of salt ◆ *1 tablespoon of breadcrumbs*
1 piece of milk chocolate

◆ Grease a deep mold of 7 inch in diameter. Dust with breadcrumbs. Preheat the oven to 360°F.
◆ Sift the ricotta cheese twice and blend with the powdered sugar, whole eggs and egg yolks. Add cinnamon, lemon peel and salt. Pour into the mold and bake in the oven for 35-40 minutes. Turn pudding onto a serving dish and let cool.
◆ Curl chocolate with a potato peeler and garnish pudding with the slivers on top and around the bottom edge.

Coffee pudding

Time needed: *25 minutes*
(plus cooling time)
Difficulty: easy

INGREDIENTS FOR 4-6 SERVINGS

2 cups of milk ◆ *4 egg yolks*
4 tablespoons of sugar
2 tablespoons of flour
1 tablespoon of instant espresso coffee
1 teaspoon of unsweetened cocoa
1 tablespoons of coffee liquor
3/4 cups of whipping cream
2 tablespoons of powdered sugar
1 oz of dark chocolate
3 grains of coffee

◆ Bring the milk to a boil. In a saucepan, whisk in the egg yolks and sugar until pale; add flour, little by little, and cocoa. Dissolve coffee in warm milk and pour one drop at a time into the egg mixture, stirring carefully.
◆ Bring to a boil on moderate heat and simmer for 8-10 minutes, stirring often. Brush a 6 inch diameter round glass mold with the liquor. Let cool then refrigerate.

Roman ricotta pudding

Coffee pudding

◆ When ready to serve, briefly dip mold in warm water and turn the pudding onto a serving dish. Whip 3 tablespoons of cream, put in a pastry bag, fitted with an indented nozzle and make a knob in the center of the pudding. Top this with coffee grains. Mix remaining cream with powdered sugar, and pour this liquid sauce around the pudding.
◆ Melt chocolate in a double boiler, pour it into a waxed paper cone and draw 2 chocolate circles on the cream sauce. Create a pattern to your taste with a toothpick.

Caramel pudding

Time needed: *1 hour and 30 minutes*
Difficulty: medium

INGREDIENTS FOR 6 SERVINGS

3/4 cup of flour ◆ *3/4 cup of sugar*
4 tablespoons of butter ◆ *3 eggs*
1/2 cup of milk ◆ *a pinch of salt*
Decoration:
20 whole walnuts ◆ *1/2 cup of sugar*
1/3 cup of whipping cream
1 tablespoon of almond oil

◆ Grease a 4-cup fluted mold. Preheat the oven to 360°F.
◆ Put the sifted flour into a saucepan and mix in the milk, a little at a time. Add 3/4 of the sugar, stirring. Cook on low heat for a few minutes, stirring until the mixture separates from the pan. Remove from heat immediately.
◆ Cook remaining sugar in 2 tablespoons of water until caramelized and golden in color (see page 19). Remove from heat and mix in the butter in pieces. Add to the flour mixture. Beat in the egg yolks one at a time. Whisk egg whites with salt to soft peaks and gently fold in the preparation.
◆ Pour into the mold and bake in a bain-marie in the oven for 1 hour. When ready, turn onto a serving dish and let cool.
◆ To decorate, cook sugar in 2 tablespoons of water until caramelized and golden in color. Remove from heat; mix the whole walnuts in the caramel and let cool on an oiled marble surface, separating each walnut from the other. Whip the cream; put in a pastry bag, fitted with an indented nozzle and top the center and sides of the pudding. Garnish with caramelized walnuts.

Caramel pudding

German orange pudding

Time needed: *40 minutes
(plus resting time)*
Difficulty: easy

INGREDIENTS FOR 6 SERVINGS

1 1/4 cup of semolina ◆ *2 cups of milk
3/4 cup of sugar* ◆ *3 egg whites
2 tablespoons of orange liquor
grated peel of 2 organic oranges
1 orange* ◆ *a few leaves of mint* ◆ *a pinch of salt*

◆ Bring the milk to a boil; pour the semolina over, little by little, stirring so as to not create any lumps. Cook on low heat for 20 minutes, stirring occasionally. Remove from heat; add sugar and orange peel. Beat the egg whites with salt to soft peaks and fold into the mixture. Bring back to a boil on low heat, stirring constantly. Remove, add the liquor and pour in a 6-cup mold previously brushed with water. Refrigerate for 5-6 hours until firm.
◆ Rinse and dry the mint leaves. Peel the orange and divide into segments, removing all white parts. When ready to serve, turn the pudding onto a dish and garnish with orange segments and mint leaves.

German orange pudding

Spanish pudding

Time needed: *1 hour and 10 minutes*
Difficulty: medium

INGREDIENTS FOR 8 SERVINGS

*1/4 lb of softened butter
1/2 cup of sugar* ◆ *7 egg yolks
4 egg whites* ◆ *1/4 cup of raisins
2 tablespoons of rum
1 8 inch sponge cake
1/4 cup of Malaga wine
3 tablespoons of apple jam
2 tablespoon of apricot jam
1 tablespoon of powdered sugar*

◆ Grease and flour a 9 inch pudding mold. Preheat the oven to 340°F. Soak raisins in the rum. Cut 3 vertical disks from the sponge cake (see page 10).
◆ In a bowl, work butter with an electric blender until smooth and creamy. Add sugar, egg yolks one at a time, apple jam and 2/3 of the drained

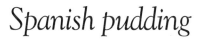

Spanish pudding

Orange pudding

raisins. Gently fold in the beaten egg whites. Pour 1/3 of the mixture into the mold. Lay a sponge cake disk over and brush with wine. Place 1/2 the remaining mixture over, followed by another sponge cake disk brushed with wine. Finish with the remaining mixture. Spread evenly and bake for about 40 minutes. Remove and let cool.
◆ Turn the pudding onto a serving dish. Cut 7 little disks from the remaining sponge cake disk. Mix powdered sugar with a little water until you have a smooth and dense glaze; brush sponge cake disks with the apricot jam previously dissolved in a double boiler. Place at the center of the pudding. Garnish with a drop of white glaze and remaining raisins.

Orange pudding

Time needed: *2 hours and 20 minutes*
Difficulty: easy

INGREDIENTS FOR 6-8 SERVINGS

4 eggs ◆ *1 1/4 cup of sugar
2 1/4 cups of flour
1/2 lb of softened butter
grated peel of 2 oranges
and 1/2 lemon
2 teaspoons of baking powder
2 tablespoons of apricot jam
7 oz of candied orange peel
a pinch of salt*

◆ Grease and flour a 6-cup deep, straight-edge pudding mold.
◆ In a bowl, work the butter with an electric blender until smooth and creamy; add sugar and continue to mix until smooth. Add egg yolks one at a time, sifted flour, baking powder and citrus peel. Beat egg whites with salt to stiff peaks and gently fold in the mixture.
◆ Pour into the mold, cover with a damp kitchen towel and cook on in a double boiler for 2 hours. Be sure that the water level is half the depth of the mold. When firm, remove from heat and turn onto a serving dish; let cool.
◆ Cut 18 small triangles from the candied peel. Cut a large disc and several little discs from the candied peel. Heat the jam with 2 tablespoons of water and brush the pudding. Form a crown of candied small discs at the base of the pudding; place the large disc on the top and triangles around the disc. Garnish the border of the pudding with the remaining triangles.

Grease and flour a cookie sheet. Preheat the oven to 360°F.

◆ Make the almond cookie dough: In a bowl, whisk in eggs, sugar and vanilla until pale and smooth. Add lemon peel and almonds. Beat egg whites with salt to stiff peaks and fold into the mixture. Place into a pastry bag and make 2 inch long sticks on the tray. Sprinkle with powdered sugar and bake in the oven for 7-8 minutes; let cool.

◆ Dissolve gelatin in a little cold water. Bring milk and split vanilla bean to a boil.

◆ In a saucepan, mix in the egg yolks and sug-

Ottoman custard

Time needed:
1 hour
(plus cooling time)
Difficulty: medium

INGREDIENTS
FOR 6-8 SERVINGS
1/2 cup of candied fruit (cherries, lemon and orange rind)
1 cup of milk ◆ 3 egg yolks
1/4 cup of sugar
1 vanilla bean
1 teaspoon of gelatin

Cookie dough:
3/4 cup of flour
1/4 cup of sugar
3 eggs
1/2 teaspoon of vanilla
grated peel of 1/2 lemon
1 teaspoon of powdered sugar
1/4 cup of blanched, chopped almonds
a pinch of salt

ar until smooth, light and creamy. Add milk through a sieve, one drop at a time. Almost bring to a boil on very low heat, stirring continuously, making sure the mixture never boils. When the custard coats a spoon, remove from heat and add gelatin, stirring until completely dissolved. Let cool.

◆ Dice 2/3 of the candied fruit and chop the baked cookie (1). Put in a bowl and add the custard (2). Pour into a fluted tube pan (3) and refrigerate for at least 4 hours.

◆ When ready to serve, dip the mold in warm water, turn onto a serving dish and garnish with the remaining candied fruit (4).

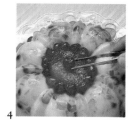

Parisian pudding

Time needed: *1 hour and 20 minutes*
Difficulty: easy

INGREDIENTS FOR 4-6 SERVINGS
2 cups of milk ◆ 1 1/3 cup of fresh cream
3 eggs ◆ 4 egg yolks ◆ 3/4 cup of sugar
grated peel of 1 orange
31/2 oz of sponge cake
1 tablespoon of raisins
1/2 cup of candied orange
3/4 cup of candied citron

◆ Grease a 6-cup straight-edge mold and line with parchment paper. Preheat the oven to 360°F.
◆ Cut the candied orange and citron into various shapes and place at the bottom and on the sides of the mold. In a bowl, mix together the sponge cake, cut in small pieces and the raisins; transfer to the mold.
◆ Bring milk, cream and orange peel to a boil. In a bowl, whisk in eggs, egg yolks and sugar. Add

Bônet

hot milk a few drops at a time. Slowly pour into the mold and bake in a bain-marie in the oven for 1 hour. Remove and cool completely.
◆ Turn onto a serving dish, remove waxed paper and refrigerate until ready to serve.

Bônet

Time needed: *1 hour and 20 minutes*
(plus cooling time)
Difficulty: medium

INGREDIENTS FOR 6-8 SERVINGS

2 cups of milk ◆ 4 eggs ◆ 2 egg yolks
1 cup of sugar ◆ 1/4 cup of cocoa
8 Amaretti ◆ 2 tablespoons of rum
a few miniature amaretti cookies

◆ Preheat an oven to 360°F.
◆ On low heat, caramelize sugar in 2 tablespoons of water until golden (see page 19). Pour into an 8 inch fluted tube pan. Turn mold in order for the caramel to cover all sides.

Ottoman custard

◆ In a bowl, whisk in the eggs and egg yolks with remaining sugar and cocoa. Bring milk to a boil and mix in the crumbled amaretti and rum. Add to the egg mixture. Pour into the mold and bake in a bain-marie (the water should be 1/2 the height of the mold) in the oven for 1 hour. Cool and refrigerate.

◆ Turn the pudding onto a serving dish, pour over the caramel left at the bottom of the mold, and garnish with the miniature amaretti.

Praline soufflé
pudding

White pudding
in caramel sauce

Time needed: *50 minutes*
(plus cooling time)
Difficulty: *medium*

INGREDIENTS FOR 6-8 SERVINGS

1 1/4 cup of blanched chopped almonds
2 cups of milk
3/4 cup of sugar
2 teaspoons of unflavored gelatin
2 cups of whipping cream
Caramel sauce:
1 cup of milk
3 egg yolks
3 tablespoons of sugar
1/2 teaspoon of cornstarch
1/2 teaspoon of vanilla
Decoration:
1 oz of white chocolate
2 oz of toasted julienne sliced almonds

◆ Dissolve the gelatin in a little cold water.

◆ Put milk, chopped almonds and sugar in a saucepan. Bring to a boil, stirring occasionally. Add gelatin and mix well, stirring. Set the almond-milk mixture until it cools. Strain through a muslin cloth, squeezing it well and let it cool. Whip the cream and gently fold into the cold almond milk and pour into a 6-inch jelly mold. Refrigerate.

◆ Prepare the caramel sauce (see page 20).

◆ Just before serving, dip mold in warm water and turn the pudding onto a serving dish. Make curls from white chocolate with an arched potato peeler, and place on the center of the pudding. Pour the caramel sauce around and surround the sauce with almond slivers.

White pudding
in caramel sauce

Praline soufflé
pudding

Time needed: *3 hours and 15 minutes*
Difficulty: *easy*

INGREDIENTS FOR 6 SERVINGS

5 eggs ◆ *3/4 cup of sugar*
1/2 cup of flour ◆ *1 1/3 cups of milk*
1 vanilla bean
1 cup of praline hazelnuts, finely chopped
2 tablespoons of rum ◆ *a pinch of salt*

◆ Grease and flour a 4-cup straight-edge glass mold. Preheat the oven to 260°F.

◆ Bring milk and vanilla bean to a boil. In a saucepan, whisk in the egg yolks and sugar. Add sifted flour, a little at a time. Add boiling milk through a sieve a few drops at a time, almost bring to a boil on low heat for 5-6 minutes, stirring continuously. Remove from heat, discard vanilla bean and add chopped hazelnuts, keeping one tablespoon aside. Add rum and stir. Let cool completely.

◆ Beat egg whites with salt to firm peaks. Fold into the cooled mixture and pour into the mold. Cover and bake in a bain-marie in the oven for 2 hours and 30 minutes. Let the pudding cool briefly, turn onto a serving dish and top with remaining chopped hazelnuts.

Simple chocolate
pudding

Time needed: *20 minutes*
(plus cooling time)
Difficulty: *easy*

INGREDIENTS FOR 4-6 SERVINGS

2 cups of milk
1/2 cup of grated dark chocolate
1/4 cup of sugar
1/2 cup of flour
3 tablespoons of butter
1 vanilla bean ◆ *1 tablespoon of raisins*
3 tablespoons of rum
3/4 cup of whipping cream

◆ Soak the raisins in 2/3 of the rum.

◆ In a saucepan, mix flour, sugar, melted chocolate, milk (a few drops at a time) and vanilla bean. Cook on low heat for 7-8 minutes, stirring constantly. Remove from heat, add 1/2 the raisins and butter in pieces. Remove vanilla bean and

Simple chocolate
pudding

pour mixture in a Zuccotto mold brushed with remaining rum. When cool, refrigerate.

◆ Just before serving, turn the pudding onto a serving dish. Fill a pastry bag, fitted with a star tube, with whipped cream and garnish with little knobs of whipped cream and a little crown of raisins around the pudding.

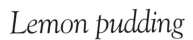

Lemon pudding

Time needed: *1 hour*
Difficulty: easy

INGREDIENTS FOR **6** SERVINGS
1 cup of flour
4 tablespoons of softened butter
3 eggs ◆ *3/4 cup of sugar* ◆ *1 lemon*
1/3 cup of milk ◆ *a pinch of salt*
3 thin slices of lemon

◆ Grease and flour an 8 inch Bundt pan. Preheat the oven to 370°F.
◆ Rinse lemon, grate peel and squeeze juice. Set aside.
◆ With an electric mixer, work butter with 2/3 of sugar until smooth and creamy. Add egg yolks one at a time, lemon juice, lemon peel, flour and milk, drop by drop. Beat egg whites with salt and gently fold into the mixture.
◆ Pour into the Bundt pan and bake in a bain-marie in the oven for 40-50 minutes until golden. Remove from oven and turn onto a serving dish. Let cool covered.
◆ Cook remaining sugar in 1/4 cup of water for 4 minutes. Dip lemon slices in syrup; set on a plate; refrigerate. Just before serving, drain and dry the lemon slices and put on the center of the pudding.

Lemon pudding

Walnut and hazelnut delight

Time needed: *1 hour and 20 minutes*
Difficulty: medium

INGREDIENTS FOR **8** SERVINGS
11/2 cup of whole walnuts
11/2 cup of shelled hazelnuts
3/4 cup of sugar ◆ *4 cups of milk*
2 1/2 cups of whipping cream
1/4 cup of hazelnut liquor
6 eggs ◆ *1 1/4 cup of semolina*
1 tablespoon of unsweetened cocoa ◆ *a pinch of salt*

Walnut and hazelnut delight

◆ Grease a 6-cup fluted tube pan and sprinkle it with sugar. Preheat the oven to 370°F. Finely chop hazelnuts and half the walnuts.
◆ Put milk, 11/2 cups of whipping cream and sugar in a pan. Bring to a boil, sprinkle semolina over and simmer for 15 minutes, stirring constantly. Remove from heat, blend in the chopped nuts, egg yolks, liquor and cocoa. Beat egg whites with salt to firm peaks and fold in.
◆ Pour into the tube pan and bake in a bain-marie for about 50 minutes. Let it cool completely. Turn onto a serving dish.
◆ Whip the remaining cream, put in a pastry bag, fitted with an indented nozzle and crown the pudding. Add the remaining whole nuts.

Portuguese custard

Time needed: *1 hour and 40 minutes*
(plus cooling time)
Difficulty: medium

INGREDIENTS FOR **6** SERVINGS
3/4 cup of sugar
3/4 cup of milk
1 1/4 cup of whipping cream
grated peel of 1 orange
6 egg yolks
2 tablespoons of White Port
Decoration:
a few pieces of candied orange peel
1 tablespoon of julienne sliced almonds
6 candied violets

◆ Preheat an oven to 320°F.
◆ Rinse orange and slice off 2 long strips of the peel. Refrigerate 6 individual molds for 1 hour.
◆ Cook 2/3 of sugar in 1 tablespoon of water until golden in color (see page 20). Remove from heat, add 4 tablespoons of boiling water a little at a time and continue to cook for 7-8 minutes. Set 2 tablespoons of this syrup aside, and cover the inside of the cold molds with the rest.
◆ Bring the milk, cream, orange peel and remaining sugar to a boil. Simmer for about 12 minutes, stirring occasionally. Remove from heat. Blend in the remaining 2 tablespoons of syrup. Add the egg yolks one at a time. Return to heat another minute, making sure it does not boil. Add the Port, mix well, pour the preparation through a sieve into the molds and

Portuguese custard

bake in a bain-marie in the oven for about 50 minutes. Refrigerate the molds for 5 hours.
◆ Dice the candied orange peel. Pass a knife in between the puddings and the molds, and turn over onto a serving dish. Insert 6 almond slivers along the border of each pudding and place the candied peel and violets in the center.

Cold pudding from Lyon

Time needed: *50 minutes*
(plus cooling time)
Difficulty: *medium*

INGREDIENTS FOR 8 SERVINGS
9 oz of savoyard cookies
1/4 cup glass of Kirsch
1/4 cup of raisins
2 cups of milk
1/2 cup of sugar
5 egg yolks
1 vanilla bean
2 teaspoons of unflavored gelatin
4 tablespoons of chestnut paste
5 Marrons Glacé
1/3 cup of whipping cream

◆ Dissolve gelatin in a little cold water and soak raisins in warm water.
◆ Warm milk and vanilla bean. In a saucepan, whisk egg yolks and sugar until smooth, light and creamy. Add boiling milk through a sieve, a few drops at a time; cook on low heat, stirring continuously making sure the mixture never boils. Remove from heat when the custard coats a spoon. Add gelatin and stir well. Add the chestnut paste.
◆ Pour a layer of custard in a 4-cup fluted tube pan and refrigerate for 10-15 minutes. Remove, coat with a layer of savoyard cookies brushed with Kirsch and a layer of raisins. Pour another layer of custard and continue alternating savoyard cookies, raisins and custard until all ingredients have been used. Keep 1 tablespoon of raisins aside.
◆ Refrigerate for 3 hours, dip briefly in warm water and turn the pudding onto a serving dish. Cut the Marron Glacé in half and place in a star shape on top of the pudding. Whip the cream, put it in a pastry bag fitted, with an indented nozzle and form a crown of puffs at the border and place a puff at the center. Garnish with remaining raisins.

American chestnut pudding

Time needed: *1 hour*
Difficulty: *easy*

INGREDIENTS FOR 4-6 SERVINGS
1 lb of chestnut
4 eggs
3 tablespoon of milk
4 tablespoons of butter
1/2 cup of sugar
a pinch of salt

◆ Grease a 4-cup tube pan. Preheat the oven to 360°F.
◆ Boil chestnuts in lightly salted water. Peel, making sure to remove the internal skin, and purée in a food processor.
◆ In a bowl, mix the purée with melted butter, milk, sugar and egg yolks. Beat egg whites with salt to stiff peaks and fold into the preparation.
◆ Pour into the mold, cover with aluminum foil and bake in the oven for about 30 minutes. Cool lightly.
◆ Turn onto a dish and serve warm or cold.

Strawberry and cream pudding

Time needed: *1 hour and 20 minutes*
(plus cooling time) ·
Difficulty: *medium*

INGREDIENTS FOR 8 SERVINGS
2 cups of milk ◆ 2 cups of whipping cream
1 vanilla bean ◆ 4 eggs
6 egg yolks ◆ 1 1/2 cups of sugar
1 lb of strawberries

◆ Preheat the oven to 370°F.
◆ In an 8-cup fluted mold, caramelize 1/3 of sugar in 2 tablespoons of water until dark in color (see page 20). Turn the mold, to cover all sides with caramel. Let cool.
◆ Bring milk, cream and vanilla to a boil. In a saucepan, whisk eggs, egg yolks and sugar. Add milk mixture through a sieve, a little at a time and stir.
◆ Rinse and dry strawberries. Keep a few large ones aside, cut remainder in half and add to egg-milk mixture. Pour into the mold and bake in a bain-marie in the oven for 45-50 minutes. When cool, refrigerate the pudding for 2 hours.

◆ Just before serving, turn onto a serving dish and garnish with remaining strawberries.

Cheese pudding

Time needed: *1 hour and 15 minutes*
Difficulty: *medium*

INGREDIENTS FOR **4** SERVINGS
1/2 cup of sugar
3 eggs
1/2 cup of ricotta
1/2 cup of mascarpone
1/2 cup of sweet condensed milk

◆ Preheat the oven to 360°F.
◆ In a 12 inch oval mold, caramelize sugar in 4 tablespoons of water until golden (see page 20). Turn mold around to cover all sides with caramel. Let cool.
◆ In a bowl, with an electric mixer, whisk eggs with 3/4 cup of water and condensed milk. Slowly mix in mascarpone and ricotta cheeses. Pour in the mold and bake in the oven for about 1 hour until the pudding has set. Remove, cool and refrigerate for at least 1 hour. Turn onto a serving dish and pour all the caramel over the pudding.

Grandma's pudding

Time needed: *1 hour and 20 minutes*
(plus resting time)
Difficulty: *medium*

INGREDIENTS FOR **4** SERVINGS
3/4 cups of rice ◆ *4 cups of milk*
1 cup of sugar
4 eggs ◆ *6 bananas* ◆ *1/3 cup of Cognac*
1/2 cup of Malaga grapes, pitted
a pinch of salt

◆ Preheat the oven to 370°F.
◆ Cut bananas into small pieces and soak in cognac for 1 hour. Soak pitted grapes in warm water.
◆ Caramelize sugar in 2 tablespoons of water until dark in color (see page 20). Pour in a 4-cup tube pan and turn mold to cover all sides with caramel.

◆ Cook the rice in its equivalent amount of water. Once the water has been absorbed completely, add warm milk, a little at a time, stirring until all absorbed, as for risotto. Stir in the remaining sugar and let the rice cool.
◆ Blend in the egg yolks. Beat egg whites with salt to firm peaks and fold in. Pour a layer of rice into the mold, followed by a layer of bananas, then another layer of rice and one of drained grapes until all ingredients have been used. Finish with a layer of rice. Bake in a bain-marie in the oven for 25 minutes.
◆ Remove from oven and set the pudding aside to cool in its mold for several hours. Turn onto a dish and serve cold.

Raspberry and blueberry pudding

Time needed: *30 minutes*
(plus cooling time)
Difficulty: *easy*

INGREDIENTS FOR **4-6** SERVINGS
1 cup of flour
3/4 cup of sugar
3 tablespoons of butter
3 eggs
1 cup of blueberries
1 cup of raspberries
1 lemon
a pinch of salt

◆ Rinse raspberries and blueberries in ice water, dry well, set 1/4 cup of each aside and mix the remainder in a food processor. Place in the refrigerator. Cut off the yellow part only of the lemon. Bring to boil 2 cups of water, butter and lemon peel. Squeeze lemon and set juice aside.
◆ In a saucepan, whisk in the egg yolks and sugar until smooth, light and creamy. Add flour and butter-water mixture passed through a sieve, a few drops at a time. Simmer on low heat for 10 minutes, stirring constantly.
◆ Remove from heat. Blend lemon juice and raspberry-blueberry pulp into the custard. Beat egg whites with salt to firm peaks and fold in. Pour into an oiled 4-cup mold, cover with aluminum foil and refrigerate for 3 hours.
◆ Just before serving, briefly dip mold in warm water; turn the pudding onto a serving dish and garnish with remaining raspberries and blueberries.

Citrus soufflé in oranges

Time needed:
1 hour
Difficulty: *medium*

INGREDIENTS
FOR 6 SERVINGS

1/2 cup of flour
1/4 cup of sugar
3 eggs ◆ 4 egg whites
7 oranges
3 tangerines
1 tablespoon of butter
3 tablespoons of Grand Marnier
1/4 cup of powdered sugar
a pinch of salt

Preheat the oven to 360°F. Rinse and dry oranges and tangerines. Grate the peel of 1 orange and 1 mandarin.

◆ Cut the cap of the 6 remaining oranges and empty them, being careful not to break the peel. Squeeze the pulp and keep 1/2 cup oz of juice. Squeeze the 2 remaining tangerines and keep 1/4 cup of juice. In a saucepan, bring citrus juice to a boil.

◆ In a saucepan, mix flour, sugar, egg, egg yolk, liquor and citrus peel. Add boiling juice and blend all ingredients carefully. Bring back to a boil on low heat, stirring until smooth.

Remove from heat, add butter and remaining egg yolk; let the mixture cool completely.

◆ Roll 6 sheets of aluminum foil into 6 rings and place on a cookie sheet. On each ring, place 1 emptied orange, individually wrapped in aluminum foil.

◆ Beat 6 egg whites with salt to firm peaks and carefully fold into the mixture. Transfer to a pastry bag and fill the emptied oranges. Bake in the oven for 25-30 minutes. Remove aluminum foil and sprinkle with powdered sugar.

Almond and ricotta soufflé

Time needed: *1 hour*
Difficulty: *medium*

INGREDIENTS FOR 4 SERVINGS
1 cup of ricotta
1/2 cup of chopped almonds
2 tablespoons of softened butter
1/2 cup of sugar
4 eggs, separated
grated peel of 1/2 lemon
1 tablespoon of flour
1 tablespoon of powdered sugar
a pinch of salt

◆ Grease and flour 4 individual soufflé molds. Preheat the oven to 360°F.
◆ In a bowl, with an electric mixer, beat butter with half the sugar until smooth, pale and creamy. Add egg yolks, one at a time, flour, lemon peel, almonds and ricotta cheese.
◆ Beat the egg whites with the salt to soft peaks; add remaining sugar and continue beating to firm peaks. Gently fold into the ricotta mixture.
◆ Pour into the molds and bake for about 30 minutes. Serve immediately, sprinkled with powdered sugar.

Almond and ricotta soufflé

Plum soufflé

Plum soufflé

Time needed: *1 hour*
Difficulty: *medium*

INGREDIENTS FOR 4 SERVINGS
1 lb of plums
1/2 cup of sugar
3 egg whites
3 tablespoons of dry red wine
1/2 lemon
a pinch of salt
1 tablespoon of vanilla flavored powdered sugar

◆ Grease 4 individual soufflé molds and sprinkle with sugar. Preheat the oven to 360°F.
◆ Rinse plums, pit and cut into 4 segments. Rinse lemon, grate peel and squeeze juice.
◆ Bring wine to a boil with 1/2 the sugar and simmer for 2 minutes. Add plums, 1 tablespoon of lemon juice and 1 of lemon peel. Continue to simmer for about 20 minutes until the plums are soft. Cool and purée in a food processor.
◆ Beat egg whites with salt to soft peaks, whip in the remaining sugar and gently fold into the plum purée.
◆ Pour into molds and bake in the oven for 30-35 minutes. Sprinkle with powdered sugar.

Citrus soufflé in oranges

Chocolate soufflé

Time needed: *50 minutes*
Difficulty: *medium*

INGREDIENTS FOR 4-6 SERVINGS

1 cup of grated bittersweet chocolate
4 eggs
1/2 cup of sugar
1 tablespoon of butter
a pinch of salt

◆ Butter a 4-cup soufflé mold. Preheat the oven to 320°F.
◆ In a double boiler, melt chocolate with butter, stirring continuously. Remove from heat; blend in sugar and egg yolks, one at a time. Set aside.
◆ Beat egg whites with salt to firm peaks and gently fold into chocolate mixture. Pour into mold and bake in the oven for 10 minutes; raise the temperature to 370°F and continue to bake for another 20 minutes.

Chocolate soufflé

Strawberry soufflé "Carême"

Time needed: *1 hour*
(plus resting time)
Difficulty: *complex*

INGREDIENTS FOR 6 SERVINGS

2 cups of ripe strawberries
1/2 cup of sugar
3 egg whites
a pinch of salt

Shortbread pastry:
1/2 cup of flour
1/4 cup of butter
1/4 cup of sugar
1 egg yolk
grated peel of 1/2 organic lemon
1 tablespoon of chopped almonds

◆ Grease 6 individual soufflé molds well.
◆ Prepare the shortbread dough (see page 12), adding the chopped almonds to it. Cover with plastic wrap and refrigerate for 30 minutes.
◆ Preheat the oven to 375 F.
◆ Roll dough very thinly; line bottom and sides of molds. Cover dough with aluminum foil and fill with uncooked beans to cook the dough blind.
◆ Bake in the oven for about 20 minutes un-

Strawberry soufflé "Carême"

Pineapple soufflé

til golden in color. Take pastry out of the molds; remove aluminum foil and beans; let the little pastry containers cool.
◆ Rinse strawberries in ice water. Purée 2/3 of strawberries with 2/3 of sugar. Beat egg whites with salt to stiff peaks and gently fold into the purée. Transfer to a pastry bag and pipe into the shortbread containers. Bake in the oven at 320°F for 25 minutes.
◆ Purée remaining strawberries with remaining sugar. Serve the soufflés hot accompanied with this sauce.

Pineapple soufflé

Time needed: *1 hour*
Difficulty: *medium*

INGREDIENTS FOR 6 SERVINGS

1/2 cup of flour
1/2 cup of sugar
3 eggs
4 egg whites
1 cup of milk
4 tablespoons of whipping cream
1 tablespoon of butter
1 lb of pineapple flesh
grated peel of 1/2 lemon
2 tablespoons of Crème de Cassis
a pinch of salt

◆ Grease a 4-cup soufflé mold and sprinkle it with sugar. Preheat the oven to 360°F.
◆ Chop pineapple into small pieces and dry it in a non-stick pan on a high heat, stirring for a few minutes. Set aside 1 tablespoon and purée the remainder in a food processor. Mix half the sugar, liquor and remaining pineapple pieces into 1/2 the purée. Pour in a sauceboat..
◆ Bring milk and cream to a boil with lemon peel. In a saucepan, mix flour, remaining sugar, egg and egg yolk. Slowly add boiling milk through a sieve, making sure all ingredients are well blended. Bring to a boil on low heat, stirring constantly, and simmer for a few minutes until smooth and creamy.
◆ Remove from heat; add the butter, the remaining egg yolk and the remaining pineapple purée.
◆ Beat 6 egg whites with salt to stiff peaks and gently fold into the mixture. Pour into mold and bake in the oven for 40 minutes. Serve with sauce on the side.

Lemon soufflé with strawberry sauce

Time needed: *1 hour*
Difficulty: *medium*

INGREDIENTS FOR 6 SERVINGS

1/2 cup of flour ◆ *3/4 cup of sugar*
1 vanilla bean ◆ *3 eggs*
4 egg whites ◆ *1 cup of milk*
4 tablespoons of heavy cream
1 tablespoon of butter
grated peel of 2 organic lemons
1/2 lb of strawberries
1 teaspoon of lemon juice
a pinch of salt

*Lemon soufflé with
strawberry sauce*

◆ Rinse strawberries in ice water, dry and purée with half the sugar and lemon juice. Pour in a sauceboat.
◆ Butter 6 individual soufflé molds and sprinkle with sugar. Preheat the oven to 360°F.
◆ Bring milk, cream and split vanilla bean to a boil. In a saucepan, whisk remaining sugar, flour, 1 egg, 1 egg yolk and lemon rind. Add boiling milk through a sieve, drop by drop and bring back to a boil on low heat, stirring constantly until smooth and creamy. Remove from heat; add butter and remaining egg yolk. Beat 6 egg whites with salt to soft peaks and fold in.
◆ Pour the mixture into molds and bake in the oven for 20-25 minutes. Serve with the strawberry sauce on the side.

Martinique soufflé

Time needed: *1 hour*
Difficulty: *medium*

INGREDIENTS FOR 6-8 SERVINGS

6 bananas ◆ *2 oranges*
1 1/4 cups of milk
1 tablespoon of cornstarch
1 tablespoon of vanilla flavored powdered sugar
1/2 cup of sugar ◆ *3 eggs*
a pinch of salt
Decoration:
1 teaspoon of powdered sugar
1 teaspoon of cinnamon
1/2 banana
1 piece of candied orange
1 tablespoon of lemon juice

Martinique soufflé

◆ Grease a 6-cup brioche mold. Preheat the oven to 360°F.
◆ Squeeze the orange juice. Peel the bananas, cut into small pieces and purée with the orange juice.
◆ In a saucepan, dissolve the cornstarch in milk on low heat for 5 minutes, stirring continuously. Set aside to cool.
◆ In the purée, add sugar, vanilla flavored powdered sugar, egg yolks and milk. Beat egg whites with salt to stiff peaks and gently fold into the mixture. Pour into mold and bake in a bain-marie in oven for about 40 minutes.
◆ To decorate, cut the peeled banana into 7 slices of the same thickness of the candied orange peel and brush with lemon juice. Cut the candied peel in 7 circles, smaller in size than the banana slices.
◆ Remove the soufflé from oven, sprinkle with a mixture of sugar and cinnamon, and garnish with the banana and orange slices

Cognac soufflé

Time needed: *1 hour and 15 minutes*
Difficulty: *medium*

INGREDIENTS FOR 6 SERVINGS

6 eggs ◆ *2 3/4 cups of milk*
3/4 cup of flour
1/2 cup of sugar
4 tablespoons of Cognac
7 tablespoons of butter
4 tablespoons of potato starch
lemon juice
a pinch of salt

◆ Grease a 8-cup soufflé mold and sprinkle it with sugar. Preheat the oven to 390°F.
◆ In a saucepan, melt the butter; blend in the flour and pour in the milk, little by little. Bring to a boil, stirring constantly. Remove from the heat; add the sugar, potato starch and cognac. Set aside to cool.
◆ Blend in the egg yolks; beat the egg whites with the salt and 2-3 drops of lemon to stiff peaks; fold in. Pour into the mold and bake in a pre-heated oven for 30 minutes increasing the temperature to 430°F halfway through. Serve immediately.

Cognac soufflé

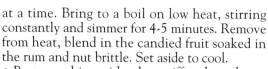

Soufflé with Grand Marnier

Time needed: *1 hour*
Difficulty: *medium*

INGREDIENTS FOR 4 SERVINGS

1/3 cup of Grand Marnier
2 tablespoons of flour ◆ *2 tablespoons of butter*
3/4 cup of warm milk
4 egg yolks ◆ *5 egg whites*
3/4 cup of sugar
a pinch of salt

◆ Butter a 4-cup soufflé mold. Preheat the oven to 360°F.
◆ In a saucepan, melt 1/2 the butter with 1/2 the flour. Add the hot milk, a little at a time, stirring constantly to avoid lumps. Stir in the sugar. Remove from heat and blend in the egg yolks, remaining butter and Grand Marnier. Let cool. Beat egg whites with salt to stiff peaks and fold in the cold mixture.
◆ Pour into mold and bake in the oven for about 25-30 minutes. Serve immediately.

Almond brittle soufflé

Time needed: *1 hour e 10 minutes*
Difficulty: *medium*

INGREDIENTS FOR 6 SERVINGS

5 eggs ◆ *3/4 cup of sugar*
2 tablespoons of flour
1 1/3 cups of milk
1 vanilla bean
5 oz of almond or hazelnut brittle
(see page 21)
3/4 cup of rum
1/2 cup of assorted candied fruit, cut in small pieces
1 tablespoon of powdered sugar
a pinch of salt

◆ Grease a 4-cup soufflé mold and sprinkle it with sugar. Preheat the oven to 360°F.
◆ Soak the candied fruit in rum for 30 minutes and finely chop the nut brittle.
◆ Bring milk and split vanilla to a boil. In a saucepan, whisk egg yolks with the sugar; add sifted flour and boiling milk through a sieve, a little

at a time. Bring to a boil on low heat, stirring constantly and simmer for 4-5 minutes. Remove from heat, blend in the candied fruit soaked in the rum and nut brittle. Set aside to cool.
◆ Beat egg whites with salt to stiff peaks and gently fold into the cool mixture. Pour into the mold and bake in the oven for 30-35 minutes. Serve sprinkled with powdered sugar.

Pear soufflé in pastry crust

Time needed: *1 hour*
(plus resting time)
Difficulty: *complex*

INGREDIENTS FOR 6 SERVINGS

1 lb of ripe pears
1/4 cup of sugar
3 tablespoons of dry white wine
3 egg whites
a pinch of salt
1 tablespoon of powdered sugar
Pastry dough:
2 cups of flour
1/4 cup of unsweetened cocoa
1/2 cup of ground almonds
1/2 cup of softened butter
1/4 cup of sugar
1 egg yolk

◆ Butter 6 individual soufflé molds.
◆ To make the pastry, sift flour and cocoa on a working surface. In the center of the flour and cocoa, put butter in pieces and egg yolk. Knead rapidly with fingertips; cover with plastic wrap and refrigerate for 30 minutes.
◆ Preheat the oven to 390°F.
◆ Roll the dough out very thinly and line the molds with it. Cover with aluminum foil and fill with dry beans. Bake in the oven for 15-20 minutes. Remove from oven and set aside to cool.
◆ Lower the oven temperature to 330°F.
◆ Peel pears, core and cut in small pieces. Cook with white wine and sugar for 15-20 minutes. Drain, cool and purée in a food processor. Fold in the egg whites, beaten with salt to stiff peaks. Place mixture into a pastry bag and pipe into pastry containers. Bake in the oven for 25-30 minutes.
◆ Serve sprinkled with powdered sugar.

Orange soufflé

Time needed: *1 hour*
Difficulty: *medium*

INGREDIENTS FOR **6** SERVINGS
1/2 cup of flour
1/4 cup of sugar
3 eggs
4 egg whites
1 cup of milk
4 tablespoons of whipping cream
1 tablespoon of butter
3 tablespoons of Grand Marnier
1 orange
1 vanilla bean
a pinch of salt

◆ Grease a 4-cup soufflé mold and sprinkle it with sugar. Preheat the oven to 360°F.
◆ Rinse and dry the orange, grate the peel and squeeze the juice.
◆ Bring the milk, cream and vanilla bean to a boil. In a saucepan, whisk flour, sugar, 1 egg, 1 egg yolk, liquor, orange peel and juice. Pour the hot milk little by little removing the vanilla bean. Blend well and bring back to a boil on low heat, stirring.
◆ Simmer for 7-8 minutes, stirring continuously until smooth and creamy. Remove from heat, add the butter and remaining egg yolk; set aside to cool.
◆ Fold in the 6 egg whites, beaten with the salt to stiff peaks. Pour into the mold and bake in the oven for 35-40 minutes.

Soufflé with mandarin liquor

Time needed: *1 hour*
(plus resting time)
Difficulty: *medium*

INGREDIENTS FOR **6** SERVINGS
1/2 small glass of Mandarin liquor
grated peel of 1 organic tangerine
1/2 cup of milk ◆ *1/2 cup of sugar*
1 tablespoon of flour
1 vanilla bean
3 eggs ◆ *a pinch of salt*

◆ Bring 1/3 cup of milk, the sugar and vanilla bean to a boil. Remove from heat; set aside covered for 20 minutes.

◆ Butter a 4-cup soufflé mold; sprinkle with sugar. Preheat the oven to 360°F.
◆ Remove vanilla bean from milk and put back on the heat. Stir in the flour dissolved in the remaining milk; bring back to a boil until cream thickens. Remove from the heat and let cool, stirring occasionally.
◆ Blend the tangerine peel, liquor and egg yolks into the cream. Gently fold in the egg whites, beaten with the salt to stiff peaks. Bake for about 40 minutes. Serve immediately.

Flemish soufflé

Time needed: *1 hour*
Difficulty: *medium*

INGREDIENTS FOR **6** SERVINGS
1/2 cup of flour
1/4 cup of sugar
3 eggs ◆ *2 egg whites*
3/4 cups of milk
4 tablespoons of heavy cream
1 tablespoon of butter
5 savoyard cookies
1/4 cup of grated dark chocolate
1/4 cup of Alchermes liquor
1 vanilla bean
1 tablespoon of powdered sugar
a pinch of salt

Crème Anglaise:
1 cup of milk ◆ *3 egg yolks*
1/2 cup of sugar
1 vanilla bean
2 tablespoons of rum

◆ Butter 6 individual soufflé molds and sprinkle with sugar. Preheat the oven to 360°F.
◆ Bring milk, cream and split vanilla bean to a boil. In a saucepan, whisk flour, sugar, 1 egg and 1 egg yolk. Add boiling milk, through a sieve, a little at a time. Bring to a boil on low heat, stirring continuously until smooth and creamy.
◆ Remove from heat and blend in the butter and remaining egg yolk.
◆ Brush the cookies with the Alchermes liquor and crumble them. Beat 4 egg whites with salt to stiff peaks and fold in the cold mixture. Pour into molds, filling them halfway. Sprinkle with a little cookie crumble and chocolate; cover with the remaining mixture. Bake in the oven for 40 minutes.
◆ Prepare the Crème Anglaise (see page 17). Sprinkle soufflé with powdered sugar and serve with Crème Anglaise.

White chocolate mousse

Time needed:
45 minutes

Difficulty: medium

INGREDIENTS FOR 8 SERVINGS
2 cups of grated white chocolate
2 tablespoons of softened butter
3 tablespoons of powdered sugar
1/2 cup of whipping cream
3 egg whites
a pinch of salt
1 piece of milk chocolate

In the top part of a double boiler, melt the white chocolate, stirring.

◆ Bring cream and powdered sugar to a boil and immediately blend in the melted chocolate.

◆ Add the butter in pieces and blend well.

◆ Place the saucepan into a bowl of cracked ice and stir until light and smooth and completely cold.

◆ Beat egg whites with salt to stiff peaks and gently fold into the mixture. Pour mousse into individual molds.

◆ To decorate, shave some milk chocolate with the aid of an arched potato peeler and place over mousse.

Lemon mousse with wild berries

Time needed: *25 minutes*
(plus cooling time)
Difficulty: medium

INGREDIENTS FOR 6-8 SERVINGS
1/3 cup of lemon juice
1/4 cup of sugar
1 tablespoon of gelatin
3/4 cup of whipping cream
2 egg whites
a pinch of salt
Sauce:
1 cup of strawberries
1 cup of blackberries
1/4 cup of sugar

◆ Dissolve the gelatin in a little cold water. Heat and dissolve the sugar in the lemon juice. Remove and add the gelatin, stirring carefully. Set aside to cool.
◆ Fold in whipped cream and egg whites, beaten with salt to stiff peaks. Brush 6 individual molds with water and fill with mousse. Refrigerate for at least 3 hours.
◆ To make the sauce, rinse the strawberries and blackberries in ice water, drain and purée with the sugar in a food processor. Pass through a sieve and transfer to a sauceboat.
◆ Just before serving, briefly dip in warm water, turn on a serving dish. Serve with sauce on the side.

Lemon mousse with wild berries

Blueberry mousse

Time needed: *25 minutes*
(plus cooling time)
Difficulty: medium

INGREDIENTS FOR 6 SERVINGS
2 cups of blueberries
1/2 cup of sugar
1 1/3 cups of whipping cream
1 teaspoon of unflavored gelatin
1 tablespoon of lemon juice

◆ Dissolve the gelatin in a little cold water.
◆ Rinse blueberries in ice water, dry and purée (keep a few aside) with sugar and lemon juice. In a double boiler, blend gelatin in blueberry purée. Whip the cream and gently fold in 2/3 of it.
◆ Pour mixture into a 4-cup fluted mold and refrigerate for 4 hours. Refrigerate remaining blueberries and whipped cream.
◆ Just before serving, briefly dip mold in warm water and turn onto a dish. Fill a pastry bag, fitted with an indented nozzle, with remaining cream and decorate base and top of mousse. Garnish with blueberries.

Blueberry mousse

White chocolate mousse

Chocolate and hazelnut mousse

Time needed: *25 minutes*
(plus cooling time)
Difficulty: *medium*

INGREDIENTS FOR 6 SERVINGS

7 oz of dark chocolate
3 tablespoons of rum
4 eggs
3/4 cup of whipping cream
1/2 cup of hazelnuts, toasted and
finely chopped
1/4 cup of sugar
a pinch of salt
a few toasted whole hazelnuts

◆ Coarsely chop the chocolate and melt in a double boiler, stir in the rum and let it cool completely.
◆ Using a whisk, incorporate the sugar; egg yolks and chopped hazelnuts into cold chocolate. Whip the cream and gently fold in 1/2 into the mixture; add egg whites, beaten with salt to stiff peaks.
◆ Pour mousse into a glass bowl or individual cups and refrigerate for 2 hours. Garnish with remaining whipped cream and whole hazelnuts.

*Chocolate and
hazelnut mousse*

◆ Dissolve gelatin in a little cold water. In a saucepan, warm the tangerine juice with grated clementine peel.
◆ In a saucepan, whisk in the egg yolks and sugar until pale and thick. Add hot juice, return to heat and almost bring to a boil on low heat, stirring continuously.
◆ Remove from heat. Add gelatin, stirring until completely absorbed. Set aside to cool.
◆ Whip the cream and gently fold into the preparation very gently. Brush a 3-cup round mold with water. Pour mixture in and refrigerate for 2 hours.
◆ To decorate, cut the candied orange peel into thin julienne strips. Peel clementines and divide into segments.
◆ In a saucepan, cook sugar and corn syrup for 7-8 minutes into a dense, transparent syrup (the thermometer should reach 250 F). Remove from heat and, with small tongs, dip clementine segments one at a time into the syrup. Drain and dry on an oiled marble surface.
◆ Just before serving, briefly dip mold in warm water and turn onto a serving dish.
◆ Garnish with a circle of marzipan leaves on top of the mousse and with caramelized clementine segments at the bottom. Complete the decoration by placing the candied orange peel strips inside the marzipan circle.

Clementine mousse

Time needed: *40 minutes*
(plus cooling time)
Difficulty: *medium*

INGREDIENTS

FOR 6-8 SERVINGS
1 cup of clementine juice
3/4 cup of sugar
1 cup of whipping cream
grated peel of 2 clementines
4 egg yolks
1 1/2 teaspoons of gelatin

Decoration:
2 clementines
1 tablespoon of corn syrup
1 cup of sugar
candied orange peel
1 tablespoon almond oil
6 confectioner's marzipan leaves

Clementine mousse

Honey mousse

Time needed: *40 minutes*
(plus cooling time)
Difficulty: *medium*

INGREDIENTS FOR 4 SERVINGS
2 cups of liquid honey
4 eggs
a pinch of salt

◆ In a saucepan, whisk in the egg yolks with honey and cook on top of a double boiler, whisking until it increases in size and becomes creamy and dense.
◆ Beat egg whites with salt to stiff peaks and gently fold into honey mixture.
◆ Pour into 4 individual bowls, cover with plastic wrap and refrigerate for 3 hours before serving.

Strawberry mousse

Time needed: *25 minutes*
(plus cooling time)
Difficulty: *medium*

INGREDIENTS FOR **4-6** SERVINGS

2 cups of strawberries
3/4 cups of sugar
1/2 cup of whipping cream
1/2 teaspoon of gelatin

Strawberry mousse

◆ Dissolve gelatin in a little cold water. Quickly rinse strawberries in ice water and dry. Keep 4 strawberries aside and purée remainder with sugar, in a food processor.
◆ In a double boiler, carefully blend gelatin into strawberry purée. Gently fold in the whipped cream and pour mixture into a 4-cup mold.
◆ Just before serving, briefly dip mold in warm water and turn mousse onto a serving dish.
◆ Finely slice remaining strawberries and place them around base of mousse.

Milk chocolate mousse

Time needed: *25 minutes*
(plus cooling time)
Difficulty: *medium*

INGREDIENTS FOR **4-6** SERVINGS

8 oz of milk chocolate
2 tablespoons of butter
1/2 teaspoon of instant coffee
3 eggs
a pinch of salt

◆ Curl milk chocolate with a potato peeler for decoration. Chop remaining chocolate, dissolve instant coffee in 3 tablespoons of warm water and melt together in a double boiler.
◆ Remove from heat; blend in the butter in small pieces and egg yolks, one at a time. Delicately fold in egg whites, beaten with salt to stiff peaks.
◆ Pour mousse into either a large bowl or individual ones. Refrigerate for at least 1 hour. Just before serving, garnish with the chocolate curls.

Pear mousse with chocolate sauce

Time needed: *30 minutes*
(plus cooling time)
Difficulty: *medium*

INGREDIENTS FOR **6** SERVINGS

6 large pears
1/3 cup of Moscato wine
(Vino Moscato d'Asti Naturale)
1/2 cup of sugar
2 teaspoons of gelatin
3/4 cups of whipping cream
juice of 1 lemon
1 tablespoon of Kirsch
3 oz of dark chocolate

Sauce:
3 oz of grated dark chocolate
1 tablespoon of butter
2 tablespoons of whipping cream
1/3 cup of milk

*Pear mousse
with chocolate sauce*

◆ Dissolve the gelatin in a little cold water.
◆ Rinse and peel the pears, core and slice. Put in a bowl with a little sugar and the lemon juice.
◆ Bring 3/4 cup of water and the Moscato wine with the remaining sugar to a boil for 5-6 minutes; add sliced pears and simmer for a further 15 minutes.
◆ Purée pears with their cooking syrup. Return to saucepan and reheat on low heat. Remove from heat and stir in the gelatin until completely dissolved. Let the mixture cool completely.
◆ Whip the cream and gently fold into the cold pear purée. Pour into 6 individual pudding molds brushed with kirsch; cover with plastic wrap and refrigerate for about 2 hours.
◆ Chop dark chocolate and melt in a double boiler. Pour onto parchment paper and spread very thinly, with a spatula. Let it harden and cut into 6 circles with a patterned edged cookie cutter.
◆ Prepare the chocolate sauce (see page 20).
◆ Just before serving, briefly dip molds into warm water and turn onto a serving dish. Top each mousse with a chocolate disk and serve accompanied with the cold chocolate sauce.

Caramel mousse

Time needed:
40 minutes
(plus cooling time)
Difficulty: medium

**INGREDIENTS
FOR 6-8 SERVINGS**
1 cup of milk
1 cup of sugar
4 egg yolks
1 1/2 teaspoon of gelatin
1 3/4 cups of whipping cream
1 vanilla bean
*1/2 teaspoon of vanilla
extract*
1 tablespoon almond oil

Dissolve gelatin in a little cold water. In a saucepan, caramelize 1/4 cup of sugar in 1 tablespoon of water until golden (see page 20). Remove from heat, stir in 1/3 cup of cream and bring to a boil until the caramel dissolves.

◆ Bring milk and vanilla bean to a boil. In a saucepan, whisk egg yolks with 1/2 cup of sugar and vanilla, until pale and thick. Remove vanilla bean from boiling milk. Add milk to egg mixture slowly. Place on low heat and almost bring to a boil, stirring constantly. Remove from heat; add gelatin, stirring constantly until completely dissolved. Stir in the caramel sauce and let the mixture cool.
◆ Whip 3/4 cup of cream and fold it into the mixture. Pour mixture into a tube pan brushed with water. Refrigerate for at least 4 hours. Caramelize remaining sugar in 2 tablespoons of water until golden (see page 20). Pour it, drop by drop, on an oiled marble surface to form small coin circles and leave to harden.

◆ Just before serving, briefly dip mold in warm water and turn on a serving dish. Whip remaining cream; put it in a pastry bag, fitted with and indented nozzle, and garnish the mousse with a crested crown of cream and the caramel coins.

Custard mousse

Time needed: *40 minutes*
(plus cooling time)
Difficulty: medium

INGREDIENTS FOR 4-6 SERVINGS

1 cup of sugar ◆ *5 egg yolks*
3 egg whites
2 1/2 cups of whipping cream
1 teaspoon of vanilla
1 pinch of salt

◆ In a saucepan, with an electric mixer, whisk the egg yolks and sugar until light and creamy. Place on a double boiler and continue to whisk until it doubles in volume, making sure the mixture never boils.
◆ Remove from heat, place saucepan over a bowl of crushed ice and whisk until the cream cools. Blend in vanilla and gently fold in the whipped cream and egg whites beaten with salt to stiff peaks.
◆ Brush an 8-cup tube pan with water. Pour preparation in pan and refrigerate for at least 4 hours.
◆ Just before serving, briefly dip pan in warm water and turn on a serving dish.
◆ As an alternative to vanilla, you may flavor the cream with liquor and garnish the mousse with whipped cream and candied fruit.

Nectarine mousse

Nectarine mousse

Time needed: *40 minutes*
(plus cooling time)
Difficulty: medium

INGREDIENTS FOR 6 SERVINGS

8 large nectarines ◆ *1/2 cup of sugar*
1 cup of whipping cream ◆ *1 teaspoon of gelatin*
3 tablespoons of dry white wine
1/4 cup of grated dark chocolate
juice of 1/2 lemon

◆ Dissolve gelatin in a little cold water. Rinse and peel 6 nectarines, pit and cut into small pieces. Simmer in white wine for 6-7 minutes, let cool and purée with sugar.
◆ Stir gelatin in a double boiler and stir into nectarine purée; cook in a double boiler for 4 minutes. Set aside to cool. Gently fold in the whipped cream and pour into 6 moistened individual pudding molds. Refrigerate for 2 hours.
◆ Just before serving, briefly dip molds into warm water and turn on individual dishes. Rinse remaining nectarines, slice thinly and dip in with lemon juice. Dry and place around each mousse. Melt chocolate in a double boiler and pour into a waxed paper cone. Draw patterns on each plate to decorate.

Caramel mousse

Persimmon mousse

Time needed: *25 minutes*
(plus cooling time)
Difficulty: *medium*

INGREDIENTS FOR 6 SERVINGS

1 lb of persimmons ◆ *3/4 cup of whipping cream*
1/2 cup of sugar
2 teaspoons of unflavored gelatin
3 confectioner's sugar flowers

Salsa:
1 lb of persimmons ◆ *1/4 cup of sugar*

◆ Dissolve gelatin in a little cold water. Peel persimmon; pit and purée in a food processor. Melt sugar in 1/4 cup of water and simmer for 5 minutes. Remove from heat and stir in the gelatin. Let syrup cool.
◆ Blend cooled syrup into persimmon purée. Gently fold in the whipped cream. Brush a 4-cup mold with water. Pour mixture in mold and refrigerate for at least 4 hours.
◆ To make the sauce, peel persimmon, pit and purée (keep 1/2 of 1 fruit aside) with sugar. Refrigerate to cool completely.
◆ Just before serving, briefly dip mold in warm water and turn onto a serving dish.
◆ Slice the 1/2 persimmon into 4 and place on the mousse. Finish garnishing the mousse with confectioner's sugar flowers. Serve with persimmon sauce.

Orange mousse with candied fruit

Time needed: *30 minutes*
(plus cooling time)
Difficulty: *medium*

INGREDIENTS FOR 6 SERVINGS

6 eggs ◆ *12 tablespoons of sugar*
3 1/4 cup of whipping cream
strained juice of 3 oranges
grated peel of 2 organic oranges
1 sachet of vanilla extract
2 teaspoons of gelatin
3 1/2 oz of candied mixed fruit, diced
1 small glass of Grand Marnier
a pinch of salt
a few candied cherries

◆ Dissolve gelatin in a little cold water.
◆ In a bowl, whisk in the egg yolks and sugar with an electric mixer until light and foamy. Add or-

ange juice, vanilla, Grand Marnier, orange peel, diced candied fruit and gelatin. Stir to mix well. Gently fold in 2/3 of whipped cream and egg whites beaten with salt to stiff peaks.
◆ Brush an 8-cup fluted tube pan with water. Pour mixture into mold and refrigerate for at least 4 hours.
◆ Just before serving, quickly dip mold in warm water, turn onto a serving dish and garnish base of mousse with crowns of whipped cream and candied cherries cut into halves.

Peach mousse with caramel sauce

Time needed: *40 minutes*
(plus cooling time)
Difficulty: *medium*

INGREDIENTS FOR 6 SERVINGS

8-10 ripe peaches
1 1/2 teaspoons of gelatin
juice of 1 lemon ◆ *3 eggs*
1 cup of sugar
1 teaspoon of vanilla powder
1/2 cup of whipping cream
a pinch of salt

Salsa:
6 ripe peaches
1 cup of sugar
1/2 teaspoon of vanilla

◆ Dissolve gelatin in a little cold water.
◆ Rinse peaches. Pit, cut into pieces and purée with lemon juice in a food processor. In a saucepan, mix egg yolks, sugar and vanilla; blend in the peach purée.
◆ Simmer mixture in a double boiler on moderate heat, stirring until dense. Make sure the custard never boils. Remove from heat; stir in the gelatin until completely mixed.
◆ Let mixture cool, stirring occasionally. Fold in the whipped cream and egg whites, beaten with salt to stiff peaks. Brush 6 individual molds with water. Pour mixture into molds and refrigerate for at least 3 hours.
◆ To make the sauce, rinse peaches, peel, pit, cut into pieces and purée. Caramelize the sugar in 5 tablespoons of water for 8-10 minutes until golden (see page 20). Transfer peaches and vanilla in a food processor; purée. Gradually add the caramel in, drop by drop, and mix together.
◆ Briefly dip individual molds in warm water; turn onto a serving dish with the caramel sauce around it.

Dark chocolate mousse with coffee cream

Time needed: *40 minutes*
(plus cooling time)
Difficulty: *medium*

INGREDIENTS FOR 6-8 SERVINGS
/2 cup of grated dark chocolate
1/4 cup of unsweetened cacao
3 tablespoons of softened butter
1/4 cup of powdered sugar
4 eggs
1 cup of whipping cream
a pinch of salt
1 teaspoon of instant coffee
white chocolate

Cream:
1 cup of milk
3 egg yolks
1/2 cup of sugar
1 vanilla bean
1 teaspoon of instant coffee

◆ Grease a 4-cup rectangular mold and line with waxed paper.
◆ Melt dark chocolate in a double boiler, pour into a bowl and stir in the sifted cocoa. Whisk egg yolks in, one at a time. Add butter in pieces, instant coffee dissolved in 2 tablespoons of warm cream and confectioner's sugar; mix well.
◆ Gently fold into the cold mixture the whipped cream, then egg whites beaten with salt to stiff peaks. Pour into mold and refrigerate for at least 12 hours.
◆ To prepare the coffee pastry cream, see page 16.
◆ Just before serving, turn mousse onto a serving dish and remove waxed paper. Shave white chocolate with a potato peeler and garnish the mousse with curls. Serve with the coffee custard.

Blackberry mousse

Time needed: *30 minutes*
(plus cooling time)
Difficulty: *medium*

INGREDIENTS FOR 6 SERVINGS
1 1/2 cups of blackberries
3/4 cup of sugar
1/2 cup of whipping cream
2 teaspoons of gelatin
1/2 teaspoon of lemon juice

1 egg white
a pinch of salt
Sauce:
1/2 cup of natural yogurt
1/3 cup of whipping cream
2 tablespoons of sugar
2 springs of mint

◆ Dissolve gelatin in a little cold water.
◆ Quickly rinse blackberries in ice water, dry and purée (set aside a few for garnish) with sugar and lemon juice. Strain purée into a bowl and set aside.
◆ Stir gelatin into purée until completely blended. Fold in the whipped cream and the egg white beaten with the salt to soft peaks. Brush a 6-cup mold with water. Pour mixture in the mold and refrigerate for at least 3 hours.
◆ To make the sauce, rinse and finely chop the mint leaves. Whip the cream to soft peaks and blend with the yogurt, sugar and mint.
◆ Just before serving, briefly dip mold in warm water and turn on a dish. Garnish with remaining blackberries and accompany with the sauce.

Avocado mousse

Time needed: *20 minutes*
(plus cooling time)
Difficulty: *easy*

INGREDIENTS FOR 8 SERVINGS
3 very ripe avocados
6 tablespoons of sugar
24 small Amaretti
Juice of 1/2 lemon

◆ Cut the avocados in half; remove the pit and purée with sugar and lemon juice in a food processor.
◆ Crumble the small amaretti, keeping 8 aside, and blend into the purée. Add 3/4 cup of whipping cream and keep mixing until mixture becomes dense.
◆ Pour mousse into 8 individual cups. Whip the remaining cream and top each mousse with a cream crown and 1 amaretto.
◆ Cover with plastic wrap to make sure the avocado purée does not become dark and refrigerate for at least 2 hours.

Dissolve gelatin in a little cold water. In a saucepan, simmer sugar and 3/4 cup of water for 10 minutes; remove from heat, add gelatin, stirring well until completely blended, and sparkling wine (1).

Fruit in spumante aspic

Time needed:
20 minutes
(plus cooling time)
Difficulty: medium

INGREDIENTS
FOR 4 SERVINGS

1/4 cup of sugar
3 teaspoons of gelatin
1 cup of dry sparkling wine
1 1/2 lb of mixed fresh fruit

◆ Peel fruits, slice and place in a large serving glass bowl (2). Arrange decoratively according to your own taste. Pour sparkling gelatin over (3) and refrigerate for 4 hours.

Banana, cherry and strawberry aspic

Time needed: *30 minutes*
(plus cooling time)
Difficulty: medium

INGREDIENTS FOR 6 SERVINGS

2 bananas ◆ *3/4 lb of ripe red cherries*
3/4 lb of strawberries
8 tablespoons of sugar
1 1/2 cups of orange juice
juice of 1 lemon
1 small glass of maraschino
4 teaspoons of gelatin

◆ Dissolve gelatin in a little cold water. Put an 8-cup pudding mold into the freezer.
◆ In a saucepan, simmer, for about 15 minutes, orange juice, lemon juice (set aside 1 table-spoon), 5 cups of water and 4 tablespoons of sugar. Remove from heat; stir in gelatin until completely blended. Let syrup cool. Pour 1/4 of syrup into the mold, turning to cover all sides. Refrigerate.
◆ Quickly rinse cherries and strawberries; drain. Peel bananas, slice and sprinkle with remaining lemon juice. Pit the cherries and slice the strawberries. Mix all fruits in a bowl with remaining sugar and maraschino. Set aside for 30 minutes.
◆ Remove mold from refrigerator and add 4 tablespoons of mixed fruits. Cover with a little gelatin and return to refrigerator to set. Continue to layer fruit and gelatin until all ingredients have been used, finishing with a layer of gelatin. Refrigerate for at least 4 hours to set.

Apricot and pistachio aspic

◆ Rapidly dip mold in warm water and turn aspic onto a serving dish.

Apricot and pistachio aspic

Time needed: *40 minutes*
(plus cooling time)
Difficulty: medium

INGREDIENTS FOR 4 SERVINGS
1 lb of apricots
1/2 cup of sugar
1/4 cup of chopped pistachios
2 teaspoons of gelatin

◆ Soak gelatin in a little cold water.
◆ Scald apricots in boiling water, drain, peel and cut into halves. Simmer apricots with the sugar in 1 1/4 cup of water for 5 minutes: drain and set aside syrup and apricots. Stir gelatin into warm syrup until completely mixed and let cool. Pour a thin layer of syrup-gelatin into 8 individual molds and refrigerate. Place 1/2 of apricots, with the hollow side upwards, in each mold on the set gelatin. Carefully layer with enough gelatin to cover the fruit and refrigerate for several hours.
◆ Once set, sprinkle with a layer of chopped pistachios. Gently pour the remaining gelatin over pistachios and refrigerate for at least 2 hours. Briefly dip molds in warm water and turn onto a serving dish.

Fruit in spumante aspic

Melon and raspberry aspic

Time needed: *50 minutes*
(plus cooling time)
Difficulty: *medium*
INGREDIENTS FOR 6-8 SERVINGS

2 large melons
2 cups of raspberries
1 organic orange
2 cups of dry white wine
1/2 cup of sugar
3 tablespoons of gelatin

◆ Dissolve gelatin in a little cold water. Seed melons and make little balls with a melon baller. Rinse raspberries in ice water and dry. Rinse and dry the orange, and slice thinly.
◆ In a saucepan, simmer sugar and 2 cups of water for 10 minutes. Remove from heat and stir in gelatin until completely blended. Stir white wine in and let cool.
◆ Pour a thin layer of gelatin in an 8-cup stainless steel mold and refrigerate. As soon as the gelatin has set, layer with raspberries, then with gelatin; return to refrigerator. Cover with a layer of melon balls and one of gelatin and return to refrigerator. Repeat until all ingredients are used, leaving space along the sides of the mold for the gelatin to run everywhere.
◆ Before covering with last layer, slide the orange slices in between the aspic and the sides of the mold, leaving half of each slice to protrude out of the mold. Cover with last layer of fruit and remaining gelatin. Return to the refrigerator and, once set, fold the protruding orange slices over the gelatin. Refrigerate for at least 3 hours.
◆ Just before serving, quickly dip in warm water and turn onto a serving dish.

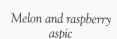

Melon and raspberry aspic

Orange and pear aspic

Orange and pear aspic

Time needed: *1 ora*
(plus cooling time)
Difficulty: *medium*

INGREDIENTS FOR 6 SERVINGS

8 large ripe pears
2 oranges
1 tablespoon lemon juice
2 tablespoons of sugar

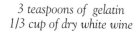

3 teaspoons of gelatin
1/3 cup of dry white wine

◆ Dissolve gelatin in a little cold water.
◆ Peel pears, core and cut into small pieces. Cook in white wine and a tablespoon of water for 10 minutes. Drain and purée. Bring purée, sugar and lemon juice to a boil. Remove from heat; add gelatin, stirring until completely blended. Let it cool.
◆ Peel the oranges (see page 28).
◆ Brush a 4-cup rectangular mold with water. Pour a layer of purée in the mold and refrigerate. As soon as it sets, cover with a layer of orange segments, followed by a little purée and another layer of oranges. Return to refrigerator. Continue this way until all ingredients are used, finishing with a layer of pear purée. Refrigerate for at least 3 hours.
◆ Quickly dip mold in warm water and turn onto a dish. Slice and serve accompanied by mixed berries.

Mixed fruit in aspic

Time needed: *1 hour*
(plus cooling time)
Difficulty: *medium*
INGREDIENTS FOR 8-10 SERVINGS

3/4 cup of pineapple
3/4 cup of raspberries
3/4 cup of red currants
3/4 cup of condensed milk
2 1/2 teaspoons of gelatin
1 cup of sugar

Decoration:
8 raspberries
1/4 cup of red currants
1/4 cup of black currants
16 mint leaves
1 teaspoon of gelatin
peel of 1/2 organic lemon
1 tablespoon of sugar

Mixed fruit in aspic

◆ Divide gelatin into 3 parts and dissolve each part in a bowl with a little water.
◆ Separately rinse raspberries and currants in ice water and dry them. In 3 different saucepans, put pineapple cut in pieces, raspberries and currants, adding 2 tablespoons of sugar to each. Cook fruits for 5-6 minutes stirring occasionally.

◆ Remove the 3 saucepans from heat, purée each fruit separately and put into 3 bowls. To each bowl, add 1/4 cup of condensed milk, and one part of the gelatin. Stir until well mixed.

◆ To decorate, dissolve gelatin in a little cold water. Rinse fruit in ice water, dry. Cook sugar and lemon peel in 1 1/4 cups of water for a few minutes. When dissolved, remove from heat and stir in gelatin until completely blended. Pour a little gelatin in a low flower-shaped mold and refrigerate.

◆ In the middle of the set gelatin layer, form a little crown of raspberries, and red and black currants. Along the edge, set red and black currants in flower patterns. Cover with a thin layer of gelatin and refrigerate.

◆ Rinse and dry mint leaves and set in a crown on the aspic. Cover with a thin layer of gelatin and return to refrigerator.

◆ Place pineapple purée in the mold over the set gelatin and refrigerate for 15 minutes; then add raspberry purée and last, the red currant purée. Refrigerate for 2 hours.

◆ When ready to serve, quickly dip mold in warm water and turn onto a serving dish.

◆ Bring white wine and 1 tablespoon of water to boil with sugar and cinnamon stick. Add apples with lemon juice and simmer for 10 minutes.

◆ Discard cinnamon and purée mixture. Return to heat; add gelatin and Calvados; cook for 2 minutes, stirring continuously. Pour in 6 shallow individual molds and refrigerate for 1 hour.

◆ To make sauce, beat egg yolks with sugar on top of a double boiler until light and creamy. Add white wine and calvados; cook, whisking until it doubles in volume. Make sure the sauce never boils. Let it cool. Carefully fold in whipped cream.

◆ Turn apple gelatins onto a serving dish, garnish with the candied lime and serve with the sauce.

*Apple aspic
with Calvados*

Apple aspic
with Calvados

Time needed: *30 minutes
(plus cooling time)*
Difficulty: medium

INGREDIENTS
FOR 6 SERVINGS

*6 Granny Smith apples
3/4 cup of sugar
1/3 cup of dry white wine
2 tablespoons of Calvados
1 tablespoon lemon juice
1 small cinnamon stick
3 tablespoons of agar-agar
1 piece of candied lime, chopped*

Calvados sauce:
*1/4 cup of Calvados
1/3 cup of dry white wine
4 egg yolks
1/3 cup of whipping cream
1/4 cup of sugar*

◆ Peel the apples, core, slice and soak in lemon juice.

Peaches in red
wine aspic

Time needed: *20 minutes
(plus cooling time)*
Difficulty: medium

INGREDIENTS FOR 4 SERVINGS
*5 peaches (or pears)
2 cups of good quality red wine
1/2 cup of sugar
3 teaspoons of gelatin
peel of 1/2 lemon*

*Peaches in red wine
aspic*

◆ Dissolve gelatin in a little cold water.

◆ Scald 4 peaches in boiling water for 1 minute; peel, slice and marinate in red wine, together with sugar and lemon peel for at least 2 hours.

◆ Drain, pour the marinating liquid in a pan, bring it to a boil, remove from heat and stir in gelatin until completely blended. Let cool completely.

◆ Pour wine gelatin into a rectangular 8-cup mold and refrigerate for 15 minutes. Cover with a layer of peaches and a thin layer of gelatin. Return to refrigerator and repeat until all ingredients are used. Refrigerate for at least 4 hours.

◆ When ready to serve, quickly dip mold in warm water, turn onto a serving dish and garnish with remaining peaches, sliced thinly.

Carefully rinse and dry lemon. Bring butter to room temperature, then whisk it with an electric mixer until creamy. Add sugar, a spoonful at a time, and continue whisking until fluffy and light. Blend in the egg yolks one at a time. Set aside.

♦ In a bowl, dissolve cornstarch in 1 tablespoon of cold milk. Pour remaining milk in a saucepan, add peel of 1/2 lemon (making sure you only cut the yellow skin; the white part would give the cream a bitter taste) and split vanilla bean. Bring to a boil and continue to boil for 5 minutes. Stir in the cornstarch. Bring to a boil and cook for about 5 minutes.

Custard flambé

Time needed:
25 minutes
Difficulty: easy

INGREDIENTS
FOR **8** SERVINGS

1 cup of sugar
8 tablespoons of softened butter
4 egg yolks ♦ 4 cups of milk
peel of 1/2 organic lemon
2 tablespoons of cocoa crème liquor
2 tablespoons of anise liquor
2 teaspoons of cornstarch
1 vanilla bean
2 tablespoons of Cognac
1/2 teaspoon of powdered cinnamon

♦ Blend a cup of hot milk mixture to butter-egg mixture. Pour all butter-egg mixture into the saucepan; return to heat. Add cocoa crème liquor and anise liquor and cook, stirring continuously, making sure the cream never boils, until it coats the back of a spoon. Let it cool a little, discard vanilla bean and pour into 8 individual cups. Refrigerate for several hours.

♦ When ready to serve, warm Cognac in a saucepan, pour a little on top of each cup, flambé and sprinkle with cinnamon.

Mascarpone cream

Time needed: *25 minutes*
(plus cooling time)
Difficulty: easy

INGREDIENTS FOR **6** SERVINGS

1/2 cup of mascarpone
2 egg yolks
1/4 cup of sugar
1 cup of milk
1/2 cup of flour
peel of 1/2 organic lemon
1 1/4 cup of whipping cream
3 tablespoons of rum
1/2 cup of toasted chopped walnuts

♦ Prepare a pastry cream with egg yolks, sugar, milk, flour and lemon peel (see page 16). Transfer to a bowl and stir in the mascarpone, rum and 2/3 of hazelnuts until well blended. Gently fold in 3/4 cup of cream, whipped to firm peaks. Refrigerate for a few hours.
♦ When ready to serve, pour into a large bowl or individual cups. Whip remaining cream, put in a pastry bag, fitted with an indented nozzle and pipe cream around the edges of the bowl. Make a rosette in the center. Garnish with remaining chopped hazelnuts.

Mascarpone cream

Strawberry Syllabub

Time needed: *25 minutes*
(plus soaking and cooling time)
Difficulty: easy

INGREDIENTS FOR **6-8** SERVINGS

3/4 cup of dry sherry
2 tablespoons of Cognac
1 1/3 cups of whipping cream
1/2 lb of strawberries
1/4 cup of sugar
peel of 1 organic lemon
1 egg white ♦ a pinch of nutmeg
6 mint leaves ♦ a pinch of salt

♦ Cut the lemon peel in a long ribbon and soak in sherry for about 12 hours.
♦ Rinse strawberries in ice water, dry and set aside 2. Of the remainder, purée 2/3 and cut the others into small pieces. Strain sherry into a bowl, stir in cognac, cream, sugar, and strawberry purée. Whip mixture with an electric mixer. Fold in the egg white beaten with salt to stiff peaks and stir in the strawberry pieces. Pour into large individual cups and refrigerate for at least 5 hours.
♦ Just before serving, gently stir the cream in the cups to fluff it up. Garnish with a strawberry slice and mint leaf.

Custard flambé

Coffee custard

Time needed: *25 minutes*
Difficulty: easy

INGREDIENTS FOR **6** SERVINGS

*3/4 cup of sugar
1 tablespoon of instant coffee
6 egg yolks
2 cups of milk
1/4 cup of flour
1/2 teaspoon of vanilla powder
1 tablespoon of coffee liquor
1 cup of whipping cream
a large piece of white chocolate*

Coffee custard

◆ Bring milk and instant coffee to boil.
◆ Prepare a pastry cream with the coffee-milk mixture, egg yolks, flour and vanilla (see page 16).
◆ Blend liquor into cooled cream and gently fold in the whipped cream. Transfer preparation to a pastry bag, fitted with a flat nozzle tube and decoratively pipe into a glass bowl. Garnish with shaved white chocolate and refrigerate.

Coffee and walnut custard

Time needed: *30 minutes*
Difficulty: easy

INGREDIENTS FOR **6** SERVINGS

*6 egg yolks
3/4 cup of milk
1/2 cup of shelled whole walnuts
1/2 cup of whipping cream
1/2 cup of sugar
3 tablespoons of instant coffee*

◆ Keep 6 whole walnuts aside and finely chop the remainder.
◆ Bring milk and instant coffee to boil.
◆ In a saucepan, mix egg yolks and sugar until well blended. Stir in the hot milk passed through a sieve, a little at a time.
◆ Put on low heat and almost bring to a boil, stirring continuously until the cream coats the back of a spoon. Remove from heat and let cool, stirring occasionally. Blend in the chopped walnuts and gently fold in the whipped cream.
◆ Pour cream into individual cups, garnishing each one with a whole walnut. Cool in the refrigerator.

Amaretto custard

Time needed: *25 minutes*
Difficulty: easy

INGREDIENTS FOR **4** SERVINGS

*4 egg yolks
4 tablespoons of sugar
8 amaretti cookies, crumbled into powder
1/3 cup of Marsala
1/2 cup of whipping cream
20 miniature amaretti cookies*

◆ On top of a double boiler, whisk egg yolks and sugar until light and creamy. Add Marsala and cook on low heat for 5-7 minutes until it doubles in volume, whisking continuously to make sure the cream never boils.
◆ Remove from heat, blend in the crumbled amaretti and let cool completely. Gently fold in the whipped cream and pour into 4 individual cups. Garnish with miniature amaretti and refrigerate.

Amaretto custard

Hazelnut cream

Time needed: *35 minutes*
Difficulty: medium

INGREDIENTS FOR **4-6** SERVINGS

*1/2 cup of toasted peeled hazelnuts
5 egg yolks ◆ 1 cup of sugar
2 cups of milk
2 teaspoons of flour
1/2 teaspoon of vanilla
1 slice of sponge cake (see page 10)
1 tablespoon of vegetable oil
1/3 cup of whipping cream*

Syrup:
*1/4 cup of sugar
1/4 cup of currants*

Hazelnut cream

◆ Cook 1/2 the sugar in 4 tablespoons of water for 3 minutes, remove from heat, add hazelnuts and stir to coat hazelnut with sandy sugar.
◆ Return to moderate heat and stir until sugar caramelizes. Pour hazelnuts onto an oiled marble surface, separating one from the other with two forks; let cool and finely chop.

Mixed berry cream

◆ Prepare cream with milk, egg yolks, remaining sugar, vanilla and flour (see page16). When cold, blend in the chopped hazelnuts, keeping 1 tablespoon aside.
◆ To make the syrup, boil sugar in 1/3 cup of water and cook for 2 minutes. Let cool. Rinse the currants in ice water, dry, purée and stir into the syrup.
◆ Pour 1/2 the hazelnut cream into a glass bowl; cover with a layer of Sponge cake. Soak cake with the currant syrup and cover with remaining hazelnut cream.
◆ Whip the cream, put it in a pastry bag, fitted with a star tube and pipe onto the cream to cover completely. Sprinkle with remaining praline hazelnuts and refrigerate.

Mixed berry cream

Time needed: *25 minutes*
Difficulty: easy

INGREDIENTS FOR 4 SERVINGS

3/4 cup of blueberries
3/4 cup of red currants
3/4 cup of strawberries
1 tablespoon lemon juice
1 tablespoon of sugar
Custard:
1/3 cup of sugar
3 egg yolks
1 cup of milk
2 teaspoons of flour
peel of 1 organic lemon

◆ Prepare a custard (see page 16) with the ingredients listed above. Let it cool, stirring occasionally to avoid a film forming on the surface. When cool, pour into 4 individual cups.
◆ Quickly rinse currants, strawberries and blueberries in ice water. Dry. Remove stems from currants and from strawberries.
◆ Put berries in a bowl, sprinkle with the lemon juice, add sugar and gently stir. Refrigerate cream and berries.
◆ Decorate with fruit over cream when ready to serve.

Chocolate custard

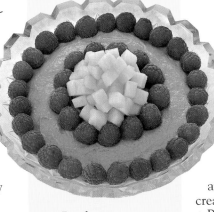

Raspberry cream with pears

Chocolate custard

Time needed: *25 minutes*
Difficulty: easy

INGREDIENTS FOR 6 SERVINGS

2 cups of milk
1/2 cup of sugar
4 egg yolks ◆ *1 tablespoon of flour*
3/4 cup of whipping cream
1/2 teaspoon of vanilla
1 cup of grated dark chocolate
2 tablespoons of maraschino

◆ Bring milk to a boil. In a saucepan, beat egg yolks with sugar; add flour and vanilla. Add hot milk, little by little. Cook on low heat for about 6 minutes, stirring continuously.
◆ Remove from heat, blend in chocolate and liquor; stir occasionally to cool. Set aside to cool. Gently fold in the whipped cream and pour the custard in a deep serving dish or glass bowl.
◆ In a double boiler, melt remaining chocolate, transfer to a parchment paper cone and garnish cream with designs of your choice.

Raspberry cream with pears

Time needed: *20 minutes*
(plus cooling time)
Difficulty: easy

INGREDIENTS FOR 4 SERVINGS

2 cups of raspberries ◆ *1/2 cup of sugar*
3/4 cup of whipping cream
juice of 1/2 lemon
2 tablespoons of Kirsch ◆ *2 pears*

◆ Peel pears, core, dice and soak in the Kirsch for 20 minutes.
◆ Rinse raspberries in ice water, dry, set a few aside to decorate and pass the remainder through a food mill. To the fruit, add sugar and lemon juice. Gently fold in the whipped cream, until blended.
◆ Pour cream into a glass bowl and refrigerate for at least 1 hour. Before serving, drain pears. Decorate cream with remaining raspberries and diced pears.

Pistachio custard

Time needed: *30 minutes*
(plus cooling time)
Difficulty: *easy*

INGREDIENTS FOR **4** SERVINGS
3/4 cup of shelled pistachios
1 cup of whipping cream
4 egg yolks ◆ *3/4 cup of sugar*
1 tablespoon of Kirsch
a pinch of salt
a few candied cherries

◆ Preheat the oven to 360 F.
◆ Scald pistachios in boiling water, peel skin off and dry in the oven. Set 1 tablespoon aside and finely chop remaining pistachios with a tablespoon of sugar.
◆ In the top of a double boiler, mix whipping cream, egg yolks, remaining sugar, chopped pistachios and salt. Stir with a wooden spoon, making sure the mixture never boils, until dense enough to coat a spoon. Let cool completely, stir in the Kirsch, pour into a glass bowl and refrigerate for at least 3 hours.
◆ When ready to serve, garnish with remaining pistachios and candied cherries, cut into small pieces.

Mascarpone zabaglione

Time needed: *25 minutes*
Difficulty: *medium*

INGREDIENTS FOR **6** SERVINGS
6 egg yolks
1/2 cup of sugar
1/2 cup of dry Marsala
1 cup of mascarpone
3 tablespoons whipping cream
1 cup of strawberries

◆ Heat 1/2 a tablespoon of Marsala with 1 teaspoon of sugar, until completely dissolved. In a saucepan, whisk egg yolks with remaining sugar until mixture is pale and creamy. Stir in hot Marsala and cook on top of a double boiler on low heat, whisking constantly until cream has doubled in volume, making sure the mixture never boils. Let the Zabaglione cool, stirring occasionally.

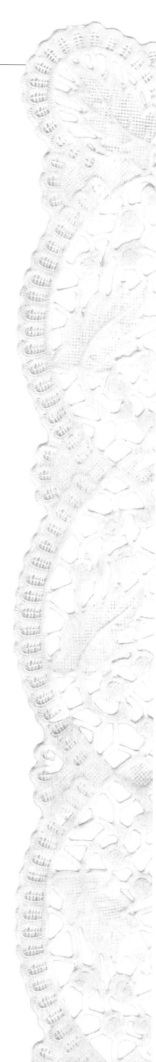

◆ Rinse strawberries in ice water, dry and cut into segments. In a bowl, lightly whisk mascarpone cheese, whipping cream and remaining Marsala; gently fold in the Zabaglione. Transfer 1/2 the strawberries in individual bowls, alternating them with layers of the Zabaglione and garnish with remaining strawberries.

Ricotta and raspberry cream

Time needed: *25 minutes*
Difficulty: *easy*

INGREDIENTS FOR **4** SERVINGS
1 cup of raspberries
1/2 cup of sugar
1 liquor glass of rum
2 eggs
2 teaspoons of vanilla flavored powdered sugar
1/2 cup of ricotta cheese
a pinch of salt

◆ Pass the ricotta through a strainer. Rinse raspberries in ice water, dry and soak in a little rum with 1 tablespoon of water.
◆ With an electric mixer, whisk egg yolks and vanilla flavored powdered sugar until creamy; add ricotta cheese and remaining rum; fold in the egg whites, beaten with the salt to stiff peaks.
◆ Place raspberries in 4 individual cups, cover with ricotta cream and refrigerate for 1 hour.
◆ For a more intense taste, you may purée half the raspberries and blend them into the cream.

Dutch wheat custard

Time needed: *20 minutes*
Difficulty: *easy*

INGREDIENTS FOR **10** SERVINGS
4 cups of milk
1/2 cup of starch
1/2 cup of sugar
1 teaspoon of vanilla
grated peel of 2 organic lemons
2 tablespoons of pistachios
1 candied lemon peel

◆ Scald the pistachios in boiling water, drain, remove skin and set half aside; chop remainder.
◆ In a saucepan, mix sugar, starch and vanilla. Add hot milk, a little at a time and blend well.

Bring to boil on low heat, stirring often; simmer for 7-8 minutes, stirring continuously. Remove from heat; add lemon peel and chopped pistachios.

◆ Pour cream into a large glass bowl or individual cups. As soon as it has cooled, garnish with remaining pistachios and slivers of candied lemon peel.

English fruit custard

Time needed: *1 hour*
Difficulty: *easy*

INGREDIENTS FOR 4 SERVINGS
*1 lb of mixed fruit
(apples, pears, cherries, currants, etc.)
1 cup of sugar
1 cup of whipping cream
3 egg yolks
2 tablespoons of melted butter*

◆ Rinse and dry pears and apples without peeling or coring. Seed grapes, pit the cherries and cook the fruits in 1/2 cup of water on low heat until tender.
◆ Pass fruit through a sieve over a pan and blend in sugar, butter, egg yolks and whipping cream. Cook on low heat until dense, stirring continuously, making sure the mixture does not boil.
◆ Pour cream into 4 individual cups and refrigerate before serving.
◆ The amount of sugar can vary depending on the fruit used. You may flavor this cream with a teaspoon of liquor to taste.

Pineapple cream

Time needed: *45 minutes*
(plus cooling time)
Difficulty: *easy*

INGREDIENTS FOR 4 SERVINGS
*1 1/4 cup of milk
4 slices of fresh pineapple
1/2 cup of flour
1/4 cup of sugar
2 egg yolks
grated peel of 1 lemon
1 1/4 cup of whipping cream
4 candied cherries*

◆ Bring milk and grated lemon peel to a boil.
◆ In a saucepan, whisk in the egg yolk and sugar until pale and creamy. Stir in flour and hot milk, a little at a time. Bring to a boil on low heat; simmer for 3-4 minutes stirring constantly. Let cool, stirring occasionally.
◆ Cut pineapple into small pieces, purée in a food processor and blend into the cream. Fold in 3/4 cup of whipped cream, pour into a large glass bowl or individual cups.
◆ Whip the remaining cream; put it in a pastry bag and crown the center of the cream. Top with a cherry.
◆ Refrigerate until ready to serve.

Almond custard

Time needed: *25 minutes*
(plus cooling time)
Difficulty: *easy*

INGREDIENTS FOR 6 SERVINGS
*1 cup of toasted almonds
1/2 cup of sugar
1 liquor glass of Amaretto di Saronno
1/4 cup of potato starch
3 egg yolks
2 egg whites
3 cups of milk
1 1/3 cups of whipping cream
1 teaspoon of vanilla
a pinch of salt*

◆ Chop the almonds; in a food processor, grind them finely.
◆ In a saucepan, bring milk and vanilla to a boil. In a bowl, whisk egg yolks and sugar until pale and creamy. Add potato starch. Mix hot milk with ground almonds; add it a little at a time to the egg mixture.
◆ Pour mixture into the saucepan in which the milk was heated, and cook on low heat, stirring until the cream is thick.
◆ Remove from heat, add the liquor and let the cream cool, stirring occasionally. Fold in the whipped cream, then fold in the egg whites beaten with salt to stiff peaks.
◆ Pour cream into individual cups, cover with plastic wrap and refrigerate for at least 3 hours before serving.

Trifle

Prepare pastry cream (see page 16). Let it cool and add the rum.

◆ Cut the cookies to line the base of a 4-cup fluted glass bowl. Brush half the cookies on both sides with the Strega liquor; brush remaining cookies on both sides with Alchermes (1, 2). Line bottom and sides of the bowl alternating the colors (3).

◆ Melt jam in 2 tablespoons of water and brush the cookies with it. Pour a layer of pastry cream into the bowl, cover with a layer of

Time needed:
35 minutes
Difficulty: easy

INGREDIENTS
PER 6-8 SERVINGS
1/2 lb of savoyard cookies
1/3 cup of Alchermes
1/3 cup of Strega liquor
2 tablespoons of apricot jam
1/2 cup of whipping cream

Pastry cream:
2 cups of milk
1/2 cup of sugar
6 egg yolks
1/4 cup of flour
rind of 1 lemon
1 tablespoon of rum

Strega flavored cookies, then with a further layer of pastry cream and one of Alchermes flavored cookies. Continue until all ingredients are used, finishing with a layer of cookies. Refrigerate.

◆ Whip the cream, transfer to a pastry bag, fitted with an indented nozzle and garnish the trifle. Refrigerate.

◆ You may vary this recipe by dividing the pastry cream in two parts and flavoring one with 2 tablespoons of melted dark chocolate.

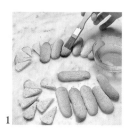 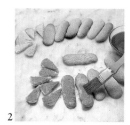

Mont Blanc

Time needed: *1 hour and 50 minutes*
Difficulty: medium

INGREDIENTS FOR 6-8 SERVINGS

2 lbs of chestnuts ◆ 2 cups of milk
1 cup of sugar ◆ a pinch of salt
1 tablespoon of unsweetened cocoa
a pinch of cinnamon ◆ 1 liquor glass of rum
3/4 cup of whipping cream
1 tablespoon of vanilla flavored
powdered sugar
4 marrons glacé, cut in halves

◆ Rinse the chestnuts, make an incision in each and boil for 15 minutes. Drain and peel, removing the internal skin. Put them in a saucepan with milk, sugar and salt. Cook for 1 hour, drain and put through a potato masher.
◆ If the purée is too soft, reheat it in a pan to dry out, stirring often. Pour into a bowl; blend in the cocoa, cinnamon and rum. Pass preparation through a potato masher, letting the puréed vermicelli drop in a dome like fashion on a serving dish.
◆ Whip the cream with vanilla flavored confectioner's sugar; put it in a pastry bag, fitted with an indented nozzle. Cover 3/4 of the chestnut with rosettes of cream and place a crown at the top.

Mont Blanc

Finish garnishing with the Marron glacé, cut in halves.

Tiramisù

Time needed: *30 minutes*
(plus cooling time)
Difficulty: easy

INGREDIENTS FOR 8-10 SERVINGS

1 lb of mascarpone ◆ 6 eggs
1 liquor glass of rum ◆ a pinch of salt
1 1/4 cup of sugar
1 lb of savoyard cookies
2 cups of (strong) espresso coffee
2 tablespoons of unsweetened cocoa

◆ With an electric mixer, beat egg yolks and sugar until pale and creamy. Blend in the mascarpone cheese and rum; gently fold in egg whites, beaten with salt to stiff peaks.
◆ Cover a rectangular tray with a layer of savoyard cookies slightly moistened with the coffee diluted in 2 teaspoons of water. Cover with an even layer of mascarpone cream. Repeat until all ingredients are used, finishing with a layer of cream. Dust with unsweetened cocoa and refrigerate for at least 4 hours.

Trifle

Chestnut pudding

Time needed: *1 hour and 25 minutes*
(plus cooling time)
Difficulty: *medium*

INGREDIENTS FOR 6 SERVINGS
2 lb of chestnuts
3 cups of milk
1/2 cup of sugar
1 vanilla bean
1/2 cup of softened butter
3 tablespoons of sweetened cocoa
2 liquor glasses of rum
3 1/2 oz of amaretti ◆ a pinch of salt
1/4 cup of toasted almonds, peeled and chopped
9 marrons glacé ◆ 1/3 cup of whipping cream

◆ Peel the chestnuts. Boil for 5 minutes, drain, remove the skin. Put in a pan with milk, sugar, vanilla and salt. Cook slowly for 1 hour. Push chestnuts through a potato masher over a saucepan and let the purée become dense on moderate heat, stirring constantly. Cool and blend in butter, cocoa, and 1 liquor glass of rum.
◆ Line a 6-cup fluted pudding mold with a moistened muslin cloth. Pour 1/3 of mixture into the mold and cover with amaretti cookies soaked in rum. Cover with half the remaining mixture, then with a second layer of amaretti and finish with remaining chestnut purée mixture. Level with a spatula.
◆ Refrigerate for at least 4 hours, turn onto a serving dish, discard the muslin cloth and garnish with almonds, whipped cream and Marron glacé.

Chestnut pudding

Caliph's hat

Time needed: *40 minutes*
(plus cooling time)
Difficulty: *medium*

INGREDIENTS FOR 8-10 SERVINGS
1 1/2 cups of grated dark chocolate
1/2 cup of grated milk chocolate
1 1/4 cup of whipping cream
1 tablespoon of sugar
5 tablespoons of rum
1/4 lb of savoyard cookies

Decoration:
3/4 cup of grated dark chocolate
3/4 cup of whipping cream

◆ In a double boiler, melt milk and dark chocolate with whipping cream and sugar, stirring well. Add 2 tablespoons of rum and let cool.
◆ Brush a 6-cup round bombe mold with 1 tablespoon of rum and pour in 1/3 of chocolate mixture. Even it out and layer with savoyard cookies brushed with rum. Cover with half the remaining chocolate mixture, form a second layer of cookies brushed with rum and cover with remaining mixture. Refrigerate for at least 3 hours.
◆ To decorate, melt chocolate in a double boiler, pour onto parchment paper and spread it out very thinly. As soon as it hardens, use a 2 inch diameter pasta cutter to cut 8 disks. Refrigerate.
◆ Quickly dip mold in warm water and turn onto a serving dish. Whip the cream; put it in a pastry bag, fitted with a large indented nozzle, and pipe a rosette around the pudding. Decorate with chocolate disks and refrigerate.

Paskha, Russian Easter pudding

Time needed: *40 minutes*
(plus cooling time)
Difficulty: *medium*

INGREDIENTS FOR 8 SERVINGS
4 cups of ricotta cheese
1/2 cup of almonds, peeled and chopped
1/2 cup of candied cherries, diced
1/2 cup of raisins
7 tablespoons of softened butter
1 tablespoon of rose water
1/2 cup of candied orange
and lime peel, diced
2 egg yolks
1/2 cup of sugar

Decoration:
1 candied orange
1 candied lemon
1 candied lime
1/4 cup of candied cherries
1 tablespoon of blueberries

◆ If the ricotta has excess milk, wrap it in a muslin cloth and hang over a bowl in a cool place for 24 hours to drain. Soak raisins in warm water.
◆ In a bowl, whisk, with an electric mixer, egg yolks and sugar until pale and creamy. Pass the well-drained ricotta through a sieve and blend with the butter, in pieces, into the egg mixture. Add the raisins, the rose water, the almonds and

*Paskha, Russian
Easter pudding*

the diced candied fruit; blend well.

◆ Line a 4-cup cylindrical mold with a muslin cloth; pour ricotta mixture and fold the cloth to encase; place a weight on top. Refrigerate for at least 12 hours. Discard the whey accumulated in the mold, open the muslin cloth and turn onto a serving dish.

◆ To decorate, thinly slice the candied orange, keeping the central slice thicker. Thinly slice the candied lemon. Cut the candied lime to form leaves and cut the candied cherries in halves. Place the lime leaves, blueberries, and cherries around the base of the pudding. Place the orange and lemon slices around the walls. Cut the thicker orange slice in half, make a vertical incision in the flesh of one of the two halves to overlap in a cross and place it on the pudding. Refrigerate.

Ricotta mousseline

Ricotta mousseline

Time needed: *1 hour and 15 minutes*
(plus cooling time)
Difficulty: **easy**

INGREDIENTS FOR 8 SERVINGS
1 chocolate sponge cake (see page 10)
1 cup of ricotta cheese
1/2 cup of mascarpone
3 eggs
1/2 cup of sugar
1/2 teaspoon of vanilla
1 liquor glass of rum
1/4 cup of candied lime and orange, diced
1/4 cup of dark chocolate, diced
a pinch of salt
1/3 cup of whipping cream

◆ On low heat, cook 1 tablespoon of sugar in 1/4 cup of water until dissolved. Add rum and let syrup cool.

◆ Line a 10-inch mold with waxed paper. Cut a circle of 1 inch in thickness from the sponge cake and place it at the bottom of the mold. Line the sides with slices of sponge cake, of 1 inch in thickness. Brush the Sponge cake with rum syrup.

◆ In a bowl, using an electric mixer, whisk egg yolks with remaining sugar and vanilla until pale and creamy. Add ricotta and mascarpone, always whisking. Blend in a tablespoon of the candied fruit and the chocolate. Fold in the egg whites, beaten with salt to stiff peaks.

◆ Fill the sponge cake box with the ricotta mixture and even it out. Cover with parchment pa-

per and refrigerate for 24 hours.

◆ When ready to serve, turn on a dish, remove the paper and garnish with rosettes of whipped cream

Zuccotto

Time needed: *1 hour and 30 minutes*
(plus cooling time)
Difficulty: **medium**

INGREDIENTS FOR 8 SERVINGS
1 sponge cake
4 cups of whipping cream
1/4 cup of sugar
3/4 cup of grated dark chocolate
1/2 cup of chocolate chips
1/2 cup of candied cherries
1/2 cup of candied lime and orange
3 tablespoons of brandy
3 tablespoons of rum
3 tablespoons of kirsch
8 tablespoons of confectioner's sugar

◆ Prepare the Sponge cake (see page 10).

◆ Line a Zuccotto mold with plastic wrap.

◆ Heat 2 cups of cream, just under the boiling point. Remove from heat; blend in the grated dark chocolate and sugar; stir until dissolved. Refrigerate.

◆ Cut sponge cake in thin slices. Sprinkle with the 3 liquors mixed with 1 tablespoon of water and line the mold with the slices.

◆ Whip remaining cream with 6 tablespoons of confectioner's sugar. Blend in the diced candied fruit. Refrigerate.

◆ When very cold, whip the cocoa flavored cream, stir in the chocolate chips, pour into the mold and level with a spatula. Pour cream with candied fruit over the chocolate. Even it and cover with slices of sponge cake moistened with liquor.

◆ Refrigerate the Zuccotto for 5 hours When ready to serve, turn onto a dish, remove plastic wrap and sprinkle with remaining confectioner's sugar.

Zuccotto

Crepes and Omelettes

Crepes ◆ Omelettes and pancakes

Apple crepes

Time needed:
1 hour (plus resting time)
Difficulty: medium

**INGREDIENTS
FOR 8 SERVINGS**
Crepes:
1 cup of flour
1 egg ◆ *1 egg yolk*
3/4 cup of milk
2 tablespoons of butter
a pinch of salt
Filling and topping:
*2 lbs of golden delicious
apples*
1/2 cup of sugar
1/3 cup of dry white wine
*2 tablespoons of
powdered sugar*
4 tablespoons of butter
*1/2 cup of peeled toasted
almonds*

Sift flour into a bowl and whisk in the egg, egg yolk, salt and milk until well blended and there are no more lumps. Set aside in a cool place for 1 hour.

◆ Butter a cookie sheet. Preheat the oven to 350°F.

◆ To make the filling, rinse apples and set 2 aside for the topping. Cut remaining apples, core and put on the cookie sheet. Cover with the wine; sprinkle with 2/3 cup of sugar and bake for 20 minutes. Remove apple sauce out of the peel with a spoon and place into a bowl.

◆ To make the crepes, lightly brush a small non-stick crepe pan with melted butter; once hot, pour in a little batter, rotating the pan to form a smooth and thin layer. Cook the crepe on moderate heat. Do not brown. Turn it over once with a spatula. Continue until all batter is used, placing the crepes on a plate.

◆ Fill each crepe with a tablespoon of apple sauce, fold over into a half moon, place on a buttered cookie sheet sprinkled with powdered sugar. Place the crepes in the preheated oven at 370°F until top is crispy.

◆ Coarsely chop the almonds. Peel remaining apples, cut into segments and sauté in a pan with remaining sugar and butter for 7-8 minutes. Place on top of the crepes and sprinkle with almonds.

Crepes with strawberry soufflé

Time needed: *1 hour
(plus resting time)*
Difficulty: medium

INGREDIENTS FOR 6 SERVINGS
Crepes:
1 cup of flour
1 tablespoon of powdered sugar
1 egg ◆ *1 egg yolk*
3/4 cup of milk
grated peel of an lemon
1 teaspoon of vanilla extract
2 tablespoons of butter
Filling:
1 lb. of strawberries
3/4 cup of sugar
2 tablespoons of kirsch
2 tablespoons of lemon juice
3/4 cup of milk
1 teaspoon of vanilla extract
1/3 cup of flour
3 eggs ◆ *a pinch of salt*
2 tablespoons of powdered sugar

*Crepes with strawberry
soufflé*

◆ Sift flour into a bowl and blend in sugar, egg, egg yolk and milk. Add citrus peel and vanilla extract and set aside in a cool place for at least 1 hour.
◆ Heat a small non-stick pan, butter it lightly and pour over a little batter, rotating the pan to form a smooth and thin layer. Cook the crepe on moderate heat. Do not brown. Turn it over once with a spatula. Continue until all batter is used, placing the crepes on a plate.
◆ To make the filling, rinse strawberries in ice water. Cook in 3/4 cup of water and 2/3 cup of sugar for 8 minutes. Let mixture cool, purée and pass through a sieve. Return to heat, stirring often until reduced by half. Remove from heat; add lemon juice and liquor.
◆ In a pan, mix in remaining sugar and egg yolks, add flour, vanilla extract and hot milk, a little at a time. Cook for 2 minutes on moderate heat, stirring continuously until dense. Add the strawberry purée and cool, stirring occasionally. Beat the egg whites with the salt until stiff and gently fold into the mixture.
◆ Butter a cookie sheet. Preheat the oven to 350°F.
◆ Place a little filling on half of each crepe; fold the other half over to close. Put the crepes next to one another on the cookie sheet, sprinkle with powdered sugar and bake for about 10 minutes until puffed up and golden. Remove from the oven and serve sprinkled with the remaining powdered sugar.

Apple crepes

Crepes Suzette

Time needed:
40 minutes
(plus resting time)
Difficulty: medium

INGREDIENTS FOR 6 SERVINGS
Crepes:
1 cup of flour
1 egg
1 egg yolk
1 cup of milk
2 tablespoons of butter
a pinch of salt

Topping:
3 tablespoons of Grand Marnier
4 tablespoons of sugar
2 tablespoons of lemon juice
6 tablespoons of orange juice
grated peel of 1 lemon
grated peel of 1 orange
1 1/2 tablespoon of butter
1/4 cup of Armagnac

Crepes Suzette

◆ Sift the flour into a bowl and whisk in the egg, egg yolk and milk into a smooth batter. Set aside in a cool place for 1 hour.
◆ Heat a small non-stick pan, butter it lightly and pour over a little batter, rotating the pan to form a smooth and thin layer. Cook the crepe on moderate heat. Do not brown. Turn it over once with a spatula. Continue until all batter is used. Place the crepes on a plate.
◆ In a saucepan, caramelize sugar with butter and citrus peel; add Grand Marnier. Put each crepe, one at a time into the pan, let them absorb the caramel on both sides, roll them up and place on a warm plate.
◆ Put the rolled crepes onto a serving tray, top with the caramelized citrus peel. Heat the Armagnac; pour onto the crepes and flambé.

Hungarian crepes

Hungarian crepes

Time needed: *1 hour*
(plus resting time)
Difficulty: medium

INGREDIENTS FOR 6 SERVINGS
Crepes:
1 cup of flour ◆ *1 egg 1 egg yolk*
1 cup of milk ◆ *2 tablespoons of butter*
a pinch of salt

Filling:
1 cup of finely chopped walnuts
1/4 cup of raisins
3 tablespoons of milk
grated peel of 1 orange
2 tablespoons of powdered sugar
1 cup of chocolate sauce (see p. 20)

◆ Soak raisins in warm water.
◆ Sift flour into a bowl and blend in the egg, egg yolk, salt and milk, a little at a time until well mixed. Set aside in a cool place for at least 1 hour.
◆ To make the filling, mix chopped walnuts with strained raisins, orange peel, powdered sugar and milk.
◆ Heat a small non-stick pan, butter it lightly and pour in a little batter, rotating the pan to form a smooth and thin layer. Cook the crepe on moderate heat. Do not brown. Turn it over once with a spatula. Continue until all batter is used. Place the crepes on a plate.
◆ Spread a little filling on each crepe and fold in four.
◆ Melt a piece of butter in a small pan and sauté the crepes. Serve with the chocolate sauce.

Imperial crepes

Time needed: *30 minutes*
(plus resting time)
Difficulty: medium

INGREDIENTS FOR 6 SERVINGS
1 1/4 cup of flour ◆ *1 1/4 cups of milk*
2 eggs ◆ *1/3 cup of sugar* ◆ *grated peel of 1 orange*
3 amaretti cookies (finely crumbled)
4 tablespoons of rum
3/4 cup of peeled and toasted hazelnuts
7 tablespoons of butter
1 tablespoon of powdered sugar

◆ Sift flour into a bowl, blend in the egg, 2 tablespoons of sugar, orange peel, amaretti, 2 tablespoons of rum and the milk, a little at a time. Set aside in a cool place for 1 hour.

◆ Heat a small non-stick pan, pour in a little batter, rotating the pan to form a smooth and thin layer. Cook the crepe on moderate heat. Do not brown. Turn it over once with a spatula. Continue until all batter is used, placing the crepes on a plate.

◆ Grind the hazelnuts with the remaining sugar, 4 tablespoons of butter in pieces and the remaining rum. Blend well.

◆ Spread a little hazelnut mixture in the center of each crepe and fold into four. In a small pan, melt remaining butter and sauté the crepes. Serve sprinkled with powdered sugar and, if you like, chocolate sauce.

Pineapple crepes flambé

Pineapple crepes flambé

Time needed: *35 minutes*
(plus resting time)
Difficulty: medium

INGREDIENTS FOR 6-8 SERVINGS
Crepes:
1 cup of flour
1 egg
1 egg yolk
1 cup of milk
2 tablespoons of butter
a pinch of salt

Filling:
1 lb. of pineapple
2 tablespoons of butter
1/4 cup of sugar
3 tablespoons of rum
5 tablespoons of pineapple juice

◆ Sift flour into a bowl and blend in the egg, egg yolk, salt and milk into a smooth batter. Rest in a cool place for 1 hour.

◆ Heat a small non-stick pan, butter it lightly and pour in a little batter, rotating the pan to form a smooth and thin layer. Cook the crepe on moderate heat. Do not brown. Turn it over once with a spatula. Continue until all batter is used; place the crepes on a plate.

◆ Cut the pineapple in 12 slices and remove the core. In a pan with the butter, sauté pineapple and sugar. Wrap each slice in a crepe.

Crepes with banana soufflé

◆ In the same pan, bring pineapple juice to a boil and simmer for 2 minutes. Place crepes in the pan and warm them up for a few minutes. Heat the rum, pour into pan and flambé.

Crepes with banana soufflé

Time needed: *1 hour*
(plus resting time)

Difficulty: medium

INGREDIENTS FOR 8 SERVINGS
Crepes:
2/3 cup of flour
4 tablespoons of butter
1 tablespoon of sugar
3/4 cup of milk
1 tablespoon of rum
1 egg
1 egg yolk

Soufflé:
3/4 cup of milk
1/3 cup of flour
3 eggs
1/4 cup of sugar
5 bananas
a pinch of salt

Sauce:
3 egg yolks
3 tablespoons of rum
3/4 cup of milk
1/3 cup of sugar
1 teaspoon of potato starch
a drop of vanilla extract

◆ Butter a cookie sheet.

◆ Sift flour into a bowl and blend in the egg, egg yolk, sugar and rum; dilute a drop at a time with milk. Add 11/2 tablespoon of melted butter. Set aside in a cool place for 1 hour.

◆ Heat a small non-stick pan, butter it lightly and pour in a little batter, rotating the pan to form a smooth and thin layer. Cook the crepe on moderate heat. Do not brown. Turn it over once with a spatula. Continue until all batter is used, placing the crepes on a plate.

◆ To make the sauce, in a saucepan mix egg yolks, sugar, potato starch and vanilla extract. Slowly pour in the boiling milk and bring to a boil on low heat, stirring constantly. Remove from heat, add rum and let it cool.

◆ To make the soufflé, peel bananas and purée. In a saucepan, mix eggs, sugar and flour; add hot milk, a little at a time and cook for 3 minutes on low heat, whisking continuously. Remove from heat, stir in the banana purée and let cool, stirring occasionally.
◆ Preheat an oven to 350°F.
◆ Cut the crepes in half to create semi-circles. Beat the remaining egg whites with salt to stiff peaks and fold into banana mixture. Spread a little of the mixture on each half crepe and roll into a cone. Put the cones on cookie sheet and bake for about 10-15 minutes until golden.
◆ Serve with the rum sauce.

Apple and apricot crepes gratiné

Time needed: *30 minutes*
Difficulty: medium

INGREDIENTS FOR 4 SERVINGS

8 ready made crepes
3 apples
3 apricots (fresh or canned)
1 1/2 tablespoons of butter
1/3 cup of sugar
1/4 cup of almond slivers

Topping:
1/2 cup of peeled, finely chopped almonds
4 tablespoons of softened butter
1/4 cup of powdered sugar
1 tablespoon of rum

◆ Peel apricots, cut in half, pit and slice thinly.
◆ Peel apples, core and dice. Sauté apples in a non-stick pan with 1 1/2 tablespoons of butter. Add apricots and sugar; cook, stirring, for about 5 minutes until the apples turn golden. Add almonds, stir and remove the pan from heat.
◆ Place a little fruit mixture on each crepe; wrap like cannelloni. Preheat the oven to 390°F.
◆ In a bowl, whisk butter until creamy. Add powdered sugar, chopped almonds and rum.
◆ Place crepes in a lightly buttered oven dish; cover with butter-almond mixture. Bake for 8-10 minutes until crisp.

Crepes with Marrons Glacés

Time needed: *40 minutes*
(plus resting time)
Difficulty: medium

INGREDIENTS FOR 6 SERVINGS
1 cup of flour
1 egg ◆ 1 egg yolk
1 cup of milk
a pinch of salt
4 tablespoons of butter
3/4 cup of marron glacé (finely chopped)
2 tablespoons of rum
1 tablespoons of powdered sugar

◆ In a bowl, mix egg, egg yolk, flour, salt and milk until well blended. Set aside in a cool place for 1 hour.
◆ Butter an ovenproof dish. Preheat the oven to 390°F.
◆ Heat a small non-stick pan, brush with a little melted butter and pour in a little batter, rotating the pan to form a smooth and thin layer. Cook the crepe on moderate heat. Do not brown. Turn it over once with a spatula. Continue until all batter is used, placing the crepes on a plate.
◆ Fill each crepe with a tablespoon of the marron glacé and fold over into a half moon. Place crepes in oven dish and brush with remaining melted butter. Sprinkle with powdered sugar and Bake for about 10 minutes until sugar has caramelized. Serve hot or lukewarm.

Crepes with bananas and chocolate

Time needed: *45 minutes*
(plus resting time)
Difficulty: medium

INGREDIENTS FOR 8 SERVINGS
Crepes:
1 cup of flour ◆ 1 egg
1 egg yolk ◆ 1 cup of milk
2 tablespoons of butter
a pinch of salt

Filling:
4 ripe bananas
1 cup of grated dark chocolate
6 tablespoons of butter
1/4 cup of brandy ◆ 1 tablespoon of sugar

◆ Sift flour into a bowl and blend in the egg, egg yolk, salt and milk into a smooth batter. Set aside in a cool place for 1 hour.
◆ Heat a small non-stick pan, butter it lightly and pour in a little batter, rotating the pan to form a smooth and thin layer. Cook the crepe on moderate heat. Do not brown. Turn it over once with a spatula. Continue until all batter is used, placing the crepes on a plate.
◆ Melt chocolate and 4 tablespoons of butter in a double boiler. Spread on each crepe, fill with sliced bananas and fold into four.
◆ Just before serving, heat remaining butter, add sugar and brandy and cook until dissolved. Sauté crepes in this sauce, place on a dish and serve.

Orange crepes with mascarpone

Time needed: *40 minutes*
(plus resting time)
Difficulty: medium

INGREDIENTS FOR 4 SERVINGS
Crepes:
1 cup of flour ◆ 1 egg
1 egg yolk ◆ 1 cup of milk
2 tablespoons of butter
a pinch of salt

Filling:
strained juice of 1 orange
1 1/2 cups of mascarpone cheese
1/4 cup of Grand Marnier
4 egg yolks ◆ 2 egg whites
1 cup of powdered sugar
a pinch of salt

◆ Sift flour into a bowl and blend in the egg, egg yolk, salt and milk into a smooth batter. Set aside in a cool place for 1 hour.
◆ Heat a small non-stick pan, butter it lightly and pour in a little batter, rotating the pan to form a smooth and thin layer. Cook the crepe on moderate heat. Do not brown. Turn it over once with a spatula. Continue until all batter is used up, placing the crepes on a plate.
◆ To make the filling, whisk egg yolks with 3/4 cup of powdered sugar until clear and creamy. Add mascarpone, liquor and orange juice. Beat egg whites with salt to stiff peaks and gently fold into mixture.
◆ Spread mixture on crepes, roll them up and place on a serving dish. Sprinkle with remaining powdered sugar.

Hazelnut crepes

Time needed: *1 hour and 20 minutes*
Difficulty: medium

INGREDIENTS FOR 4 SERVINGS
Crepes:
1 cup of flour ◆ 1 egg
1 egg yolk ◆ 1 cup of milk
a pinch of salt ◆ 2 tablespoons of butter

Filling:
1 3/4 cups of shelled hazelnuts
1 cup of ricotta cheese
4 tablespoons of honey
2 eggs ◆ 4-5 tablespoons of milk

Topping:
1 cup of heavy cream
2 tablespoons of powdered sugar
cinnamon

◆ Preheat the oven to 390°F.
Sift flour into a bowl and whisk in egg, egg yolk, salt and milk into a lump-free batter. Set aside in a cool place for 1 hour.
◆ Spread hazelnuts onto a cookie sheet and toast them in the oven for a few minutes. Rub with a kitchen towel to remove the skin. Grind in a food processor.
◆ With an electric mixer, whisk honey, eggs and ricotta. Mix in ground hazelnuts and add a few tablespoons of milk to obtain a smooth mixture.
◆ Heat a small non-stick pan, butter it lightly and pour in a little batter, rotating the pan to form a smooth and thin layer. Cook the crepe on moderate heat. Do not brown. Turn it over once with a spatula. Continue until all batter is used up, placing the crepes on a plate.
◆ Raise oven temperature to 420°F and butter a rectangular ovenproof dish.
◆ Fill crepes with the ricotta-hazelnut mixture, roll them up like cannelloni and place them, one next to the other in the oven dish. Slightly warm the cream; pour over the crepes and sprinkle with powdered sugar and cinnamon. Bake for 10-15 minutes. Serve warm or cold.

American soufflé pancakes

Time needed: *35 minutes*
Difficulty: *easy*

INGREDIENTS FOR **6** SERVINGS
4 eggs
1 cup of milk
1 cup of flour
1/2 cup of sugar
3 tablespoons of orange juice
3 tablespoons of butter
1 tablespoon of powdered sugar
1 cup of strawberries

◆ Butter 4 individual oven dishes. Preheat the oven to 400°F.
◆ Whisk eggs with the flour, milk, sugar, orange juice and melted butter until smooth.
◆ Warm oven dishes in the oven. Turn down the oven to 350°F. Pour 1/4 of the mixture in each dish and bake for 15-20 minutes or until fluffy and golden.
◆ Rinse strawberries in ice water, dry and slice.
◆ Remove pancakes from the oven, sprinkle with powdered sugar and cover with strawberry slices.

American soufflé pancakes

Pancakes

Time needed: *25 minutes*
Difficulty: *easy*

INGREDIENTS FOR **4** SERVINGS
1 egg
1 cup of buttermilk
2 tablespoons of melted butter
1 1/4 cups of flour
1 tablespoon of sugar
1 teaspoon of baking powder
1/2 teaspoon of salt

◆ Whisk all ingredients with an electric mixer.
◆ Heat a large non-stick pan. With a spoon, pour in enough batter to form thick discs. Cook until its surface is covered with bubbles. Turn with a spatula and cook other side until golden. Continue until all batter is used up, placing the pancakes on a plate, one on top of the other.
◆ Fruits can be added to the basic pancake recipe. Pancakes are served for breakfast, with maple syrup or a fruit sauce.

Apple soufflé omelette

Apple soufflé omelette

Time needed: *40 minutes*
Difficulty: *easy*

INGREDIENTS FOR **6** SERVINGS
3 golden delicious apples
4 tablespoons of butter
6 eggs
3/4 cup of sugar
a pinch of cinnamon
a pinch of salt

◆ Peel apples, core and slice thickly. In a saucepan, melt 3 tablespoons of butter and cook apples for about 5 minutes, stirring often. Add cinnamon and 1/4 cup of sugar; sauté apples on high heat until golden, stirring gently.
◆ Preheat the oven to 350°F.
◆ In a bowl, whisk the egg yolks with the remaining sugar until pale and thick. Beat egg whites with salt to stiff peaks and fold into egg yolks. Melt 1 1/2 tablespoons of butter in a 9-inch cake pan, pour in the egg mixture and cook for 1 minute on a low heat. Transfer to the oven and bake for 10-15 minutes.
◆ Place omelet on a serving dish and top with apple slices.
◆ You may substitute the apples with other fruit.

Pear soufflé omelette

Time needed: *25 minutes*
Difficulty: *easy*

INGREDIENTS FOR **4** SERVINGS
2 pears
3 tablespoons of butter
3 tablespoon of brown sugar
grated peel of 2 lemons
4 eggs
1 egg white
2 tablespoons whipping cream
1/3 cup of sugar
a pinch of salt

◆ Butter an ovenproof dish and preheat the oven to 360°F.
◆ Peel pears, core and slice. Cook in a saucepan with butter, stirring occasionally. Add brown

sugar and lemon peel.
- In a bowl, whisk eggs with whipping cream. Beat egg whites with salt to soft peaks; add a little sugar and continue to whisk. Keep adding sugar and whisking it until all sugar has been used. Gently fold into the egg and cream mixture.
- Put the pear slices in the oven dish, pour the egg mixture over and bake in preheated oven for 4-5 minutes until top is crisp.

Glazed omelette in orange liquor

Time needed: *30 minutes*
Difficulty: *medium*

INGREDIENTS FOR 4 SERVINGS
8 eggs
4 tablespoons of orange marmalade
4 tablespoons of butter
1/3 cup of sugar
grated peel of 1 orange
3 tablespoons of orange liquor
2 tablespoons of milk
2 tablespoons of powdered sugar

Sauce:
1/4 cup of sugar
1/2 cup of whipping cream
juice of 1 orange

- For the sauce, caramelize the orange juice and sugar on a low heat. Remove from heat, whisk caramel, add whipping cream a little at a time and return to very low heat until the caramel is completely dissolved.
- In a bowl, beat eggs with grated orange peel, milk, liquor and sugar. Heat 1 tablespoon of butter in a non-stick pan; pour 1/4 of the egg mixture, stirring rapidly. Once the omelet has reached the right consistency, push it towards the edge of the pan; spread over 1 tablespoon of marmalade and with a spatula fold the omelet over. Slide it onto a serving plate. Make 3 other omelets the same way. Sprinkle with powdered sugar. Bring a skewer to red heat and use it to trace a "grill" design on the surface of the omelets. Serve hot with the orange sauce.

Glazed omelette in orange liquor

Viennese omelette

Time needed: *40 minutes (plus resting time)*
Difficulty: *medium*

INGREDIENTS FOR 4 SERVINGS
3/4 cup of milk
11/4 cups of flour
2 eggs
2 tablespoons of butter
3 tablespoons of sugar
grated peel of 1/2 lemon
g pinch of salt
1 tablespoon of powdered sugar
1 liquor glass of Grand Marnier

Filling:
1/2 cup of apricot or peach jam
1/4 cup of grated dark chocolate
3 tablespoons of milk

- For the filling, mix jam with chocolate and milk.
- Beat egg yolks with sugar; add melted butter, lemon peel, sifted flour and milk. Set aside for 1 hour.
- Butter an ovenproof dish and preheat the oven to 375°F.
- Beat egg whites with salt to stiff peaks and gently fold in the batter. Heat a small non-stick pan, butter it lightly and pour in a little batter to form a smooth and thin layer. Cook the omelet for about 2 minutes on each side. Continue until all batter is used.
- Spread a thin layer of filling on each omelet, roll them up and put in the oven dish.
- Sprinkle with powdered sugar and bake for a few minutes until golden. Pour the heated Grand Marnier over, flambé and serve hot.
- Suggestion: For the filling, you may substitute the jam with fresh fruit. Rinse, dry and peel 1/2 lb. of peaches and pit. Slice and put in a saucepan with 4 tablespoons of sugar. Cook for 10-15 minutes, let cool. When cooled, mix in with the chocolate.

Viennese omelette

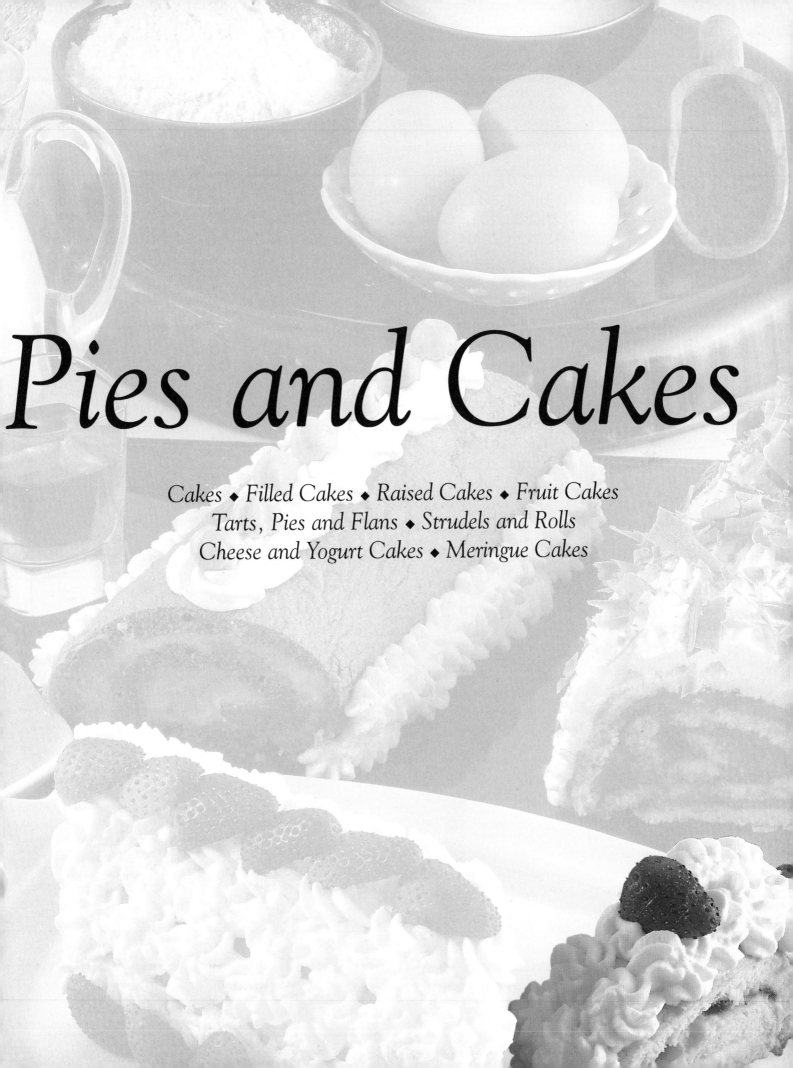

Pies and Cakes

Cakes ◆ Filled Cakes ◆ Raised Cakes ◆ Fruit Cakes
Tarts, Pies and Flans ◆ Strudels and Rolls
Cheese and Yogurt Cakes ◆ Meringue Cakes

Butter and flour an 8-inch cake pan. Preheat the oven to 370°F.

◆ Scald almonds in boiling water, drain, dry, peel and chop finely.

◆ Place hazelnuts on a cookie sheet and toast in the oven for 5 minutes. Transfer to a kitchen towel and scrub to peel. Chop finely.

◆ With a potato peeler, grate chocolate; make some curls for decoration.

◆ In a saucepan, heat coffee; add grated chocolate and melt, stirring continuously.

Quick almond and hazelnut cake

Time needed: *1 hour*
Difficulty: *easy*

INGREDIENTS
FOR 6-8 SERVINGS

1/2 cup of chopped blanched almonds
1/2 cup of chopped hazelnuts
5 oz of bittersweet chocolate
4 eggs
1/2 cup of sugar
1/2 cup of strong espresso coffee
2 tablespoons of flour
3 tablespoons of butter
1/4 cup of milk chocolate
1 tablespoon of cocoa
a pinch of salt
whole almonds and hazelnuts

◆ In a bowl, whisk egg yolks and sugar until pale and creamy. Add melted chocolate, chopped hazelnuts, chopped almonds, flour and melted butter; mix well until all ingredients are blended. Beat egg whites and salt to firm peaks; delicately fold in mixture.

◆ Pour mixture into cake pan and bake for 25-30 minutes. Remove from oven and let cool in pan for 10 minutes.

◆ Turn cake onto a serving dish. Cover with sifted cocoa; decorate with almonds, hazelnuts and chocolate curls.

Almond cake I

Time needed: *1 hour and 40 minutes*
Difficulty: *easy*

INGREDIENTS FOR 6-8 SERVINGS

1 1/2 cups of chopped blanched almonds
3/4 cup of softened butter
1 1/2 cups of powdered sugar
7 eggs
1 teaspoon of rose extract
1 1/4 cups of flour
a pinch of salt

◆ Grease and flour a 12-inch pizza pan. Preheat the oven to 360°F. In a food processor, grind almonds to a fine paste, adding a few drops of water so the almonds do not become too oily.
◆ In a bowl, whisk butter and sugar. Add egg yolks one at a time. Mix in almond paste, rose extract and flour. Beat eggs and salt to stiff peaks; fold into batter.
◆ Pour batter into pizza pan. Bake for 35-40 minutes.
◆ Turn cake onto a platter and serve cold.
◆ This cake can be served topped with cream. The rose extract can be replaced by amaretto liquor.

Chocolate "Pandolce"

Chocolate "Pandolce"

Time needed: *1 hour*
Difficulty: *easy*

INGREDIENTS FOR 6-8 SERVINGS

3/4 cup of flour ◆ *7 tablespoons of softened butter*
3/4 cup of grated chocolate
3/4 cup of sugar ◆ *4 eggs*
1 teaspoon of baking powder
1/2 cup of chopped blanched almonds
a pinch of salt
1/2 cup of white chocolate
1/4 cup of milk chocolate

◆ Grease and flour a 12-inch cake pan. Preheat the oven to 350°F. In a bowl, whisk butter and sugar until creamy. Add egg yolks, one at a time. Mix in flour, baking powder, almonds and chocolate. Beat egg whites and salt to firm peaks and fold into mixture.
◆ Pour batter in cake pan and bake for 30-35 minutes. Remove from oven and turn onto a serving plate.
◆ Separately melt white and milk chocolates in a double boiler. Cool.
◆ Spread white chocolate on the center of the cake. Put milk chocolate in a waxed paper cone and decorate cake.
◆ Set aside for 24 hours.

Quick almond and hazelnut cake

Milk cake

Time needed: *1 hour and 30 minutes*
(plus time to soak the bread)
Difficulty: easy

INGREDIENTS FOR 4-6 SERVINGS

12 slices of day-old bread
3 cups of milk ◆ *6 amaretti*
6 tablespoons of sugar
2 tablespoons of cocoa
1/2 cup of raisins
1 tablespoon of pine nuts ◆ *2 eggs*
1 teaspoon of vanilla extract
4 tablespoons of brandy
6 tablespoons of unsalted butter
1/2 cup of blanched almonds
2 tablespoons of breadcrumbs

◆ Soak the slices of bread in the warmed up milk for 30 minutes. Soak the raisins in water. Lightly butter a 10 inch springform mold and dust with the breadcrumbs. Preheat the oven to 350°F.
◆ With a wooden spoon, stir the soften bread. Add the sifted cocoa, the vanilla extract, the sugar, the pine nuts, the crushed amaretti, the brandy, the drained raisins and the eggs. Mix very well.
◆ Melt remaining butter and mix into the bread preparation. Pour preparation into springform mold. Cover with the blanched almonds.
◆ Cook in the oven for 50-60 minutes. Remove from oven and invert the cake immediately onto a serving plate. Cool before serving.

Creole rice cake

Time needed: *1 hour and 20 minutes*
Difficulty: easy

INGREDIENTS FOR 6-8 SERVINGS

2 cups of milk
3 eggs, separated
1 cup of rice (not parboiled)
1/2 cup of sugar
6 tablespoons of softened butter
1/2 cup of grated bittersweet chocolate
1/2 cup of raisins
1/2 cup of rum
1 tablespoon of powdered sugar
2 tablespoons of chopped
candied orange peel ◆ *a pinch of salt*

Milk cake

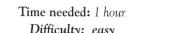

Creole rice cake

Pistachio cake

◆ Cover the bottom of a loaf pan with parchment paper. Butter and flour. Preheat the oven to 350°F.
◆ In a bowl, soak raisins in the rum. Boil the rice in the milk for 30 minutes; remove from heat and let it cool. Transfer to a food processor and mix until creamy.
◆ In a large bowl, mix the creamy rice mixture with the egg yolks, the butter in small pieces and the sugar. When all ingredients are blended, add the strained raisins, the chocolate and the candied orange. Whip the egg whites with the salt to stiff peaks and add delicately to the preparation.
◆ Pour the preparation in the loaf pan and bake for 35-40 minutes.
◆ Invert the cake onto a serving plate and remove the parchment paper. Let it cool. Dust with the powdered sugar and if you wish, you can decorate with candied orange and chocolate.

Pistachio cake

Time needed: *1 hour*
Difficulty: easy

INGREDIENTS FOR 6 SERVINGS

1/2 cup of unbleached flour
1 cup of sugar
4 eggs
6 tablespoons of butter
1 teaspoon of baking powder
1/2 cup of milk
1 tablespoon of peach jam
1 1/2 cups of peeled, chopped pistachios
a pinch of salt

◆ Butter and flour a 10-inch cake pan. Preheat the oven to 350°F.
◆ Beat the egg yolks with the sugar and when pale, add the melted butter. Mix in the flour and the milk, a little at a time. Continue mixing with a whisk until blended. Add the baking powder and 1/2 cup of chopped pistachios.
◆ Beat the egg whites with the salt to stiff peaks. Delicately fold them into the batter, until all blended.
◆ Pour the preparation into the cake pan and bake for 40-45 minutes. Remove from oven and turn onto a rack.
◆ Cool completely and transfer to a serving dish.
◆ Brush the cake with the peach jam and cover the top with the remaining chopped pistachios.

Plum cake

Time needed: *1 hour and 10 minutes*
Difficulty: easy

INGREDIENTS FOR **6-8** SERVINGS
2 1/2 cups of flour
1 cup of sugar
3/4 cup of butter
7 eggs
1 cup of raisins
1/2 cup of chopped mixed candied fruits
1 teaspoon of baking powder
2 teaspoons of vanilla extract
grated peel of 1 lemon
4 tablespoons of rum
Strips of candied fruits
1 tablespoon of powdered sugar

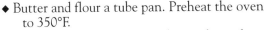

Plum cake

◆ Cover the bottom of a loaf pan with parchment paper and let paper extend over the sides. Butter and flour. Preheat the oven to 350°F.
◆ Soak raisins in the rum. In a large bowl, work the butter with the sugar until creamy and light. Add the eggs, one by one, mixing well after each addition. Add the vanilla, the flour and the baking powder. Mix well and add the drained raisins, the candied fruits and lemon peel.
◆ Pour the preparation in the cake pan and bake for 45-50 minutes. Turn and cool on a rack. Dust with the powdered sugar and garnish with strips of candied fruits.

Pumpkin spice cake

Pumpkin spice cake

Time needed: *1 hour and 25 minutes*
Difficulty: easy

INGREDIENTS FOR **8** SERVINGS
1 lb of pumpkin
3 cups of flour
1 1/4 cups of sugar
1 cup of raisins
a pinch of salt
3 eggs
4 tablespoons of olive oil
2 teaspoons of powdered cloves
2 teaspoons of cinnamon
1 teaspoon of powdered cardamom
1 teaspoon of baking powder
1 tablespoon of powdered sugar

◆ Butter and flour a tube pan. Preheat the oven to 350°F.
◆ Slice the pumpkin and spread on a buttered cookie sheet. Bake the pumpkin for 15 minutes or until tender. Pass through a food mill or mix in a food processor.
◆ In a large bowl, mix flour with salt, cinnamon, powdered cloves, cardamom and baking powder. Add pumpkin, eggs, raisins, sugar and olive oil. Mix everything until the batter is smooth.
◆ Pour preparation into the cake pan. Bake for 55-60 minutes.
◆ Remove from oven and transfer to a rack to cool. Dust with powdered sugar.

Potato and raisin cake

Time needed: *1 hour*
Difficulty: easy

INGREDIENTS FOR **6** SERVINGS
1 lb of cooked potatoes,
passed through a food mill
8 tablespoons of butter
3/4 cup of sugar ◆ *5 amaretti*
2 tablespoons of candied citron
3 tablespoons of raisins
7 eggs ◆ *grated peel of 1 lemon*
a pinch of cinnamon
a pinch of salt ◆ *4 amaretti*
3 tablespoons of candied cherries
2 tablespoons of powdered sugar
1 tablespoon of apricot jam

◆ Butter and flour a 12 inch springform pan. Preheat the oven to 325°F.
◆ Melt the butter. Chop the amaretti and the candied citron. Rinse and dry raisins.
◆ In a large bowl, mix the puréed potatoes with 4 eggs, adding 1 at a time. Add 3 egg yolks and the sugar; blend well. Add the melted butter, the amaretti, the citron, the raisins, the lemon peel and the cinnamon. Mix well to make a smooth batter.
◆ Whip 3 egg whites with salt to stiff peaks. Fold them delicately into the batter. Pour into the pan. Bake for 45-50 minutes. Turn onto a serving plate and cool.
◆ Dust the top of the cake with powdered sugar. Brush the 4 amaretti with warmed-up apricot jam. Place them in the middle of the cake with the candied cherries. Serve warm or cold.

Potato and raisin cake

Mantova cake

Time needed: *1 hour and 20 minutes*
Difficulty: *easy*

INGREDIENTS FOR **6** SERVINGS
1 cup of blanched chopped almonds
1 1/4 cups of flour
1 1/2 cups of fine corn flour
1 cup of sugar
2 teaspoons of vanilla extract
grated peel of 1 lemon
2 egg yolks
7 tablespoons of butter
7 tablespoons of vegetable shortening

◆ Butter a 12 inch cake pan. Preheat the oven to 350°F.
◆ On a work surface, sift the flour. Make a well in the middle and add the almonds, sugar (keeping aside 2 tablespoons), lemon peel, egg yolks, butter, shortening and vanilla.
◆ Work the mixture with fingertips: You will not get a smooth dough but a rough and dry preparation. Transfer to the cake pan and bake for 50-55 minutes.
◆ As soon as taken out of the oven, shake the pan to undo the cake and transfer it to a platter. Dust with the remaining sugar.
◆ This cake can keep for a week, wrapped in aluminum foil.

Sweet polenta cake

Time needed: *1 hour and 20 minutes*
Difficulty: *easy*

INGREDIENTS FOR **6-8** SERVINGS
2 1/2 cups of fine ground corn flour
3/4 cup of chopped dried figs
3/4 cup of raisins
1 teaspoon of vanilla
1 apple
4 tablespoons of butter
1/2 cup sugar
juice of 1/2 lemon
juice of 1 orange
3 tablespoons of extra virgin olive oil
2 tablespoons of milk
2 teaspoons of baking powder
1 tablespoon of powdered sugar
a pinch of salt

◆ Butter and flour a square cake pan. Preheat the oven to 350°F.
◆ Soak raisins in warm water. Peel the apple, cut

in quarters and thinly slice. Melt butter.
◆ In a large bowl, mix the sifted flour with baking powder, vanilla, strained raisins, figs, apples, sugar, salt, lemon juice and orange juice until well blended. Add olive oil, milk and melted butter; mix well. Pour batter into cake pan. Bake for 40-45 minutes. Remove from oven and turn onto a rack to cool. Serve dusted with powdered sugar.

Angel food cake

Time needed: *1 hour and 20 minutes*
Difficulty: *easy*

INGREDIENTS FOR **6** SERVINGS
1 cup of flour
1 cup of sugar
8 egg whites
2 teaspoons of baking powder
1 teaspoon of vanilla extract
1 teaspoon of almond extract
a pinch of salt

◆ You will need a 10-inch tube pan, ungreased. Preheat the oven to 325°F.
◆ Sift flour and baking powder 3 times. In a large bowl, whip the egg whites with a pinch of salt to firm peaks; delicately add the sugar, vanilla and almond extracts; keep whipping until very firm. Delicately incorporate the flour with a spoon, with folding movements from the bottom to the top.
◆ When the batter is smooth, pour it into the ungreased tube pan and bake for about 1 hour.
◆ Remove from oven and turn the cake pan onto a rack; set to cool. Remove cake pan only when cake has cooled completely.

Small hazelnut cake

Time needed: *1 hour*
Difficulty: *easy*

INGREDIENTS FOR **4** SERVINGS
3/4 cup of toasted chopped hazelnuts
3/4 cup of sugar
6 egg whites
1 tablespoon of powdered sugar
a pinch of salt

◆ Cover the bottom of a loaf pan with parchment paper. Grease and flour the paper. Preheat the oven to 350°F.

◆ In a bowl, beat the egg whites with the salt until frothy. Add the sugar, one spoon at a time and continue beating until peaks are stiff. Delicately add the hazelnuts. Pour the preparation into the prepared pan.

◆ Bake for 35-40 minutes. Remove from oven, turn onto a plate, remove parchment paper and dust with powdered sugar.

Fantasia cake

Time needed: *1 hour and 20 minutes*
Difficulty: *easy*

INGREDIENTS FOR 6 SERVINGS
2 cups of flour
1/4 cup of boiling water
1/2 cup of sugar
8 tablespoons of honey
1/2 teaspoon of baking soda
1/2 cup of raisins
1/2 cup of blanched almonds
1/2 cup of pine nuts
1/3 cup of candied citron
1/3 cup of candied orange
1/3 lb of bittersweet chocolate
1 teaspoon of aniseeds
1 pinch of cinnamon
1 pinch of salt

◆ Grease a 12 inch cake pan. Preheat the oven to 350°F.

◆ Soak raisins in warm water. Cut the pieces of candied orange in thick slices and the candied citron in small pieces. With a heavy knife, cut the bittersweet chocolate in small pieces.

◆ In a large bowl, mix together honey, sugar, baking soda, aniseeds and boiling water. Add flour and mix with a wooden spoon. Add strained raisins, almonds, pine nuts, citron, chocolate, cinnamon and salt.

◆ Pour preparation in the cake pan, level the batter and place candied orange on top decoratively.

◆ Bake for 40 minutes. The cake should be golden brown. Remove from oven and turn onto a serving plate. Serve cold.

◆ This traditional cake from the region of Bologna can be kept for a few months tightly wrapped in aluminum foil. It results in a very compact cake and should be served in thin slices.

Oxford cake

Time needed: *1 hour and 35 minutes*
Difficulty: *easy*

INGREDIENTS FOR 6-8 SERVINGS
1 cup of flour ◆ 1 cup of corn flour
2 cups of softened butter
1 cup of sugar ◆ 5 eggs
1 cup of diced candied citron
1 teaspoon of baking soda
1/4 cup of Cognac
3 pieces of candied citron
1 candied cherry

◆ Grease a charlotte mold and line with parchment paper; grease again. Preheat the oven to 325°F.

◆ In a small bowl, soak the diced candied citron in the Cognac.

◆ In a bowl, beat the butter with the sugar until smooth and creamy. Add the eggs, one at a time. Add the diced citron, the flour, the corn flour and the baking soda; mix well. Pour the batter into the cake pan and bake for about 1 hour and 20 minutes. Remove and cool completely before turning onto a plate.

◆ To decorate the cake, slice the candied citron in round petals that you put around the candied cherry to form a flower.

Lemon donut cake

Time needed: *1 hour*
Difficulty: *easy*

INGREDIENTS FOR 6 SERVINGS
3/4 cup of sugar
6 eggs, separated
1 lemon ◆ 1 cup of flour
1 tablespoon of powdered sugar
a pinch of salt

◆ Grease and flour a large tube pan. Preheat the oven to 325°F.

◆ Grate the peel of the lemon and press the juice. Set aside.

◆ In a large bowl, mix egg yolks with sugar until creamy and light. Add lemon peel and lemon juice; continue beating for 3 minutes. Incorporate flour and, at the end, the egg whites, beaten with the salt to stiff peaks.

◆ Pour preparation into the tube pan. Bake for 35-40 minutes. Turn the cake onto a plate and dust with the powdered sugar.

Grease a 12-inch quiche pan. Preheat the oven to 375°F.

◆ Soak the raisins in the grappa. Peel the apple and chop it. Chop the dried figs and the candied fruit.

◆ In a large saucepan, mix the flour and the sugar together. Cooking on low heat, slowly stir in enough hot water to get a thick polenta.

◆ Cook for 20 minutes. Add the butter, the

Epiphany cake

Time needed:
1 hour and 15 minutes
Difficulty: easy

INGREDIENTS FOR 6 SERVINGS

3 cups of corn flour
2 cups of flour
1 1/2 cups of butter
1 cup of sugar
1/2 cup of raisins
1/2 cup of candied citron
1/2 cup of candied pumpkin
10 dried figs
1 apple
a pinch of aniseeds
1/4 cup of grappa
1 teaspoon of baking powder

raisins with the grappa, the aniseeds, the apple, the candied fruits and the figs.

◆ Cook, stirring for another 15 minutes.

◆ Add the baking powder, and passing it through a sieve, transfer the mixture to the prepared pan. Bake in the preheated oven for 20 minutes or until a golden crust has formed over the cake.

◆ This cake can be served warm or completely cold.

Nuremberg cake

Time needed: *1 hour and 30 minutes*
Difficulty: easy

INGREDIENTS FOR 8-10 SERVINGS
5 cups of flour
2 1/2 cups of sugar
4 eggs
3/4 cup of sliced almonds
1/2 teaspoon of cinnamon
a pinch of allspice
1/2 cup of candied orange peel
1/2 cup of candied citron
2 teaspoons of baking powder
grated peel of 1 lemon

◆ Grease and flour 4 individual pie pans. Preheat the oven to 400°F.
◆ Chop all candied fruit finely. In a bowl, beat the eggs with the sugar. Sift flour and baking powder; slowly add to the eggs, stirring. Add almonds, candied fruits, cinnamon, allspice, lemon peel and stir well.
◆ Pour batter in the 4 prepared pans and bake for 15 minutes. Lower the heat to 325°F and cook for 40 minutes.
◆ Remove from oven, let cool completely and turn onto serving dishes.

Irish whisky cake

Time needed: *1 hour and 20 minutes*
(plus 2 hours soaking)
Difficulty: easy

INGREDIENTS FOR 6 SERVINGS

2 cups of flour
3/4 cup of softened butter
1 cup of sugar ◆ *2 eggs*
1/2 cup of raisins
1 orange
4 tablespoons of Irish whisky
2 teaspoons of baking powder
powdered sugar

Irish whisky cake

◆ Grease and flour a 12-inch cake pan. Preheat the oven to 375°F.
◆ Remove all peel from orange and soak in the whisky for 2 hours. Soak raisins in warm water for 20 minutes, drain and soak in the whisky with orange peel.
◆ In a bowl, whisk sugar and butter; add eggs, one at a time; add sifted flour and baking powder. Mix well. Remove and discard orange peel from whisky. Add whisky and raisins to batter.
◆ Pour batter into prepared pan and bake for 45-50 minutes.
◆ Remove from oven, turn onto a serving plate and sprinkle with powdered sugar.

Epiphany cake

Carrot cake

Time needed: *1 hour and 30 minutes*
Difficulty: easy

INGREDIENTS FOR 4-6 SERVINGS

1 lb of carrots
1 1/4 cups of flour
7 tablespoons of softened butter
1 cup of blanched chopped almonds
1 cup of sugar
1/2 cup of milk ◆ 3 eggs
1/4 teaspoon of baking powder
1 egg white
grated peel of 1 organic orange
1/4 teaspoon of cinnamon
a pinch of salt
powdered sugar

◆ Grease and flour a 10-inch cake pan. Preheat the oven to 350°F.
◆ Trim, peel and finely shred carrots.
◆ In a bowl, whisk butter and sugar until very creamy. Add the orange peel and cinnamon carefully. Mix in the eggs, one at a time.
◆ Add flour, chopped almonds and baking powder to the mixture. Stir in the milk. Beat eggs white and salt to stiff peaks. Delicately fold in the shredded carrots and egg white.
◆ Pour batter in prepared cake pan and bake for 35-40 minutes.
◆ Cool cake completely in pan before turning it onto a serving plate. Dust with powdered sugar and serve.

Carrot cake

Margaret cake

Time needed: *1 hour and 30 minutes*
Difficulty: easy

INGREDIENTS FOR 6 SERVINGS

3 cups of flour ◆ 8 eggs
1 1/2 cups of softened butter
2 1/2 cups of vanilla sugar
1 1/2 cups of grated bittersweet chocolate
2 cups of chopped walnuts
1/4 cup of amaretto liquor
a pinch of salt
powdered sugar
8 half walnuts

Margaret cake

◆ Grease and flour a 10-inch cake pan. Preheat the oven to 350°F.
◆ In a bowl, whisk butter until creamy; add egg yolks, one at a time. Whisk in the sugar, chocolate, chopped walnuts and liquor. Beat egg whites and salt to stiff peaks and fold in the batter.
◆ Sift flour and baking powder; delicately mix to the batter. Pour into the prepared pan.
◆ Bake cake for 55-60 minutes. Remove from oven, cool in the pan and turn onto a serving dish.
◆ Cover cake with sifted powdered sugar and decorate with walnuts.

Honey cake

Time needed: *1 hour and 10 minutes*
Difficulty: easy

INGREDIENTS FOR 6 SERVINGS

10 tablespoons of honey
3 cups of flour
1 cup of heavy cream
3/4 cup of hot milk
1/2 cup of sugar
1/2 cup of candied orange and lemon peel
2 teaspoons of baking powder
1/2 teaspoon of aniseeds
1/4 teaspoon of powdered clove
1/4 teaspoon of nutmeg
1/2 teaspoon of cinnamon
a pinch of salt

◆ Grease a loaf pan. Preheat the oven to 350°F.
◆ Dice the candied orange and lemon peel.
◆ In a bowl, whip the cream with 8 tablespoons of honey, sugar, chopped candied peel and all spices.
◆ Sift flour, baking powder and salt. Add to the cream mixture a little at a time. Stir in the hot milk to have a very thick batter.
◆ Pour batter in prepared pan and bake for 45 minutes. Remove and cool in pan.
◆ Turn cake onto a serving platter and brush with remaining honey.
◆ Instead of being brushed on cake, the honey can be diluted in 1/4 cup of warm rum and poured onto the hot cake. Rum-soaked raisins can also be added to the batter.

Genoa cake with coffee and pine nuts

Time needed: *1 hour*
Difficulty: easy

INGREDIENTS FOR 6-8 SERVINGS
2 cups of flour
3/4 cup of softened butter
1 cup of sugar
5 tablespoons of milk ◆ 2 eggs
2 tablespoons of instant espresso
1/2 cup of pine nuts
1/4 cup of raisins
1/4 cup of chopped walnuts
2 teaspoons of baking powder
a pinch of salt
powdered sugar

◆ Grease and flour a 10-inch cake pan. Preheat oven to 375°F.
◆ Soak raisins in warm water.
◆ In a bowl, whisk butter and sugar until creamy. Slowly add milk, egg yolks, sifted flour, baking powder, coffee, 2/3 of pine nuts, drained raisins and chopped walnuts. Mix well. Beat egg whites with salt to stiff peaks and fold into the batter.
◆ Pour batter in the cake pan and bake for 40 minutes in the oven. Cool the cake in pan. Turn onto a serving plate.
◆ Cover with sifted powdered sugar and decorate with remaining pine nuts.

Genoa cake with coffee and pine nuts

Amaretti cake

Time needed:
1 hour and 15 minutes
Difficulty: easy

INGREDIENTS FOR 8 SERVINGS
2 cups of amaretti
1 1/2 cups of flour
1 1/2 cups of potato starch
3/4 cup of sugar
10 tablespoons of butter ◆ 3 eggs
grated peel of one organic lemon
a pinch of salt
2 tablespoons of Marsala
1 teaspoon of baking powder
powdered sugar
6 amaretti
1 tablespoon of apricot jelly

Amaretti cake

◆ Grease and flour a 12-inch cake pan. Preheat the oven to 350°F.
◆ In a saucepan, melt butter and crush 2/3 of amaretti. Set aside.
◆ In a bowl, whisk egg yolks and sugar until pale and creamy. Add the melted butter and amaretti. Slowly add the flour, baking powder, potato starch and grated lemon peel. Beat egg whites and salt to stiff peaks; fold into the batter. Soak remaining amaretti in the Marsala.
◆ Pour 1/2 the batter into the cake pan. Place amaretti over and cover with remaining batter. Bake for 40-50 minutes. Turn onto a rack to cool.
◆ Sprinkle cake with powdered sugar. Melt apricot jelly and brush on 6 amaretti; decorate cake.

Edinburgh cake

Time needed: *1 hour and 45 minutes*
Difficulty: easy

INGREDIENTS FOR 6 SERVINGS
4 cups of flour
1 1/2 cups of butter
1 cup of sugar
1 cup of molasses
4 eggs
1 teaspoon of cinnamon
1 teaspoon of nutmeg
1/4 teaspoon of powdered clove
1 cup of chopped pitted dates
1/2 cup of chopped walnuts
1/2 cup of milk (as necessary)
a pinch of salt

◆ Grease and flour an 8-inch cake pan. Preheat oven to 350°F.
◆ In a bowl, sift flour, baking powder, salt, sugar and spices. Mix the dates and walnuts in.
◆ In a saucepan, warm molasses and melt butter. Beat eggs and add to the flour with molasses and butter. Stir in a little milk at a time, so the batter is not too fluid.
◆ Pour mixture in cake pan and bake for 30 minutes. Lower the temperature to 320°F and continue baking for 45 minutes.
◆ This spice cake can be stored in aluminum paper in a cool and dry place for several weeks.

181

Hazelnut "schiacciata"

Time needed: *55 minutes*
Difficulty: *easy*

INGREDIENTS FOR 6 SERVINGS
1 cup of unbleached flour
1/2 cup of corn flour
1/2 cup of toasted chopped hazelnuts
8 tablespoons of softened butter
1/2 cup of sugar
grated peel of one organic lemon
4 tablespoons of honey
1 egg yolk
1 tablespoon of powdered sugar

◆ Grease and flour a 10-inch cake pan. Preheat oven to 320°F.
◆ On a work surface, pour both flours into a mound with hazelnuts. In the center, add sugar, butter in small pieces, egg yolk, grated lemon peel and honey. Rapidly mix the ingredients with your fingertips.
◆ Transfer the dough into the cake pan, pressing to level.
◆ Bake for 30-35 minutes. Turn the "schiacciata" onto a rack and cool.
◆ Sprinkle with powdered sugar and serve in small portions.

Candied fruit baba

Time needed: *1 hour and 30 minutes*
Difficulty: *easy*

INGREDIENTS FOR 6-8 SERVINGS
2 1/2 cups of flour
3/4 cup of sugar
3/4 cup of softened butter
1/2 cup of blanched almonds
1/2 cup of candied cherries
1/2 cup of chopped dates
1/3 cup of milk
1/4 cup of raisins
1/4 cup of honey
1 jumbo egg
1 teaspoon of baking powder
4 tablespoons of apricot jelly
a pinch of salt

◆ Grease and flour a large baba mold. Preheat the oven to 360°F.
◆ In a large bowl, sift flour and baking powder. Add salt and sugar.
◆ Whisk in the butter, honey, egg and milk. When the batter is creamy and smooth, add dates and candied cherries.
◆ Pour batter into the mold. Sprinkle decoratively with almonds and raisins. Bake for 50-60 minutes.
◆ The cake is ready when a skewer inserted in the middle comes out clean. Remove from oven and turn onto a serving plate. Melt apricot jelly and brush the baba. Cool before serving.

Bermuda cake

Time needed: *1 hour*
Difficulty: *easy*

INGREDIENTS FOR 6 SERVINGS
7 tablespoons of butter
3/4 cup of sugar
2 cups of flour
2 teaspoons of baking powder
3/4 cup of fresh cream (or sour cream)
1/2 cup of candied citron
3/4 cup of raisins
1/2 teaspoon of cinnamon
1/4 teaspoon of nutmeg

◆ Grease and flour a loaf pan. Preheat the oven to 350°F.
◆ Soak raisins in warm water. Let the butter soften at room temperature. Finely chop the candied citron.
◆ Whisk butter until creamy; add sugar and whisk until light and creamy. Sift flour with baking powder and add to butter mixture. Stir the cream in.
◆ Drain and dry raisins. Roll raisins and citron in flour. Stir into batter, adding cinnamon and nutmeg.
◆ Pour batter into prepared pan and bake for 40-45 minutes or until a skewer inserted in the middle comes out clean and dry. Cool cake in pan. Turn onto a serving plate and serve cold.

Sand cake

Time needed: *1 hour and 40 minutes*
Difficulty: easy

INGREDIENTS FOR **6-8** SERVINGS
1 1/2 cups of softened butter
1 cup of sugar
1 1/2 cups of potato starch
3/4 cup of flour
3 eggs
2 egg yolks
grated peel of one organic lemon
2 teaspoons of vanilla sugar

◆ Line a 12-inch springform pan with parchment paper, grease and flour. Preheat oven to 350°F.
◆ In a bowl, whisk butter until creamy and light. Add egg yolks one at a time; add egg, whisking constantly. Add sugar, flour, potato starch and grated lemon peel.
◆ Pour the batter in pan and bake for 35-40 minutes.
◆ Cool completely before opening springform pan. Transfer cake to a serving plate and dust with vanilla sugar.
◆ This cake is even better if served two days later. Keep it wrapped in aluminum paper in a cool dry place.

Maraschino cake

Time needed: *1 hour and 20 minutes*
Difficulty: easy

INGREDIENTS FOR **8** SERVINGS
3 cups of flour
1 1/2 cups of softened butter
1/4 cup of Maraschino
1 1/4 teaspoons of baking powder
6 egg yolks
4 egg whites
1/2 cup of blanched, chopped almonds
1 teaspoon of vanilla
3/4 cup of sugar
1/2 cup of Maraschino cherries
a pinch of salt

◆ Grease a 10-inch cake pan and cover bottom and sides with chopped almonds. Preheat the oven to 360°F.

◆ Whisk butter with sugar. Add egg yolks one at a time. Cut cherries in half and stir into mixture. Sift flour and baking powder; add to mixture. Add Maraschino and vanilla. Beat egg whites and salt to firm peaks. Delicately fold into batter. Pour batter in cake pan and bake for 45-50 minutes. Remove from oven and leave cake in pan for 10 minutes. Turn onto a serving plate. Serve cold.

November cake

Time needed: *1 hour and 15 minutes*
Difficulty: medium

INGREDIENTS FOR **12-14** SERVINGS
1/2 lb of bittersweet chocolate
8 tablespoons of butter
3 eggs
3/4 cup of sugar
1/2 cup of flour
1/2 cup of shelled hazelnuts
4 tablespoons of Grand Marnier
a pinch of salt
1/2 teaspoon of baking powder
1 tablespoon of powdered sugar

◆ Line a springform pan with buttered parchment paper. Preheat the oven to 370°F.
◆ Place hazelnuts on a cookie sheet and toast in the oven for 5 minutes. Remove and immediately rub with a towel to remove skin; grind finely in a food processor.
◆ Chop chocolate and melt with butter in a double boiler. Mix well and remove from heat. In a bowl, mix egg yolks and 1/2 cup of sugar with an electric mixer until pale and creamy. Stir in chocolate mixture. Sift flour and baking powder and mix in. Stir in Grand Marnier and ground hazelnuts.
◆ In another bowl, beat egg whites and salt to soft peaks. Add remaining sugar a little at a time and beat to firm peaks. Delicately fold 1/3 of egg whites to chocolate batter. Fold in remaining egg whites.
◆ Pour batter in prepared pan and bake for 35-40 minutes. Remove and leave in pan for 10 minutes. Turn onto cake rack to cool completely.
◆ Transfer cake to a serving plate and dust with sifted, powdered sugar.

Line a low 12-inch cake pan with the wafers. Preheat the oven to 400°F.

◆ Place walnuts and almonds on a cookie sheet; toast in the oven for 5-6 minutes. Remove from the oven and coarsely chop. In a large bowl, mix the walnuts, almonds, candied citron, candied orange, allspice, coriander and cinnamon. Stir in the flour.

◆ Lower the oven to 350°F.

◆ In a saucepan, cook the powdered sugar (keep 1 tablespoon aside) and honey in 1 tablespoon of water on low heat, stirring continuously so the mixture does not stick to the pan. When mixture starts boiling, immerse a skewer in the syrup and drop it immediately

Panforte

Time needed:
1 hour
Difficulty: *easy*

**INGREDIENTS
FOR 6-8 SERVINGS**
*1 cup of flour
3/4 cup of powdered sugar
3/4 cup of honey
3/4 cup of walnuts
1 1/2 cups of blanched
almonds
1/4 cup of sliced,
candied citron
1 1/2 cups of sliced,
candied orange
1/2 teaspoon of cinnamon
1/4 teaspoon of allspice
1 teaspoon of powdered
coriander
1 teaspoon of vanilla sugar
15 large wafers*

in ice water. If the sugar forms a soft ball, it is ready.

◆ Remove saucepan from heat and pour syrup in the flour-fruit preparation, mixing well to incorporate all ingredients.

◆ Pour this mixture in the cake pan. Level with a wet knife. Sprinkle with remaining tablespoon of sugar. Bake for 25-30 minutes.

◆ Do not overbake. The panforte should not brown. Remove from oven and turn onto a rack. Cut off any wafers that sticks out from the sides and dust with vanilla sugar. Serve cold. Panforte can be kept for several weeks, stored in a metal box.

Belgian cake

Time needed: *55 minutes*
Difficulty: *easy*

INGREDIENTS FOR 6-8 SERVINGS
*1 1/4 cups of flour
9 tablespoons of softened butter
4 eggs ◆ 3/4 cup of sugar
grated peel of 2 organic oranges
powdered sugar
1 candied violet
1/2 cup of sliced almonds*

◆ Grease a 10-inch cake pan and line bottom and sides with almonds. Preheat oven to 350°F.
◆ In a bowl, mix butter, flour and grated orange peel, until well blended. Roll out mixture on a work surface and cut in 1/2-inch cubes.
◆ In another bowl, beat eggs and sugar until frothy. Mix in the butter-flour cubes until blended.
◆ Pour batter in the cake pan and bake for 35-40 minutes. Turn cake onto a rack and cool.
◆ Dust decoratively with powdered sugar and set a candied violet in the center.

Belgian cake

Burgundy cake

Burgundy cake

Time needed: *1 hour*
Difficulty: *easy*

INGREDIENTS FOR 6 SERVINGS
*1 1/3 cups of flour
1/2 cup of softened butter
2 organic oranges
2 eggs
1/2 teaspoon of vanilla
1/2 cup of powdered sugar
1 egg white
grated peel of one organic orange
1 tablespoon of orange juice
1 teaspoon of Kirsch*

◆ Grease and flour a 12-inch cake pan. Preheat the oven to 375°F.
◆ Rinse and dry oranges. Cut off peel (without any of the white pith) and chop it finely. Press the juice in a bowl.
◆ In a bowl, whisk butter and sugar until it is smooth, pale and thick. Mix in the orange juice. Slowly stir in the eggs, the flour, baking powder and the chopped orange peel.

Panforte

◆ Pour in the cake pan and bake for 30-40 minutes. Cool cake completely before turning onto a plate.
◆ In a bowl, mix egg white, orange juice, powdered sugar and Kirsch to a smooth icing paste. Spread icing all over cake.
◆ Sprinkle with grated orange peel and refrigerate until icing has solidified.

Dundee cake

Time needed: *2 hours and 30 minutes*
Difficulty: easy

INGREDIENTS FOR 6 SERVINGS

1/2 cup of currants
1/2 cup of raisins
1/2 cup of Malaga raisins
1/4 cup of candied orange peel
2 eggs
2 cups of flour
7 tablespoons of butter
3/4 cup of sugar
1/2 cup of shelled almonds
1 teaspoon of baking powder
grated peel of one organic orange or lemon
1/4 teaspoon of cinnamon
1/4 cup of brandy
1/4 teaspoon of nutmeg
a pinch of salt

◆ Grease and flour a 10-inch cake pan. Preheat the oven to 370°F.
◆ Bring butter to room temperature. Chop candied orange peel finely.
◆ Scald almonds in boiling water, drain, peel and chop.
◆ Sift flour with baking powder, salt, nutmeg and cinnamon.
◆ Soak currants and raisins in warm water for 5 minutes. Drain, dry and pass in flour.
◆ In a bowl, whisk butter and sugar until creamy and smooth. Alternating, mix in the eggs and the flour mixture. Add raisins, currants, grated orange peel, candied peel, almonds and brandy. The batter should be thick.
◆ Pour batter in cake pan and bake for 50-60 minutes.
◆ This cake should be served cold.

Corn flour and almond cake

Almond cake

Corn flour and almond cake

Time needed: *1 hour*
Difficulty: easy

INGREDIENTS FOR 8 SERVINGS

1 1/2 cups of flour
1/2 cup of unbleached flour
1 cup of softened butter
1/2 cup of sugar ◆ 2 eggs
6 tablespoons of milk
grated peel of one organic lemon
3/4 cup of blanched, chopped almonds
1/2 cup of raisins
1 1/2 teaspoons of baking powder
1 tablespoon of powdered sugar

◆ Grease and flour a 10-inch cake pan. Preheat the oven to 375°F.
◆ Soak raisins in warm water until soft, drain, dry and toss them in flour.
◆ In a bowl, whisk butter and sugar until creamy. Add eggs, one at a time. Sift flour and baking powder; add to mixture. Mix in milk, lemon peel, almonds and raisins. Mix all ingredients well. Pour batter in cake pan and bake for 1 hour.
◆ Turn the cake onto a rack and cool completely. Transfer to a plate and dust with powdered sugar.

Almond cake II

Time needed: *1 hour and 20 minutes*
Difficulty: easy

INGREDIENTS FOR 6-8 SERVINGS

2 1/2 cups of blanched almonds
1 1/2 cups of sugar
4 eggs ◆ 2 organic oranges
2 tablespoons of orange jam
3 tablespoons of candied orange peel

◆ Butter a 12-inch cake pan, line the bottom with parchment paper, butter again and flour. Preheat the oven to 350°F.
◆ Rinse and dry oranges; grate peel of 1 orange and press juice of both.
◆ Toast the almonds in the oven. Set aside 1/4 cup. Grind the remainder.
◆ In a bowl, whisk egg yolks and sugar until creamy and pale. Add ground almonds, orange peel and juice. Beat egg whites and salt to firm

peaks. Fold in the preparation. Pour batter in cake pan.
◆ Bake for 50-60 minutes. Turn cake onto a rack, remove parchment paper and cool completely.
◆ Coarsely chop remaining almonds. Slice the candied orange peel in julienne.
◆ On low heat, melt the orange jam in 1 tablespoon of water. Brush cake with jam, press almonds around sides and decorate with sliced orange peel.

Swiss egg white cake

Time needed: *1 hour and 10 minutes*
Difficulty: *easy*

INGREDIENTS FOR 6 SERVINGS

1 cup of flour
6 egg whites
3/4 cup of sugar
1/2 cup of raisins
1/4 cup of candied cherries
1/4 cup of candied citron
4 fresh apricots
5 tablespoons of butter
a pinch of salt
powdered sugar

Decoration:
5 candied cherries
candied citron

◆ Grease and flour a 12-inch cake pan. Preheat the oven to 400°F.
◆ Soak raisins in warm water. Pit the apricots and dice. Drain raisins, dry, set 1 teaspoon aside and roll remainder in flour. Chop candied cherries in half and candied citron finely.
◆ In a bowl, beat egg whites and salt to stiff peaks. Whisk in sugar. Delicately fold in the flour, candied fruit, apricots, raisins and melted butter.
◆ Pour batter in pan. Bake for 45-50 minutes. Remove from oven, turn onto a plate and cool.
◆ Dust cake with powdered sugar. Cut cherries in half. Decorate cake with remaining raisins, cherries and candied citron cut into leaf shapes.

Swiss egg white cake

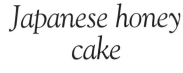

Japanese honey cake

Time needed: *1 hour and 10 minutes*
Difficulty: *easy*

INGREDIENTS FOR 6-8 SERVINGS
10 tablespoons of honey
4 eggs
1 cup of sugar
3 cups of flour
1 teaspoon of baking powder
powdered sugar

◆ Grease and flour a 12-inch cake pan. Preheat the oven to 350°F.
◆ In a bowl, whisk egg whites with sugar and honey. Slowly add the flour and baking powder, whisking until well mixed.
◆ Cool the cake in pan. Turn onto a serving plate and sprinkle with sifted powdered sugar.

Castagnaccio

Time needed: *45 minutes*
Difficulty: *easy*

INGREDIENTS FOR 6-8 SERVINGS
3 cups of chestnut flour
1/2 cup of raisins
1/2 cup of pine nuts
1 branch of rosemary
3/4 cup of milk
a pinch of salt
2 tablespoons of extra virgin olive oil

◆ Brush a 14-inch pizza pan with a little extra virgin olive oil. Preheat the oven to 350°F.
◆ Soak raisins in warm water until soft. Tear off the leaves from rosemary.
◆ Sift flour and salt in a large bowl. Slowly mix in milk and 1 cup of water, stirring well to eliminate any lumps.
◆ Pour batter in prepared pan. Sprinkle with drained raisins, pine nuts and rosemary. Drizzle with extra virgin olive oil. Bake for 25-30 minutes.
◆ Turn castagnaccio onto serving plate and serve warm or cold.

Castagnaccio

Grease and flour a cookie sheet. Preheat the oven to 400°F.

◆ Put pâte à choux in a pastry bag, fitted with a straight tube. Make a donut shape on the cookie sheet with pâte à choux..

◆ Bake for 40 minutes. Cool.

◆ Rinse strawberries in ice water, dry and slice. Keep aside a few whole strawberries for decoration.

◆ Bring milk and lemon peel to boil. Set aside.

◆ In a saucepan, mix egg yolks with sugar. Add flour and slowly mix in the hot milk. Stirring constantly, bring cream to boil and

Baba surprise

Time needed:
1 hour and 20 minutes
Difficulty: medium

**INGREDIENTS
FOR 4-6 SERVINGS**
*2 cups of pâte à choux
(see page 11)
grated peel of 1 lemon
3/4 cup of milk
2 egg yolks
3 tablespoons of sugar
1/2 cup of flour
3 tablespoons of whipped
cream
3/4 lb of strawberries
2 tablespoons of butte*

Decoration:
*1/2 cup of powdered sugar
1 egg white
a few drops of Alchermes*

cook for 7 minutes.

◆ Cool cream, stirring from time to time. Blend in sliced strawberries and whipped cream.

◆ Slice the baba (donut) in half with a serrated knife. Spread pastry cream on the bottom layer and garnish with a few remaining strawberries.

◆ Mix powdered sugar, egg whites and Alchermes to get a glossy and smooth icing. Brush on the top part of the baba.

◆ When icing has solidified, put top part of baba on top of the cream. Decorate with strawberries.

Truffled orange cake

Time needed: *1 hour and 15 minutes*
Difficulty: medium

INGREDIENTS FOR 8-10 SERVINGS
*1 cup of flour
1/2 cup of potato starch
1/2 cup of cocoa ◆ 6 eggs
6 tablespoons of butter
3/4 cup of sugar
1 teaspoon of vanilla*

Syrup:
*1 cup of sugar
grated peel of one organic orange
3 tablespoons of Grand Marnier*

Ganache:
*3 cups of chopped bittersweet chocolate
1 1/2 cups of heavy cream
3 tablespoons of Grand Marnier*

Decoration:
*1 tablespoon of cocoa
2 tablespoons of chocolate chips
1 large piece of white chocolate
2 tablespoons of sliced candied orange peel*

*Truffled orange
cake*

◆ Grease and flour a 12-inch cake pan. Preheat the oven to 200°F.
In a saucepan, melt the butter. In a bowl, whisk eggs and sugar, with an electric mixer, until pale and creamy. Delicately add flour, starch, cocoa, vanilla and melted butter, stirring.
◆ Pour batter in the pan and bake for 40 minutes. Turn cake onto a rack and cool.
◆ Make the ganache: In a double boiler, melt chocolate in the cream. Cool and add Grand Marnier. When cold, whisk mixture with an electric mixer, until doubled in volume.
◆ Prepare the syrup: boil 3/4 cup of water with sugar and orange peel. Cook for 2-3 minutes. Remove from heat, add Grand Marnier and set aside to cool.
◆ Slice the cake in two circles. Brush one circle with the syrup; spread 1/3 of ganache over it; cover with a second layer of cake and brush with syrup. Cover with remaining ganache.
◆ To decorate, put a small circle of waxed paper in center of cake. Powder cake with sifted cocoa. Remove paper. Grate white chocolate curls and place on center of cake with candied orange peel. Press chocolate chips around cake.

Baba surprise

Zabaglione pie

Time needed: *1 hour and 20 minutes*
Difficulty: medium

INGREDIENTS FOR 8-10 SERVINGS

1/2 cup of flour
1/2 cup of potato starch
1/2 cup of sugar
3 eggs
4 tablespoons of butter

Filling:
5 egg yolks
3/4 cup of Marsala
1/2 cup of white wine
3 tablespoons of flour
1 cup of heavy cream
4 tablespoons of Grand Marnier

Decoration:
1/2 cup of bittersweet chocolate
1/2 cup of heavy cream

Zabaglione pie

◆ Grease and flour a 12-inch round cake pan. Preheat the oven to 350°F.
◆ In a bowl, whisk eggs and sugar with an electric mixer, until pale and thick. Sift flour and potato starch; delicately mix in egg mixture. Stir in the melted butter.
◆ Pour into the cake pan and bake for 30-40 minutes. When ready, turn cake onto a rack and cool.
◆ Prepare the filling: In a saucepan, heat wine and Marsala. In a bowl, mix egg yolks and sugar with a wooden spoon. Stir in the flour and, slowly, the hot wine. Transfer to a saucepan and stirring continuously, bring to a boil. Cook cream for 3-4 minutes on low heat. Cool cream completely, mixing from time to time.
◆ Slice cake in half. Brush 1 circle with Grand Marnier and cover with 1/3 of filling cream. Cover with the second circle, brush with Grand Marnier and cover cake with cream.
◆ To decorate, melt chocolate and cream in a double boiler. Pour in a paper cone and design a chocolate spiral on cake. With a toothpick, starting at the center, draw lines through the chocolate circles.
◆ Transfer to a serving plate and refrigerate.

The duke's cake

Time needed: *1 hour*
Difficulty: medium

INGREDIENTS FOR 8-10 SERVINGS

5 egg whites
3/4 cup of sugar
1 teaspoon of vanilla
1 cup of ground toasted almonds
a pinch of salt

Filling:
4 egg whites
1/2 cup of sugar
1 1/4 cups of softened butter
a pinch of salt
1 tablespoon of rum
1/2 cup of bittersweet chocolate
1 tablespoon of instant espresso coffee

Syrup:
1/4 cup of water
1/4 cup of sugar
1 orange peel
2 tablespoons of Cointreau

Decoration:
3/4 cup of heavy cream
1/4 lb of milk chocolate
1 tablespoon of apricot jelly

◆ Grease 3 cake pans. Line bottoms with parchment paper, butter again and flour. Preheat the oven to 400°F.
◆ In a bowl, beat egg whites and salt, with an electric mixer, to soft peaks; add sugar and vanilla; beat to firm peaks. Fold in the almonds.
◆ Divide in the 3 cake pans. Bake for 15 minutes. Turn off oven, open door and cool in the oven. Turn circles onto a rack to cool completely.
◆ For the filling, make a classic butter cream (see page 17).
◆ Divide butter cream in 3 bowls. To one add rum; to the other, add melted chocolate; to the last, add coffee melted in 1 tablespoon of water.
◆ In a saucepan, boil water, sugar, orange peel for 3 minutes. Cool and mix in Cointreau.
◆ Put one circle of meringue on a serving plate. Brush with a little syrup and cover with rum but-

The duke's cake

ter cream. Cover with the second circle, brush with syrup and cover with chocolate butter cream. Cover with last meringue, brush with syrup and cover with coffee cream.

◆ Whip the cream and spread over coffee butter cream. Make little milk chocolate curls and sprinkle over cream. Refrigerate.

◆ Cut a long piece of waxed paper.

◆ Melt leftover milk chocolate in a double boiler and spread over the strip of waxed paper.

◆ Remove cake from refrigerator. Brush sides of cake with melted apricot jelly. Envelop cake in the chocolate strip, the waxed paper on the outside. Refrigerate. Before serving, remove waxed paper.

Fernand Point cake

Fernand Point cake

Time needed: *1 hour and 20 minutes*
Difficulty: **medium**

INGREDIENTS FOR **6-8** SERVINGS
1 1/4 cups of flour
1 cup of softened butter
4 eggs ◆ *1 1/2 cups of sugar*
1 cup of grated bittersweet chocolate
a pinch of salt

Butter cream:
1 cup of chopped milk chocolate
1 cup of chopped bittersweet chocolate
1/2 cup of heavy cream
5 tablespoons of butter
1 tablespoon of rum

Decoration:
1/4 lb of bittersweet chocolate
1 tablespoon of powdered sugar

◆ Grease a 12-inch cake pan. Line with parchment paper. Grease again and flour. Preheat the oven to 350°F.

◆ In a bowl, whisk butter and 1/3 of sugar. Add egg yolks, one at a time and remaining sugar. Whisk until pale and creamy. Add grated chocolate and flour. Beat egg whites and salt to firm peaks; fold into mixture.

◆ Pour into cake pan and bake for 55-60 minutes. Turn onto a rack to cool. Peel off paper.

◆ For the butter cream, melt both chocolates in a double boiler with cream and butter. Cool and mix in rum.

◆ Cover cake completely with this butter cream, keeping 2 tablespoons aside.

◆ Grate bittersweet chocolate in tiny rolls. Use to cover cake. Dust with powdered sugar.

◆ Using a fork, decorate sides of cake with leftover butter cream.

Swiss almond cake

Time needed: *1 hour and 20 minutes*
Difficulty: **medium**

INGREDIENTS FOR **8-10** SERVINGS
6 eggs ◆ *3 egg yolks*
3/4 cup of sugar
1 cup of cornstarch
1 cup of flour
1/2 cup of finely chopped toasted almonds
6 tablespoons of butter
1 teaspoon of vanilla

Filling:
1 cup of sugar
3/4 cup of almonds
3 egg whites
1/2 tablespoon of lemon juice
1 tablespoon of almond oil
14 tablespoons of butter
2 tablespoons of Maraschino
a pinch of salt

Decoration:
1/2 cup of toasted slivered almonds
1 tablespoon of cocoa

◆ Grease and flour a 10-inch cake pan. Preheat the oven to 375°F.

◆ Melt butter on low heat. In a bowl, whisk eggs, egg yolks, sugar and vanilla with an electric mixer until creamy. Sift flour and cornstarch together; add to mixture with almonds and melted butter.

◆ Pour in cake pan and bake for 40 minutes. Turn onto a rack and cool.

◆ Prepare the filling. With sugar, almonds, lemon juice, and almond oil, prepare an almond brittle (see page 21) and, when cold, chop it finely. With the remaining ingredients, prepare a butter cream (see page 17). Fold in almond brittle and Maraschino.

◆ Slice the cake in two circles. Spread a circle with 1/3 of prepared filling. Cover with the second circle and spread remaining filling all over the cake.

Swiss almond cake

▶

◆ Decorate with the slivered almonds. Place strips of cardboard on the cake and sprinkle cocoa over the uncovered surface. Remove strips before serving.

Hazelnut cream cake

Time needed: *1 hour and 20 minutes*
Difficulty: *medium*

INGREDIENTS FOR 6-8 SERVINGS
1/2 cup of flour
1/4 cup of potato starch
1/2 cup of sugar ◆ *4 eggs*
3/4 cup of chopped pralined hazelnuts
2 tablespoons of Kirsch ◆ *a pinch of salt*
Filling:
1 1/4 cups of toasted chopped hazelnuts
1/2 cup of sugar ◆ *2 cups of milk*
1/2 cup of flour ◆ *5 egg yolks*
1/2 teaspoon of vanilla
grated peel of one organic lemon
Decoration:
3/4 cup of coarsely chopped toasted hazelnuts
1/2 cup of heavy cream
12 praline hazelnuts
a few mint leaves
1 tablespoon of apricot jelly

◆ Grease and flour a 10-inch cake pan. Preheat the oven to 350°F.
◆ In a bowl, beat egg yolks and sugar until pale and creamy. Sift flour and potato starch; add to egg yolks with praline hazelnuts and Kirsch. Beat egg whites and salt to firm peaks; fold into mixture.
◆ Pour into cake pan and bake for about 40 minutes. Turn onto a rack and cool.
◆ Prepare the filling, following the directions for pastry cream (see page 16). Fold hazelnuts in and let cool.
◆ Slice the cake into three circles. Spread the bottom circle with half the filling. Cover with the second circle. Spread the remaining filling and top with the last circle.
◆ Warm up the jelly with a tablespoon of water and brush evenly over the whole cake. Gently press over it the chopped hazelnuts.
◆ Whip the cream. Transfer to a pastry bag, fitted with a star tube and make eight little rosettes at the border of the cake and a large one in the center.
◆ Decorate the mounds with pralined hazelnuts and mint leaves.

Graz chocolate cake

Time needed: *1 hour and 10 minutes*
(plus refrigeration time)
Difficulty: *medium*

INGREDIENTS FOR 8-10 SERVINGS
1 1/4 cups of flour
10 tablespoons of softened butter
1/4 cup of powdered sugar
1 teaspoon of vanilla
6 eggs
1 cup of chopped bittersweet chocolate
3/4 cup of sugar
a pinch of salt
Cream:
1 cup of heavy cream
1/2 cup of chopped milk chocolate
Syrup:
1/4 cup of sugar
2 tablespoons of rum
Decoration:
1 1/4 cups of chopped white chocolate
1/2 cup of chopped bittersweet chocolate
3 oz of milk chocolate

◆ The day before, melt chocolate with heavy cream in a double boiler and refrigerate for 12 hours.
◆ Grease and flour a 10-inch spring cake pan. Preheat the oven to 350°F.
◆ Melt in a double boiler the bittersweet chocolate. In a bowl, whisk butter, sugar and powdered sugar until creamy.
◆ Add the egg yolks, one at a time and melted chocolate, stirring. Fold in flour and vanilla. Beat egg whites and salt to firm peaks; fold into mixture.
◆ Pour into cake pan and bake for 35-40 minutes. Turn onto a rack and cool.
◆ Make the syrup: Cook sugar in 1/4 cup of water for about 3 minutes. Cool; stir in the rum.
◆ Whip the refrigerated cream-chocolate mixture and set aside 2 tablespoons for decoration.
◆ Slice cake in 2 circles. Brush bottom circle with rum syrup and spread with half cream-chocolate mixture. Top with remaining circle, brush with remaining rum syrup and cover with remaining cream-chocolate mixture. Refrigerate.
◆ To decorate, shave milk chocolate. In a double boiler, melt white chocolate, evenly spread over cake and refrigerate. When white chocolate is solid, spread the 2 tablespoons of chocolate cream around sides of cake and gently press chocolate shavings.
◆ In a double boiler, melt bittersweet chocolate,

pour it on marble surface and when solid, cut out a flower for the center of cake. Pour remaining melted chocolate in a waxed paper cone and decorate with lines of chocolate.

Austrian raspberry cake

Time needed: *1 hour and 20 minutes (plus refrigeration time)*
Difficulty: *medium*

INGREDIENTS FOR 8 SERVINGS
*1 cup of powdered sugar
1 cup of flour
1 tablespoon of bitter cocoa powder
3/4 cup of finely chopped toasted hazelnuts
9 egg whites
a pinch of salt*

Filling:
*1 lb of raspberries
1 1/2 cups of heavy cream
3 tablespoons of powdered sugar*

Decoration:
*1/2 cup of heavy cream
5 candied violets
1/2 cup of raspberries*

◆ Line 2 cookie sheets with parchment paper and with a pencil draw three 10-inch circles. Preheat the oven to 300°F.
◆ In a large bowl, whisk egg whites and salt to stiff but not dry peaks. Add sugar by the spoonful, whisking after each addition. Fold in hazelnuts, flour and cocoa. Pour batter onto the 3 circles. Bake for 40 to 45 minutes until golden on the outside but still soft on the inside. Cool on a wire rack.
◆ For the filling wash raspberry in ice water and dry on a towel. Whip cream with powdered sugar.
◆ Place one cake circle on a serving plate. Spread over 1/3 of whipped cream and a layer of raspberry. Cover with another circle, a layer of cream, a layer of raspberry, and finish with the last cake circle and whipped cream. Refrigerate for 12 hours.
◆ For the decoration, whip cream to stiff peaks. Using a pastry bag fitted with a star tip pipe rosette of whipped cream around the border of cake and in the center. Decorate the border rosette with raspberry and the center with candied violets.

Ukrainian cake

Time needed: *1 hour and 30 minutes (plus resting time)*
Difficulty: *medium*

INGREDIENTS FOR 8-10 SERVINGS
*1/2 cup of poppy seeds
4 eggs
1 1/2 cups of sugar
1 cup of sour cream
3 cups of flour
3 teaspoons baking powder
a pinch of salt*

Cream:
*1 cup of chopped bittersweet chocolate
3 tablespoons of heavy cream
2 egg yolks
1/4 cup of sugar
6 tablespoons of butter, softened
1 teaspoon of cocoa*

Decoration:
*1/2 cup of chopped bittersweet chocolate
1/2 cup of heavy cream
1 tablespoon of powdered sugar
2 tablespoons of poppy seeds*

◆ Grease and flour a 10-inch springform cake pan. Preheat the oven to 350°F.
◆ Soak poppy seeds 15 minutes in hot water. Drain, dry on a towel and place in the oven on a piece of parchment paper to dry completely, shaking the seeds from time to time.
◆ With an electric mixer, beat eggs and sugar for about a minute and add sour cream. Fold in flour, poppy seeds, baking powder and salt. Pour into cake pan and bake for 45-50 minutes. Turn cake onto a wire rack and let cool.
◆ Prepare the filling: In a double boiler, melt chocolate in cream. In a bowl, whisk egg yolks and sugar; add butter in pieces and cocoa. Fold in the melted chocolate and refrigerate for about 30 minutes.
◆ Cut cold cake in half and spread bottom half with filling. Top with remaining cake half.
◆ For the decoration, in double boiler, melt chocolate; spread to a thickness of 1/4 inch on a sheet of parchment paper . When set, cut out 8 little disks.
◆ Dust cake with powdered sugar, arrange chocolate disks along the border and decorate them with a rosette of whipped cream and few poppy seeds.

Grease and flour a 10-inch cake pan.

♦ In a bowl, whisk butter and sugar until creamy and smooth. Beat in egg yolks, one at a time.

♦ Melt chocolate in a double boiler and, when cool, fold into butter mixture. Gradually add flour and beat egg whites to firm peaks and fold into batter.

♦ Pour batter into cake pan and bake for approximately 40 minutes.

♦ Turn onto a rack and cool. Slice cold cake

Sacher torte

Time needed:
1 hour and 30 minutes
Difficulty: medium

**INGREDIENTS
FOR 6 SERVINGS**
*3/4 cup of softened butter
3/4 cup of sugar
6 eggs
1 cup of bittersweet chocolate
1 1/2 cups of flour
1/2 cup of apricot jam*

Decoration:
*1/4 cup of powdered sugar
2 tablespoons of butter
2-3 tablespoons of milk
8 oz of bittersweet chocolate*

in half horizontally and spread bottom half with 1/3 of warmed apricot jam. Cover with remaining cake half and spread remaining jam over top and side.

♦ For decoration, chop 3/4 of the chocolate and melt in a double boiler with butter, sugar, and milk, stirring constantly. Cool briefly and pour over the cake; spread evenly.

♦ Melt the remaining chocolate in a double boiler and pour into a paper cone. In chocolate, write the name that made this torte famous: SACHER.

Cake with lemon icing

Time needed: *1 hour and 15 minutes*
Difficulty: medium

INGREDIENTS FOR 8-10 SERVINGS
*1/2 cup of flour ♦ 3 eggs
2 tablespoons of potato starch
1/2 cup of sugar
6 tablespoons of melted butter
1 teaspoon of vanilla*

Cream:
*4 egg yolks
4 tablespoons of softened butter
1/2 cup of sugar
juice of 3 lemons*

Syrup:
*1/4 cup of sugar
3 tablespoons of Maraschino
grated peel of 1/2 lemon*

Glaze:
*3/4 cup of sugar
1 organic lemon
2 tablespoons of chopped pistachios*

♦ Grease and flour a 10-inch cake pan. Preheat the oven to 350°F.

*Cake with
lemon icing*

♦ In a large bowl, whisk eggs and sugar until light and creamy. Sift flour and potato starch; fold into egg mixture. Stir in vanilla and melted butter.
♦ Pour into cake pan and bake for 35-40 minutes. Turn onto a wire rack and cool.
♦ For the filling, in a double boiler, whisk egg yolks and sugar until pale and creamy. Remove from heat; add lemon juice. Return to heat and stir until mixture has thickened sufficiently to coat the back of a spoon; do not boil.
♦ Remove from heat; add butter, a tablespoon at a time, stirring after each addition. Cool completely.
♦ Make the syrup: In a saucepan, boil sugar and lemon peel in 1/2 cup of water for 2 minutes. Cool. Add rum and Maraschino.
♦ Make the icing: Wash and dry lemon; grate the peel and press the juice. In a bowl, mix powdered sugar with grated lemon peel and 2 tablespoons of juice until mixture is thick and smooth.
♦ Slice cold cake in half horizontally and brush bottom half with syrup; spread filling evenly. Cover with remaining cake half and brush with remaining syrup.
♦ Cover cake with lemon icing, spreading with a spatula, and garnish with pistachios.
♦ Transfer to a serving plate and refrigerate until icing is set.

Sacher torte

"Mascotte" cake

Time needed: *1 hour and 20 minutes*
Difficulty: *medium*

INGREDIENTS FOR 6-8 SERVINGS
1/2 cup of flour
2 tablespoons of cornstarch
3/4 cup of sugar ◆ *4 eggs*
2 tablespoons of Kirsch
a pinch of salt
3/4 cup of pralined almonds

Filling:
14 tablespoons of softened butter
1/2 cup of sugar
1 egg white ◆ *a pinch of salt*
1/2 cup of chopped bittersweet chocolate

Decoration:
1/2 cup of powdered sugar
2 tablespoons of butter
1 tablespoon of milk
3/4 cup of chopped bittersweet chocolate
12 almond slivers ◆ *lemon juice*
1/2 cup of chopped toasted almonds

◆ Grease and flour a square 8-inch cake pan. Preheat the oven to 370°F.
◆ With an electric mixer, whisk egg yolks and sugar until pale and creamy. Slowly add flour and potato starch, chopped pralined almonds and Kirsch. Beat egg whites and salt to firm peaks; fold into mixture.
◆ Pour batter in pan; bake for 30-40 minutes. Turn on cake rack and cool.
◆ Prepare filling (see butter cream recipe on page 17). Set aside 1/3 of the butter cream for decoration. Melt the chocolate and stir into remaining butter cream.
◆ Slice cake in 3 circles. Place one on a serving plate, spread with half of the chocolate cream. Cover with another cake circle and spread with remaining chocolate cream. Cover with the last cake circle.
◆ Cover sides of cake with white butter cream and press the chopped walnuts to stick.
◆ In a double boiler, melt chocolate with butter, milk and 2/3 of powdered sugar. Spread evenly on top of cake. Arrange 3 almond slices at each corner of cake.
◆ Mix remaining powdered sugar with a few drops of lemon juice; pour into a waxed paper cone and decorate, writing in the center, the name "Mascotte."

"Mascotte" cake

Success cake

Time needed: *2 hours*
Difficulty: *medium*

INGREDIENTS FOR 8-10 SERVINGS
3/4 cup of egg whites
3/4 cup of sugar
1 teaspoon of vanilla
1 cup of ground almonds
a pinch of salt

Cream:
1/2 cup of egg white
1/2 cup of sugar
3/4 cup of softened butter
a pinch of salt
1 tablespoon of cocoa
2 tablespoons of Maraschino

Decoration:
/4 cup of almonds
1 tablespoon of apricot jam
1 tablespoon of powdered sugar
3 pralined almonds

◆ Grease and flour a cookie sheet and draw three 8-inch circles. Preheat oven to 200°F.
◆ Beat egg whites with vanilla and salt to soft peaks, adding sugar, 1 teaspoon at a time; continue beating until the mixture stands in stiff peaks. Gently fold in chopped almonds and using a pastry bag fitted with plain tube, pipe rings into the 3 circles filling them completely.
◆ Bake for 1 hour and 30 minutes. Cool on a wire rack.
◆ Preheat the oven to 360°F.
◆ Prepare butter cream (see page 17). Divide in two. To one, add cocoa and to the other, add the Maraschino.
◆ With a very sharp knife, cut 3 equal circles. On a serving plate, place 1 circle and spread with chocolate butter cream. Cover with another circle, cover with Maraschino butter cream and finish with the third circle.
◆ Lightly toast almonds in the oven and chop coarsely.
◆ Warm apricot jelly with a spoonful of water; brush top of cake. Cover cake with chopped almonds. In the center of cake, make a triangle with the powdered sugar. Decorate with the 3 pralined almonds in the middle.

Success cake

Madrilena cake

Time needed: *1 hour and 15 minutes*
(plus refrigeration time)
Difficulty: medium

INGREDIENTS FOR 8 SERVINGS
4 eggs
1 egg yolk
1/2 cup of sugar
2 tablespoons of heavy cream
1/2 cup of cornstarch
1/2 cup of flour
1 teaspoon of vanilla
a pinch of salt

Filling:
1 cup of milk ◆ 4 egg yolks
2 cups of heavy cream
1/2 cup of sugar
3 teaspoons of almond milk
2 teaspoons of unflavored gelatin

Decoration:
1/2 cup of sugar
1 teaspoon of lemon juice
3/4 cup of heavy cream
1 tablespoon of oil

◆ Grease and flour four 10-inch cake pans. Preheat oven to 375 °F.
◆ In a bowl, with an electric mixer, whisk 5 egg yolks and 1/2 the sugar until pale and creamy. Add cream, sifted flour and vanilla.
◆ In another bowl, beat egg whites and salt to soft peaks. Continue to beat, adding 1 teaspoon of sugar at a time, to stiff peaks. Gently mix in cornstarch and fold into egg yolk mixture.
◆ Pour 1/4 of mixture into each cake pan, spreading it in an even layer. Bake for 15 minutes. Turn onto a rack and cool.
◆ For the filling, soften gelatin in a little water. Bring milk to boil. In a saucepan, beat egg yolks and sugar until thick. Slowly beat milk into egg mixture. Cook on low heat, stirring until mixture has thickened sufficiently to coat the back of a spoon; do not boil. Remove from heat; add gelatin and mix well. Strain into clean bowl. Cool and fold in almond milk and whipped cream.
◆ On a serving plate, place a layer of cake; spread with a thin layer of filling. Cover with another layer of cake and spread again with filling. Cover with a third cake and finish with the filling. Refrigerate for about 2 hours.

Madrilena cake

◆ For the decoration, cook sugar and lemon twice to get a light caramel; spread evenly on the top of fourth cake. Out of the center of this fourth cake, cut a 4-inch circle.
◆ With an oiled knife, cut the remaining caramelized cake into 9 triangles.
◆ When ready to serve, place the caramelized disk in the center of the cake. Using a pastry bag fitted with a star tube, pipe 9 rosettes of whipped cream along the side of the cake. Gently place the 9 caramelized triangles on top of the 9 rosettes.

Millefeuille with cream

Time needed: *1 hour*
Difficulty: complex

INGREDIENTS FOR 6-8 SERVINGS
1 lb of puff pastry (see page 12)
3 tablespoons of powdered sugar

Pastry cream:
2 egg yolks
1/4 cup of sugar
2 cups of milk
2 tablespoons of flour
1 teaspoon of vanilla
grated peel of 1/2 organic lemon

◆ Preheat the oven to 425°F.
◆ Prepare the pastry cream (see page 16). Cool.
◆ Roll out puff pastry to 1/8-inch thickness. Cut out three 10-inch circles. Brush a baking sheet with water. Lifting carefully, place circles and trimmings on baking sheet. Prick all over with a fork and bake until lightly golden.
◆ Dust with powdered sugar and return to oven until golden-brown. Remove from oven and cool on a wire rack.
◆ Trim edges with a very sharp knife to make all circles even.
◆ Place one pastry circle on a serving plate and spread with 1/2 of pastry cream. Lay another circle on top and spread with remaining pastry cream. Top with remaining circle.
◆ Crush pastry trimmings and press into sides of millefeuille. Dust with powdered sugar.

Millefeuille with cream

Cointreau millefeuille

Time needed: *1 hour and 20 minutes*
Difficulty: *complex*

INGREDIENTS FOR 4-6 SERVINGS
1 lb of puff pastry (see page 12)
2 cups of milk ◆ *5 egg yolks*
1/2 cup of sugar ◆ *1/2 cup of flour*
1 teaspoon of vanilla
2 tablespoons of chopped toasted hazelnuts
2 tablespoons of Cointreau
1 1/2 cups of whipping cream
powdered sugar

◆ Preheat the oven to 425°F.
◆ Roll puff pastry out to a 1/8-inch thickness. Cut out five 10-inch squares. Brush a cookie sheet with water; place squares on sheet and prick all over with a fork. Bake for 15-20 minutes.
◆ Prepare the cream: In a saucepan, beat egg yolks and sugar. Add flour, vanilla and hot milk. Cook on low heat 5-6 minutes, stirring continuously. Pour cream into two bowls. Let it cool and stir to cool completely. In one bowl, add chopped hazelnuts, and in the other, add the Cointreau.
◆ Whip the cream and gently fold half into the hazelnut preparation and the rest into the liquor preparation.
◆ Trim edges of pastry squares. Spread a section with half of hazelnut cream; cover with another section of pastry; spread with half of Cointreau cream. Continue this way, finishing the millefeuille with a pastry section.
◆ Refrigerate. Just before serving, dust with powdered sugar.

Torino cake

Time needed: *1 hour and 15 minutes*
Difficulty: *medium*

INGREDIENTS FOR 8-10 SERVINGS
1 cup of flour ◆ *1/2 cup of sugar* ◆ *3 eggs*
4 tablespoons of butter
1/3 cup of toasted hazelnuts
Syrup:
1/4 cup of sugar ◆ *3 tablespoons of rum*
Decoration:
1 1/4 cups of whipping cream ◆ *10 pistachios*
1 cup of chopped marrons glacés
3 tablespoons of apricot jam
1/2 cup of powdered sugar
a few drops of rum ◆ *1 egg white*

◆ Grease and flour an 8-inch square cake pan. Preheat oven to 350°F. Chop hazelnuts finely.
◆ In a bowl, using an electric mixer, beat eggs and sugar until thick and pale. Fold in sifted flour flour, hazelnuts and melted butter. Pour into cake pan and bake for 30-40 minutes. Turn onto a rack and cool.
◆ Make the syrup: Cook sugar in 1/2 cup water for about 2-3 minutes. Cool and mix in the rum.
◆ Whip the cream. Cut cake in half crosswise. Brush bottom half with a little syrup. Spread with half of whipped cream. Arrange 1/2 the marrons glacés over whipped cream. Top with remaining cake half and brush with the rest of syrup.
◆ Place the remaining whipped cream in a star-tip pastry bag and refrigerate.
◆ Melt jam with a tablespoon of water and spread a thin layer over the whole cake.
◆ In a bowl, beat egg whites and rum, adding powdered sugar little at a time until it becomes a smooth paste. Spread evenly over the cake. Garnish border and center with remaining marrons glacés.
◆ Place the cake on serving plate. With the remaining whipped cream, make rosettes at the base and in the center. Cut pistachios in half and garnish corners and center.

Cream cake

Time needed: *2 hours*
Difficulty: *medium*

INGREDIENTS FOR 8-10 SERVINGS
1 1/2 cups of flour
1/2 cup of cornstarch
1 cup of softened butter
1 cup of sugar ◆ *1 teaspoon of vanilla*
1 1/2 cups of bittersweet chocolate
5 eggs
1/2 cup of chopped toasted almonds
2 teaspoons of baking powder
1/4 cup of rum ◆ *a pinch of salt*
Filling and decoration:
1 1/2 cups of whipping cream
1 teaspoon of instant coffee
3 tablespoons of powdered sugar
1 tablespoon of apricot marmalade
6 oz of bittersweet chocolate

◆ Grease and flour a 12-inch cake pan. Preheat the oven to 350°F.
◆ In a bowl, beat butter and sugar; add vanilla and continue beating, until creamy and smooth.
◆ Melt chocolate in a double boiler. Cool lightly and add to butter mixture. Add eggs, salt, and

rum stirring after each addition. Fold in sifted flour, cornstarch, baking powder, and chopped almonds. Pour into cake pan and bake 50-55 minutes. Turn onto a rack and cool completely.

◆ Prepare the filling: Warm 2 tablespoons of whipping cream; add the instant coffee and dissolve; stir into remaining cream and refrigerate.

◆ Heat jam with 2 tablespoons of water. Slice cake crosswise in 3 sections. Spread bottom with half of jam. Whip cream and sugar to stiff peaks and spread 1/3 over jam layer. Cover with another section of cake, spread with jam and 1/3 whipped cream. Top with the third section.

◆ Cover the whole cake with remaining whipped coffee cream, keeping 2 tablespoons aside.

◆ Shave some of the chocolate and press gently to make it stick to the sides of cake. Melt the remaining chocolate in a double boiler and transfer to a paper cone. Draw criss-cross lines on top of the cake.

◆ Transfer the remaining whipped cream to a pastry bag, fitted with a star tube. Pipe out a border of rosettes around edge of the cake.

Marrons glacés Napoleon

Time needed: *1 hour*
Difficulty: *complex*

INGREDIENTS FOR 6-8 SERVINGS

10 oz of puff pastry (see page 12)

Cream:
1 cup of coarsely chopped marrons glacés
2 tablespoons of Maraschino
1/2 cup of milk
1 1/4 cups of heavy cream

Decoration:
1 tablespoon of powdered sugar
3 marrons glacés
1/2 cup of chopped bittersweet chocolate

◆ Preheat the oven to 400°F.

◆ Roll out puff pastry to a 1/8 inch-thick rectangle and cut in 5 equal rectangular sections. Place on baking sheet brushed with water and bake 15 minutes.

◆ For the cream, mix the marrons glacés, Maraschino and milk, in a food processor. Fold in the whipped cream. Spread a pastry section with a thin layer of cream. Top with another section, another layer of cream and continue the process, finishing with pastry. Dust with powdered sugar.

◆ In a double boiler, melt chocolate. Brush chocolate on the inside of a paper cupcake. Spread the remaining chocolate on a sheet of parchment paper and cut out four leaves. Cool. Remove the paper cup and place the little chocolate basket in the center of the pastry. Arrange in the basket the marrons glacés and around them, a crown of chocolate leaves. Garnish each corner of the mille-feuille with half a marron glacé.

Chocolate triumph

Time needed: *1 hour and 15 minutes*
Difficulty: *medium*

INGREDIENTS FOR 8-10 SERVINGS

1 cup of unsweetened cocoa
2 cups of flour
2 teaspoons of baking powder
3/4 cup of chopped bittersweet chocolate
1 cup of softened butter ◆ *1 1/2 cups of sugar*
3 egg yolks ◆ *5 egg whites*
3/4 cup of whipping cream
2 tablespoons of dark rum
a pinch of salt

Filling and decoration:
1 3/4 cups of chopped bittersweet chocolate
13 tablespoons of softened butter
4 eggs ◆ *a pinch of salt*

◆ Grease a 10-inch cake pan and dust with cocoa. Preheat the oven to 375°F.

◆ In a bowl, dissolve 3 tablespoons of cocoa with 1/2 cup of hot water. In a double boiler, melt chocolate. Add to the cocoa mixture.

◆ In a bowl, using an electric mixer, whisk butter and sugar until creamy; add egg yolks and continue beating for 2 minutes. Fold in melted chocolate, baking powder, cream, rum and flour. Beat egg whites and salt to firm peaks; fold into chocolate mixture.

◆ Pour into prepared cake pan and bake 35 minutes. Turn onto a rack and cool completely.

◆ For the filling, melt chocolate and butter in a double boiler. Remove from heat and mix in egg yolks, one at a time. Beat egg whites and salt to firm peaks; fold into chocolate mixture.

◆ Cut the cake crosswise in 3 circles. Spread the first circle with 1/3 of chocolate cream and top with another circle; spread with 1/2 of the remaining cream, finish with the last circle of cake.

◆ Cover the entire cake with the remaining cream and press "wavy" patterns all over the cake, using the concave side of a spoon.

Mocha cake

Time needed:
1 hour and 15 minutes
Difficulty: medium
INGREDIENTS
FOR **6-8** SERVINGS
1/2 cup of sugar
1/2 cup of cornstarch
*2 tablespoons of softened
butter*
6 eggs
*1/4 cup of finely chopped
almonds*
*1 tablespoon of apricot jam
a pinch of salt*

Butter Cream:
2 egg whites
1/4 cup of sugar
*6 tablespoons of butter,
softened*
1 teaspoon of coffee liquor

Syrup:
1/4 cup of sugar
1 teaspoon of coffee liquor

Decoration:
1 cup of powdered sugar
1 egg white
1 teaspoon of instant coffee
20 coffee beans

Grease and flour a 9-inch cake pan. Preheat the oven to 325°F.

◆ In a bowl, whisk eggs and sugar until light. Add, a little at a time, cornstarch, almonds, and butter. In a separate bowl, whisk egg whites and salt to firm peaks; fold into mixture.

◆ Pour preparation into cake pan and bake for 40 minutes. Turn onto a rack and cool completely.

◆ Prepare the butter cream with the ingredients listed above (see page 17). Add coffee liquor. Make the syrup: Cook on low heat the sugar in 1/2 cup water for 2-3 minutes. Cool and mix in the rum. Heat jam and a tablespoon of water until jam is melted.

◆ Cut cold cake in two layers; brush bottom half with syrup, and spread with cream **(1)**.

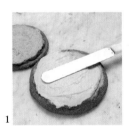

Cover with remaining cake half. Brush with syrup and spread with jam.

◆ For the decoration, dissolve instant coffee in a teaspoon of warm water. In a bowl, whisk egg whites and powdered sugar to obtain a thick shiny glaze; add a few drops of coffee.

◆ Place cake on a wire rack and spread evenly with icing **(2)**, keeping a few tablespoons aside. Refrigerate.

◆ To the remaining icing, add the leftover coffee. Transfer the mixture into a parchment cone. Pressing gently on the cone, make rows of little drops at the base of the cake, around the border, and on 1/3 of the top **(3)**. Garnish the rest with coffee beans set on a drop of icing.

◆ Keep in a cool place until ready to serve.

Duchess cake

Time needed: *1 hour
(plus resting time)*
Difficulty: medium

INGREDIENTS FOR **6-8** SERVINGS
2 cups of flour ◆ 1/2 cup of sugar
15 tablespoons of butter
3/4 cup of finely chopped toasted almonds
1 egg yolk

Filling:
3 egg yolks ◆ 1/4 cup of sugar
1/2 cup of flour
1 cup of milk
2 teaspoons of vanilla
1/4 cup of apricot jam

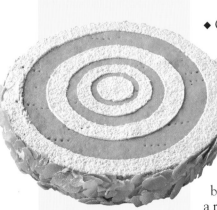

Duchess cake

Decoration:
1/4 cup of slivered almonds
1 tablespoon of powdered sugar

◆ Grease and flour 3 cookie sheets. Preheat the oven to 350°F.

◆ On a work surface, place flour and almonds in a mound; make a well in the center; add butter cut in pieces, sugar, and egg yolk. Mix lightly, using fingertips. Make a ball, cover with plastic wrap and refrigerate for about 30 minutes.

◆ Divide the dough into 3 equal parts. Roll out each part into a 10-inch circle. Place on cookie sheets, prick all over with a fork, and bake for 15-18 minutes until golden. Turn onto a rack and cool completely.

◆ For the filling prepare a pastry cream (see page 16). Cool, stirring it once in a while.

Mocha cake

♦ Spread the first circle with apricot jam; cover with second circle, spread with cream, and too with the third circle. With a spatula, spread the cream that comes out on the sides of cake. Stick sliced almonds all around.

♦ In a cardboard the same size of the cake, cut off 6 circular bands 3/4-inch-wide and a central 1-inch circle. Place the circular bands on the cake at regular interval. Dust with powdered sugar. Carefully remove the cardboard and keep in a cold place until ready to serve.

Hungarian cake

Time needed: *1 hour*
(plus cooling time)
Difficulty: medium

INGREDIENTS FOR 6-8 SERVINGS
1/2 cup of chopped poppy seeds
1/4 cup of chopped walnuts
1/2 cup of flour
4 eggs ♦ 1/2 cup of sugar
2 teaspoons of vanilla
a pinch of salt
a pinch of cinnamon
a pinch of nutmeg

Pastry Cream:
3/4 cup of chopped toasted walnuts
5 egg yolks ♦ 3/4 cup of sugar
2 cups of milk ♦ 1/2 cup of flour
2 teaspoons of vanilla

Decoration:
2/3 cup of whipping cream
2 tablespoons of poppy seeds

♦ Grease and flour a 10-inch cake pan. Preheat the oven to 375°F.

♦ In a bowl, using an electric mixer, whisk eggs and sugar until light and creamy. Fold in poppy seeds, walnuts, flour, vanilla, cinnamon, and nutmeg. Whisk egg whites and salt to firm peaks; delicately fold into mixture.

♦ Pour into cake pan and bake for approximately 40 minutes. When cool, turn onto a rack and cool completely.

♦ Prepare the pastry cream (see page 16). When cold, mix in the chopped walnuts.

♦ Cut cold cake in 2 circles. Turn bottom half on serving plate and spread with 1/3 of cream. Top with remaining cake half and cover with cream.

♦ Refrigerate cake for about 1 hour.

♦ To decorate, whip cream to stiff peaks. Using a

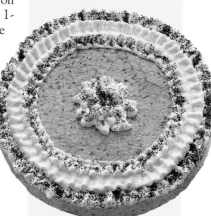

Hungarian cake

pastry bag fitted with a straight tube, pipe out 3 concentric circles around the border of cake and a big rosette in the center. Garnish with poppy seeds.

Old Parisian cake

Time needed: *1 hour and 10 minutes*
Difficulty: medium

INGREDIENTS FOR 20 SERVINGS
1 cup of flour ♦ 3/4 cup of cornstarch
6 eggs ♦ 3 tablespoons of melted butter
2 teaspoons of vanilla ♦ 3/4 cup of sugar

Cream:
1 cup of chestnut purée
4 eggs ♦ 1/2 cup of sugar
3/4 cup of whipping cream
4 tablespoons of rum

Syrup:
1/2 cup of sugar ♦ 4 tablespoons of rum

Decoration:
3/4 cup of whipping cream
3 chopped marrons glacés
3 tablespoons of chopped pistachios

♦ Grease and flour a 10-inch cake pan and a 4-cup charlotte mold. Preheat the oven to 375°F.

♦ In a bowl, using an electric mixer, whisk eggs and sugar until light and creamy. With a wooden spoon, fold in the sifted flour, cornstarch, and melted butter. Pour 2/3 of mixture into pan and the rest into charlotte mold. Bake for approximately 35 minutes. Turn onto a rack and cool completely.

♦ Prepare the cream: Whisk eggs and sugar until light and creamy. Fold in chestnut purée and rum. In separate bowls, whip cream and egg whites to stiff peaks. Gently fold both into chestnut mixture.

♦ Make the syrup: Boil sugar in 3/4 cup of water for 3 minutes. Cool briefly and mix in the rum.

♦ Cut the larger cake in 2 circles and the tall one crosswise into 3 layers. Brush one large cake layer with a little syrup, spread with cream, cover with the other cake layer and brush with syrup. Proceed the same way with the tall cake. Cover both cakes with the remaining cream. Arrange on a serving plate, placing the tall cake in the center of the larger one.

♦ Whip cream until stiff. Transfer to a pastry bag fitted with a star tube; pipe out rosettes of

Old Parisian cake

whipped cream as illustrated in the picture.
◆ Arrange pistachios on the border of the larger cake and chopped marrons glacés on top of the taller one.

Mimosa cake

Time needed: *1 hour*
Difficulty: *medium*

INGREDIENTS
FOR 8-10 SERVINGS
1/2 cup of cornstarch
2/3 cup of flour
4 tablespoons of butter
1/2 cup of sugar ◆ *3 eggs* ◆ *2 egg yolks*
1 tablespoon of powdered sugar

Pastry Cream:
5 egg yolks ◆ *1/2 cup of sugar*
1/2 cup of flour ◆ *2 cups of milk*
2 teaspoons of vanilla
1/3 cup of chopped toasted hazelnuts
3/4 cup of whipping cream

Syrup:
1/2 cup of sugar ◆ *1 teaspoon of rum*
peels of orange and lemon

◆ Grease and flour a 9-inch cake pan. Preheat the oven to 360°F.
◆ Melt butter in a small saucepan. In a bowl, using an electric mixer, whisk eggs, egg yolks, and sugar until light and creamy. With a wooden spoon, gently fold in the flour and cornstarch sifted together; add melted butter.
◆ Pour mixture into cake pan and bake for approximately 30 minutes. Turn onto a rack and cool completely.
◆ Prepare a pastry cream (see page 16). Cool and fold in hazelnuts and whipped cream. Refrigerate.
◆ Make the syrup: Boil 3/4 cup of water, add lemon and orange peels, sugar and cook for 3 minutes. Cool briefly and mix in the rum.
◆ Slice cake into 4 layers. Keep one as it is. Make the others smaller: 8, 7, and 6 inch respectively in diameter. Save the trimmings. Brush the larger layer with syrup and spread with pastry cream. Proceed the same way with the other cake layers placing the smaller one on the top in order to make the shape of a dome. Cover the entire cake with the remaining cream.
◆ Crumble cake trimmings and spread all over the cake pressing lightly with your hands. Dust with powdered sugar.

Mimosa cake

Dobos cake

Time needed: *1 hour and 15 minutes*
Difficulty: *complex*

INGREDIENTS FOR 8 SERVINGS
4 eggs
1 egg yolk
2 tablespoons of heavy cream
1/2 cup of cornstarch
1/2 cup of flour
2 teaspoons of vanilla
a pinch of salt

Mousse:
1 cup of chopped milk chocolate
12 tablespoons of butter
4 eggs
a pinch of salt

Decoration:
1/2 cup of sugar
1 tablespoon of lemon juice

◆ Grease and flour 6 round baking sheets. Preheat the oven to 350°F.
◆ In a bowl, using an electric mixer, whisk 5 egg yolks and 1/4 cup of sugar until light and creamy.
◆ Fold in heavy cream, flour, and vanilla. Beat 4 egg whites and salt to firm peaks; add 1/4 cup of sugar and, whisking, add the cornstarch. Gently mix the egg yolk mixture with the egg white preparation.
◆ Divide the mixture in 6 parts and pour it in separate baking sheets. Bake approximately 15 minutes until golden. Turn onto a rack and cool. Trim the 6 circles so they are all the same size.
◆ To make the mousse, melt chocolate and butter in a double boiler. Remove from heat. Cool slightly. Mix in egg yolks and when cold, fold in egg whites whipped with salt to firm peaks.
◆ Spread a circle with mousse, cover with the second circle and then another layer of mousse. Continue until you use 5 circles. You will need one circle and some mousse for decoration. Refrigerate the cake.
◆ On low heat, cook sugar and lemon juice to have a golden caramel. Spread the circle set aside with caramel and cut, with a sharp knife, in 12 equal size wedges.
◆ Shortly before serving, place 12 rosettes of mousse around the border of cake to help arranging the wedges at a slight angle. See picture. Do not place the cake in the refrigerator because the caramel would soften.

Dobos cake

203

Milano torte

Time needed: *1 hour*
Difficulty: *medium*

INGREDIENTS FOR **6-8** SERVINGS
2/3 cup of flour ◆ *1/2 cup of sugar*
5 tablespoons of butter
3 eggs ◆ *grated peel of 1 orange*

Filling:
2 cups of milk
1 cup of toasted hazelnuts
3/4 cup of sugar
1/2 cup of flour ◆ *5 egg yolks*
2 teaspoons of vanilla
2 tablespoons of apricot jam
1 tablespoon of almond extract

Decoration:
11 cup of chopped bittersweet chocolate
2/3 cup of powdered sugar
2-3 tablespoons of milk ◆ *2 tablespoons of butter*
1/3 cup of toasted almonds, halved

◆ Grease and flour a square 9-inch square cake pan. Preheat the oven to 350°F.
◆ In a bowl, using an electric mixer, whisk eggs, sugar and orange peel until light and creamy. Gently fold in flour and melted butter.
◆ Pour mixture into cake pan and bake for 30-40 minutes. Turn onto a rack and cool completely.
◆ Prepare the filling caramelizing 1/2 cup of sugar with 4 tablespoons of water following the directions for brittle on page 21. When completely cool, chop finely.
◆ Bring milk to boil. In a saucepan, whisk egg yolks and sugar until light and creamy. Stir in flour, vanilla, and milk, a little at a time. Bring to boil and cook, stirring continuously, for 7-8 minutes.
◆ Remove from heat, cool and add the chopped hazelnut brittle.
◆ Slice the cake in three layers. Spread bottom layer with 1/2 filling, cover with second layer, spread with rest of filling and top with the third cake layer.
◆ Heat apricot jam with 2 tablespoons of water. Pour it and spread over the whole cake.
◆ In a double boiler, melt chocolate with butter and powdered sugar. Pour over cake and spread evenly with a spatula.
◆ To decorate, arrange the half almonds on top and base of cake.

Coffee napoleons

Time needed: *1 hour*
Difficulty: *complex*

INGREDIENTS FOR **6-8** SERVINGS
10 oz of puff pastry
(see page 12)
3/4 cup of strong coffee
1/2 cup of sugar
3 tablespoons of cornstarch
1/4 cup of rum
1/4 cup of whipping cream
1/2 cup of toasted hazelnuts
almond oil

Decoration:
1 tablespoon of powdered sugar
3/4 cup of chopped bittersweet chocolate
10 coffee beans

◆ Preheat the oven to 400°F.
◆ Roll out puff pastry to a 1/8-inch-thick and place on a baking sheet, previously brushed with water. Prick dough all over with a fork and bake for 15 minutes. Turn onto a rack and cool. Cut with a sharp knife into 4 rectangles of equal size.
◆ For the cream melt 1/4 cup of sugar with 4 tablespoons of water, on low heat.
◆ When sugar is golden, stir into hazelnuts. Mix well, remove from heat and pour on a lightly oiled marble surface. When cool grind it and place in a saucepan with coffee, the remaining sugar, and cornstarch dissolved in a tablespoon of water.
◆ Bring to boil and cook for 4 minutes, stirring continuously. Cool and mix in rum and whipped cream.
◆ Spread a rectangle with a layer of cream, cover with another rectangle and continue alternating rectangles and cream. Top with a rectangle.
◆ In a double boiler, melt chocolate and spread on wax paper to 1/8-inch-thick. Cool and cut into 1/4-inch-wide strips.
◆ Dust the entire pastry with sifted powdered sugar and garnish with chocolate strips placed diagonally.
◆ Melt the chocolate trimmings and pour in a paper cone. Decorate by squeezing drops of melted chocolate on the pastry and cover each drop with a coffee bean.

Orange napoleons

Time needed: *1 hour*
Difficulty: complex

INGREDIENTS FOR 6-8 SERVINGS
*10 oz of puff pastry
(see page 12)
2 egg yolks
1/4 cup of sugar
1 cup of milk
1/3 cup of flour
2 teaspoons of vanilla
2 organic oranges
4 tablespoons of butter*

Decoration:
*1/2 cup of sugar
1 tablespoon of powdered sugar
1 tablespoon of almond extract*

◆ Preheat the oven to 425°F. Brush a cookie sheet with water.
◆ Roll out puff pastry in a large 1/8-inch-thick rectangle. Cut into 5 equal-size rectangles. Place on baking sheet. Prick all over with a fork.
◆ Bake for approximately 15 minutes until golden brown. Turn onto a rack and cool. With a sharp knife trim the pastry rectangles.
◆ Rinse and dry oranges. Cut out peel from one orange and placed in milk. Bring milk to boil.
◆ In a saucepan, whisk egg yolks and sugar until light and creamy. Mix in flour, vanilla, and hot milk passed through a strainer. Place mixture on medium heat and, stirring constantly, bring to boil. Reduce heat and cook for 7-8 minutes. Cool, stirring once in a while.
◆ Grate the peel and squeeze the juice of an orange. Add to warm cream. Add butter, a tablespoon at a time, stirring after each addition.
◆ Spread a rectangle of dough with cream. Cover with another rectangle. Continue alternating pastry rectangles and cream. Top with a pastry rectangle.
◆ Cut off pith of first orange and separate in segments. Cook sugar with 3 tablespoons of water until golden. With small tongs, dip orange segments in caramelized sugar, one at the time. Cool on an oiled marbled surface.
◆ To draw squares on the cake, place a griddle on the top and dust the entire surface with powdered sugar. Garnish with the caramelized orange sections.

Almond cream cake

Time needed: *1 hour and 20 minutes*
Difficulty: medium

INGREDIENTS FOR 10-12 SERVINGS
*1/2 cup of flour
1/2 cup of finely chopped almonds
1/4 cup of almond paste
4 eggs ◆ 1 egg yolk
12 tablespoons of butter
3/4 cup of sugar ◆ 2 teaspoons of vanilla
a pinch of salt
grated peel of one organic lemon
a pinch of cinnamon*

Syrup:
1 tablespoon of sugar ◆ 1 tablespoon of rum

Butter Cream:
*1 cup of almond paste ◆ 1 tablespoon of rum
1 egg white ◆ 6 tablespoons of butter
a pinch of salt ◆ 1/4 cup of sugar*

Decoration:
*1 cup of chopped milk chocolate
3/4 cup of pralined almonds
1 tablespoon of apricot jam*

◆ Grease and flour a 10-inch cake pan. Preheat the oven to 350°F.
◆ Crumble almond paste and in a bowl, mix well with egg yolks. Add butter cut in small pieces, 1/2 cup of sugar, cinnamon, vanilla, and lemon peel. Whisk egg whites and salt to firm peaks and fold into mixture. Add remaining sugar, flour and almonds, folding delicately.
◆ Pour into cake pan and bake for 45-50 minutes. Turn onto a rack and cool completely. Cut cake in 2 circles.
◆ Make the syrup: Boil sugar in 2 tablespoons of water for 2 minutes. Cool and mix in the rum.
◆ To prepare the cream, follow the directions for classic butter cream (see page 17), adding almond paste and rum.
◆ Brush bottom half of cake with half of the syrup, spread with cream. Top with remaining cake circle. Brush with remaining syrup. Melt apricot jam with 1 tablespoon of water. Brush over the entire cake.
◆ In a double boiler, melt chocolate and pour it over cake. Using a spatula, spread the chocolate sauce over the entire cake. Decorate with pralined almonds and keep refrigerated until ready to serve.

Orange and chocolate napoleon

Time needed: *1 hour*
(plus infusion time)
Difficulty: *complex*

INGREDIENTS
FOR **8** SERVINGS

*1/4 lb of puff pastry
(see page 12)
2 organic oranges
3/4 cup of chopped bittersweet chocolate
6 egg yolks
3/4 cup of sugar
2 cups of milk
1/4 cup of flour
1/2 teaspoon of vanilla*

Decoration:
*1 tablespoon of powdered
sugar
1/4 cup of sugar
1 organic orange*

Ondley day before making this dessert, rinse and dry the orange for decoration.

◆ With a sharp knife, cut out two 3/4-inch slices from the center of the orange. Cut the peel in 2 opposite sides and fold in from one end to the other, leaving attached in the middle. From remaining peel, cut two 1/2-inch circles. Place in a deep dish.

◆ In a saucepan, cook sugar with 1/2 cup of water for 3 minutes and pour onto orange and peel. Set aside to infuse for 24 hours.

◆ The next day, preheat the oven to 420°F. Roll out puff pastry to thin 20x12-inch rectangles. Set aside in a cool place for 1 hour. Brush a cookie sheet with water; transfer dough rectangle to cookie sheet and prick with a fork. Slice in 3 equal-size rectangles and bake for 12-15 minutes. Delicately remove from cookie sheet.

◆ To make the cream, rinse and dry oranges.

Grate peel from 1 orange. Cut off peel from the other orange; slice it in thin strips and scald twice in boiling water; drain well. Boil milk with grated orange peel.

◆ In a saucepan, whisk egg yolks and sugar; add sifted flour, vanilla and slowly pour in the hot milk. Cook for 8 minutes, on low heat, whisking constantly.

◆ Remove from heat; add the butter, cut in small pieces, the drained orange peels and the chocolate. When chocolate is melted, stir in the juice of one orange.

◆ Spread half the cream on a rectangle of dough and cover with a second rectangle. Dust with sifted powdered sugar.

◆ Drain the orange slices and peel from their syrup and dry carefully. Place slices on the napoleon and the peel circles on the center of oranges.

Strawberry wedding cake

Time needed: *55 minutes*
(plus infusion time)
Difficulty: *medium*

INGREDIENTS FOR **14-16** SERVINGS
*2 recipes of sponge cake (see page 10)
1 3/4 lbs of strawberries
2 cups of heavy cream
1/4 cup of powdered sugar*

Pastry Cream:
*2 cups of milk ◆ 6 egg yolks
1/2 cup of sugar
1/2 cup of flour
peel of one organic lemon
2 tablespoons of Maraschino
3/4 cup of heavy cream*

Syrup:
*1/4 cup of sugar
4 tablespoons of Maraschino*

*Strawberry
wedding cake*

Decoration:
*4 organic oranges
1 cup of chopped white chocolate
1/4 lb of strawberries
4 tablespoons of sugar*

◆ Rinse and dry 2 oranges. With a small orange peeler, remove all peel in tiny strips; roll strips around metal tubes. Arrange tubes in a deep dish with a weight on top.

◆ In a saucepan, boil 3/4 cup of water with 4 tablespoons of sugar, for 2 minutes; pour over orange peel strips. From the other 2 oranges, remove 1/4-inch-wide strips and place them in the dish. Set aside for 6 hours.

◆ To prepare the pastry cream, follow instructions on page 16, using the ingredients listed above. Cool completely, stirring often and add the Maraschino. Delicately fold in the whipped cream.

◆ To make the syrup, boil 1/2 cup of milk with the sugar, for 3 minutes. Cool completely and stir in the Maraschino.

◆ Rinse the strawberries in ice water; drain, dry and cut in half.

Orange and chocolate napoleon

◆ Slice both sponge cakes (one 8-inch and the other, 10-inch) in 2 layers. Brush one of the largest layers with a little syrup, cover with a layer of pastry cream and a layer of strawberries. Cover with equal-size layer of cake. Brush again with a little syrup and spread 2 tablespoons of pastry cream in the center. Place a smaller circle of sponge cake in the center; brush with syrup and cover with remaining pastry cream. Cover with half the strawberries and the last circle of sponge cake. Brush with the remaining syrup.

◆ Whip cream with powdered sugar and spread 2/3 all over the cake. Transfer remaining cream to a pastry bag, fitted with a star tube and pipe out rosettes around the upper and lower layers of cake.

◆ In a double boiler, melt the white chocolate; pour onto a marble surface, spreading it to 1/4-inch-thick. When chocolate hardens lightly, cut out strips, form into small cones and refrigerate.

◆ Remove orange peels from syrup and dry them. Roll the large strips into rosebuds and place in white chocolate cones. Place on top of cake, with the thin orange strips to form a bouquet. Refrigerate until ready to serve.

*Chocolate
orange cake*

Chocolate
orange cake

Time needed: *1 hour*
Difficulty: *medium*

INGREDIENTS FOR 6 SERVINGS
3/4 cup of flour
1/2 cup of sugar
3 eggs
2 tablespoons of melted butter
1 teaspoon of vanilla
Syrup:
1/4 cup of sugar
2 tablespoons of Grand Marnier
Cream:
3/4 cup of chopped chocolate
2 tablespoons of butter
3 egg yolks
2 egg whites
2 tablespoons of sugar
3 tablespoons of candied orange peel
2 tablespoons of orange marmalade
a pinch of salt

◆ Butter and flour an 8-inch cake pan. Preheat the oven to 360°F.

◆ In a bowl, with an electric mixer, whisk eggs

and sugar until thick and frothy. Mix in flour, vanilla and melted butter.
Pour batter in cake pan and bake for 30 minutes. Turn cake onto a rack and set aside to cool.

◆ For the syrup, cook sugar in 1/4 cup of water, until completely dissolved. Cool slightly and stir in Grand Marnier.

◆ For the cream, melt chocolate and butter in a double boiler. Remove from heat and whisk in egg yolks, one at a time.

◆ Beat egg whites and salt to soft peaks, add sugar and beat to firm peaks. Fold into chocolate mixture and refrigerate for 30 minutes.

◆ Slice sides of cake to make it square; slice horizontally. Brush one layer with syrup. Spread marmalade over it and cover with a second layer of cake. Brush with syrup and spread with chocolate cream (on top and part of sides). Decorate with orange peel.

Paris - Brest

Time needed: *1 hour*
Difficulty: *medium*

INGREDIENTS FOR 6-8 SERVINGS
1 recipe for pâte à choux (see page 11)
Cream:
4 egg yolks
3/4 cup of sugar
1 cup of milk
2 tablespoons of flour
1/2 teaspoon of vanilla
grated peel of 1/2 organic lemon
1/4 cup of toasted hazelnuts
1/4 cup of heavy cream
3 tablespoons of butter

Decoration:
3/4 cup of heavy cream
1/4 cup of pearl sugar
2 tablespoons of sliced almonds

◆ Grease and flour a cookie sheet. Preheat the oven to 375°F.

◆ Prepare the pâte à choux and transfer to a pastry bag, fitted with a large plain tube.

◆ Trace an 8-inch circle on the cookie sheet and pipe out the dough over it. Pipe out a second circle inside the first one and a third circle on top of the first two.

◆ Sprinkle the wheel of dough with pearl sugar and the almonds. Bake for 20-25 minutes or until raised and golden. Remove and cool.

◆ With egg yolks, sugar, milk, vanilla, flour and

Paris - Brest

lemon peel, prepare a pastry cream (see page 16).
◆ Remove from heat; add chopped hazelnuts and butter, stirring well until mixture is cold. Whip the cream and fold into mixture. Refrigerate.
◆ Open the wheel in 2 circles, slicing just under top to remove a "hat." Transfer pastry cream to a pastry bag and fill the bottom part of the wheel.
◆ Whip the cream and transfer to a pastry bag, fitted with a large star tube. Pipe out over pastry cream. Cover with top part of wheel. Transfer to a serving plate and refrigerate.

Viennese walnut cake

Time needed: *1 hour and 25 minutes*
Difficulty: medium

INGREDIENTS FOR 8-10 SERVINGS
1/2 cup of softened butter
1 cup of finely chopped walnuts
1/2 teaspoon of vanilla
grated peel of one organic lemon
a pinch of cinnamon
7 eggs
4 oz of sponge cake (see page 10)
3/4 cup of sugar

Filling:
1/8 cup of egg whites
1/2 cup of sugar
3/4 cup of softened butter
a pinch of salt
1/2 cup of chopped walnuts
2 tablespoons of rum

Decoration:
1/4 cup of walnuts
3/4 cup of chopped chocolate
5 tablespoons of whipping cream

◆ Grease and flour a 10-inch cake pan. Preheat the oven to 350°F.
◆ Crumble sponge cake and mix with chopped walnuts.
◆ In a bowl, whisk butter, sugar, vanilla, lemon peel and cinnamon until creamy. Add egg yolks, one at a time, and the sponge-cake-walnut mixture. Beat eggs to firm peaks and fold into batter.
◆ Pour batter into cake pan. Bake for 55-60 minutes. Turn cake onto a rack, cool and slice in 3 circles.
◆ Prepare filling (see butter cream recipe on page

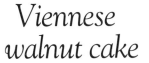

Viennese walnut cake

17). To the cool mixture, add chopped walnuts and rum.
◆ Set aside 2 tablespoons of butter cream in a pastry bag, fitted with a star tube. Spread 1/3 of butter cream on a cake circle; cover with the second circle and spread with half the remaining butter cream; cover with the last cake circle. Spread butter cream on top and sides of the cake. Refrigerate.
◆ To decorate, in a double boiler, melt chocolate in cream. Spread evenly on the cake and refrigerate it until solid.
◆ Place cake on a serving dish. With a sharp knife, cut thin strips out of the chocolate topping; place walnuts in these incisions.
◆ With leftover whipped cream, decorate center and sides of cake.

Pistachio croquembouche

Time needed: *1 hour and 15 minutes*
Difficulty: complex

INGREDIENTS FOR 8-10 SERVINGS
1 recipe for pâte à choux (see page 11)
Cream:
1/2 cup of milk
2 egg yolks
1/4 cup of flour
1/4 cup of sugar
1/4 cup of shelled pistachios
3/4 cup of heavy cream

Decoration:
1 cup of sugar
1 tablespoon of lemon juice

◆ Grease and flour a cookie sheet. Preheat the oven to 400°F.
◆ Prepare the pâte à choux; transfer to a pastry bag, fitted with a plain tube. Pipe out small balls of dough on the cookie sheet.
◆ Bake for 20 minutes or until choux have raised and are golden. Remove from the oven and cool.
◆ With milk, egg yolks, flour and sugar, prepare a pastry cream (see page 16) and cool completely.
◆ Scald pistachios in boiling water; drain, peel and chop.
◆ Whip the cream and fold into pastry cream; add pistachios.
◆ Make a small hole in each choux. Pour pastry cream into a pastry bag, fitted with a small tube ▶

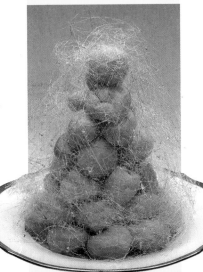

Pistachio croquembouche

and fill choux.

◆ Cook half of sugar in 2 tablespoons of water, and a few drops of lemon juice, on low heat, until lightly golden. Remove from heat.

◆ Dip every choux, one at a time, in the caramel. Place them on a serving plate, in a circle. Continue to add all choux, in concentric circles, forming a cone. The caramel holds the choux together.

◆ Place a piece of waxed paper on work surface. At each end of paper, place 2 upside down glasses, supporting 2 wooden spoons across the paper.

◆ In a saucepan, cook remaining sugar with 2 tablespoons of water and 3 drops of lemon juice, on moderate heat.

◆ When caramel is golden, remove from heat. Dip a fork into the caramel; lift, forming strings of sugar, over and across the two wooden spoons.

◆ Continue the caramel web until all is used. Delicately lift the caramel string and place around the croquembouche.

◆ To use a simpler method, make the caramel and, with a fork, drop strings of caramel from top to bottom of croquembouche. Finish with candied violets.

Saint-Honoré

Time needed: *50 minutes*
Difficulty: *medium*

INGREDIENTS FOR 6-8 SERVINGS
1/2 lb of puff pastry (see page 12)
8 choux (see page 11)
one 10-inch circle of sponge cake,
1-inch thick (see page 10)
3/4 cup of heavy cream, whipped

Saint-Honoré cream filling:
5 egg yolks
1/2 cup of sugar
2 cups of milk
1/2 cup of flour
1/2 teaspoon of vanilla
grated peel of one organic lemon
1 3/4 cups of whipped cream
2 tablespoons of dry Marsala
1/2 cup of cocoa

Syrup:
1/4 cup of sugar
organic orange and lemon peel
1 teaspoon of rum

Caramel:
1/2 cup of sugar

◆ Preheat the oven to 410°F. Brush a cookie sheet with water.

◆ Roll out puff pastry in a 12-inch circle. Transfer to a cookie sheet; prick with a fork and bake for 15 minutes. Cool completely.

◆ Prepare filling. Bring to boil milk and grated lemon peel. In a bowl, whisk egg yolks and sugar; add vanilla and flour. Pass boiling milk through a sieve and stir into mixture.

◆ Return mixture to saucepan, bring just to a boil and cook on low heat for 7-8 minutes, stirring.

◆ Add Marsala and divide cream in 2 bowls. In the first bowl, mix the cocoa. When completely cool, fold in half of whipped cream into each bowl. Refrigerate both.

◆ Make the syrup: In a saucepan, bring to boil 1/2 cup of water, sugar and citrus peel; cook for 2 minutes. Cool and add rum.

◆ With a sharp knife, equalize the circles of puff pastry and the sponge cake (in two 12-inch circles). Set cut-out pieces aside.

◆ Fill 4 choux with chocolate cream and 4 choux with plain cream.

◆ In a saucepan, cook sugar with 1/2 teaspoon of water, until golden. Dip top of choux in caramel.

◆ Spread a thin layer of plain cream on puff pastry. Cover with sponge cake and brush with syrup.

◆ Cover all cake with chocolate cream; crumble leftover sponge cake and stick to sides of cake.

◆ Arrange choux on top of cake, around the edges, alternating with rosettes of whipped cream. Decorate with rosettes of remaining plain cream.

Niçois cake

Time needed: *1 hour and 15 minutes*
Difficulty: *medium*

INGREDIENTS FOR 10-12 SERVINGS
1/2 cup of chopped hazelnuts
1/2 cup of chopped almonds
1/2 cup of sugar
1/2 teaspoon of vanilla
grated peel of one organic orange
2 tablespoons of flour
5 tablespoons of softened butter

4 eggs ◆ 3 egg yolks
a pinch of salt

Filling:
1 1/4 cups of chopped milk chocolate
1/2 cup of heavy cream
3 eggs
1/4 cup of sugar
2 tablespoons of rum
1/2 cup of chopped hazelnuts
a pinch of salt

Decoration:
5 egg whites
1/2 cup of sugar
3/4 cup of softened butter
a pinch of salt
grated peel of one organic orange
1 tablespoon of Grand Marnier
1 tablespoon of Alchermes
1/4 cup of chopped chocolate
1 large strawberry

◆ Grease and flour a 12-inch cake pan. Preheat the oven to 375°F.
◆ In a bowl, whisk egg yolks and sugar until pale and creamy. Sift flour over mixture; add vanilla, almonds, hazelnuts, orange peel and butter, stirring well. Beat eggs and salt to firm peaks and fold into batter.
◆ Pour batter in cake pan and bake for 35-40 minutes. Cool on a rack and slice in 3 circles.
◆ Melt milk chocolate in a double boiler. In a stainless steel saucepan, whisk egg yolks and sugar until frothy; add milk chocolate and cream. Cook until cream thickens and coats a spoon. Cool; stir in rum and chopped hazelnuts. Beat egg whites and salt to firm peaks; fold into mixture.
◆ Spread 1/2 the filling on a cake circle. Cover with second cake circle and spread remaining filling. Cover with the last cake circle.
◆ With egg whites, sugar, butter and salt, prepare butter cream (see page 17); add orange peel. Set aside 2 tablespoons of butter cream. To the remaining butter cream, add Grand Marnier and Alchermes. Spread half of this pink cream on top and sides of cake.
◆ Place cake on a serving dish. Pour remaining pink cream in a pastry bag, fitted with a small star tube. Decorate lower and upper sides of cake with ribbons of pink cream.
◆ Pour remaining pink cream in a paper cone; in another cone, pour 2 tablespoons of white cream; in another cone, pour the melted chocolate. Gently piping out, decorate with strips of alternating color.
◆ With melted chocolate, make small chocolate circles and place them on cake, over 4 segments of strawberry.

Rosolio cake

Time needed: *1 hour and 20 minutes*
Difficulty: medium

INGREDIENTS FOR 8-10 SERVINGS
3/4 cup of ground blanched almonds
6 eggs ◆ 3/4 cup of sugar
1/2 cup of potato starch ◆ a pinch of salt

Cream:
2 egg whites ◆ 1/2 cup of sugar
5 tablespoons of softened butter
a pinch of salt
1/2 lb of chopped fresh pineapple
1 teaspoon of lemon juice

Syrup:
1/4 cup of sugar
3 tablespoons of rosolio liquor

Decoration:
2 tablespoons of apricot jelly
6 peeled pistachios, sliced in half
1/2 cup of candied cherries, quartered
2 tablespoons of sliced candied tangerine peel
1/2 cup of almond paste
1 1/4 cups of powdered sugar
1 egg white ◆ 1 tablespoon of rosolio liquor

◆ Grease and flour a 12-inch cake pan. Preheat the oven to 350°F.
◆ In a bowl, with an electric mixer, whisk 2 eggs, 4 egg yolks and sugar until pale and thick. Add almonds and potato starch. Beat egg whites and salt to firm peaks; fold into mixture.
◆ Pour batter in cake pan. Bake for 35-40 minutes. Cool and turn onto a work surface.
◆ In a pan, cook pineapple and 2 tablespoons of sugar for 8 minutes. Cool and purée.
◆ Make the syrup: Bring to boil the sugar with 2 tablespoons of water and cook for 3 minutes. Cool and stir in rosolio liquor.
◆ Slice cake in 2 circles. Brush lower layer with rosolio syrup; spread with pineapple butter cream. Cover with other cake circle and brush with rosolio syrup.
◆ Melt apricot jelly and spread on top and around sides of cake. Place cake on a baking rack.
◆ In a bowl, whisk egg whites, rosolio liquor and 1 cup of powdered sugar. Cover cake with rosolio icing and refrigerate.
◆ Sprinkle work surface with powdered sugar; roll out almond paste. Cut out oval forms to decorate sides of cake. Brush with apricot jelly and stick to cake.
◆ Decorate with pistachios, cherries and tangerine peel.

Grease and flour a cookie sheet. Soak raisins in rum.

◆ Dissolve yeast in 2 tablespoons of warm water. In a saucepan, warm milk, butter and sugar, stirring to dissolve. Cool and add yeast.

◆ In a bowl, sift flour and salt; add 3 eggs and yeast mixture. Mix well and knead for 20 minutes to get a smooth and elastic dough, that does not stick to your hands.

◆ Cover and set aside in a warm place for 30-40 minutes. Deflate and knead again for 5 minutes, to stop rising. Return to bowl; cover with a humid kitchen towel and refrigerate for 12 hours.

Stollen

Time needed:
1 hour and 20 minutes
(plus rising time)
Difficulty: *medium*
INGREDIENTS
FOR 8 SERVINGS
5 cups of flour
3/4 cups of butter
2 tablespoons of peeled
almonds
2 tablespoons of
slivered almonds
1/4 cup of sugar
2 teaspoons of yeast
1/2 cup of milk ◆ 4 eggs
1/2 cup of raisins
1/2 cup of mixed candied
fruit
1/4 cup of rum
a pinch of salt
1 tablespoon of
powdered sugar

◆ Scald peeled almonds; drain, peel and chop. Dice candied fruit.

◆ Add drained raisins, candied fruit and chopped almonds to dough; knead lightly. Form a long bread and set on cookie sheet.

◆ Make a cut 1/4-inch deep all along the top of the bread. Set aside to rise for 80-90 minutes. Preheat the oven to 375°F.

◆ Brush bread with beaten egg and sprinkle with slivered almonds. Bake for 50-60 minutes. Cool and dust with powdered sugar.

Sicilian braid

Time needed: *1 hour and 15 minutes*
(plus rising time)
Difficulty: *medium*

INGREDIENTS FOR 6-8 SERVINGS
3 cups of flour
2 eggs
1 egg yolk
7 tablespoons of butter
3 tablespoons of sugar
1 1/2 teaspoons of yeast
6 tablespoons of milk
a pinch of salt

Filling:
3/4 cup of candied fruit
1 cup of almond paste
1 teaspoon of cinnamon

◆ Grease and flour a cookie sheet.

Sicilian braid

◆ Dissolve yeast in 1 tablespoon of warm water. In a saucepan, heat milk, butter and sugar. Cool and stir in yeast. In a bowl, mix flour, salt, eggs and yeast mixture, with a wooden spoon. With your hands, knead vigorously until dough is smooth and elastic, and detaches from sides of bowl. Cover with towel and set aside in a warm place for 30-40 minutes.

◆ Punch dough and knead for 3 minutes. Return to bowl, cover and refrigerate for 12 hours.

◆ For the filling, chop candied fruit and divide in 3 parts. With the almond paste, make three 7 inch long, thin rolls.

◆ On a work surface, knead dough for 1 minute. Divide in 3 parts and roll out 3 rectangles. On each one, place candied fruit and a tube of almond paste, sprinkled with cinnamon. Roll rectangles onto themselves; press sides to close. With these 3 rolls, make a braid.

◆ Transfer braid to cookie sheet. Set aside to raise for 1 hour or until doubled.

◆ Preheat the oven to 350°F. Brush braid with beaten egg yolk and bake for 35-40 minutes. Cool completely.

Stollen

Almond "kranz"

Time needed: *1 hour*
(plus rising time)
Difficulty: *medium*

INGREDIENTS FOR 6 SERVINGS
1/2 lb of puff pastry (see page 12)
3 1/4 cups of flour
7 tablespoons of butter
2 eggs
1/4 cup of sugar
2 teaspoons of yeast
3 tablespoons of milk
a pinch of salt

Filling and decoration:
1 1/2 cups of chopped blanched almonds
1/2 cup of sugar
1 egg
1 egg yolk
1 tablespoons of milk
2 tablespoons of pearl sugar

Almond "kranz"

◆ For the dough, see kranz recipe on page 220.
◆ In a bowl, mix almonds, sugar, egg yolk and milk. Divide mixture in 5 parts. Beat egg with a fork.
◆ Make rectangles of dough, as indicated in the kranz recipe. Place a layer of filling on each layer of dough; proceed as in kranz recipe. Brush with beaten egg and sprinkle with pearl sugar. Bake as indicated.

Pandoro

Time needed: *1 hour and 15 minutes*
(plus rising time)
Difficulty: *medium*

INGREDIENTS FOR 8 SERVINGS
3 cups of flour
3/4 cup of softened butter
3/4 cup of sugar
2 teaspoons of yeast
1/4 cup of heavy cream
grated peel of one organic lemon
1 egg
5 egg yolks
2 tablespoons of powdered sugar
1/2 teaspoon of vanilla

Pandoro

◆ Grease and flour a pandoro pan. In a bowl, mix yeast, 1 tablespoon of sugar, 1 egg yolk and 2 tablespoons of flour in 1 tablespoon of warm water. Form in a pattie and set aside to raise for 2 hours.

◆ On a work surface, mix half the flour with sugar, yeast patty, 3 egg yolks and 1/4 c ups of butter. Knead mixture and form a ball. Place dough in a floured bowl, cover with a kitchen towel and set aside for 1 hour. Mix raised dough with remaining flour and sugar, 1 egg yolk and whole egg. Knead vigorously and set aside to raise, covered, for 2 hours.
◆ Return dough to floured work surface. Mix in lemon peel, vanilla and, a little at a time, the cream. With a rolling pin, form a rectangle; place remaining butter, in pieces, on dough; fold in 3. Roll again and fold in 3. Set aside for 30 minutes.
◆ Place dough in pandoro pan (it will fill half) and let rise, in a warm place, for 30 minutes (dough will raise to fill mold). Preheat the oven to 400°F. Bake for 20 minutes; lower heat to 350°F and bake for 30 minutes. Turn pandoro onto a rack and sprinkle with sugar.

Pan de mei

Time needed: *1 hour*
(plus rising time)
Difficulty: *medium*

INGREDIENTS FOR 8 SERVINGS
2 cups of coarse corn flour
2 cups of fine corn flour
1 cup of flour
2 teaspoons of yeast
6 tablespoons of melted butter
1 cup of sugar
3 beaten eggs
2 tablespoons of dried sambuca flowers
1/4 cup of milk
a pinch of salt

◆ Grease and flour a cookie sheet. Dissolve yeast in warm milk and mix with flour. Cover and let raise for 20 minutes.
◆ On a work surface, place the two corn flours and mix with eggs, butter, salt, yeast mixture, 3/4 cup of sugar and 1 tablespoon of dried sambuca flowers. If the dough is too dry, add a few teaspoons of milk. Form into a ball, cover and set aside to rise for 1 hour.
◆ Preheat the oven to 370°F.
◆ Divide the dough into 8 balls. Place on cookie sheet. Sprinkle with dried sambuca flowers and remaining sugar. Bake for 25-30 minutes.

Belgian raisin brioche

Time needed: *1 hour and 30 minutes (plus rising time)*
Difficulty: medium

INGREDIENTS FOR 6-8 SERVINGS
3/4 cup of raisins
3/4 cup of currants
5 cups of flour
2 teaspoons of yeast
1 1/2 cups of warm water
3/4 cup of brown sugar
3/4 cup of softened butter
2 eggs
a pinch of salt
1/4 teaspoon of cinnamon

◆ Grease a cookie sheet. Rinse and dry raisins. Dissolve yeast in 1/4 cup of warm milk and set aside for 30 minutes.
◆ In a large bowl, mix flour, salt and dissolved yeast; cover and set aside for 3 hours in a warm place.
◆ Mix butter, sugar, eggs, raisins and cinnamon in dough. Knead vigorously, slowly adding remaining milk, a little at a time, until dough is smooth. Cover bowl and set aside for 2 hours in a warm place. Preheat the oven to 375°F.
◆ Place dough on cookie sheet, rolled into a long bread shape. Bake for 1 hour or until brioche has browned.

Bee's nest

Time needed:
1 hour and 15 minutes (plus rising time)
Difficulty: medium

INGREDIENTS FOR 6-8 SERVINGS
3 cups of flour
6 tablespoons of softened butter
1/2 cup of sugar
2 teaspoons of yeast
3 egg yolks
5 tablespoons of milk
a pinch of salt

Filling:
1 cup of chopped bittersweet chocolate
1 egg white
3/4 cup of chopped walnuts

Bee's nest

◆ Grease and flour a 10-inch round cake pan. On a work surface, sift flour into a mound. In the middle, add dissolved yeast, egg yolks, sugar, salt and butter; mix well and knead until dough is smooth and elastic. Cover with a towel and set aside to raise in a warm place, for 45 minutes.
◆ Prepare the filling: Mix chocolate with egg white and melt in a double boiler. Remove from heat and stir in walnuts.
◆ With a rolling pin, roll dough to 1/4-thick. Cut out long wide strips. Spread every strip with filling and roll on itself into rolls. Slice each roll in 1/2 1inch pieces; place next to each other in the cake pan. Set aside to rise for 40 minutes, in a warm place. Preheat the oven to 375°F.
◆ Bake for 40-45 minutes. Turn onto a serving dish. Serve warm.

Kugelhopf

Time needed: *1 hour and 30 minutes (plus rising time)*
Difficulty: medium

INGREDIENTS FOR 4 SERVINGS
3 1/2 cups of flour
1 tablespoon of yeast
1/2 cup of warm milk
6 tablespoons of melted butter
1/2 cup of sugar
3 eggs, lightly beaten
1/2 cup of blanched slivered almonds
3/4 cup of raisins, soaked in warm water
grated peel of one organic lemon
1 tablespoon of powdered sugar
a pinch of salt

Kugelhopf

◆ Grease a 6-cup Kugelhopf mold.
◆ Melt yeast in warm milk. In a bowl, sift 1/2 cup of flour; mix with dissolved yeast, cover and set aside in a warm place until doubled in volume.
◆ Sift the remaining flour on a work surface into a mound. In the center, add yeast mixture, eggs, sugar, butter, salt, drained raisins, lemon peel and almonds. Mix well and knead for 10 minutes; place in prepared mold. Cover and set aside to rise until dough reaches top of mold. Preheat the oven to 375°F.
◆ Bake for 50-60 minutes. Cool and sprinkle with powdered sugar.
◆ If served as a dessert, the Kugelhopf can be served with a fruit or chocolate sauce.

Crown brioche

Time needed: *1 hour and 15 minutes*
(plus rising time)
Difficulty: *medium*

INGREDIENTS FOR **8** SERVINGS
3 cups of flour
7 tablespoons of softened butter
3/4 cup of sugar
1/2 cup of milk
2 teaspoons of yeast
1/2 cup of diced candied fruit
1/2 cup of raisins
2 eggs
grated peel of one organic lemon
a pinch of salt

Decoration:
1 egg
1 tablespoon of pearl sugar
a few peeled almonds

◆ Butter and flour a 12-inch tube pan.
◆ Soak raisins in warm water. Dissolve yeast in warmed milk. On a work surface, sift flour and keep 1 tablespoon aside. Add the yeast, eggs, sugar, salt, butter and lemon peel. Knead mixture until dough is smooth, elastic and does not stick to fingers.
◆ Cover dough with a kitchen towel and set aside to raise, in a warm place, for 1 hour. Knead again for 5 minutes; work in the drained raisins and candied fruit. Divide dough in 3 equal parts; roll in cylinders and make a long braid; bring the ends together to form a crown.
◆ Preheat oven to 375°F. Place braid in the prepared pan and set aside to raise, in a warm place, until dough has doubled. Brush with the beaten egg and sprinkle with pearl sugar and almonds.
◆ Bake for 50-55 minutes. Turn onto a rack and cool before serving.

Candied fruit twist

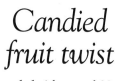

Time needed: *1 hour and 20 minutes*
(plus rising time)
Difficulty: *medium*

INGREDIENTS FOR **6-8** SERVINGS
3 cups of flour ◆ *2 eggs*
7 tablespoons of butter ◆ *3 tablespoons of sugar*
1 1/4 teaspoons of yeast
6 tablespoons of milk ◆ *a pinch of salt*

Filling:
1/4 cup of raisins
1/4 cup of diced candied orange and citron
1/8 cup of candied cherries
1/4 cup of diced dried apricots

Decoration:
1 egg ◆ *6 candied cherries*
2 dried apricots
candied orange and citron

◆ Grease and flour a cookie sheet.
◆ In a saucepan, heat milk with butter and sugar. Cool lightly and add the yeast previously diluted in cold water.
◆ In a bowl, sift flour and salt; mix with eggs and the milk mixture. Knead the dough and floured board for 20 minutes, until dough is smooth and elastic. Cover with a towel and let it rise, in a warm place, for 30 minutes.
◆ Knead dough again for a few minutes and place in a large bowl. Refrigerate for at least 12 hours, covered with a humid cloth.
◆ To prepare filling, mix all candied fruits. Roll out dough in a large rectangle.
◆ Cut rectangle in half; spread fruits in the center of the dough strips and fold them into 2 rolls. Twist the 2 rolls in a spiral and place it on the cookie sheet. Cover and set aside to rise for 1 hour, or until doubled in volume.
◆ Preheat the oven to 375°F.
◆ Brush the twist with beaten egg. Cut apricots in quarters and slice candied fruits; place them in the folds of the twists. Bake for 45 minutes. Remove from oven and cool completely before serving.

Copenhagen cake

Time needed: *1 hour and 15 minutes*
(plus rising time)
Difficulty: complex

INGREDIENTS FOR 8-10 SERVINGS
3 cups of flour
1/4 cup of butter
2 teaspoons of yeast
1/8 cup of sugar
1/4 cup of milk
a pinch of salt
2 tablespoons of apricot jelly
2 tablespoons of raisins

◆ Butter and flour a 12-inch cake pan.
◆ In a saucepan, heat milk, 2 tablespoons of butter, salt and sugar. Dissolve yeast in 2 tablespoons of cold water and add to milk mixture. In a bowl, sift the flour and stir in the yeast mixture. Mix rapidly and knead lightly. Form a loaf and set aside for 30 minutes.
◆ Work the remaining butter into a 6-inch square. Cover with plastic wrap and refrigerate. On a floured surface, roll dough into a 10-inch square. Remove butter from refrigerator; place between 2 sheets of plastic wrap and beat lightly with a rolling pin to soften it. Place it in the middle of dough and fold 4 corners over it.
◆ Roll out with the rolling pin into a rectangle; fold in 3, give it a 1/4 turn and roll again. Fold in 3, cover loosely with plastic wrap and refrigerate for 1 hour. Again, roll dough in a rectangle; fold in 3, cover with plastic wrap and refrigerate for 2 hours (or overnight).
◆ Roll dough to 1/4 inch thickness. Cut out a 12 inch circle and place in the cake pan. Roll remaining dough in a rectangle and cut into strips. Turn strips into spirals and place around dough base. Sprinkle with raising. Set aside to rise for 30-40 minutes, in a warm place.
◆ 10 minutes before the end of rising time, preheat oven to 350°F. Bake for 45 minutes. Melt apricot jelly and brush all over the cake.

Kirsch brioche

Time needed: *1 hour*
(plus rising time)
Difficulty: medium

INGREDIENTS FOR 8 SERVINGS
3 cups of flour ◆ *3 tablespoons of sugar*
1 teaspoon of yeast ◆ *6 tablespoons of milk*
3 eggs ◆ *8 tablespoons of butter*
a pinch of salt ◆ *1 tablespoon of pearl sugar*

Filling and Syrup:
1/4 cup of apricot marmalade
1/4 cup of black currants
1/4 cup of sugar ◆ *3 tablespoons of Kirsch*

◆ Butter and flour a 4x8-inch rectangular mold.
◆ In a saucepan, heat milk; add butter, cut in pieces, and sugar; mix well until all ingredients are dissolved. Cool. Stir in the yeast, dissolved in 2 tablespoons of warm water. In a bowl, sift the flour; add salt, 2 eggs and yeast mixture. Knead vigorously for 20 minutes, until the dough is smooth and elastic, and it detaches itself from the sides of the bowl.
◆ Cover with a kitchen towel and set aside in a cool place for 30 minutes. Punch dough and knead briefly; return to bowl (it will fill 1/3) and refrigerate for 12 hours, covered with a humid kitchen towel.
◆ Briefly work the dough once more; place in the prepared mold and let rise for 1 hour, or until volume has doubled.
◆ Ten minutes before the end of rising time, preheat the oven to 400°F.
◆ Brush dough with remaining egg, lightly beaten. Sprinkle with pearl sugar. Bake for 30 minutes. Turn brioche onto a rack, cool and slice in 3 layers.
◆ Prepare the syrup: Cook the sugar with 1/2 cup of water, cool and add Kirsch. Brush one layer of brioche with syrup; spread with apricot marmalade. Cover with the second layer of brioche; brush it with syrup; spread with marmalade and top with last layer of brioche. Serve warm.

Butter a tall round mold. Line with parchment paper and carefully butter the paper.

◆ Soak raisins in warm water.

◆ Dissolve yeast in 2 teaspoons of warm water and mix with 1 cup of flour.
Form into a ball; with a knife, make a cross on top; let it raise, in a warm place, for 20 minutes.

◆ In a large bowl, mix the raised yeast ball with 1/2 the flour and a little warm water. Set aside to raise.

◆ Preheat the oven to 350°F.

Panettone

Time needed: *1 hour (plus rising time)*
Difficulty: medium

INGREDIENTS FOR 12 SERVINGS

*7 cups of flour
3/4 cup of butter
4 teaspoons of yeast
3/4 cup of sugar
6 egg yolks
1 teaspoon of salt
1 1/2 cups of raisins
1/4 cup of candied orange peel
1/4 cup of candied citron
grated peel of one
organic lemon*

◆ Dice the candied orange and citron peel.

◆ When dough has doubled, mix with remaining flour, melted butter, beaten egg yolks, sugar, lemon peel and salt. Add as much warm water as needed. Knead dough for 10-12 minutes; add the strained raisins and candied peel.

◆ When dough is smooth, place in the mold (it should fill 1/2) and let raise until it reaches top of mold. Cut a cross on top of dough and brush with melted butter. Bake for 45-50 minutes.

Filled Savarin

Time needed: *1 hour and 15 minutes (plus rising time)*
Difficulty: medium

INGREDIENTS FOR 6 SERVINGS
*1 1/4 cups of flour
1/4 cup of softened butter
1/4 cup of sugar
1 teaspoon of yeast
2 eggs
grated peel of 1/2 organic lemon
a pinch of salt
2 tablespoons of milk
1 tablespoon of apricot jelly*

Filling:
*1/3 cup of sugar
3 egg yolks
1 cup of milk
1/3 cup of flour
1 teaspoon of vanilla
peel of 1/2 organic lemon
3/4 cup of whipped cream
1 tablespoon of Grand Marnier
2/3 lb of wild strawberries*

Syrup:
*1/2 cup of sugar
3 tablespoons of Grand Marnier
peel of one organic orange and one organic lemon
1 vanilla bean
2 cloves*

Filled Savarin

◆ Butter and flour a 6-cup mold. Dissolve yeast in warmed milk.

◆ In a bowl, sift the flour; add yeast, sugar, butter, salt, lemon peel and the eggs, one at a time. Knead vigorously until dough is elastic. Place in a bowl, cover and set aside in a warm place until dough has doubled. Transfer dough in prepared mold and let it rise until it reaches top of mold. Ten minutes before the end of the raising time, preheat the oven to 380°F.

◆ Bake for 40-45 minutes. Remove from oven and cool in the mold.

◆ To prepare the filling, make a pastry cream (see page 16), cool it and stir in the Grand Marnier and 3/4 cup of whipped cream.

◆ To make the syrup, cook 1 cup of water, sugar, orange and lemon peel, split vanilla bean and cloves for 3 minutes. Cool and stir in the Grand Marnier.

◆ Rinse the wild strawberries in ice water; set aside 1/2. Slice the upper part of the Savarin; with a knife, remove the inside of the Savarin without piercing the bottom. In this cavity, pour a layer of pastry cream and a layer of strawberries, another layer of cream and so on, until all ingredients have been used.

◆ Close the Savarin with cut-off top; soak with the syrup. Turn onto a serving plate and pour leftover syrup on top.

◆ In a double boiler, melt the apricot jelly and brush the Savarin. Place remaining whipped cream on top of Savarin; decorate with wild strawberries.

Panettone

Orange Savarin

Time needed: *1 hour and 50 minutes*
(plus rising time)
Difficulty: medium

INGREDIENTS FOR 8-10 SERVINGS
2 1/2 cups of flour
1/3 cup of softened butter
1/3 cup of sugar
1 teaspoon of yeast ◆ *4 eggs*
grated peel of one organic lemon
a pinch of salt
1/4 cup of raisins
1/4 cup of milk
2 tablespoons of Grand Marnier

Syrup:
1 cup of sugar
2 organic oranges
1 tablespoon of Grand Marnier
1 tablespoon of apricot jelly

Icing and Decoration:
1/2 cup of powdered sugar
1 tablespoon of orange juice
1 egg white
3/4 cup of heavy cream
6 strawberries
7 raspberries

◆ Butter and flour a 10-inch tube pan. Dissolve yeast in warm milk.
◆ Soak raisins in Grand Marnier for 30 minutes. In a bowl, sift the flour; stir in the yeast, butter, sugar, salt, lemon peel and the eggs, one at a time. Knead vigorously until dough is elastic and it detaches itself from the sides of the bowl. Drain raisins, dry and roll in flour; add to the dough.
◆ Cover dough with a towel and set aside in a warm place, until doubled.
◆ Preheat the oven to 400°F.
◆ Transfer dough to prepared pan. It should fill 3/4 of pan. Set aside in a warm place until the dough reaches top of pan. Bake for 40 minutes; remove from oven and cool in its pan.
◆ To prepare the syrup, boil 2 cups of water with the sugar and the peel from 2 oranges. Cook for 3 minutes, remove from heat and stir in the Grand Marnier. Pour hot syrup on Savarin to soak completely. Turn onto a rack and brush with apricot jelly, melted in 1 tablespoon of hot water.
◆ To prepare the icing, whisk the egg white with orange juice; slowly add sugar until the icing is thick and fluid. Pour on the Savarin and refrigerate.
◆ Transfer Savarin to a serving dish. Rinse and

Orange Savarin

dry strawberries and raspberries. Dice 1 strawberry and slice the remainder. Whip the cream; transfer to a pastry bag, fitted with a star tube; decorate the base and the center of Savarin. Decorate with strawberries and raspberries.

Kranz

Time needed: *1 hour*
(plus rising time)
Difficulty: medium

INGREDIENTS FOR 6 SERVINGS
3/4 lb of puff pastry (see page 12)
3 cups of flour
7 tablespoons of butter
1/4 cup of sugar
2 eggs
1 teaspoon of yeast
1/8 cup of milk
a pinch of salt

Filling and Decoration:
1 1/2 cups of raisins
2 cups of diced candied fruits
1/4 cup of pearl sugar
1 egg
1/4 cup of rum

◆ Butter and flour a cookie sheet. Soak raisins and candied fruit in rum.
◆ Mix 2 tablespoons of flour and salt with yeast in warmed milk; make a small dough ball and place in a bowl covered with warm water. When dough has doubled, it will float. Drain, dry and place in the center of remaining flour. Add sugar, egg and butter cut in pieces. Knead vigorously until dough is elastic and place in a bowl; with a knife, cut a cross on top of dough, cover with a towel and set aside until dough has doubled.
◆ Preheat the oven to 360°F.
◆ Knead this dough again; roll it and divide in 3 equal rectangles. Roll out puff pastry dough in 3 equal-sized rectangles.
◆ Drain raisins and candied fruits; divide in 5 portions. Brush all 6 pieces of dough with beaten egg. Spread raisins and fruits on 5 rectangles, leaving one rectangle of pastry dough without. Starting with the raised dough, place all rectangles one over the other, finishing with the puff pastry dough. Gently press with a rolling pin. Turn dough like a screw and brings ends under.
◆ Place kranz on the prepared cookie sheet; brush with beaten egg and sprinkle with pearl sugar. Bake for 40 minutes.

Kranz

Bavarian ring cake

Time needed:
1 hour and 20 minutes
(plus rising time)
Difficulty: medium

INGREDIENTS FOR **6-8** SERVINGS
2 1/2 cups of flour
7 tablespoons of softened butter
1/3 cup of sugar
1 teaspoon of yeast
4 eggs
grated peel of one organic lemon
a pinch of salt
1/8 cup of milk

Syrup:
1 cup of sugar
peel of 1 organic orange and 1 organic lemon
1/2 cup of Maraschino

Decoration:
1 cup of heavy cream
2 tablespoons of apricot jelly
1/2 cup of peeled and chopped almonds

◆ Butter and flour a 12-inch tube pan. Dissolve yeast in warm milk.
◆ In a bowl, sift the flour and add yeast, butter, sugar, salt, lemon peel and the eggs, one at a time. Knead energetically until dough is smooth and soft. Set aside in a warm place to rise until doubled. Transfer dough to prepared pan and let rise until dough reaches top of pan.
◆ Ten minutes before the end of rising time, preheat the oven to 375°F. Bake for 40 minutes. Let cool in the pan.
◆ To prepare the syrup, cook sugar in 2 cups of water, and orange and lemon peels, for 3-4 minutes. Remove from heat and add Maraschino, keeping 2 tablespoons aside. Through a sieve, pour hot syrup on dessert. Turn onto a serving dish.
◆ Melt the apricot jelly in remaining Maraschino; brush on cake. Whip cream and fill the center of cake. Cover cream and bottom of cake with chopped almonds. Keep refrigerated until ready to serve.

Bavarian ring cake

Luxemburg Savarin

Luxemburg Savarin

Time needed:
1 hour and 15 minutes
(plus rising time)
Difficulty: medium

INGREDIENTS FOR **6-8** SERVINGS
1 1/4 cups of flour
7 tablespoons of softened butter
5 egg yolks
1/8 cup of milk
1/4 cup of sugar
a pinch of salt

Syrup:
1/2 cup of sugar
1/2 cup of Kirsch

Decoration:
5 tablespoons of apricot jelly
3/4 cup of whipping cream
1/3 lb of blackberries

◆ Butter and flour a 10-inch tube pan. Dissolve yeast in warm water.
◆ In a bowl, mix the sifted flour with yeast, butter cut in small pieces, sugar, salt and egg yolks. Knead vigorously until dough is elastic. Cover with a kitchen towel and set aside to rise until it has doubled. Transfer dough to pan (it should fill 3/4) and let rise until it reaches top of pan. Ten minutes before the end of rising time, preheat the oven to 400°F.
◆ Bake Savarin for 40 minutes; remove from oven and set aside to cool in the baking pan.
◆ Prepare syrup: Bring to boil 1 cup of water with the sugar and cook for 2 minutes. Remove from heat and add Kirsch. Pour syrup on Savarin.
◆ Turn Savarin onto a serving dish and brush with melted apricot jelly. Rinse blackberries in ice water and dry. Transfer whipping cream to a pastry bag, fitted with a star tube and decorate Savarin with rosettes of cream and blackberries.

Hazelnut crown

Time needed: *1 hour and 20 minutes (plus rising time)*
Difficulty: *medium*

INGREDIENTS FOR 6-8 SERVINGS
3 cups of flour
2 eggs
7 tablespoons of butter
3 tablespoons of sugar
1 teaspoon of yeast
1/4 cup of milk
a pinch of salt

Filling and Decoration:
1 cup of milk
3 egg yolks
1/4 cup of sugar
1 1/4 cups of toasted, coarsely chopped nuts
1/4 cup of walnuts
3 tablespoons of rum
2 tablespoons of apricot jelly

◆ Butter and flour a cookie sheet.
◆ In a saucepan, heat milk with sugar and butter, cut in small pieces. Cool briefly and add the yeast, previously dissolved in 2 tablespoons of warm water. In a bowl, sift the flour; add egg and salt; mix with a wooden spoon. Knead dough vigorously for 20 minutes, until dough is smooth and elastic, and it detaches itself from the bowl. Cover with a kitchen towel and set aside to raise, in a warm place, for 30 minutes.
◆ Knead again for 5 minutes and transfer to a large bowl. Cover with a humid kitchen towel and refrigerate for at least 12 hours.
◆ To make the filling, melt sugar in the milk. Add nuts and hazelnuts; bring to boil. Remove from heat, rapidly stir in the egg yolks and cool; add rum.
◆ Roll out dough in a rectangle; spread filling mixture in the middle. Roll dough in a long cylinder and bring ends together to seal into a donut shape. With scissors, cut into top of donut in a zig-zag pattern. Place a ball of aluminum paper in the center of donut. Set aside to rise for 1 hour.
◆ Ten minutes before the end of raising time, preheat the oven to 350°F. Bake for 40-45 minutes. Cool completely and brush with apricot jelly, dissolved in a double boiler.

Dresden stollen

Time needed: *1 hour and 15 minutes (plus rising time)*
Difficulty: *medium*

INGREDIENTS FOR 6 SERVINGS
3 1/2 cups of flour
2 teaspoons of yeast
9 tablespoons of butter
1/3 cup of sugar
2 eggs
1 egg yolk
3 cups of milk
1/4 cup of currants
1/4 cup of raisins
2 oz of candied citron
2 oz of candied orange peel
2 oz of shelled bitter almonds
2 oz of shelled almonds
a pinch of nutmeg
2 ground cloves
a pinch of mace
grated peel of one organic lemon
1 tablespoon of vanilla
a pinch of salt

◆ Butter and flour a cookie sheet. Soak raisins and currants in warm water.
◆ Dissolve yeast in 1 cup of warm milk; add 1 cup of flour. Cover with a kitchen towel and set aside for 30 minutes in a cool place.
◆ Bring butter to room temperature. Scald both types of almonds in boiling water; drain, peel and chop. Dice candied orange peel and candied citron.
◆ In a bowl, mix 7 tablespoons of butter with the sugar; stir in the eggs, egg yolk, lemon peel, salt and all spices. Add remaining flour and milk to the mixture; mix in the yeast mixture. Knead dough on work surface until smooth; add the drained currants and raisins, candied fruits and almonds. Set aside, covered, for 20 minutes.
◆ Preheat the oven to 425°F. In the lower part of the oven, place a small baking dish filled with water: this will help bake the "stollen" perfectly.
◆ Form dough into an oblong-shaped bread. Place on cookie sheet and set aside for about 10 minutes.
◆ Bake for 40 minutes. Melt remaining butter. Remove bread from oven and brush with melted butter. Sprinkle with vanilla sugar and serve.

Artusi baba

Time needed: *1 hour*
(plus rising time)
Difficulty: *medium*

INGREDIENTS FOR **4** SERVINGS
2 1/2 cups of flour
3 teaspoons of yeast
1/2 cup of milk
5 tablespoons of butter
1/4 cup of powdered sugar
2 eggs
1 egg yolk
1/2 cup of raisins
1 tablespoon of candied citron
1/4 cup of heavy cream
1/8 cup of Marsala
1 tablespoon of powdered sugar
a pinch of salt

◆ Butter and flour a tall 6-cup mold. Soak the raisins in warm water; chop the candied citron. Let butter soften at room temperature.
◆ Melt yeast in warm water and mix with 1/2 cup of flour. Cover and let rise in a warm place for 30 minutes.
◆ In a large bowl, mix the remaining flour, eggs, egg yolk, sugar, salt and butter, cut in small pieces, until dough is smooth.
◆ Add the mixed yeast, cream, Marsala and rum. Knead vigorously, beating the dough in the bowl, until it is light and elastic, and it detaches itself from the sides of the bowl. Mix in the raisins and the candied citron. Cover and let rise for at least 20 minutes.
◆ Transfer mixture in the prepared mold (it should fill half of it), cover and let rise for 2 hours. Twenty minutes before the end of rising time, preheat the oven to 400°F.
◆ When the dough has risen to the top of the mold, bake for 20-25 minutes. When top of baba has browned, turn off the oven and leave the baba inside. Turn baba onto a serving plate and dust with vanilla sugar.
◆ This baba can be soaked in this rum syrup: melt 6 tablespoons of sugar in 1 cup of water, with one large lemon peel; when the sugar has dissolved, add 3/4 cup of rum.

Crown cake from Valtellina

Time needed: *1 hour and 10 minutes*
(plus rising time)
Difficulty: *medium*

INGREDIENTS FOR **6-8** SERVINGS
4 cups of flour
1/2 lb of butter
3 eggs
2/3 cup of sugar
1/2 lb of dried figs
1/2 lb of shelled hazelnuts
1/2 lb of raisins
1/2 cup of candied citron
2 teaspoons of yeast
3 tablespoons of milk
a pinch of salt

Decoration:
1/2 cup of pralined hazelnuts

◆ Preheat the oven to 400°F.
◆ Butter and lightly flour an 8-inch tube pan.
◆ Soak raisins in warm water. Let butter soften at room temperature. Dice dried figs and candied citron.
◆ Toast the hazelnuts in the preheated oven; peel them, rubbing in a kitchen towel and chop. Turn off oven. Dissolve yeast in warm milk.
◆ On a work surface, sift the flour and add yeast, sugar, salt, and butter, cut in small pieces. Knead vigorously until dough is smooth. Cover with a kitchen towel and let rise in a warm place for 1 hour.
◆ Knead the dough for 5 minutes. Mix in the strained raisins, the candied citron, the chopped hazelnuts and figs.
◆ Transfer dough in the prepared pan (it should fill about 2/3) and set aside in a warm place to raise, until dough reaches border of pan (about 40 minutes). Ten minutes before the end of cooking time, preheat the oven to 375°F.
◆ Bake for 50-60 minutes.
◆ Turn dessert on a rack and cool completely. Place on a serving dish and decorate with the pralined hazelnuts.

Butter an oven dish and dust with breadcrumbs. Preheat the oven to 400°F.

◆ Soak raisins in brandy for 20 minutes. Peel apples, core and chop coarsely. Spread apples and strained raisins in prepared dish.

◆ On a work surface, sift the flour; add sugar and butter, cut in small pieces.

◆ With your fingertips, knead ingredients in-

Old England

Time needed: *1 hour*
Difficulty: easy
INGREDIENTS
FOR 8 SERVINGS

8 apples
1/2 cup of raisins
1/2 lb of cold butter
1/4 cup of brandy
3/4 cup of sugar
1 3/4 cups of flour
breadcrumbs

to a mixture that resembles coarse meal. This can be done very easily and quickly in a food processor.

◆ Spread this mixture over the apples and raisins. Bake for 35-40 minutes.

◆ Bring this dessert directly from the baking dish. It can be served hot or warm.

Irish apple and potato cake

Time needed: *1 hour and 10 minutes*
Difficulty: easy

INGREDIENTS FOR 4 SERVINGS
4 apples ◆ *1 lb of potatoes*
1 cup of flour ◆ *4 tablespoons of butter*
2 tablespoons of sugar ◆ *a pinch of cinnamon*
1 tablespoon of vanilla sugar ◆ *a pinch of salt*

◆ Wash potatoes; cook in salted water. Peel, while hot, and pass through a food mill onto a work surface. Add the flour and mix until dough is smooth.
◆ Split dough in 2 equal parts; roll out in 2 equal circles.
◆ Peel the apples, core and slice thinly.
◆ In a skillet, the size of the dough circles, melt half the butter.
◆ Delicately put in a circle of dough; cover with sliced apples and the remaining butter cut in small pieces. Sprinkle with sugar and cinnamon. Cover with second circle of dough, pressing the sides to close the pie. Cook on low heat.
◆ When pie is golden on the underside, turn it, like a frittata and let it brown on the other side. This whole process should take 30 to 40 minutes.
◆ Slide the pie on a serving dish, dust with vanilla sugar and serve. To decorate, use a few slices

of apple and mint leaves.
◆ This simple but delicious pie can be served with a fruit sauce or a few scoops of ice cream.

Viennese black cherry cake

Time needed: *1 hour and 10 minutes*
Difficulty: easy

INGREDIENTS FOR 4 SERVINGS
3/4 lb of black cherries
1 1/2 cups of flour
3/4 cup of sugar
12 tablespoons of butter
4 eggs
1 cup of peeled almonds
a pinch of salt

◆ Butter an 8x10-inch baking pan. Preheat the oven to 350°F.
◆ Remove stem from the cherries, rinse and dry. Finely grind the almonds.
◆ In a bowl, mix sugar, flour and melted butter. Add the egg yolks, one by one, and the ground almonds. Whisk egg whites and salt to stiff peaks; delicately fold into mixture.
◆ Pour mixture in prepared pan; cover with cherries. Bake for 35-40 minutes. Turn cake onto a serving dish and serve warm or cold.

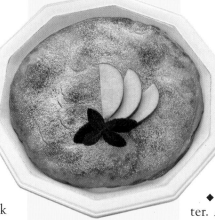

Irish apple and potato cake

Old England

Grape clafoutis

Time needed: *1 hour*
Difficulty: easy

INGREDIENTS FOR 6 SERVINGS
3/4 lb of white grapes
3/4 lb of red grapes
3 eggs ◆ *2 cups of flour*
8 tablespoons of melted butter
2/3 cup of sugar
1 teaspoon of baking powder

Topping:
a few white and red grapes
2 oz of apricot jelly

Grape clafoutis

◆ Brush a 10-inch cake pan with a little melted butter; sprinkle with flour.
◆ Preheat the oven to 390°F.
◆ Rinse and dry grapes; cut in half and seed.
◆ Sift the flour in a bowl and blend in the baking powder, sugar, eggs and melted butter until smooth. Mix in the grapes. Pour the batter in the cake pan and even it out with a spatula. Bake for 35-40 minutes. Cool for 5 minutes before transferring it onto a serving plate.
◆ In a double boiler, melt the jelly; brush the cake with a little jelly. Garnish with grapes, placing them around the border and in the center of cake. Brush with remaining jelly.
◆ You may substitute the grapes with apples, pears, plums, cherries or other fruits of your choice.

Caramelized fruit cake

Time needed: *1 hour*
Difficulty: easy

INGREDIENTS FOR 6-8 SERVINGS
2 cups of flour
1 1/2 cups of sugar
3/4 cup of melted butter
1/2 teaspoon of baking powder
4 eggs ◆ *11 oz of apricots*
11 oz of apples ◆ *11 oz of pears*

◆ Preheat the oven to 340°F. On low heat,

Caramelized fruit cake

caramelize 3/4 cup of sugar with 2 tablespoons of water in an 8-inch cake pan (see page 19). Rotate the cake pan to evenly cover the bottom and sides with the caramelized sugar.
◆ Scald the apricots in boiling water, peel, cut in half and pit. Peel the apples and pears, core and cut into 4 segments.
◆ Whip 4 tablespoons of butter and spread on the cold caramel. Place the fruits in the cake pan, alternating apples, pears and apricots. In a bowl, whisk 3/4 cup of butter with 3/4 cup of sugar using an electric mixer; add the eggs, the sifted flour and baking powder.
◆ Pour batter over the fruits in the cake pan and bake for 35-40 minutes. Remove from the oven, transfer onto a dish and serve warm or cold.

Fruit pastiche

Time needed: *1 hour*
(plus cooling time)
Difficulty: easy

INGREDIENTS FOR 6 SERVINGS
7 oz of savoyard cookies
5-7 apricots in syrup
18 candied cherries
2 apples
2 tablespoons of raisins
3 eggs
1/2 cup of sugar
2 cups of milk
2 tablespoons of rum
1/2 cup of whipping cream

◆ Line a rectangular 10x4-inch loaf pan with parchment paper. Preheat the oven to 360°F.
◆ Cut the apricots in half and pit. Peel the apples, core and slice.
◆ In a bowl, whisk the eggs with the sugar; a little at a time, add milk and rum.
◆ Line the apricots at the bottom of the loaf pan, covering the empty spaces with the cherries. Cover with a layer of savoyard cookies, a layer of apples and one of raisins. Finish with a layer of savoyard cookies. Pour the egg and milk mixture on top.
◆ Bake in a bain-marie in the oven for 40 minutes. Cool and refrigerate for at least 2 hours.
◆ Transfer the pastiche onto a serving dish and top with rosettes of whipped cream.

Fruit pastiche

Cake with grapes

Time needed: *1 hour and 10 minutes*
Difficulty: medium

INGREDIENTS FOR 6 SERVINGS
1 lb of ripe green and red grapes
2 tablespoons of semolina
2 cups of milk
4 tablespoons of butter ◆ 3 eggs
2 tablespoons of dark rum
1/2 cup of sugar
a pinch of salt

◆ Butter and flour a 12-inch cake pan and preheat the oven to 360°F.
◆ Gently rinse the grapes, remove stems and set a handful aside. Cut the remainder in half and seed.
◆ In a saucepan, bring milk to a boil. Add semolina and cook for 10-15 minutes, stirring constantly.
◆ Remove from heat; blend in the butter, 3 egg yolks, sugar and rum; add the grape halves.
◆ In a bowl, beat egg whites with salt to stiff peaks and gently fold into the semolina mixture. Pour into the cake pan and bake for 40-50 minutes, until raised and golden.
◆ Remove from the oven, cool for 10 minutes, then transfer onto a serving dish.
◆ Garnish with the whole grapes, forming a bunch. Serve cold.

Cake with grapes

Whole-wheat pear cake

Time needed: *1 hour*

Difficulty: easy
2 lbs of pears
1/2 cup of flour
1/2 cup of whole wheat flour
1/2 cup of sugar
1 teaspoon of baking powder
2 eggs ◆ 1/4 cup of milk
1 tablespoon of lemon juice
1 tablespoon of powdered sugar

◆ Butter and flour a cake pan and preheat an oven to 350°F.

Whole-wheat pear cake

◆ Peel the pears, core, slice and soak in the lemon juice.
◆ Whisk the egg yolks and sugar with an electric mixer, until pale and creamy. Mix in the sifted flours, baking powder, the milk and pear slices. Beat egg whites with salt to stiff peaks and gently fold into the mixture. Pour into the cake pan.
◆ Bake for 40-45 minutes. Transfer the cake onto a serving dish and cool. Sprinkle with powdered sugar.

Fig, walnut and orange cake

Time needed: *1 hour and 10 minutes*
Difficulty: easy

INGREDIENTS FOR 6 SERVINGS
1 1/4 cups of flour
4 tablespoons of melted butter
1/2 cup of sugar
1 egg
1/2 teaspoon of baking soda
5 tablespoons of milk
1/2 lb of fresh figs
1/2 cup of finely chopped walnuts
1/2 tablespoon of one organic orange peel
1 teaspoon of vanilla

Decoration:
2 tablespoons of apricot jelly
1 tablespoon of finely chopped walnuts
1/2 cup of fresh figs

◆ Butter and flour a tube pan. Preheat the oven to 350°F.
◆ Peel the figs, slice and cook with 1/4 cup of sugar on moderate heat for 8-10 minutes. Cool completely.
◆ Beat the butter and remaining sugar until creamy; add the egg. Mix in the sifted flour, baking soda, milk, figs, walnuts, orange peel and vanilla until well blended.
◆ Pour the mixture into the pan, cover with aluminum foil and bake for 30 minutes. Remove the aluminum foil and continue to bake for another 20 minutes. Turn the cake onto a grid.
◆ To decorate, peel the figs and cut into segments. Brush the cake with the jelly, diluted in a double boiler. Sprinkle with the chopped walnuts and transfer onto a serving dish. Fill the hole with the fig segments.

Fig, walnut and orange cake

Kirsch apricot cake

Time needed: *1 hour*
Difficulty: easy

INGREDIENTS FOR 6-8 SERVINGS
1 lb of fresh apricots (or 14 oz of canned apricots)
8 tablespoons of melted butter
1 1/4 cups of flour
4 eggs
1/4 cup of Kirsch
1 teaspoon of vanilla
1 teaspoon of baking powder
1 tablespoon of breadcrumbs
1 tablespoon of powdered sugar
1 pinch of salt

◆ Grease a 10 x 5 inch rectangular cake pan and sprinkle with breadcrumbs. Preheat the oven to 375°F.
◆ Rinse and dry the apricots, pit and cut into thin rings. Whisk the butter with egg yolks, sugar and vanilla until pale and creamy. Mix in the Kirsch, sifted flour and baking powder. Beat eggs with salt to stiff peaks and fold into the mixture.
◆ Pour 2/3 of the mixture into the cake pan, layer with apricots, pour over the remaining mixture and cover with the remaining apricots. Bake for about 40 minutes. Transfer onto a serving dish and sprinkle with powdered sugar.

Date cake

Time needed: *1 hour and 30 minutes*
Difficulty: easy

INGREDIENTS FOR 6 SERVINGS
1 2/3 cups of flour
1/2 cup of sugar
1/2 cup of dates
6 tablespoons of softened butter
1/4 cup of milk
1 tablespoon of honey
2 eggs
1 teaspoon of baking powder
a pinch of salt

◆ Grease and flour a rectangular 6-cup loaf pan. Preheat the oven to 375°F.

◆ On a work surface, mix in flour, baking powder, sugar, honey and butter in pieces.
◆ Crumble with your hands and put in a large bowl (or pulse in an electric mixer until it resembles coarse meal).
◆ Beat eggs with milk and salt; pour onto the crumbled mixture, stirring vigorously until smooth. Pit the dates and finely chop. Mix into the mixture and pour it into the loaf pan.
◆ Bake for about 50 minutes. Transfer the cake onto a rack and cool.

Apple walnut cake

Time needed: *1 hour and 20 minutes (plus infusion time)*
Difficulty: easy

INGREDIENTS FOR 6-8 SERVINGS
2 lbs of apples
2 cups of flour
1/2 cup of sugar
2 egg yolks
4 tablespoons of butter
3/4 cup of milk
1/4 cup of Cognac
1/4 cup of whole walnuts
1/4 cup of raisins
4 crumbled amaretti
1 teaspoon of vanilla-flavored powdered sugar
1/2 teaspoon of baking powder
grated peel of 1/2 organic lemon
1 tablespoon of breadcrumbs

Decoration:
1 tablespoon of powdered sugar
1/8 cup of raisins
1 apple
2 tablespoons of sugar
1 whole walnut

◆ Grease an 8-inch cake pan and sprinkle with breadcrumbs. Preheat the oven to 350°F.
◆ Peel the apples, core and slice thinly.
◆ Whisk egg yolks, sugar and butter in pieces. Mix in the sifted flour and baking powder a little at a time; add the milk, cognac and lemon peel.
◆ Pour half of the mixture into the cake pan; cover with half of the apples, sprinkle with the amaretti, a few raisins, walnuts and vanilla-fla-

vored powdered sugar. Spread over a second layer of apples, sprinkle with the remaining ingredients and cover with the remaining batter. Bake for 40-45 minutes. Remove from the oven and cool completely.

◆ To decorate, peel the apple, core and slice thinly.

◆ On low heat, dissolve the sugar in 3 tablespoons of water. Macerate the apples in syrup for 1 hour. Place a 3-inch cardboard circle on the cake. Sprinkle with powdered sugar and remove the cardboard circle. Top with drained and dried apples and complete the decoration with the raisins and whole walnut.

Banana delight

Time needed: *1 hour and 10 minutes*
Difficulty: easy

INGREDIENTS FOR 8 SERVINGS
1 1/2 lbs of bananas (ripe and firm)
1/2 lb of savoyard cookies
4 amaretti
1/2 cup of sugar
5 eggs
8 tablespoons of butter
juice of 1 lemon
a pinch of salt
1 tablespoon of breadcrumbs

◆ Butter a 12-inch cake pan and sprinkle with breadcrumbs. Preheat the oven to 350°F.

◆ Grind the cookies. Peel the bananas, slice and mix with lemon juice.

◆ Whisk butter and sugar until smooth and creamy. Mix in the egg yolks, one at a time and the ground cookies. Beat egg whites with salt to stiff peaks; fold into the mixture. Gently mix in the banana slices and pour the mixture into the cake pan. Bake for 45 minutes, remove from the oven and transfer onto a serving dish.

◆ To decorate, peel the banana, slice and mix with lemon juice.

◆ Brush the entire cake with the jelly, melted in a double boiler. Drain the banana slices, cut some of them in half and place in a crown at the base of the cake. Place the whole slices and mint leaves on the cake; brush the fruit with the remaining jelly.

Orange cake

Time needed: *1 hour and 20 minutes*
Difficulty: easy

INGREDIENTS FOR 6-8 SERVINGS
2 cups of flour
3/4 cup of sugar
8 tablespoons of butter
3 eggs
a pinch of salt
2 organic oranges
1/2 teaspoon of baking powder

Syrup:
2 oranges
1/3 cup of sugar

Decoration:
1 orange
1/4 cup of slivered almonds

◆ Grease a 10-inch cake pan. Preheat the oven to 350°F.

◆ Bring the butter to room temperature. Thoroughly rinse the oranges, dry, grate the peel and squeeze the juice.

◆ With an electric mixer, whisk egg yolks with sugar until pale and creamy. Stirring continuously, slowly add flour, baking powder; butter in pieces, orange peel and orange juice.

◆ Beat egg whites with salt to stiff peaks and gently fold into the mixture.

◆ Pour batter into the prepared cake pan and bake for 35-40 minutes. Remove from the oven, transfer onto a rack and cool completely.

◆ Make the syrup: Squeeze the juice of two oranges and bring it to boil with sugar, in a small saucepan. Cook for a few minutes until syrup is transparent. Pour it, still hot, onto the cake and spread it out evenly with a spatula.

◆ To decorate, peel the orange to the fruit (see page 28) and cut it in very thin slices. Garnish the cake with the orange slices and place a crown of slivered almonds on the border.

Preheat the oven to 350°F. Peel pears and mangos; cut into 1-inch-thick slices.

◆ In a bowl mix 6 tablespoons of butter with 1/3 cup of sugar. Spread the mixture in the bottom of a cake pan **(1)**. Layer with the fruit, alternating pear and mango slices, overlapping them slightly. Put the cake pan on a low heat, rotating it and remove from heat, when the sugar starts to caramelize.

◆ In a bowl, whisk egg and egg yolk with re-

Mango and pear cake

Time needed: *1 hour*
Difficulty: easy
INGREDIENTS
FOR 6-8 SERVINGS

12 tablespoons of
softened butter
1 1/2 lbs of pears
1 lb of mango
3/4 cup of sugar
1 egg
1 egg yolk
1/2 cup of milk
2 cups of flour
1 1/2 teaspoons of baking
powder
a pinch of salt

maining sugar, salt and remaining butter cut in pieces; add the sifted flour and baking powder, stirring continuously **(2)**.

◆ Pour this batter over the fruit in the cake pan **(3)** and bake for 30-35 minutes.

◆ Remove from the oven and turn onto a dish. Serve warm or cold.

Pineapple and walnut cake

Time needed: *1 hour and 15 minutes*
Difficulty: easy

INGREDIENTS FOR 6 SERVINGS
3 1/2 cups of flour ◆ 2/3 cup of sugar
1 teaspoon of baking powder ◆ 3 eggs
1 can of pineapple in syrup
2/3 cup of coarsely chopped walnuts
1 teaspoon of vanilla
7 tablespoons of butter
1/2 cup of milk
1/2 cup of pineapple syrup (from can)
a pinch of salt

◆ Grease and flour a 10-inch cake pan. Preheat the oven to 350°F.
◆ Beat egg yolks with sugar and butter until creamy. Mix in the flour, a little at a time, alternating it with the milk and pineapple syrup. Mix in the baking powder, chopped walnuts, vanilla and pineapple cut in small pieces. Beat egg whites with salt to stiff peaks; gently fold into the batter.
◆ Pour batter into the cake pan and bake for 45-50 minutes.
◆ Remove from the oven, cool completely and transfer onto a serving dish.

Peach sunburst cake

Peach sunburst cake

Time needed: *1 hour and 15 minutes*
Difficulty: easy

INGREDIENTS FOR 8-10 SERVINGS
2 lbs of peaches ◆ 3 1/2 cups of flour
3/4 cup of softened butter
4 eggs ◆ 1 1/4 cups of sugar
1 teaspoon of baking powder
1 teaspoon of cinnamon

Decoration:
6 crumbled amaretti
1 tablespoon of apricot jelly

◆ Grease and flour a 12-inch cake pan. Preheat the oven to 350°F.
◆ Scald the peaches in boiling water, peel and slice.
◆ In a bowl, whisk butter with 1 cup of sugar until creamy. Mix in the eggs, then the sifted flour and baking powder. Pour into the cake pan; cover with the peach slices in a sunburst pattern. Mix remaining sugar with cinnamon; sprinkle over peaches. Bake for 50-60 minutes.
◆ Remove from heat and transfer onto a serving dish. Brush with the apricot jelly, melted in a double boiler. Place the crumbled amaretti around the border of the cake.

Mango and pear cake

Soft pear cake

Time needed:
1 hour and 10 minutes
Difficulty: easy

INGREDIENTS FOR 6 SERVINGS
2 lbs of pears
1 cup of flour
3 eggs
1/2 cup of sugar
1/2 teaspoon of baking powder
1/4 cup of milk
juice of 1 lemon
1 teaspoon of powdered sugar
a pinch of salt

◆ Butter and flour a cake pan. Preheat the oven to 360°F.
◆ Peel the pears, core and thinly slice. Put them in a bowl with the lemon juice and sprinkle with 1/4 cup of sugar.
◆ Beat the egg yolks with the sugar until pale and creamy; mix in the sifted flour, baking powder and milk. Drain the pears from their liquid and mix into the soft batter. Beat egg whites with salt to stiff peaks and fold into the batter. Pour batter into the cake pan and bake for about 50 minutes.
◆ Remove from the oven and transfer onto a dish. Serve warm or cold, sprinkled with powdered sugar.

Périgord fruit cake

Time needed: *1 hour*
Difficulty: easy

INGREDIENTS FOR 6-8 SERVINGS
1 1/4 cups of flour
1 lb of pears
1/3 cup of raisins
3 eggs
1/3 cup of sugar
4 tablespoons of melted butter
1/3 cup of milk
1 teaspoon of baking powder
grated peel of one organic lemon
1 tablespoon of rum
1 tablespoon of lemon juice
1/2 a tablespoon of powdered sugar

Soft pear cake

Périgord fruit cake

◆ Grease and flour a deep 6-cup cake pan. Preheat the oven to 370°F.
◆ Peel the pears, core, slice and soak in the lemon juice.
◆ Rinse and dry the raisins. In a bowl, mix the sifted flour and baking powder with sugar, lemon peel and eggs. Add milk a little at a time; stir in rum and melted butter, then mix in the pear slices and raisins.
◆ Pour batter into the cake pan and bake for 40-45 minutes. Remove from heat, transfer onto a serving dish, cool and sprinkle half of the cake with powdered sugar.
◆ You may substitute the pears with other fruits according to season and taste.

Cake from Gascony

Time needed: *1 hour and 20 minutes*
Difficulty: easy

INGREDIENTS FOR 6 SERVINGS
4 Golden Delicious apples
3/4 cup of softened butter
1 3/4 cups of flour
3/4 cup of sugar ◆ *2 eggs*
1 teaspoon of nutmeg
1 teaspoon of cinnamon
1 cup of ground walnuts
1 teaspoon of vanilla
a pinch of salt

Decoration:
1 apple
1 tablespoon of powdered sugar
3/4 cup of dry white wine

◆ Butter and flour a cake pan. Preheat the oven to 350°F.
◆ Peel the apples, core and grate them. In a bowl, whisk the butter and sugar with an electric mixer; whisk in the eggs. Mix in the sifted flour, vanilla, cinnamon, nutmeg and salt; blend well. Mix in the apples and nuts. Pour the batter into the cake pan and bake for about 50 minutes.
◆ Peel the apple, slice and cut it into 30 small squares of 1/4-inch each side. Soak in the wine for 20 minutes.
◆ Transfer the cake onto a serving dish. Let cool and sprinkle with the powdered sugar. Garnish the center of the cake with the drained and dried apple squares in a checkered pattern.

Cake from Gascony

Fruit salad cake

Time needed: *1 hour*
Difficulty: easy

INGREDIENTS FOR **6** SERVINGS
10 tablespoons of butter
2 cups of flour
3/4 cup of sugar
4 eggs
grated peel of one organic lemon
1 teaspoon of baking powder
1 banana
1 apple
3/4 cup of strawberries
2 pineapple slices
1 peach
2 tablespoons of apricot jam
1 liquor glass of brandy
2 tablespoons of white wine
a pinch of salt

◆ Grease and flour a 12-inch cake pan. Preheat the oven to 400°F.
◆ Peel the banana, apple and peach. Core the apple and pit the peach; dice all fruits. Rinse and dice strawberries. Cut the pineapple in small pieces. Melt the butter on very low heat. In a bowl, mix fruits with jam, brandy and white wine.
◆ In a bowl, sift flour and baking powder; add butter, egg yolks, sugar and lemon peel. Beat vigorously; mix in the fruit salad. Beat egg whites with salt to stiff peaks and fold into batter. Pour batter into the cake pan and bake for 35-40 minutes.
◆ Remove from the oven, transfer onto a dish and serve warm or cold.

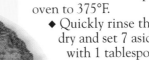

Fruit salad cake

Blueberry star cake

Blueberry star cake

Time needed: *1 hour and 10 minutes*
Difficulty: easy

INGREDIENTS
FOR **6-8** SERVINGS
2 1/2 cups of blueberries
4 eggs ◆ *4 egg yolks*
1 3/4 cups of flour ◆ *1/2 cup of sugar*
2 tablespoons of cornstarch
a pinch of mace
7 tablespoons of butter ◆ *1 teaspoon of vanilla*
grated peel of one organic lemon
1/3 cup of slivered almonds
1/8 cup of powdered sugar

◆ Grease a star shaped cake pan. Preheat the oven to 375°F.
◆ Quickly rinse the blueberries in ice water, dry and set 7 aside. Sprinkle the remainder with 1 tablespoon of flour. Melt butter on low heat; add vanilla and lemon peel.
◆ In a double boiler, mix the eggs, egg yolks and sugar. As soon as the mixture warms and the sugar is dissolved remove from heat; whisk with an electric mixer until tripled in volume. Mix in the sifted flour, cornstarch and mace; stir in the melted butter and blueberries.
◆ Pour the batter into the cake pan, sprinkle with the slivered almonds and bake for 35-40 minutes. Let the cake rest for 10 minutes in the pan; turn onto a serving dish and cool.
◆ Sprinkle with powdered sugar and garnish with remaining blueberries.

Prague blueberry cake

Time needed: *1 hour*
Difficulty: easy

INGREDIENTS FOR **8** SERVINGS
3 cups of blueberries ◆ *1 1/3 cups of flour*
1/2 cup of softened butter
3 eggs ◆ *1/2 cup of sugar*
1 tablespoon of Cointreau
grated peel of one organic orange
a pinch of salt

Decoration:
1/4 cup of raspberries
1/2 cup of blueberries
1 tablespoon of apricot jelly

◆ Grease and flour a rectangular loaf pan. Preheat the oven to 350°F.
◆ Quickly rinse the blueberries in ice water, drain and dry.
◆ In a bowl, using an electric mixer, whisk sugar and egg yolks until creamy. Mix in the liquor and orange peel. Beat egg whites with salt to stiff peaks; fold into the mixture alternating with the flour. Pour batter into the loaf pan; top with blueberries. Bake for about 45 minutes.
◆ To decorate, quickly rinse the blueberries and raspberries in ice water, dry. Brush the top of the cake with jelly, dissolved in a double boiler; garnish with the berries and brush with remaining jelly.

Prague blueberry cake

Grease a 12-inch quiche pan.

◆ Make the shortbread dough following the instructions and refrigerate for 1 hour, covered with plastic wrap. After 30 minutes, preheat the oven to 350°F.

◆ Roll out the dough into a thin sheet and line the cake pan, pinching the dough with a fork, around the edges.

◆ Line the dough with parchment paper and cover with dry beans. Bake for 15-20 minutes. Remove from the oven, discard the paper and beans and cool completely.

Lieges cake

Time needed:
*1 hour and 30 minutes
(plus resting time)*
Difficulty: medium
INGREDIENTS
FOR 6-8 SERVINGS

*1 recipe for shortbread pastry
(see page 12)
5 egg yolks
2 tablespoons of flour
1 cup of warm milk
6 tablespoons of sugar
2 tablespoons of brandy
10 tablespoons of whipped
cream
6 cups of blueberries
1/2 cup of raspberry jelly*

◆ In a saucepan, whisk eggs with sugar. Stir in the flour and warm milk until well blended. Cook in a double boiler, until mixture thickens, stirring constantly. Do not boil. Transfer saucepan on a bowl of ice and stir until mixture is thick and cold. Mix in the brandy and 6 tablespoons of whipped cream.

◆ Mix the rinsed and dried blueberries with the raspberry jelly. Pour half the custard into the cooked pastry box; cover with half the blueberries; cover with remaining custard and top with a layer of blueberries. Decorate with whipped cream and refrigerate for at least 2 hours before serving.

American pumpkin pie

Time needed: *1 hour and 20 minutes
(plus resting time)*
Difficulty: medium

INGREDIENTS FOR 6-8 SERVINGS
*2 cups of flour
7 tablespoons of cold butter
1 egg yolk
1 pinch of salt*

Filling:
*2 lbs of pumpkin
3/4 cup of sugar ◆ 3 eggs
1 tablespoon of flour
1 teaspoon of cinnamon
1/4 teaspoon of powdered ginger
a pinch of nutmeg
1/4 teaspoon of ground clove
1/3 cup of milk
3 amaretti
grated peel of one organic lemon*

Decoration:
*1/4 cup of candied pumpkin
3 tablespoons of whipped cream
a few mint leaves*

◆ Butter and flour a 12-inch pie pan. Preheat the oven to 400°F.

*American
pumpkin pie*

◆ In a food processor, mix the flour, butter and salt until the mixture resembles coarse meal. Beat the egg yolk with 2-3 tablespoons of ice water and add to the mixture. Pulse until you have a ball of dough. (To make the dough by hand, put the flour into a mound on a work surface, place pieces of butter in the center and working with your fingertips or with a fork, crumble the butter into the flour until the mixture resembles coarse meal. Beat the egg with 2-3 tablespoons of water and with your fingertips, rapidly mix it into the dough until you have a smooth ball of dough) Refrigerate for 30 minutes, covered with plastic wrap.

◆ To make the filling, peel the pumpkin; cut into 2-inch-thick slices. Place on a cookie sheet and bake for 30 minutes. As soon as the pumpkin is soft, purée; pour into a bowl; mix in the sugar, ginger, nutmeg, clove, cinnamon, lemon peel and milk. Lower the oven temperature to 350°F.

◆ Roll out the pastry dough into a thin sheet, line the pie pan, prick with a fork and sprinkle with the crumbled amaretti. Pour in the pumpkin mixture and bake for 50 minutes. Cool and transfer onto a serving dish.

◆ To decorate, cut 9 circles of candied pumpkin and 9 other smaller circles. Rinse and dry the mint leaves. Place 8 large pumpkin circles around the border of the cake and the last one in the center. Pipe a little whipped cream on each circle and top with a smaller circle. Garnish with the mint leaves. Keep in a cool place until ready to serve.

Lieges cake

"Patissière" tart

Time needed: *1 hour*
(plus resting time)
Difficulty: medium

INGREDIENTS FOR 8-10 SERVINGS
1 recipe for shortbread pastry (see page 12)
1 1/3 cups of milk
5 egg yolks
1/2 cup of sugar
1/2 cup of flour
1 vanilla bean
grated peel of 1/2 organic lemon
1 sugar rose
6 small sugar leaves

◆ Grease and flour a 12-inch pie pan.
◆ Make the shortbread pastry, form into a ball, cover with plastic wrap and refrigerate for 1 hour. After 30 minutes, preheat the oven to 360°F.
◆ Prepare a pastry cream (see page 16), with milk, 4 egg yolks, sugar, flour, lemon peel and vanilla bean. Let cool, stirring occasionally.
◆ Roll out the pastry dough into a thin sheet, line the pie pan and keep the trimmings aside. Prick the pastry sheet with a fork. Pour the pastry cream in the pie. Roll 1-inch-wide strips with the pastry trimmings and criss-cross over the cream. Brush the strips with the remaining, lightly beaten egg yolk. Bake for 30-35 minutes.
◆ Remove from the oven. Cool lightly and transfer onto a serving dish. Garnish with the sugar leaves and sugar rose.

Cherry puff pastry tart

Cherry puff pastry tart

Time needed: *2 hours*
(plus resting time)
Difficulty: complex

INGREDIENTS FOR 6-8 SERVINGS
12 oz of puff pastry (see page 12)
3/4 lb of ripe cherries
3 oz of marzipan
1/2 cup of finely chopped toasted hazelnuts
1 egg white
2 tablespoons of Kirsch
2 tablespoons of butter
2 tablespoons of sugar

◆ Preheat the oven to 400°F.
◆ Thoroughly rinse the cherries, pit and cut into half. In a bowl, mix the marzipan with the egg white, chopped hazelnuts and 1 tablespoon of Kirsch.
◆ Roll out the puff pastry into a thin sheet and cut a 10-inch circle. Brush a 10-inch pie dish with water; line with dough and prick dough with a fork. Spread the hazelnut-marzipan mixture in pie and cover with the half cherries in concentric circles.
◆ Bake for 15-20 minutes. Remove from the oven. Transfer immediately onto a serving dish and drizzle remaining Kirsch on the pie.
◆ Cook sugar in 3 tablespoons of water until thick. Mix in the butter and brush over the cherries. Serve warm.

Leopard cake

Time needed: *1 hour*
(plus resting time)
Difficulty: medium

INGREDIENTS FOR 10 SERVINGS
1 recipe for shortbread pastry (see page 12)
5 eggs ◆ *3/4 cup of sugar*
1 2/3 cups of toasted chopped almonds
1/4 cup of "Passito di Pantelleria" wine
1 teaspoon of vanilla
1 tablespoon of powdered sugar
1 candied cherry ◆ *a pinch of salt*

◆ Butter a 10-inch springform pan.
◆ Make the shortbread dough, form into a ball and refrigerate for 1 hour, covered with plastic wrap. After 30 minutes, preheat the oven to 350°F.
◆ Roll out 2/3 of the shortbread dough into a thin sheet, line the cake pan and prick dough with a fork.
◆ In a bowl, with an electric mixer, whip egg yolks and sugar. Mix in the almonds, vanilla and wine. Beat egg whites with salt to stiff peaks and delicately fold into the mixture. Pour into the pan.
◆ Roll out the remaining shortbread dough into a thin sheet and place over the filling, trimming it and sealing the edges carefully. Prick the top of the cake with a fork; decorate with a few leaves and bake for 40-45 minutes.
◆ Serve the cake cold, sprinkled with powdered sugar and garnished with the candied cherry in the center.

Leopard cake

Peach pie

Time needed: *2 hours*
Difficulty: **complex**

INGREDIENTS FOR **6-8** SERVINGS
1/2 recipe for puff pastry (see page 12)
1/3 cup of toasted ground almonds
2 lbs of peaches (ripe and firm)
1 tablespoon of apricot jelly
1/4 cup of toasted thinly slivered almonds

◆ Preheat the oven to 375°F.
◆ Scald the peaches in boiling water for 2 minutes, peel, pit and cut into 4 segments.
◆ Roll out the puff pastry into a thin sheet. Brush a 10-inch pie pan with water; line with dough and prick dough with a fork. Sprinkle with the ground almonds and cover with the peach segments in a sunburst fashion. Bake for 30-35 minutes.
◆ Transfer the pie onto a serving dish, brush with the jelly, melted in a double boiler. Decorate with the slivered almonds around the border and in the center. Serve warm or cold.

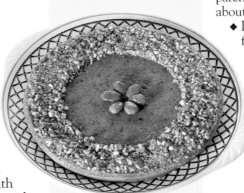

Praline cake
Alain Chapel

Praline cake Alain Chapel

Time needed: *1 hour*
(plus resting time)
Difficulty: **medium**

INGREDIENTS FOR **6-8** SERVINGS
2 cups of flour
3/4 cup of sugar
1 cup of peeled almonds
3/4 cup of whipping cream
a pinch of salt
1 tablespoon of almond oil
1 tablespoon of apricot jelly

◆ Butter and flour an 8-inch pie pan.
◆ In a food processor, mix in the flour, butter and salt until mixture resembles coarse meal. Pulsing, add 2-3 tablespoons of ice water to form a ball of dough. Immediately cover with plastic wrap and refrigerate for 30 minutes. Preheat the oven to 350°F.
◆ Cook sugar with 3 tablespoons of water and praline the almonds (see page 21). Pour onto an oiled marble surface. Before they cool, separate 6

almonds with a fork and set aside. When the remainder has cooled, finely chop 2/3 of it and coarsely chop 1/3.
◆ Roll out the pastry dough into a thin sheet; line the pie pan. Prick dough with a fork, cover with parchment paper and fill with dry beans. Bake for about 15 minutes.
◆ In a bowl, mix the whipping cream with the finely chopped almonds, pour into the baked dough; level with a spatula and return to the oven for another 15 minutes.
◆ When cool, transfer the cake onto a serving dish. Brush around the border with the jelly, melted in a double boiler. Sprinkle the border with the coarsely chopped almonds and top the center of the cake with 6 whole almonds.

Pine nut cake

Time needed: *1 hour*
(plus resting time)
Difficulty: **medium**

INGREDIENTS FOR **6-8** SERVINGS
2/3 recipe for shortbread pastry (see page 12)
1 1/2 cups of chopped pine nuts
3/4 cup of sugar
4 egg whites
7 tablespoons of softened butter
1/2 cup of potato starch
a pinch of salt

Decoration:
1/4 cup of pine nuts
1 tablespoon of apricot jelly
8 sugar beads

◆ Butter and flour a 10-inch pie pan.
◆ Prepare the shortbread pastry dough adding 1/4 cup of chopped pine nuts. Cover with plastic wrap and refrigerate for 1 hour. After 30 minutes, preheat the oven to 350°F.
◆ Roll out the dough into a thin sheet; line the pie pan and prick dough with a fork. Cover with a sheet of parchment paper and fill with dry beans. Bake for 10-12 minutes. Remove the beans and paper.
◆ In a bowl, beat the butter with sugar until creamy; mix in the potato starch and the remaining chopped pine nuts. Beat egg whites with salt to stiff peaks and fold into the mixture. Pour into the pastry crust and level. Decorate with pine nut flowers and bake for 25 minutes.

Pine nut cake

▶

♦ When cold, transfer the cake onto a serving dish. Brush with the jelly, melted in a double boiler. Decorate each pine nut flower with a sugar bead.

Basque cherry tart

Time needed: *1 hour and 30 minutes*
(plus resting time)
Difficulty: medium

INGREDIENTS FOR 6-8 SERVINGS
1 recipe for shortbread pastry (see page 12)
1 cup of sugar
4 egg yolks
1 cup of milk
2 tablespoons of flour
1 lb of cherries
1/8 teaspoon of vanilla
juice and grated peel of one organic lemon
1 tablespoon of powdered sugar
1 tablespoon of apricot jelly

♦ Butter and flour an 8-inch pie pan.
♦ Prepare the shortbread pastry dough, shape into a ball and refrigerate for 1 hour, covered with plastic wrap. After 30 minutes, preheat the oven to 350°F.
♦ Prepare a pastry cream (see page 16) with milk, lemon peel, egg yolks, sugar, flour and vanilla. Let cool, stirring occasionally.
♦ Rinse and dry the cherries, pick out 4 of the best ones and set them aside. Pit the remaining cherries and cut in half. Mix them with lemon juice and remaining sugar; cook in a saucepan for 15 minutes on low heat. Let mixture cool and stir into the pastry cream.
♦ Roll out 2/3 of the shortbread pastry dough into a thin sheet; line the pie pan, prick dough with a fork and pour the cherry mixture in pie pan. Roll out the remaining shortbread pastry dough, lay it over the filling and pinch the edges to seal. Brush the surface of the cake with the remaining lightly beaten egg yolk and trace decorative lines with the back of a fork. Bake for 50 minutes.
♦ Remove from the oven. When cool, transfer onto a serving dish and sprinkle the border with powdered sugar. Dip the remaining cherries in the jelly, melted in a double boiler, and place on the center of the cake.

Abetone mountain tart

Time needed: *1 hour and 20 minutes*
(plus resting time)
Difficulty: medium

INGREDIENTS FOR 8 SERVINGS
1 recipe for shortbread pastry (see page 12)
1 1/4 cups of sugar
3 1/2 cups of peeled chopped almonds
1 cup of grated bittersweet chocolate
4 eggs
1/2 cup of espresso coffee
1/3 cup of whipping cream
a pinch of salt
1 tablespoon of powdered sugar
1/4 cup of praline almonds

♦ Butter and flour a 10-inch pie pan.
♦ Prepare the shortbread pastry dough, form a ball and refrigerate for 1 hour, covered with plastic wrap. After 30 minutes, preheat the oven to 350°F.
♦ Roll out the shortbread pastry dough into a thin sheet; line the cake pan and prick dough with a fork. Melt the chocolate in coffee on low heat. Remove from heat and mix in the whipping cream. Beat egg yolks and sugar with an electric mixer until creamy. Mix in the chopped almonds and melted chocolate. Beat egg whites with salt to stiff peaks and gently fold into mixture.
♦ Pour the mixture in pie and bake for about 1 hour. Remove from the oven, let cool and transfer onto a serving dish. Place a 5-inch cardboard circle over the center of the pie and sprinkle powdered sugar around the cardboard. Remove cardboard and garnish the center of the pie with pralined almonds.

Melon puff pastry tart

Time needed: *2 hours*
Difficulty: complex

INGREDIENTS FOR 4 SERVINGS
6 oz of puff pastry (see page 12)
1 melon of about 1 1/2 lbs
1/3 cup of sugar ♦ *1 vanilla bean*
1/4 cup of crumbled dry cookies
1/8 cup of apricot jelly
1 marzipan flower

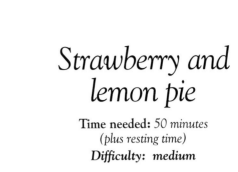

◆ Roll out the puff pastry dough into a thin sheet. Cut into a 12-inch circle and place in a 10-inch greased pie pan. Prick the dough with a fork.
◆ Peel the melon, seed and cut into regular and thin slices. Cook melon slices for 10 minutes with sugar and vanilla bean.
◆ Preheat the oven to 375°F.
◆ Sprinkle the puff pastry with the crumbled cookies. Drain the melon slices; place over the cookie crumbs clock-wise in a sunburst fashion. Form a second layer, smaller in the center, placing the slices anti-clock wise.
◆ Bake for about 25 minutes, until the pastry is golden. Transfer onto a serving dish. Brush the melon slices with the apricot jelly, melted in a double boiler. Decorate the center of the tart with the marzipan flower.

Blackberry and raspberry tart

Time needed: *1 hour*
(plus resting time)
Difficulty: *medium*

INGREDIENTS FOR **10** SERVINGS
1 recipe for shortbread pastry (see page 12)
4 cups of blackberries
2/3 cup of raspberries
3 tablespoons of apricot jelly

Pastry Cream:
1 1/2 cups of milk
3 egg yolks ◆ *1/3 cup of sugar*
1/3 cup of flour
grated peel of 1/2 organic lemon
1 tablespoon of Kirsch

◆ Butter and flour a 12-inch pie pan.
◆ Prepare the shortbread dough, form into a ball and refrigerate for 30 minutes, covered with plastic wrap.
◆ Prepare a pastry cream (see page 16) with the above listed ingredients; remove from heat, mix in the Kirsch and cool completely.
◆ Preheat the oven to 350°F.
◆ Quickly rinse the raspberries and blackberries in ice water, and dry. Roll out the pastry dough into a thin sheet; line the pie pan. Prick dough with a fork. Pour the pastry cream in dough; cover with the raspberries and blackberries and bake for 30-35 minutes.
◆ Transfer the tart onto a serving dish and let it cool. Melt the jelly in a double boiler and brush the fruits.

Strawberry and lemon pie

Time needed: *50 minutes*
(plus resting time)
Difficulty: *medium*

INGREDIENTS FOR **12** SERVINGS
1 recipe for shortbread pastry (see page 12)
Filling:
2/3 cup of flour
2/3 cup of sugar
2 tablespoons of butter
2 eggs
3 organic lemons
a pinch of salt

Decoration:
2/3 cup of strawberries
2 tablespoons of strawberry jelly
3 candied violets

◆ Butter and flour a 12-inch pie pan.
◆ Prepare the shortbread dough, form into a ball and refrigerate for 30 minutes, covered with plastic wrap.
◆ Preheat the oven to 350°F.
◆ Roll out the pastry dough and line the pie pan. Prick dough with a fork. Cover it with a sheet of parchment paper and fill it with dry beans so the pastry does not puff up during baking. Bake for about 20 minutes, until golden. Remove from the oven, discard the paper and beans and cool completely.
◆ To make the filling, bring to boil 1 cup of water with butter and the entire peel of one lemon. Squeeze the juice of all the lemons. In a saucepan, whisk egg yolks and sugar; mix in the flour and add, a little at a time, through a sieve, the boiling water-butter mixture. Bring to boil on low heat and simmer for 10 minutes, stirring continuously. Remove from heat; add the lemon juice. Beat egg whites with salt to stiff peaks and fold into the mixture.
◆ Transfer the shortbread crust onto a serving dish. Brush the bottom with a little jelly, melted in a double boiler and pour filling into pie. Rinse the strawberries in ice water, drain, dry and slice thinly. Place along the border and in the center of the cake to form a star. Brush with the remaining jelly; decorate with candied violets and refrigerate until ready to serve.
◆ You may vary the decoration by adding kiwis or alternating circles of kiwi and strawberries, which add a pleasant colorful effect.

239

American apple pie

Time needed:
1 hour and 30 minutes
(plus resting time)
Difficulty: medium

INGREDIENTS
FOR 6 SERVINGS

3 cups of flour
10 tablespoons of cold butter
a pinch of salt
2 lbs of Granny Smith apples
3/4 cups of sugar
a pinch of nutmeg
1/2 teaspoon of cinnamon
grated peel of one organic lemon
1 tablespoon of flour
2 tablespoons of butter

Butter a 12-inch pie pan. Preheat the oven to 400°F.

◆ In a food processor, mix flour, butter in pieces and salt until mixture resembles coarse meal. Pulsing, add, one at a time, a few tablespoons of ice water until dough forms a ball. (To make the dough by hand, put the flour and knobs of butter onto a work surface, crumble the butter into the flour with your fingertips or with a fork; add the water working rapidly.) Refrigerate for 30 minutes, covered with plastic wrap.

◆ Peel the apples, core and dice into 1/2-inch cubes. In a bowl, mix apples, sugar, nutmeg, cinnamon, lemon peel and flour.

◆ Roll out the pastry dough into a thin circle and line the pie pan. Prick dough with a fork, cover with the apples and sprinkle with pieces of butter. Roll out the remaining dough into a second circle. Place over the apples, seal the edges well and prick the top circle.

◆ Bake for 45-50 minutes. Remove from oven and serve warm or cold.

◆ Accompanied with vanilla ice cream, the pie becomes an "Apple pie à la mode".

Wild cherry tart

Time needed: *1 hour*
(plus resting time)
Difficulty: medium

INGREDIENTS FOR 6 SERVINGS
1 recipe for shortbread pastry (see page 12)
1 lb of wild cherry jam
1 egg yolk

◆ Butter and flour a 10-inch pie pan.
◆ Prepare the shortbread pastry, form into a ball and refrigerate for 1 hour, covered with plastic wrap. After 30 minutes, preheat the oven to 350°F.
◆ Roll out 2/3 of the pastry dough into a thin sheet, line the pie pan and prick dough with a fork. Spread with the jam. With remaining dough, make strips and cover pie, criss-crossing the strips. Brush with the lightly beaten egg yolk and bake for 40 minutes.
◆ Cool completely and transfer onto a serving dish.
◆ The type of jam can vary according to taste : orange, plum, peach or other fruit jam.

Wild cherry tart

Pear tart

Time needed: *2 hours*
Difficulty: complex

INGREDIENTS FOR 6-8 SERVINGS
2/3 recipe for puff pastry (see page 12)
3-4 William pears
5 tablespoons of sugar
3 tablespoons of butter
juice of 1/2 lemon
1 tablespoon of pear grappa

◆ Preheat the oven to 400°F.
◆ Roll out the puff pastry dough into a thin sheet and cut it into a 10-inch circle. Brush a cookie sheet with water; place dough on it. Prick dough with a fork.
◆ Peel the pears, core, slice thinly and toss in the lemon juice. Sprinkle the pastry disk with 1 tablespoon of sugar and cover with the pear slices in concentric circles, starting from the edge. Sprinkle with another tablespoon of sugar and with 1 1/2 tablespoons of butter in pieces.
◆ Bake for about 25 minutes, then transfer onto a serving dish and drizzle with grappa. Cook remaining sugar in 3 tablespoons of water for a few minutes. Stir in the remaining butter until melted. Brush the surface of the tart with this syrup. Serve warm.

Pear tart

American apple pie

Walnut and raisin tart

Time needed: *1 hour*
(plus resting time)
Difficulty: medium

INGREDIENTS FOR 8-10 SERVINGS
1 recipe for shortbread pastry (see page 12)
4 tablespoons of softened butter
1/3 cup of sugar
5 eggs
1 1/2 cups of raisins
1 1/2 cups of finely chopped walnut
1 teaspoon of vanilla
1 teaspoon of unsweetened cocoa

◆ Butter and flour a 14-inch pie pan. Soak the raisins in warm water.
◆ Prepare the shortbread dough, form into a ball and refrigerate for 30 minutes, covered with plastic wrap. After 30 minutes preheat the oven to 375°F.
◆ In a bowl, whisk butter and sugar; mix in the eggs one at the time. Add the drained raisins, walnuts and vanilla.
◆ Roll out the dough into a thin sheet and line the pie pan. Prick dough with a fork, pour in the walnut-raisin mixture and bake for about 40 minutes. Let cool and transfer onto a serving dish. Carefully sprinkle the border and center with the cocoa.

Walnut and raisin tart

Tarte Tatin

Time needed: *1 hour*
Difficulty: medium

INGREDIENTS FOR 8 SERVINGS
1 1/4 cups of sugar
12 tablespoons of butter
5-6 Granny Smith apples
2 tablespoons of Calvados
2 cups of flour
1 egg
3-4 tablespoons of milk
2 cups of whipping cream

◆ Preheat the oven to 375°F. Peel the apples, core and slice thinly.
◆ In a heat-resistant 12-inch pie pan, on low heat, caramelize 2/3 cup of sugar in 4 tablespoons

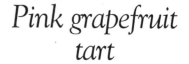

Tarte Tatin

of butter. Place the apple slices in a sunburst fashion over the caramelized sugar, sprinkle with remaining sugar and Calvados.
◆ With a fork, crumble the remaining butter in the flour; mix in the egg and milk and rapidly knead with your fingertips. Roll out the dough into a 14-inch circle and place it over the apples. Bake for 30-35 minutes, until golden. Immediately turn the cake onto a dish and serve warm, accompanied with lightly whipped cream.

Pink grapefruit tart

Time needed: *1 hour*
(plus resting time)
Difficulty: medium

INGREDIENTS FOR 6-8 SERVINGS
1 recipe for shortbread pastry (see page 12)
2 eggs
6 1/2 tablespoons of sugar
5 tablespoons of butter
juice of 2 pink grapefruits
a pinch of salt
4 pink grapefruits

◆ Butter and flour a 12-inch pie pan.
◆ Prepare the shortbread dough, form into a ball and refrigerate for 30 minutes, covered with plastic wrap. After 30 minutes, preheat the oven to 375°F.
◆ Roll out the pastry dough into a thin sheet and line the pie pan. Prick dough with a fork. Cover with a sheet of parchment paper and fill with dry beans. Bake for about 20 minutes. Remove from oven and raise the temperature to 450°F.
◆ In a double boiler, whisk egg yolks and sugar. Place on low heat and continue to whisk for 3 minutes. Add the butter, one piece at a time, whisk for another 3 minutes and add the grapefruit juice. Cook for another 5 minutes; cool. Beat egg whites with salt to stiff peaks and fold into the custard.
◆ Pour into the pastry crust and bake for 3 minutes until top is golden.
◆ Peel the grapefruit to the fruit and separate in segments, cutting the larger ones into half lengthwise; place on the tart in concentric circles.

Pink grapefruit tart

Lyonnaise tart

Time needed: *2 hours and 20 minutes*
Difficulty: *complex*

INGREDIENTS FOR 8 SERVINGS
*1/2 recipe for puff pastry
(see page 12)
1 lb of Golden Delicious apples
1 lb of apricots
1/2 cup of sugar
2 tablespoons of cornstarch
juice and grated peel of one organic lemon
1/2 teaspoon of vanilla
1 egg
1 tablespoon of powdered sugar*

◆ Peel the apples; cores and dice. In a non-stick saucepan, cook with 6 tablespoons of sugar, lemon juice and lemon peel on medium heat for 20 minutes. Add the cornstarch dissolved in 1 tablespoon of water and cook for 3 minutes. Preheat the oven to 375°F.
◆ Rinse the apricots, pit and cut into small pieces. Cook on medium heat in a non-stick saucepan with remaining sugar for 10 minutes. Add the apricots to the apple mixture and mix in the vanilla.
◆ Roll out 2/3 of the pastry dough into a 1/4-inch-thick circle; line a 10-inch pie pan. Roll out the remaining dough and cut into 1-inch-wide strips. Pour the fruit mixture onto the pastry, leaving an uncovered edge of 1/2-inch all around. Brush the edge with the beaten egg. Cover with pastry strips, criss-crossing; brush with the egg.
◆ Bake for 30-35 minutes. Serve the tart warm, sprinkled along the edge with powdered sugar.

Orange peel tart

Time needed:
*1 hour and 20 minutes
(plus resting time)*
Difficulty: *medium*

INGREDIENTS FOR 8 SERVINGS
*1 portion of shortbread pastry (see page 12)
1 lb of organic oranges
1 1/4 cups of sugar
1 1/4 cups of whipping cream
4 eggs ◆ 1 tablespoon of lemon juice*

Lyonnaise tart

Orange peel tart

Apricot sunburst

Decoration:
*peel of 2 organic oranges
1/2 cup of sugar*

◆ Prepare the decoration one day ahead. Cut the peel (without any pith) of oranges into as many disks as possible of 1-inch diameter. Scald twice for 2 minutes each time, drain and put in a bowl. Cook the sugar in 3/4 cup of water for 7 minutes, pour this syrup over the orange disks and infuse for 24 hours.
◆ Butter and flour a shallow 10-inch cake pan.
◆ Prepare the shortbread pastry, form into a ball and refrigerate for 1 hour, covered with plastic wrap. After 30 minutes, preheat the oven to 360°F.
◆ Rinse the oranges, grate the peel and set aside. Peel the oranges to the fruit, with a small sharp knife; slice, then cut into small pieces. In a saucepan, cook on low heat the sugar, lemon peel and half the orange peel for 30 minutes. In a bowl, beat eggs, whipping cream and remaining orange peel and add to the warm orange mixture.
◆ Roll out the dough into a thin sheet; line the cake pan and prick bottom with a fork. Pour the orange mixture in the pie crust and bake for 40 minutes. Cool. Drain the orange disks from the syrup and place on the edges and center of the cold tart.

Apricot sunburst

Time needed: *1 hour
(plus resting time)*
Difficulty: *medium*

INGREDIENTS FOR 8-10 SERVINGS
*1 portion of shortbread pastry (see page 12)
1 lb of apricots
3 tablespoons of apricot jelly*

◆ Butter and flour a cookie sheet.
◆ Prepare the shortbread pastry, form into a ball and refrigerate for 1 hour, covered with plastic wrap. After 30 minutes, preheat the oven to 320°F.
◆ Scald the apricots in boiling water and set aside.
◆ Roll out the dough into a thin sheet, and cut out a 10-inch disk. Place it on the cookie sheet and prick it with a fork. Roll out the dough scrapings, divide into 2-inch wide strips and cut into small regular rectangles. Attach the triangles all around the border of the disk to form sunrays. ▶

◆ Peel apricots, cut into half, pit, thinly slice and put on the disk in concentric circles. Bake for 35-40 minutes. Cool and transfer onto a serving dish. Brush the fruit with the apricot jelly, previously dissolved in a double boiler.

Pistachio tart

Time needed: *1 hour*
(plus resting time)
Difficulty: *medium*

INGREDIENTS FOR 10 SERVINGS
1 portion of shortbread pastry (see page 12)
Filling:
3 cups of milk
6 egg yolks
2/3 cup of flour
10 tablespoons of sugar
3 tablespoons of chopped candied citron
1 1/2 cups of peeled, chopped pistachios
1 tablespoon of Kirsch
Decoration:
3 oz of dark chocolate
1/2 cup of peeled pistachios
1/3 cup of whipping cream

◆ Butter and flour a pie pan.
◆ Prepare the shortbread pastry, form into a ball and refrigerate for 30 minutes, covered with plastic wrap.
◆ Preheat the oven to 350°F.
◆ To make the filling, first bring the milk to a boil. In a bowl, beat the egg yolks and sugar, stir in the chopped pistachios, flour and boiling milk, a little at a time. Return to saucepan and bring to a boil on low heat. Cook for about 7-8 minutes, stirring constantly to avoid lumps. When cool, add the Kirsch and candied citron.
◆ Roll out the dough into a thin sheet and line pie pan. Prick with a fork, pour in the pistachio mixture and bake for 30-35 minutes. Cool completely.
◆ To decorate, whip the cream. Chop the dark chocolate into small pieces; melt it in a double boiler, pour into a waxed paper cone and draw 2 circles on the edge of the tart. Trace a grid that you will garnish with whipped cream rosettes, piped from a pastry bag, fitted with an indented nozzle. Top each rosette with a pistachio and refrigerate the tart until ready to serve.

Pineapple tart

Time needed: *1 hour and 10 minutes*
(plus resting time)
Difficulty: *complex*

INGREDIENTS FOR 8 SERVINGS
1 portion of shortbread pastry (see page 12)
1/4 cup of biscotti
1/4 cup of sugar
1/4 cup of brown sugar
3 tablespoons of melted butter
1 fresh pineapple of 4 lbs in weight
3 tablespoons of apricot jelly
1/3 cup of raisins
3 tablespoons of Grand Marnier
1 tablespoon of powdered sugar

◆ Butter and flour a pie pan. Soak the raisins in the Grand Marnier.
◆ Prepare the shortbread pastry, form into a ball and refrigerate for 1 hour, covered with plastic wrap. After 30 minutes, preheat the oven to 350°F.
◆ Peel the pineapple carefully, slice and core. Leave 1 slice whole and cut the others in half.
◆ Roll out the dough into a thin sheet and line the pie pan. Prick bottom with a fork; sprinkle with 1/2 the crumbled biscotti and the drained raisins. Layer with the 1/2 slices of pineapple in a circle and place the whole slice in the center. Fold the edges of the pastry dough towards the inside and sprinkle the fruit with both kinds of sugar, mixed together, the remaining crumbled biscotti and melted butter.
◆ Bake the tart in the oven for 50 minutes. When cool, transfer onto a serving dish, brush with the apricot jelly dissolved in a double boiler and sprinkle the edge of the tart with powdered sugar.

Lemon tart

Time needed: *50 minutes*
(plus resting time)
Difficulty: *medium*

INGREDIENTS FOR 8-10 SERVINGS
1 portion of shortbread pastry (see page 12)
1/2 cup of sugar
3 eggs

4 tablespoons of flour
1/2 teaspoon of baking powder
8 tablespoons of lemon juice
2 tablespoons of grated lemon peel
powdered sugar

◆ Butter and flour a shallow rectangular cake pan.
◆ Prepare the shortbread pastry, form into a ball and refrigerate for 1 hour, covered with plastic wrap. After 30 minutes, preheat the oven to 350°F.
◆ Roll out the dough into a thin sheet and line the cake pan. Prick with a fork. Cover the bottom with a sheet of parchment paper and fill with dried beans. Bake for about 25 minutes. Remove and discard the beans and paper; let the pastry crust cool.
◆ In a bowl, sift flour with baking powder; add eggs, sugar, lemon juice and lemon peel; mix well. Pour the mixture into the shortbread crust and bake for another 30-35 minutes.
◆ When ready, transfer the tart onto a serving dish and let it cool. Serve sprinkled with powdered sugar.

Sour cherry and custard tart

Time needed: *1 hour and 30 minutes*
(plus resting time)
Difficulty: *medium*

INGREDIENTS FOR 8 SERVINGS
1 portion of shortbread pastry (see page 12)
4 egg yolks
6 1/2 tablespoons of sugar
2 cups of milk
1/3 cup of flour
peel of one organic lemon
1/2 teaspoon of vanilla
1 1/2 cups of drained sour cherries in syrup
1/4 cup of crumbled biscotti

◆ Butter and flour a 10-inch springform pan.
◆ Prepare the shortbread pastry, form into a ball and refrigerate for 1 hour, covered with plastic wrap. After 30 minutes, preheat the oven to 350°F.
◆ With the milk, lemon peel, egg yolks, sugar, flour and vanilla, prepare a pastry cream (see page 16). Let cool.
◆ Roll out 3/4 of the dough into a thin sheet and line the springform pan and prick dough with a fork. Sprinkle the bottom with the crumbled bis-

cotti; pour 1/2 the pastry cream over and layer with the sour cherries, keeping 2 tablespoons aside. Cover with the remaining pastry cream. Roll out the remaining dough, cut into long strips and criss-cross over the pastry cream. Place a sour cherry in each space of the grid.
◆ Bake for about 50-60 minutes. Transfer onto a dish and serve cold.

Grape and fig tart

Time needed: *1 hour*
(plus resting time)
Difficulty: *medium*

INGREDIENTS FOR 8 SERVINGS
1 portion of shortbread pastry (see page 12)
5 egg yolks
1/2 cup of flour
5 tablespoons of sugar
1 1/4 cups of white dry wine
1 small bunch of white grapes
1 small bunch of red grapes
6 figs
2 tablespoons of apricot jelly

◆ Butter and flour a pie pan.
◆ Prepare the shortbread dough, form into a ball and refrigerate for 1 hour, covered with plastic wrap. After 30 minutes, preheat the oven to 400°F.
◆ Roll out the dough into a thin sheet and line the pie pan. Prick dough with a fork. Cover the bottom with parchment paper and fill with dried beans. Bake for about 20 minutes, remove the beans and paper and let the pastry crust cool. As soon as it is cool, remove beans and paper; transfer the pastry crust onto a serving dish.
◆ In a saucepan, beat the egg yolks and sugar until pale; mix in the flour, a little at a time. Heat the white wine, without letting it boil and pour it, a little at a time into the egg mixture. Bring this custard to a boil on low heat and cook for 2 minutes, stirring constantly.
◆ Peel the figs and cut into segments. Rinse and dry both kinds of grape. Pour the wine custard into the pastry crust, top with the grapes and figs and brush the fruit with the apricot jelly, dissolved in a double boiler.

Preheat the oven to 375°F. Bring the milk to a boil.

◆ In a saucepan, beat the egg yolks and sugar; mix in 1/2 tablespoon of cornstarch and the vanilla; slowly add the boiling milk. Bring to boil on low heat and cook for 7-8 minutes, stirring constantly to prevent lumps from forming. Let cool.

◆ Scald the almonds in boiling water, peel, toast, and grind.

◆ In a bowl, beat butter and sugar until creamy, mix in the almonds, 2 eggs, the remaining cornstarch and rum; blend into the custard.

◆ Roll out the puff pastry dough into a very thin sheet and cut into two 10-inch circles. Place one circle onto a moistened cookie sheet and brush the border with the remain-

Pithiviers

Time needed: *2 hours (plus resting time)*
Difficulty: complex

INGREDIENTS
FOR 8 SERVINGS
12 1/2 oz of puff pastry (see page 12)
3 eggs
3 egg yolks
1/4 cup of sugar
1 cup of milk
1 tablespoon of cornstarch
a pinch of vanilla
8 tablespoons of butter
2/3 cup of powdered sugar
3/4 cup of peeled almonds
1 tablespoon of rum

Decoration:
1 1/2 oz of dark chocolate
3 confectioner's candied violets

ing beaten egg. Pour the custard in the center of the circle, cover with the other dough circle and press around the edges to seal. Brush with the beaten egg. Press the border lightly toward the center, making a decorative round edge pattern. With a knife, press curved lines from center to edges. Refrigerate for 30 minutes and raise the oven temperature to 390F.

◆ Bake for 30-35 minutes until golden, then transfer onto a serving dish.

◆ To decorate, break the chocolate, melt it in a double boiler, put into a waxed paper cone and trace thin lines over the top of the pastry in curves from the center. Underline the chain on the border with a chocolate line around the whole pie. Place the confectioner's candied violets in the center of the cake.

Sweet potato pie with meringue

Time needed: *1 hour and 20 minutes (plus resting time)*
Difficulty: medium

INGREDIENTS FOR 6 SERVINGS
6 tablespoons of butter
1 1/2 cups of flour
a pinch of salt

Filling:
9 oz of sweet potatoes
1/2 cup of brown sugar
4 tablespoons of whipping cream
2 egg yolks
1/2 teaspoon of cinnamon
1/2 teaspoon of ginger
1 clove (crushed)
a pinch of nutmeg
a pinch of salt ◆ *1 egg white*
1/3 cup of sugar
grated peel of one organic lemon
1 tablespoon of powdered sugar

Sweet potato pie
with meringue

◆ Butter a 10-inch pie pan.
◆ In a food processor, mix the flour, butter in pieces and salt until the mixture is crumbly. Add 2-3 tablespoons of ice water while pulsing, to form a ball of pastry dough. Refrigerate for 30 minutes, covered with plastic wrap. Preheat the oven to 350°F.
◆ To make the filling, rinse the potatoes, put them in a saucepan, cover with cold water and bring to a boil. Cook for 30-40 minutes until tender. Peel, mash and let them cool. Mix in the brown sugar, whipping cream, egg yolks, cinnamon, ginger, clove, nutmeg and salt until well blended.
◆ Roll out the dough into a thin sheet and line the pie pan; prick bottom with a fork. Pour in the potato mixture and bake for 35-40 minutes. Let cool.
◆ With an electric mixer, beat egg whites with salt to soft peaks. Continue beating, adding the sugar a little at a time and the grated lemon peel.
◆ In a pastry bag, fitted with a star tube, place beaten egg white and pipe a meringue onto the pie; sprinkle with powdered sugar and put in a very hot oven (425°F) for a few minutes until golden. Serve cold, sprinkled with brown sugar.

Pithiviers

Torta frangipane

Time needed: *2 hours*
Difficulty: complex

INGREDIENTS FOR 8 SERVINGS
3/4 lb of puff pastry (see page 12)
1/2 cup of flour
1/4 cups of sugar
3 eggs
2 tablespoons of softened butter
1 tablespoon of milk
a pinch of vanilla
1/2 cup of peeled ground almonds
1 tablespoon of powdered sugar

◆ Preheat the oven to 350°F.
◆ Roll out 1/2 of the puff-pastry dough into a thin sheet. Brush a 10-inch pie pan with water. Line the pie pan with dough and prick bottom with a fork.
◆ With an electric mixer, whisk the eggs, butter and sugar until creamy; mix in the flour, almonds, vanilla and milk; pour into the cake pan.
◆ Roll out 1/2 of the remaining dough into a thin 10-inch circle. Place over the egg mixture and seal the edges, pinching with your fingers. Brush the surface of the pie with a little of the remaining egg. Roll out the remaining dough and cut into little triangles, place them over the pie and brush them with the remaining beaten egg.
◆ Bake for 30-40 minutes. Remove from the oven, sprinkle with powdered sugar and replace in a very hot oven for just a few minutes, until the sugar has caramelized. Transfer onto a dish and serve warm.

Torta frangipane

Gascony tart

Time needed: *1 hour and 20 minutes*
(plus resting and marinating time)
Difficulty: medium

INGREDIENTS FOR 6 SERVINGS
1 1/2 cups of flour ◆ 1 egg yolk
6 tablespoons of softened butter
1/3 cup of finely chopped walnut

Filling:
1 lb of apples ◆ 1/2 cup of sugar
1/3 cup of Armagnac or brandy
1 egg yolk
1 tablespoon of apricot jam

Gascony tart

◆ Butter and flour a 10-inch pie pan. On a work surface, put the flour into a mound, make a well in the center and place pieces of butter, walnuts and egg yolks. Knead rapidly, form a ball and refrigerate for 1 hour, covered with plastic wrap.
◆ Peel the apples, slice, put in a bowl with brandy and sugar; set aside to macerate for 1 hour. After 30 minutes, preheat the oven to 350°F.
◆ Roll out 2/3 of the dough into a thin sheet. With it, line the pie pan and prick dough with a fork. Brush with the jam and layer with the drained apple slices. Roll out the remaining dough and cover the apples, sealing the edges carefully. Make a small hole in the center, garnish with the pastry trimmings and brush with the beaten egg yolk. Bake for 40-45 minutes.
◆ In a saucepan, boil the apple macerating liquid until reduced by half. Remove the cake from the oven and pour the syrup into the pie crust hole. Serve cold.

Dried fig and honey pie

Time needed: *1 hour*
(plus resting time)
Difficulty: medium

INGREDIENTS FOR 6-8 SERVINGS
1/3 portion of pastry dough (see page 14)
1 cup of dried figs
2/3 cup of peeled almonds
1/3 cup of raisins
2 tablespoons of honey

Dried fig and honey pie

◆ Butter and flour a pie pan.
◆ Prepare the pastry dough, form into a ball and refrigerate for 1 hour, covered with plastic wrap. After 30 minutes, preheat the oven to 360°F.
◆ Slice the figs and almonds; put in a saucepan with the raisins and honey. Cook on low heat for 10 minutes, stirring continuously.
◆ Divide the pastry dough in half, one half larger then the other. Roll out the larger one into a thin sheet and line the pie pan; prick with a fork. Fill with the fig mixture. Roll out the remaining dough into a slightly thinner sheet and with it, cover the fig mixture, sealing the edges carefully.
◆ Prick the surface of the pie and decorate it with pastry leaves made from the dough trimmings. Bake for 35-40 minutes. Serve cold.

Mango tart

Time needed: *1 hour*
(plus resting time)
Difficulty: *medium*

INGREDIENTS FOR 8-10 SERVINGS
1 portion of shortbread pastry
(see page 12)
3 mangos
2 1/3 cups of milk
2/3 cup of sugar
7 egg yolks
1/2 cup of flour
grated peel of 1/2 an organic lemon
1/2 teaspoon of vanilla
2 tablespoons of apricot jelly

Mango tart

◆ Butter and flour a 12-inch pie pan.
◆ Prepare the short bread pastry, form into a ball and refrigerate for 1 hour, covered with plastic wrap. After 30 minutes, preheat the oven to 375°F.
◆ Thinly roll out the shortbread pastry dough and line the pie pan. Prick the bottom with a fork; cover with parchment paper and fill with dried beans. Bake in a pre-heated oven for 20-25 minutes; remove the beans and paper and let the pastry crust cool.
◆ Peel the mangos, pit, thinly slice half of them and dice the remainder.
◆ Make a pastry cream (see page 16) with the milk, lemon peel, egg yolks, sugar, flour and vanilla.
◆ When cool, mix in the diced mango and pour into the pastry crust. Place the slices of mango in the center and all around the edges of the pie. Melt apricot jelly in a double boiler; brush mango. Serve cold.

Ricotta tart

Time needed: *1 hour and 30 minutes*
(plus resting time)
Difficulty: *medium*

INGREDIENTS FOR 8 SERVINGS
1 portion of shortbread pastry (see page 12)
1 cup of ricotta
1 cup of milk
2 egg yolks
1/4 cup of sugar
1/3 cup of flour
1/2 teaspoon of vanilla
grated peel of 1/2 organic lemon
2 tablespoons of powdered sugar

Ricotta tart

◆ Butter and flour a 12-inch pie pan.
◆ Prepare the pastry dough, form a ball and refrigerate for 1 hour, covered with plastic wrap. After 30 minutes, preheat the oven to 350°F. Make a pastry cream (see page 16) with the milk, egg yolks, sugar, flour and vanilla. Remove from heat and mix in the ricotta cheese and grated lemon peel.
◆ Thinly roll out the pastry dough, line the pie pan and set the trimmings aside. Prick the bottom with a fork and pour in the ricotta mixture. From the trimmings, roll out strips and place them over the filling criss-crossing. Fold the edges of the pastry over strips and bake for about 1 hour.
◆ Remove from the oven and transfer onto a dish. Serve cold, sprinkled with powdered sugar.

Torta bavarese

Time needed: *1 hour*
(plus resting and marinating time)
Difficulty: *medium*

INGREDIENTS FOR 8 SERVINGS
1 portion of shortbread pastry (see page 12)
7 oz of mascarpone cheese
1/2 cup of sugar ◆ *2 eggs*
1 Granny Smith apple ◆ *juice of half lemon*

Decoration:
2 Granny Smith apples
1/4 cup of sugar ◆ *1/3 cup of white wine*

◆ Butter and flour a springform pie pan.
◆ Prepare the shortbread pastry dough, form a ball and refrigerate for 30 minutes, covered with plastic wrap. Preheat the oven to 350°F.
◆ Thinly roll out the dough and line the pie pan. Prick the dough with a fork and bake for 6-8 minutes. Let it cool completely.
◆ To make the filling, peel the apple, core, thinly slice and soak in lemon juice. Whisk the mascarpone cheese and sugar; mix in the eggs one by one. Add the apple and lemon juice. Pour the mixture into the pasty crust; return it in the oven to 340°F. Bake for about 20 minutes, remove from the oven and let the tart cool completely.
◆ Put the wine and sugar into a saucepan. Cut the 2 apples in half, core and with a melon baller, form into small balls. Soak them in the wine and sugar for 30 minutes. Cook the apple balls in the wine on high heat, until caramelized. Arrange the caramelized apples on the tart, starting from the center.

Bavarian tart

Peach and plum upside down cake

Time needed: *2 hours*
Difficulty: *complex*

INGREDIENTS FOR 6 SERVINGS
1/2 lb of puff pastry (see page 12)
1 1/2 lbs of peaches
1 lb of blue plums
8 tablespoons of softened butter
1/2 cup of sugar

◆ Preheat the oven to 360°F.
◆ Scald the peaches in boiling water, peel and slice into 4-6 segments. Rinse the plums and cut into 4 segments.
◆ Spread the butter on the bottom of a 10-inch cake pan and sprinkle with sugar. Layer with the fruit, alternating peaches and plums. Place the cake pan on low heat, rotating it often until the sugar caramelizes. Let it cool.
◆ Thinly roll out the pastry dough and cut it into a circle slightly larger than the cake pan. Lay it over the fruit and fold the edges inside. Prick with a fork.
◆ Bake for 15-20 minutes until golden. Turn the pie over onto a dish. Serve warm or cold.

Amaretto tart

Time needed: *1 hour and 30 minutes*
(plus resting time)
Difficulty: *medium*

INGREDIENTS FOR 8 SERVINGS
1 portion of shortbread pastry (see page 12)
1/2 lb of ricotta cheese
1/2 cup of crumbled amaretti
2 oz of grated dark chocolate
1/3 cup of raisins
3 egg yolks
1 egg white
1/3 cup of sugar
1 liquor glass of amaretto liquor

◆ Butter and flour a 12-inch pie pan. Soak the raisins in warm water.
◆ Prepare the shortbread pastry dough, form a ball and refrigerate for 1 hour, covered with plastic wrap. After 30 minutes, preheat the oven to 350°F.
◆ In a bowl, mix the amaretti with the amaretto liquor. Strain the ricotta cheese through a sieve, and add into the bowl. Stir in the egg yolks, sugar, raisins and grated chocolate; mix well.

◆ Roll out the pastry dough and line the pie pan (setting the trimmings aside); prick the bottom with a fork. Pour the ricotta mixture on the crust, even it out and decorate with the pastry trimmings. Brush the edges of the tart with a little beaten egg white and bake for 40-45 minutes. Let the tart cool before transferring it onto a serving dish.

Hazelnut pie

Time needed: *1 hour and 20 minutes*
(plus resting time)
Difficulty: *medium*

INGREDIENTS FOR 8 SERVINGS
1 2/3 cup of flour
1/3 cup toasted finely chopped hazelnuts
7 tablespoons of softened butter
3 egg yolks ◆ *1/2 cup of sugar*
grated peel of 1/2 organic lemon
1/3 cup /30 g of toasted hazelnuts
a pinch of salt

Filling:
1 1/2 cups of toasted finely chopped hazelnuts
3/4 cup of whipping cream
2/3 cup of sugar
2 tablespoons of honey

◆ Butter and flour a pie pan.
◆ Put the flour into a mound on a work surface, make a well in the center and add butter, sugar, eggs, chopped hazelnuts, salt, egg yolks and lemon peel. Mix rapidly with fingertips and refrigerate dough ball for 1 hour, covered with plastic wrap.
◆ Preheat the oven to 360°F.
◆ To make the filling, cook the sugar in 1 tablespoon of water until caramelized (see page 19). Add the whipping cream and stir to completely dissolve the caramel; stir in the honey and chopped hazelnuts. The mixture should not be very thick.
◆ Roll 2/3 of the pastry dough into a thin sheet, line the pie pan and prick the bottom with a fork. Pour the filling in pie pan and even it out. Roll out the remaining pastry dough, lay over the filling, trim and pinch the edges to seal. Roll out the pastry trimmings and cut into leaves. Trace a grid on the surface of the pie with a knife; brush the grid with the remaining beaten egg and garnish the edges alternating pastry leaves and whole hazelnuts.
◆ Bake for 45-50 minutes. Let the pie cool completely before transferring it onto a serving dish.

Kiwi flan

Time needed: *1 hour*
(plus resting time)
Difficulty: *medium*

INGREDIENTS FOR **8-10** SERVINGS
1 portion of shortbread pastry
(see page 12)
12 kiwis
1 1/4 cups of heavy cream
2/3 cup of powdered sugar
2 eggs
1/4 cup of plum acquavit

◆ Butter and flour a 12-inch pie pan.
◆ Prepare the shortbread pastry dough, form a ball and refrigerate for 1 hour, covered with plastic wrap. After 30 minutes, preheat the oven to 350°F.
◆ Thinly roll out the pastry dough and line the pie pan. Prick the dough with a fork, cover with a sheet of parchment paper and fill with dry beans. Bake for 20-25 minutes; remove from the oven, discard the beans and paper. Let the pastry crust cool completely.
◆ Peel the kiwis, slice and place in layers over the pre-cooked pastry crust. In a bowl, beat the eggs with 1/2 of the sugar, the heavy cream and the acquavit. Pour mixture over the kiwi slices. Return to oven for another 20 minutes.
◆ Remove from the oven, cover the border with aluminum foil, sprinkle the filling with the remaining powdered sugar. Replace the flan in the oven for 3-4 minutes under the grill to caramelize the sugar. Serve warm.

Strawberry sand cake

Time needed: *45 minutes*
(plus resting time)
Difficulty: *medium*

INGREDIENTS FOR **6-8** SERVINGS
1 lb of strawberries
1 1/2 cups of flour
1/4 cup of ground almonds
1/3 cup of sugar
7 tablespoons of softened butter
1 egg yolk
grated peel of half organic lemon
1/4 cup of raspberry jelly

◆ Butter and flour a pie pan.
◆ Put the flour, almonds and sugar into a mound on a work surface; make a well in the center and add butter, egg yolk and lemon peel. Knead rapidly and form a ball of dough. Refrigerate for 1 hour, covered with plastic wrap. After 30 minutes, preheat the oven to 375°F.
◆ Thinly roll out the pastry dough, line the pie pan and prick dough with a fork. Cover dough with parchment paper and fill with dry beans to keep the shape whilst cooking. Bake for 20-25 minutes; remove from the oven, discard the beans and paper. Let the pastry crust cool completely.
◆ Melt the raspberry jelly in a double boiler. Rinse the strawberries in ice water, dry and cut into thin vertical slices. Transfer the pastry crust onto a serving dish; brush the inside with part of the jelly and top with the strawberries in concentric circles. Brush the fruit with the remaining jelly.

Rhubarb pie

Time needed: *1 hour*
(plus resting time)
Difficulty: *medium*

INGREDIENTS FOR **4** SERVINGS
1/2 portion of shortbread pastry
(see page 12)
1 1/2 lbs of tender rhubarb stalks
3/4 cup of sugar
grated peel of 1 organic lemon

Decoration:
3/4 cup of whipped cream
1 piece of rhubarb stalk about 2 inches long

◆ Butter and flour an 8-inch pie pan.
◆ Prepare the shortbread pastry dough, form a ball and refrigerate for 1 hour, covered in plastic wrap. After 30 minutes preheat the oven to 360°F.
◆ Rinse the rhubarb, remove its filaments and cut into 2-inch long pieces. Cook with the sugar in a non-stick saucepan for 20 minutes. Remove from heat and stir in the lemon peel.
◆ Thinly roll out the shortbread pastry dough, line the pie pan and prick dough with a fork. Pour the rhubarb in the pie and bake for 20-30 minutes. Remove from the oven and transfer onto a serving dish. Let the tart cool completely.
◆ Put the whipped cream in a pastry bag, fitted with a star tube; pipe cream rosettes in the middle and around the edges of the tart. Rinse and dry the rhubarb, dice and place in the center of the tart.

California tart

Time needed:
1 hour and 50 minutes
Difficulty: easy

**INGREDIENTS
FOR 6 SERVINGS**
*1 1/2 cups of flour
6 tablespoons of cold butter
3 tablespoons of sour cream
3/4 cup of brown sugar
1/4 teaspoon of powdered
ginger
a pinch of nutmeg
a pinch of salt*

Filling:
*1 1/2 lb of Granny Smith
apples
5 tablespoons of sour cream
3/4 cup of sugar
3 egg yolks
1 tablespoon of flour
1 teaspoon of vanilla*

Butter a 10-inch springform pan. Preheat the oven to 350°F..

◆ In a food processor, briefly whisk the flour, butter, sour cream, 1 tablespoon of brown sugar, ginger, nutmeg and salt, until mixture resembles coarse meal (1).

◆ Line the bottom of the cake pan with 2/3 of the mixture, pressing (2). In a bowl, place the other 1/3 of the mixture with the remaining brown sugar and refrigerate.

◆ Peel the apples, cut in half, core and place them in the pie, to cover bottom (3).

◆ In a food processor, mix the sugar, sour cream, egg yolks, flour and vanilla, pour the batter all around the apples and cover with the refrigerated crumbled sugar mixture (4).

◆ Bake for 60-70 minutes, until the apples are tender. Transfer unto a dish and serve with a bowl of sweetened sour cream on the side.

Linzer torte

Time needed: *1 hour*
(plus resting time)
Difficulty: medium

INGREDIENTS FOR 8 SERVINGS
*1 1/2 cups of flour
10 tablespoons of softened butter
3 hard-boiled egg yolks
1/8 cup of peeled almonds
1/4 cup of powdered sugar
a pinch of cinnamon
1 teaspoon of rum
1 1/4 cups of raspberries
3 Golden delicious apples
1/4 cup of sugar
1 organic lemon
a few almonds slivers
1 teaspoon of jam*

◆ Butter and flour a 10-inch cake pan and preheat the oven to 375°F.
◆ Bring the butter to room temperature. Scald the almonds in boiling water, drain, peel and spread onto a cookie sheet. Toast them in the oven and grind.
◆ In a bowl, put the flour, butter, crumbled egg

Linzer torte

yolks, almonds, 1/2 the powdered sugar, cinnamon and rum. Mix with the tip of your fingers as rapidly as you can to form a ball. Refrigerate the dough ball for 1 hour, covered in plastic wrap. Cut the lemon peel (without the pith) and finely chop it; squeeze the lemon juice.
◆ Peel the apples, cut into small pieces and cook with the sugar and lemon peel for about 20 minutes, stirring occasionally. Let the mixture cool. In a food processor, mix the raspberries and sugar for 1 minute. Cook on moderate heat until dense, stirring occasionally. Press through a sieve and mix with the applesauce.
◆ Preheat the oven to 400°F.
◆ Divide the pastry dough in 2 parts, one larger then the other. Roll out the larger one into a thin sheet, line the cake pan and pour the raspberry-applesauce on dough. Roll out the remaining pastry dough; cut it into strips and crisscross over the filling. Fold the dough at the edges over the strips to seal. Bake for about 20 minutes. Remove from the oven and transfer warm onto a serving dish. Sprinkle with the remaining powdered sugar. Top the center with the slivered almonds to form a flower, making it stick with jam.

California tart

Academy apple tart

Time needed: *2 hours*
Difficulty: *complex*

INGREDIENTS FOR 8 SERVINGS
*1/2 lb of puff pastry
(see page 12)
2 lbs of apples
3/4 cup of sugar
1/2 teaspoon of vanilla
1/3 cup of milk
1/2 cup of whipping cream
3 eggs
1 tablespoon of flour
1/3 cup of raisins
juice of 1 lemon
4 tablespoons of butter*

◆ Preheat the oven to 350°F.
◆ Thinly roll out the dough. Brush a deep pie dish with water. Line it with dough. Prick dough with a fork.
◆ Peel the apples, core, dice and put in a bowl with raisins; mix with lemon juice.
◆ With an electric mixer, whisk 2 eggs, vanilla and 1/2 cup of sugar until frothy. Blend in the milk and whipping cream; mix in the flour and raisins. Pour mixture into the cake pan and bake for about 30 minutes.
◆ In a small bowl, beat the remaining egg and sugar; mix in the melted butter and pour over the cake. Continue to bake for another 15 minutes. Transfer onto a dish. Cool completely before serving.

Umbrian tart

Umbrian tart

Time needed:
*1 hour and 30 minutes
(plus resting time)*
Difficulty: *medium*

INGREDIENTS FOR 8 SERVINGS

1 portion of shortbread pastry (see page 12)

Pastry cream:
*1/4 cup of sugar
1 cup of milk
2 egg yolks
1/3 cup of flour
peel of one organic lemon*

Filling:
*1 1/3 cups of toasted, ground almonds
3/4 cup of sugar
1 egg
3 egg yolks
4 tablespoons of melted butter
grated peel of one organic lemon*

Decoration:
*1 tablespoon of powdered sugar
12 peeled almonds
1 candied cherry*

◆ Butter and flour a 10-inch pie pan.
◆ Prepare the shortbread pastry dough, form a ball and refrigerate for 1 hour, covered in plastic wrap. After 30 minutes, preheat the oven to 350°F.
◆ Prepare a pastry cream (see page 16) with the ingredients listed above. Let cool.
◆ To make the filling, whisk the egg with the egg yolks and sugar until creamy. Mix in the almonds, lemon peel and melted butter.
◆ Thinly roll out the pastry dough; line the pie pan and set the trimmings aside. Prick the dough with a fork. Spread a layer of pastry cream and cover with the filling. Form 2 long cylinders with the pastry trimmings. Twist them and lay them around the edge of the pie. Bake for 50-60 minutes and let cool completely.
◆ Cut a piece of cardboard decoratively and lay it over the tart. Sprinkle with powdered sugar. Remove cardboard and complete the decoration with almonds and candied cherries.

Pear flan

Pear flan

Time needed: *1 hour
(plus resting time)*
Difficulty: *medium*

INGREDIENTS FOR 6 SERVINGS
*1/2 recipe for shortbread pastry
(see page 12)
2 pears
2 eggs
4 tablespoons of milk
3 tablespoons of finely chopped almonds
1/4 cup of sugar
1 tablespoon of Kirsch*

◆ Butter and flour a 10-inch pie pan.
◆ Prepare the pastry dough, form a ball and refrigerate for 1 hour, covered in plastic wrap. After 30 minutes, preheat the oven to 350°F.

◆ Thinly roll out the pastry dough, line the pie pan and prick dough with a fork. In a bowl, mix the almonds, sugar, eggs, milk and Kirsch. Peel the pears, cut into segments and place on dough in a sunburst pattern. Pour the batter over the pears and bake for 25-30 minutes. Transfer the flan onto a serving dish and let it cool completely.

◆ To make the decoration, rinse and dry the pear. Cut the peel into vertical segments, starting from the bottom of the fruit to just over half of its length, leaving the peel attached to its upper section. Cut and discard the bottom section of the peeled pear, leaving just enough so the peel stays attached to the upper part of the pear. Dissolve 1/4 cup of sugar in 1/3 cup of boiling water, cook the pear with its peel in the syrup for 2 minutes; drain.

◆ Sprinkle the flan with powdered sugar and place the pear in the center, folding the peel to form petals.

Rice tart

Rice tart

Time needed: *1 hour and 15 minutes (plus resting time)*
Difficulty: medium

INGREDIENTS FOR 6-8 SERVINGS
1/2 portion of pastry dough (see page 14)
grated peel of 1/2 organic orange
2 cups of milk
1/2 cup of Baldo or Arborio rice
1/3 cup of whipping cream
1/3 cup of sugar
1/2 cup of raisins
1/2 cup of finely copped dates
grated peel of 1/2 organic orange
1/2 teaspoon of cinnamon
4 egg yolks
1/2 teaspoon of vanilla
a few drops of rose water
1 tablespoon of powdered sugar

◆ Butter and flour a 10-inch pie pan.
◆ Prepare the pastry dough with the orange peel, cover in plastic wrap and refrigerate for 1 hour. After about 30 minutes, preheat the oven to 350°F. Soak the raisins in warm water.
◆ Thinly roll out the pastry dough, line the pie

pan and prick the bottom of dough with a fork. Cover with parchment paper, fill with dry beans and bake for 10 minutes. Remove the paper and beans and continue to bake for another 10 minutes. Let the pastry crust cool.

◆ In a saucepan, bring the milk to a boil, add the rice and cook for 10-12 minutes until the milk is completely absorbed. Mix in the whipping cream, sugar, raisins, dates, orange peel and cinnamon; bring to a boil.

◆ Remove from the heat and blend in the egg yolks, vanilla and rose water. Pour the filling into the pastry crust and sprinkle with powdered sugar.

◆ Bake the tart for 20-25 minutes; transfer onto a dish and serve warm..

Pavia tart

Time needed: *1 hour*
Difficulty: easy

INGREDIENTS FOR 6-8 SERVINGS
1/2 cup of potato starch
1 cup of flour
10 tablespoons of butter
2 eggs
2 egg yolks
1/3 cup of raisins
grated peel of one organic lemon
2/3 cup/100 g of peeled almonds
3 tablespoons of apricot jelly

◆ Butter and lightly flour a pie pan.
◆ Scald the almonds in boiling water, peel and chop coarsely. Soak the raisins in rum. Bring the butter to room temperature.
◆ Sift the flour and potato starch on a work surface into a mound; make a well in the center; add butter, eggs and egg yolks, the grated lemon peel, raisins and rum. Knead until well blended. Spread evenly in the pie pan and sprinkle with chopped almonds, leaving 1/2 in. free all around the edge.
◆ Bake the tart for 40-45 minutes. Let it cool completely.
◆ Transfer it, cold, to a serving dish. Melt the apricot jelly in a double boiler and brush it onto the surface of the tart.

Pavia tart

Butter a cookie sheet. Soak the raisins in warm water. Prepare the pasty dough and let it rest in a warm bowl for 30 minutes.

◆ In a bowl, with an electric mixer, whisk butter, sugar, egg yolks and lemon peel. Mix in the ricotta cheese, bread pushed through a sieve (1), raisins and breadcrumbs.

◆ Preheat the oven to 350°F. On a clean and floured cloth, roll the dough in a 1/4-inch thick rectangle. Passing your floured hands underneath the dough, pull it until very thin

Ricotta strudel

Time needed:

1 hour and 45 minutes
Difficulty: complex
INGREDIENTS
FOR 6-8 SERVINGS

1 recipe for strudel pastry
(see page 13)
1 1/2 lbs of ricotta
2 tablespoons of breadcrumbs
the soft part of 3 bread rolls
soaked in milk
4 tablespoons of softened
butter
1 cup of sugar
3/4 cup of raisins
3 eggs
2 egg yolks
grated peel of 1/2 organic
lemon
a pinch of salt
melted butter

being careful to not break it; cut out the thicker edges.

◆ Whisk the egg whites and salt to stiff peaks; fold them into the ricotta mixture (2); spread the mixture onto the sheet of dough (3), leaving 1 inch free around the edges. Roll the strudel over with the help of the cloth; seal the edges and slide strudel onto the cookie sheet. Brush it with the melted butter (4) and bake for 1 hour. Serve warm.

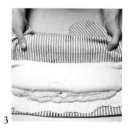

Pineapple rolls

Time needed: *1 hour*
Difficulty: medium

INGREDIENTS FOR 8 SERVINGS
1 portion of almond cookie dough
(see page 11)
Cream:
1/2 pineapple
3/4 cups of sugar
1 cup of milk
2 egg yolks
1/3 cup of flour
1/2 teaspoon of vanilla
grated peel of 1/2 organic lemon

Decoration:
2 tablespoons of apricot jelly
2 peeled pineapple slices
1/4 cup of sugar
a few pineapple leaves

◆ For the decoration, core 2 pineapple slices, divide each slice into 5 segments and place them in a bowl. Cook the sugar in 1/3 cup of water for 1 minute, pour the boiling syrup over the pineapple and set aside for 12 hours.

Pineapple rolls

◆ Butter a cookie sheet and line it with a buttered and floured sheet of parchment paper. Preheat the oven to 350°F.
◆ Prepare the mixture for the almond cookie dough. Spread it evenly onto the cookie sheet and bake for 15-20 minutes. Turn the cake onto a humid kitchen cloth and roll the pastry in the cloth; remove the paper. Let it cool.
◆ To make the filling, peel the pineapple, core and cut into pieces. Cook in a saucepan with 1/3 cup of sugar for 15-20 minutes; let it cool. Prepare the pastry cream (see page 16) with the milk, egg yolks, lemon peel, remaining sugar, flour and vanilla. Let it cool, stirring often.
◆ Purée 2/3 of the cooked pineapple and mix it into the custard. Unroll the pastry, cover with pastry cream, leaving 1/2-inch free all around the edges. Cover with the remaining pineapple pieces. Reroll the pastry on itself.
◆ For the decoration, drain the pineapple from the infusing syrup and dry it. Brush the pastry with apricot jelly dissolved in a double boiler and cut it into 10 slightly slanted slices. Put them in a circle on a serving dish and top each slice with a syrupy pineapple segment. Place 1 pineapple leave between each slice. In the center form a flower with the pieces of the 2 remaining pineapple slices.

Ricotta strudel

Chestnut rolls

Time needed: *45 minutes*
Difficulty: medium

INGREDIENTS FOR 6 SERVINGS
*1 recipe for cookie dough
(see page 11)
6 tablespoons of chestnut jam
2 tablespoons of rum
1 tablespoon of melted butter
2 tablespoons of crystallized sugar
potato starch*

◆ Line a cookie sheet with a buttered sheet of aluminum foil and sprinkle with potato starch. Preheat the oven to 350°F.
◆ Prepare the cookie dough. Spread on the cookie sheet and bake for 20-25 minutes. Turn the pastry onto a kitchen towel, sprinkled with crystallized sugar. Remove the aluminum foil.
◆ Mix the chestnut jam with the rum and melted butter and spread on the pastry rectangle. Using the towel, form a tight roll and slide it onto a serving plate. Let the roll rest for 4-5 hours before slicing.
◆ The chestnut jam can be replaced by any other fruit jam.

Chestnut rolls

Apple strudel

Time needed: *1 hour and 35 minutes*
Difficulty: complex

INGREDIENTS FOR 6-8 SERVINGS
*1 recipe for strudel pastry
(see page 13)
6 tablespoons of butter
1/2 cup of sugar
2 lbs of apples
4 tablespoons of brandy
1 tablespoon of breadcrumbs
a pinch of cinnamon
grated peel of 1/2 organic lemon
1/2 cup of raisins
1/2 cup of pine nuts
1 tablespoon of powdered sugar*

◆ Butter and flour a cookie sheet. Soak the raisins in warm water.
◆ Prepare the strudel pastry, place in a warm bowl, cover and let it rest for 30 minutes.
◆ For the filling, peel the apples, core and slice thinly. In a bowl, toss apples with brandy. In a

pan, roast the breadcrumbs. Melt the butter in a small saucepan. In a bowl, mix the sugar, cinnamon and lemon peel.
◆ Preheat the oven to 360°F.
◆ Put the pastry on a clean floured cloth and roll it out into a 1/4-inch thick rectangle. Spread the dough until very thin by pulling underneath it with your floured hands, being careful to not tear it. Trim the thicker edges. Brush the sheet of dough with the melted butter (keeping a little aside) and sprinkle with breadcrumbs, leaving 1 inch free space all around the edges. Spread the apples, drained raisins, pine nuts and sugar mixture onto the pastry sheet.
◆ Roll up the strudel using the cloth; seal it well along the edges. Gently slide it onto the cookie sheet, brush with the remaining melted butter and bake for about 1 hour. Serve warm, sprinkled with powdered sugar.

Fig roll

Time needed: *1 hour*
Difficulty: medium

INGREDIENTS FOR 8 SERVINGS
*4 1/2 cups of flour
1/2 cup of sugar
1 1/2 lbs of fresh figs
8 tablespoons of melted butter
2 eggs
a pinch of salt
1/3 cup of raisins
1/2 cup of peeled ground almonds
1/2 cup of peeled ground hazelnuts
1/2 cup of ground walnuts
1 teaspoon of baking powder
1/3 cup of milk
grated peel of 1/2 organic lemon
3 tablespoons of rum*

◆ Butter and flour a cookie sheet. Preheat the oven to 350°F.
◆ Soak the raisins in the rum. Peel the figs and slice thinly. In a bowl, mix the figs, walnuts, almonds, hazelnuts and raisins.
◆ On a work surface, sift the flour and baking powder in a mound; make a well in the center; add butter, sugar, salt, milk, 1 egg and lemon peel. Knead until well blended.
◆ Roll out the dough onto a floured cloth into a very thin rectangle. Spread fig mixture on dough, leaving 1 inch free space around the edges. Roll the pastry using the cloth and seal it well along

Fig roll

the edges. Place the roll onto the cookie sheet; bring the two ends together to form a donut and brush with the remaining lightly beaten egg.

◆ Bake for about 40 minutes. Let the roll cool before slicing and serving.

Chocolate and apricot roll

Time needed: *1 hour*
(plus cooling time)
Difficulty: *medium*

INGREDIENTS FOR 8 SERVINGS
4 eggs
3/4 cup of sugar
1/3 cup of flour
2 tablespoons of unsweetened cocoa
1 teaspoon of baking powder
a pinch of salt

Filling:
1 lb of apricots
1 lb of ricotta cheese
4 egg yolks
3/4 cup of powdered sugar
grated peel of 1/2 organic lemon
2 tablespoons of Grand Marnier
2 tablespoons of unsweetened cocoa

Decoration:
3/4 cup of whipping cream
1/4 cup of dried apricots
2 oz of dark chocolate

◆ Line a cookie sheet with a buttered sheet of parchment paper. Preheat the oven to 375°F.
◆ In a bowl, using an electric mixer, whisk egg yolks, sugar and 2 tablespoons of water until pale and creamy. Stir in the sifted flour, baking powder and cocoa. Beat egg whites with salt to stiff peaks and gently fold them into the mixture. Pour onto the cookie sheet and bake for about 20 minutes. Turn cake onto a humid kitchen towel; remove the paper and roll the pastry up in the cloth.
◆ To make the filling, pit the apricots and cut them into small pieces. Pass the ricotta cheese through a sieve and mix it with the egg yolks, powdered sugar, Grand Marnier and lemon peel. Unroll the dough and cover it with ricotta mixture leaving 1 inch free space all around the edges. Cover with the apricot pieces, roll up the cake and refrigerate for 2 hours.
◆ To decorate, rinse and dry the dried apricots and cut into small sticks. Grate the chocolate. Sprinkle the cake with cocoa. Whip the cream, put it in a pastry bag, fitted with a star tube and pipe 4 strips onto the cake. Decorate with little mounds of grated chocolate and dried apricot sticks. Refrigerate until ready to serve.

Chocolate and apricot roll

Plum cream roll

Time needed: *1 hour*
Difficulty: *medium*

INGREDIENTS FOR 8-10 SERVINGS
4 1/2 cups of flour
3/4 cups of sugar
3/4 lb of prunes
8 tablespoons of butter
2 eggs
1/3 cup of raisins
1/3 cup of peeled chopped almonds
1/3 cup of toasted chopped hazelnuts
1/4 cup of chopped walnuts
1 teaspoon of baking powder
1/3 cup of milk
grated peel of half organic lemon
3 tablespoons of rum
a pinch of salt

◆ Butter and flour a cookie sheet. Preheat the oven to 350°F.
◆ Soak the raisins in the rum. Pit the prunes and put them with 1/4 cup of sugar in a saucepan barely covered with water. Cook for 10-15 minutes, drain and purée. In a bowl, mix the prune purée with the chopped almonds, hazelnuts, walnuts and drained raisins.
◆ Melt the butter in a saucepan on very low heat.
◆ On a work surface, sift the flour, baking powder and salt into a mound; make a well in the center and add remaining sugar, melted butter, milk, egg and lemon peel.
◆ Knead well and place the dough on a floured cloth. Roll out into a very thin rectangle. Spread the prune mixture on dough, leaving 1 inch free space around the edges. Roll the pastry up with the help of the cloth and seal it well along the edges. Slide the roll onto the cookie sheet.
◆ Brush the cake with the remaining lightly beaten egg and bake for 40-45 minutes. Carefully and gently detach the roll from the cookie sheet. Let it cool completely before serving.

Plum cream roll

259

Sweet roll

Time needed: *1 hour*
Difficulty: *medium*

INGREDIENTS FOR **6** SERVINGS

2 1/2 cups of flour
3 tablespoons of potato starch
2 tablespoons of baking powder
a pinch of salt
8 tablespoons of butter in pieces
1/4 cup of sugar
1 egg
1/2 cup of Marsala
14 oz of jam of your choice
1 tablespoon of vanilla-flavored powdered sugar
1 egg white

◆ Butter and flour a cookie sheet. Preheat the oven to 375°F.
◆ On a work surface, sift the flour, potato starch, baking powder and salt into a mound; make a well in the center and add butter, sugar, egg and Marsala. Knead briefly and roll out into a thin rectangle. Spread the jam on the dough, leaving a 1 inch empty space around the edges. Roll the pastry up pulling the ends together to form a donut.
◆ Place onto the cookie sheet, brush with the lightly beaten egg white and bake for 40-45 minutes. Cool.
◆ Transfer onto a serving dish and sprinkle with the vanilla-flavored powdered sugar..

Cream strudel

Time needed: *1 hour and 20 minutes*
Difficulty: *complex*

INGREDIENTS FOR **6-8** SERVINGS

1 recipe for strudel pastry (see page 13)
2 cups of whipping cream
6 egg yolks
1/2 cup of sugar
3/4 cup of flour
2/3 cup of peeled chopped almonds
1/2 cup of raisins
1 1/4 oz of candied chopped citron
a pinch of cinnamon
3 tablespoons of melted butter
1 tablespoon of powdered sugar

◆ Butter and flour a cookie sheet.
◆ Prepare the pastry dough, cover and let it rest in a warm bowl for 30 minutes.
◆ Preheat the oven to 350°F.

◆ To make the custard, bring the whipping cream to a boil. In a saucepan, mix the egg yolk and sugar; add flour and cinnamon, then the boiling cream, a little at a time. Bring to a boil on moderate heat and cook for 7-8 minutes stirring continuously to avoid lumps. Let the custard cool, stirring occasionally.
◆ Rinse and dry the raisins; stir them into the mixture with the candied citron and chopped almonds.
◆ Put the pastry dough on a floured cloth and roll it out into a 1/4 in. thick rectangle. Pass your floured hands underneath the dough, pulling to spread it until very thin carefully, to not tear it. Trim the thicker edges.
◆ Spread the custard on dough, leaving 1 inch free space around the edges. Roll the pastry up in a cloth and seal it well along the edges. Slide the roll onto the cookie sheet.
◆ Brush with melted butter and bake for about 1 hour. When warm, transfer it onto a serving dish and sprinkle with powdered sugar.

Fruit filled tea roll

Time needed: *1 hour*
Difficulty: *medium*

INGREDIENTS FOR **6** SERVINGS

6 cups of flour
3 eggs
6 tablespoons of sugar
2 cups of strong tea
4 tablespoons of softened butter
1 teaspoon of baking powder
4 tablespoons of breadcrumbs
1/2 lb of strawberries
1/2 lb of pitted apricots
1/2 cup of Maraschino
1 teaspoon of cinnamon

◆ Butter and flour a cookie sheet. Preheat the oven to 350°F.
◆ Cut fruits into small pieces and soak in Maraschino with 1/2 teaspoon of cinnamon and 2 tablespoons of sugar. On a work surface, put the flour in a mound; form a well in the middle and add 2 eggs, remaining cinnamon, baking powder, 3 tablespoons of sugar, butter and tea. Knead vigorously until smooth. Divide into 4 pieces and roll 4 very thin sheets of the same size.
◆ Sprinkle one sheet with breadcrumbs and 1/4 of the fruit; repeat the process for the other 3 sheets of pastry, laying them one on top of the

other. Roll the stacked sheets of pastry tightly and place it on the cookie sheet.
◆ Brush with the remaining egg and sugar, lightly beaten together, and bake for 30 minutes. Raise the temperature to 400°F and continue to bake for 10-15 minutes. Serve cold.

Chocolate chip cream roll

Time needed: *50 minutes*
(plus cooling time)
Difficulty: *medium*

INGREDIENTS FOR **6** SERVINGS
4 eggs ◆ *1/3 cup of flour*
1/2 cup of sugar
1 1/4oz of unsweetened cocoa
1/2 teaspoon of baking powder
1 tablespoons of vanilla-flavored powdered sugar
1/3 cup of whipping cream
a pinch of salt

◆ Line a cookie sheet with a buttered and floured sheet of parchment paper. Preheat the oven to 375°F.
◆ In a bowl, with an electric mixer, whisk egg yolks, sugar and 1 tablespoon of water until pale and creamy. Mix in the flour, cocoa and baking powder. Beat egg whites with salt to stiff peaks and fold into the mixture. Spread onto the cookie sheet and bake for 16-18 minutes.
◆ Turn cake onto a lightly humid cloth and roll the pastry in the cloth. When cold, unroll the pastry. Whip the cream with the vanilla-flavored powdered sugar; spread on cake and roll up once more. Refrigerate the cake for 2 hours and slice just before serving.

Apulian strudel

Time needed: *1 hour and 20 minutes*
Difficulty: *medium*

INGREDIENTS FOR **8-10** SERVINGS
3 cups of flour
1/3 cup of extra virgin olive oil
1/3 cup of dry white wine
a pinch of salt
grated peel of 1/2 organic lemon ◆ *1 egg*
Filling:
1 2/3 cups of peeled almonds
2 3/4 cups of raisins ◆ *3/4 cups of sugar*
1/3 cup of extra virgin olive oil
1 1/4 oz of cinnamon ◆ *1/4 cup of Maraschino*

◆ Brush a cookie sheet with oil. Preheat the oven to 350°F.
On a work surface, put the flour in a mound, make a well in the center and break in the egg. Pour in the wine and oil; add the salt and lemon peel.
Knead until the dough is smooth and elastic; cover with a cloth and let it rest for 30 minutes.
To make the filling, soak the raisins in the Maraschino. Toast the peeled almonds in the oven. Coarsely chop them.
On a floured work surface, roll out the dough into a thin rectangle. Sprinkle with the sugar, almonds, drained raisins and cinnamon. Drizzle with the oil, roll up and bring the ends together to form a donut. Put onto the cookie sheet, brush with a little oil and bake for 50-60 minutes. Serve cold.

Grape strudel

Time needed: *2 hours and 15 minutes*
Difficulty: *complex*

INGREDIENTS FOR **6** SERVINGS
1 lb of puff pastry (see page 12)
2 lbs of blue grapes
3 tablespoons of breadcrumbs
6 tablespoons of butter
3/4 cup of sugar
a pinch of cinnamon
1 egg
1 tablespoon of powdered sugar

◆ Butter and flour a cookie sheet. Preheat the oven to 400°F.
◆ Rinse the grapes, cut in half and seed. Mix them with 1/2 cup of sugar and cinnamon. Roast the breadcrumbs in 5 tablespoons of butter until golden.
◆ On a floured cloth, roll out the puff pastry into a thin but even rectangle. Sprinkle with the roasted breadcrumbs and the grapes in sugar and cinnamon leaving a 1 in. free space all along the edges. Roll the pastry dough up in the cloth. Seal the edges with care.
◆ Slide the strudel onto the cookie sheet. In a bowl, beat the egg with the remaining sugar and melted butter; brush the surface of the cake with this mixture.
◆ Bake for about 40 minutes, brushing it again with the egg mixture a couple of times during the baking time.
◆ Carefully and gently detach the strudel from the cookie sheet and transfer it onto a dish. Serve cold or warm, sprinkled with powdered sugar.

Chestnut log

Time needed:
1 hour and 15 minutes
Difficulty: medium
Ingredients
for 6 servings
4 eggs ◆ *4 tablespoons of sugar*
4 tablespoons of unsweetened cocoa
2 tablespoons of flour
1 1/2 cups of heavy cream
10 chopped Marrons Glacé
3 tablespoons of chestnut jam
1 tablespoon of Cognac
1 tablespoon of chocolate chips
a pinch of salt

Butter and flour a cookie sheet and line it with a buttered and floured sheet of parchment paper. Preheat the oven to 375°F.

◆ With an electric mixer, whisk the egg yolks and sugar for 2-3 minutes until pale and creamy. Mix in the flour and cocoa. Beat the egg whites with the salt to stiff peaks and gently fold into the egg and cocoa mixture.

◆ Roll the batter to 1/2-inch thick onto the cookie sheet and bake it for 18-20 minutes or until done. Turn it over onto a lightly moistened cloth, remove the paper and roll it up into the cloth.

◆ Whip the cream and mix in the jam dis-solved in cognac: Unroll the pastry, spread it with the cream, keeping a little aside and reroll the pastry.

◆ Cover the cake with the remaining cream, and top it with the pieces of Marron Glacé and the chocolate chips.

◆ This roll can also be filled with a pastry cream: Prepare a pastry cream (see page 16) and while still hot, melt in 3 1/2 oz of chopped dark chocolate. Let it cool and mix in chopped praline hazelnuts. Garnish the roll with a little chocolate cream and a few praline hazelnuts or chocolate chips.

Lemon roll

Time needed: *50 minutes*
(plus cooling time)
Difficulty: medium

Ingredients for 6-8 servings
1 portion of almond cookie dough
4 egg yolks
1/2 cup of sugar
3 tablespoons of lemon juice
2 tablespoons of butter
Decoration:
1 tablespoon of powdered sugar
3 tablespoons of whipped cream
1 tablespoon of candied cherries

◆ Line a cookie sheet with a buttered and floured sheet of parchment paper. Preheat the oven to 400°F.
◆ Prepare the almond cookie dough; place it onto the cookie sheet and bake for about 15 minutes. Turn onto a humid cloth, discard the paper and roll the pastry in the cloth. Let it cool.
◆ To make the custard, whisk the egg yolks and sugar in a double boiler until pale and creamy. Mix in the lemon juice and continue to cook, always stirring, until the custard becomes dense and coats a spoon (make sure the mixture never boils). Add pieces of butter and let it cool.
◆ Unroll the pastry, spread with the custard, reroll and refrigerate for 1 hour.
◆ To decorate, sprinkle the roll with powdered sugar, slice and place on a serving dish. Garnish each slice with a rosette of whipped cream and 1/2 candied cherry.

Lemon roll

Wild berry strudel

Time needed:
1 hour and 20 minutes
Difficulty: complex

Ingredients for 6-8 servings
1 recipe for strudel pastry (see page 13)
1 cup of wild strawberries
2 1/2 cups of blackberries
1 cup of very fresh ricotta
6 tablespoons of melted butter
2 egg yolks
2 tablespoons of powdered sugar
grated peel of an organic lemon
1 tablespoon of breadcrumbs
a pinch of cinnamon

◆ Butter and flour a cookie sheet.
◆ Prepare the strudel pastry, place in a warm bowl, cover and let it rest for 30 minutes. Preheat the oven to 350°F.
◆ Rinse the strawberries and blackberries in ice ▶

Chestnut roll

water. Push the ricotta cheese through a sieve and mix it with the egg yolks, powdered sugar (except for 1 tablespoon), lemon peel and cinnamon.

◆ On a floured cloth, roll out the pastry dough in a 1/4 in. thick rectangle. Pass your floured hands underneath the dough to pull it out very thinly, being careful not to tear it. Trim the thicker edges. Brush the sheet of dough with a little melted butter, sprinkle with breadcrumbs and spread with the ricotta mixture, leaving a 1 in. free space all around the edges. Top the ricotta mixture with the strawberries and blackberries.

◆ Roll up the strudel in the cloth, seal around the edges and slide it onto the cookie sheet. Brush it with the melted butter and bake for about 1 hour. Remove from the oven. As soon as it is cool, transfer it onto a dish, sprinkle with remaining powdered sugar and serve cold.

Gubana

Gubana

Time needed: *1 hour and 45 minutes*
(plus resting time)
Difficulty: complex

INGREDIENTS FOR **8-10** SERVINGS
2 1/2 cups of flour
1 egg yolk
15 tablespoons of softened butter
7 tablespoons of white wine
a pinch of salt

Filling:
1 1/2 cups of chopped walnuts
1/4 cup of peeled chopped almonds
2 tablespoons of peeled pine nuts
2 tablespoons of chopped candied
orange and citron peel
1/3 cup of raisins ◆ *1 egg*
grated peel of one organic lemon
grated peel of one organic orange
3 tablespoons of Marsala
2 tablespoons of sugar
2 tablespoons of honey
a pinch of cinnamon
1/8 teaspoon powdered clove
a pinch of salt

Decoration:
1/2 tablespoon of powdered sugar
10 thinly sliced almonds
4 thin stripes of candied citron
4 raisins

*Apricot and
ricotta strudel*

◆ Soak the raisins in Marsala. On a work surface, sift the flour into a mound and make a well. Add the wine and salt; knead to form a ball. Slit a cross over the top, cover with a cloth and let it rest for 15 minutes. Then roll the dough out into a square, 12 inches per side.

◆ Press the butter between 2 sheets of plastic wrap, forming a square of 7 inches per side and place it in the center of the dough. Fold the pastry over the butter to cover it and roll with a rolling pin to obtain a 24 in. long rectangle. Fold the dough in 3, and starting from the short side, reroll it out into a 24-inch long rectangle. Refold it in 3, wrap it in transparent foil and refrigerate for 30 minutes. Repeat this process 3 times, always returning the dough to the refrigerator for 30 minutes.

◆ Preheat the oven to 325°F.

◆ To make the filling, mix the candied citron and orange, pine nuts, almonds, lemon peel, orange peel, raisins, honey, sugar, cinnamon and clove; blend in the egg yolk. Beat egg white with salt to stiff peaks and fold in.

◆ On a floured cloth, roll out the pastry dough into a 20 x 10 inch rectangular sheet. Spread with the filling and fold over, sealing the ends. Roll up into a spiral, place onto a cookie sheet, brushed with water. Brush the roll with beaten egg yolk. Bake for 45-50 minutes. As soon as it is cool, sprinkle with powdered sugar and transfer it onto a serving dish. Garnish with flowers made with almond slivers and candied citron.

Apricot and ricotta strudel

Time needed: *1 hour and 20 minutes*
Difficulty: complex

INGREDIENTS FOR **6-8** SERVINGS
1 recipe for strudel pastry (see page 13)
1 lb of apricots
1 3/4 cups of ricotta
6 tablespoons of melted butter
4 egg yolks
1/2 cup of powdered sugar
grated peel of one organic lemon
1 tablespoon of breadcrumbs

◆ Rinse the apricots, pit and slice thinly. Pass the ricotta cheese through a sieve and mix with egg yolks, powdered sugar and lemon peel.

◆ On a floured cloth, roll out the pastry dough to a 1/4-inch thick rectangle. Pass your floured hands underneath the dough to pull it out very thinly, being careful not to tear it. Trim the thicker edges. Brush the sheet of dough with a little melted butter; sprinkle with breadcrumbs. Spread with the ricotta mixture, leaving 1 inch free space all around the edges. Cover the ricotta mixture with the apricot slices.

◆ Roll up the strudel in the cloth, seal around the edges and slide it onto the cookie sheet. Brush it with the melted butter and bake for about 1 hour. Remove from the oven. Serve cold.

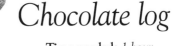

Coffee cream roll

Coffee cream roll

Time needed: *1 hour*
(plus cooling time)
Difficulty: medium

INGREDIENTS FOR 8 SERVINGS

1 recipe for cookie dough (see page 11)
Filling:
3/4 cup of espresso coffee
3/4 cup of sugar
3/4 oz of potato starch
1/4 cup of rum
1/4 cup of whipping cream
2/3 cup of toasted hazelnuts
almond oil

Decoration:
1/4 cup of chopped milk chocolate
20 coffee beans
1 tablespoon of powdered sugar

◆ Butter a cookie sheet and line it with a buttered and floured sheet of parchment paper. Preheat the oven to 350°F.

◆ Prepare the cookie dough. Roll it out into an even sheet of dough into the cookie sheet and bake for 15-20 minutes. Turn cake onto a lightly humid cloth, discard the paper and roll the pastry in the cloth. Let it cool.

◆ For the filling, cook 1/2 cup of sugar in 4 tablespoons of water and follow the instructions for the hazelnut brittle (see page 21). As soon as it is cold, grind the brittle and put it in a saucepan with the coffee, remaining sugar and potato starch dissolved in 1 tablespoon of water. Bring to a boil and cook for 4-5 minutes, stirring constantly. Let it cool.

Chocolate log

◆ Whip the cream and fold it with the rum into the filling. Unroll the pastry, leaving it on the cloth and spread the filling on top. Roll the cake up, sprinkle with powdered sugar and transfer onto a serving dish. Melt the chocolate in a double boiler, put it in a parchment paper cone and pipe chocolate rosettes on the top of the roll. Decorate the rosettes with coffee beans and refrigerate the roll for 2 hours.

Chocolate log

Time needed: *1 hour*
(plus cooling time)
Difficulty: medium

INGREDIENTS FOR 8 SERVINGS

1 recipe for cookie dough (see page 11)
1/4 cup of rum

Cream:
4 egg whites ◆ *1/2 cup of sugar*
3/4 cup of softened butter
1/2 cup of chopped bittersweet chocolate

Decoration:
5 oz/150g chopped bittersweet chocolate
1/3 cup of whipping cream
sugar flowers

◆ Butter a cookie sheet and line it with buttered and floured parchment paper. Preheat the oven to 350°F.

◆ Prepare the cookie dough; roll it out into the cookie sheet and bake for about 20 minutes. Turn it over onto a humid cloth, remove the paper and roll up the cake in the cloth.

◆ Make a classic butter cream with the ingredients mentioned above (see page 17), mix in the chocolate, melted in a double boiler.

◆ Unroll the dough; brush it with the rum diluted in a little water and spread with the cream. Roll the pastry up and refrigerate for 3 hours, wrapped in the cloth. Remove the cloth, cut one end, (slanted) and put both pieces on a grid.

◆ To decorate, melt the chocolate in a double boiler and pour it over the 2 rolls. When the chocolate has hardened, transfer the larger role onto a serving dish, and place the smaller one next to it. Design patterns on the chocolate with a fork. Fill a pastry bag, fitted with a star tube with the whipping cream and pipe rosettes at the bottom ends of the chocolate log. Garnish with the sugar flowers.

Cheesecake

Butter a pie pan. Preheat the oven to 350°F.

♦ In a saucepan, melt the butter on a very low heat.

♦ Grind the crackers; mix with the sugar (or honey) and melted butter (1), until well blended.

♦ Put this mixture into the pie pan and press with your fingertips to make it stick to the bottom and sides (2).

Time needed: *1 hour*
Difficulty: easy
INGREDIENTS
FOR 8 SERVINGS
1 cup of Graham crackers
7 tablespoons of butter
1/4 cup of sugar or honey

Filling:
1 lb of cream cheese
4 tablespoons of whipping cream
grated peel and juice of one organic lemon
3 eggs
1/2 cup of sugar
1 teaspoon of vanilla
a pinch of salt

Decoration:
3/4 cup of whipping cream
1 teaspoon of lemon juice
1/4 cup of sugar

♦ To make the filling, whisk the cheese with the whipping cream, mix in the lemon juice and lemon peel, eggs, salt, sugar and vanilla. (3). Pour into the cake pan (4) and bake for 35-40 minutes.

♦ To decorate, whisk 1/3 cup of whipping cream with the lemon juice and sugar until it becomes thick. Spread the mixture onto the warm cake and replace in the oven to 450°F for 5 minutes. Cool. Just before serving, whip the remaining cream, put it in a pastry bag and pipe a crown around the border of the cake.

Apple cheesecake

Time needed: *1 hour and 15 minutes (plus cooling time)*
Difficulty: medium

INGREDIENTS FOR 10-12 SERVINGS

1 cup of Graham crackers
1/4 cup of walnuts
7 tablespoons of butter
2 tablespoons of brown sugar
1/2 teaspoon of cinnamon
Filling:
1/2 lb of Philadelphia type cream cheese
1/2 cup of flour ♦ *4 eggs* ♦ *2 egg yolks*
3/4 cup of whipping cream
1 tablespoon of lemon juice
2 tablespoons of Calvados
1 teaspoon of vanilla ♦ *1 tablespoon of sugar*
Decoration:
4 tablespoons of butter
3/4 cups of brown sugar
2 tablespoons of whipping cream
2 tablespoons of milk
2 tablespoons of Calvados
1 lb of Golden Delicious apples

Apple cheesecake

♦ Butter a springform pan. Preheat the oven to 400°F.
♦ Lightly toast the walnuts in the oven then chop them. In a saucepan, melt the butter on very low heat.
♦ Grind the crackers; mix with the melted butter, walnuts, brown sugar and cinnamon. Put this mixture into the cake pan and press with your fingertips to make it stick to the bottom and sides.
♦ To make the filling, whisk the whipping cream with the lemon juice until it becomes thick. With an electric mixer, whisk the cream cheese with brown sugar. Stir in the flour, eggs, egg yolks, 1/2 the sour cream and Calvados. Spread the mixture in the springform pan and bake for 15 minutes. Lower the temperature to 325°F and continue to bake for about 30 minutes.
♦ Mix the remaining cream preparation with the vanilla and the tablespoon of sugar, spread the mixture over the hot cake and replace in the oven to 400°F for 5 minutes. Let it cool. Refrigerate for 12 hours.
♦ For the decoration, peel the apples, core and slice. In a saucepan cook the butter, sugar, whipping cream, milk and Calvados to obtain a syrup. In this syrup, cook the apples until tender but still whole. Cool lightly and use to decorate the cake.

Cheesecake

Hazelnut cake

Time needed: *1 hour*
Difficulty: easy

INGREDIENTS FOR **6-8** SERVINGS
1 cup of ground toasted hazelnuts
3 1/2 oz of ricotta cheese
8 tablespoons of softened butter
1/2 cup of sugar
4 eggs
grated peel of 1/2 organic lemon
a pinch of salt

Decoration:
1 tablespoon of powdered sugar
2 tablespoons of apricot jam
1/4 cup of grated dark chocolate

◆ Butter and flour a 12-inch cake pan. Preheat the oven to 360°F.
◆ With an electric mixer, whisk the butter and sugar until creamy. Mix in the eggs, strained ricotta , hazelnuts and lemon peel. Beat the egg whites with the salt to stiff peaks and fold them in gently. Pour the mixture into the cake pan and bake for about 40 minutes. Let the cake cool completely before transferring it onto a serving dish.
◆ Melt the apricot jelly in a double boiler and brush it over the cake. Top the whole surface of cake with grated chocolate and dust with powdered sugar.

Hazelnut cake

Cherry ricotta cake

Cherry ricotta cake

Time needed: *1 hour and 10 minutes (plus resting time)*
Difficulty: medium

INGREDIENTS FOR **8** SERVINGS
shortbread pastry recipe (see page 12)
1 lb of black cherries
12 1/2 oz of ricotta
1 cup of sugar
2 tablespoons of Maraschino
2 egg whites
1 tablespoon of apricot jelly

◆ Butter and flour a 12-inch pie pan.
◆ Prepare the shortbread pastry, form into a ball

and refrigerate for 1 hour, covered with plastic wrap. After 30 minutes, preheat the oven to 350°F.
◆ Rinse and dry the cherries; pit them. Set 4 1/2 oz aside for decoration. Strain the ricotta cheese through a sieve; whisk it with the sugar, Maraschino and egg whites. Refrigerate the mixture for 1 hour. Roll out the short pastry dough into a thin sheet, line the pie pan and prick with a fork. Cover with a sheet of parchment paper and fill with dried beans. Bake for 15 minutes. Remove the beans and paper and let the dough cool slightly.
◆ Cover the pastry crust with cherries, pour the ricotta mixture to cover cherries. Return to the oven for another 30 minutes. Remove from the oven and transfer onto a serving dish.
◆ Melt the apricot jelly in a double boiler. With the cherries set aside, make a crown all along the border of the pie and a smaller one at the center. Brush the cherries with jelly and refrigerate until ready to serve.

Yogurt cake

Time needed: *1 hour*
Difficulty: easy

INGREDIENTS FOR **6** SERVINGS
2 1/2 cups of flour
9 tablespoons of softened butter
1 cup of sugar
2 eggs
4 tablespoons of milk
1 teaspoon of baking powder
5 oz of full fat yogurt
grated peel of one organic lemon
1 tablespoon of lemon juice
a pinch of salt
1 tablespoon of powdered sugar
1 teaspoon of cinnamon

◆ Butter and flour a 10-inch pie pan. Preheat the oven to 360°F.
◆ In a large bowl, with an electric mixer, whisk the butter and sugar until creamy. Stir in the eggs, one at a time; add the yogurt, mixed with the milk, the sifted flour, the baking powder, the grated lemon peel and the lemon juice.
◆ Beat egg whites with salt to stiff peaks and gently fold them into the mixture. Pour the batter into the pie pan and bake for 45-50 minutes.
◆ Transfer the cake onto a serving dish; sprinkle

Yogurt cake

with the powdered sugar. Cover cake with a sheet of paper with cut-out patterns of your choice; through a sieve sprinkle with the cinnamon and carefully remove the paper.

Apricot ricotta cake

Time needed: *1 hour*
(plus cooling time)
Difficulty: *medium*

INGREDIENTS FOR 6-8 SERVINGS
3 eggs
2/3 cup of sugar
1 sachet of vanilla flavored powdered sugar
1 cup of flour
2 oz of potato starch
1 teaspoon of baking powder
grated peel of one organic lemon

Filling:
1 lb 2oz of ricotta cheese
1 cup of sugar
grated peel and juice of one organic lemon
3/4 cup of whipping cream
1 1/2 lb of apricots
5 tablespoons of Kirsch
1 tablespoon of powdered sugar
2 tablespoons of peeled pine nuts

◆ Butter a 10-inch springform pan and line it with a buttered and floured sheet of parchment paper. Preheat the oven to 370°F.
◆ With an electric mixer, whisk the egg yolks, sugar and 2 tablespoons of water until light and creamy. Stir in the sifted flour, baking powder and potato starch; stir in the lemon peel, vanilla flavored powdered sugar. Beat the egg whites with the salt to stiff peaks and fold them in gently. Pour the mixture into the springform pan and bake for 30-35 minutes. To make the filling, strain the ricotta cheese through a sieve and mix it with the lemon juice, sugar and 2 tablespoons of Kirsch. Gently fold in the whipped cream.
◆ Scald the apricots in boiling water, peel and pit; slice into 4 segments. Soak them for 15-20 minutes in the remaining Kirsch.
◆ Remove the cake from the pan and cut into 2 circles. Replace the bottom circle into the cake pan, and brush with the apricots soaking liquid. Cover with half of the filling; cover with the apricots and layer with the remaining filling. Top

Apricot ricotta cake

Whole wheat yogurt cake

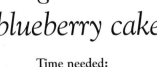

Yogurt and blueberry cake

with the other cake circle, press lightly and refrigerate for 2 hours.
◆ Remove spring form. Transfer the cake onto a serving dish, sprinkle with powdered sugar and decorate the center with a little pistachio.

Whole-wheat yogurt cake

Time needed: *1 hour and 20 minutes*
Difficulty: *easy*

INGREDIENTS FOR 8 SERVINGS
3 1/2 cups of whole wheat flour
12 tablespoons of softened butter
3 eggs
6 tablespoons of honey
1 teaspoon of cinnamon
1 teaspoon of grated nutmeg
1/4 teaspoon powdered cloves
7 oz of full fat yogurt
1 teaspoon of baking powder

Decoration:
1 1/4 cups of whipping cream
3 tablespoons of honey

◆ Butter and flour a 10-inch cake pan. Preheat the oven to 360°F.
◆ With an electric mixer, whisk the butter and honey until creamy. Stir in the eggs, the sifted flour and baking powder, the spices and finally the yogurt. Blend the ingredients well; pour the mixture into the cake pan and bake for about 1 hour.
◆ To decorate, whip the cream, and with half or it, cover the cake. Fill a pastry bag, fitted with a star tube with the remainder and draw 9 small circles of cream, in each circle place a teaspoon of honey. Top the cake with cream rosettes.

Yogurt and blueberry cake

Time needed:
1 hour and 30 minutes
(plus cooling time)
Difficulty: *medium*

▶

269

INGREDIENTS FOR 8-10 SERVINGS
1/2 portion of shortbread pastry (see page 12)
2 lb of full fat yogurt
2/3 cups of milk
3/4 cups of sugar
1 oz of unflavored gelatin
4 egg yolks
juice of 1 lemon
3 cups of blueberries

◆ Butter and flour a springform pan. Preheat the oven to 390°F.
◆ Prepare the shortbread pastry dough and refrigerate for 30 minutes.
◆ Roll out the dough into a disk, line the cake pan and prick it with a fork. Bake for 18-20 minutes.
◆ Soak the gelatin in cold water and bring the milk to a boil. In a saucepan whisk the egg yolks and sugar until light and creamy. Bring to a boil on low heat, stirring continuously and add gelatin. Remove from heat, let it cool and blend in the yogurt and lemon juice.
◆ Rinse blueberries in ice water, dry and set 1 tablespoon aside. Layer the cake alternating yogurt cream and blueberries until all the ingredients are used up. Finish with a layer of cream. Refrigerate the cake for about 4 hours, then decorate with the remaining blueberries and serve.

Ricotta coffee cake

Time needed: *1 hour and 20 minutes*
(plus resting time)
Difficulty: *medium*

INGREDIENTS FOR 8 SERVINGS
1 1/2 cups of flour
6 tablespoons of melted butter
1/4 cup of sugar
30 ground walnuts
1 egg yolk

Filling:
7 oz of mascarpone cheese
5 oz of ricotta
3 1/3 oz of powdered sugar
2 eggs
2 tablespoons of unsweetened cocoa
1 tablespoon of instant coffee

Decoration:
1 tablespoon of cocoa
1 tablespoon of powdered sugar
30 coffee beans

◆ Butter a 10-inch cake pan and line with a sheet of buttered parchment paper. Preheat the oven to 360°F.
◆ Put the sifted flour in a mound on a work surface, make a well in the center and put the ground walnuts, melted butter, sugar and egg yolk. Knead rapidly, cover the dough with plastic wrap and refrigerate for 30 minutes.
◆ Put the dough in a cake pan and spread it evenly, pressing with the back of a spoon. Cover with a sheet of parchment paper and fill with dried beans. Bake for 15 minutes. Remove the beans and paper and let the pastry crust cool completely.
◆ To make the filling, strain the ricotta cheese through a sieve and mix it with the mascarpone, the cocoa and sugar. Add the instant coffee dissolved in a tablespoon of hot water. Whisk in the egg yolks, one by one. Pour the mixture into the pastry crust and replace in the oven to 325°F for 20 minutes. Cool completely.
◆ To decorate, sprinkle the cold cake with sifted cocoa. Place over it a sheet of paper with cut out patterns and sprinkle with powdered sugar. Remove the paper and complete the decoration with the coffee beans.

Sicilian "cassata"

Time needed: *1 hour and 30 minutes*
(plus cooling time)
Difficulty: *medium*

INGREDIENTS FOR 6-8 SERVINGS
14 oz of sponge cake (see page 10)
1 lb of ricotta
14 oz chopped mixed candied fruit
1 1/4 cups of sugar
3 1/2 oz of apricots jelly
1 tablespoon of orange water
1 liquor glass of Maraschino
1 teaspoon of vanilla
2 tablespoons of peeled pistachios
1/2 cup of chopped dark chocolate
1 cup of powdered sugar
1 egg white
a few drops of lemon juice

◆ Butter a 10-inch cake pan and line with parchment paper.
◆ Cut the sponge cake into 1/2 inch slices and with them line the bottom and sides of the cake pan, attaching the slices together with a little apricot jelly.
◆ Strain the ricotta cheese through a sieve. On a low heat dissolve the sugar with the vanilla in 2 tablespoons of water until warm. Whisk the ri-

cotta cheese. Add 3/4 of the candied fruit and the chocolate pieces; add the orange water, the pistachios cut in half and the Maraschino. Mix well and pour the mixture into the cake pan. Cover with more sponge cake slices. Refrigerate for about 2 hours.

◆ Lightly beat the egg whites with a few drops of lemon juice. Sift in the powdered sugar and mix until thick and smooth. Turn the Cassata onto a serving dish, brush with the remaining jelly, melted in a double boiler, and cover with the sugar glaze. Garnish with the remaining candied fruit.

Baked Sicilian "cassata"

Time needed: *1 hour*
(plus resting time)
Difficulty: medium

INGREDIENTS FOR 8 SERVINGS
a recipe for shortbread pastry (see page 12)
14oz of ricotta cheese
4 1/2 oz of powdered sugar
1 teaspoon of vanilla
1 1/2 oz of dark chocolate
1 1/2 oz of milk chocolate
3 1/2 oz of candied orange and citron peel

Decoration:
1 1/4 oz of chopped dark chocolate
1 1/4 oz of chopped milk chocolate
1 1/4 oz of chopped white chocolate
1 1/4 oz of candied cherries
1 1/4 oz of candied citron
2 oz of candied orange
1 tablespoon of apricot jelly

◆ Butter and flour a 10-inch pie pan.
◆ Prepare the shortbread pastry, form into a ball and refrigerate for 1 hour, covered with plastic wrap. After 30 minutes, preheat the oven to 360°F.
◆ Cut the milk chocolate and dark chocolate into small pieces. Cut the candied orange and citron peel into small pieces. Strain the ricotta through a sieve and whisk it with the sugar and vanilla until creamy. Mix in the chopped chocolate and citrus peel.
◆ Roll out the short bread pastry dough into a thin sheet and line the pie pan. Cover with a sheet of parchment paper and fill with dried beans. Bake for 20 minutes. Remove from the oven; let it cool; remove and discard the beans and paper. Transfer onto a serving dish. Fill the pastry crust with the ricotta mixture and even it

out.
◆ To decorate cut the candied cherries, orange and lemon peel into thin strips. Melt the 2 types of chocolate separately in a double boiler and spread them thinly on a sheet of parchment paper. Let the chocolate harden and cut into strips.
◆ Top the cake with the candied fruit and chocolate strips. Brush with the apricot jelly, melted in a double boiler. Refrigerate until ready to serve.

Chocolate and ricotta cake

Time needed: *40 minutes*
(plus resting time)
Difficulty: medium

INGREDIENTS FOR 6 SERVINGS
3 1/2 oz of biscotti
8 tablespoons of butter
14oz of ricotta cheese
3/4 cups of sugar
1 teaspoon of vanilla
2/3 cup of shelled almonds
1/2 small cup of espresso coffee
4 1/2 oz of dark chocolate
3/4 cup of whipping cream

◆ Butter a 10-inch shallow springform pan.
◆ In a saucepan, melt the butter on very low heat. Grind the cookies in a food processor and mix with the melted butter. Line the cake pan with the ground cookie and butter mixture, pressing to make it stick. Refrigerate for 1 hour.
◆ Scald the almonds in boiling water, drain and peel. Toast them in a preheated oven for a few minutes. Cool then chop finely.
◆ Strain the ricotta cheese through a sieve; whisk in with the sugar and vanilla until smooth. Divide the ricotta mixture into 2 separate bowls and refrigerate.
◆ Cut the dark chocolate into pieces; melt it in a double boiler with the coffee. Cool lightly and stir into one of the two bowls of ricotta. Stir the chopped almonds into the other bowl of ricotta.
◆ Whip the cream; fold half of it into one bowl of ricotta and the other half into the second bowl. Put the two ricotta mixtures into two pastry bags, fitted with star tubes and fill the cookie crust with circles, alternating the colors. Place rosettes between the crowns in alternating colors.
◆ Open the springform pan, slide the cake onto a serving dish and refrigerate until ready to serve.

271

Neapolitan pie

Soak the wheat kernels in water for 3 days, changing the water every 24 hours. (If using canned wheat sprouts, follow the instructions on the label.)

♦ Dice the candied orange and citron.

♦ Prepare the shortbread pastry dough, form into a ball and refrigerate for 1 hour, covered with plastic wrap.

♦ Drain the wheat sprouts; cover with cold water and cook for 15 minutes on medium heat. Drain and return to pot adding milk, a teaspoon of sugar and a pinch of cinnamon; bring to a boil. Lower heat to medium and cook until milk is absorbed. Let it cool.

♦ Butter a 12-inch springform pan. Preheat the oven to 350°F. Strain the ricotta through a sieve. With an electric mixer, whisk it with the egg yolks, sugar, cinnamon, lemon peel

Time needed: *2 hours (plus soaking and resting time)*
Difficulty: *medium*
INGREDIENTS
FOR 8-10 SERVINGS

a recipe for shortbread pastry (see page 12)
8 oz of durum wheat kernels
1 lb of ricotta cheese
1 cup of sugar
1/2 cup of candied orange and citron
1 teaspoon of orange water
1/2 teaspoon of cinnamon
2 cups of milk
grated peel of 1/2 organic lemon
4 eggs
a pinch of salt
2 tablespoons of powdered sugar

and orange water until creamy.

♦ Fold in the cooked wheat sprouts and diced orange and citron pieces.

♦ Roll out 2/3 of the shortbread pastry dough very thinly and line the springform pan. Beat the egg whites with salt to stiff peaks and fold it into the ricotta mixture. Pour it into the cake pan.

♦ Roll out the remaining shortbread pastry dough. Slice into 1-inch-wide strips and crisscross them onto the ricotta mixture.

♦ Fold the edges of the dough together, pressing with your fingertips and bake for 1 hour. Remove from oven.

♦ When cold, transfer onto a serving dish and sprinkle generously with the powdered sugar.

Yogurt and orange cake

Time needed: *1 hour and 30 minutes*
Difficulty: *easy*

INGREDIENTS FOR 8-10 SERVINGS
3 cups of flour
3 eggs
2/3 cup of walnuts
1 teaspoon of baking powder
juice and grated peel of one organic orange
1 1/2 cups of sugar
1 cup of extra virgin olive oil
3 1/2 oz of full fat yogurt
3 cloves
a pinch of nutmeg
a pinch of salt

Decoration:
7 oz of powdered sugar
grated peel of 1 organic orange
1 teaspoon of apricot jelly
1 teaspoon of vanilla
5 oz of candied orange peel

Yogurt and orange cake

♦ Butter and flour a cake pan. Preheat the oven to 370°F.
♦ Lightly toast the walnuts in a preheated oven. Cool completely and finely chop. Grind the cloves.
♦ Sift the flour and baking powder into a bowl. Stir in the chopped walnuts, ground cloves, nutmeg, sugar and salt. With an electric mixer, whisk in the eggs, orange peel and orange juice, oil and yogurt. Mix until all is blended
♦ Pour the mixture into the prepared cake pan and bake for 50 minutes. Transfer the cake onto a cake rack and cool completely.
♦ Brush the top of the cake with the apricot jelly, melted in a double boiler. In a bowl, mix the powdered sugar, orange peel and vanilla in 2 tablespoons of water. Cover the cake with this thick glaze.
♦ Cut the candied orange peel with cutters of different shapes and decorate the base and top of the cake. Let the glaze dry in a cool place before serving.

Neapolitan pie

Cheese and lemon cake

Time needed: *1 hour and 30 minutes*
Difficulty: easy

INGREDIENTS FOR **6** SERVINGS
3 cups of flour
1 teaspoon of baking powder
1/2 cup of cream cheese
10 tablespoons of softened butter
3 eggs
2/3 cups of sugar
juice and grated peel of an organic lemon
a pinch of salt
1 teaspoon of vanilla
1 tablespoon of powdered sugar
1 1/4 oz of candied citron

◆ Butter a 10-inch tube pan. Preheat the oven to 360°F.
◆ In a bowl, beat the cream cheese. Add butter, sugar and beat in the eggs one at a time. Mix in the lemon peel, lemon juice, sifted flour and baking powder, vanilla and salt. Pour into the cake pan and bake for about 1 hour. Transfer the cake onto a rack and cool completely.
◆ Thinly slice the candied citron, then cut into small triangles. Sprinkle the cake with powdered sugar and decorate with candied citron triangles.

Cheese and lemon cake

Ricotta and raisin cake

Time needed:
1 hour and 15 minutes
Difficulty: medium

INGREDIENTS FOR **6-8** SERVINGS
1 lb of ricotta
5 eggs
grated peel of an organic lemon
1/3 cup of sugar
3 tablespoons of breadcrumbs
a tablespoon of rum
1/4 cup of raisins
1 tablespoon of powdered sugar
2 teaspoons of cinnamon
a pinch of salt

◆ Butter a 10-inch cake pan and line the bottom with a sheet of buttered parchment paper. Sprinkle with a little breadcrumb. Preheat the oven to

Ricotta and raisin cake

325°F.
◆ Soak the raisins in rum. Strain the ricotta cheese through a sieve and mix it with the egg yolks, sugar and lemon peel. Add the strained raisins and breadcrumbs. Beat the egg whites with salt to stiff peaks, and fold them in the ricotta mixture. Pour into the cake pan and bake for 50 minutes.
◆ Transfer the cake onto a serving dish, remove the paper and cool. Sprinkle with cinnamon, cover with patterned cardboard cuttings, and through a sieve sprinkle with powdered sugar. Gently remove the cardboard.

Greek ricotta cake

Time needed: *1 hour and 15 minutes*
Difficulty: medium

INGREDIENTS FOR **6-8** SERVINGS
2 1/2 cups of flour ◆ *1 egg*
1 tablespoon of olive oil
1 tablespoon of sugar
a pinch of cinnamon
a pinch of salt

Filling:
1 lb of ricotta cheese
1/2 cup of sugar
1/2 cup of milk
1 teaspoon of vanilla
2 eggs ◆ *1 egg yolk*
1/2 teaspoon of cinnamon
2 tablespoons of melted butter
1 teaspoon of vanilla

◆ Butter a 10-inch springform pan. Preheat the oven to 360°F.
◆ Put the flour in a mound onto a work surface and make a well in the center. Add the egg, oil, sugar, cinnamon and salt. Knead, adding a little water, until smooth and light. Roll out into 2 disks, one slightly larger then the other. With the larger one, line the cake pan.
◆ Press the ricotta cheese through a sieve and mix in the eggs, sugar, milk, vanilla and cinnamon.
◆ Pour the mixture into the cake pan and cover with the remaining pastry disk, sealing the edges. Brush the top of the cake with the melted butter and bake for 40-45 minutes.
◆ When pie is cool, sprinkle with powdered sugar and serve warm or cold.

Frozen meringue

Time needed: *2 hours*
(plus time to freeze)
Difficulty: complex

INGREDIENTS FOR **6** SERVINGS
3 meringue discs 9 inch in diameter (see page 25)
1 lb of nougat ice cream
1 lb of chocolate ice cream
1 1/4 cups of whipping cream
3 oz of nougat

◆ Line a 10-inch springform pan with parchment paper.
◆ Place a meringue disk into the spring form and cover with a 1/2-inch thick layer of nougat ice cream. Cover the ice cream with another meringue disk and cover it with chocolate ice cream. Top with the third meringue disk and put in the freezer for 2 hours.
◆ Finely chop the nougat and whip the cream. Transfer the cake onto a serving dish, remove the paper, and cover completely with some of the whipped cream. With a fork, trace some lines all around the side of the cake, to decorate.
◆ Fill a pastry bag, fitted with a star tube, with the remaining cream and form a spiral crown on the top of the cake. Pipe cream rosettes at the base. Sprinkle the chopped nougat within the spiral.

Frozen meringue

Two color fruit meringue

Time needed: *2 hours*
Difficulty: complex

INGREDIENTS FOR **6** SERVINGS
1 recipe for zabaglione (see page 17)
3 egg whites
5 oz of powdered sugar
a pinch of salt ◆ *2 red oranges*
2 kiwi ◆ *2 tablespoons of sugar*
5 candied cherries
1 liquor glass of Grand Marnier

◆ Butter a shallow non-stick pie pan. Preheat the oven to 215°F.
◆ Beat the egg whites, salt and sugar following the instructions for meringue (see page 25). Pour the meringue mixture into the pie pan and bake for 2 hours, covering with aluminum foil during the last 30 minutes of baking.

◆ Peel the kiwis, slice and cut in half. Peel the oranges to the fruit and remove segments (see page 28). Put all fruit on a plate and cover with sugar and Grand Marnier.
◆ Prepare the Zabaglione and let it cool.
◆ Gently turn over the meringue onto a rack. Cool. Transfer onto a serving dish, cover it with the zabaglione and top with the well-drained fruit. Garnish with the candied cherries.

Pink meringue cake with wild strawberries

Time needed: *1 hour*
(plus time for the meringue)
Difficulty: complex

INGREDIENTS FOR **6-8** SERVINGS
3 meringue discs (see page 25)
2 cups of milk ◆ *6 egg yolks*
1/2 cup of sugar ◆ *2/3 cup of flour*
1 teaspoon of vanilla
1 1/2 cups of whipping cream
grated peel of 2 organic oranges
3/4 cup of wild strawberries

Decoration:
3/4 cup of whipping cream
1 tablespoon of powdered sugar
50 wild strawberries

◆ In a saucepan, beat the egg yolks and sugar. Slowly add the flour and vanilla, a little at the time; mix in the boiling milk, little by little. Bring to a boil on low heat and cook for 7-8 minutes stirring continuously. Pour the custard in two bowls; cool, stirring occasionally to avoid the formation of a skin on top. In one bowl, mix the grated orange peel.
Whip the cream, divide in two parts, mix one part with the orange custard and the other part with the remaining custard. Rinse strawberries and dry. Keep a few aside; mix remainder to the regular custard.
Put a meringue disk onto a serving dish and spread with the orange custard. Cover with a second disk and spread it with the strawberry custard. Cover with the third disk.
To decorate, purée the strawberries with the powdered sugar, mix with the cream and whip it until stiff. Top the cake with the whipped strawberry cream and garnish with a few strawberries.

*Pink meringue cake
with wild strawberries*

275

Raspberry meringue cake

Line 2 shallow cake pans with parchment paper. Preheat the oven to 215°F.

◆ Beat the egg whites, salt and sugar following the instructions for meringue (see page 25).

◆ Fill a pastry bag, fitted with a smooth tube, with the meringue mixture; pipe it out in a spiral to cover the bottom of both cake pans.

◆ Bake for about 2 hours, covering with aluminum foil during the last 30 minutes until white, dry and light.

Time needed:
2 hours and 30 minutes
Difficulty: complex
INGREDIENTS
FOR 6 SERVINGS
3 egg whites
3/4 cups of sugar
a pinch of salt
1 1/2 cups of whipping cream
2 1/2 cups of raspberries
2 tablespoons of powdered sugar

◆ Rinse the raspberries in ice water and dry them. Whip the cream with 2 tablespoons of powdered sugar. Place a meringue disk on a serving dish, spread over the whipped cream, layer with 1/3 of the raspberries, cover with the second meringue disk and put in the freezer for 1 hour.

◆ In a food processor, purée the remaining raspberries coarsely. Serve with the meringue cake.

Meringue with wild berries

Time needed: *2 hours*
Difficulty: complex

INGREDIENTS FOR 4 SERVINGS
2 tablespoons of strawberry jelly
3 cups of strawberries, raspberries and blueberries
2/3 cup of peeled ground almonds
1/3 cup of sugar ◆ *1/3 cup of flour*
3 egg whites
1 1/4 oz of powdered sugar
a pinch of salt

Meringue:
3 egg whites ◆ *1/2 cup of sugar*
a pinch of salt

Pastry cream:
1/3 cup of sugar ◆ *3 egg yolks*
1 cup of milk ◆ *1 vanilla bean*
1/2 teaspoon of cornstarch

Sauce:
1 cup of raspberries
1/3 cup of sugar
1 tablespoon of lemon juice

◆ Butter a cookie sheet and line the bottom with parchment paper. Preheat the oven to 375°F.
◆ Beat the egg whites with the salt to stiff peaks; blend in the sugar, flour, almonds and powdered sugar. Pour the mixture onto the cookie sheet in-

Meringue with wild berries

to a thin layer and bake for 10-15 minutes.
◆ Remove the pastry from the cookie sheet, discard the paper, and let the pastry cool.
◆ Line the cookie sheet with parchment paper and on the paper, draw 4 circles, each of 4 inches in diameter. Lower the oven temperature to 215°F.
◆ Beat the egg whites, salt and sugar following the instructions for meringue (see page 25).
◆ Fill a pastry bag, fitted with a smooth tube with the meringue mixture, and pipe it out around the circumference of the 4 circles drawn on the parchment paper. Substitute the pastry bag tube with a star one and pipe rosettes on the edges of the circles to form a crown. Bake for 1 hour and 30 minutes.
◆ To make the custard, bring the milk to a boil with the vanilla bean. In another saucepan, whisk the egg yolks and sugar; add the cornstarch. Add the boiling milk through a sieve, a little at a time. On low heat, almost bring to a boil, stirring constantly until the custard films a spoon.
◆ To make the sauce, quickly rinse the raspberries in ice water and dry. Purée with the sugar and lemon juice in a food processor. Strain through a sieve.
From the pastry, cut 4 circles of 4 inches in diameter with a round cutter. Place on individual plates and brush with the jelly, dissolved in a double boiler. Spread with the custard.
◆ Rinse the berries in ice water, dry and place over the custard alternating strawberries, raspberries and blueberries. Cover with the meringue circles and place over the remaining berries. Serve with the raspberry sauce.

Raspberry meringue cake

Ices and Frozen Desserts

Ice Cream ◆ Semifreddo ◆ Bombes and Cassata ◆ Granite
Sorbets ◆ Frozen desserts

Pine nut ice cream

Time needed:
40 minutes
Difficulty: medium

**INGREDIENTS
FOR 4-6 SERVINGS**

2 cups of milk
1 tablespoon of heavy cream
5 egg yolks
3/4 cup sugar
1 tablespoon of white rum
1 vanilla bean
1/2 cup of pine nuts
1/4 cup of almonds
1/3 cup of pistachios

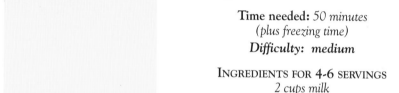

Preheat the oven at 400 F. Scald almonds in boiling water; drain and peel. Toast pine nuts in oven; grind pine nuts with almonds. Add heavy cream and mix.

◆ Preheat the oven at 400 F. Scald almonds in boiling water; drain and peel. Toast pine nuts in oven; grind pine nuts with almonds. Add heavy cream and mix.

◆ In a saucepan, bring milk to a boil; add split vanilla bean. In a bowl, mix egg yolks with sugar, stirring with a wooden spoon until creamy. Add warm milk, a little at a time, passing it through a sieve. Transfer mixture to a saucepan, and almost bring to a boil on low heat. As soon as the cream thickens and coats the back of a spoon, add the nut cream. Set aside to cool, stirring from time to time.

◆ Transfer mixture to ice cream machine and follow the manufacturer's instructions. When ice cream is ready, mix in the rum. Freeze until serving time.

◆ Scald pistachios for 1 minute in boiling water; drain and peel. Transfer ice cream in individual bowls and decorate with pistachios.

Pineapple ice cream

Time needed: *40 minutes*
(plus freezing time)
Difficulty: medium

INGREDIENTS FOR 4 SERVINGS
2 cups milk
4 egg yolks
4/5 cup of sugar
1 vanilla bean
1 large pineapple
1/4 cup butter

◆ Prepare a crème anglaise (see page 17) with milk, vanilla, egg yolks and 3/4 cup of sugar. Set aside to cool, stirring often.
◆ Peel pineapple, slice, core and cut slices in triangles. In a non-stick pan, melt butter and cook pineapple for 3 minutes. Add remaining sugar, mixing often. Cook another 3 minutes. Remove from heat and let cool. Chop 1/2 the pineapple triangles, keeping the other 1/2 for decoration.
◆ Mix chopped pineapple with the crème anglaise and transfer to ice cream machine, following the manufacturer's instructions. Place ice cream in a 3-cup mold and freeze for 24 hours.
◆ To serve, quickly dip mold in warm water; turn ice cream onto a serving dish and decorate with pineapple triangles.

Apricot ice cream

Apricot ice cream

Time needed: *50 minutes*
(plus freezing time)
Difficulty: medium

INGREDIENTS FOR 4-6 SERVINGS
2 cups milk
4 egg yolks
3/4 cup sugar
1 vanilla bean
8 apricots
1 piece of candied citron

◆ Prepare a crème anglaise (see page 17) with milk, vanilla, egg yolks and 2/3 of sugar. Set aside to cool, stirring often.
◆ Rinse apricots and scald them in boiling water for 2 minutes. Drain them, peel, pit and slice. Transfer to a saucepan and cook over medium heat for 15 minutes with remaining sugar, stirring from time to time. Remove from heat, keep 1 tablespoon aside and purée remainder in a food processor. Set aside to cool.
◆ In a bowl, mix cold apricot purée with crème anglaise and transfer to ice cream machine; follow the manufacturer's instructions.
◆ Dice apricots you set aside and cut candied citron in the shape of a leaf. Freeze ice cream in an airtight container. To serve, place ice cream in individual bowls; decorate with apricot and citron leaves.

Pine nut ice cream

Pistachio ice cream

Time needed: *20 minutes*
Difficulty: *medium*

INGREDIENTS FOR 4-6 SERVINGS

2 cups of milk
5 egg yolks
3/4 cup of sugar
1 vanilla bean
3/4 cup of pistachios

◆ Scald pistachios for 2 minutes in boiling water; drain and peel them. Chop 1 tablespoon for decoration and grind the remainder in a food processor.
◆ Prepare a crème anglaise (see page 17) with milk, vanilla, egg yolks and 2/3 of sugar. Set aside to cool, stirring often. Remove from heat and add ground pistachios. Set aside to cool, stirring from time to time.
◆ Transfer mixture to the ice cream machine, following the manufacturer's instructions. Distribute ice cream in individual bowls and sprinkle with chopped pistachios.

Pistachio ice cream

Vanilla ice cream

Time needed: *30 minutes*
Difficulty: *medium*

INGREDIENTS FOR 4-6 SERVINGS

2 cups of milk
5 egg yolks
3/4 cup of sugar
1 vanilla bean
a few small cookies

◆ In a saucepan, bring milk and split vanilla bean to a boil. In a bowl, whisk egg yolks and sugar. When the mixture is pale and creamy, add warm milk, a little at a time, passing it through a sieve. Transfer mixture in a saucepan and almost bring to a boil, stirring often. When the cream coats the back of a spoon, remove from heat and set aside to cool, mixing well.
◆ Transfer the mixture to ice cream machine and follow the manufacturer's instructions. If you are not serving ice cream immediately, freeze in an airtight container. Distribute in bowls and decorate with the cookies

Vanilla ice cream

Yogurt ice cream

Time needed: *20 minutes*
Difficulty: *easy*

INGREDIENTS FOR 4 SERVINGS

1 cup of yogurt
1 cup of fresh cream
3/4 cup of sugar
1 teaspoon of Cognac
fresh fruit
mint leaves

◆ In a saucepan, heat cream and sugar on moderate heat. When sugar has melted, remove from heat and set aside to cool, stirring often. Add yogurt and Cognac, incorporating the ingredients well.
◆ Transfer to ice cream machine, following the manufacturer's instructions.
◆ When it is ready, transfer ice cream in a pastry bag fitted with a large nozzle and pipe in a large serving bowl or individual cups. Decorate as you wish with fresh fruit and mint leaves.

American cold punch

Time needed: *40 minutes*
Difficulty: *easy*

INGREDIENTS FOR 4-6 SERVINGS

1/2 cup of white rum
2 cups of milk
3/4 cup of Cognac
1 cup of Champagne (or dry sparkling wine)
1/2 cup of sugar
2 eggs
a pinch of salt

◆ In a bowl, whisk egg yolks and sugar until pale and creamy. Add a little at a time milk, rum, Cognac and Champagne, stirring well. Transfer mixture in the ice cream machine, following the manufacturer's instructions.
◆ In a bowl, beat egg whites with salt to soft peaks. Transfer punch in a bowl and delicately fold in egg whites. Serve immediately in parfait glasses..

American cold punch

Chocolate chip
ice cream

Time needed: *35 minutes*
Difficulty: easy

INGREDIENTS FOR **4-6** SERVINGS
3/4 cup of fresh cream
1 1/4 cup of milk
3/4 cup of sugar
1/2 cup of grated dark chocolate

◆ In a saucepan, heat cream, milk and sugar on moderate heat. When sugar has melted, remove from heat and let cool, stirring from time to time.
◆ Transfer to ice cream machine, following the manufacturer's instructions.
◆ In a double boiler, melt chocolate. When ice cream is almost ready, dip a fork in the chocolate and let it run over the ice cream, while the machine is activated.
◆ Serve ice cream in individual bowls. If you will not serve it immediately, keep the ice cream in an airtight container in the freezer.

*Chocolate chip
ice cream*

Chocolate
ice cream

Time needed: *20 minutes*
Difficulty: medium

INGREDIENTS FOR **4-6** SERVINGS
2 cups of milk
5 egg yolks
3/4 cup of sugar
3/4 cup of grated dark chocolate
1 vanilla bean
1 piece of bittersweet chocolate

◆ Prepare a crème anglaise (see page 17) with milk, vanilla, egg yolks and sugar. Remove from heat. Add grated dark chocolate and mix until chocolate has melted. Set aside to cool, stirring from time to time.
◆ Transfer the cold mixture in ice cream machine and follow the manufacturer's instructions. Place the ice cream in a stainless steel mold and keep in the freezer.
◆ When ready to serve, quickly dip mold in warm water and turn the ice cream onto a serving dish. With a potato peeler, shave the dark chocolate and place curls on the ice cream.

Walnut ice cream

*Hazelnut or almond
ice cream*

Walnut
ice cream

Time needed: *35 minutes*
Difficulty: medium

INGREDIENTS FOR **4-6** SERVINGS
2 cups of milk
4 egg yolks
3/4 cup of sugar
3/4 cup of ground walnuts
1 vanilla bean
a few whole walnuts

◆ Prepare a crème anglaise (see page 17) with milk, vanilla, egg yolks and sugar. Cool.
◆ When the crème will be cold, mix in the ground walnuts. Transfer to the ice cream machine, following the manufacturer's instructions.
◆ Place the ice cream in a large serving bowl or in parfait glasses; decorate with whole walnuts.

Hazelnut or
almond ice cream

Time needed: *50 minutes*
Difficulty: medium

INGREDIENTS FOR **4-6** SERVINGS
2 cups of milk
4 egg yolks
3/4 cup of sugar
1/2 cup of hazelnuts or almonds
1 vanilla bean

◆ Preheat the oven at 350 F.
◆ Prepare a crème anglaise (see page 17) with milk, vanilla, egg yolks and sugar. Set aside to cool, stirring often.
◆ Lightly toast the hazelnuts in the oven. Brush with a clean kitchen towel and remove the peel (if you use almonds, just toast them lightly). Keep 2 tablespoons aside and grind the remainder in a food processor.
◆ Add the ground hazelnuts (or almonds) to the cold mixture. Transfer to the ice cream machine, following the manufacturer's instructions.
◆ Place the ice cream in parfait glasses and decorate each with the whole hazelnuts (or the almonds) set aside.

Honey
ice cream

Time needed: *50 minutes*
Difficulty: *medium*

INGREDIENTS FOR **4-6** SERVINGS
2 cups of milk
5 egg yolks
1/4 cup of sugar
Grated peel of 1/2 lemon
3/4 cup of honey
2 tablespoons of almonds
1/2 cup of whipped cream
3 candied cherries

◆ Preheat the oven to 350 F.
◆ Prepare a crème anglaise (see page 17) with milk, vanilla, egg yolks and sugar. Set aside to cool, stirring often.
◆ Add honey to the cold mixture and transfer to the ice cream machine, following the manufacturer's instructions.
◆ Lightly toast the almonds in the oven and set aside to cool. Dice the candied cherries. Whip the cream and refrigerate.
◆ Distribute the ice cream in individual bowls and decorate each with rosettes of whipped cream, cherries and almonds.

Coffee
ice cream

Time needed: *40 minutes*
Difficulty: *medium*

INGREDIENTS FOR **4-6** SERVINGS
2 cups of milk ◆ *4 egg yolks*
3/4 cup of sugar
2 teaspoons of instant coffee
3 teaspoons of rum

◆ In a bowl, whisk egg yolks and sugar. Add warm milk a little at a time and simmer on low heat, stirring often, until the mixture coats the back of a spoon. Add the coffee and, when it is all melt, add the rum. Set aside to cool, stirring from time to time.
◆ Transfer the cold mixture to ice cream machine, following the manufacturer's instructions.
◆ Place the ice cream in individual bowls. If you will not use it immediately, keep the ice cream in an airtight container in the freezer.

Caramel
ice cream

Time needed: *40 minutes*
Difficulty: *medium*

INGREDIENTS FOR **4-6** SERVINGS
2 cups of milk
4 egg yolks
1 cup of sugar
almond oil

◆ In a high-side saucepan, melt 1/2 cup of sugar with 5-6 tablespoons of water on moderate heat (see page 19). When the sugar is golden, remove from heat and whisk in 4 tablespoons of cold water. Add the milk and bring to boil, mixing so that the caramel melts completely.
◆ With an electric mixer, whisk the egg yolks with 1 tablespoon of sugar and add the caramel-milk mixture, a little at a time. In a bain-marie, cook the mixture without bringing it to boil, until it will coat the back of a spoon. Set aside to cool, stirring from time to time. Transfer to the ice cream machine, following the manufacturer's instructions.
◆ Simmer the remaining sugar, dissolved in a little water, on low heat, until it will be golden. Pour onto an oiled marble surface, let it become dense and coarsely chop.
◆ Distribute the ice cream in individual bowls and decorate with chopped caramel pieces.

Cinnamon
ice cream

Time needed: *20 minutes*
Difficulty: *medium*

INGREDIENTS FOR **4-6** SERVINGS
2 cups of milk
5 egg yolks
3/4 cup of sugar
20 g of powdered cinnamon
1 vanilla bean

◆ Prepare a crème anglaise (see page 17) with milk, vanilla, egg yolks and sugar. Let cool.
◆ When the cream is completely cold, transfer to the ice cream machine and follow the manufacturer's instructions.
◆ Serve the ice cream in individual cups.

Nougat ice cream

Time needed: *40 minutes*
Difficulty: medium

INGREDIENTS FOR 4-6 SERVINGS
2 cups of milk ◆ *4 egg yolks*
1/2 cup of sugar
1 vanilla bean
160 g of nougat

◆ In a saucepan, bring the milk and the split vanilla bean to a boil. In a bowl, mix the egg yolks and the sugar together; add the warm milk, a little at a time, passing it through a sieve. Transfer the mixture in a saucepan and almost bring to a boil, stirring often. When the mixture coats the back of a spoon, remove from heat and set aside to cool, stirring from time to time.
◆ When the mixture is cold, transfer to the ice cream machine and follow the manufacturer's instructions. Finely chop 130 g of nougat and add it to the ice cream, towards the end of mixing time.
◆ Coarsely chop the remaining nougat and sprinkle on the ice cream, when ready to serve.

Chestnut ice cream

Time needed: *50 minutes*
Difficulty: medium

INGREDIENTS FOR 4-6 SERVINGS
2 cups of milk ◆ *4 egg yolks*
3/4 cup of sugar
3/4 cup of ready-to-use chestnut cream
1 vanilla bean
1/4 cup of grated dark chocolate

◆ Prepare a crème anglaise (see page 17) with milk, vanilla, egg yolks and sugar. While still warm, add chestnut cream. Set aside to cool, stirring from time to time.
◆ Transfer the mixture to the ice cream machine and follow the manufacturer's instructions. When it is ready, place the ice cream in the freezer with 4 individual bowls.
◆ In a double boiler, melt chocolate and transfer in a parchment paper cone. Distribute the ice cream in iced bowls and pipe out little chocolate decorations.

Ice cream with Cognac

Time needed: *45 minutes*
Difficulty: easy

INGREDIENTS FOR 4 SERVINGS
3/4 cup of fresh cream
11/4 cup of milk
3/4 cup of sugar
1 teaspoon of Cognac

◆ In a saucepan, whisk milk, cream and sugar on moderate heat; mix until sugar is completely melted. Remove from heat and set aside to cool, stirring from time to time with a wooden spoon. When the mixture is cold, add the Cognac.
◆ Transfer the mixture to the ice cream machine and follow the manufacturer's instructions. When it is ready, distribute the ice cream in individual glasses or in a large serving bowl.

Zabaglione ice cream

Time needed: *40 minutes*
Difficulty: medium

INGREDIENTS FOR 4-5 SERVINGS
1/2 cup of fresh cream
1/4 cup of Marsala
1/4 cup of white wine
4 egg yolks
1/2 cup of sugar
1 vanilla bean

◆ In a saucepan, heat cream, Marsala, wine and split vanilla bean. In a bowl, whisk egg yolks and sugar with an electric mixer. When the mixture will be creamy, add the warm cream, after discarding the vanilla bean.
◆ In a double boiler, simmer the mixture on low heat, without bringing to a boil, until it coats the back of a spoon. Remove from heat and set aside to cool, stirring from time to time.
◆ Transfer the cold mixture in the ice cream machine and follow the manufacturer's instructions. Place the ice cream in a larger bowl or in parfait glasses.
◆ If you will not use it immediately, place the ice cream in an airtight container in the freezer.

Semifreddo with strawberry sauce

Time needed:
45 minutes
(plus freezing time)
Difficulty: medium

**INGREDIENTS
FOR 10-12 SERVINGS**
2 cups of heavy cream
3/4 cup of sugar
8 egg yolks
1/4 teaspoon of vanilla
3 strawberries

Sauce:
1 lb of strawberries
3/4 cup of sugar
1/4 cup of Aurum liquor
grated peel of 1 lemon

In a saucepan, mix sugar and 4 cups of water; bring to boil and cook on low heat for 7-8 minutes or until the syrup is transparent and thick.

◆ In a bowl, with an electric mixer, beat egg yolks and vanilla until frothy. Beat in the hot sugar syrup; continue mixing until the mixture is cool.

◆ Delicately blend in the whipped cream. Pour mixture in a 4-cup mold and store in the freezer for 3 hours.

◆ To make the sauce, rinse strawberries in ice water; dry on a towel and remove stems. Set aside 3 strawberries.

◆ In a food processor, mix strawberries with sugar, Aurum and lemon peel, until creamy. Pour in a sauce boat and refrigerate.

◆ Before serving, quickly dip bowl in hot water, turn onto a serving dish and decorate. Slice 2 of the remaining strawberries, fan and set in the middle of the semifreddo. Top with the last strawberry. Serve with the sauce.

◆ The same sauce can be prepared with other fruits: raspberries, apricots, peaches, pineapples or others. Decorate the semifreddo with the chosen fruit.

Frozen chocolate soufflé

Time needed: *40 minutes*
(plus freezing time)
Difficulty: medium

INGREDIENTS FOR 6-8 SERVINGS
1/2 cup of grated dark chocolate
3/4 cup of sugar ◆ *5 egg yolks*
2 cups of heavy cream
1 teaspoon of cocoa
1 chocolate decorative piece

◆ In a double boiler, melt chocolate.
◆ Cook sugar in 1/2 cup of water for 7-8 minutes. In a bowl, beat egg yolks, with an electric mixer, until frothy. Slowly add sugar syrup, mixing continuously until the mixture is cool. Blend in the melted chocolate and, very delicately, fold in the whipped cream.
◆ Wrap the exterior of a 4-cup soufflé mold with aluminum foil, 2 or 3 inches higher than the mold. Pour the chocolate mixture in the mold and store in the freezer for at least 4 hours.
◆ Before serving, delicately remove aluminum foil, dust with sifted cocoa and set a decorative piece of chocolate on top of the soufflé.

Frozen chocolate soufflé

Kirsch parfait

Time needed: *40 minutes*
(plus freezing time)
Difficulty: medium

INGREDIENTS FOR 6 SERVINGS
3/4 cup of sugar
5 egg yolks
2 cups of heavy cream
4 tablespoon of kirsch
1/4 cup of candied cherries
1/4 cup of candied citron

◆ Bring sugar and 1/2 cup of water to a boil and cook for 7-8 minutes; the syrup will be transparent and thick.
◆ Whisk egg yolks until frothy. Slowly add hot syrup, whisking constantly until the mixture is cool. Add kirsch and delicately blend in the whipped cream. Pour into a square 3-cup mold. Store in the freezer for at least 3 hours.
◆ Before serving, quickly dip mold in hot water. Turn onto a serving plate. Slice in thick slices and decorate with strips of candied citron and cherries.
◆ The same recipe can be made with Grand Marnier instead of the kirsch and garnished with strips of candied orange.

286

Semifreddo with strawberry sauce

Zabaglione semifreddo

Time needed: *50 minutes*
(plus freezing time)
Difficulty: medium

INGREDIENTS FOR 4-6 SERVINGS

8 egg yolks
3/4 cup of dry marsala
1 cup of sugar
1 1/2 cup of heavy cream
1/4 cup of candied orange peel
1 piece of candied citron

◆ With egg yolks, marsala and sugar, prepare a zabaglione (see page 17); set aside to cool, stirring often.
◆ Whip the cream and mix into the cold zabaglione. Pour into a 4-cup mold and freeze it for 3-4 hours.
◆ Before serving, quickly dip mold in hot water and turn onto a plate. Decorate with a circle of candied citron and orange peel. Refrigerate for 20 minutes before serving.

Frozen strawberry mousse

Time needed: *40 minutes*
(plus freezing time)
Difficulty: medium

INGREDIENTS FOR 4-6 SERVINGS

1 lb of strawberries
2 1/4 cup of sugar
1/4 cup of white
1 cup of heavy cream
2 pieces of candied citron
a pinch of salt

◆ Rinse 3/4 of the strawberries in ice water, dry and remove the stems. In a food processor, purée them with half the sugar.
◆ Cook 1/4 cup of sugar with a few drops of water for 5-6 minutes. In a bowl, beat egg whites, salt and remaining sugar with an electric mixer. Slowly add hot syrup, mixing constantly until the mixture is cool. Delicately blend into the puréed strawberries.

Zabaglione semifreddo

Frozen strawberry mousse

Gianduia parfait

◆ Whip 2/3 of the cream and mix into strawberry preparation. Pour in a 4-cup low mold and set in freezer for at least 4 hours.
◆ Before serving, quickly dip mold in hot water. Turn onto a serving plate. Refrigerate.
◆ Cut leaves of citron. Rinse remaining strawberries, dry and remove the stems. Set 1 whole strawberry aside, cut 3 in quarters and slice the rest. Whip the remaining cream. Transfer to a pastry bag, fitted with a star tube and decorate the mousse. Distribute the strawberries in a decorative way. Garnish with candied citron leaves.

Gianduia parfait

Time needed: *50 minutes*
(plus freezing time)
Difficulty: medium

INGREDIENTS FOR 6-8 SERVINGS

1/2 cup of sugar
5 egg yolks
1/4 cup of grated bittersweet chocolate
2 1/4 cups of heavy cream
1/2 cup of finely chopped praline hazelnuts
1 praline hazelnut

◆ In a double boiler, melt chocolate.
◆ Cook sugar with 1/4 cup of water for 7-8 minutes. In a bowl, whisk egg yolks, with an electric mixer until frothy. Add hot sugar syrup, mixing constantly, until the mixture cools completely. Mix in the chopped praline hazelnuts.
◆ Divide this cream in 2 bowls. To one, add the melted chocolate. Whip 2 cups of heavy cream and divide in 2 parts. Half should be mixed in the chocolate cream and the other half into the light cream.
◆ Pour the light cream into a 3-cup mold and level it. Delicately pour the chocolate cream over and transfer the mold to the freezer for at least 3 hours.
◆ Before serving, quickly dip mold in hot water. Turn onto a serving dish.
◆ Whip remaining heavy cream, transfer to a pastry bag and decorate the base and the top of the parfait. Top with hazelnut.

Frozen pineapple soufflé

Time needed: *50 minutes*
(plus freezing time)
Difficulty: medium

INGREDIENTS FOR 8 SERVINGS
3 cups of pineapple
1/2 cup of sugar
5 egg yolks
2 cups of heavy cream
3 slices of pineapple
1 pomegranate

◆ Dice pineapple and cook for 5-6 minutes to dry lightly. Purée in a food processor. Cook sugar with 1/4 cup of water for 7-8 minutes.
◆ In a bowl, whisk egg yolks, with an electric mixer until frothy. Slowly add sugar syrup, whisking continuously until the mixture is cool. Blend in the puréed pineapple and whipped cream. Pour into a 6-cup rectangular mold and store in the freezer for at least 4 hours.
◆ Before serving, dip mold in hot water. Turn onto a serving plate. Dry the 3 pineapple slices, slice 6 diamonds and cut the rest in pieces. Place the diamonds on top and pieces around dessert. Cover with grains of pomegranate.

Frozen pineapple soufflé

Lime semifreddo

Time needed: *40 minutes*
(plus freezing time)
Difficulty: medium

INGREDIENTS FOR 6 SERVINGS
3/4 cup of lime juice
1 1/3 cup of sugar
5 egg yolks
Grated peel of 3 limes
2 cups of heavy cream
2 limes

◆ In a saucepan, reduce lime juice by 1/3. Cook 2/3 of sugar in 1/4 cup of water for about 10 minutes.
◆ In a bowl, whisk egg yolks with an electric mixer until frothy. Slowly add hot sugar syrup, whisking constantly until the mixture is cool. Add reduced lime juice and lime peel; very delicately

Lime semifreddo

blend in the whipped cream. Pour into a 4-cup mold and store in the freezer for at least 3 hours.
◆ Rinse and dry 2 limes. Slice very thinly and place in a bowl. Cook remaining sugar in 3/4 cup of water for 2 minutes. Pour this syrup over lime slices and refrigerate.
◆ Before serving, quickly dip mold in hot water. Turn semifreddo onto a serving dish. Drain the lime slices on a kitchen towel. Place decoratively around the semifreddo, covering the whole dessert. It is better to refrigerate the semifreddo for 30 minutes before serving it.

Jamaican semifreddo

Time needed: *1 hour*
(plus freezing time)
Difficulty: medium

INGREDIENTS FOR 8 SERVINGS
3/4 cup of sugar
5 egg yolks
1/4 cup of grated bittersweet chocolate
2 cups of heavy cream
1/2 cup of chopped pralined hazelnuts
1/4 cup of orange juice
grated peel of 2 oranges
1 1/2 teaspoons of instant coffee
1 tablespoon of milk
1 piece of milk chocolate

Ice cream:
2 cups of milk
4 egg yolks
3/4 cup of sugar
1 cup of chopped bittersweet chocolate
1 vanilla bean

◆ Prepare the chocolate ice cream (see page 283). Line the sides of a 4-cup rectangular mold with ice cream and place in the freezer.
◆ On medium heat, reduce orange juice by half. Dissolve coffee in milk. In a double boiler, melt chocolate. Cook sugar in 1/4 cup of water for 7-8 minutes. In a bowl, whisk egg yolk, with an electric mixer, until frothy. Slowly add sugar syrup, whisking constantly until the mixture is cool.
◆ Divide the mixture in 3 bowls. To the first bowl, mix in the melted chocolate and the chopped hazelnuts. To the second bowl, add the ▶

Jamaican semifreddo

orange juice and the orange peel. To the third bowl, add the dissolved coffee. Whip the cream and delicately mix 1/3 into each bowl.

◆ In the cold mold, pour the chocolate cream and level with a spatula. Very delicately pour the coffee cream over, and the orange cream over the coffee cream. Set aside in the freezer for 4 hours.

◆ Before serving, quickly dip mold into hot water. Turn onto a serving plate. With a potato peeler, make curls with the piece of milk chocolate and decorate the semifreddo.

Frozen Amaretto brick with hot chocolate

Time needed: *50 minutes*
(plus freezing time)
Difficulty: *medium*

INGREDIENTS FOR 8 SERVINGS
1 lb of Amaretti
1 1/2 cups of heavy cream
3 teaspoons of instant coffee
2 egg yolks
1/2 cup of powdered sugar
1/4 lb of dried biscotti
1 teaspoon of vanilla
3/4 cup of whipped cream
1/4 cup of amaretto liquor
a pinch of salt

Cream:
3/4 cup of chopped bittersweet chocolate
1 tablespoon of cornstarch
3 tablespoons of sugar
2 cups of milk
2 tablespoons of butter

◆ Coarsely chop the Amaretti and biscotti. In a bowl, mix with egg yolks, sugar, vanilla, heavy cream and coffee (dissolved in 1/4 cup of warm water). Add a pinch of salt and mix all ingredients well. Delicately fold in the whipped cream. Pour the preparation in a 6-cup rectangular mold and store in the freezer for at least 4 hours.

◆ To make the cream, melt chocolate in a double boiler. Add sugar, butter and cornstarch; mix well. Slowly add milk, whisking constantly until the cream thickens. Set aside, leaving the cream in the double boiler to keep warm.

◆ To serve, quickly dip mold in hot water. Turn the brick over a serving dish. Slice and serve with hot chocolate cream on the side.

Coffee cups of parfait

Time needed: *40 minutes*
(plus freezing time)
Difficulty: *medium*

INGREDIENTS FOR 6-8 SERVINGS
1/4 cup of sugar
3 egg yolks
1 1/4 cup of heavy cream
1 1/2 tablespoon of instant espresso coffee
2 tablespoons of milk

◆ Dissolve 1 tablespoon of coffee in warm milk. Cook sugar in 3 tablespoons of water for 7-8 minutes. In a bowl, whisk egg yolks, with an electric mixer, until frothy. Slowly add hot sugar syrup, whisking constantly, until the mixture is cool. Add dissolved coffee. Whip 2/3 of heavy cream. Very delicately fold in the whipped cream. Pour preparation into individual coffee cups and freeze for 2 hours.

◆ Dissolve the remaining coffee in the remaining warm cream and refrigerate for 1 hour.

◆ To serve, whip the coffee-flavored cream, transfer to a pastry bag, fitted with a star tube and decorate every cup of parfait.

Orange peel parfait

Time needed: *40 minutes*
(plus soaking and freezing time)
Difficulty: *medium*

INGREDIENTS FOR 6 SERVINGS
1 cup of sugar
5 egg yolks
1 cup of orange juice
2 cups of heavy cream
2 oranges
6 candied violets

◆ Wash and dry the oranges; remove the peel in long and thin strips; set aside in a bowl. Cook 1/2 cup of sugar in 3/4 cup of water for 2 minutes and pour the syrup over orange peels and soak for 24 hours.

◆ Bring the orange juice to a boil and let it reduce by half. In another saucepan, cook the remaining sugar with 1/4 cup of water for 10 minutes or until the syrup is thick.

◆ In a bowl, whisk the egg yolks until frothy; slowly add the sugar syrup and continue whisking until cool. Mix in the reduced orange juice.
◆ Drain orange peels from the liquid, dry them and coarsely chop. Whip the cream and delicately fold into mixture; add the chopped orange peels. Brush a 4-cup mold with water; pour mixture in mold and freeze for at least 4 hours.
◆ To serve, quickly dip mold in hot water. Turn onto a serving dish and decorate with candied violets

Chestnut semifreddo with rum sauce

Time needed: 40 minutes
(plus freezing time)
Difficulty: medium

INGREDIENTS FOR 6-8 SERVINGS
3/4 cup of chestnut cream
4 eggs, separated
1/2 cup of sugar
1 1/4 cup of heavy cream
4 tablespoons of rum
5 chopped Marrons Glacés
1/4 cup of peeled pistachios
a pinch of salt

Sauce:
1 cup of milk
3 egg yolks
1/2 cup of sugar
1 small vanilla bean
3 tablespoons of rum

◆ In a bowl, whisk egg yolks and sugar with an electric mixer until creamy and pale. Mix in the chestnut cream, rum and chopped marrons glacés. Whip 2/3 of the cream and fold it into the egg mixture. Beat egg whites to stiff peaks and delicately fold into the mixture. Pour into a round pan and freeze for at least 3 hours.
◆ Prepare a vanilla sauce with milk, egg yolks, sugar and vanilla (see page 19), add rum and stir until cool.
◆ To serve, quickly dip mold into hot water. Turn onto a serving dish. Whip the remaining cream and transfer to a pastry bag, fitted with a star tube. Decorate the semifreddo with whipped cream and the chopped marrons glacés. Pour the sauce around the semifreddo.

Frozen hazelnut soufflé

Time needed: 40 minutes
(plus freezing time)
Difficulty: medium

INGREDIENTS FOR 6 SERVINGS
3/4 cup of sugar ◆ *5 egg yolks*
1 1/4 cup of shelled hazelnuts
2 cups of heavy cream
4 candied violets

◆ Preheat the oven at 375 F and toast the hazelnuts. Scrub with a kitchen towel to peel. Finely grind 1 cup and coarsely chop 1/4 cup of hazelnuts.
◆ Mix the sugar with 1/4 cup of water, bring to a boil and cook for 7-8 minutes or until syrup is thick. Whisk egg yolks until frothy. Slowly add the sugar syrup, mixing constantly until the mixture is cool. Add the finely ground hazelnuts and fold in the whipped cream.
◆ Line the outside of a 6-cup mold with aluminum paper; the paper crown should be higher than the mold. Pour the mixture in the mold and freeze for 3 hours.
◆ To serve, remove the paper and press the chopped hazelnuts around the sides of the soufflé. Decorate with candied violets.

Parfait Rothschild

Time needed: 30 minutes
(plus freezing time)
Difficulty: medium

INGREDIENTS FOR 6 SERVINGS
3/4 cup of sugar ◆ *5 egg yolks*
2 cups of heavy cream ◆ *1/4 cup of kirsch*
1 cup of chopped candied fruit

◆ Set aside 1 tablespoon of candied fruit and soak the remainder in a bowl with the kirsch.
◆ Cook sugar with 1/4 cup of water for 7-8 minutes. In a bowl, whisk egg yolks, with an electric mixer, until frothy. Slowly add sugar syrup, whisking constantly until mixture is cold. Mix in the candied fruit and kirsch. Delicately fold in the whipped cream. Pour mixture in a 4-cup pudding mold and freeze for 3 hours.
◆ To serve, quickly dip mold in hot water. Turn the parfait onto a serving dish and garnish with 1 tablespoon of candied fruit.

Freeze 1 empty 5-cup bombe mold.

◆ Cook sugar with 3/4 cup of water for 8-10 minutes or until syrup is thick and transparent.

◆ Peel bananas, slice and soak in the sugar syrup for 30 minutes (**1**). In a food processor, mix banana and syrup. Add 1/2 cup of heavy cream (**2**) and pour into ice cream machine. Follow the manufacturer's instructions.

Banana plombières

Time needed:
50 minutes
(plus freezing time)
Difficulty: medium

INGREDIENTS
FOR 6-8 SERVINGS
1 lb of bananas
1/2 cup of chopped candied pineapple
3/4 cup of heavy cream
1 cup of sugar

◆ Line the sides and the bottom of a mold with banana ice cream (**3**). Mix the remaining ice cream with candied pineapple and fill the bombe (**4**). Level and freeze for at least 3 hours.

◆ To serve, quickly dip the mold in hot water. Turn the bombe mold onto a cold serving dish and freeze. Whip the cream and decorate the bombe before serving.

Ice cream brick

Time needed: *15 minutes*
(plus freezing time)
Difficulty: medium

INGREDIENTS FOR 6 SERVINGS
1/2 lb of chocolate ice cream (see page 283)
1/2 lb of vanilla ice cream (see page 282)
1/4 cup of pine nuts
1/4 cup of peeled pistachios
1/2 cup of heavy cream

◆ Freeze a 4 x 6-inch rectangular mold for 10 minutes.
◆ Line the cold mold with lightly softened chocolate ice cream, spreading it with a spatula. Return to the freezer.
◆ In a bowl, work the vanilla ice cream with a spoon to soften it. Whip the cream and fold into the ice cream. Add the pistachios and pine nuts.
◆ Pour the vanilla mixture into the mold and level it with a spatula. Return to the freezer for at least 4 hours.
◆ To serve, quickly dip mold in hot water. Turn onto a cold serving dish and slice.

Ice cream brick

Frozen bombe

Time needed: *40 minutes*
(plus freezing time)
Difficulty: medium

INGREDIENTS FOR 4 SERVINGS
1 1/4 lb of ice cream, any flavor
1 cup of sugar
1 cup of heavy cream
5 egg yolks
3 tablespoons of liquor, any flavor
1/2 cup of chopped candied fruit

◆ Freeze a 3-cup bombe mold for 1 hour.
◆ Line the cold mold with the lightly softened ice cream, leaving the middle empty. Transfer to a freezer.
◆ Cook sugar with 1/4 cup of water for 7-8 minutes. Add liquor. In a bowl, whisk egg yolks with an electric mixer until frothy. Slowly add the hot sugar syrup, mixing continuously until the mixture is cold.
◆ Whip the cream and delicately fold into the egg mixture. Add the candied fruit. Pour into the empty cavity of the bombe mold. Cover with aluminum foil and return to freezer for at least 2 hours.
◆ To serve, quickly dip mold in hot water. Turn onto a cold serving plate.

Banana plombières

Orange and pineapple sorbet bombe

Time needed: *1 hour and 30 minutes*
(plus freezing time)
Difficulty: *medium*

INGREDIENTS FOR **6-8** SERVINGS
Pineapple sorbet:
1/2 lb of pineapple
1/2 cup of sugar
1 egg white
juice of 1/2 lemon
Orange sorbet:
1 1/2 cup of orange juice
1/2 cup of sugar
1 egg white
Decoration:
2 slices of pineapple
1 orange
1 tablespoon of whipped cream
1 sugar flower

◆ Freeze a 3-cup ice cream mold.
◆ Prepare the pineapple sorbet (see page 302).
When ready, transfer to the cold mold and line its sides, leaving a space in the center. Return to the freezer.
◆ Prepare the orange sorbet (see page 302). When ready, remove the mold from the freezer and fill the center with the orange sorbet. Level and return to the freezer for at least 2 hours.
◆ Cut the pineapple slices in pieces; peel the orange down to the fruit and separate in segments; refrigerate.
◆ To serve, quickly dip mold in hot water. Turn the bombe onto a cold serving plate and decorate with the fruits, the whipped cream and the sugar flower.

Pistachio cassata

Time needed: *1 hour and 15 minutes*
(plus freezing time)
Difficulty: *medium*

INGREDIENTS FOR **6** SERVINGS
1 1/2 cup of mixed candied fruit
1/2 cup of heavy cream
1/4 cup of Cognac
1 egg white
1 tablespoon of powdered sugar
a pinch of salt

Orange and pineapple sorbet bombe

Ice cream:
3/4 cup of shelled pistachios
5 egg yolks
4 cup of whole milk
1 cup of sugar

◆ Place a 4-cup round cassata mold in the freezer.
◆ Put the chopped candied fruit and the Cognac in a bowl and set aside.
◆ Prepare the pistachio ice cream (see page 282). Line the interior of the cold mold with ice cream, leaving it empty in the middle. Return to the freezer.
◆ Whip the cream and refrigerate. Beat egg white with salt, using an electric mixer until frothy; add sugar and keep whisking to firm peaks. Delicately fold the firm egg white into the whipped cream. Drain candied fruit and add to cream.
◆ Fill center of the ice cream mold, level and return to freezer for at least 3 hours. To serve, quickly dip mold in hot water and turn onto a cold serving plate. Slice in 6 large pieces and serve.

Raspberry and watermelon bombe

Time needed: *1 hour and 15 minutes*
(plus freezing time)
Difficulty: *medium*

INGREDIENTS FOR **4-6** SERVINGS
Sorbet:
3 cups of watermelon
1/4 cup of sugar
1 teaspoon of lemon juice

Parfait:
1/2 cup of sugar ◆ *3 egg yolks*
1 cup of heavy cream
2 1/2 cups of raspberries

◆ Place a 4-cup bombe mold in the freezer.
◆ For the sorbet, pass the watermelon through a food mill and cook with the sugar on medium heat for 7-8 minutes, or until it reduces to 2/3. Refrigerate the mixture, stirring often. Mix in the lemon juice and pour into the ice cream machine. Follow the manufacturer's instructions.
◆ Line the interior of the cold bombe with the watermelon sorbet and return to the freezer.
◆ To make the parfait, rinse raspberries in ice water, dry and mix half in a food processor with 1 tablespoon of sugar. Pass through a sieve, cook un-

Raspberry and watermelon bombe

til reduced to 2/3 and set aside to cool. Cook the leftover sugar with 2 tablespoons of water for 7-8 minutes. In a bowl, whisk the egg yolks with an electric mixer until frothy. Slowly add sugar syrup, mixing constantly until the mixture is cold. Blend in the raspberry mixture; fold in the whipped cream and a few whole raspberries.

◆ Pour the parfait in the center of the bombe mold; level and return to the freezer for at least 2 hours.

◆ To serve, quickly dip the bombe mold in hot water. Turn onto a cold serving plate and decorate with remaining raspberries.

Principessa bombe

Time needed: *1 ora*
(plus freezing time)
Difficulty: *complex*

INGREDIENTS FOR 8-10 SERVINGS

Ice cream:
2 cups of whole milk
4 egg yolks ◆ 1 cup of sugar
1 vanilla bean
1 1/2 lb of pineapple
2 tablespoons of butter

Semifreddo:
1 cup of sugar ◆ 3 egg yolks
1 cup of heavy cream
2 cups of raspberries

Decoration:
1/2 cup of chopped toasted hazelnuts
1/2 cup of grated bittersweet chocolate

◆ Place a 6-cup bombe mold in the freezer.
◆ Prepare the pineapple ice cream (see page 280), and while it is in the ice cream machine, prepare the semifreddo.
◆ Rinse the raspberries in ice water, dry them and mix in a food processor with 1 tablespoon of sugar. Cook the mixture and reduce it to 2/3, stirring with a spoon. Set aside to cool.
◆ Cook remaining sugar in 3 tablespoons of water for 7-8 minutes. In a bowl, whisk egg yolks with an electric mixer until frothy. Slowly add sugar syrup, whisking constantly until the mixture is cold. Stir in the raspberry purée and delicately fold in the whipped cream.
◆ Line the bombe mold with pineapple ice cream. Fill the center with the raspberry semifreddo. Level and place in the freezer for at least 2 hours.

Principessa bombe

◆ To decorate, melt the chocolate in a double boiler. Transfer to a wax paper cone and design abstract forms on a sheet of wax paper; refrigerate. Detach the chocolate forms from the paper and arrange them decoratively, gluing the forms together with drops of chocolate.
◆ To serve, quickly dip bombe mold in hot water. Turn bombe onto a cold platter. Press the chopped hazelnuts on the base of the bombe and the chocolate decoration on top.

Frozen coffee bombe

Time needed: *3 ore*
(plus freezing time)
Difficulty: *medium*

INGREDIENTS FOR 8 SERVINGS

Coffee ice cream:
4 egg yolks ◆ 3/4 cup of sugar
2 cups of whole milk
2 tablespoons of instant espresso coffee
3 tablespoons of rum

Chocolate ice cream:
1 cup of whole milk
2 egg yolks ◆ 1/4 cup of sugar
1 1/2 cup of grated bittersweet chocolate
1 vanilla bean

Hazelnut ice cream:
1 cup of whole milk ◆ 2 egg yolks
1/4 cup of sugar
1/2 cup of shelled hazelnuts
1 vanilla bean

Decoration:
some coffee grains

◆ Place a 6-cup mold in the freezer.
Prepare the coffee ice cream (see page 284), the chocolate ice cream (see page 283) and the hazelnut ice cream (see page 283).
With a spatula, line the cold mold with the coffee ice cream and return to the freezer for 20 minutes. Pour chocolate ice cream at the bottom of the center. Level with a spatula and return to the freezer. When the hazelnut ice cream is ready, pour it over the chocolate ice cream and cover with aluminum foil. Place in the freezer for at least 3 hours.
To serve, quickly dip mold in hot water. Turn onto a cold serving plate and decorate with coffee grains.

Frozen coffee bombe

Tea granita

Time needed:
45 minutes
(plus refrigeration time)
Difficulty: easy

**INGREDIENTS
FOR 4-6 SERVINGS**

*2 cups of water
1 teaspoon of tea leaves
3/4 cup of sugar
1 orange and 1 lime
4 teaspoons of rum
1/2 teaspoon of vanilla
a few mint leaves*

Bring 1 1/2 cup of water to boil. In a teapot, place the tea leaves; add boiling water and infuse for 10 minutes

◆ Pass the tea through a sieve and set aside to cool completely.

◆ Thoroughly wash the orange and the lime; dry with a kitchen towel then grate the peel and extract the juice.

◆ In a saucepan, place remaining water, the sugar and the grated peels of the orange and the lime. On low heat, bring to boil for 5-6

minutes, until the sugar will be completely melt and the syrup will be dense and transparent.

◆ Remove from the heat. Mix the syrup with the tea, the vanilla, the orange juice and the lime juice. Set aside to cool.

◆ Transfer the mixture to the ice cream machine following the manufacturer's instructions.

◆ Serve the granita immediately in parfait glasses, decorating with the mint leaves.

Strawberry granita

Time needed: *45 minutes*
Difficulty: easy

INGREDIENTS FOR 6 SERVINGS
*1/2 lb of strawberries ◆ juice of 2 lemons
juice of 1 orange ◆ 1 1/4 cup of sugar*

◆ Cook the sugar in 1 cup of water for 3 minutes, until the syrup is dense and transparent. Set aside to cool.
◆ Rinse and dry the strawberries and remove their stems. Purée in a food processor. Add the orange juice, the lemon juice and the cold syrup to the mixture.
◆ Transfer the mixture to the ice cream machine and follow the manufacturer's instructions. Serve in parfait glasses.

Brachetto granita

Time needed: *30 minutes*
Difficulty: easy

INGREDIENTS FOR 4-6 SERVINGS
*1 cup of Brachetto wine
3/4 cup of sugar ◆ 1 cinnamon stick
1 bunch of red currants
1 bunch of black currants*

◆ On moderate heat, boil the sugar and the cinnamon stick in 1 cup of water for 5 minutes, until the syrup is dense and transparent. Set aside to

Brachetto granita

cool and remove the cinnamon.
◆ Mix the wine to the syrup and transfer the mixture to the ice cream machine, following the manufacturer's instructions.
◆ Rinse the currants in cold water, dry them and remove the seeds. Place the granita in a large bowl or in individual cups; serve immediately, decorated with currants.
◆ The Brachetto wine can be substituted by other sweet wine or with apple or pear cider.

Peach granita

Time needed: *50 minutes*
Difficulty: easy

INGREDIENTS FOR 6 SERVINGS
*500 g of peaches ◆ 1 1/4 cup of sugar
1/4 teaspoon of cinnamon
1 tablespoon of lemon juice*

◆ On moderate heat, boil the sugar and the cinnamon stick in 1 cup of water for 5 minutes, until the syrup is dense. Set aside to cool.
Rinse the peaches and remove the pits; slice them and purée in a food processor. Mix with the lemon juice and the syrup; transfer to the ice cream machine, following the manufacturer's instructions. Place the granita in parfait glasses and serve immediately.
Peaches can be substituted by apricots: Scald them in boiling water and peel them. Do not use the lemon juice.

Tea granita

Raspberry liquor granita

Time needed: *40 minutes*
Difficulty: easy

INGREDIENTS FOR 4-6 SERVINGS
3/4 cup of raspberry liquor
3/4 cup of raspberry syrup ◆ *1/4 cup of sugar*

◆ Boil the sugar in 1 1/2 cup of water for 5 minutes, until the syrup is dense and transparent. Set aside to cool completely. When cool, mix the syrup and the raspberry liquor in the mixture. Transfer to the ice cream machine, following the manufacturer's instructions.
◆ Place the granita in a large bowl or in individual cups and serve immediately.

Orange granita

Time needed: *50 minutes*
Difficulty: easy

INGREDIENTS FOR 6 SERVINGS
1 lb of oranges
1 1/4 cup of sugar ◆ *juice of 1 lemon*

◆ Cook on low heat the sugar and the orange peel in 1 1/4 cup of water for 30 minutes. Remove the peel and set aside to cool.
◆ Press the oranges and mix the juice with the lemon juice, the sugar syrup and 1 glass of water. Transfer to the ice cream machine, following the manufacturer's instructions.
◆ Serve the granita immediately, in individual cups.

Lemon granita

Time needed: *45 minutes*
(plus refrigeration time)
Difficulty: easy

INGREDIENTS FOR 4 SERVINGS
3/4 cup of sugar
juice and grated peel of 4 organic lemons

◆ Cook the sugar in 1/2 cup of water for 5 minutes, until the syrup is dense and transparent. Add the lemon juice and the lemon peels; set aside in the refrigerator for 30 minutes, then pass the mixture through a sieve over a bowl.

Raspberry liquor granita

Chocolate granita with cream

Coffee granita

◆ Transfer the cold mixture in the ice cream machine and follow the manufacturer's instructions. Serve the granita in parfait glasses.

Chocolate granita with cream

Time needed: *45 minutes*
Difficulty: easy

INGREDIENTS FOR 6 SERVINGS
130 g of dark chocolate
1/2 cup of sugar ◆ *1/2 cup of milk*
1 cup of fresh cream ◆ *1 small bunch of mint*

◆ Finely chop the chocolate and place in a bowl. Cook the sugar in _ cup of water for 5 minutes, until the syrup is dense and transparent. Transfer to the bowl with the chocolate; cover for 1 minute, then mix with a spoon to melt the chocolate. Add the milk and the cream. Set aside to cool.
◆ Transfer the chocolate mixture in the ice cream machine and follow the manufacturer's instructions. When it is ready, serve the granita in parfait glasses, decorating with mint leaves.

Coffee granita

Time needed: *40 minutes*
Difficulty: easy

INGREDIENTS FOR 4-6 SERVINGS
9 tablespoons of coffee
3/4 cup of sugar
1/2 cup of fresh cream
a few coffee grains

◆ Cook the sugar in 1 cup of water for 3 minutes, until the syrup is dense and transparent. Set aside to cool.
Whip the cream and refrigerate.
Mix the coffee in the cold syrup and transfer to the ice cream machine, following the manufacturer's instructions.
Transfer the ice cream in a large bowl or in individual cups. Place the whipped cream in a pastry bag, fitted with a large star tube and decorate the granita with rosettes. Top each cup with a coffee grain. A variation would be to double the quantity of whipped cream and place a layer of whipped cream in the cup, followed by one layer of granita and topping it with rosettes of cream.

Pink grapefruit sorbet with mint

Time needed: *45 minutes*
Difficulty: **easy**

INGREDIENTS FOR **6-8** SERVINGS
5 pink grapefruits
3/4 cup of sugar
2 teaspoons of mint syrup
1 egg white
a few mint leaves

◆ Cook the sugar with 3 tablespoons of water for 5 minutes. Let cool and mix with mint syrup.
◆ Using a sharp knife, peel the grapefruits and cut into segments. Keep the segments of 1 grapefruit in the refrigerator to use for decoration; purée the others. Mix the sugar syrup in and set aside for 30 minutes. Transfer to the ice cream machine and follow the manufacturer's instructions. Halfway through the blending, add the egg white.
◆ Serve the sorbet in a large bowl or in parfait glasses, garnished with remaining grapefruit segments and mint leaves.

Pink grapefruit sorbet with mint

Frozen tea punch

Time needed: *40 minutes*
Difficulty: **easy**

INGREDIENTS FOR **4-6** SERVINGS
2 cups of tea, already prepared
2 1/2 cups of Champagne or spumante
1 1/4 of sugar
1/4 cup of rum
1 egg white
juice and peel of one organic lemon and one organic orange
1/4 cup of candied orange and lemon peel

◆ Transfer the cold tea, sugar and Champagne to a bowl; stir to melt the sugar completely. Add juice and peel of fruits; set preparation aside for 30 minutes.
◆ Pass mixture through a sieve and transfer to ice cream machine, following the manufacturer's instructions. Halfway through the blending, add the egg white and rum.
◆ Cut the candied orange and lemon peel thinly. Serve the sorbet in a large bowl or cold individual cups, garnished with candied fruit peel.

Pear sorbet

Time needed: *30 minutes*
Difficulty: **easy**

INGREDIENTS FOR **4** SERVINGS
1 lb of William pears
1/2 cup of sugar
1 egg white
1 teaspoon of pear grappa

◆ Cook the sugar in 1/2 cup of water for 7-8 minutes and let syrup cool.
◆ Wash the pears, peel, core and slice. Purée with grappa and sugar syrup, until mixture is smooth.
◆ Transfer to ice cream machine, following manufacturer's instructions. Halfway through the blending, add the egg white.
◆ Serve immediately in Champagne glasses. The sorbet can be kept in the freezer in an airtight container.

Pear sorbet

Lemon sorbet

Time needed: *30 minutes*
Difficulty: **medium**

INGREDIENTS FOR **4** SERVINGS
4 large lemons
3/4 cup of sugar
1 egg white

◆ Cook the sugar in 1/2 cup of water for 10 minutes and set aside to cool.
◆ Wash lemons and dry. Cut the top part and empty the inside with a grapefruit knife. Using a spoon, remove all pulp, without making a hole through the skin; set pulp and juice aside in a bowl. Place the emptied lemons and their tops in the freezer.
◆ Pass juice and pulp through a food mill and mix with the sugar syrup. Transfer to ice cream machine, following manufacturer's instructions. Halfway through the blending, add the egg white.
◆ Fill the emptied lemons with the sorbet, cover with their tops and return to freezer for at least 30 minutes before serving.

Lemon sorbet

Champagne sorbet

Time needed:
30 minutes
Difficulty: easy

INGREDIENTS
FOR 4 SERVINGS
1 1/2 cup of Champagne
1 cup of sugar
1 green apple
1 teaspoon of lemon juice
1 egg white

Bring to boil the sugar in 1 cup of water on moderate heat. Cook for 2-3 minutes until the sugar has melted and the syrup is transparent. Transfer to a bowl and set aside to cool.

◆ Rinse the green apple, peel, core and press in a juice extractor to keep the apple juice.

◆ Add lemon juice, apple juice and Champagne to the cold sugar syrup. Transfer to ice cream machine, following manufacturer's instructions. Halfway through the blending, add the egg white.

◆ Transfer sorbet mixture in a pastry bag, fitted with an oblong tube and fill a large bowl, or individual glasses. Serve immediately.

Bellavista iced melon

Time needed: *40 minutes*
Difficulty: medium

INGREDIENTS FOR 6 SERVINGS
1 melon
100 g of sugar
1 egg white

◆ In a saucepan, bring to boil the sugar in 1/2 cup of water on moderate heat. Cook for 2-3 minutes, stirring until the sugar has melted and the syrup is transparent. Remove from heat and set aside to cool.
◆ Rinse and dry melon. Cut the top part. With a melon baller, make 8 balls; refrigerate. Using a spoon, remove remaining flesh from melon and set aside. Discard seeds.
◆ Cut the borders of the emptied melon decoratively and refrigerate it.
◆ Purée the melon flesh, add cold sugar syrup and transfer to ice cream machine, following manufacturer's instructions. Halfway through the blending, add the egg white.
◆ Fill the cold emptied melon with the sorbet. Decorate with the melon balls. Cover with melon top and keep in the freezer. When ready to serve, place in a large bowl filled with crushed iced and garnish with mint leaves.

Bellavista iced melon

Strawberry sorbet

Time needed: *25 minutes*
Difficulty: easy

INGREDIENTS FOR 4 SERVINGS
3/4 lb of strawberries
juice of 1/2 lemon ◆ *3/4 cup of sugar*
1 egg white ◆ *4 mint leaves*

◆ Cook the sugar in 1/2 cup of water for 5 minutes and set aside to cool.
◆ Rinse strawberries, dry and remove stems. In a food processor, purée with lemon juice. Pass purée through a sieve. Mix with the cold sugar syrup and transfer to ice cream machine, following manufacturer's instructions. Halfway through the blending, add the egg white.
◆ Distribute the sorbet in cold individual cups and garnish with mint leaves.

Blueberry sorbet

Time needed: *30 minutes*
Difficulty: easy

INGREDIENTS FOR 4 SERVINGS
3/4 lb of blueberries
juice of 1/2 lemon
3/4 cup of sugar
1 egg white

◆ Cook the sugar in 1/2 cup of water for 5 minutes and set aside to cool.
◆ Rinse blueberries in iced water, dry, keep 4 aside ▶

Champagne sorbet

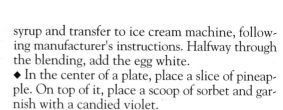

for decoration and purée the remainder in a food processor with lemon juice. Pass purée through a sieve. Add the cold sugar syrup and transfer to ice cream machine, following manufacturer's instructions. Halfway through the blending, add the egg white.

◆ Distribute the sorbet in cold individual cups and garnish each with a blueberry.

Peach sorbet with red wine

Time needed: *40 minutes*
Difficulty: *easy*

Ingredients for 4 servings
6-8 peaches
2 1/4 cup of water
1/2 cup of sugar
juice and peel of one organic lemon
1/2 cup of red wine
1 egg white

◆ Rinse, peel and chop the peaches. Cook on low heat for 15 minutes with water, lemon peel, lemon juice and sugar. Remove lemon peel and purée the mixture in a food processor. Add the red wine and set aside to cool.

◆ Transfer to ice cream machine, following manufacturer's instructions. Halfway through the blending, add the egg white.

◆ Distribute the sorbet in cold individual cups.

Pineapple sorbet

Time needed: *30 minutes*
Difficulty: *easy*

Ingredients for 6 servings
3/4 lb of pineapple
1/2 cup of sugar
1 egg white
juice of 1/2 lemon
6 slices of pineapple
6 candied violets

◆ Cook the sugar in 1/2 cup of water for 5 minutes and set aside to cool.

◆ Dice the pineapple and purée with lemon juice. Pass the purée through a sieve, add cold sugar

syrup and transfer to ice cream machine, following manufacturer's instructions. Halfway through the blending, add the egg white.

◆ In the center of a plate, place a slice of pineapple. On top of it, place a scoop of sorbet and garnish with a candied violet.

Papaya sorbet

Time needed: *30 minutes*
Difficulty: *easy*

Ingredients for 6 servings
1 lb of papaya
1/2 cup of sugar
1 egg white

◆ Cook the sugar in 1/2 cup of water for 5 minutes and set aside to cool.

◆ Peel papaya, seed, slice and purée. Mix the purée with cold sugar syrup and transfer to ice cream machine, following manufacturer's instructions. Halfway through the blending, add the egg white.

◆ Distribute the sorbet in a large bowl or in cold individual cups, garnished with an almond paste rose. The sorbet can be kept in an airtight container in the freezer, if not served immediately.

Orange sorbet

Time needed: *40 minutes*
(plus refrigeration time)
Difficulty: *easy*

Ingredients for 4 servings
4 large oranges
3/4 cup of sugar
1 egg white
2 tablespoons of candied orange

◆ Cook the sugar in 1/2 cup of water for 10 minutes and set aside to cool.

◆ Rinse and dry oranges. Cut the top part off and set aside.

◆ With a grapefruit knife, empty the oranges, being careful not to pierce the orange skin. Place the emptied oranges and their tops in the freezer.

◆ In a food processor, purée the orange flesh. Mix 3/4 lb of orange purée with the sugar syrup. Transfer to ice cream machine, following manufacturer's instructions. Halfway through the blending, add the egg white.

◆ Distribute the sorbet in the emptied oranges, covering with their tops and return to the freezer for 30 minutes. When ready to serve, decorate with candied orange.

Antilles cup

Time needed: *15 minutes*
Difficulty: medium

INGREDIENTS FOR 4 SERVINGS
4 tablespoons of chestnut cream
2 cups of vanilla ice cream (see page 282)
1 cup of bittersweet chocolate
2 tablespoons of slivered almonds
6 tablespoons of whipped cream
candied violets

◆ Melt chocolate in a double boiler and keep warm.
◆ Mix chestnut cream with 4 tablespoons of whipped cream so the mixture is just striped. Transfer to a cold serving bowl (or individual bowls). Top with 4 ice cream scoops. Drizzle with melted chocolate.
◆ Put the remaining whipped cream in a pastry bag and decorate the ice cream. Sprinkle with almonds and candied violets.

Magic apples

Time needed: *20 minutes*
(plus freezing time)
Difficulty: medium

INGREDIENTS FOR 4 SERVINGS
4 "golden" apples
1 lb of pear sorbet (see page 299)
3 cups of chopped bittersweet chocolate
3 tablespoons of candied citron

◆ Wash apples, peel and slice in half. Empty center of apples. Fill cavities with pear sorbet and place other half of apple over (to recreate an unsliced apple). Freeze for 30 minutes.
◆ Melt chocolate in a double boiler. Dip frozen apples in chocolate. Set on a piece of waxed paper and return to freezer.
◆ Pour remaining melted chocolate on waxed paper, forming little tubes (like apple stems). Cut candied citron in leaf shapes. With a warmed knife, make a little whole at the top of every apple; insert chocolate stem and candied leaf. Keep frozen until ready to serve.

Snow ball

Time needed: *40 minutes*
(plus freezing time)
Difficulty: medium

INGREDIENTS FOR 6-8 SERVINGS
2 lbs of vanilla ice cream
(see page 282)
3 cups of heavy cream
2 tablespoons of kirsch
3/4 cup of candied violets
3/4 cup of chopped mixed candied fruit
2 tablespoons of powdered sugar

◆ Soak candied fruit in kirsch for 20 minutes. In a bowl, mix ice cream with candied fruit and kirsch. Fill two parts of a round ice cream mold; press them together and freeze for 3 hours. Another way would be to use two spheric bowls and cover with aluminum foil.
◆ Whip cream with powdered sugar. Transfer to a pastry bag, fitted with a star tube.
◆ Dip mold in hot water and transfer ice cream to a serving dish (or bring the two spheric ice creams together in one ball). Cover the whole "ball" with the whipped cream. Decorate with the candied violets. Freeze for 30 minutes before serving.

Creole charlotte

Time needed: *1 hour*
(plus freezing time)
Difficulty: medium

INGREDIENTS FOR 6 SERVINGS
1/4 lb of savoyard cookies ◆ *3/4 cup of Alchermes*
1 lb of chocolate ice cream (see page 283)
1 lb of vanilla ice cream (see page 282)
1 lb of pistachio ice cream (see page 282)
3 cups of chopped chocolate
4 tablespoons of butter

◆ Line a Zuccotto mold with savoyard cookies; soak with Alchermes and 1/2 teaspoon of water. Fill bottom part with pistachio ice cream. Cover with vanilla ice cream and top with chocolate ice cream. Finish with savoyard cookies (soaked in liquor) and freeze.
◆ Melt chocolate and butter in a double boiler. To serve, turn the charlotte onto a plate and cover with melted chocolate.

Chestnut bag

Time needed:
*1 hour and 15 minutes
(plus freezing time)*
Difficulty: complex

**INGREDIENTS
FOR 6 SERVINGS**
*One 8-inch meringue circle
(see page 25)*
Ice cream:
*1 cup of milk
2 egg yolks
1/2 cup of sugar
1 vanilla bean
2 tablespoons of rum*

Parfait:
*1/2 cup of sugar
3 egg yolks
1 cup of heavy cream
1 cup of chestnut cream
2 chopped Marron Glacé*

Decoration:
*12 oz of almond paste
2 teaspoons of cocoa
2 teaspoons of ground pistachios
a pinch of saffron
1 tablespoon of powdered sugar
1/2 cup of chopped bittersweet chocolate*

In a saucepan, boil milk and vanilla bean.

◆ In a bowl, mix egg yolks and sugar with a wooden spoon until creamy. Slowly add hot milk, through a sieve. Return mixture to saucepan and, stirring, almost bring to a boil. When cream coats a spoon, remove from heat and let cool, stirring from time to time.

◆ Mix rum into cool preparation. Pour mixture in ice cream machine and follow the manufacturer's instructions. When ready, spread ice cream on the sides of a Zuccotto mold, leaving its center empty. Freeze for 1 hour.

◆ For the parfait, boil 1/2 cup of water with sugar in a saucepan. Reduce heat and cook for 7-8 minutes or until syrup is thick and transparent. In a bowl, whisk egg yolks with an electric mixer until frothy. Slowly add sugar syrup, whisking until mixture is cold.

◆ Mix in chestnut cream, chopped Marron Glacé and whipped cream. Pour parfait into the frozen ice cream mold. Top with the meringue circle and press lightly. Return to freezer for 1 hour.

◆ To decorate, scald the pistachios in boiling water. Dry and grind in a food processor. Gently work the almond paste and divide in 3 parts of 8 oz, 4 oz, and 2 oz. To the 8 oz part, add cocoa. To the 4 oz part, add the pistachios. Dilute saffron in a drop of water and add to the 2 oz part.

◆ Dust work surface with sugar and roll the green almond paste. Cut many leaves out of the paste and set aside.

◆ Roll out the yellow almond paste and cut 3 long strips and 2 small strips.

◆ Roll out the chocolate almond paste and cut a circle (**1**).

◆ Remove mold from freezer, quickly dip in hot water and turn ice cream in the middle of chocolate almond paste circle. Close paste around ice cream (**2**), leaving an opening at the top, like a little bag.

◆ Place the strip of yellow almond paste (**3**) like a ribbon around the bag. With the other strips, make a bow and press onto the bag.

◆ Open the top of the bag and bring down over the yellow ribbon (**4**).

◆ Melt bittersweet chocolate in a double boiler. Transfer to a wax paper cone. Design lines of chocolate around borders of opening and ribbon (see page 305). Place dessert on a serving dish and freeze.

◆ Before serving, remove dessert from freezer and fill top of bag with Marron Glacé and green almond paste leaves.

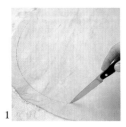
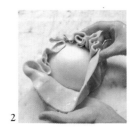

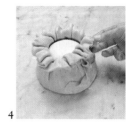

Chestnut bag

Three-flavor brick

Time needed: *15 minutes*
(plus freezing time)
Difficulty: *medium*

INGREDIENTS FOR 12-14 SERVINGS

2 lbs of pistachio ice cream
(see page 282)
2 lbs of hazelnut ice cream
(see page 283)
2 lbs of chocolate ice cream
(see page 283)
Decoration:
1/2 cup of chopped bittersweet
chocolate
1/2 cup of heavy cream
15 hazelnuts
20 peeled pistachios

Three-flavor brick

♦ In a large square mold, spread the pistachio ice cream. Over it, spread the hazelnut ice cream and finally the chocolate ice cream. Cover with aluminum foil and freeze for at least 3 hours.
♦ Melt chocolate in a double boiler. Whip the cream and put in a pastry bag, fitted with a small star tube.
♦ Quickly dip mold in warm water and turn onto a cold serving dish. Place a rosette of whipped cream and circles in the middle of the ice cream brick. Decorate with hazelnuts and pistachios.
♦ Pour melted chocolate in a waxed paper cone and artistically decorate frozen dessert. Keep in freezer until ready to serve.

Igloo

Time needed: *1 hour*
(plus freezing time)
Difficulty: *complex*

INGREDIENTS FOR 6 SERVINGS

2 cups of milk
4 egg yolks
3/4 cup of sugar
3/4 cup of ground almonds
1 vanilla bean

Decoration:
1 cup of whipping cream
1/2 cup of chopped white chocolate
1/4 cup of chopped milk chocolate

Igloo

♦ Make a crème anglaise with milk, egg yolks, sugar and vanilla (see page 17). When cold, add ground almonds. Pour into ice cream machine and follow manufacturer's instructions.
♦ Pour the ice cream in a 4-cup Zuccotto mold and freeze for 2 hours.
♦ To decorate, melt white and milk chocolates, separately, and keep warm over hot water. Whip the cream.
♦ Quickly dip ice cream mold in warm water and turn onto a cold plate. Spread 2/3 of whipped cream all over ice cream. Put remaining whipped cream in a pastry bag, and build the igloo door. With a toothpick, draw circles around the igloo. Pour white chocolate in a waxed paper cone and draw lines on the igloo (to look like igloo bricks).
♦ Pour milk chocolate in another cone and cover the entry of the igloo. Keep dessert in freezer until ready to serve.

Imperial cup

Time needed: *35 minutes*
Difficulty: *medium*

INGREDIENTS FOR 4-6 SERVINGS

1/2 lb of strawberry ice cream
1/2 lb of chocolate ice cream
12 savoyard cookies
2 tablespoons of brandy
1/2 cup of toasted almonds
3/4 cup of heavy cream
1/2 cup of flakes of bittersweet chocolate
1/4 cup of sugar
1 teaspoon of almond oil

♦ Cook sugar in 2 tablespoons of water for 3 minutes. Stir in almonds quickly (they will be covered with sandy sugar) and continue cooking, on medium heat, until sugar is caramelized.
♦ Pour the almonds on a marble surface, brushed with almond oil, and cool. Coarsely chop.
♦ Whip the cream and put in a pastry bag, fitted with a star tube. Refrigerate.
♦ In a cold clear bowl, spread strawberry ice cream. Brush savoyard cookies with brandy and place over ice cream. Cover with chocolate ice cream. Sprinkle with almond brittle and decorate with whipped cream rosettes. Freeze until ready to serve.

Frozen Ondine cake

Time needed: *2 hours*
(plus freezing time)
Difficulty: complex

INGREDIENTS FOR 10 SERVINGS

Chocolate ice cream:
2 cups of whole milk
5 egg yolks
3/4 cup of sugar
1-1/4 cups of chopped bittersweet chocolate
1 vanilla bean

White chocolate ice cream:
1 cup of heavy cream
3/4 cup of whole milk
1/2 cup of sugar
3/4 cup of chopped white chocolate
1 tablespoon of Cognac

Pudding:
2 cups of milk
3 eggs
2 egg yolks
3/4 cup of sugar
1 teaspoon of vanilla

Frozen Ondine cake

◆ Preheat the oven to 375 F.
◆ Prepare the pudding. In a bowl, mix the egg yolks, the sugar and the vanilla. Add the milk. Pour this mixture in a 6-cup mold. Cook in a bain-marie in the preheated oven for 1 hour. Cool the pudding and refrigerate for at least 1 hour.
◆ For the chocolate ice cream, prepare a crème anglaise with the milk, the egg yolks, the sugar and the vanilla bean (see page 17), mixing the ingredients until the chocolate is melted; set aside to cool. Transfer to the ice cream machine, following the manufacturer's instructions. When the ice cream is ready, transfer 2/3 of it in a round 8-cup mold. Place the mold, and the remaining ice cream, in the freezer.
◆ For the white chocolate ice cream, bring the cream, the sugar and the milk to a boil. Remove from heat when the sugar is melted. Stir in the white chocolate and set aside to cool, stirring from time to time. Add the cognac. Pour the mixture in the ice cream machine and follow the manufacturer's instructions. When it is ready, place the ice cream in the freezer.

◆ Turn the pudding in the middle of the chocolate ice cream. Cover the sides and the top, spreading the remaining chocolate ice cream. Return to the freezer for 2 hours.
◆ Turn the frozen pie onto a cold serving plate. Transfer the softened white chocolate ice cream to a pastry bag, fitted with a rose tube and decorate the top and the sides of the pie in a wavy pattern. Keep the pie in the freezer until ready to serve.

Frozen amaretti and chocolate brick

Time needed: *20 minutes*
(plus freezing time)
Difficulty: medium

INGREDIENTS FOR 10 SERVINGS
1 1/2 cups of heavy cream
2 cups of ground amaretti
1 1/2 cups of grated chocolate
3 eggs
1 tablespoon of instant coffee
1 tablespoon of sugar
a pinch of salt

Decoration:
10 amaretti
2 tablespoons of heavy cream
4 candied violets
1 tablespoon of apricot jelly

Frozen amaretti and chocolate brick

◆ Melt chocolate in a double boiler. Remove from heat and mix in the coffee and egg yolks. Cool. Beat egg whites and salt to firm peaks and fold into the chocolate mixture.
◆ In a bowl, whip the cream with sugar and stir in the ground amaretti.
◆ Line the bottom of a rectangular mold with waxed paper. Spread in half of the whipped cream mixture. Cover with all the chocolate mixture. Pour the remaining whipped cream over. Refrigerate for at least 4 hours.
◆ Soak a long knife in hot water. Pass the blade of the knife around the brick and turn the frozen dessert onto a cold plate. Whip the cream and decorate the brick, adding the amaretti and the candied violets. Refrigerate for 30 minutes before serving.

Fried Desserts

Fritters ◆ Krapfen and Donuts ◆ Filled fritters
Choux ◆ Carnival Fritters

In a saucepan, mix 1 cup of water, Cognac, sugar and salt; bring to a boil. Remove from heat and add flour. Mix well and return to heat. Stir until mixture forms a ball and detaches itself from sides of saucepan. Brush work surface with oil. Transfer mixture onto work surface and rest for 15 minutes.

◆ Vigorously work dough and roll out several times until elastic and smooth. From long sticks of dough and cut into 3-inch pieces.

Zeppole

Time needed:
1 hour and 20 minutes
Difficulty: medium

**INGREDIENTS
FOR 6-8 SERVINGS**
*6 cups of flour
2 tablespoons of sugar
1 tablespoon of Cognac
a pinch of salt
2 tablespoons of powdered
sugar*

Close both ends of sticks to form donuts. Prick dough with a fork.

◆ Fry donuts in hot oil until golden. Drain on paper towel. Serve hot, sprinkled with powdered sugar.

Fried bananas
with coffee sauce

Time needed: *1 hour and 15 minutes*
Difficulty: medium

INGREDIENTS FOR 6 SERVINGS

*5 bananas (not too ripe)
1 1/2 cups of flour
1 egg
1/2 cup of milk
2 teaspoons of baking powder
4 tablespoons of sugar*

Sauce:
*1 cup of espresso coffee
1/2 cup of sugar
2 tablespoons of potato starch
3 tablespoons of butter
3 tablespoons of cold coffee
1/4 cup of rum*

◆ In a bowl, mix 1 cup of flour with baking powder, salt and sugar. Add egg, milk and melted butter. Stir to get a smooth but not liquid batter.
◆ Peel bananas and slice thickly. Lightly flour and dip in batter. Fry bananas in boiling oil until golden, a few at a time. Drain on paper towels.
◆ For the sauce, melt sugar in a saucepan. Stir in espresso coffee, potato starch and cold coffee, until it thickens. Remove from heat. Add butter and rum.
◆ Serve fried bananas with coffee sauce.

*Fried bananas
with coffee sauce*

Barcelona twists

Barcelona
twists

Time needed: *1 hour
(plus raising time)*
Difficulty: medium

INGREDIENTS FOR 6-8 SERVINGS

*7 cups of flour
6 eggs
grated peel of 1 organic lemon
1/2 cup of milk
1/2 cup of softened butter
2 teaspoons of yeast
a pinch of salt
peanut oil for frying
2 tablespoons of powdered sugar*

◆ Dissolve yeast in warm milk. Sift flour on a work surface, make a well in the middle and add, milk, butter, salt, eggs and lemon peel. Work dough until smooth.
◆ Knead vigorously for 20 minutes, beating it against table until smooth and elastic. Put in a large bowl, cover with a towel and set aside overnight.
◆ The next day, divide dough in pieces and roll out in long strips. Roll strips, pinching with fingers so they stay put. Fry in hot oil until golden. Drain on paper towel. Serve hot sprinkled with powdered sugar.

Zeppole

Apricot fritters

Time needed: *50 minutes*
(plus resting time)
Difficulty: *medium*

INGREDIENTS FOR 6-8 SERVINGS

1 3/4 cups of flour
2 eggs
1/2 cup of dry white wine
3 tablespoons of butter
2 tablespoons of sugar
1 lb of apricots
a pinch of salt
peanut oil for frying
1 tablespoon of powdered sugar

◆ In a bowl, mix flour, egg yolks, melted butter and sugar. Slowly stir in the wine. Set aside for 1 hour.
◆ Wash apricots; scald in boiling water for a few seconds, drain and peel. Slice in half and pit (if too tart, sprinkle with sugar).
◆ Beat egg whites and salt to stiff peaks; fold into batter. Delicately dip apricots in batter and fry in hot oil, a few at a time, until golden. Drain and serve hot sprinkled with powdered sugar

Apricot fritters

Marzipan circles

Time needed: *40 minutes*
Difficulty: *complex*

INGREDIENTS FOR 6-8 SERVINGS

1 brioche
1 cup of almond paste
1/2 cup of candied orange peel
1 tablespoon of Grand Marnier
2 cups of milk
4 eggs
1 teaspoon of vanilla sugar
peanut oil for frying

Cinnamon cream:
1 cinnamon stick
1/4 cup of sugar
3/4 cup of heavy cream

◆ With a cookie cutter, slice 1-inch thick pieces in brioche. In a bowl, crumble almond paste and mix with Grand Marnier and chopped candied peel. Spread mixture on half of brioche slices. Top with other half, like sandwiches.

Marzipan circles

◆ In a saucepan, cook sugar in 1/2 cup of water for 2-3 minutes. Add cinnamon stick and cook for 3 minutes.
◆ Remove from heat, cool and discard cinnamon stick. Whip cream lightly; add 2 tablespoons of syrup and continue beating. Refrigerate.
◆ In a bowl, beat eggs, vanilla sugar and milk with a fork. Dip sandwiches in mixture and fry in hot oil until golden. Drain on paper towel. Serve cold with cinnamon cream.

Oriental fried cream

Time needed: *1 hour*
Difficulty: *medium*

INGREDIENTS FOR 6-8 SERVINGS

3 cups of milk
1 cup of sugar
1 1/2 cups of corn flour
1/2 cup of semolina
a pinch of salt
4 tablespoons of butter
2 eggs
1/4 cup of raisins
1/4 cup of pine nuts
1/4 teaspoon of vanilla
grated peel of 1/2 an organic lemon
1 cup of breadcrumbs
peanut oil for frying

◆ Soak raisins in warm water.
◆ In a saucepan, boil milk, sugar and 1 cup of water. Add salt, flour and semolina, stirring constantly. Cook for 20 minutes until mixture is smooth. Remove from heat. Add butter, eggs, drained raisins, pine nuts, vanilla and lemon peel, mixing well.
◆ Pour batter on humid work surface. Level with a spatula and cool.
◆ Cut batter in squares; pass in breadcrumbs and fry in hot oil until golden. Drain and serve.

Oriental fried cream

Semolina fritters

Time needed: *1 hour*
Difficulty: *medium*

INGREDIENTS FOR 6-8 SERVINGS

*2 cups of semolina
1 cup of chopped almonds
2 cups of milk
4 eggs
grated peel of one organic lemon
1/2 cup of sugar
1 tablespoon of powdered sugar
2 tablespoons of breadcrumbs
peanut oil for frying*

◆ In a saucepan, boil milk with 1 tablespoon of sugar. Sprinkle on the semolina, and continue cooking for 20 minutes, stirring. Remove from heat, add 2 eggs, sugar, almonds and lemon peel.
◆ Transfer dough to a marble surface, spread and cool.
◆ Beat remaining eggs. With cookie cutters, slice dough and pass into beaten eggs and then in breadcrumbs.
◆ Fry in hot peanut oil until golden. Drain and sprinkle with powdered sugar.

Semolina fritters

Apple fritters

Apple fritters I

Time needed: *1 hour*
(plus resting time)
Difficulty: *medium*

INGREDIENTS FOR 6-8 SERVINGS

*2 lbs of apples
5 tablespoons of sugar
juice of one lemon
1/4 teaspoon of cinnamon
3 tablespoon of Maraschino
peanut oil for frying
powdered sugar*

Batter:
*1 3/4 cup of flour
2 eggs
3 tablespoons of butter
3/4 cup of wine
3 tablespoons of sugar
a pinch of salt*

◆ In a bowl, mix flour, egg yolks, melted butter and sugar. Add wine and set aside for 1 hour.
◆ Peel apples, core and slice. Soak in lemon juice and Maraschino. Sprinkle with sugar and cinnamon. Marinate for 30 minutes.
◆ Beat egg whites and salt to firm peaks and fold into batter. Drain apples, dip in batter and fry in hot oil until golden. Drain on paper towel. Transfer to serving dish and dust with powdered sugar

Sweet Greek fritters

Time needed: *1 hour*
Difficulty: *medium*

INGREDIENTS FOR 8 SERVINGS
*1 1/2 cups of rice (not parboiled)
3/4 cups of milk
1/2 cup of sugar
a pinch of salt
1/2 teaspoon of anise seeds
4 tablespoons of butter
1/2 cup of flour
4 eggs
3 tablespoons of raisins
1/4 teaspoon of cinnamon
2 tablespoons of breadcrumbs
peanut oil for frying
2 tablespoons of powdered sugar*

◆ Soak raisins in warm water.
◆ Boil rice for 15 minutes, drain and rinse under cold water. Return to saucepan with milk and bring to boil. Cook until milk is absorbed, stirring often. Remove from heat. Add sugar, cinnamon, butter and anise seeds. Cool. Beat egg whites and salt to stiff peaks and fold into rice mixture.
◆ Form small balls with mixture. Roll in breadcrumbs and fry in hot oil. Drain on paper towel and serve hot, sprinkled with powdered sugar.

*Sweet Greek
fritters*

Carrot and nut fritters

Time needed: *50 minutes*
Difficulty: **medium**

INGREDIENTS FOR **6** SERVINGS
1/2 lb of carrots
1/2 cup of softened butter
3/4 cups of sugar
1 egg
1 1/2 cups of flour
1 teaspoon of baking powder
a pinch of salt
1/2 cup of chopped walnuts
peanut oil for frying
2 tablespoons of powdered sugar

◆ Peel and rinse carrots. Cook or steam, drain and pass through a food mill.
◆ In a bowl, whisk butter, salt and sugar until creamy. Add egg, flour and baking powder, alternating with carrot purée. Add nuts and mix well.
◆ Form little balls the size of a nut. Fry in hot oil until golden. Drain on paper towel and serve hot, sprinkled with powdered sugar.

Apple fritters II

Time needed: *1 hour*
Difficulty: **easy**

INGREDIENTS FOR **6** SERVINGS
4 apples
1/4 cup of sugar
grated peel of 1/2 organic lemon
1 teaspoon of cinnamon
2 eggs
1 cup of breadcrumbs
1/4 cup of vanilla sugar
peanut oil

◆ Preheat the oven to 350 F.
◆ Peel apples, slice and place on a cookie sheet. Bake for 15 minutes; purée in a food processor. Mix purée with sugar, lemon peel, cinnamon, 1 egg and 2/3 cups of breadcrumbs.
◆ Form little balls of mixture. Pass in beaten egg and then in remaining breadcrumbs. Fry in hot oil until golden. Drain on paper towel and serve with vanilla sugar.

Pineapple fritters

Time needed: *50 minutes*
(plus resting time)
Difficulty: **medium**

INGREDIENTS FOR **6** SERVINGS
1 pineapple
juice of 2 lemons
2 tablespoons of powdered sugar
peanut oil for frying

Batter:
2 cups of flour
2 eggs
3/4 cups of milk
3 tablespoons of butter
1/4 cup of sugar
a pinch of salt

◆ In a bowl, mix flour, egg yolks, melted butter and sugar. Slowly stir in milk and set aside for 2 hours.
◆ Peel pineapple and slice. With a small cookie cutter, cut off hard center of pineapple. Soak slices in lemon juice for 30 minutes.
◆ Beat egg whites and salt to firm peaks and fold into batter. Drain pineapple slices; dip in batter and fry in hot oil until golden. Drain on paper towel and serve sprinkled with powdered sugar.

Medlar fritters

Time needed: *50 minutes*
Difficulty: **medium**

INGREDIENTS FOR **6-8** SERVINGS
1 lb of medlar fruits
1 3/4 cups of flour
2 eggs
3/4 cups of white wine
2 tablespoons of Maraschino
2 tablespoons of butter
1/4 cup of sugar
a pinch of salt
peanut oil for frying
1 tablespoon of powdered sugar

◆ In a bowl, sift flour and mix with egg yolks, melted butter, sugar and Maraschino. Slowly add wine, stirring to blend well. Set aside for 1 hour.
◆ Rinse fruits, peel, slice in half and pit.

◆ Beat egg whites and salt to stiff peaks and fold into batter. Dip medlar fruits in batter and fry in hot oil until golden. Drain on paper towel and serve sprinkled with powdered sugar.

Potato and orange patties

Time needed: *1 hour*
Difficulty: *medium*

INGREDIENTS FOR **4** SERVINGS
1/2 cup of flour
1/2 lb of potatoes
3 tablespoons of softened butter
1/2 cup of sugar
grated peel of one organic orange
1 egg yolk
a pinch of salt
peanut oil for frying
1 tablespoon of powdered sugar

◆ Wash potatoes and cook. Drain, peel and mash. Set aside to cool.
◆ In a bowl, mix mashed potatoes with butter, sugar, flour, egg yolk, salt and orange peel. Flour your hands and for patties with mixture. To make equal patties, form them with a round cookie cutter.
◆ Heat oil and fry patties until golden. Drain on paper towel and sprinkle with powdered sugar

Chinese fritters

Time needed: *45 minutes*
Difficulty: *medium*

INGREDIENTS FOR **6-8** SERVINGS
1 cup of red soy bean flour
1 cup of rice flour
1 cup of flour
3/4 cup of sugar
5 tablespoons of butter
1/2 cup of sesame seeds
peanut oil for frying

◆ In a saucepan, mix soy bean flour with 3/4 cup of water, stirring with a wooden spoon. Add sugar. Bring to a boil; reduce heat and cook until mixture is thick. Remove from heat and stir butter in.
◆ On a work surface, put flour and rice flour. Add 1/2 cup of water and work to get a soft dough.
◆ Form little balls of soy mixture. Sprinkle work surface with flour and roll out a cylinder with 2-flour mixture. Slice the cylinder in 1-inch pieces. Flatten to make circles. Envelop every soy mixture ball in a circle of dough. Pass in sesame seeds, pressing so seeds stick.
◆ Fry in hot oil until golden. Drain on paper towel and serve immediately.

Chestnut flour fritters

Time needed: *50 minutes*
Difficulty: *medium*

INGREDIENTS FOR **6-8** SERVINGS
4 cups of chestnut flour
1/4 cup of rum
1/2 cup of raisins
1/2 cup of pine nuts
2 egg whites
a pinch of salt
1 tablespoon of flour
peanut oil for frying
1 tablespoon of powdered sugar

◆ Soak raisins in warm water.
◆ In a bowl, sift chestnut flour and add rum and a few teaspoons of warm water. Mix with a wooden spoon until batter is smooth. Drain and dry raisins. Roll in flour and add to batter. Stir pine nuts in. Beat egg whites and salt to stiff peaks and fold into batter.
◆ Fry spoonfuls of batter in hot oil.
◆ Drain on paper towel and serve sprinkled with powdered sugar.

On a work surface, mix flour, semolina, sugar and salt. Make a well in the middle and pour in warmed extra virgin olive oil with the white wine (1). Work ingredients into a smooth dough, adding water if needed.

◆ Roll out dough and slice in long strips (2). Fold sides of strips together and turn into spirals (3). Transfer to a cookie sheet to dry.

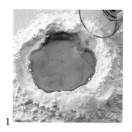

1

2

Apulian fritters

Time needed:
1 hour and 15 minutes
Difficulty: *medium*

INGREDIENTS
FOR 6-8 SERVINGS
5 cups of flour
1 cup of semolina
7 tablespoons of extra virgin olive oil
1 tablespoon of sugar
a pinch of salt
1/4 cup of white wine
peanut oil for frying
2 cups of dessert wine from Apulia
1/4 cup of white wine
3 tablespoons of sliced almonds

◆ Fry the fritters in hot oil, turning them to brown on both sides. Drain on paper towels (4).

◆ In a saucepan, bring to boil white wine and dessert wine. Place the fritters in the wine mixture and, when it boils again, remove fritters. Drain on paper towel and sprinkle with almonds.

3

4

Corynthian fritters

Time needed: *50 minutes*
Difficulty: *medium*

INGREDIENTS FOR 6-8 SERVINGS
1 1/2 cups of flour
9 tablespoons of butter
4 eggs
3/4 cup of raisins
1 teaspoon of vanilla
a pinch of salt
peanut oil for frying
2 tablespoons of powdered sugar
1 teaspoon of cinnamon

◆ Soak raisins in warm water.
◆ In a saucepan, bring to boil 3/4 cups of water, butter, salt and vanilla. Remove from heat. Add flour all at once and stir with a wooden spoon. Return to heat and cook for a few minutes until dough forms a ball. Transfer to a bowl, cool lightly and add eggs, one at a time, with an electric mixer. Stir in the drained raisins.
◆ Make small balls of dough and fry in hot oil until golden. Drain on paper towels and sprinkle with powdered sugar and cinnamon, mixed together.

Corynthian fritters

Fried pastry cream

Fried pastry cream

Time needed: *1 hour*
Difficulty: *medium*

INGREDIENTS FOR 6 SERVINGS
1 3/4 cups of flour
2 cups of milk
1 egg
8 egg yolks
1/2 cup of sugar
1/2 teaspoon of vanilla
1/2 cup of raisins
1/2 cup of chopped candied citron
5 tablespoons of butter
1/4 cup of powdered sugar
peanut oil for frying

◆ With 1 cup of flour, milk, egg yolks, sugar and vanilla, prepare a pastry cream (see page 16). Remove from heat and stir in butter. Cool and mix in raisins and citron.
◆ Brush a marble surface with water. Spread mixture onto marble; cool until it solidifies. Slice with diamond shape cutter.
◆ Dip diamonds in the beaten egg, pass in flour and fry in hot oil until golden. Drain on paper towel and sprinkle with powdered sugar. Serve hot.

Apulian fritters

Preheat the oven at 375 F. Scald almonds in boiling water, drain and peel. Dry them in oven for a few minutes and chop coarsely.

♦ Crumble amaretti.

♦ In a bowl, mix ricotta, eggs, amaretti, 2 tablespoons of vanilla sugar, sifted flour, baking powder and cinnamon until well blended.

♦ Make small balls with mixture.

1

2

Filled ricotta fritters

Time needed:
40 minutes
Difficulty: medium

INGREDIENTS FOR 6-8 SERVINGS

1 lb of ricotta
2 eggs
5 amaretti
2 tablespoons of vanilla sugar
1 cup of flour
1/4 teaspoon of cinnamon
1 teaspoon of baking powder
4 tablespoons of apricot jam
1/2 cup of chopped chocolate
1/4 cup of almonds
peanut oil for frying

♦ With the back of a spoon, press the center of balls to form a cavity (1); fill some with apricot jam (2) and others with a few pieces of chocolate and almonds. Close the balls (3), turning them in the palm of your hands. Fry in hot oil.

♦ Drain on paper towel (4) and sprinkle with remaining sugar.

3

4

Ricotta donuts

Time needed: *1 hour*
(plus resting time)
Difficulty: medium

INGREDIENTS FOR 6-8 SERVINGS
1/2 lb of ricotta
3 cups of flour
1 egg yolk
1/2 cup of sugar
2 teaspoons of yeast
4 tablespoons of milk
grated peel of one organic lemon
peanut oil for frying
2 tablespoons of powdered sugar

♦ Dissolve the yeast in warm milk.
♦ In a bowl, mix ricotta, egg yolk and sugar. Add flour, dissolved yeast and grated lemon peel. Stir to blend well. Set aside for 1 hour in a warm place.
♦ With dough, form donuts and fry in hot oil. Drain on paper towel and serve sprinkled with powdered sugar.

Oltrepo fritters

Oltrepo fritters

Time needed: *1 hour*
Difficulty: medium

INGREDIENTS FOR 6-8 SERVINGS
2 1/2 cups of flour
1/4 cup of sugar
6 tablespoons of milk
6 tablespoons of Marsala
2 eggs
1/2 cup of raisins
1/2 teaspoon of vanilla
a pinch of salt
peanut oil for frying
1/2 cup of vanilla sugar

♦ Soak raisins in warm water for 10 minutes. Drain and flour.
♦ In a bowl, sift 2 cups of flour, baking powder and salt. Mix in eggs, sugar, milk, Marsala and raisins.
♦ Drop spoonfuls of batter into hot oil; fry until puffed up and golden. Drain, roll in vanilla sugar and serve.

Filled ricotta fritters

Tunisian yoyos

Time needed: *1 hour*
(plus resting time)
Difficulty: *medium*

INGREDIENTS FOR 4 SERVINGS
3 cups of flour
3 eggs
3 tablespoons of extra virgin olive oil
1 teaspoon of baking powder
1/2 cup of powdered sugar
a pinch of baking soda
a pinch of salt
peanut oil for frying
3 tablespoons of chopped blanched almonds
3 tablespoons of chopped walnuts
3 tablespoons of chopped hazelnuts
1 teaspoon of vanilla sugar

Syrup:
1 1/2 cups of powdered sugar
2 tablespoons of rose water
juice of one lemon

Venetian fritters

◆ On a work surface, sift flour, baking powder and baking soda. Make a well in the center; add eggs, olive oil, powdered sugar and salt. Work ingredients until dough is smooth. Set aside in a floured bowl for 30-40 minutes.
◆ On low heat, cook powdered sugar, rose water and lemon juice until syrup is thick.
◆ Roll dough to 1-inch thickness and with a cookie cutter, cut out circles; make wholes in the middle with a thimble.
◆ Fry circles in hot oil until puffed up and golden. Drain on paper towel. Dip donuts in syrup and roll in almonds, walnuts, hazelnuts and vanilla sugar.

Venetian fritters

Time needed: *1 hour*
(plus rising time)
Difficulty: *medium*

INGREDIENTS FOR 6 SERVINGS
3 cups of flour
1 cup of milk
2 teaspoons of yeast
1/2 cup of sugar
4 tablespoons of butter

3 eggs
1/2 cup of raisins
1/4 cup of pine nuts
grated peel of one lemon
2 tablespoons of rum
a pinch of salt
peanut oil for frying

◆ Soak raisins in warm water. Dissolve yeast in milk.
◆ In a large bowl, with an electric mixer, whisk eggs and 1/4 cup of sugar until frothy. Add melted butter, dissolved yeast, drained raisins, pine nuts, lemon peel and rum. Mix well. Add sifted flour and salt; mix vigorously. Set aside in a warm place until doubled in volume.
◆ Drop spoonfuls of mixture in hot oil. When golden, drain on paper towel. Roll in remaining sugar and put on a serving plate.

Krapfen

Time needed: *50 minutes*
(plus rising and rising time)
Difficulty: *medium*

INGREDIENTS FOR 8-10 SERVINGS
4 1/2 cups of flour
2 teaspoons of yeast
1 1/4 cup of milk
6 tablespoons of softened butter
6 egg yolks
3/4 cup of sugar
grated peel of one organic lemon
1 teaspoon of vanilla
1/2 cup of apricot jam
2 tablespoons of rum
peanut oil for frying

Krapfen

◆ Dissolve yeast in warm milk. Add vanilla.
◆ In a large bowl, mix flour, 1/2 cup of flour, lemon peel, egg yolks and salt. Add dissolved yeast and butter; mix well. Turn mixture on a work surface and knead for 20 minutes until dough is elastic. Put dough in a large bowl, cover and set aside in a warm place for 2 hours.
◆ Knead dough for 2 minutes and refrigerate for 3 to 12 hours.
◆ Mix apricot jam with rum. Roll dough on a floured board and cut into strips. On half of the strips, drop spoonfuls of jam, 1 1/2 inch from one

another. Cover with the other half of strips; press around jam to make dough stick. With a cookie cutter, cut round "raviolis." Set aside to rise for 1 hour.
◆ Fry the krapfen in hot oil until golden. Drain on paper towel and sprinkle with remaining sugar.

Chocolate donuts

Time needed: *50 minutes*
Difficulty: *medium*

INGREDIENTS FOR 6-8 SERVINGS
2 1/2 cups of flour
1 egg
1/2 teaspoon of baking soda
1/2 teaspoon of cinnamon
a pinch of salt
1/2 cup of sugar
1/2 cup of chopped bittersweet chocolate
2 tablespoons of butter
2 tablespoons of heavy cream
1 teaspoon of lemon juice
peanut oil for frying
1 tablespoon of vanilla powdered sugar

◆ In a double boiler, melt chocolate.
◆ In a bowl, sift flour, baking soda, cinnamon and salt. Mix in egg, sugar, melted chocolate, cream, milk and lemon juice, until well blended.
◆ Transfer mixture onto floured work surface; roll dough to 1/4 inch.
◆ With a cookie cutter, cut out circles of dough. Cut out the center of each circle with a thimble. With the "holes," make little balls.
◆ Fry donuts and holes in hot oil. Drain on paper towel and serve hot sprinkled with powdered sugar.

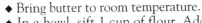

Chocolate donuts

Small donuts

Time needed: *1 hour*
(plus rising time)
Difficulty: *medium*

INGREDIENTS FOR 4 SERVINGS
2 cups of flour
1/4 cup of sugar
4 tablespoons of butter
1 teaspoon of yeast
2 egg yolks
1/2 cup of milk
grated peel of one organic lemon
peanut oil for frying
1 tablespoon of powdered sugar

◆ Bring butter to room temperature.
◆ In a bowl, sift 1 cup of flour. Add yeast, dissolved in 1/4 cup of warm milk. Stir ingredients slowly, incorporating remaining flour, until well blended. If too dense, add a few teaspoons of milk. Set bowl aside in a warm place until doubled in volume.
◆ In a bowl, using an electric mixer, whisk sugar, softened butter, egg yolks, lemon peel and remaining milk, until light and creamy.
◆ Incorporate to dough. Turn onto floured board and knead until smooth and elastic. Return to the bowl, cover with a cloth and set aside to raise for 1 hour.
◆ Return dough to work surface. Roll long little tubes. Press ends of tubes together and set aside to raise for 15 minutes.
◆ Fry donuts in hot oil until golden.
◆ Drain on paper towel and sprinkle with powdered sugar. Serve hot.

Small donuts

Bring butter to room temperature. Crumble amaretti.

◆ On work surface, sift flour, sugar and salt into a mound. In the center, put 1 egg, egg yolk, butter, lemon peel and maraschino.

◆ Work all ingredients, slowly adding the white wine, to get a smooth and soft dough. Cover with plastic wrap and refrigerate for 30 minutes.

◆ Scald peaches for 1 minute in boiling water. Immerse in ice water and peel. Cut in half, pit and slice.

Peach fritters

Time needed: *1 hour (plus resting time)*
Difficulty: *medium*

INGREDIENTS
FOR 8-10 SERVINGS
2 1/2 cups of flour
2 eggs ◆ 1 egg yolk
1 tablespoon of sugar
grated peel of one organic lemon ◆ a pinch of salt
2 tablespoons of maraschino
2 tablespoons of butter
dry white wine
peanut oil for frying
2 tablespoons of powdered sugar

Filling:
1 1/2 lb of peaches
3/4 cup of brown sugar
10 amaretti

◆ In a saucepan, cook peaches and sugar on medium heat for 15 minutes. Remove from heat. Mix in amaretti and cool.

◆ On work surface, roll out dough very thin and cut in two parts. Beat 1 egg and brush on half of dough. Drop little mounds (1/2 teaspoon) of peaches on dough, 2 inches apart. Cover with other half of dough and press lightly between peach mounds.

◆ With a flower cookie cutter, cut around mounds of filling. Fry in hot oil. Drain on paper towel and serve hot, sprinkled with powdered sugar.

Pear fritters

Time needed: *1 hour*
Difficulty: *complex*

INGREDIENTS FOR 6-8 SERVINGS

1/3 lb of puff pastry (see page 12)
1 lb of pears
1/2 cup of sugar ◆ 1 egg
peanut oil for frying

Sauce:
1 cup of apple jam
1 tablespoon of white rum

Pear fritters

◆ In a double boiler, melt apple jam and rum. Set aside.
◆ Peel and dice pears; cook with sugar and 2 tablespoons of water for 25 minutes. Cool.
◆ Roll out pastry dough thinly. With a cookie cutter, cut off circles. Brush around sides of half of the circles, with beaten egg. Drop 1 teaspoon of pear compote in the center and cover with other circles.
◆ Fry rissoles in hot oil until golden. Drain on paper towel. Sprinkle with powdered sugar and serve with sauce.

Fried plum gnocchi

Time needed: *1 hour*
Difficulty: *medium*

INGREDIENTS FOR 6 SERVINGS

1 lb of potato
2 1/2 cups of flour
1 egg
2 tablespoons of milk
3 tablespoons of sugar
1/2 lb of plums
a pinch of salt
peanut oil for frying
2 tablespoons of powdered sugar

◆ Cut plums, pit and quarter. Cook potatoes, drain, peel and mash.
◆ On work surface, sift 2 cups of flour. In the center, make a well and add potatoes, egg, sugar, milk and salt. Work ingredients until dough is soft. Form little 3-inch-long sticks; form long balls and fill with a teaspoon of plums. Close well around filling.
◆ Roll gnocchi in flour and fry in hot oil. Drain on paper towel and serve hot, sprinkled with powdered sugar.

Peach fritters

Fried apple tortelli

Time needed: *1 hour*
Difficulty: **medium**

INGREDIENTS FOR 6-8 SERVINGS
3 cups of flour
1/4 cup of sugar
3 eggs
4 tablespoons of softened butter
grated peel of one organic lemon
2 tablespoons of Kirsch
a pinch of salt
peanut oil for frying
1 tablespoon of powdered sugar

Filling:
2 large apples
1/4 cup of sugar
2 tablespoons of raisins
1 tablespoon of Kirsch

◆ Soak raisins in warm water.
◆ Peel apples, core, dice and cook with sugar and 1/4 cup of water on low heat for 20 minutes. Cool and add drained raisins and Kirsch.
◆ On a work surface, sift flour in a mound. In the center, add sugar, salt, lemon peel, butter, eggs and Kirsch. Blend ingredients into a smooth dough. Roll out into a thin sheet and, with a fluted cookie cutter, cut out circles.
◆ Drop 1 teaspoon of apple mixture on half of the circles. Brush sides of circle with water. Cover with other half of circles and gently press around filling. Fry tortelli in hot oil. Drain on paper towel and sprinkle with powdered sugar.

Sicilian cannoli

Time needed: *1 hour*
(plus resting time)
Difficulty: **complex**

INGREDIENTS FOR 6-8 SERVINGS
1 1/2 cups of flour
1 teaspoon of instant espresso coffee
1 teaspoon of cocoa
1 teaspoon of sugar

Fried plum gnocchi

Fried apple tortelli

Sicilian cannoli

a pinch of salt
1 teaspoon of white wine vinegar
2 tablespoons of butter (or shortening)
1 egg white
dry white wine or Marsala
2 tablespoons of powdered sugar

Filling:
3/4 lb of ricotta
1/2 cup of sugar
a few drops of orange flower water
2 tablespoons of chopped candied orange
1/4 cup of chopped bittersweet chocolate

◆ On a work surface, sift flour into a mound. In the center, add butter, salt, sugar, vinegar, cocoa and coffee. Mix ingredients, adding enough wine to make dough. Knead until smooth and elastic. Set aside for 30 minutes, covered with plastic wrap.
◆ Roll out dough and, with a large cookie cutter, cut out circles, until all dough is used. Brush cannoli molds with oil; place a circle of dough in, brush with beaten egg white and cover with a second circle of dough. Repeat for all cannoli. Fry in hot oil. Drain on paper towel.
◆ In a bowl, mix ricotta, sugar and orange water, with an electric mixer, until creamy. Add all other filling ingredients and refrigerate for 30 minutes.
◆ Fill cannoli with ricotta mixture a few minutes before serving and dust with powdered sugar.

Sebadas

Time needed: *1 hour*
(plus resting time)
Difficulty: **medium**

INGREDIENTS FOR 6-8 SERVINGS
2 1/2 cups of flour
2 eggs
1 egg white
1 tablespoon of sugar
grated peel of 1/2 organic lemon
2 tablespoons of butter
dry white wine
1/4 cup of anise liquor
1 tablespoon of Marsala
2/3 lb of young sheep's milk cheese
1 cup of chestnut honey
a pinch of salt
peanut oil for frying
3 tablespoons of powdered sugar

◆ On work surface, sift flour and salt into a mount. In the center, add eggs, butter, lemon peel and Marsala. Work ingredients into a smooth dough. Set aside in a cool place for 30 minutes, covered with plastic wrap.

◆ With a rolling pin, roll out dough very thinly. With a cookie cutter, cut out circles. Slice cheese and cut out circles in cheese slices, smaller than dough circles. Brush half dough circles with beaten egg white; cover with cheese circles; brush with Marsala and sprinkle with sugar. Top with other half of circles, pressing sides carefully with fingers.

◆ Fry the sebadas in hot oil until golden on both sides. Drain on paper towel and sprinkle with powdered sugar. Serve hot with warm honey.

Sebadas

Fried ravioli filled with chestnut cream

Time needed: *1 hour*
Difficulty: **medium**

INGREDIENTS FOR **6-8** SERVINGS
3 cups of flour
1/4 cup of sugar
3 eggs
4 tablespoons of softened butter
grated peel of one organic lemon
2 tablespoons of maraschino
a pinch of salt
peanut oil for frying
1 tablespoon of powdered sugar

Filling:
1 cup of chestnut purée
1/4 cup of sugar
1 teaspoon of cocoa
2 teaspoons of maraschino

◆ On work surface, sift flour into a mound. In the center, add sugar, salt, lemon peel, butter, eggs and maraschino. Work ingredients into a smooth dough. Roll out dough with a rolling pin (or pasta machine) to 1/2-inch. Slice large strips of dough.

Fried ravioli filled with chestnut cream

Fritter filled with prunes in Port wine

◆ Prepare the filling: In a bowl, mix chestnut purée, sugar, cocoa and maraschino. Drop teaspoons on half of the strips of dough, 3 inches apart. Cover with remaining strips. Press around filling to seal. Cut raviolis in triangles.

◆ Fry in hot oil. Drain on paper towel. Transfer to a plate and serve cold, sprinkled with powdered sugar.

Fritters filled with prunes in Port wine

Time needed: *1 hour*
(plus refrigerating time)
Difficulty: **medium**

INGREDIENTS FOR **6** SERVINGS
2 cups of flour
7 tablespoons of butter
2 egg yolks
2 tablespoons of milk
1/4 cup of sugar

Filling:
20 prunes
1/2 cup of powdered sugar
2 cloves
1 cup of red wine
1/2 cup of Port
1 egg
peanut oil for frying

◆ On work surface, sift flour into a mound. In the center, add butter, sugar, and egg yolks. Work ingredients rapidly with fingertips into a coarse mixture. Mix in milk. Transfer to a bowl, cover with plastic wrap and refrigerate.

◆ For filling, cook prunes with wine, Port, 1/4 cup of sugar and cloves for 15-20 minutes. Cool prunes in their liquid (better if prepared 7 days in advance). Drain, pit and chop.

◆ Roll out dough thinly and cut out circles with cookie cutter. In center of circles, drop 1 spoonful of prunes. Brush sides of circles with beaten egg. Fold circles in half-moons; press to seal.

◆ Fry in hot oil until golden. Drain on paper towel and serve warm, sprinkled with powdered sugar.

Fried tortelloni filled with ricotta

Time needed: *1 hour*
Difficulty: *medium*

INGREDIENTS FOR 6-8 SERVINGS
3 cups of flour
1/2 cup of sugar
1/4 cup of dry white wine
4 tablespoons of softened butter
grated peel of one organic lemon
a pinch of salt ◆ *1 egg*
peanut oil for frying

Filling:
1/2 lb of ricotta
3 egg yolks
1/2 cup of sugar
1/4 teaspoons of cinnamon
2 tablespoons of rum

◆ For filling, whisk ricotta and sugar, with an electric mixer until creamy. Add egg yolks, cinnamon and rum.
◆ On work surface, sift flour into a mound. In the center, add sugar, salt, lemon peel, butter and egg. Mix, adding wine, until dough is smooth and firm. Roll out dough very thinly with a rolling pin or a pasta machine) into 2-inch squares.
◆ In the center of every square, place 1 teaspoon of filling. Fold dough to form triangles. Press sides to seal well and bring ends together to form tortelloni.
◆ Fry in hot oil until golden. Drain on paper towel and transfer to a plate. Dust with powdered sugar and serve hot or warm.

Fried ravioloni filled with pineapple

Time needed: *1 hour*
Difficulty: *medium*

INGREDIENTS FOR 6-8 SERVINGS
3 cups of flour
1/2 cup of sugar
1/4 cup of dry white wine
4 tablespoons of softened butter
grated peel of one organic lemon
a pinch of salt ◆ *1 egg*
peanut oil for frying
2 tablespoons of powdered sugar

Filling:
1 cup of ricotta
1/2 lb of pineapple flesh
1/4 cup of sugar
3 egg yolks
1/4 cup of maraschino

◆ For filling, chop pineapple and dry in a kitchen towel. In a bowl, with an electric mixer, whisk ricotta, sugar, egg yolk and maraschino until creamy. Stir in the pineapple.
◆ On work surface, sift flour into a mound. In the center, add sugar, salt, lemon peel, butter and egg. Work ingredients, slowly adding wine, into a soft dough. Roll out dough very thinly with a rolling pin to 2-inch wide strips. On half the strips, drop spoonfuls of filling. Cover with other half of strips. Press with fingers around filling to seal and cut the ravioloni.
◆ Fry in hot oil until golden. Drain on paper towel. Serve hot or warm, sprinkled with powdered sugar.

Quince filled frittelle

Time needed: *1 hour*
(plus resting time)
Difficulty: *medium*

INGREDIENTS FOR 6 SERVINGS
2 1/2 cups of flour
a pinch of salt
1 tablespoon of sugar ◆ *1 egg*
4 tablespoons of softened butter
peanut oil for frying
2 tablespoons of powdered sugar

Filling:
3/4 cup of quince jam
1/4 cup of raisins ◆ *1 egg*
3/4 cup of chopped almonds,
walnuts and hazelnuts

◆ Soak raisins in warm water.
On work surface, sift flour into a mound. In the center, add sugar, salt, butter and egg. Mix, adding 5-6 tablespoons of warm water. Knead until dough is smooth and elastic. Cover with kitchen towel and set aside for 30 minutes.
For filling, in a bowl, mix quince jam, drained raisins and all nuts.
Roll out dough thinly and slice into 2-inch squares. Brush half the squares with beaten egg. Drop a teaspoon of filling in their center. Cover with other half of squares. Press sides to seal well. Fry in hot oil until golden. Drain on paper towel, dust with powdered sugar and serve hot.

St. Joseph's fritters

Time needed: *45 minutes*
Difficulty: *medium*

INGREDIENTS FOR **6-8** SERVINGS
Pâte à choux:
3 cups of flour
8 tablespoons of butter
1 cup of water
2 tablespoons of sugar
1 teaspoon of vanilla
10 eggs
1/2 cup of powdered sugar

◆ With flour, butter, water, sugar, vanilla and eggs, prepare a pâte à choux (see page 11).
◆ Drop spoonfuls of dough into hot oil (pull off dough with two spoons). Turn fritters in oil so they swell and brown on all sides. Drain on paper towels. Sprinkle with powdered sugar and serve warm.

Creole banana fritters

Time needed: *50 minutes*
Difficulty: *easy*

INGREDIENTS FOR **6** SERVINGS
1 1/2 cups of flour
1 ripe banana
1/2 cup of sugar
1 egg
juice of one lemon
2 tablespoons of milk
1/4 cup of rum
1/4 teaspoon of vanilla
3/4 teaspoon of baking powder
peanut oil for frying
2 tablespoons of powdered sugar

◆ Peel banana. Slice and purée with lemon juice, sugar and rum.
◆ In a bowl, mix sifted flour, egg, milk, vanilla and baking powder. Stir in the banana purée, until well blended.
◆ Drop spoonfuls of batter into hot oil. Fry until golden. Drain on paper towels. Sprinkle with powdered sugar.

Malaga Choux

Time needed: *1 hour and 15 minutes*
(plus resting time)
Difficulty: *complex*

INGREDIENTS FOR **8-10** SERVINGS
Pâte à choux:
1 1/2 cups of flour
8 tablespoons of butter
3/4 cup of water
6 eggs
1/2 teaspoon of vanilla
a pinch of salt

Filling:
2 egg yolks
1/4 cup of sugar
1 cup of milk
1/4 c up of flour
grated peel of one organic lemon
1/2 cup of raisins
2 tablespoons of Port

Batter:
2 cups of flour
2 eggs
3/4 cup of milk
2 tablespoons of butter
1/4 cup of sugar
a pinch of salt
peanut oil for frying
2 tablespoons of powdered sugar

◆ Grease and flour a cookie sheet.
◆ For the batter, in a bowl, mix flour, egg yolks, melted butter and sugar. Slowly add milk and set aside in a warm place for 2 hours.
◆ With the ingredients above, prepare a pâte à choux (see page 11). Preheat the oven to 200 F.
◆ Transfer pâte à choux in a pastry bag, fitted with a straight tube. Pipe out small choux on a cookie sheet, away from each other. Bake for 20 minutes. Remove and cool.
◆ Rinse raisins, drain and soak in Port. With egg yolks, sugar, milk, flour and lemon peel, prepare a pastry cream (see page 16). Cool and stir in raisins and Port.
◆ Make a small hole in choux with the point of a knife. Transfer cream into pastry bag and fill choux.
◆ Beat egg whites and salt to stiff peaks. Fold in batter. Dip choux in batter and fry in hot oil until golden. Drain on paper towel. Serve hot, sprinkled with powdered sugar.

327

Puffed litchi fritters

Time needed: *1 hour*
(plus resting time)
Difficulty: *medium*

INGREDIENTS FOR 6-8 SERVINGS
1 lb of litchi
1/2 cup of sugar
1/2 cup of flour
peanut oil for frying
2 tablespoons of powdered sugar

Batter:
2 cups of flour
2 eggs
3/4 cup of milk
2 tablespoons of butter
2 tablespoons of sugar
a pinch of salt

◆ Prepare batter. In a bowl, mix sifted flour, egg yolks, melted butter, sugar and milk. Set aside in a warm place for 2 hours.
◆ Peel litchis; cut in half and pit. Mix with sugar and set aside for 1 hour.
◆ Beat egg whites and salt to stiff peaks. Gently fold into batter. Drain litchis, pass in flour and dip in batter. Fry in hot oil.
◆ When golden, drain on paper towel. Serve warm, sprinkled with powdered sugar.

Choux

Choux

Time needed: *1 hour*
Difficulty: *medium*

INGREDIENTS FOR 4 SERVINGS
1 1/2 cups of flour
5 tablespoons of butter
1 tablespoon of sugar
1 cup of water
5 eggs
3 tablespoons of vanilla sugar
peanut oil for frying

Crème anglaise:
3/4 cup of sugar
5 egg yolks
1 cup of milk
peel of 1/2 organic lemon

◆ For cream, bring to boil milk and lemon peel. In a stainless steel bowl, whisk egg yolks and sugar, with an electric mixer, until pale and thick. Slowly add the hot milk and cook in a double boiler until cream is thick and coats the back of a spoon. Do not boil.
◆ With the flour, butter, water, sugar and eggs, prepare a pâte à choux (see page 11). Transfer to a pastry bag, fitted with a small straight tube. Pipe out small amounts of dough into hot oil and fry until golden.
◆ Drain on paper towels. Sprinkle with powdered sugar and serve with crème anglaise.

Neapolitan puff pastry

Time needed: *50 minutes*
Difficulty: *medium*

INGREDIENTS FOR 8 SERVINGS
2 1/2 cups of flour
4 eggs
2 egg yolks
2 tablespoons of softened butter
1 teaspoon of sugar
peanut oil for frying

Decoration:
3/4 cup of honey
grated peel of two organic oranges
1/4 cup of candied citron
1/4 cup of candied orange
1/4 cup of colored sugar

◆ Chop candied fruits. On a work surface, sift flour into a mound. In the center, add butter, eggs, egg yolks and sugar. Mix well to prepare a smooth dough. Form cylinders and cut into 1/2-inch slices.
◆ Fry slices in hot oil until golden. Drain on paper towel.
◆ In a saucepan, mix honey, orange peel and 2/3 of candied fruits. Cook on low heat. Add the fritters and stir, with a wooden spoon, until honey is completely absorbed.
◆ Place fritters in a pyramid, on a serving plate and cool. Decorate with remaining candied fruits and colored sugar.

Neapolitan puff pastry

Lyonnaise fritters

Time needed: *1 hour*
(plus resting time)
Difficulty: *medium*

INGREDIENTS FOR **6-8** SERVINGS
5 cups of flour
2 eggs
2 egg yolks
2 tablespoons of sugar
grated peel of one organic lemon
1 teaspoon of baking powder
a pinch of salt
1/4 cup of grappa
6 tablespoons of softened butter
peanut oil for frying
2 tablespoons of powdered sugar

◆ On a work surface, sift flour and baking powder in a mound. In the center, add eggs, egg yolks, salt, butter, sugar, lemon peel and grappa. Mix ingredients into a smooth and soft dough. Cover with plastic wrap and set aside for 2 hours.
◆ Roll out dough thinly and cut into squares. Make a cut in the center of all squares. Fry in hot oil until golden.
◆ Drain fritters on paper towel. Serve sprinkled with powdered sugar.

Lyonnaise fritters

Chiacchiere a girandola

Time needed: *1 hour*
(plus resting time)
Difficulty: *medium*

INGREDIENTS FOR **6** SERVINGS
3 cups of flour
2 eggs
6 tablespoons of heavy cream
6 tablespoons of dry white wine
2 tablespoons of sugar
a pinch of salt
peanut oil for frying
2 tablespoons of powdered sugar

◆ On a work surface, sift flour in a mound. In the center, add eggs, sugar, cream, wine and salt. Mix slowly to get a smooth and light dough. Set aside

Chiacchiere a girandola

in a cool place for 1 hour, covered with plastic wrap.
◆ Roll out dough very thinly with a rolling pin (or a pasta machine) and cut with a round cookie cutter. Press the center of circles with a finger, twisting the circles delicately.
◆ Fry the "chiacchiere" in hot oil until golden. Drain on paper towel and sprinkle with powdered sugar.

Gale

Time needed: *1 hour*
(plus resting time)
Difficulty: *medium*

INGREDIENTS FOR **8-10** SERVINGS
5 cups of flour
2 eggs
2 egg yolks
2 tablespoons of sugar
grated peel of one organic lemon
a pinch of salt
dry white wine
1/4 cup of maraschino
2 tablespoons of softened butter
peanut oil for frying
2 tablespoons of powdered sugar

◆ On a work surface, sift flour and salt in a mound. In the center, add eggs, egg yolks, butter, sugar, lemon peel and maraschino. Mix ingredients, adding wine, to get a soft and smooth dough. Set aside in a cool place for 30 minutes.
◆ Roll out dough very thinly with a rolling pin or a pasta machine. Cut in strips and then in diamonds. Make a cut in the middle of the dough. Fold one point into the cut to form the "gale."
◆ Fry in hot oil until golden. Drain on paper towel and sprinkle with powdered sugar.
◆ These fritters change names, depending on the regions of Italy: cenci, frappe, galani, crostoli, nastri and others.

Carnival roses

Time needed: *40 minutes*
(plus resting time)
Difficulty: medium

INGREDIENTS FOR 6-8 SERVINGS
1 1/2 cups of flour
2 egg yolks
1 egg white
1 tablespoon of sugar
1 tablespoon of Marsala
2 tablespoons of softened butter
a pinch of salt
peanut oil for frying

Decoration:
1/2 cup of heavy cream
15-20 candied cherries
2-3 tablespoons of almonds
2 tablespoons of honey

Carnival roses

◆ Preheat the oven to 375°F.
◆ On a work surface, sift flour, sugar and salt into a mound. In the center, add egg yolks, butter and Marsala. Mix ingredients to get a firm dough. Cover with plastic wrap and set aside for 30 minutes.
◆ Scald almonds in boiling water. Drain, peel and place on a cookie sheet. Dry in the oven without toasting. Cool and chop.
◆ On a work surface, roll out dough very thinly. Cut out circles with large cookie cutter, until all dough is used. On all circles, make a cross-cut, from sides to center without cutting the center. Brush half the circles with beaten egg white. Cover with other half of circles, so the cuts do not overlap. Press in center.
◆ In a saucepan with high sides, fry circles; keep them in oil with a long wooden spoon. When puffed up and golden, drain on paper towel.
◆ Melt honey and brush on sides of fried roses. Roll in chopped almonds. Fill roses with whipped cream and candied cherries. Serve.

Kirsch fritters

Time needed: *1 hour*
(plus resting time)
Difficulty: medium

INGREDIENTS FOR 10-12 SERVINGS
5 cups of flour
6 tablespoons of butter
4 egg yolks
1/4 cup of sugar
4 tablespoons of heavy cream
2 tablespoons of Kirsch
a pinch of salt
peanut oil for frying
2 tablespoons of powdered sugar

◆ On a work surface, sift flour into a mound. In the center, add salt, sugar, butter, egg yolks, Kirsch and cream. Mix ingredients to get a smooth and soft dough. Cover with plastic wrap and set aside for 30 minutes.
◆ Roll dough thinly and slice into free forms. Fry in hot oil until golden. Drain on paper towel and sprinkle with powdered sugar.

Castagnole

Time needed: *50 minutes*
Difficulty: medium

INGREDIENTS FOR 4 SERVINGS
1/2 cup of sugar
3 tablespoons of rum
2 eggs
6 tablespoons of butter
powdered sugar
a pinch of salt
1/2 teaspoon of vanilla
peanut oil for frying

◆ In a bowl, whisk eggs and sugar. Add melted butter, rum and, a little at a time, the flour sifted with the baking powder. Mix well and form small cylinders; slice and make balls in the palms of your hands.
◆ Fry in hot oil until golden. Drain on paper towel. Serve hot, sprinkled with powdered sugar.

Kirsch fritters

Decorating techniques

The Basics ◆ Floral Decoration
Geometric Decoration ◆ Creative Decoration

Decorating with whipped cream

◆ Decorating with whipped cream is easy and always guarantees beautiful results. The first thing to do is to whip the heavy or whipping cream correctly (see page 29) and refrigerate it for 30 minutes. Spread the cream with a flat spatula, all over the cake. It can then be decorated with almonds, hazelnuts, pralines, chocolate chips or other.

◆ If you wish to decorate a cake elaborately, fill a pastry bag, fitted with a star tube; press the bag, in short movements, forming a crown of rosettes around the cake. (1) Mix a few drops of Alchermes to the rest of the whipped cream and decorate the center of pink rosettes. (2) You can change the color by adding various liquors.

◆ Another kind of decorative effect can be done by piping out vertical strips of whipped cream around the cake. (3) Then proceed by piping out rosettes to cover the top of the cake. (4)

◆ With a straight tube, you can easily design little squares of cream, giving a basket wave impression. (5) To make stars, simply use a small star tube. (6)

◆ To decorate the classic Saint Honoré, use a special "drop" tube. (7)

◆ Adding a few teaspoons of cocoa or, better, cold melted chocolate to the whipped cream (8), you will get a lovely chocolate cream that can be used to cover a cake, alternating white and brown decorations. (9) With a round tube, you can make small decorations, particularly used in miniature desserts.

Decorating with chocolate

◆ Chocolate is one of the most used ingredients for decorating big and small cakes with different kinds of designs that are always impressive. The designs made should be left to harden in a cool place but not in a refrigerator so the chocolate does not lose its sheen.

Delicate ornamental decoration

◆ Draw the design on waxed paper. Melt some bittersweet chocolate in a bain-marie; pour into a parchment paper cone and trace over the design drawn on the waxed paper (1).

◆ Let the chocolate harden in a cool place; then delicately remove with a thin spatula (2). Use to decorate small cakes.

Leaves

◆ Choose fresh, thick leaves that are preferably chemical-free. Wash them, dry on a towel and refrigerate for one hour. In a double boiler, melt some bittersweet chocolate. With a paint brush, apply a coat of melted chocolate on the leaves (3) and refrigerate until chocolate is solid. Delicately pull back from the stem end (4) and keep chocolate leaves in a cool place. Use to decorate pies, semifreddo and cakes.

Roses

◆ In a double boiler, melt chocolate; transfer to a marble surface, spread with a spatula and cool. With a slightly bent round cookie cutter, scrape chocolate to make curved strips (5).
◆ Roll a strip to form the center of a rose; place other strips around, bending certain pieces to make the petals (6).

Decorating with marzipan

◆ Decorated with almond paste, desserts can be very impressive. After kneading it briefly, roll out marzipan between 2 sheets of plastic wrap or on a work surface, lightly dusted with cornstarch or powdered sugar to prevent it from breaking.
◆ To cover a cake, first brush the entire surface of cake with melted fruit jelly. Roll the thin marzipan sheet on a rolling pin and place it on the cake. Delicately press with hands to make marzipan stick to the cake. Trim any excess with a sharp knife (1) and keep trimmings for decora-

tion.
◆ Natural products (instead of chemical food colorants) can be used to color marzipan: Ground pistachios or powdered Japanese green tea for a green paste; a few drops of Alchermes for a pink paste (2) or even a pinch of saffron to make the paste yellow.

Special script

◆ Prepare a strip of marzipan, shape with a small knife and curl the sides parchment-like (3); write the message with melted chocolate piped out of a parchment paper (4).

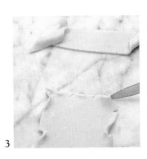

Hazelnut flowers

◆ Praline the hazelnuts (see page 21). Roll out the marzipan 1/16 of an inch to 1/8 of an inch thick and slice it with a serrated pastry wheel (5). Brush one serrated side with melted milk chocolate; place a hazelnut on the strip and roll the marzipan (6). Make several flowers the same way and attach 3 together to form a bouquet; garnish with little leaves.

Roses

◆ Prepare different color marzipan: Light pink, dark pink and green. Roll light pink and pink pastes in 2 thin sheets. Cut out 5 small pieces from the first one and 2 pieces from the second sheet; make little cones which will become the buds. With 2 cookie cutters of different sizes, cut out small and large circles. Flatten the tip of each circle to form the external part of the petals and pinch them around the bud, one at a time, starting with the smaller ones to the largest ones (7). Lightly fold the flatten ends of the petals to open the rose (8). Garnish with leaves, cut out from the green paste.

7

8

Carnations

◆ Prepare pink marzipan, roll out thinly and cut out strips, pinching to form the petals (9). Press several petals together and lightly cut with the point of a sharp knife to give it the carnation look (10).

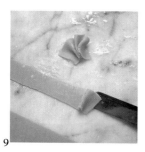
9

10

Parchment paper cone

◆ This cone is a precious tool for it permits elegant writing and miniature cake decorations. You can find it already made in specialty shops or make it yourself, with parchment paper, as explained in the following illustrations:

◆ Fold a rectangle of parchment paper diagonally and cut, with a long knife, into 2 rectangles (1). Roll one rectangle into a cone (2). Make a small indentation, folding the paper inward to secure the cone (3). Fold down the top to even out the borders of the cone (4). With the other triangle you can make another cone. Fill the cone with the prepared cream (5); close it, folding each side and rolling down the paper (6). Slice the tip of the cone with scissors (7), making the hole according to the type of decoration needed. Press on the cone to pipe out cream.

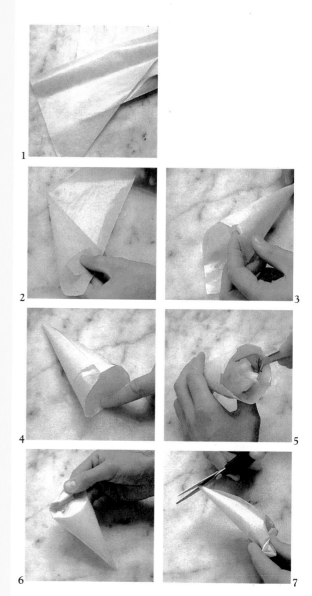

Decoration made of butter cream, chocolate and strawberry segments for a Niçois cake.

Hazelnut and almond flowers

INGREDIENTS

2 tablespoons of cocoa
15 almonds
3 hazelnuts
3 oz. of milk chocolate
3 oz. of bittersweet chocolate
1/4 cup of sugar
1 tablespoon of almond oil
3 tablespoons of apricot jelly

◆ Scald the almonds and peel them. On a cookie sheet, toast the hazelnuts in a preheated oven and peel, rubbing them in a kitchen towel.

◆ In a saucepan, cook the sugar with 1 tablespoon of water for 3 minutes. Remove from heat, add almonds and hazelnuts; mix with wooden spatula until nuts are covered with a sandy mixture. Return to low heat, and mixing, cook until sugar is caramelized.

◆ Pour mixture on an oiled marble surface (1). Working fast, with 2 forks, detach almonds and hazelnuts from each other.

◆ Brush sides of cake with melted apricot jelly. With a potato peeler, cut small strips of bittersweet chocolate and press them around the cake to stick to the apricot jelly.

◆ Completely dust the cake with sifted cocoa (2). Place cake on a serving dish. With a potato peeler, cut long strips of milk chocolate (3).

◆ To decorate the top of the cake, make flowers with hazelnuts and almond petals (4) and use chocolate strips as stems (5).

White chocolate Magnolia

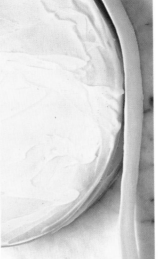

INGREDIENTS
*3/4 lb of chopped
white chocolate
1/4 cup of chopped
bittersweet chocolate
1 large piece o
candied orange peel*

◆ Cut two 4-inch wide strips of waxed paper, long enough to fit around the cake. In a double boiler, melt the white chocolate. With a spatula, thinly spread it on the waxed paper strip (**1**).
◆ Set aside to harden very slightly. Chocolate should still be foldable when it is placed around the cake (**2**), with paper on the exterior. Press delicately and refrigerate cake until chocolate is hard. Delicately remove waxed paper.
◆ Pour leftover melted chocolate on a marble surface and spread thinly. If chocolate is too hard, melt it again. Slice in short strips and lightly fold with a spatula to create large folds (**3**). Refrigerate until hard and place on top of the cake, in concentric circles (**4**).
◆ With a cookie cutter, cut a circle in the orange peel; place in the center of the chocolate decoration. In a double boiler, melt bittersweet chocolate; brush the sides of all white chocolate petals with it (**5**). Refrigerate cake until ready to serve.

Candied
fruit leaves

INGREDIENTS

*1/4 lb of marzipan
(see page 23)
2 oz of candied citron peel
5 oz of candied orange peel
1/4 cup of chopped
bittersweet chocolate
3 candied cherries
1 tablespoon of apricot jelly*

◆ Melt apricot jelly in 1 tablespoon of water; brush all over cake. Slice the candied citron in long strips. With an oval cookie cutter, cut the candied orange. Slice those ovals in half with a sharp knife. (1)

◆ In a double boiler, melt chocolate; pour into a parchment paper cone and, pressing lightly, decorate the candied orange pieces. (2)

◆ Roll the marzipan and cut into a circle, large enough to cover the top of the cake. (3) With the melted chocolate, decorate all along the sides of the marzipan circle.

◆ Delicately place the orange peel leaves, 3 by 3, on the marzipan (4), with a cherry in the center. Finish the decoration with the candied citron strip. (5). Place on a serving dish and refrigerate.

Lemon sunflowers

1

2

3

4

INGREDIENTS

2 organic lemons
1 organic orange
1 3/4 cups of sugar
lemon juice
2 teaspoons of gelatin

5

◆ Wash and dry a lemon; cut off regular strips of peel, from top to bottom of lemon. Cut the lemon in thin slices and place in a bowl. In a saucepan, mix 1/4 cup of sugar and 1 cup of water; cook for 3 minutes. Pour syrup on lemon slices and macerate for at least 6 hours.

◆ Wash the second lemon and the orange. With a potato peeler, cut off peel and thinly slice. Put orange and lemon peel strips in 2 saucepans. Cover with water, bring both to boil and drain. Repeat this operation twice to eliminate any bitter taste. Drain peel strips and return to their saucepans. To each, add 5 tablespoons of water and 1/4 cup of sugar; bring to boil. Reduce heat and cook for 15 minutes, mixing from time to time, until peels are transparent and liquid is almost all evaporated. Drain and separate peels; place on a rack to dry.

◆ Melt gelatin in a little water. In a saucepan, bring to boil the lemon juice and remaining sugar; cook until completely dissolved. Remove from heat and add gelatin; mix well and cool.

◆ In a springform pan, place a layer of cooked cake (1); spread with the lemon gelatin (2) and refrigerate until gelatin is set. Unmold and place on a serving dish and decorate with candied lemon peels to form a basket design. (3) With the candied orange peels, design the stems coming out of the basket. (4) Place the drained and dried lemon slices to form the flowers. (5) Refrigerate until ready to serve.

This decoration is made for a lemon gelatin on a layered cake. The dessert should be made in a springform mold to retain its shape.

343

Apricot daisies

INGREDIENTS

1/2 cup of apricot jelly
1 cup of powdered sugar
1 egg white
a few drops of lemon juice
1/2 cup of sugar
2 tablespoons of cocoa
2 apricots
1/8 cup of peeled pistachios

◆ For the royal icing, in a bowl, mix the egg white with the lemon juice. Slowly add the sifted powdered sugar and stir until mixture is smooth.

◆ Melt apricot jelly with 1 tablespoon of hot water. Brush jelly on the cake (a cake filled with fruits, prepared in a springform mold and not yet unmolded). Pour icing on cake (keeping 2 tablespoons aside), spread and refrigerate until set (1).

◆ Scald apricots, drain, rinse under ice water and peel. Slice in two and pit. In a saucepan, cook sugar and 2 tablespoons of water for 3 minutes.

When sugar has melted, add apricot halves and cook for 3 minutes, on low heat. Drain and cool completely.

◆ Scald the pistachios for 1 minute; peel and halve. Mix cocoa with the remaining icing (2) and pour into a parchment paper cone.

◆ Open the springform pan; transfer cake on a serving dish. Place apricot halves on the cake (3). With chocolate icing, trace petal designs around apricots to form 4 daisies (4). With the chocolate icing, bring stems together and decorate with pistachio "leaves" (5).

Flower cake

1

2

3

4

INGREDIENTS

5 egg whites
a pinch of salt
3/4 cup of sugar
1/2 lb of butter
2 tablespoons of candied cherries
3 tablespoons of Alchermes

5

◆ With egg whites, salt, sugar and butter, prepare a classic butter cream (see page 17). Add the Alchermes, mixing well.

◆ On a cardboard circle, design a 6-petal flower. Place cardboard on cake and trim all around with a very sharp knife. (1) Spread half of butter cream all over cake, evenly. (2)

◆ In the center of the cake, trace a 3-inch circle. Transfer remaining butter cream to a pastry bag fitted with a star tube. Pipe out rosettes around the traced circle (3), all along the "petals" (4) and around the bottom of the cake.

◆ Transfer remaining butter cream in a small parchment paper cone and pipe out 5 thin lines on each petal. (5) To finish, place the candied cherries in the center. Refrigerate until ready to serve.

This is a splendid decoration for a simple or layered cake.

347

Giant flower
with fruits

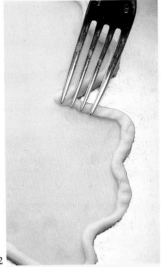

Ingredients

1 recipe of puff pastry (see
page 12)
1 recipe of pastry cream (see
page 16)
3/4 lb of raspberries
1/2 lb of strawberries
1 small mango
1 white peach
2 tablespoons of blueberries
3 tablespoons of apricot jelly

◆ Roll out the puff pastry and place on a cookie sheet. On a cardboard, draw a 6-petal flower and place it on the dough. Cut out dough following cardboard patterns (**1**). With remaining dough, from a long strip and place it around the petals and in the center of the flower. Press lightly with a fork (**2**) and prick dough all over.

◆ Cook the pastry flower in a preheated oven at 400 F, for 15-20 minutes, or until golden. Trans-fer to a serving plate and cover with pastry cream.

◆ Quickly rinse raspberries, strawberries and blueberries and dry them. Peel the peach and the mango; slice them thinly. Place raspberries at the end of the petals, then the sliced strawberries (**3**) around the pie. Arrange mango slices (**4**) and peach slices. Fill the center with the blueberries (**5**). In a double boiler, melt the apricot jelly and brush over the fruits. Serve immediately.

Rose branch

1

2

3

4

INGREDIENTS

*14 oz of marzipan
(see page 23)
2 tablespoons of Alchermes
1/2 cup of peeled pistachios
2 tablespoons of cocoa
4 tablespoons of apricot jelly
powdered sugar*

5

◆ Divide the marzipan in 1 piece of 6 oz, 1 piece of 4 oz, and 2 pieces of 2 oz. Place in 4 different bowls.

◆ Scald pistachios, peel and grind. Mix the pistachios to a portion of 2 oz of marzipan. To the other 2 oz portion, mix the cocoa. To the 4 oz portion of marzipan, add the Alchermes. Knead all four marzipan, separately, with your fingertips to soften and mix colors perfectly.

◆ Dust a work surface with powdered sugar. Roll out white marzipan and cut out a circle to fit top of cake. In a double boiler, melt apricot jelly.

◆ Place cake on a serving dish and brush top with melted apricot jelly. Cover with the marzipan circle. Roll out the pink marzipan; pull off 3 small pieces to form 3 small cones, that will be the centers of roses. With 2 cookie cutters, make large

and small circles. With a spatula, flatten on sides of the circles (1) to form the petals.

◆ Press the small petals to the base of the cones with your fingertips (2), placing the thin parts upwards. Attach larger petals, folding the upper parts toward the exterior (3). Complete roses.

◆ With the cocoa marzipan, make a long stick, that will be the stem. Roll out the green marzipan and, with the large cookie cutter, cut out circles; cut in half, placing the cutter in the middle to make leaves. With a small knife, trace veins on the leaves (4). Place the stem, leaves and roses on the cake (5).

This elegant decoration is especially good on a charlotte or over a layered cake.

Cream and chocolate triangles

Ingredients

2 1/2 cups of heavy cream
1 tablespoon of powdered sugar
2 cups of chopped milk chocolate
1/4 cup of chopped bittersweet chocolate
1 tablespoon of peeled pistachios
i

◆ Scald the pistachios, drain and peel. In a double boiler, melt the milk chocolate (see page 20).
◆ Pour the melted chocolate on a marble surface (or on a cookie sheet) and spread 1/4-inch thick. When cool, cut out 1-1/2-inch circles, using a cookie cutter (1) and set aside until hard.
◆ Whip the cream with the powdered sugar, keeping 2 tablespoons aside. Cover the entire cake with 1/3 of cream.
◆ In a double boiler, melt bittersweet chocolate in 2 tablespoons of cream. Cool completely and mix with 1/3 of remaining whipped cream, whisking delicately until completely mixed.

◆ Stick the milk chocolate circles around the cake (2). Transfer the whipped cream and the chocolate cream in 2 pastry bags, fitted with star tubes. Pipe out a large rosette in the center of the cake (3). Starting at the rosette, pipe out 8 strips of rosettes with the chocolate cream (4). With the white cream, pipe out rosettes in between the chocolate strips (5). Decorate with pistachio halves and refrigerate until ready to serve.

This delicious decoration can be used not only for a simple or filled cake, but also for an ice-cream cake.

Chocolate and hazelnut
chess board

1

2

3

INGREDIENTS

*2 tablespoons of apricot jelly
1 cup of chopped white chocolate
1 cup of chopped bittersweet
chocolate
1 cup of chopped hazelnut
brittle (see page 21)*

4

5

◆ In a saucepan, melt the apricot jelly with 1 tablespoon of water and brush on a rectangular
cake.
◆ In a double boiler, melt white chocolate (see
page 20). With a spatula, spread on top of cake
(1) and refrigerate until hard.
◆ In a double boiler, melt bittersweet chocolate.

Pour into a parchment paper cone and, pressing
lightly, draw a line around the cake edges. Trace
3 parallel chocolate lines (2) and 4 crossing lines
to form 10 boxes. (3) Fill 3 boxes with melted
chocolate (4) and 5 with the chopped hazelnut
brittle, alternating.

Raspberry and white chocolate stripes

INGREDIENTS

1/2 lb of raspberries
4 oz of white chocolate
1 cup of chopped bittersweet chocolate
1/2 cup of heavy cream
2 tablespoons of apricot jelly

◆ In a saucepan, heat the cream. In another saucepan, put 2/3 cup of bittersweet chocolate, pour the hot cream over and stir until completely melted. Cool. With an electric mixer, whisk the chocolate mixture. Spread it over a rectangular cake, as in this example for a layered cake (**1, 2**).

◆ In a double boiler, melt remaining bittersweet chocolate (see page 20). Pour into a parchment paper cone and pipe out diagonal lines on the cake (**3**), dividing in 3 large spaces and 3 thinner ones. Refrigerate cake until chocolate is hard.

◆ Rinse raspberries in ice water and dry them. With a potato peeler, make little curls from the white chocolate. Place curls on the large strips, on top of the cake (**4**). Fill the thin spaces with raspberries (**5**).

◆ In a double boiler, melt the apricot jelly; brush over raspberries.

Wild berry rhombus

1

2

3

4

INGREDIENTS

1/8 cup of red currants
1/8 cup of blueberries
9-12 wild strawberries
8 mint leaves
2 tablespoons of apricot jelly
3 tablespoons of powdered sugar

5

◆ Quickly rinse all fruits in ice water. (1) Dry them and gently clean the mint leaves.

◆ On a cardboard, cut five 2-inch squares. Place 1 square on the middle of cake and the 4 others around, angles touching the middle square. Sprinkle sifted powdered sugar all over top of cake (2); remove the cardboard squares to get 5 squares without sugar.

◆ With small tweezers, place wild strawberries in the middle square (3), the blueberries in opposite squares and the currants in the other squares. Brush fruits with melted apricot jelly. Decorate with mint leaves. (5) Keep in a cool place until ready to serve.

This decoration goes very well with a pie or fruit cake.

Strawberry and cream cross

INGREDIENTS

6-7 large strawberries
3/4 cup of whipping cream
3 tablespoons of apricot jelly
1/4 lb of Margherita cake
(see page 10)

◆ Keep aside one slice of Margherita cake and 3 large strawberries (1).

◆ Crumble the slice of Margherita cake and pass through a fine sieve. Quickly rinse the strawberries in ice water, dry and slice.

◆ Melt apricot jelly in 1 tablespoon of water; brush over the square cake, filled with pastry cream and strawberries (2). Sprinkle the cake, crumble over and around cake (3).

◆ Whip the cream and transfer to a pastry bag,

fitted with a star tube. Pipe out cream decoratively in 2 crossing strips on top of cake (4). In each triangle and in the middle, pipe out a cream rosette and decorate with sliced strawberries. Place sliced strawberries on the cream strips (5) and refrigerate until ready to serve.

A simple decoration for a summer cake filled with strawberries or pastry cream.

Raspberry and pear arrows

Ingredients

2 pears
1/2 lb of raspberries
*3 tablespoons of
apricot jelly*
*1/2 cup of still
Moscato d'Asti*

◆ Prepare cake with savoyard **(1)** and raspberry compote layers **(2)**.
In a double boiler, melt the apricot jelly; brush top of layered cake **(3)**.
In iced water, quickly rinse the berries, dry and set aside in a bowl. Peel the pears. With a melon baller, cut out balls, the size of the raspberries; place in a bowl with the Moscato d'Asti **(4)**.
With tweezers, delicately place the raspberries and pear balls on the cake, alternating colors to make arrows **(5)**.
Brush all fruits with melted apricot jelly. Refrigerate.

363

Mango and strawberry triumph

1

2

3

4

INGREDIENTS

1 cup of whipped cream
1 mango
2 large strawberries
2 tablespoons of powdered
sugar

5

◆ Generously sprinkle cake with sifted powdered sugar.

◆ Peel mango, cut in half and slice thinly (1). Place in the middle of the pie in concentric circles (2). keep 4 equal-size slices aside.

◆ Place whipped cream in a pastry bag fitted with a star tube. Pipe out for large rosettes in the mango circle. Place 4 strawberry segments between cream and place 4 remaining slices of mango (3)

on the cream rosettes. Pipe out rosettes of cream around the mango circle (4); and 8 other large rosettes over this circle. Delicately place strawberry segments on the rosettes (5). Refrigerate until ready to serve.

This simple and quick decoration is better over a layered cake filled with pastry cream.

Imperial eagle

INGREDIENTS

2 tablespoons of apricot jelly
1 1/2 cups of chopped bitter-
sweet chocolate
1/2 cup of powdered sugar
1 cup of chopped milk choco-
late
1/4 cup of chopped white
chocolate
2 tablespoons of butter
3 tablespoons of milk

◆ Melt the apricot jelly in 1 tablespoon of water; brush all over cake.

◆ In a double boiler, melt the bittersweet chocolate with the butter, milk and sugar, stirring continuously. Pour melted chocolate on cake and spread with a spatula. Pour remaining melted chocolate in a parchment paper cone and decorate the base of cake, the corners and around top of cake (1). Refrigerate until chocolate is hard.

◆ In a double boiler, melt milk chocolate; pour into a parchment paper cone and draw the emblem of the tsars on the cake (2, 3). To make it easier, draw emblem on a cardboard, cut it out and place on cake before drawing in chocolate.

◆ In a double boiler, melt the white chocolate; pour into a parchment paper cone and decorate (4, 5). Set aside in a cool place until set.

This particular and difficult decoration is for a layered cake and an important occasion.

Chocolate
treble clef

1

2

3

4

INGREDIENTS

*1/2 cup of chopped
milk chocolate
1/4 cup of chopped
white chocolate*

5

◆ Prepare a rectangular chocolate cake (this decoration looks better on that shape) and slice it in 3 layers.
◆ Return the bottom part to the cake pan. Cover with a layer of ganache (see page 18) **(1)** and cover with a second layer of cake **(2)**. Spread half of the remaining ganache and top with last cake layer. Refrigerate until ganache is set. Transfer cake to a serving dish. Cover top, spreading an even layer of the remaining ganache.
◆ In a double boiler, melt milk chocolate; pour into a parchment paper cone. Pressing lightly, trace 5 long thin chocolate lines from one end of the cake to the other **(3)**. Set aside to set.
◆ In a double boiler, melt the white chocolate; pour into a parchment paper cone. Pressing lightly, draw a treble clef **(4)** and a few musical notes **(5)**. Refrigerate until ready to serve.

Chocolate and almond lace

1

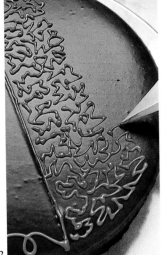

2

3

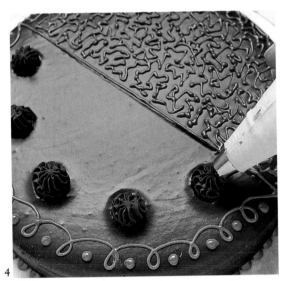

4

INGREDIENTS

*2 tablespoons of
apricot jelly
1 1/4 cups of chopped
bittersweet chocolate
1/2 cup of chopped
milk chocolate
1/2 cup of powdered sugar
4 tablespoons of
softened butter
5 pralined almonds
(see page 21)*

5

◆ Melt apricot jelly in 1 tablespoon of water and brush all over the prepared cake.

◆ In a double boiler, melt the bittersweet chocolate and stir in the butter. Remove from heat and stir in the powdered sugar and, a little at a time, 3 to 4 tablespoons of water, or enough to make the mixture smooth and you can spread it. Pour mixture on the cake and spread it with a spatula. With a pastry comb or a fork, make lines around the border of the cake. Transfer cake to a serving dish.

◆ In a double boiler, melt milk chocolate; pour into a parchment paper cone. Pressing lightly, draw a chocolate line on top of cake, slightly off center, and a curly border on the largest half (**1**). Pipe out a filigree design on the opposite part (**2**) and drops of chocolate between the curls of the border (**3**) and all along the bottom of the cake.

◆ Transfer the remaining chocolate in a pastry bag, fitted with a star tube and pipe out 5 rosettes at equal distance from each other (**4**). Delicately place a pralined almond on every rosette (**5**).

This impressive decoration can cover a simple or layered cake.

Pistachio and cream
butterfly

INGREDIENTS
1/4 lb of butter
1/2 cup of whipping cream
2 cups of chopped
bittersweet chocolate
1 cup of chopped
pistachios

◆ In a saucepan, put the chocolate and the melted butter; cook on low heat until mixture is smooth and shiny. Pour on the cake and spread on top and around cake (1). Refrigerate for at least 30 minutes.

◆ Scald the pistachios, peel and chop coarsely. Set aside 15 whole pistachios. Remove cake from refrigerator and gently press chopped pistachios around the sides (2).

◆ Whip the cream and transfer to a pastry bag, fitted with a large star tube. In the center of the cake, pipe out 6 mounds. Change tube to a smaller star tube and pipe out rosettes, drawing butterfly wings (3). With a spoon, fill wings with chopped pistachios (4).

◆ Delicately place whole pistachios to decorate butterfly body (5). Refrigerate until ready to serve.

This quick and simple way to decorate a cake is used to cover simple cakes.

Cluster of grapes

1

2

3

4

INGREDIENTS

1 cluster of red grapes
3 candied orange peels
2 candied citron pieces

5

◆ Rinse the grapes, dry and slice thinly, removing any seeds (**1**). With tweezers, place slices of grapes, on the prepared cake, partially overlaying them (**2**). Continue until the design of the grape bunch is finished (**3**).
◆ Place the candied orange peels and candied citron to form the stem and the leaves of the grapes (**4**). Place a thin curled orange peel over the citron leaves (**5**).

This decoration was designed for a grape pudding or panna cotta, but can also be used on any cake covered with royal icing.

375

Cream festoons
on marzipan

1

2

3

4

INGREDIENTS

*1 lb of marzipan
(see page 23)
2 tablespoons of Alchermes
3/4 cup of whipping cream
2 tablespoons of apricot jelly
2 tablespoons of powdered
sugar*

5

◆ Add the Alchermes to the plain marzipan (1) and mix with your fingertips until completely absorbed. Sprinkle a work surface with powdered sugar; roll out marzipan to 1/8-inch sheet (2).

◆ Melt apricot jelly with 1 tablespoon of water; brush all over the prepared cake. Delicately cover the cake with marzipan sheet, pressing lightly with the palm of your hands to make it stick. Trim any excess marzipan around the base of the cake (3).

◆ Whip the cream and transfer to a pastry bag, fitted with a star tube. Pipe out a crown of rosettes around the upper edge of cake. Draw a star of rosettes on top of cake with a rosette in its middle (4). Decorate the sides of the cake (5). It is preferable to design the star, on top of the cake, pressing lightly with the tip of a small knife, before piping out the cream.

This splendid classic type of decoration covers a multi-layered cake, for a very special occasion.

Chocolate ornament

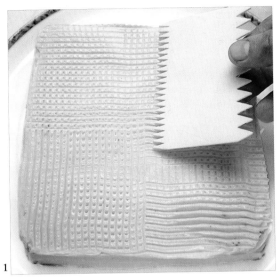

1

2

3

4

INGREDIENTS

12 tablespoons of butter
1/2 cup of sugar
4 egg whites
a pinch of salt
grated peel of
1 organic orange
2 tablespoons of dry sherry
3/4 cup of chopped
bittersweet chocolate

5

◆ With butter, sugar, egg whites and salt, prepare a classic butter cream (see page 17) and mix in the dry sherry and the orange peel. Set 1/4 of the butter cream aside; with a spatula, spread the remaining butter cream all over prepared cake. Place cake on a serving dish. With a pastry comb, draw lines on top of the cake (1). Refrigerate until set.

◆ On a piece of cardboard, draw an ornament 5-inch tall and 2-1/2-inch at the base. In a double boiler, melt the bittersweet chocolate; pour into a parchment paper cone. Place the cardboard ornament cut-out on a large piece of waxed paper and draw 4 times. Pipe out chocolate on the emblem design (2); make 3 more identical emblems on the waxed paper. Pipe out a full square of melted chocolate (on waxed paper). Set aside until hard.

◆ Remove cake from refrigerator. Place remaining butter cream in a pastry bag, fitted with a small star tube. Pipe out rosettes around top, bottom and corners of cake (3). Remove chocolate squares from waxed paper and place in the center of the cake (4). Delicately remove waxed paper from chocolate emblems. With the cone filled with melted chocolate, place tiny drops on each rosettes (5); draw a cross on the chocolate square to fix the chocolate emblems upright. Refrigerate until ready to serve.

This is a very impressive decoration for a layered orange cake.

Index